OPERATIONS STRATEGY

Nigel Slack

Michael Lewis

FINANCIAL TIMES
Prentice Hall

An imprint of **Pearson Education**

Harlow, England · London · New York · Reading, Massachusetts · San Francisco · Toronto · Don Mills, Ontario · Sydney
Tokyo · Singapore · Hong Kong · Seoul · Taipei · Cape Town · Madrid · Mexico City · Amsterdam · Munich · Paris · Milan

Pearson Education Limited

Edinburgh Gate
Harlow
Essex CM20 2JE

and Associated Companies throughout the world

Visit us on the World Wide Web at:
www.pearsoneduc.com

First published 2002

ISBN 0 273 63781 9

British Library Cataloguing-in-Publication Data
A catalogue record for this book is available from the British Library

Library of Congress Cataloguing-in-Publication Data
Slack, Nigel.
    Operations strategy/Nigel Slack, Michael Lewis.
        p. cm.
        Includes bibliographical references and index.
        ISBN 0–273–63781–9
            1. Production management. I. Lewis, Michael. II. Title.

    TS155 .S563 2001
    658.5--dc21

                                          2001033632

10 9 8 7 6 5 4 3 2 1
05 04 03 02 01

Typeset in 9½/12pt Stone by 3
Printed by Ashford Colour Press Ltd., Gosport

Contents

Foreword

By Rupert Gasser, Executive Vice President, Nestlé S.A.

After the fabulous success of the outstanding book *Operations Management* by Nigel Slack and his team, it is a great pleasure for me to now introduce another work of equally high standing by Nigel Slack and Michael Lewis on *Operations Strategy*.

Through increasing globalisation, operations are spanning large regions. Therefore a company's operations are, as a consequence, ensuring supply across multiple countries, cultures and functions and have therefore to be approached with a long-term strategy in view. The content of this book mirrors the great tasks that many industries are facing in the process of globalisation.

More specifically, this text reflects the challenges that the world's largest and most diversified food company – Nestlé – is facing every day to reconcile the performance of its operations to the requirements of the markets.

Whilst Nestlé aims at high operational performance standards across its world-wide factory systems, the continuous development of its network of factories to the changing business and trade environment also ensures operational effectiveness. This optimisation of operations performance and effectiveness became possible through the elimination of trade barriers, changes in the relative importance of transport costs, outsourcing and improvements in technology – and it is managed through an *Operations Strategy* approach.

Nestlé's redesign of its industrial structure aims to create the optimal industrial platform for long term, capital efficient and profitable growth. In so doing, we are defining the role of factories. For example, from local to regional production centres or from multi-product to single product manufacturing sites. Such changes will aim to optimally deploy new technologies, improve our international supply chains and effectively manage the day to day running of our operations. In this way the design and implementation of an appropriate *Operations Strategy* affects all parts of our organisation in an essential way and is therefore a core competence.

Operations Strategy superbly illustrates those broad, principle-defining and long-term issues which are the concern of operations *strategy*. As such it complements the more operational, immediate, tangible and specific issues which define operations *management*.

Nigel Slack and Michael Lewis's *Operations Strategy* makes highly interesting reading on a subject which is of paramount importance to any corporation. I am convinced that this book will contribute to a more comprehensive approach to operations strategy by tomorrow's management all over the world.

RUPERT GASSER
Executive Vice-President, Nestlé S.A.

Preface

What's in a name? Well, for a concept like Operations Strategy, quite a lot actually. Depending on the punctuation you use or even the order of the words, one could be referring to the longer-term impact of day-to-day operations, the medium-term direction of a narrowly defined organisational function, or the much more nebulous interaction between all operational resources and external requirements. It is this latter interpretation that forms the focus for this book.

Introduction

Just as some physical objects are so big that it can be difficult to see their whole, some concepts are so broadly based that they can be difficult to define. Operations strategy, as we see it, is like this. Indeed one might argue that it is because it is so all-embracing that it becomes easy to dismiss the significance of the subject. Yet operations strategy lies at the heart of how organisations manage their strategic intent in practice, and is the context within which managers make strategic decisions. The following are just some of the decisions with which operations strategy is concerned:

- How should the organisation satisfy the requirements of its customers?
- What intrinsic capabilities should the organisation try to develop as the foundation for its long-term success?
- How specialised should the organisation's activities become?
- Should the organisation sacrifice some of its objectives in order to excel at others?
- How big should the organisation be?
- Where should the organisation locate its resources?
- When should it expand or contract, and by how much?
- What should it do itself and what should it contract out to other businesses?
- How should it develop relationships with other organisations?
- What type of technology should it invest in?
- How should it organise the way it develops new products and services?
- How should it bind together its resources into an organisational structure?
- How should the organisation's resources and processes be improved and developed over time?
- What guiding principles should shape the way any organisation formulates its operations strategies?

All these questions are not merely important, they are fundamental. No organisation, whether large or small, for-profit or not-for-profit, in the services or manufacturing sector, international or local, can ignore such questions. Operations strategy is central, ubiquitous, and vital to any organisation's sustained success.

The aim of this book

This book aims to provide a treatment of operations strategy which is clear, well structured, and interesting. It seeks to apply some of the ideas of operations strategy to a variety of businesses and organisations. The text provides a logical path through the key activities and decisions of operations strategy as well as covering the broad principles which underpin the subject and the way in which operations strategies are put together in practice.

More specifically, the text aims to be:

- Balanced in its treatment of the subject. In addition to taking the orthodox 'market-led' approach to operations strategy, the book also provides an alternative but complementary 'resource-based' perspective.

- Conceptual in the way it treats the decisions, activities and processes which together form an organisation's operations strategy. Although some examples are quantified, the overall treatment in the book is managerial and practical.

- Comprehensive in its coverage of the more important ideas and issues which are relevant to most types of business. In any book covering such a broad area as operations strategy, one cannot cover everything. However, we believe that the more important issues are all addressed.

- Grounded in the various bodies of knowledge which underpin operations strategy. Theory boxes are included in most chapters, introducing concepts and principles, often from other academic disciplines, which illuminate the particular operations strategy issue being discussed.

- International in the examples which are used. Out of over 70 boxes describing practical operations strategy issues, around 35 per cent are from Europe, 35 per cent from the USA and 30 per cent are either from elsewhere in the world, or are generally 'global'.

Who should use this book?

This book is intended to provide a broad introduction to operations strategy for all students who wish to understand the strategic importance and scope of the operations function; for example:

- Undergraduates on business or technical degrees (although we assume a prior knowledge of the basics of operations management).

- MBA students should find that it both links and integrates their experience and study of operations management with their core studies in business strategy.

- Postgraduate students on other specialised Masters degrees should find that it provides them with a well-grounded approach to the subject.

- Executives will also be able to relate the practical and pragmatic structure of the book to the more conceptual and theoretical issues discussed within the structure.

Distinctive features

Clear structure

The book employs coherent models of the subject that run through each part of the text and explain how the chapters fit into the overall subject. Key questions set the scene at the beginning of each chapter and also provide a structure for the summary at the end of each chapter.

Illustration based

The study of operations, even at a strategic level, is essentially a practical subject and cannot be taught in a purely theoretical manner. Because of this, we have used both abstracted examples and 'boxed' examples which explain some issues faced by real operations.

Theory boxes

Operations strategy is a practical subject which is driven by theoretical ideas. Most chapters contain one or more theory boxes which explain the underpinning ideas which have contributed to our understanding of the issues being discussed.

Case exercises

Every chapter includes a short case exercise which has ample content to serve as the basis for a formal case de-brief but is also sufficiently concise to be used as a simple 'in-class' illustration.

Selected further reading

Every chapter ends with a list of further reading which takes the topic covered in the chapter further, or treats some important related issues.

Web site

A web site is available which helps students to develop a firm understanding of the issues covered in the book and provides lecturers with pedagogical assistance. There is also a teacher's manual available. These resources can be found at www.booksites.net/slack.

Acknowledgements

There are not many books on Operations Strategy. There are a few on Manufacturing Strategy which cover many of the topics we explore in this book, but exclusively in a manufacturing context. Even those books in operations strategy tend to be overwhelmingly manufacturing in the scope of their coverage. Also, it is relatively unusual to attempt to balance market-based and resource-based concepts in the same book. For all these reasons, this book is different. Therefore, more than is usual, we have been influenced by academics and practitioners from a wide range of disciplines and industries. In listing those whom we would like to thank, we include not only the friends and colleagues who have made a direct contribution to the way this book was put together, but also to those people who have particularly influenced us (and whose ideas we have often unashamedly plundered, although hopefully always acknowledged). We express our gratitude to all who helped us, but especially Pär Åhlström of Stockholm School of Economics, David Barnes of the Open University, David Bennett of Aston University, John Bessant of Brighton University, Peter Bircher of Aston University, Ruth Boaden of the University of Manchester Institute of Science and Technology, Mike Bourne of Cranfield University, Sarah Caffyn of Brighton University, Paul Coghlan of Trinity College Dublin, Henrique Correa of FGV São Paulo, Roland van Dierdonck of the University of Ghent, Kasra Ferdows of Georgetown University, Vic Gilgeous of Nottingham University, Keith Goffin of Cranfield University, Lynda Graham of Warwick University, Mike Gregory of Cambridge University, Terry Hill of Templeton College, Oxford, Christer Karlsson of Stockholm School of Economics, Shaun Macdonald of Warwick University, Bart McCarthy of Nottingham University, John Mills of Cambridge University, Chris Morgan of Cranfield University, Andy Neely of Cranfield University, Alistair Nicholson of London Business School, Nick Oliver of Cambridge University, Ken Platts of Cambridge University, Martin Spring of UMIST, Mike Sweeney of Cranfield University, Ann Vereecke of the University of Ghent, and Chris Voss of London Business School.

Our academic colleagues in the Operations Management Group at Warwick Business School also helped both by contributing ideas and by creating a lively and stimulating work environment. Our thanks go to Joy Batchelor, Hilary Bates, Alan Betts, Stuart Chambers, Simon Croom, Mike Giannakis, Bob Johnston, Mike Shulver, Rhian Silvestro, Bridget Sullivan-Taylor, Ram Venuprasad, Paul Walley and Adrian Watt.

We are also grateful to many friends, colleagues and company contacts. In particular, thanks go to John Banyard of Severn Trent, Christopher Cook of Insignia, Mark Fisher and Peter Norris of the Royal Bank of Scotland, David Garman of TDG plc, Rupert Gasser, Tyko Persson and Hans Meyer of Nestlé, Gillian McGrattan and Steven Edmunds of Grant Thornton, Philip Godfrey and Cormack Campbell of OEE, and John Tyley of Lloyds TSB.

Mary Walton is secretary to our group at Warwick Business School. She will claim that she did not contribute to this book. In fact her cheerful disposition and (largely forlorn) efforts to keep us organised have contributed more than she could imagine.

The team from Pearson Education provided their usual highly professional support. Particular thanks to Penelope Woolf (now of Oxford University Press), Anna Herbert, John Yates, Simon Lake, Alison Kirk, Stuart Hay, Laura Graham, Suki Cheyne, David Harrison, Mary Lince and Annette Abel.

Every word of this book, together with many words which were discarded during the writing process, were word processed by Angela Slack. The task of typing and retyping the manuscript, providing PowerPoint versions of all the illustrations, organising the writing process and generally making some kind of sense of eccentric word processing styles was a truly amazing effort. We owe Angela our thanks for her effort and her (almost) infinite patience.

Finally, and most importantly, we would like to thank our wives, Angela and Helen, for their forbearance and their unwavering support.

Publisher's acknowledgements

1

THE NATURE OF OPERATIONS STRATEGY

Part 1 of this book introduces the idea of operations strategy and the dual influences of market requirements and operations resource capabilities which it has to reconcile. It draws the distinction between the *content* and *process* of operations strategy and it explains how operations strategy changes over time. In addition, it describes how trade-offs between operations performance objectives are at the heart of the strategic reconciliation which is the main objective of operations strategy.

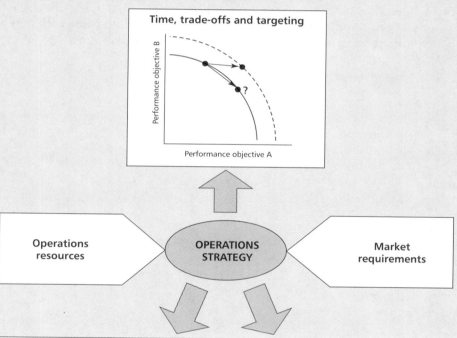

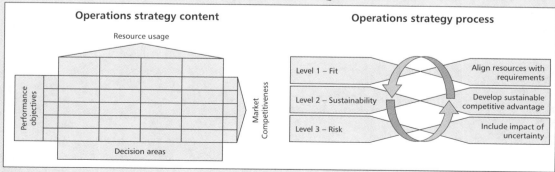

Continued overleaf

Continued from previous page

- Chapter 1 defines operations strategy in terms of the reconciliation between market requirements and operations resources.

- Chapter 2 distinguishes between the content and process of operations strategy and briefly introduces both areas.

- Chapter 3 looks at three interrelated issues which affect reconciliation – how operations change over time, how operations deal with trade-offs, and how trade-offs can be used to understand 'targeted', or focused, operations.

Operations strategy – the two perspectives

Introduction

Operations strategy sounds at first like a contradiction. How can 'operations', which is generally concerned with the *day-to-day* creation and delivery of goods and services, be *strategic*? 'Strategy' is usually regarded as the antithesis of those day-to-day routines and activities which are the responsibility of operations managers. But the way in which a firm's operations resources are managed is increasingly seen as being central to its long-term strategic success. Operations *does* have a strategic role. Nor is 'strategic' operations management merely a matter of doing the operational things well so as not to hold back more important strategic decisions. Operations strategy should certainly prevent strategic decisions being frustrated by poor operational implementation, but it should also be able to ensure that the management of operations resources can itself provide advantage. The influence of an organisation's aspirations for its operations as well as the operations function's ability to contribute to strategic positioning are both fundamental to its long-term success. Both issues are also undeniably strategic. In order to take this argument further this chapter will first draw the distinction between *operations* and *operational* and, by doing so, distinguish between *operations management* and *operations strategy*. It will also discuss how *manufacturing strategy* has developed into the broader *operations strategy* by treating all types of business, whether they provide products or services, or some mixture of the two. Most importantly, it will set out our approach to operations strategy. This sees operations strategy as an attempt to reconcile two sets of pressures. One derives from the requirements of the markets in which the firm operates. The other comes from the intrinsic characteristics of its resources – what they can and can't do. Figure 1.1 illustrates this idea.

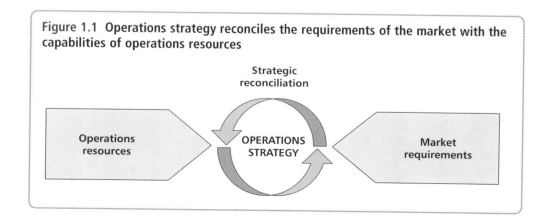

Figure 1.1 Operations strategy reconciles the requirements of the market with the capabilities of operations resources

Strategic reconciliation

Operations resources → OPERATIONS STRATEGY ← Market requirements

KEY QUESTIONS

- *What is the difference between operations management and operations strategy?*
- *Does operations strategy have meaning for all kinds of organisations?*
- *How does operations strategy differ from the more conventional subject of manufacturing strategy?*
- *How do the requirements of the market influence the way operations resources are managed?*
- *How can the intrinsic characteristics and capabilities of operations resources influence market position?*

The 'new' approach to operations

The theory and practice of operations used to be something of a Cinderella subject, without the glamour of Marketing or the professional solidity of Accounting. No longer. Many of the fashionable new ideas in management, such as Total Quality Management (TQM), benchmarking, ISO9000, Supply Chain Management (SCM), 'lean' thinking, Business Process Re-engineering (BPR) and so on, are centred around and within the operations function. Partly because of this, professional and academic journals teem with articles on the importance of operations. Perhaps most significantly, a recent survey of the world consultancy market[1] showed that the largest single slice of the market (32%) was devoted to 'operations and process management'. If the area where companies are spending their money is a reflection of perceived importance for business success, then operations management is seen as an area of considerable untapped potential. So why has operations management become so appealing? Partly it is because managers have realised that 'that is where the money is'. Getting operations to work effectively can give the twin benefits of improved efficiency, thus reducing costs, while also providing the improved quality and service which increases revenue. Partly also it is a growing recognition of the *strategic* importance of operations.

All this attention has had its effect on the way the management of operations is seen both by practitioners and by academics. There are more people studying the subject of course, but, more interestingly, there also have been qualitative changes in how the subject is treated. In the remainder of this chapter we examine three emerging themes which characterise this 'new' approach to operations:

- 'Operations' is not always 'operational' – operations management has an important strategic dimension.
- 'Operations' is not limited to manufacturing – it concerns the production of both products and services in any type of operation whether they are for-profit or not-for-profit.
- 'Operations' is the part of the organisation where the requirements of the market and the capabilities of the organisation's resources have to be reconciled. In fact this is the main task of operations strategy.

This last point is particularly important and forms the underlying rationale of the whole book.

Operations strategy

'Operations' is not always 'operational'

The boundary between what is regarded as operations *strategy* and what is regarded as operations *management* is often not clear. In fact it can never be absolutely clear because an important element in operations strategy is the capabilities that resources and processes demonstrate on a routine day-to-day basis. Nevertheless, although operations management and operations strategy cannot be totally separated, they do have different characteristics and treat issues in a different manner.

Operations management

Operations management is the activity of managing the resources and processes that produce and deliver goods and services. Every organisation, whether for-profit or not-for-profit, has an operations function because every organisation produces some mix of goods and services, even if the operations function is not called by this name.[2] All operations have inputs, some of which are *transformed* by the processes in the operation. These *transformed* resources are some combination of physical materials, information and customers. So, predominantly, a television factory processes materials, a firm of accountants processes information, while a theatre processes customers. The *transforming* resources act on the transformed resources. These are usually classified into the physical *facilities* (buildings, machines, equipment, computers, etc.) and the human resources (*staff*) who operate, support and manage the processes. While operations, such as an aluminium smelter, mainly produce products with only a peripheral service element, others, such as a psychotherapy clinic, produce almost pure service with few, if any, physical products. But most operations lie in between these extremes and produce both products and services. The total operations function of any organisation is comprised of smaller units, departments and processes which themselves are smaller versions of the whole operation. Operations management is concerned largely with the way in which these processes are managed. Typical tasks include designing processes, choosing and maintaining process technologies, designing the jobs of the operation's staff, planning and controlling activities, ensuring quality standards, improving operations performance, and so on.

Operations strategy

By contrast, operations strategy is concerned less with individual processes and more with the total transformation process that is the whole business. If it is a large business, its relationship is with other parts of the corporation to which it may belong and with the commercial environment outside the business. It is concerned with how the competitive environment is changing and what the operation has to do in order to meet current and future challenges. It is also concerned with the long-term development of its operations resources and processes so that they can provide the basis for a sustainable advantage. The decisions taken as part of a company's operations strategy are considered strategic because they:

- are widespread in their effect and so are significant in the part of the organisation to which the strategy refers;
- define the position of the organisation relative to its environment;
- move the organisation closer to its long-term goals.

But a 'strategy' is more than a single decision, it is a *total pattern of the decisions*. A company's operations strategy, therefore, is shown in the pattern of decisions that the organisation takes to develop its operations resources. Such decisions include the magnitude and nature of its total capacity, the way in which it relates to customers, competitors, suppliers and partner operations, its approach to acquiring or developing process technology, the way in which it organises and develops its resources, and so on.

Definition – part one

We are now at a point where we can start building towards a working definition of operations strategy. We will extend this definition twice during the remainder of this chapter.

> Operations strategy is the total pattern of decisions which shape the long-term capabilities of an operation and their contribution to overall strategy.

Operations strategy vs. operations management

Perhaps the best way to describe this is by taking an example of a well-known and successful operation – Singapore Airlines. We can then examine its operations management and operations strategy issues.

Singapore Airlines[3]

In spite of periodic hiccups, caused by wars and economic cycles, the growth in airline passenger transport has been remarkable. By the late 1990s more than 1.5 billion passengers were being carried every year, with this figure set to double by 2010 according to some forecasts. It is surprising then, that so few airlines seem to be able to make serious profits. One notable exception is Singapore International Airlines (SIA), one of the most consistently profitable airlines in the world, the winner of numerous service quality awards and an industry leader in service innovation. In the 1970s SIA was the first airline to introduce complimentary drinks, a choice of meals and free headsets in its economy class. During the 1980s, with its personalised service from flight attendants and constant communication between the pilot and passengers, the airline was successful in differentiating itself with superior service. In the early 1990s business class travellers could utilise the first global in-flight telephone, together with fax and online services on SIA's Megatop Boeing 747s.

  By the mid-1990s SIA had begun a two-year programme to install a new in-flight entertainment system for passengers in all its Megatop B747s. This offered 22 channels of video entertainment, 12 digital audio channels, 10 Nintendo video games, destination information, a telephone at every seat, teletext news service, an interactive in-flight shopping facility and – for business and first class passengers – audio and video programmes on demand. In the late 1990s new services included online hotel, airline, car hire and restaurant booking services – for a fee. Another money-maker for SIA is 'in-flight gaming' with electronic one-armed bandits and other casino specials. Interactive entertainment systems allow passengers to gamble between the safety demonstration and the film. Recent innovations include armrest portals for client's PC notebooks to access the

Internet. In 1990, Singapore Airlines were investing just $1,800 per seat for their systems. By 2000, the cost was around $10,000. Typically, that equates to a spend of around $3–5 million per aircraft on such technology – or around some $100 million across the fleet – with the investment written off over three to five years. Nor is SIA's investment limited to in-cabin technology. It has a history of purchasing and operating long-range, state-of-the-art aircraft, while balancing the increase in its operational capacity with the opening up of new routes. It has also balanced its purchases, with Boeing and Airbus getting equal attention. At the same time the company sells aircraft on a regular basis, so that cash can be generated and the fleet constantly renewed. An example is its 1988 sale of operationally fit aircraft, including 747s, which brought the airline $110 million for investment in new Boeing 747-400s and Airbus A340s.

SIA's subsidiaries and divisions include Silkair, providing local and tourist flights, a cargo operation, and Singapore Air Terminal Services (SATS) which provides ground services such as baggage handling, check-in and ticketing. The maintenance operation, with over 40 maintenance bays, spun off as an independent unit in 1992, also provides services to other airlines and has joint venture agreements with Pratt and Whitney, the US engine manufacturer, and the Japanese Taiko Engineering with whom it operates a maintenance operation in Xiamen, China. In its passenger operations, alliances enhance geographical reach. The idea is to extend operational frontiers without incurring major capital costs, while winning customer support by offering seamless travel. Alliances with Air New Zealand and Ansett increased links with Australasia. The alliance in 1997 with Lufthansa increased operational capabilities in Europe through giving reciprocal rights to Lufthansa at Singapore's Changi Airport. Similarly, the 1998 alliance with South African Airlines has extended the operational range of SIA in Africa.

Changi, one of the worlds most efficient airports, is the company's home. It is also its cargo hub. Around 30 per cent of the airline's revenues come from cargo operations. The cargo infrastructure at Changi boasts a state-of-the-art system which can make an online booking from any one of the 75 cities where the airline has cargo offices and use data warehousing to help keep track of the various shipments in transit. An Internet site allows cargo shippers to generate their own airway bills. The 'super-hub', Terminal 5, handles cargo extremely efficiently through the use of specialist equipment.

For most of its recent history SIA has been clear on its strategic approach: *'Offer our customers the very best services, cut our costs to the bone and generate a surplus to continue the unending process of renewal.'* But the first of these objectives has always been what SIA's Managing Director, Dr Cheon Choong Kong, called *'the importance of the passengers. So the only way to meet the customers' need is to consider every detail about service.'* This means both getting the major decisions on structure and investment right, and never underestimating the importance of the attention to detail. SIA knows that what makes the difference between 'good' service and 'excellent' service can be something as simple as installing double castor wheels on the cabin carts, which eases and speeds the service of meals.

Operations management and operations strategy at Singapore Airlines

In a global, busy enterprise like Singapore Airlines, there are many operations management decisions taken every day. They might include such things as the following:

- scheduling aircrew to flights so as to provide efficient use of staff, accommodate individual staff preferences and fall well within safety regulations;
- devising procedures and training to continuously improve the quality of service provided by air and ground staff;
- designing the internal customer 'service level agreements' between the various parts of the airline such as passenger flights, cargo, terminal services, maintenance, etc.;

- reducing the on-ground time for aircraft between flights;
- scheduling the timing and extent of aircraft maintenance episodes;
- managing the delivery of refreshments to aircraft, etc.

For Singapore Airlines operations strategy issues will be somewhat different. They might include such things as the following:

- determining the number and type of aircraft which form the capacity of its long-haul passenger, its local Silkair and its cargo operations, and timing purchase options with aircraft suppliers;
- deciding the relative balance of investment in aircraft, in-flight services, terminal facilities, cargo warehouses and handling equipment, etc.;
- defining the organisational structure, commercial relationship and boundaries between the various parts of the group;
- the approach to choosing which non-core services (such as food preparation, cleaning services, maintenance, etc.) to subcontract and which to keep in-house;
- configuring the location and scope of the group's maintenance operations, etc.

With Singapore Airlines operations strategy is not different from operations management in terms of the functional area it inhabits, or even necessarily the managers

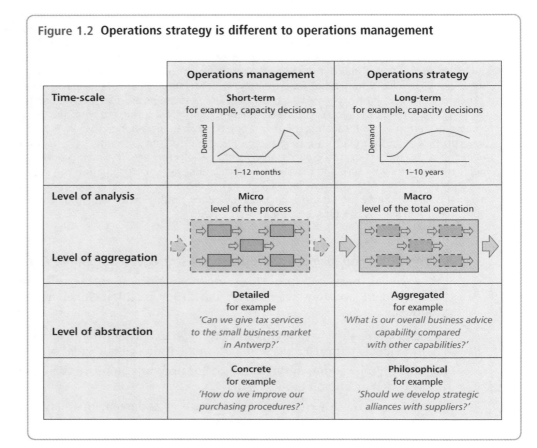

Figure 1.2 Operations strategy is different to operations management

	Operations management	Operations strategy
Time-scale	**Short-term** for example, capacity decisions *Demand / 1–12 months*	**Long-term** for example, capacity decisions *Demand / 1–10 years*
Level of analysis Level of aggregation	**Micro** level of the process	**Macro** level of the total operation
Level of abstraction	**Detailed** for example *'Can we give tax services to the small business market in Antwerp?'*	**Aggregated** for example *'What is our overall business advice capability compared with other capabilities?'*
	Concrete for example *'How do we improve our purchasing procedures?'*	**Philosophical** for example *'Should we develop strategic alliances with suppliers?'*

who practise it. Operations strategy is concerned with more or less the same set of resources as operations management and has broadly similar objectives. The difference is one of perspective. Whereas operations management deals with relatively immediate, narrow, specific and often tangible issues, operations strategy is more far-reaching, broader, generalised and treats the underlying principles. The difference between the operations management and operations strategy perspectives can be summarised in terms of time-scale, level of analysis, level of aggregation and level of abstraction. See Figure 1.2.

Top-down and bottom-up

So, operations strategy is longer term, higher level, more aggregated and more abstract than operations management. But how does it fit into the pattern of decision making and development within an organisation? One view (the more traditional) is that operations strategy is one of several *functional strategies* which are governed by decisions taken at the top of the organisational tree and which set the overall strategic direction of the organisation. This is essentially a 'top-down' approach to the management of operations.

Top-down – operations strategy interprets higher-level strategy

If the organisation is a large, diversified corporation, its *corporate strategy* will consist of decisions about what types of business the group wants to be in, in what parts of the world it wants to operate, what businesses to acquire and what to divest, how to allocate its cash between its various businesses, and so on. Within the corporate group, each business unit will also need to put together its own *business strategy*. This will set out its individual mission and objectives as well as defining how it intends to compete in its markets. Similarly, within the business each function will need to consider what part it should play in contributing to the strategic and/or competitive objectives of the business by developing a *functional strategy* which guides its actions within the business. So, in the 'top-down' view, these three levels of strategy – corporate, business and functional – form a hierarchy, with business strategy forming the context of functional strategies and corporate strategy forming the context of business strategies.

For example, a manufacturer of metrology instruments is part of a group which contains several high-tech companies. It has decided to compete by being the first in the market with every available new product innovation. Its operations function, therefore, needs to be capable of coping with the changes that constant innovation will bring. It must develop processes which are flexible enough to manufacture novel parts and products. It must organise and train its staff to understand the way products are developing so that they can put in place the necessary changes to the operation. It must develop relationships with its suppliers which will help them to respond quickly when supplying new parts. Everything about the operation, its technology, staff, and its systems and procedures, must, in the short term, do nothing to inhibit the company's competitive strategy.

Bottom-up – operations strategy contributes day-to-day experience

The 'top-down' perspective provides an orthodox view of how functional strategies *should* be put together. But in fact the relationship between the levels in the strategy hierarchy is more complex than this. Although it is a convenient way of thinking about strategy, this hierarchical view does not represent the way strategies are always formulated. When any group is reviewing its corporate strategy, it will also take into account the circumstances, experiences and capabilities of the various businesses that form the group. Similarly, businesses, when reviewing their strategies, will consult the individual functions within the business about their constraints and capabilities. They may also incorporate the ideas that come from each function's day-to-day experience.

Therefore an alternative view to the top-down perspective is that many strategic ideas emerge over time from actual experiences. Sometimes companies move in a particular strategic direction because the ongoing experience of providing products and services to customers at an operational level convinces them that it is the right thing to do. There may be no high-level decisions examining alternative strategic options and choosing the one that provides the best way forward. Instead, a general consensus emerges, often from the operational level of the organisation. The 'high level' strategic decision making, if it occurs at all, may confirm the consensus and provide the resources to make it happen effectively. This idea of strategy being shaped by experience over time is sometimes called the concept of *emergent strategies*. Strategy gradually becomes clearer over time and is based on real-life experience rather than theoretical positioning. Indeed, strategies are often formed in a relatively unstructured and fragmented manner to reflect the fact that the future is at least partially unknown and unpredictable.

This view of operations strategy is perhaps more descriptive of how things really happen, but at first glance it seems less useful in providing a guide for specific decision making. Yet while emergent strategies are less easy to categorise, the principle governing a bottom-up perspective is clear: shape the operation's objectives and action, at least partly, by the knowledge it gains from its day-to-day activities. The key virtues required for shaping strategy from the bottom up are an ability to learn from experience and a philosophy of continual and incremental improvement.

For example, the manufacturer of metrology instruments discovers that continual product innovation both increases its costs and confuses its customers. The company's designers therefore work out a way of 'modularising' their product designs so that one part of the product can be updated without interfering with the design of the main body of the product. This approach becomes standard design practice within the company. Note that this strategy has emerged from the company's experience. No top-level board decision was probably ever taken to confirm this practice, but nevertheless it emerges as the way in which the company organises its designs.

Top-down and bottom-up

In reality, functional strategies such as operations strategy involve elements of both the top-down and bottom-up views (Figure 1.3). Any business strategy is usually evaluated in terms of its making sense in the context of its overall corporate strategy. Nor can any functional strategy, especially operations strategy which includes most of the organisation's assets, afford to be in conflict with the business's overall strategy. Yet the strategic direction of any organisation will be strongly influenced by day-to-day experiences. Not only will operational issues set practical constraints on business strategy (which in turn influences corporate strategy), more significantly,

Figure 1.3 Top-down and bottom-up perspectives of strategy

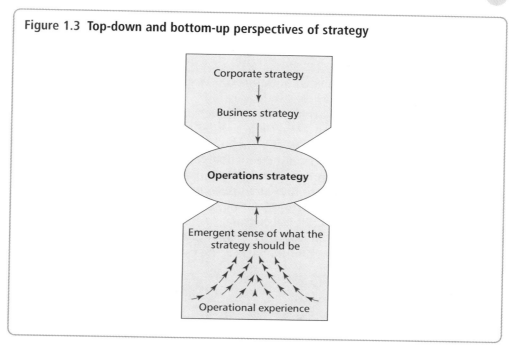

day-to-day experiences can be exploited to provide an important contribution to overall strategy. To this extent the top-down model of operations is a reminder that there must be *alignment* between higher- and lower-level strategies.

From 'manufacturing strategy' to 'operations strategy'

The second point of difference for the new approach to operations is the inclusion of all types of operation rather than just those that manufacture physical products. It is clearly misguided to imagine that issues which were traditionally seen as important in manufacturing can have no relevance in service organisations. Both manufacturing and service use processes to transform inputs into outputs. Both have to design their processes, plan how the resources within the processes will be used, control their day-to-day activities, and pay attention to how process performance can be improved. Furthermore, in most developed economies, service sectors account for the clear majority of economic activity. If that were not enough, there is genuine difficulty in separating manufacturing and services. This is what *The Economist* had to say about it:[4]

> ... persisting in using the 'industrial economy' name for rich nations helps to maintain the myth that industry is superior to services – i.e. that the production of material goods, as opposed to ephemeral services, is the only true source of wealth and jobs. Given that service accounts for two-thirds of jobs in the industrial economies, it might be more apt to call them the service economies. But even that would be simplistic. The service sector lumps together vastly disparate activities: from programming to policing to prostitution. The only thing services have in common is what they are not: things that you can drop on your toe. And the old division between goods and services has been blurred by information technology and corporate reorganisation. If a software program is sold as a computer disc it

counts as a manufactured good; if it is sold on-line, it is a service. Even in manufacturing, around two-thirds of jobs no longer involve making things, but are in service areas such as design, finance, advertising or marketing. Newspapers are officially counted in the manufacturing sector, yet few journalists see a factory floor.

This prompts a further question, 'do service and manufacturing operations share the same set of operations strategy issues?' The box on Nestlé and Wal-Mart illustrates some operations strategy issues which might be considered in these two different types of operation – the largest international food processing company and the largest retailer in the world. The purpose here is not to provide an exhaustive list of what operations strategy means for these two companies. Nor is it to demonstrate that their two approaches to operations strategy are identical. But it does show that broadly they do face the same issues. It is our contention that all types of business, whether service or manufacturing, can be usefully analysed in terms of a common set of objectives and decision areas (shown in **bold** in the box). These will be formally identified later in this chapter and described more fully in the next chapter. For now, it is the commonality of the categories that we are stressing.

Nestlé[5]

Founded back in 1866, Nestlé is now the world's largest food company with sales of over 70 billion Swiss Francs (CHF) per year and a market capitalisation of over CHF117 billion. Both its sales and operations are spread worldwide with about a third of sales in Europe, a third in North and South America, and a third over the rest of the world. Its worldwide operations include 522 factories and a total workforce of almost a quarter of a million people. Its food, beverage, nutrition, pet care, and cosmetics products (more than 8500 in all) are sold in more than 100 countries around the world.

Nestlé's almost obsessive attention to product quality reflects not only the company's sense of responsibility to its customers but also the damage which can easily be caused to any food company by poor product quality. It also needs to keep tight control over its operating costs, so that its prices can remain competitive. Likewise, product innovation is seen as a way of affirming its brand values. This is why Nestlé annually invests more than CHF800 million in research and development. Also, ever-increasing levels of delivery service are being demanded by its major trade customers such as Wal-Mart.

The company's **capacity** policy is influenced by the need to have plants relatively close to its markets for fast delivery and freshness. Yet to

Wal-Mart[6]

Wal-Mart is the world's largest and most successful retailer. Founded by Sam Walton in 1962 and floated on the stock market in 1970, the company now has sales in excess of $140 billion. Wal-Mart's initial strategy was simple – to open out of town stores, selling a range of household items at heavily discounted prices, in areas where there was little or no competition. Its stores, still operating with exceptionally low prices, now dominate most American towns with around 3000 stores employing over 600,000 people. Increasingly too they have a major international presence, with acquisitions in Germany, Britain, Canada, Mexico, Argentina, Brazil and China.

The company's competitive strategy is based primarily on very low prices. Next comes quality of service, with company staff (called associates) having to promise to 'put the customer first'. Prices were kept low originally through aggressive purchasing, with buyers scouring the world for low-cost suppliers. As the company has grown, however, prices have also been kept low by lean operations practices.

Many of the company's smaller stores have been replaced by high **capacity** 'Supercentres' with 170,000 to 200,000 square feet of space.

keep costs down it must also get the maximum utilisation out of its capacities and benefit from economies of scale. Recently, trade liberalisation and increasing regional economic integration have allowed the company to concentrate production in larger units supplying entire regions.

Supply network issues can be complicated by the fact that many of its customers (the large supermarkets) are also competitors, manufacturing a growing range of products under their own brands. Nevertheless, Nestlé must maintain the best possible supply service to its supermarket customers through its logistics management. Equally important are its raw material and packaging supplies, accounting for 28 per cent and 9.5 per cent of total operating costs respectively. One problem is the sometimes considerable fluctuations in the costs of raw materials. For example, in 1997 cocoa bean prices varied from 50 to 80 cents per pound, while green coffee prices varied even more dramatically between 80 and 200 cents per pound.

Nestlé spends usually in excess of CHF3 billion per year on its **process technology**. This expenditure is partly driven through the company's desire for continual product innovation, rigid adherence to health and safety standards, and the increasing costs of maintaining its environmental policy.

As far as the **development and organisation** of its resources is concerned, the requirements of its ever-changing world markets require a knowledge and respect for local values and desires. Therefore, Nestlé has made decentralisation one of its basic principles, with offices, factories and research centres throughout the world. This retention of local knowledge is also helped by Nestlé's policy of promoting from within the company where possible. Nevertheless, sharing knowledge and experience on a worldwide level is also important. To help this process the company's training centre, by the banks of Lake Geneva, organises hundreds of seminars every year.

These give economies of scale and attract customers from a wide area. Smaller pockets of demand can be mopped up through the company's smaller in-town stores.

Wal-Mart is best known for its ruthless pursuit of **supply network** efficiencies. In the 1970s the company introduced state-of-the-art automated shipping centres which cut shipping costs, and computerised stock control systems which speed up reordering and shipping processes. Its most revolutionary move was handing over some responsibility for managing the supply of its stores to its leading suppliers in each category. This cuts its own overhead and reduces the amount of stock held in the pipeline between supplier and store.

Process technology innovations include state-of-the-art store sales monitoring systems which are able to track every aspect of which products are selling where, so as to monitor consumer buying patterns as well as streamline its buying and distribution networks. The company was even amongst the first to introduce bar-code scanning technology which, in its day, improved productivity by more than 50 per cent.

As part of its **development and organisation** policies Wal-Mart says that it carries on Sam Walton's legacy of encouraging employees to contribute ideas as to how stores can be improved. There are also profit-sharing schemes and staff are encouraged to invest in the company. Wal-Mart claim that they have produced more millionaire staff than any other company through this policy. However, the company has also been criticised for being anti-union and having a 'disposable' workforce mentality. About one-third of Wal-Mart's workers in the States are temporary.

Operations strategy in non-profit organisations

We have already used terms such as *competitive advantage, markets* and *business,* all of which are usually associated with companies in the for-profit sector. The question is whether operations strategy is a concept of relevance to organisations whose purpose is not primarily to earn profits in order to make a financial return for their owners. Are the issues associated with strategically managing the operations resources of, say, an animal welfare charity, research organisation, government department, or university, the same as those in profit-making institutions? Of course most for-profit organisations do not always devise operations strategies *exclusively* to maximise profitability. For example, considerations of the unemployment impact on a local area may make a company reluctant to close a site, even in the face of a strong economic case. However, here we need to distinguish between the short and long terms. Whereas the company may not close down a site the moment it becomes unprofitable, it is unlikely to keep it open for ever in spite of mounting losses. To do so would be irresponsible to its investors. A non-profit organisation on the other hand may choose to sustain poor or negative economic returns in the long term in order to pursue other, non-economic, objectives.

The implication of this for operations strategy is that judging the attractiveness of a strategic resource option is more complex and involves a mixture of economic objectives and objectives related to the values, social, environmental, or policy objectives of the organisation. Because of this there may be a greater chance of operations decisions being made under conditions of conflicting objectives (often the economic versus the value-based). Managing such conflicts is a particular concern to the operations part of the organisation because it is at this level that they become evident. So, for example, it is the operations staff in a children's welfare department who have to face the conflict between the cost of providing extra social workers and the risk of a child not receiving adequate protection. Because of this direct connection between operations decisions and the conflicts between strategic objectives there is also a tendency for decision making to be more overtly (and rightly) political.

Not all non-profit organisations are the same. But they all have to make the same set of decisions as for-profit organisations. They need to decide their level of operating capacity, invest in technology, contract out some of their activities, devise performance measures, improve their operations performance, and so on. The vast majority of the topics covered in this treatment of operations strategy have relevance to all types of organisation, including non-profit.

Definition – part two

We should now add to the working definition of operations strategy to emphasise its inclusiveness.

> **Operations strategy is the total pattern of decisions which shape the long-term capabilities of *any type* of operation and their contribution to overall strategy.**

Requirements, resources and reconciliation

Many authors have proposed their own ideas of what constitutes an operations strategy (usually for a manufacturing audience). Several of these authors are represented in the further reading section at the end of this chapter. Their ideas and definitions differ, sometimes significantly, but three 'themes' do emerge as enjoying wide support amongst both practitioner and academic writers.

● *Market influence* – The first theme is that any operations strategy should reflect the intended market position of the organisation. Companies compete in different ways, that is, their intended market positions differ. Some may compete primarily on cost, others on the excellence of their products or services, others on high levels of customer service, others on customising their products and services to individual customer needs, and so on. The operations function must respond to this by providing the ability to perform in a manner appropriate for the intended market position of the company.

● *Resource influence* – The second theme is that the success of competitive strategy is not just a matter of selecting the 'current' market position and then 'adjusting' the operation's various resources and processes to fall in line. Operations resources are often complex to manage and have an inertia which cannot be overcome instantly in order to correspond to changes in competitive stance. More positively, the resources and processes within an operation constitute a set of *competences* or *capabilities* which is capable of being harnessed and exploited in the marketplace.

● *Vision* – The third theme is that operations strategy should provide a 'vision' (also described as the operations 'task' or 'mission') for the operation. This 'vision' may be relatively 'down to earth' in the form of a pragmatic plan which describes how products and services are produced and delivered. Alternatively, it may be expressed in the form of an abstract 'philosophy' which conceptually links strategic 'ends' with operations 'means'.

Operations strategy – market and resource perspectives

These first two themes may seem to be in conflict. How can an organisation's operations strategy be shaped by the requirements of its market position but at the same time be developing and exploiting the competences of its operations resources, so that they can play a significant part in determining that very market position? Neither idea is obviously false. The manner in which any business develops its operations resources needs to reflect how the company wants to compete in the market. But also any company would be foolish if it did not exploit any exceptional competences it may have by reflecting them in the way it positioned itself in its markets. So does market position shape operations resources, or vice versa?

   The market and resource perspectives represent different approaches to operations strategy certainly, but that does not mean that operations managers should not attempt to reconcile them. It is possible to imagine an organisation which has both a market position which is itself desirable and yet maintains this market position through the contribution of its superior operations resources capabilities. Indeed satisfying market requirements, and therefore sustaining an attractive market position, directly through operations resource capabilities, would seem to be the ultimate aim of any operations strategy. Such a reconciliation of the two ideas will not be easy, it may take time and it will be subject to constant revision as both markets and operations resources change. Nonetheless, it is at the heart of what most practitioners of operations strategy are trying to achieve.

Definition – final part

Before going on to examine these two perspectives more closely, we can include this concept of their reconciliation into the final version of our definition of operations strategy.

> Operations strategy is the total pattern of decisions which shape the long-term capabilities of any type of operation and their contribution to overall strategy, *through the reconciliation of market requirements with operations resources.*

The market perspective on operations strategy – 'outside in'

Developing an understanding of markets is usually thought of as the domain of the marketing function, whose specialists employ tools and techniques designed to access customer and consumer opinions and preferences. Indeed the activity of marketing is often partly defined as the process that 'identifies and anticipates' customer requirements.[7] The main approach it uses to do this is 'market segmentation' (see the Theory Box on market segmentation). While the marketing process should include an appreciation of how products and services are created and delivered to customers, the marketing orientation is primarily 'market facing'. Its job is to bring information about markets from outside, into the organisation. One consequence of this is that the concepts, language and, to some extent, philosophy used by the marketing function to help them understand markets are not always useful in guiding operations activities. Descriptions of market needs developed by marketing professionals usually need 'translating' before they can be used in an operations strategy analysis.

Theory Box | Market segmentation[8]

Market segmentation is primarily a way of understanding markets so as to match a company's marketing efforts to its customers' requirements. It approaches this by viewing heterogeneous markets as a collection of smaller, more homogeneous, markets. Usually this is done by assessing the needs of different groups of potential users in terms of the needs which will be satisfied by the product or service. Segmentation variables help to classify these needs, either by examining various characteristics of customers, or by classifying their responses to a particular product or service. Customer characteristic segmentation variables include such things as age, gender, family size, education, national origin, social class, and so on. Customer response segmentation variables include the benefits that customers may be looking for, brand loyalty, purchase behaviour, product or service image, and so on. The purpose of segmentation is usually to ensure that the product or service specification, its price, the way it is promoted and how it is channelled to customers are all appropriate to customer needs. However, it can also be used to identify new market opportunities and to check for any changes in a market's characteristics. Most importantly, it is the prerequisite to choosing the target market at which the company's products or services will be aimed. As such, market segmentation is central to the objective of achieving a *fit* between any organisation's strengths and the requirements of its markets.

Translating market characteristics

At the heart of most marketing-based approaches is the 'segmenting, targeting, positioning' (STP) concept. The idea is straightforward – rather than compete for the business of every possible type of customer, it is necessary to identify the most attractive parts of the market which can be served effectively. This involves dividing the market into distinct groups of customers with different needs (segmentation), measuring the attractiveness of each of these market groups or segments and deciding which ones to engage with (targeting), and deciding on a viable competitive position to adopt in each target market (positioning).[9] However, market segmentation is primarily a way of trying to understand complex markets by subjecting them to multiple dimensions of classification.

The influence of competitors

How an organisation chooses to position itself in its market will depend on how it feels it can achieve some kind of advantage over its competitors. This, of course, will depend on how its competitors have themselves adopted market positions. Although one particular segment of a market may look, in itself, attractive, the number of other companies competing in it could deter any new entrants. That is, unless a company sees itself as being able to make its products or services more attractive to customers, even in the face of the competition from other firms, it is probably not worth entering a market.

Example

For example, a garment manufacturer segmenting the market primarily by 'age' may choose to target part of the 'youth market'. It is attracted to this market partly because it is large and growing and partly because it believes that competitors have been sluggish in exploiting its potential. It plans to introduce stylish and innovative designs and promote them through celebrity endorsements. This will require an adaptive and flexible operation to keep up with the fast-changing fashion market as well as an ability to coordinate complex product launches. In this case the 'translation' logic goes something like the following:

(a) Age is a major influence on purchasing behaviour in our market.

(b) We have chosen to target the broad youth market (as opposed to more specialist niches such as youth sportswear).

(c) Competitors have been relatively conservative in this market and have not exploited the potential for a series of short-term promotions which build brand image.

(d) We can differentiate ourselves from competitors by offering fashionable styling, celebrity endorsements and attractive point-of-sale merchandising.

(e) Therefore, we need to be able to get new products to market faster than competitors, be able to introduce variants of a product range to reflect endorsement deals, change the mix of products supplied to the market as it becomes evident which colour/style combinations prove popular, and be able to coordinate the delivery of launch quantities of products and merchandising materials to a wide range of retail outlets timed to match with marketing campaigns.

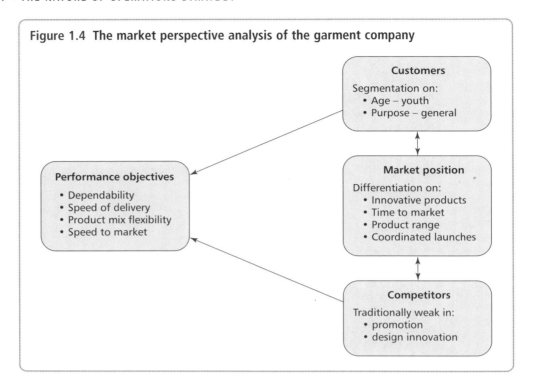

Figure 1.4 The market perspective analysis of the garment company

(f)   Operations therefore, needs to prioritise time-to-market, high product mix flexibility and volume flexibility, together with fast and dependable delivery performance.

Although these are somewhat simplified statements, they demonstrate a path of increasing specificity, with increasing meaning to the operations function of the business.

Not all businesses work through this logic in such a systematic way. Nor is it intended to be a prescription as such. It is an example, however, of how the market-operations *translation* process can work. Figure 1.4 summarises this company's analysis.

Performance objectives

The last stage of analysis in Figure 1.4 needs more explanation. This is the stage that identifies the generic *performance objectives* for the operation. That is, the aspects of operations performance that satisfy market requirements and therefore that the operation is expected to pursue. Many authors on operations (or more frequently, manufacturing) strategy have defined their own set of performance objectives. No overall agreement exists on either the terminology to use when referring to these objectives or what they are. They are referred to variously as 'performance criteria', operations 'strategic dimensions', 'performance dimensions', 'competitive priorities', 'strategic priorities'. Here, we will be using the term *performance objectives*. While there are differences between authors as to exactly what these performance dimensions are, there are some commonly used categories. Here, we will use a set of five performance objectives which have meaning for any type of operation (though obviously their relative priorities will differ). Within these five we will subsume the other dimensions. They are:

- Quality
- Speed
- Dependability
- Flexibility
- Cost

Each will be examined in more detail in Chapter 2.

Summarising the market perspective on operations strategy

We are now in a position to summarise the influence of a company's market aspirations on operations strategy. Traditionally this has been the starting point for any operations strategy analysis, primarily because it fits neatly into conventional approaches to strategic analysis which, likewise, emphasise market positioning. It is based on the following points:

- Companies make choices (implicit or explicit) as to which customers in which part of the market they wish to attract.
- Competitors partly define the competitive environment in which the company tries to attract these customers.
- A company's market position defines how it wishes to attract customers relative to their competitors.
- The operations function of any company, therefore, must devote itself to providing those aspects of performance driven by customer needs and competitor activity, which support its market position.
- Different customer needs, competitor actions, and therefore market positions, will require different types of performance from operations.
- Similarly, if a company's market position changes over time, it will likewise require its operation to change its performance objectives in order to keep market requirements aligned with operations performance.

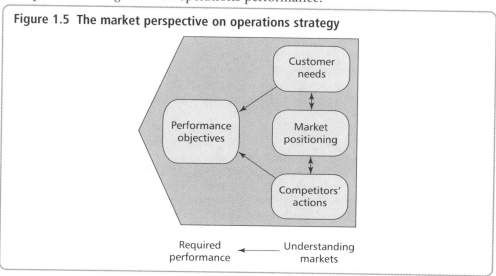

Figure 1.5 The market perspective on operations strategy

Figure 1.5 illustrates this 'outside-in' logic. The box on First Direct gives an example of one financial services business which devised its operation specifically to target one particular market.

Telephone banking with First Direct[10]

In the late 1980s and early 1990s, the financial services industry in Europe was in the middle of a period of substantial change. Competition, especially between the retail banks, was fiercer than it had ever been before. Not only were the banks busy designing new services with the intention of holding on to their existing customers and, if possible, expanding the customer base, they were also competing by reducing their prices.

'The domestic retail bank of the time was like a desert. It needed some rain to bring it back to life. Banking was believed to be a mature sector, wherein differentiation was only possible on the basis of price. This was not a sustainable means of achieving competitive advantage. Price changes were mirrored by competitors and led to price wars. Eventually all the banks ended up at equilibrium, but financially worse off . . . inertia was huge. There was a perception that all banks were the same.' (Kevin Newman, CEO, First Direct)

In 1988, a development team at Midland Bank in the UK (now part of the Hong Kong and Shanghai Banking Corporation – HSBC) wrestled with the issue of customers' deep-rooted frustration with the traditional banking system. It was given the task of creating a bank that revolved around the customer and offered outstanding service and access. Market research had shown that the traditional branch network was under threat:

● One in five people had not visited their bank in the last month.
● Fifty-one per cent said they would rather visit their branch as little as possible.
● Forty-eight per cent had never met their branch manager.
● Twenty-seven per cent wished they were able to conduct more business with the bank over the telephone.
● Eighty-five per cent of people preferred to talk to a person rather than a computer.

The results of this market research led to the conclusion that a viable market position for a bank could be achieved by the launch of a full person-to-person banking service, available over the telephone 24 hours a day, 7 days a week, 365 days a year. This concept was not new. It was first used back in 1985 by Första Sparbanken in Sweden, with a service called Första Direkt. They set up what has become a blueprint for the many followers. In order to meet the requirements of this potential market, Midland decided that they needed a totally new operation, organised and located quite separately from their existing businesses, with its own systems, culture and operations philosophy. On 1 October 1989, First Direct opened its doors for business. To emphasise the continuous nature of its service, doors were opened at one minute past midnight on a Sunday. Over ten years later First Direct has revolutionised UK banking. Not only is it profitable, many banks around the world have tried a 'me-too' copy of the operation. Its success is put down to being able to target the key aspects of performance for its market – speed ('because most people would rather be doing other things with their time'), convenience ('busy people don't want to have to pre-book appointments'), value for money and quality of service. Although a typical High Street branch can offer a wider range of services than a telephone-based system, it cannot match its access – at First Direct an average call is answered within 20 seconds at any time of the day or night. Nor can the branch network match it on cost. A telephone-based bank secures a 30–40 per cent cost advantage over High Street banks in addition to large savings in operating overheads (premises and staff). First Direct also designs its operations to minimise costs. For example, customer calls are recorded in order to keep written information down to a minimum.

First Direct's operations are centred around three large call centres in the North of England and Scotland. As time has progressed, they have become more efficient at using their capacity. A ratio of customers to staff of under 200:1 when it first opened has risen to around 300:1 ten years later. This is partly due to economies of scale but also due to its flexibility. Because of the shift patterns essential for a 24-hour business, it is important that the physical environment is as flexible as possible. Employees have moveable shelves containing stationery and paperwork which they can easily pull up to any free desk. Within its call centres, large electronic score boards flash the number of customers on hold and the time they have been waiting. In this way customer demand and staff scheduling are coordinated on a minute-by-minute basis. In addition, customers are not only a recipient of service, but also an active participant in its delivery. Wherever possible First Direct utilises the customer to save time and provide additional capacity. So, for example, new customers are given a standard joining pack which guides them through the changeover process, which they then carry out themselves, saving time and paperwork, and, again, contributing to the operation's very low costs.

First Direct were also a pioneer in the banking sector in their innovative use of information technology. The initial handling of account applications is dealt with live on screen. The system goes through credit checks and automatically dials out for a credit reference while potential customers' details are being taken. This reduces time for the operators and means that customers can be given approval (or otherwise) faster. First Direct's information systems build profiles of their customers, which allows a picture of customers' behavioural patterns to be built up over time. In this way the bank is able to target its services to customer needs. Indeed targeting markets is an underlying theme at First Direct. By developing its operations resources in such a way as to target those customers who value its low-cost, friendly, fast and constantly available services, the company has grown fast. In ten years it has taken around a million customers from its more traditional rivals and, although precise levels of profit are not disclosed, has made a significant contribution to HSBC's overall profits.

The resource perspective on operations strategy – 'inside out'

The market perspective may be seen conventionally as the domain of the marketing function, but the resource perspective lies clearly within the operations function's traditional area of responsibility. Indeed in most organisations, the majority of its resources or assets will be the direct responsibility of its operations function. It is not surprising, then, that long-term resource management is often regarded as the underlying rationale for operations strategy. What is surprising, though, is that the problem is again one of translation. The approach and terminology which are useful for understanding the properties and attributes of a firm's resources are not necessarily appropriate to clarify the nature of the decisions which shape those resources. In some ways the translation process follows the same logic as we used to describe the market perspectives. We start from a position of trying to understand 'what is there'. Here though it is not the totality of the market but the totality of the resources owned by (or available to) the operation and the way they form the operation's processes. Similarly, just as we needed to translate this broad understanding into specific and concrete performance objectives ('what we want to be able to do'), we now need to translate a broad understanding of the nature of our resources and processes into specific and concrete operations strategy decisions ('what actions we are going to take'). Once again, to achieve this translation we need a concept to bridge the gap between the sometimes fuzzy understanding of 'what is there' and the necessarily more specific 'what should we do?' stages. When considering the market perspective we used *market position* to help us translate market understanding into performance objectives. From the operations resource perspective we use the concept of *operations capabilities*.

Operations resources and processes

Conventionally, operations management theory distinguishes between *transforming* and *transformed* resources, as we mentioned earlier. Transforming resources are seen as the 'building blocks' of the operation. They can be categorised as:

- *facilities* – the 'hard' physical assets of the operation such as land, buildings, equipment and machinery, and process technology generally;
- *staff* – the human resources who operate, maintain, plan and manage the operation. (Note we use the term 'staff' to describe all the people in the operation at any level.)

Transformed resources are the inputs to the operation which are converted or transformed in some way. These are usually some mix of

- *materials*,
- *information*, and
- *customers*.

A straightforward listing of an operation's transforming and transformed resources provides only the first step in understanding the operation. It is rather like trying to describe an automobile by listing its component parts. To understand how an operation works we need to examine the interaction between its various transforming and transformed resources. For example, how different types of physical facilities, such as machines, workstations and so on, are positioned relative to each other. How the operation's staff divide their tasks between themselves. How staff and facilities are combined. Most importantly, how transformed resources flow, in some kind of sequence, through the transforming resources. These arrangements of resources constitute the *processes* of the operation. These processes are the way in which the operation actually operates. The way things happen. To return to the automobile analogy, processes are the mechanisms that power, steer and control its performance. Yet even a full technical explanation of an automobile's mechanisms does not convey either the full extent of how it performs on the road or its style, feel and 'personality'. Similarly, any view of an operation that limits itself to a description of its obvious tangible resources and processes fails to move our knowledge of the operation beyond the most basic level. Any audit of a company's resources and processes needs to include the organisation's *intangible* resources.

Intangible resources

To understand the value of the intangible resources that a company possesses, simply look to how it is valued by those who invest in it. The difference between the market value of a company and the value of its physical assets is, in part, explained by the company's intangible assets. These are the factors which may not be directly observable but are nonetheless significant in enabling any company to function. So, for example, a company's *reputation* (or in a more managed sense, its *brand*) is often of immense importance to a firm's success, yet may be difficult to define precisely. However, if a brand is closely identified with a distinguishing name, symbol, trademark or visual design, it may be valued in monetary terms, especially when a brand is sold independently of the operation's (tangible) resources. Just because a resource is intangible does not necessarily mean it cannot be traded. Other intangible resources, although having real value to a firm, are less easy to trade. They are in that sense *less tangible*.

Generally, intangible resources include such things as:

● supplier relationships, contracts and mutual understanding of how suppliers are managed;

● knowledge of, and experience in, dealing with technology sources and labour markets;

● process knowledge relating to the day-to-day production of products and services;

● new product and service development skills and procedures;

● contacts and relationships in the market which enable an understanding of market trends and more specific customer needs.

Theory Box **Valuing intangible resources[11]**

Accountants have considerable trouble when dealing with intangible resources (or invisible assets as they are sometimes called). Even the more tradeable assets such as patents, copyrights, licensing agreements and brand names can be valued as part of a company's capital in its financial accounts only under very strict conditions. Including such investments as research and development in a company's assets is generally not allowed because of the difficulty in precisely associating future benefits from the investment. Those assets which are even less tangible, such as 'knowledge' or 'intellectual capital', cannot be formally counted at all. Yet intangible assets are often the reason for a firm's success. Bill Gates, the head of Microsoft, points out that '. . . *our primary assets, which are our software and software development skills, do not show up in the balance sheet at all'*.

Investors, however, seem to be willing to place a value on intangible assets. In most stock markets around the world the gap between a company's formal 'book' value and its value on the stock market (judged by what investors are willing to pay for a share in the company) is getting wider. The 20 years up to 1993 saw a doubling of the average gap between book and market values. Table 1.1 shows some examples.

Table 1.1 **Book and market values in selected companies (market values as of 31 May 1998)**

Company	Book value $bn	Market value $bn	Market to Book value
Merck	12.6	139.9	11.1 to 1
Johnson & Johnson	12.4	92.9	7.4 to 1
DuPont	11.3	87.0	7.7 to 1
Dow Chemical	7.7	21.8	2.8 to 1

The gap between market and book value, which is at least partly explained by the extent of a company's investment in intellectual capital, is important because it is useful to be able to assess the return on investments in such intangible assets. Whereas investing in machinery

▶

uses well-tried techniques to judge return, there is more difficulty doing the same for investments in, for example, research and development, or developing employee knowledge or
training. A few organisations, such as the Swedish financial company Skandia, publish
details of their investment in intellectual capital in their financial accounts, but this is rare.
Yet in many growth industries, such as financial services, software and consulting, the
money spent on employees each year is equal to, or more than, the total capital employed
within the company.

One problem in formally counting intellectual capital as part of a company's total assets
is that much of its intellectual capital can walk out of the company's doors. For example, as
Internet companies boomed in the late 1990s, the experts, who constituted much of the
companies' value, had an inconvenient habit of leaving to start their own company or join
smaller, faster-growing outfits for more money. Disney's fledgling Internet business was
plagued by this in its early years. In parts of the financial services industry the problem was
even more severe. April 1999 saw a whole team of expert analysts decamping *en masse* from
Deutsche Bank to Goldman Sachs, carrying their precious experience and knowledge with
them in their heads.

Example

A company that produces specialist packaging for medical products uses sophisticated polymer
extrusion machines which produce heat-resistant transparent film (which is stable when heat
sterilised). It then forms the film into 'bubble packs'. All this must take place in extremely clean
conditions to conform to prescribed industry hygiene regulations. The company's experience
has enabled it to develop a knowledge of how to use its process technology in such a way as
to produce exceptionally consistent products, a key competitive factor in this industry. This
knowledge has been learned over several years of using the equipment under a wide range
of conditions. The details of how to use the process technology have been codified into an
operating manual but many of the *finer* details of how to 'tweak' the equipment are in the
heads of the small team of staff who operate the equipment. Some small changes have also
been made to the equipment itself by the company's process engineers working with the staff
who operate the process. The result of this is a manufacturing process which not only gives
consistent quality, it also produces less waste and can even maintain quality and productivity
when the equipment is switched to making different types of product. Because of these capabilities the products are successful and profitable in their market, and the company has higher
than average returns on its investments.

Consider some points from this simple example:

● A straightforward audit of the operation's tangible assets invested in its processes
would not describe adequately their contribution to competitive success. The tangible assets are the equipment and the base skills of the staff who operate the
equipment. Both of these are probably available in the open market for any competitor to buy. Behind the tangible assets, though, are a number of intangibles:
the process knowledge and experience of the operators, the experience and
expertise of the process engineers, the cooperative and productive relationship
between the process engineers and the operators, and the minor adjustments
made to the equipment itself.

● The real value of the operation's intangible assets may be much greater than those
of its tangible assets. It is the intangible assets here which are directly responsible
for the company's competitive advantage. Yet their formal worth is unlikely to be

reflected on the company's balance sheet. (The modification to the equipment may even have reduced its resale value!)

- All of these intangible assets are *firm specific*. That is, they are a function of how that particular firm's operations have developed under their own circumstances. They are not freely available for competitors to buy.

- The intangible assets were *developed over time*. They were a result, not of a dramatic change in direction, but of long experience and a process of *learning*. Put another way, in the development of operations processes, history matters.[12] The current competitive advantage enjoyed by the company is a result of a stream of learning and accumulated knowledge over time.

- The real power of these intangible resources is only realised when several streams of learning are brought together in a coordinated manner. So, for example, the modifications to the equipment may not reach their full value (even with the operating manual) unless they are combined with the intrinsic skills of the operators. The process knowledge of the process engineers will only be effective when combined with the creative relationship which has been developed between themselves and the process operators, and so on.

Processes and routines

Notice how many of the issues concerning intangible assets involve not so much what an operation *has* but what it *does*. In other words, it is when the resource 'building blocks' are arranged into processes that their full potential starts to be realised. However, to appreciate an operation fully it is necessary to define its processes in as wide a manner as possible and include both formal and informal processes. All operations have documented procedures to formalise their regular activities, such as 'generating orders', 'fulfilling orders', 'developing new products and services', and so on. But they also have ways of getting things done which are less formally documented. For example, the formal process for designing new financial services in a retail bank may involve formal consultation with the bank's Information Technology group at a particular stage in the process. Over the years, however, the service designers may have adapted the practice of talking with the Information Technology staff informally before they start the formal new service design process. Indeed there is a whole network of relationships between the service designers and other parts of the bank. The effectiveness of these informal practices depends on the relationships between individual staff, shared values and understandings of the bank's overall objectives, a wealth of tacit (non-articulated) knowledge accumulated by individuals, an understanding of 'who knows what' and 'who can get things done', and so on. To capture fully the nature and nuances of this informal process is beyond any simple process analysis.

Yet it is these informal arrangements of a company's resources that go a long way to explaining the effectiveness of its operations. Not that the formal processes are unimportant. It is the combination of formal and informal processes, explicit and tacit knowledge, the intrinsic attributes of the company's resources and the way in which these resources are deployed that describes an operation's abilities. The collective term for both formal and informal processes is the *routines* of the firm. The concepts of *intangible* (or invisible) resources and of *routines* are central to what is sometimes called the 'resource-based view' of strategic management (see the Theory

Box on the resource-based view of the firm). This view is particularly important in operations strategy because it highlights how many of a firm's intangible resources are embedded in its routines. And the management of most of the value-adding processes and routines, as we noted earlier, is the prime task of operations management. The resource-based view also allows us to make the link between an organisation's resources and processes and its *capabilities*.

Theory Box Resource-based view of the firm

Although it is now one of the most influential current theories in operations (and business) strategy, the resource-based view (RBV) of the firm has its origins in early economic theory. Some of the initial works in strategic management also included consideration of the firm's internal resources.[13] The 'SWOT' (strengths/weaknesses, opportunities, threats) approach saw competitive advantage as exploiting the opportunities raised in the competitive environment using the firm's strengths, while neutralising external threats and avoiding being trapped by internal weaknesses. While one school of thought, the 'environmental' school, focused on a firm's opportunities and threats, the other, the 'resource based', focused on firm's strengths.[14] Each school is grounded on different economic theories. The environmental approach adopted neo-classical economics, and more specifically industrial organisations (IO) theory,[15] whereas the resource-based theory has many similarities to the 'Austrian school', which stresses the importance of entrepreneurship, and behavioural economics.

The two schools of thought differ in the way they explain why some companies outperform others over time – what strategists call a 'sustainable competitive advantage' (SCA). Through the 1970s and 80s, the dominant school, the environmental school, saw a firm's performance as being closely related to the industrial structure of its markets. In this view, key strategic tasks centred on competitive positioning within industrial sectors. This firm itself is seen as an allocater of resources between different product-market opportunities. The implication of this is that a firm should analyse the forces present within the environment in order to assess the profit potential of the industry, and then design a strategy that aligns the firm to the environment. The 'resource-based' explanation of why some companies manage to gain sustainable competitive advantage, by contrast, focuses on the role of the resources which are (largely) internal to the company's operations. Put simply, 'above average' performance is more likely to be the result of the *core capabilities* (or competences) inherent in a firm's resources than its competitive positioning in its industry.

The RBV also differs in its approach to how firms protect any competitive advantage they may have. The environmental view sees companies as seeking to protect their competitive advantage through their control of the market. For example, by creating *barriers to entry* through product differentiation, or making it difficult for customers to switch to competitors, or controlling the access to distribution channels (a major barrier to entry in gasoline retailing, for example, where oil companies own their own retail stations), and so on. By contrast, the RBV sees firms being able to protect their competitive advantage through *barriers to imitation*, that is by building up 'difficult-to-imitate' resources. Thus the resources which a firm possesses are closely linked to its ability to outperform competitors. Certain of these resources are particularly important, and can be classified as 'strategic' if they exhibit the following properties.[16]

- *They are scarce* – Unequal access to (or information about) resources can lead to their uneven distribution amongst competing firms. In this way scarce resources such as specialised production facilities, experienced engineers, proprietary software, etc. can underpin competitive advantage. So, for example, if a firm did not have good foresight (or luck) in acquiring a strategic resource when its value was not known and therefore inexpensive, it will have to acquire it when its market value has grown. The resource will have become more expensive and the returns of investing in the resource will be diminished.

- *They are imperfectly mobile* – Some resources are difficult to move out of a firm. For example, resources that were developed in-house, or are based on the experience of the company's staff, or are interconnected with the other resources in the firm, cannot be traded easily. As a result, the advantages which they create are more likely to be retained over time.

- *They are imperfectly imitable and imperfectly substitutable* – These critical dimensions help define the overall sustainability of a resource-based advantage. It is not enough only to have resources which are unique and immobile. If a competitor can copy these resources or, less predictably, replace them with alternative resources, then their value will quickly deteriorate. Again, the more the resources are connected with tacit knowledge and routines embedded within the firm, the more difficult they are for competitors to understand and to copy. By contrast some resources may be very public but yet still difficult to copy. The competitive importance of 'brand' can be largely explained through these two dimensions.

Capabilities and competences

Within operations management the 'common sense' notion that most companies consider themselves to be particularly good at some specific activities, but try to avoid head-to-head competition in others, has long been accepted. The terms *distinctive capabilities* or *distinctive competence* are used to describe those unique aspects of operations through which the firm competes. While the concept of capability or competence remains somewhat ambiguous (and the words themselves are often used interchangeably), the central idea is very close to the resource-based view of the firm, namely that externally unobservable (within-firm) factors are at least as important as observable industry market (between-firm) factors in determining competitive advantage.

It is important to be careful as to how capabilities are seen. The idea is not that developing resource-based capabilities is a substitute for sensible market positioning (even though they may be a better predictor of sustainable competitive advantage). Rather the idea is that its operations capabilities can allow a company to take up an attractive market position and can protect it from competitive threat. Many of these operations capabilities derive from the way resources are deployed to form processes, and the fit that these resulting processes have with the firm's strategy within its markets. Furthermore, the sustainability of any market advantage to which capabilities contribute will depend upon the advantage not being 'competed away' too quickly. This also depends upon the nature of the competitive environment. For example, a computer chip company, such as Intel, might, at any point in time, possess a significant capability-based performance advantage over its competitors. Yet in such a hyper-competitive market its advantage may be 'competed away' relatively quickly. Here sustainability would be measured in months rather than years. This does not mean that such competences are not worth developing. A resource-based advantage is still exceptionally valuable. It is the time-scale on which we judge 'sustainability' that is short compared with other industries.

Capabilities, then, are:

> those combinations of organisational resource and process that together underpin sustainable competitive advantage for a specific firm competing in a particular product/service market. The advantage thus conferred is based upon key processes being better than, or different from, rivals and sustainable (the duration of which is dependent upon the industry sector) because the underlying strategic resources are rare, difficult to copy, difficult to create a substitute for and difficult to move.

The boxed example on South African Breweries gives an example of a company whose market strategy is at least partly dictated by its acquired capabilities.

South African Breweries (SAB)[17]

The business of producing and distributing consumer products such as food, drink and household items has become increasingly consolidated, with a handful of companies taking most of the world market. So, for example, the top four soft drink companies together have 78 per cent of the world market (Coca-Cola alone accounts for a massive 50 per cent). The surprising exception is the beer industry where the top four companies still have only 20 per cent of the world market. Even then, the largest, Anheuser-Busch, sells 85 per cent of its beers in the USA, its home market. Several factors explain this. Beer used to have a relatively short shelf life and has a low value to weight ratio, so is relatively expensive to transport long distances. Also, consumers have different tastes around the world. Notwithstanding a few global premium beers, the majority of consumers prefer beers produced to local tastes. Significantly, the economies of scale in brewing are such that medium-sized breweries (0.5 to 1.0 hectolitres per year) can compete against the giants such as Brazil's Brahma Breweries 6 million decolitres per year plant.

In these conditions South African Breweries (SAB) has been thriving. Founded in 1895 in Johannesburg, it has since grown to be the world's fourth-largest brewer and third-biggest con-glomerate in Africa. As well as producing a massive 98 per cent of all the beer sold in its native South Africa, it has expanded globally, especially in the rest of sub-Saharan Africa, China, Central and Eastern Europe. Outside South Africa it operates in a total of 18 countries with 30 clear beer breweries, whose capacity totals 30.5 million hectolitres, and 22 sorghum beer (popular in many parts of Africa) breweries with 8.5 million hectolitres of capacity.

In recent years the company has expanded, not by building new capacity, but either by buying existing local companies or through joint venture partnerships, usually with the backing of the host government. Often it buys controlling stakes in newly privatised state breweries, a strategy it has used in Tanzania, Zambia, Mozambique, Hungary and China. Globally, the beer industry may not be consolidating fast but at a national level there are rarely more than a handful of companies. Typically, the top two companies share 80 per cent of a national beer market. Thus SAB can dominate a local market by acquiring underperforming, but high market share, companies and applying its highly professional operations expertise to their production, distri-bution and marketing operations.

SAB's particular competence is the ability to enter an underdeveloped but high volume market, adapt to its specific operating conditions, and quickly develop world-class operations standards, low-cost facilities and efficient distribution networks. Furthermore, it can achieve these charac-teristics of developed-country brewing in developing-country conditions. SAB has not tried to muscle-in on developed Western European markets. Rather it concentrates on doing what others find difficult – overcoming poor infrastructure, unreliable communications, sometimes less than helpful officialdom, natural disasters, labour unrest, even political revolutions. Although the specific problems in each country may be different, the skills and procedures which the company has developed on the back of its experience have helped it to move quickly down the learning curve at each new acquisition. Its expertise lies in adapting its operations to suit local economic and cultural conditions. Even before it enters a new market SAB sends in both technical and marketing/distribution teams. Local managers are trained at SAB's training institute and considerable effort is put into capturing the learning its expatriate and local managers gain at each new acquisition. So, for example, Hungary acts as a hub of knowledge and expertise for developing the company's new Central European operations until they reach the SAB standards of quality and operating efficiency. Should difficulties arise (not unknown in such unpredictable markets) the company has SWAT teams of technical specialists it can send in. Even so, the business is inevitably risky. The collapse of the Russian economy in 1998, and the resulting squeeze on profit margins, caused the company to write down its beer-making assets in Russia from $85 million to $15 million before they had even started production.

Dynamic capabilities

Resource-based capabilities can provide a robust defence against competitive attack and protect existing competitive advantages. However, any approach exclusively based around defensive barriers to imitation will offer only a static view of a company's operations strategy. Any assessment of *sustainable* competitive advantage will include these barriers to imitation, but must also explore the dynamic efforts a firm makes to improve what it currently does well on a continuous basis and how it intends to innovate for the future. The underlying mechanisms that allow a firm to build up advantage from the way it changes what it 'has' and what it 'does' are called *dynamic capabilities*.[18] Dynamic capabilities will be built up from the firm's resources and processes, and be mediated by external market influences. Crucially, however, the development and application of capabilities will be driven by how managers make judgements about the firm and its future. The practical problem is that a firm's capabilities are often not obvious; they are 'hidden' deep within its organisational processes and composed of tacit components such as skills and experience. Managers sometimes may find it difficult to identify or articulate exactly why the firm is able to reconfigure its capabilities over time.

Example

The original business of a small theatre lighting company was devoted to designing lighting arrangements for theatrical and entertainment events. The company could also supply any specialist lighting equipment that was necessary. Soon they realised that there was considerable potential to hire equipment independently of their lighting design service. Soon the hire business, which specialised in technically advanced lighting, sound and control equipment, was larger than the original lighting design business. As it grew, its customer base shifted to include commercial companies who needed equipment (and often lighting designs) for sales promotion events, conferences, displays and exhibitions. The company's history and experience of advising theatrical producers allowed them to understand how to translate someone else's vision into theatrical reality. Furthermore, their lighting and sound technicians were experienced at re-programming equipment and configuring equipment to fit almost any concept their clients wanted. These skills, combined with an intimate network of contracts with equipment and software suppliers, enabled the company to outperform competitors and eventually dominate this (for them) new market. In order to maintain its competitive advantage it opens new sites in a number of locations where existing and potential customers are located, all of which have a resident lighting and sound design expert. The company also developed a virtual reality simulation which helped demonstrate to potential customers how a set might look. This simulation was developed in consultation with key equipment suppliers, to utilise their expertise. In order to make all equipment readily available at all sites it installed a computer-based equipment tracking and scheduling system which was integrated across all sites. The company also organised periodic 'state of play' conferences where all staff discussed their experiences of serving clients. Some suppliers and customers were invited to these meetings.

Consider this example and how its resources have helped it to compete so effectively. It has gone through a set of experiences which has enabled it to 'translate' an understanding of its resources to a set of operations strategy decisions. The translation logic goes something like this.

(a) We have a set of equipment which is sophisticated and useful in the theatre lighting business.

(b) We also have some staff who have sound and lighting design expertise.

(c) As a company we have developed a reputation for being able to take a theatre director's 'vision' for a production, and using our knowledge of available equipment, make it reality or even improve on the original vision.

(d) What allows us to do this so well is the way we have 'grown up together' and are able to understand all the stages of satisfying customers, from an understanding

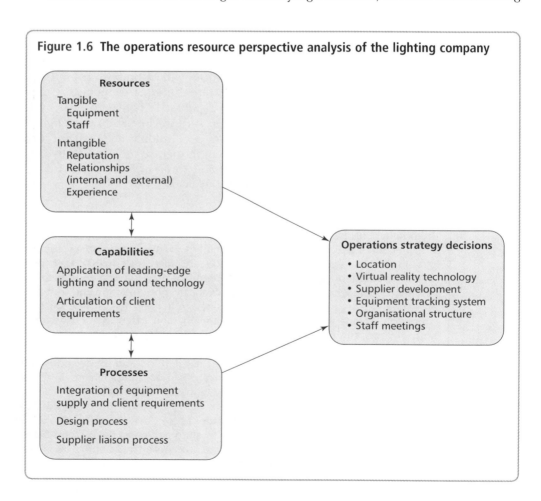

Figure 1.6 The operations resource perspective analysis of the lighting company

Resources

Tangible
 Equipment
 Staff

Intangible
 Reputation
 Relationships
 (internal and external)
 Experience

Capabilities

Application of leading-edge lighting and sound technology

Articulation of client requirements

Processes

Integration of equipment supply and client requirements

Design process

Supplier liaison process

Operations strategy decisions

• Location
• Virtual reality technology
• Supplier development
• Equipment tracking system
• Organisational structure
• Staff meetings

of what equipment is available right through to managing the design, installation, operating and dismantling of the production.

(e) This combination of an ability to handle and adapt novel and sophisticated equipment, together with well-developed client relations skills and the integration of these processes, make the company particularly attractive to commercial customers. These become the company's main market.

(f) In order to consolidate and sustain this competitive position, the company makes a number of decisions as to how its resources are to be managed.

Figure 1.6 summarises this 'resources perspective' logic for the company.

Decision areas

This last stage – the operations strategy decisions – needs some explanation. In practice, operations management attempts to influence how it operates by making decisions. Earlier we discussed how these decisions ranged from the operational to the strategic. The strategic decisions which directly (if not always exclusively) concern operations managers can be grouped together under a number of headings. Different writers on operations strategy use slightly different groupings and refer to them collectively in slightly different ways, such as operations policy areas, sub-strategies or operations tasks. We shall refer to them throughout this book as *operations strategy decisions* or *decision areas*.

The groupings of decision areas which we shall use are:

- capacity, including facilities in general;
- supply networks, including purchasing and logistics;
- process technology, which either produces, or assists the production of, products and services;
- development and organisation.

These will be more fully explained in Chapter 2.

Summarising the operations resources perspective

We can now summarise the operations resources perspective on operations strategy. Although looking at operations strategy in this way is relatively new, writers in the subject have always emphasised the centrality of resource-based decisions. Including it here in so explicit a manner could be seen as a 'rebalancing' of the subject, so as to provide a counterpoint to the traditionally dominant market perspective. Put simply, an operations resource perspective on operations strategy is based on the following points:

- A major influence on how successful any company is in its markets is the nature and characteristics of its resources (what the company has).

- The potential inherent in resources is realised largely in the way the company arranges its resources into processes (what a company does).

- Some of the most important resources a company possesses are intangible – things such as the reputation of the company in its markets, the tacit knowledge possessed by its staff, the learning embedded in its processes and the relationships within and outside its boundaries.

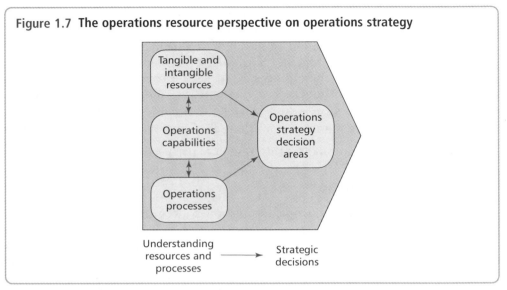

Figure 1.7 The operations resource perspective on operations strategy

● Some resources and processes are particularly influential in determining a competitive advantage (the strategic resources). Strategic resources are those which are particularly *scarce,* or cannot be *moved* out of the company, or cannot be *imitated,* or for which no *substitute* can be found.

● Strategic resources give the company a set of *core capabilities or competences* with which it can establish, excel and protect itself in its markets.

● Maintaining and improving these core capabilities is, in itself, one of the key tasks of operations management. The mechanisms by which this is done are the dynamic capabilities of the operation and are shaped by the nature of management decision making.

● In operations strategy these decisions can be grouped into those relating to capacity, supply networks, process technology, and development and organisation.

Figure 1.7 illustrates this operation resources perspective.

Bringing the two perspectives together

The two perspectives on operations strategy which we have outlined need not necessarily conflict. Nor are they 'alternative' views of how operations strategy should be formulated. Operations managers can hold both views simultaneously. They represent two starting points for understanding the nature, scope and rationale of operations strategy. Bringing both views together exposes the dilemmas inherent within the operations strategy. A company may find that its intended market position is matched exactly by the capabilities of its operations resources, the strategic decisions made by its operations managers having, over time, generated precisely the right balance of performance objectives to achieve a sustainable competitive advantage in its markets. Then again, it may not. In fact, the picture in most organisations is often not well understood and, where it is understood, the capabilities of its operations resources are unlikely to be in perfect alignment with

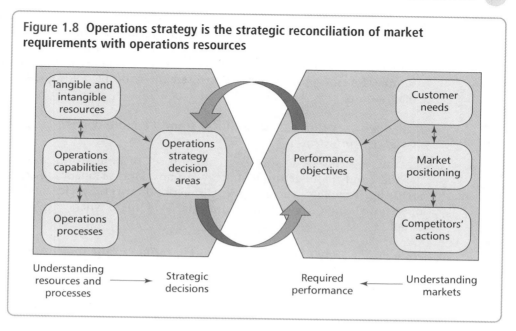

Figure 1.8 Operations strategy is the strategic reconciliation of market requirements with operations resources

the requirements of its markets. The objective of operations strategy is to attempt this alignment over time without undue risk to the organisation. Operations managers must attempt to do this through the process of reconciliation, a process which is ongoing and iterative.

Because of the complexity and uncertainty inherent in the operations resources and the dynamic nature of most markets, it is also a particularly complex and challenging process. Figure 1.8 illustrates the story so far. Chapter 2 will discuss this process of reconciliation further and the remainder of the book looks in more detail at how reconciliation can be attempted.

SUMMARY ANSWERS TO KEY QUESTIONS

What is the difference between operations management and operations strategy?

Although operations strategy is concerned with the same type of resources and issues as operations management, the perspective is different. Operations strategy operates on a longer time-scale, years rather than days or months. The level of analysis is usually higher; it is concerned primarily with the whole organisation rather than the constituent parts of the operation. Also, decisions are made with more aggregated data rather than with the detailed data used in operations management. Finally, operations strategy is concerned with a greater level of abstraction, dealing in overall concepts and approaches rather than specific localised solutions.

Does operations strategy have meaning for all kinds of organisations?

Operations strategy is the total pattern of decisions which shape the long-term capabilities of any kind of operation and their contribution to overall strategy, through the ongoing reconciliation of market requirements and operation resources. All businesses have markets, all businesses own or deploy resources, therefore all businesses are concerned with the reconciliation of markets and resources. Terminology may have to be changed for different types of operation (for example, for non-profit organisations) but the concept holds good for any kind of organisation.

How does operations strategy differ from the more conventional subject of manufacturing strategy?

It is more inclusive. It applies a common set of frameworks and concepts (often derived from manufacturing strategy) to any kind of operation, service or manufacturing. Arguably, there is less difference between service and manufacturing operations when viewed at a strategic level than when viewed in operational detail.

How do the requirements of the market influence the way operations resources are managed?

Generally the two important elements within markets are customers and competitors. The concept of market segmentation is used to identify target markets which have a clear set of requirements and where a company can differentiate itself from current, or potential, competitors. On the basis of this, the company takes up a *market position*. This market position can be characterised in terms of how the company wishes to compete for customers' business. By grouping competitive factors into clusters under the heading of generic *performance objectives* (quality, speed, dependability, flexibility and cost), market requirements are translated into a form useful for the development of the operation.

How can the intrinsic characteristics and capabilities of operations resources influence market position?

Over time, an operation may learn how to do some things particularly well. It acquires distinctive capabilities, or competences, on the basis of the accumulation of decisions and experiences taken over time. These capabilities are often embedded within a company's intangible resources and within the operating practices of its processes. That is, they concern both what the operation has and what it does. Operations shapes these capabilities (consciously or unconsciously) through the way it makes a whole series of decisions over time. These decisions can be grouped under the headings of capacity, supply network, process technology, and development and organisation. A legitimate aim of any operation's function must be to develop strategic competences which will enable the company to develop a sustainable competitive advantage in its markets.

CASE EXERCISE – What would you do?

Hagen Style

'Hagen Style' was one of the most successful direct marketing companies in Europe, selling kitchen equipment, tableware, containers, small gadgets, salad bowls and so on. Founded around forty years ago as a manufacturer of plastic kitchenware, it originally sold its products through department stores. However, soon it had evolved into a pioneering direct marketing operation which sold its products (only about half of which were now manufactured by itself) through a network of local representatives. Working from home, they were recruited to service a geographic area, usually within a one-hour drive. In total the company had almost 10,000 representatives although only around 70 per cent of them were 'active'. Representatives would sell from door-to-door or at places of work, community centres, clubs, etc. and consolidate their orders on a weekly basis. Hagen would receive their orders, pack and dispatch them so that the representatives could deliver to their customers in less than one week. Most representatives still mailed their order to Hagen using pre-printed forms and pre-paid envelopes, some faxed their orders and a growing number posted their consolidated orders by Internet. Whereas many representatives now used the Internet to place orders, most of their customers were not amongst those who would have access to, or be comfortable using, this way of placing orders. Most of Hagen Style's products were 'value' items of reasonable quality with standard rather than innovative design.

Orders were received at one of Hagen Style's two distribution centres (staggered through the week so as to smooth demand on the centres). Both centres, one in Dortmund near the company's head office, the other, just outside Munich, used the same processes, perfected over many years. First, the representatives' orders were keyed in to the company's information system (or checked if they came through the Internet, as mistakes by representatives were still common using this medium). This information was fed down to the warehouse where each representative's order (usually containing 20 to 50 individual items) was packed. Much of the packing process was standardised and automatic. A standard-sized box was automatically loaded on a moving belt conveyor and, as it proceeded down the belt, automatic dispensers, each loaded with one of the higher selling products, deposited items in the box. At the end of the belt, if an order was complete, as around 45 per cent were, the box would be automatically check weighed (to ensure that no items had missed the box), the delivery note inserted, filler put in the box to prevent damage in transit, sealed, and addressed. Those boxes which needed additional items packing (usually these were less popular or large items which would not fit the automatic dispensers) were automatically routed on to a manual line where operators would complete the packing process. At the end of the packing lines were the loading bays where boxes would be loaded onto the trucks for their journey to the representatives. The packing sequence fed down to the warehouse was calculated so as to ensure that all boxes for a certain area arrived at the correct loading bay just in time for dispatch on the correct truck.

Kurt Meyer, Hagen Style's vice president of distribution, was proud of his distribution centres:

'It is no exaggeration to say that we run one of the slickest order fulfilment operations in the world. Years of investment and improvement have gone into perfecting it.

Certainly industry benchmarking studies show that we are significantly superior to similar operations. We have lower costs per order, far fewer packing errors, and faster throughput times from order receipt to dispatch. Our information system, transportation and warehouse people have together created a great system. Our main problem is that the operation was designed for high volumes but the direct marketing business using representatives is, in general, on a slow but steady decline.'

Kurt's anxiety over future business was shared by all the company's management. Direct selling using door-to-door representatives was regarded as an old-fashioned market channel. Traditional customers were moving towards using catalogues, TV shopping channels, or just buying from supermarkets and discount stores, most of which now stocked the type of products in which Hagen Style specialised. Recently even Hagen Style, bowing to the inevitable, had started selling a limited range of its products through selected discount stores and was planning to sell through a catalogue operation. It reckoned that it could maintain, or even improve, its product margins selling through these channels. The problem was how to distribute their products to these new channels. Should they modify their existing fulfilment operation or subcontract the business to specialist carriers? And what would happen to their distribution centres?

This posed a problem for Kurt:

'Although our system is great at what it does, the downside is that it would find it difficult to cope with very different types of order. Moving into the catalogue business will mean dealing with a far greater number of individual customers, each of whom will place relatively small orders for one or two items. Our IT systems, packing lines, and dispatch arrangements are not designed to cope with that kind of order. We would have the opposite problem delivering to discount stores. There, relatively few customers would place large orders for a relatively narrow range of products. As far as I am concerned, it would be better to concentrate on what we know. For example, I have been talking with Lafage Cosmetics who sell their products in a very similar way to our traditional business. They have always been envious of our fulfilment operation and have indicated that they would be willing to subcontract most of their order fulfilment to us. I am sure we could still get profitable business by utilising our distribution skills for the substantial number of companies who still need our kind of service.'

Further reading

Hamel, G. and C.K. Prahalad (1994) *Competing for the Future*, Harvard Business School Press.

Hayes, R.H. and G. Pisano (1994) 'Beyond world class: The new manufacturing strategy', *Harvard Business Review*, January–February.

Hayes, R.H. and S.C. Wheelwright (1984) *Restoring Our Competitive Edge: Competing through manufacturing*, Wiley.

Hayes, R.H., G.P. Pisano and D.M. Upton (1996) *Strategic Operations: competing through capabilities: text and cases*, The Free Press.

Hayes, R.H., S.C. Wheelwright and K.B. Clark (1988) *Dynamic Manufacturing: Creating the learning organisation*, The Free Press.

Hill, T. (1993) *Manufacturing Strategy: the strategic management of the manufacturing function*, 2nd edn, Macmillan.

Kay, J. (1993) *Foundations of Corporate Success*, Oxford University Press.

Mintzberg, H. and J. Quinn (1990) *The Strategy Process, Concepts, Contexts, and Cases*, Prentice Hall.

Nelson, R.R. (1991) 'Why do firms differ, and how does it matter?', *Strategic Management Journal*, Vol. 12.

Peteraf, M. (1993) 'The cornerstones of competitive advantage: a resource-based view', *Strategic Management Journal*, Vol. 14.

Porter, M.E. (1985) *Competitive Advantage: Creating and sustaining superior performance*, The Free Press.

Prahalad, C.K. and G. Hamel (1990) 'The core competence of the corporation', *Harvard Business Review*, May–June.

Skinner, W. (1978) *Manufacturing in the Corporate Strategy*, Wiley.

Stalk, G., P. Evans and L. Shulman (1992) 'Competing on capabilities: the new rules of corporate strategy', *Harvard Business Review*, March–April.

Voss, C.A. (ed.) (1992) *Manufacturing Strategy – Process and Content*, Chapman and Hall.

Wernerfelt, B. (1984) 'A resource-based theory of the firm', *Strategic Management Journal*, No. 5.

Whittington, R. (1993) *What is Strategy – and Does It Matter?*, Routledge.

Notes on the chapter

1 *The Economist*, 22 March 1997.

2 In some organisations the operations manager could be called by some other name. For example, he or she might be called the 'fleet manager' in a distribution company, or the 'administrative manager' in a hospital, or the 'store manager' in a supermarket.

3 Singapore Airlines published information, including web site. 'Singapore Airlines keeps its lead', *Asian Wall Street Journal*, 12 November 1997. Lewis, P. (1997) 'SIA Ponders', *Flight International*, 26 March; Chen, Yung-hang (1999) 'Singapore Airlines', Internal report, Warwick Business School.

4 'Name calling and its perils', *The Economist*, 6 May 1995.

5 Nestlé published information, including www.nestlé.com.

6 Sources: Company reports and Benoit, B. (2000) 'Wal-Mart finds German failure hard to swallow', *Financial Times*, 12 October.

7 Leverick, F., quoting the Chartered Institute of Marketing definition, in *The Concise Blackwell Encyclopedia of Management*, entry on 'Marketing', Cooper, C.L. and Argyris C. (eds), 1998.

8 Kotler, P. (1991) *Marketing Management*, 7th edn, Prentice-Hall International.

9 Kotler, P., op. cit.

10 Sources: *Financial Times*, 'Banking on the phone for free', 8 November 1997; First Direct, 'Nutshell – a guide to an innovative bank', 2001.

11 See Bantis, N., N.C. Dragonetti, K. Jacobsen, and G. Roos, (1999) 'The Knowledge toolbox: a review of tools available to measure and manage tangible resources', *European Management Journal*, Vol. 17, No. 4.

12 Teece, D. (1982) 'Towards an economic theory of the multiproduct firm', *Journal of Economic Behavior and Organization*, Vol. 3.

13 Learned, E.C., C. Christensen, K. Andrews, and W. Guth, (1969) *Business Policy: Text and Cases*, Irwin, Homewood IL.

14 Penrose, E. (1959) *The Theory of the Growth of the Firm*, Blackwell, Oxford.

15 Bain, J.S. (1968) *Industrial Organization*, Wiley, New York.

16 Barney, J. (1991) 'The resource-based model of the firm: Origins, implications and prospects; and firm resources and competitive advantage', *Journal of Management*, Vol. 17, No. 1.

17 Sources: Company information; Maitland, A. (2000) 'A troubled history is no small beer', *Financial Times*, 19 December.

18 See Teece, D.J. and Pisano, G. (1994) 'The dynamic capabilities of firms: an introduction', *Industrial and Corporate Change*, Vol. 3, No. 3.

The content and process of operations strategy

Introduction

In the first chapter of the book we defined what *we* mean by the two perspectives which constitute the twin forces on operations strategy, namely market requirements and operations resources. We also introduced some of the practical and theoretical issues raised when the strategic role of operations is considered. In this chapter we shall focus on two aspects of reconciliation between market requirements and operations resources. These are what have become known as the *content* and the *process* of operations strategy. 'Content' means the collection of decisions which are made (deliberately or by default) within the operations strategy domain. In effect these are the *elements* of operations strategy with which the reconciliation process is concerned. 'Process' means the way in which operations strategies are (or can be) formulated. It is a reflection both of what operations managers *should do* and what they *actually do* in practice. It is important to establish these two concepts of content and process at this stage because they have dictated the overall structure of this book. Part 2 is directed entirely to content issues, while Part 3 is concerned with issues of process.

Figure 2.1 restates our overall model of operations strategy with the areas which will be examined in this chapter shaded.

Figure 2.1 Topics in operations strategy treated in this chapter

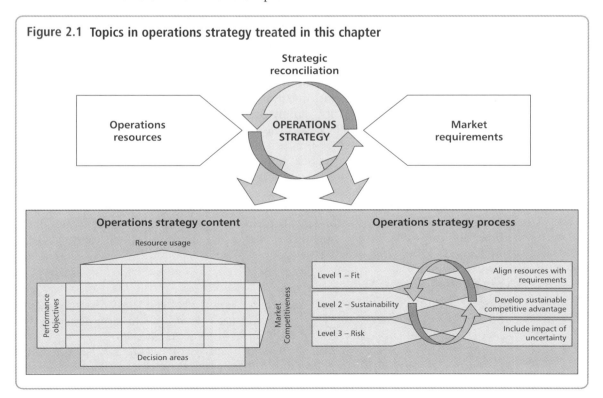

Requirements, resources and reconciliation

Operations strategy is the attempt to *reconcile* the *requirements* of the market with the operations' underlying *resources*. This is actually a very complex interaction. Partly the complexity lies in the difficulty most organisations have in clarifying either the nature of market requirements or the characteristics of their operations resources. Sometimes this is simply because not enough effort is put into clarifying their intended markets. Some operations strategies are formulated without the context of a well-understood market and/or business strategy. But, even in better-managed companies, market requirements may be unclear. For example, a company may compete in many different markets which exhibit sometimes subtle, but nevertheless important, differences in their requirements. Furthermore, markets are dynamic. Neither customers nor competitors are totally predictable. Customer behaviour may change for reasons which become clear only after the event. Competitor reaction, likewise, can be unpredictable and sometimes irrational. Above all, it is important to understand that the links between customers, competitors and market positioning are not always obvious. Market positioning is not an exact science and the strategic reconciliation process of operations strategy may have to take place under conditions of both uncertainty and ambiguity. The operations resources side of the equation may be equally unclear. Businesses do not always know the value, abilities, or performance of their own resources and processes. Notwithstanding the popularity of the 'core competence' concept in recent years, organisations frequently find difficulty in identifying what are, could be, or should be, their core competences. More significantly, the resources and processes within the operation are not deterministically connected, like some machine where adjustments to levers of control lead inexorably to a predictable and precise change in the behaviour of the operation. The cause–effect mechanisms for most operations are, at best, only partially understood.

Content and process

In order to understand the nature of reconciliation between market requirements and operations resources, many writers on strategy draw a distinction between two sets of issues, one concerned with content, the other with process.

Content is concerned with the strategic decisions which shape and develop the long-term direction of the operation and form the 'building blocks' of an operations strategy. To determine the content of its operations strategy an operation needs to do two things:

● Decide on the nature and relative *priority of its performance objectives*. Should it concentrate on being particularly good at quality or speed or dependability or flexibility or keeping cost down, or some combination of two or more of these?

● Decide on the policies and plans which determine the overall approach it wishes to adopt for the *specific decision areas* of the operation.

The *process* of operations strategy refers to the procedures which are, or can be, used to formulate those operations strategies which the organisation should adopt. Process determines how an operation pursues the reconciliation between its market requirements and operations resources in practice. Several methods of devising operations strategies have been suggested. Most consultancy companies have developed their own frameworks, as have several academics.

The first, and largest part of this chapter, introduces the *content* of operations strategy, while the second introduces issues concerned with the operations strategy *process*.

A word of warning is appropriate here, though. There is, in reality, significant overlap between content and process. As we shall see later in this chapter, part of the 'content' of operations strategy is concerned with the organisational structure and responsibility relationships within the operations function, as well as the development of the operation's approach to performance measurement and improvement. Yet each of these issues has a direct impact on how the organisation formulates its own operations strategies, that is, its operations strategy process. Furthermore, the exact nature of the process of strategy formulation adopted by any organisation will depend on which of the 'content' decision areas is deemed particularly important. Nevertheless, despite the overlap, it is conventional to treat content and process separately. More importantly it allows us to examine the set of issues associated with each in a logical manner.

Content – performance objectives

Let us remind ourselves of what performance objectives are. They are the dimensions of an operation's performance, with which it will attempt to satisfy market requirements. Their purpose is to articulate market requirements in a way that will be useful to operations. However, before we can pursue the idea of performance objectives further we must take a step back in order to consider market positioning and how *competitive factors* are used to describe positioning.

Competitive factors

A company may try to articulate its position in the market in a number of ways. It might compare itself with a competitor, for example 'We wish to offer a wider range of products than Gap, but not be as expensive as Donna Karan'. Alternatively they might associate themselves with the needs of a particular customer group. For example, 'We wish to provide a level of service and attention which discerning business people expect when they stay at our hotels'. Either way,

Table 2.1 Competitive factors for two operations grouped under their generic performance objectives

Mortgage services *Associated competitive factors include . . .*	Performance objectives	Steel plant *Associated competitive factors include . . .*
● Professionalism of staff ● Friendliness of staff ● Accuracy of information ● Ability to change details in future	**Quality**	● Percentage of products conforming to their specification ● Absolute specification or products ● Usefulness of technical advice
● Time for call centre to respond ● Prompt advice response ● Fast loan decisions ● Fast availability of funds	**Speed**	● Lead-time from enquiry to quotation ● Lead-time from order to delivery ● Lead-time for technical advice
● Reliability of original promise date ● Customers kept informed	**Dependability**	● Percentage of deliveries 'on time, in full' ● Customers kept informed of delivery dates
● Customisation of terms, such as duration/life of offer ● Cope with changes in circumstances, such as level of demand	**Flexibility**	● Range of sizes, gauges, coatings etc. possible ● Rate of new product introduction ● Ability to change quantity, composition and timing of an order
● Interest rate charged ● Arrangement charges ● Insurance charges	**Cost**	● Price of products ● Price of technical advice ● Discounts available ● Payment terms

they finish up defining market position in terms of a number of dimensions, for example range, price, quality of service, etc. These dimensions on which a company wishes to compete are called *competitive factors*. Different words will be used for different types of operation and their relative importance will change depending on how the company wishes to compete. Nevertheless, their common characteristic is that they describe the things that a customer can see or experience. Table 2.1 illustrates this idea for two contrasting operations. This clusters the competitive factors for each operation into the five generic performance objectives which they represent.

It is worth making a few points about how we are using this idea of performance objectives:

● First, note that the two operations we have used as examples in Table 2.1 have a different view of each of the performance objectives. So, for example, the mortgage service sees quality as being at least as much about the manner in which their customers relate to their service as it does about the absence of technical errors. The steel plant, on the other hand, while not ignoring quality of service, primarily emphasises product-related technical issues. Different operations will see quality (or any other performance objective) in different ways, and emphasise different aspects. Broadly speaking though, they are selecting from the same pool of factors which together constitute the generic performance objective, in this case 'quality'.

● Each of the performance objectives represents a cluster of competitive factors grouped together for convenience. Sometimes operations may choose to re-bundle, using slightly different headings. For example, it is not uncommon in some service operations to refer to 'quality of service' as representing all the competitive factors we have listed under quality *and* speed *and* dependability. In practice, the issue is not so much one of universal definition but rather consistency within one, or a group of operations. At the very least it is important that individual companies have it clear in their own minds what list of generic performance objectives is appropriate to their business, what competitive factors each represents, and how each competitive factor is to be defined.

● Cost is different from the other performance objectives. While most competitive factors are clear manifestations of their performance objectives, the competitive factors of *price* are related to the *cost* performance objective. So, an improvement in cost performance does not necessarily mean a reduction in the price charged to customers. Firms who achieve lower costs may choose to take some, or all, of the improvement in higher margins rather than reduce prices.

Performance objectives

It is worth examining each of the five performance objectives in a little more detail. Not to present any precise definitions, but rather to illustrate how the terms, quality, speed, dependability, flexibility and cost, may be used to mean slightly different things depending on how they are interpreted in different operations.

Quality

Many definitions of quality refer to the 'specification' of a product or service, usually meaning *high specification*; as in 'the Mercedes-Benz S Class is at the quality end of the market . . .'. Quality can also mean *appropriate specification*; meaning that the products and services are 'fit for purpose', they do what they are supposed to do. 'Fit for purpose' quality includes two concepts which are far more usefully treated separately. One is the level of the product or services *specification*, the other is whether the operation achieves *conformance* to that specification.

Specification quality is also a multidimensional issue. We needed to use several aspects of specification in the automobile example above, even to reach a crude indication of what type of car is being produced. So any product or service needs to use several dimensions of specification to define its nature. These dimensions can be separated into 'hard' and 'soft' aspects of specification quality. Hard dimensions are those concerned with the evident and largely objective aspects of the product or service. Soft dimensions are associated with aspects of personal interaction between customers and the product (or more usually) service. Table 2.2 identifies some hard and soft dimensions of specification quality, though each list will change depending on the type of product or service being considered.[1]

Conformance quality is more a concern of the operation itself. It refers to the operation's ability to produce goods and services to their defined specification reliably and consistently. This is not always a simple matter of yes it can, or no it cannot.

Table 2.2 Examples of hard and soft dimensions of specification quality

'Hard' dimensions of specification quality	*'Soft' dimensions of specification quality*
e.g.	e.g.
● Features	● Helpfulness
● Performance	● Attentiveness
● Reliability	● Communication
● Aesthetics	● Friendliness
● Security/safety	● Courtesy
● Integrity	
Etc.	Etc.

Rather the issue is often a matter of how closely the operation can achieve the product or service specification consistently. Here there is a difference between hard and soft dimensions of specification. Generally the conformance to soft dimensions of quality is more difficult to measure and more difficult to achieve. This is largely because soft dimensions, being related to interpersonal interaction, depend on the response of individual customers relating with individual staff.

Speed

At its most basic, speed indicates the time between the beginning of an operations process and its end. It is an elapsed time. This may relate to externally obvious events; for example, from the time when the customer requests a product or service, to the time when the customer receives it. Or it may be used internally in the operation; for example, the time between when material enters an operation and when it leaves fully processed. As far as operations strategy is concerned we are usually interested in the former. Part of this elapsed time may be the actual time to 'produce the product or service' (the 'core' processing time). It may also include the time to clarify a customer's exact needs (for example, designing a product or service), the 'queuing' time before operations resources become available, and after the core processing, the time to deliver, transport and/or install the product or service. Figure 2.2 illustrates some of the significant 'process' times which signify the steps in customer response for two operations – a hospital and a software producer. One issue for these organisations' operations is how to define the speed of delivery. Clearly, limiting it to the elapsed time taken by the core process (though this is the part they can most directly control) is inadequate. From the customers' view the total process starts when they become aware that they may need the product or service and ends when they are completely satisfied with its 'installation'. Some may even argue that, given the need continually to engage the customer in other revenue-generating activities such as maintenance or improvement, the process never ends.

Dependability

The term dependability here is used to mean keeping delivery promises – honouring the delivery time given to the customer. It is the other half of total delivery performance along with delivery speed. The two performance objectives are often linked in some way. For example, theoretically, one could achieve high dependability merely by quoting long delivery times. In which case the difference between the expected delivery time and the time quoted to the customer is being used as an

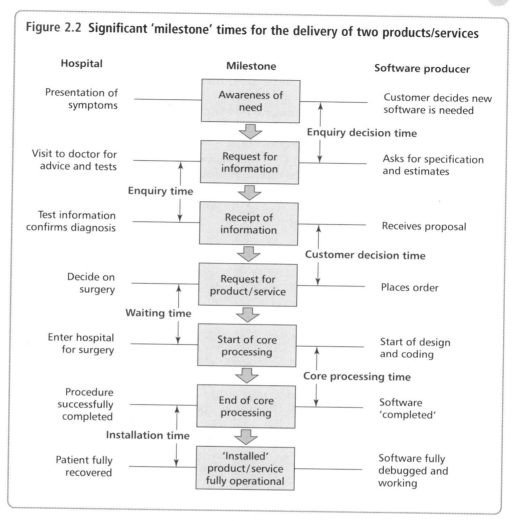

Figure 2.2 Significant 'milestone' times for the delivery of two products/services

insurance against lack of dependability within the operation. However, companies that try to absorb poor dependability inside long lead-times can finish up being poor at both. There are two reasons for this. First, delivery times tend to expand to fill the time available. Attempting to discipline an operation to achieve delivery in two weeks when three are available is unambitious and allows the operation to relax its efforts to use all the available time. Second, long delivery times are often a result of slow internal response, high work-in-progress, and large amounts of non-value-added time. All of these can cause confusion, complexity and lack of control, which are the root causes of poor dependability. Good dependability can often be helped by fast throughput, rather than hindered by it.

In principle, dependability is a straightforward concept:

$$\textbf{dependability} = \textbf{due delivery time} - \textbf{actual delivery time.}$$

When delivery is on time, the equation should equal zero. Positive means it is early and negative means it is late. What, though, is the meaning of 'due time'? It could be the time originally requested by the customer or the time quoted by the operation. Also, there can be a difference between the delivery time scheduled by Operations and that promised to the customer. Delivery times can also be changed, sometimes by customers, but more often by the operation. If the customer wants a new delivery time, should that be used to calculate delivery performance? Or if the operation has to reschedule delivery, should the changed delivery time be used? It is not uncommon in some circumstances to find four or five arguable due times for each order. Nor is the actual delivery time without its complications. When, for example, should the product or service be considered to have been delivered? Here we are facing a similar issue to that posed when considering speed. Delivery could be when the product or service is produced, when the customer receives it, when it is working, or when they are fully comfortable with it. Then there is the problem of what is late. Should delivery to the promised minute, hour, day, week or even month be counted as on time?

Flexibility

The word 'flexibility' means two different things. One dictionary definition has flexibility meaning the 'ability to be bent'. It is a useful concept which translates into operational terms as the ability to adopt different states – take up different positions or do different things. So one operation is more flexible than another if it can do more things – exhibit a wide *range* of abilities. For example, it might be able to produce a greater variety of products or services, or operate at different output levels. Yet the range of things an operation can do does not totally describe its flexibility. The same word is also used to mean the ease with which it can move between its possible states. An operation that moves quickly, smoothly and cheaply from doing one thing to doing another should be considered more flexible than one that can only achieve the same change at greater cost and/or organisational disruption. Both the cost and time of making a change are the 'friction' elements of flexibility. They define the *response* of the system – the condition of making the change. In fact, for most types of flexibility, time is a good indicator of cost and disruption, so response flexibility can usually be measured in terms of time.

So the first distinction to make is between *range flexibility* – *how much* the operation can be changed; and *response flexibility* – *how fast* the operation can be changed.

The next distinction is between the way we describe the flexibility of a whole operation and the flexibility of the individual resources which, together, make up the system. *Total operations flexibility* is best visualised by treating the operation as a 'black box' and considering the types of flexibility which would contribute to its competitiveness. For example:

- *product or service flexibility* – the ability to introduce and produce novel products or services or to modify existing ones;
- *mix flexibility* – the ability to change the variety of products or services being produced by the operation within a given time period;
- *volume flexibility* – the ability to change the level of the operation's aggregated output;
- *delivery flexibility* – the ability to change planned or assumed delivery dates.

Each of these types of total operations flexibility has its range and response components, described in Table 2.3.

Table 2.3 The range and response dimensions of the four types of total operations flexibility

Total operations flexibility	Range flexibility	Response flexibility
Product/service flexibility	The range of products and services which the company has the design, purchasing and operations capability to produce.	The time necessary to develop or modify the products or services and processes which produce them to the point where regular production can start.
Mix flexibility	The range of products and services which the company produces within a given time period.	The time necessary to adjust the mix of products and services being produced.
Volume flexibility	The absolute level of aggregated output which the company can achieve for a given product or service mix.	The time taken to change the aggregated level of output.
Delivery flexibility	The extent to which delivery dates can be brought forward.	The time taken to reorganise the operation so as to replan for the new delivery date.

Performance objectives at Burger King[2]

Founded by James W. McLamore and David Edgerton in 1954, Burger King is now the number two burger restaurant in the United States. With annual sales in excess of $10 billion, it has more than 8000 US and around 3000 international outlets. Over 92 per cent of these are franchised. In 1999 Burger King announced a 'transformation' of its restaurant operations. As well as a changed image, this also involved a new kitchen system and improvements to its other operations processes. The future success of Burger King relies partly, said commentators, on its ability to continue delivering excellent service through world-class operations. This means excelling in its key operations performance objectives.

● *Quality* – Burger King is proud of the quality of its food, especially its flame grilled 'Whopper'. This process, according to Paul Clayton, BK's US President, is an important point of product differentiation. 'If it's done right, the Whopper tastes better than any other burger in the marketplace.' However, achieving this result does rely on the burger being cooked as it should be. Quality is very much dependent on conformance in restaurant processes. Quality of service is also important and it will include aspects such as the cleanliness of stores, and the friendliness and helpfulness of staff.

● *Speed of service* – This is a particularly important performance objective in the restaurant sector popularly known as 'fast food'. It is especially important to Burger King because 'drive-thru' service accounts for around 50 per cent of Burger King's business, while 'take-out' business (where speed is also a key issue) represents another 15 per cent.

● *Dependability* – This refers to Burger King's reliability of service. Although hardly ever happening, if a drive-thru is closed or fries run out, customers would be understandably upset; they take the availability of the full range of services for granted. Dependability could also be taken to refer to the reliability of the whole customer experience; no matter which Burger King restaurant is visited, customers expect the same style of décor, product range, queuing and

▶

ordering arrangements. In this sector customers can come to rely on knowing how to behave inside the operation.

- *Flexibility* – This could refer to both volume and mix flexibility. For example, volume flexibility gives restaurants the ability to cope with sudden increases in demand. Mix flexibility indicates the variety of meals which can be ordered by a customer. Unlike some rivals, Burger King say that there are 1024 ways in which a customer can order the Whopper.

- *Cost* – Although Burger King does not compete by being the very cheapest in the market, it does offer value, so cost is important. This not only means the efficient use of raw materials to avoid excessive wastage, it also includes the transaction costs of providing facilities and labour to serve customers.

Cost

Cost is here treated last, not because it is the least important performance objective, but because it is the most important. To companies that compete directly on price, cost will be clearly their major performance objective. The lower the cost of producing their products and services, the lower can be the price to their customers. Yet even companies that compete on things other than price will be interested in keeping their costs low. Other things being equal, every euro, dollar or yen removed from an operation's cost base is a further euro, dollar or yen added to its profits. Not surprisingly, low cost is a universally attractive objective.

Here we are taking a broad definition of 'cost' as it applies in operations strategy. In this broad definition, cost is any financial input to the operation that enables it to produce its products and services. Conventionally, these financial inputs can be divided into three categories:

- *Operating expenditure* – the financial inputs to the operation needed to fund the ongoing production of products and services. It includes expenditure on labour, materials, rent, energy, etc. Usually the sum of all these expenditures is divided by the output from the operation (number of units produced, customers served, packages carried, etc.) to give the operation's 'unit cost'.

- *Capital expenditure* – the financial inputs to the operation that fund the acquisition of the 'facilities' which produce its products and services. It includes the money invested in land, buildings, machinery, vehicles, etc. Usually the funding for facilities is in the form of a lump sum 'outflow' investment followed by a series of smaller inflows of finance, in the form of either additional revenue or cost savings. Most methods of investment analysis are based on some form of comparison between the size, timing and risks associated with the outflow and its consequent inflows of cash.

- *Working capital* – the financial inputs needed to fund the time difference between regular outflows and inflows of cash. In most operations, payments must be made on the various types of operating expenditure which are necessary to produce goods and services before payment can be obtained from customers. Thus funds are needed to bridge the time difference between payment out and payment received. The length of this time difference, and therefore the extent of the money required to fund it, is largely influenced by two processes – the process that handles the day-to-day financial transactions of the business, and the operations process itself which produces the goods and services. The faster the financial process can get payment from customers and the more it can negotiate credit delays to its suppliers, the shorter the gap between money going out and money coming in, and the less working capital is required. Similarly, the faster the operations process can move materials through the operation, the shorter the gap between obtaining the materials and having products and services ready for sale. This argument may also apply to information processing or even customer processing operations if operating expenditure is associated with the information or customers entering and progressing through the operation process.

Internal and external effects

The whole idea of generic performance objectives is that they can be clearly related to some aspects of external market positioning, through their connection with competitive objectives, and can be clearly connected to the internal decisions which are made concerning the operations resources. Because of this, it is worthwhile examining each of the performance objectives in terms of how they affect market position outside the operation and operations resources inside the operation. Table 2.4 identifies some of these effects. What is interesting is that whereas the consequences of excellent performance outside the operation are specific and direct, the consequences inside the operation are more interdependent. So, for example, a high performance in terms of speed of delivery outside the operation gives clear benefits to

Table 2.4 Internal and external benefits of excelling at each performance objective

Operations resources *Potential internal* *benefits include ...*	*Performance objective*	*Market requirements* *Potential external* *benefits include ...*
• Error-free processes • Less disruption and complexity • More internal reliability • Lower processing costs	**Quality**	• High specification products and services • Error-free products and services • Reliable products and services
• Faster throughput times • Less queuing and/or inventory • Lower overheads • Lower processing costs	**Speed**	• Short delivery/queuing times • Fast response to requests
• Higher confidence in the operation • Fewer contingencies needed • More internal stability • Lower processing costs	**Dependability**	• On-time delivery/arrival of products and services • Knowledge of delivery times
• Better response to unpredicted events • Better response to variety of activities • Lower processing costs	**Flexibility**	• Frequent new products and services • Wide range of products and services • Volume adjustments • Delivery adjustments
• Productive processes • Higher margins	**Cost**	• Low prices

customers who value short delivery times for products or queuing times for services. If an operation competes on speed of delivery, then it will need to develop the speed objective inside its operations. Internally, fast throughput time will presumably help it to achieve short delivery times to its external customers. However, there are other benefits which may come through fast throughput times inside the operation. Materials, information or customers moving rapidly through an operation can mean less queuing, lower inventory levels, a lower need for materials, information or customers to be organised and tracked through the process. All this adds up to lower processing costs in general. This gives operations strategy one of its more intriguing paradoxes. Even if a performance objective has little value *externally* in terms of helping the company to achieve its desired market position, the operation may still value high performance in that objective because of the *internal* benefits it brings.

Market positions and priorities

If, as is likely, an operation produces goods or services for more than one customer group, it will need to determine a separate set of competitive factors, and therefore,

---

Figure 2.3 Different product groups require different performance objectives

	First/Business class	Economy class
Services	First/Business-class cabin, airport lounges, pick-up service	Economy cabin
Customers	Wealthy people, business people, VIPs	Travellers (friends and family), vacation takers, cost-sensitive business travels
Service range	Wide range, may need to be customised	Standardised
Rate of service innovation	Relatively high	Relatively low
Volume of activity	Relatively low volume	Relatively high volume
Profit margins	Medium to high	Low to medium
Main competitive factors	Customisation, extra service, comfort features, convenience	Price, acceptable service
Performance objectives	Quality (specification and conformance), Flexibility, Speed	Cost, Quality (conformance)

different priorities for the performance objectives for each group. For example, one of the most obvious differences to be found within an airline's activities is that between the operations supporting business and first-class travellers on one hand, and those supporting economy-class travellers on the other. This is shown in Figure 2.3.

Underlying this type of analysis is the pre-eminence of customers' needs (or expectations) as a guide to operations objectives. Customers' needs are rarely static, however. They will change with customers' own circumstances and they will respond to whatever products and services are available. What is regarded as acceptable performance at one point in time can be rendered inadequate by a competitor raising its own, and possibly the whole industry's, standards. Nevertheless, the main point is that an operation can define its intended market position, and therefore its competitive stance, in terms of the five performance objectives. Figure 2.4 illustrates this.

Order-winning and qualifying competitive factors

One way of determining the relative importance, or at least the different nature, of competitive factors is to distinguish between what are sometimes called 'order-winning' and 'qualifying' factors.[3] Although not a new idea, it is a particularly useful one. Different authors use different terms, so order-winners can also be called competitive edge factors, critical or primary factors, motivating factors, enhancing factors, and so on. Qualifiers sometimes go under the names hygiene factors or failure preventors.

- *Order-winning factors* are things that directly and significantly contribute to winning business. They are regarded by customers as key reasons for purchasing the product or service. They are, therefore, the most important aspects of the way a company defines its competitive stance. Raising performance in an order-winning factor will either result in more business or improve the chances of gaining more business.

- *Qualifying factors* may not be the major competitive determinants of success, but are important in another way. They are those aspects of competitiveness where the operation's performance has to be above a particular level just to be considered by the customer. Below this 'qualifying' level of performance the company probably won't even be considered by many customers. Above the 'qualifying'

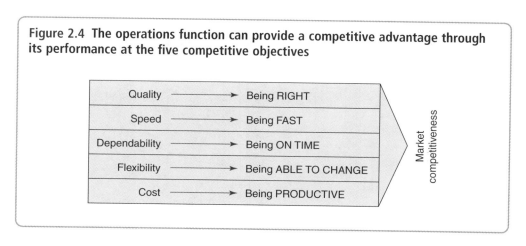

Figure 2.4 The operations function can provide a competitive advantage through its performance at the five competitive objectives

level, it will be considered, but mainly in terms of its performance in the order-winning factors. Any further improvement in qualifying factors above the qualifying level is unlikely to gain much competitive benefit.

To order-winning and qualifying factors can be added *less important factors* which are those that are neither order-winning nor qualifying. They do not influence customers in any significant way. They are worth mentioning here only because they may be significant in other parts of the operation's activities.

The benefits from order-winners and qualifiers

The distinction between order-winners and qualifiers does illustrate the important point that competitive factors differ, not only in their relative importance, but also in their nature. This is best thought of as how the competitive benefit, which is derived from a competitive factor, varies with how well an operation performs in delivering that competitive benefit. In other words, it is an indication of the benefits an operation gains by being good at different aspects of performance. Figure 2.5 shows the benefits from order-winners and qualifiers as performance levels vary. No matter how well an organisation performs at its qualifiers, it is not going to achieve high levels of competitive benefits. The best that it can usually hope for is neutrality. After all, customers expect these things, and are not going to applaud too loudly when they receive them. They are the givens. However, if the organisation does not achieve satisfactory performance with its qualifiers, it is likely to result in considerable dissatisfaction amongst customers – what in Figure 2.5 is termed as negative competitive benefit. In effect, there is a discontinuity in the benefit function. This is different from an order-winner which can achieve negative or positive competitive benefit, depending on performance, and whose benefit function is far more linear. The advantage of order-winners (and why they are called order-winners) is that high levels of performance can provide positive competitive benefit, and hence more orders. Less important objectives are similar to order-winners only in so much as

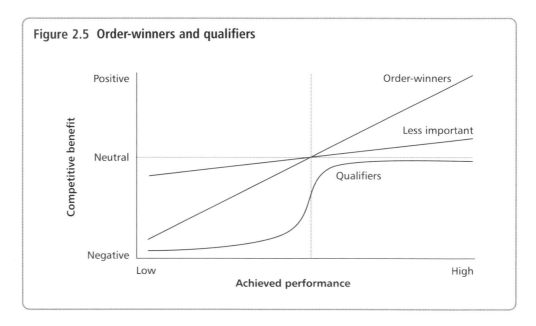

Figure 2.5 Order-winners and qualifiers

they have no discontinuity in their benefit function, but they are not as competitively significant.

Criticisms of the order-winning and qualifying concepts

Not everyone agrees with the idea of categorising competitive factors as order-winners or qualifiers. There are two major criticisms:[4]

(a) The idea of order-winners and qualifiers is based on how potential purchasers of services and products behave when considering a single transaction. Increasingly though, purchasers of both consumer and 'industrial' services and goods do not consider a single transaction but rather think in terms of longer-term relationships. Some purchasers may be willing to accept occasional lapses in performance in either order-winners or qualifiers because they wish to preserve the long-term relationship with their supplier. So the relationship itself both transcends the idea of order-winners and qualifiers and becomes the major order-winning competitive factor itself.

(b) The original interpretation of the order-winner/qualifier concept is based on considering past sales data, including the reaction of individual customers for individual orders. A more traditional, market-based, approach would treat far larger groups of customers in its segmentation procedures.

Prioritising performance objectives

Initially it may seem that the most important influence on the prioritisation of competitive factors must be the needs and expectations of customers within the target market. When we examined differences between first/business class and economy class for the airline in Figure 2.3, it was the expectation of different customer groups that defined the set of competitive factors and therefore the set of generic performance objectives on which the airline places *importance*. But there is also a further influence on prioritisation, namely the company's *performance* against its competitors. So, for example, in the case of an airline, one may (arguably) believe that price

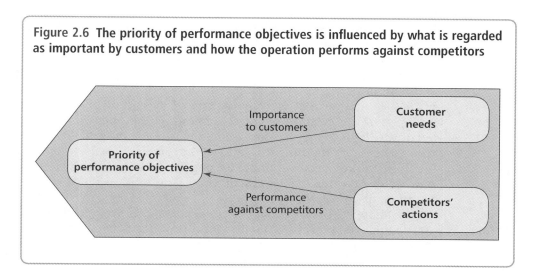

Figure 2.6 The priority of performance objectives is influenced by what is regarded as important by customers and how the operation performs against competitors

is the most important competitive factor and therefore cost the most important performance objective for economy class travel. However, it could be that an airline has a considerable cost advantage over its rivals, and it can therefore set prices well below any competitor. Its quality of service, however, may be particularly poor when compared to competitors. In terms of prioritising its performance objectives, although cost is important to customers, quality levels are poor compared with its competitors. Therefore, it would be sensible perhaps to prioritise quality. In other words, it is both the relative importance of competitive factors, as judged by *customers* in target markets, *and* the current performance of an operation, as judged against *competitor* performance, that drives priorities, the highest priority being given to competitive factors which are both important to customers and where performance is poor compared to competitors. See Figure 2.6. We shall return to this idea of prioritisation being governed by importance to customers and performance against competitors in Chapter 11.

Content – operations strategy decision areas

In Chapter 1 we identified a number of operations strategy decision areas. These were the sets of decisions which operations managers (with others) needed to take in order to manage the resources of the operation in the long term. These decision areas were identified as:

● capacity, including facilities in general;

● supply networks, including purchasing and logistics;

● technology, the process technology which produces goods and services;

● development and organisation of the operation's processes.

Such a list can be justified in terms of operations practice alone. All these decision areas will be familiar to managers in a wide variety of operations. Furthermore, although there are some differences between authors, most of those who write on operations strategy use a very similar list. Custom, practice and familiarity, therefore, dictate that we should do the same. However, it is possible to support this intuitive list of decision areas with a slightly more rigorous approach. To do this let us indulge in some simple ratio analysis.

Essentially, ratio analysis is an attempt to decompose a fundamental ratio of some element of performance into other ratios by inserting the same measure on the top and bottom of the resulting ratios. The idea is to split the fundamental ratio into other measures so that we can understand how it is built up. The best-known examples of this occur in financial accounting. Here we will do it in a slightly different way by inserting measures which have some meaning in an operations context. We are not proposing this ratio analysis as a practical analysis tool. Rather it is intended to provide some underpinning for each decision area. Figure 2.7 shows how we can do this for the fundamental ratio of profit divided by total assets, or return on assets (ROA).[5]

The simple ROA ratio, profit over total assets, is broken down into 'profit/output' and 'output/total assets'. This first ratio (in effect, average profit) can be further broken down into average revenue minus average cost. Operations affects the former through its ability to deliver superior levels of competitive performance

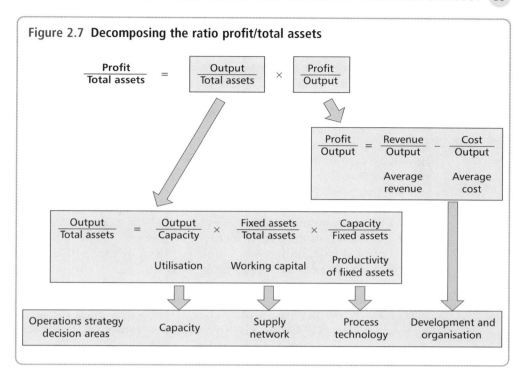

Figure 2.7 **Decomposing the ratio profit/total assets**

(better quality, speed, dependability and flexibility). It affects the latter through the more productive use of its resources (lower costs). These are the two measures which have been seen as the great operations balancing act, keeping revenue high through standards of service and competitive pricing while keeping costs low. Both are a function of an organisation's success in achieving an effective and efficient operation through its *development and organisation decisions*. These attempt to ensure that improvement and learning continually reduce costs, while the performance of products and services and its level of service to customers are continually increased.

The other part of the decomposed ROA ratio – output/total assets – represents the output being produced for the investment being put into the operation. It is shown in Figure 2.7 broken down into three ratios, 'output/capacity', 'fixed assets/total assets' and 'capacity/fixed assets'.

'Output/capacity', or the *utilisation* of the operation, is determined by the balance of demand on the operation and its long-term ability to meet that demand. To improve ROA, utilisation needs to be as close to 1 as possible. To do this, either demand must be generated to match capacity, or the operation must develop an ability to adjust its capacity to match demand. This ratio is largely a function of an organisation's *capacity decisions*. Has it managed to balance the provision of capacity with demand (output) and can it change its capacity to meet changing levels of demand?

'Fixed assets/total assets' is a ratio partially governed by the *working capital* requirements of the business. The smaller the working capital required by the operation, the closer fixed assets is to total assets. For the operations function, working capital minimisation is often a matter of reducing the inventories in its supply network, a function of an organisation's *supply network decisions*. Can the supply network maintain appropriate delivery of its products and services without carrying excessive levels of inventory?

'Capacity/fixed assets' is sometimes called *the productivity of fixed assets*. It is a measure of how much the operation has had to spend in order to acquire, or develop, its capacity. To some extent this is determined by the skill of the operation's designers and technologists. An operation that achieves the required capacity levels without needing large amounts of capital expenditure will have a better ratio than the operation that has 'thrown money at the problem'. This ratio is largely a function of an organisation's *process technology decisions*. Has it invested wisely in appropriate process technologies, which can create a sufficient volume of appropriate products and/or services, without excessive capital expenditure?

Obviously this is not a totally clean categorisation. In some way all the decision areas will have some impact on all the ratios. For example, a company's development and organisation strategy includes such issues as how improvement is encouraged, how the organisation's structure works and how performance is measured. This will affect many of these ratios. Its main focus, however, is likely to be on improving average profit, by reducing costs through operations efficiency and increasing revenue through improved operations effectiveness at delivering its products and services. All of Part 2 of this book is devoted to these decision areas. Chapter by chapter, each one will be discussed in terms of the cluster of individual decisions represented by the area, the alternatives between which choices are made, and the consequences of choice on the performance objectives. However, it is useful at this point to identify briefly the nature of each decision area.

Two important points come from this ratio analysis. The first is that the operations function can influence ROA in more ways than keeping operational costs down (although clearly this is important). Operations also influences ROA through its impact on revenue generation, volume flexibility, imaginative and economical design of the process, and tight inventory management. The second point is that we can identify the four groups of operations strategy decision areas which are most associated with each part of this interconnecting pattern of ratios:

Capacity

Capacity is usually taken to mean the ability of an operation, or business, to achieve a particular level of activity or output. This is often measured as output per unit of time. Broadly speaking, there are two sets of questions to be answered regarding capacity strategy. The first concerns how capacity should be configured across the operation. It includes questions such as 'what should be the overall level of capacity?', 'how many sites should the capacity be distributed across, and what size should they be?', 'should each site be engaged in a broad mixture of activities, or should they specialise in one or two?', 'exactly where should each site be located?', and so on. The second broad issue concerns how capacity is changed over the long term. Questions here include 'when should changes be made to overall capacity levels?', 'how big should each change in capacity be?', 'how fast should capacity expansion or reduction be pursued?', and so on.

Chapter 4 will deal with the decisions concerning capacity configuration. Chapter 5 will deal with those concerning the management of capacity change.

Supply networks

No single operation exists in isolation. All are part of an interconnected network of other operations, including customers, customers' customers, suppliers, suppliers' suppliers, distribution operations, and so on. All operations need to consider their position in this network, both to understand how the dynamic forces within the network will affect them, and to decide what role they wish to play in the network. We can divide supply network issues into two groups. The first is concerned with the behaviour of whole networks and how individual operations try to manage their position within the network. Decisions here include such things as 'how much of the network do we wish to own?', 'how can we gain an understanding of our competitive position by placing it in a network context?', 'how do we predict and cope with dynamic disturbances and fluctuations within the network?', 'should we attempt to manage the network in different ways depending on the types of market we are serving?', and so on. The second set of issues concern the more detailed management of the relationships with immediate suppliers and customers, especially suppliers. This issue is usually called supplier development. This includes questions such as 'how many suppliers should we have?', 'what should be the nature of our relationship with our suppliers, purely market-based or long-term partnerships?', 'what are the appropriate ways of managing different types of supplier relationships?', and so on.

Chapter 6 will deal with the nature of relationships in supply networks. Chapter 7 will deal with the overall behaviour of supply networks.

Process technology

There are two types of process technology. The first type is what we all recognise as the equipment, machines and processes which act on transformed resources to convert them into finished products and services. This includes such things as the machines inside factories, the aircraft that transport an airline's customers, and the information technology that processes bank statements in a retail bank. But there is also another kind of process technology, which may not directly produce core products and services, but does, indirectly, help the transformation process. This type of technology is usually information processing technology, and would include a manufacturing business's enterprise resource planning (ERP) systems, the airline's staff scheduling, meal ordering and passenger management systems, and the bank's internal balance reconciliation systems.

Chapter 8 will deal with both these types of process technology. Chapter 9 will deal with how process technologies are chosen and implemented.

Development and organisation

After capacity is configured, supply relationships settled and process technology installed, the operation must be run on a day-to-day basis. While the actual running of the operation itself is an operations management rather than an operations strategy issue, there is a set of broad- and long-term decisions which must be made governing how the operation is run. We call this set of decisions development and organisation. Development concerns how we enhance and improve the processes within the operation over time. Organisation refers to the way in which resources are clustered together within the business and how reporting relationships are organised between the clusters. We devote three chapters to these areas: one to the organisation of the day-to-day processes within the operation, one to the way in which these processes can be improved over time and one that looks at both development and organisation within the processes which design and develop products and services.

Chapter 10 will deal with the operation's role and organisation, Chapter 11 with operations development and Chapter 12 with product and service development and organisation.

General Motors puts (most of) its eggs in one basket[6]

Any successful operations strategy needs to consider carefully how *all of the four decisions areas* can contribute to its market objectives. It also needs to get an appropriate balance between the emphasis placed in each area and consider the sequence of all the decisions it will have to take. Over reliance on one decision area is usually a mistake. What is now regarded as a classic failure to do these things was General Motors' huge investments in process technology during the 1980s. The largest of the United States automobile manufacturers, General Motors had traditionally used its size and economies of scale to dominate the industry. But at the beginning of the 1980s, under pressure from Japanese manufacturers, the company had endured its first loss since 1921 by running a deficit of $763 million in one year. Technology, it was decided, would be the answer. During the 1980s GM invested a staggering $80 billion modernising its worldwide operations. Included in this was $2.5 billion spent buying a computer services firm to bolster its drive for computerisation and $5.2 billion to buy Hughes Aircraft for its leading edge product and process technology. Further billions were spent on robots, automated guided vehicles, laser-based measurements systems, and so on. Typifying this policy, the Hamtramck plant in Detroit was built to provide a state-of-the-art, fully automated facility which replaced two older plants. *'Technology leadership,'* said GM's Chairman, *'is what will keep us ahead in world competition.'*

The policy was a disaster. Some industry experts held that at least 20 per cent of GM's spending on new technology was wasted. Costs remained high, quality was a continual problem, and much of the technology either did not work, or came in over budget and late. A year after the Hamtramck plant was opened it was still unreliable and producing at only half the rate that had been planned. The company eventually conceded that Hamtramck was probably 'over-automated'.

Ironically, while all this was happening, GM had a perfect example of how to do it right. In 1983 they had struck a deal with Toyota to form a new joint venture called New United Motor Manufacturing Inc. (NUMMI) at an old GM factory in California. Under the influence of Toyota, this factory was run in a very different way to what was happening elsewhere at GM. The emphasis here was on quality, team work, inventory reduction, and getting the methods of production right. Only when the process was satisfactory was money spent on sophisticated process technology. By 1990, the company, which had traditionally taken around half the American car market, had a market share of 35 per cent.

Figure 2.8 illustrates these categories of operations strategy decisions. Between them they define the scope and nature of the resource base of any organisation. Once again though, the boundaries between operations strategy decisions in these four areas is not clean. For example, decisions on capacity location are influenced by the choice of suppliers in the supply network, the extent of vertical integration is determined partly by the nature of the process technologies involved, the organisation structure of the operation is influenced by the size of operating locations, and so on. Furthermore, the exact nature of the decisions will depend on the nature of the organisation. However, this relatively straightforward categorisation allows the

Figure 2.8 The four categories of operations strategy decision areas

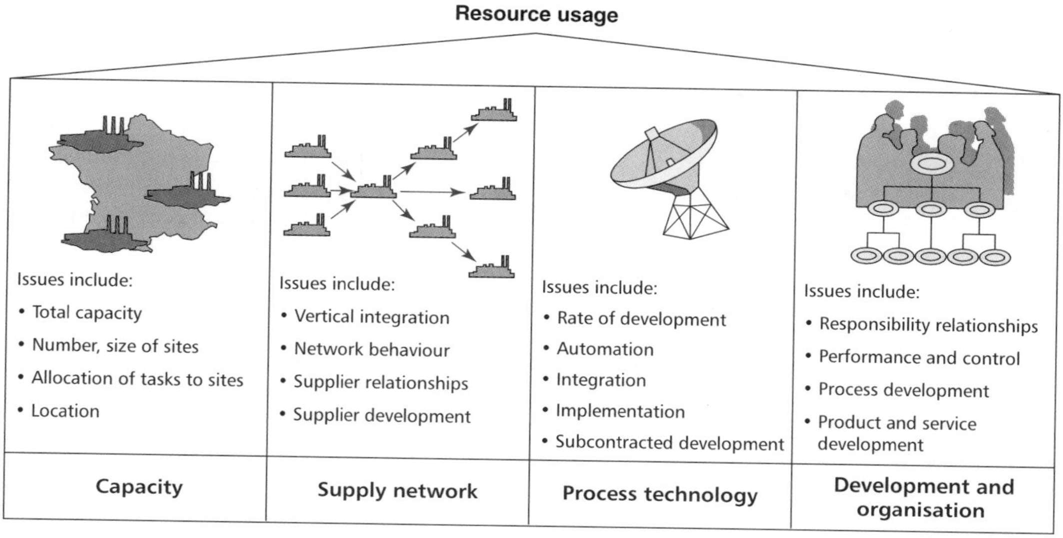

Resource usage

Issues include: • Total capacity • Number, size of sites • Allocation of tasks to sites • Location	Issues include: • Vertical integration • Network behaviour • Supplier relationships • Supplier development	Issues include: • Rate of development • Automation • Integration • Implementation • Subcontracted development	Issues include: • Responsibility relationships • Performance and control • Process development • Product and service development
Capacity	**Supply network**	**Process technology**	**Development and organisation**

examination of each set of decisions in turn, even if it is necessary to remind ourselves continually of the interconnections between them. Table 2.5 sets out some typical decisions which need to be taken in two very different types of operation, clustered under the four areas.

Structural and infrastructural decisions

A distinction is often drawn in operations strategy between the strategic decisions that determine an operation's structure, and those that determine its infrastructure. *Structural* issues primarily influence the physical arrangement and configuration of the operation's resources. Infrastructural strategy areas influence the activities that take place within the operation's structure. This distinction in operations strategy has been compared to that between 'hardware' and 'software' in a computer system. The hardware of a computer sets limits to what it can do. Some computers, because of their technology and their architecture, are capable of higher performance than others, although those computers with high performance are often more expensive. In a similar way, investing in advanced process technology and building more or better facilities can raise the potential of any type of operation. But the most powerful computer can only work to its full potential if its software is capable of exploiting the potential embedded in its hardware. The same principle applies with operations. The best and most costly facilities and technology will only be effective if the operation also has an appropriate infrastructure which governs the way it will work on a day-to-day basis.

However, a simple dichotomy between structural and infrastructural decisions is perhaps too much of a simplification. Not that the distinction itself is inappropriate. What is at fault is the tendency to categorise decision areas as being either entirely

Table 2.5 Some decisions in each decision area for an hotel chain and an automobile manufacturer

Hotel chain	Decision area	Automobile manufacturer
• How many rooms and other facilities should each hotel have? • Should each hotel have the same set of facilities? • Where should our hotels be located? • How do we manage the long-term expansion or contraction of capacity in each region?	**Capacity**	• How big should each plant be? • Should we focus all production on one model on a single site? • Where should each site be located? • How do we manage the long-term expansion or contraction of overall capacity?
• What activities should we be performing in-house and what should we buy in? • Do we develop franchise opportunities on our sites? • Should we form alliances with other vacation or travel companies?	**Supply networks**	• What parts should we be making in-house and what should we buy in? • How do we coordinate deliveries from our suppliers? • Should we form long-term supply alliances? • How many 'first tier' suppliers should we have?
• To what extent should we be investing in multi-functional information systems? • Should all information systems be linked to a central system?	**Process technology**	• What processes should be receiving investment for automation? • How can investment in technology increase our flexibility while keeping costs low? • Should our process technologies be integrated?
• How can we integrate new services features smoothly into our existing operation? • What should be the reporting responsibility relationships within and between hotels? • Should we promote company-wide improvement initiatives? • How do we make sure sites learn from each other?	**Development and organisation**	• How can we bring new products to market quickly? • Should we develop products on common platforms? • How do we manage product variety? • What should be the reporting responsibility relationships within and between sites? • Should we promote company-wide improvement initiatives? • How do we make sure sites learn from each other?

Operations strategy decision areas at Burger King[7]

Although 92 per cent of its restaurants are owned and operated by independent franchisees, Burger King must make sure that its own resources and those of its franchisees are used effectively. From its world headquarters in southern Miami-Dade County, Florida, the company takes operations strategy decisions which affect its over 10,000 restaurants and hundreds of suppliers.

- *Capacity* – The number and location of its outlets has a very significant effect on Burger King's sales and costs. It is important for the company to have its outlets situated conveniently for its potential customers without having them so close to each other that they could take each other's business. Burger King, like many other similar companies, is expanding through 'co-branding' outlets in convenience stores, gas stations, etc. Burger King is also expanding rapidly internationally because this is where the highest growth potential lies.

- *Supply networks* – It is important for Burger King to establish close and trusting relationships with both their franchisees and their suppliers. A key issue with franchisees is the balance between company-owned stores and franchised stores. Company-owned stores allow Burger King to gain first-hand the experience which allows them to understand their customers and operations intimately. Franchised stores allow expansion while reducing the need for capital expenditure. Supplier relationships are also important. Burger King has several long-term supplier relationships. For example, its long-term relationship with Coca-Cola involved the drinks company investing an estimated $30 million in equipment installed in Burger King's restaurants for its new frozen-slush drinks. The company does not have a conventional purchasing department, as such; it uses an independent purchasing cooperative which operates separately from the rest of the company. Restaurant Service Inc. is the sole purchasing entity for both corporate and franchised units.

- *Process technology* – Burger King has invested heavily in new kitchen equipment such as its flame-broiler grill. Computerised technology is used to monitor the cooking process to ensure consistent high quality and enable one member of staff to cook a variety of products for one customer at the same time. Computerised order confirmation units with images displaying side-order options are used at drive-thrus to improve order accuracy which, according to research, is of the utmost importance to these customers.

- *Development and organisation* – Learning how best to make changes in its operation without disturbing its franchisees is an important issue for Burger King. This is why they often trial new equipment and operating routines in their 43 company-owned stores in Orlando and Reno in the US. Sales data and customer response, as well as operations issues, can be analysed before new procedures are rolled out through their outlets. In this way they can also prove to cautious franchisees that new procedures really do work. The company also has network-wide improvement and training systems which allow high standards to be maintained throughout their branded stores and ensure that smaller franchisees have the opportunity to learn from each other.

structural or entirely infrastructural. In reality all the decision areas have both structural and infrastructural implications. Capacity strategy, since it is concerned with the physical size and location of operations, is mainly a structural issue. However, both size and location can affect the organisation's reporting relationships systems and procedures. Similarly, supply network decisions have much to do with the configuration of an operation's resources in terms of what the organisation chooses to perform in-house and what it chooses to buy in. But buying products and services from outside the organisation implies the need for infrastructural support for communications and the development of relationships. Process technology, likewise, has

Figure 2.9 Operations strategy decision areas are partly structural and partly infrastructural

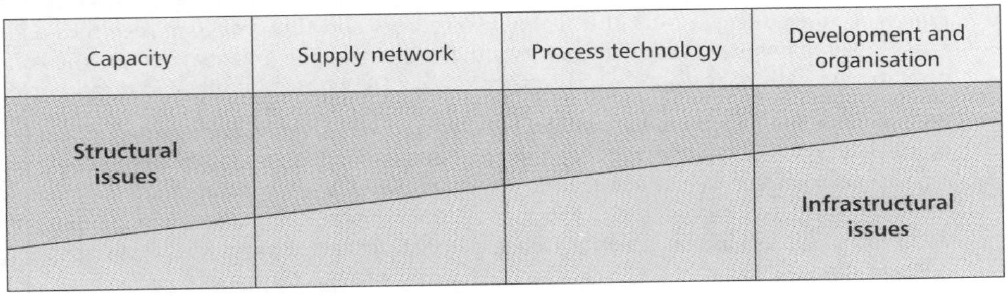

Capacity	Supply network	Process technology	Development and organisation
Structural issues			
			Infrastructural issues

its structural aspects. The physical size, shape and attributes of process technology partly determine the physical form of the operation. Much of an operation's process technology, though, will be devoted to driving the systems, procedures and monitoring systems that form its infrastructure. Even decisions within the development and organisation category, while primarily being concerned with infrastructure, can have structural elements. A set of reporting relationships embedded within an organisational structure may reflect different locations and different process technologies. It is usually best to consider a spectrum with, at one end, capacity-related decisions which are largely structural, and, at the other end, development and organisation-related decisions which are largely infrastructural, as illustrated in Figure 2.9.

The operations strategy matrix

We can now bring together two sets of ideas (and two diagrams – Figures 2.2 and 2.8) and, in doing so, we also bring together the two perspectives of (a) market requirements and (b) operations resources to form the two dimensions of a matrix. This *operations strategy* matrix is shown in Figure 2.10. It describes operations strategy as the intersection of a company's performance objectives with its decision areas. The process of reconciliation between the two perspectives takes place within and between these intersections. It emphasises the intersections between *what* is required from the operations function (the relative priority given to each performance objective), and *how* the operation tries to achieve this through the set of choices made (and the capabilities which have been developed) in each decision area. We shall be treating each decision area and the way in which they impact on performance objectives in the next part of this book.

Using the operations strategy matrix

The complexity of attempting to make decisions in each of the matrix intersections should not be underestimated. Nevertheless, the operations strategy matrix can, at the very least, be considered a checklist of the issues which are required if an oper-

Figure 2.10 The operations strategy matrix

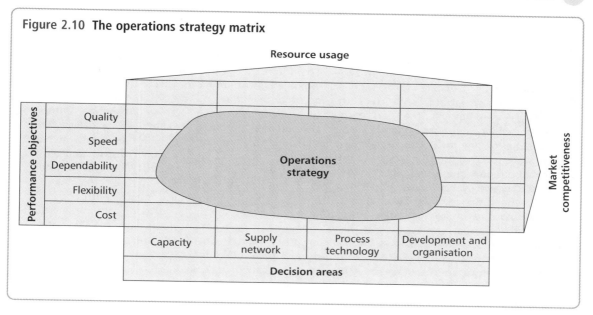

ations strategy is to be successfully formulated. Any operation which claims to have an operations strategy will presumably be able to have some kind of story to tell for each of the intersections. It should be able to explain exactly how capacity strategy is going to affect quality, speed, dependability, flexibility or cost. It should be able to explain exactly how flexibility is influenced by capacity, supply network, process technology, and development and organisation decisions, and so on. In other words, the matrix helps operations strategies to be *comprehensive*. Also, it is unlikely that all the intersections on the matrix will necessarily be of equal importance. Some intersections will be more *critical* than others. Which intersections are critical will, of course, depend on the company, and the nature of its operations, but they are likely to reflect the relative priority of performance objectives and those decisions areas that affect, or are affected by, the company's strategic resources.

The idea of the operations strategy matrix will be used more extensively in Part 3 of the book, where we treat the *process* of operations strategy. For now, the box on Seven-Eleven Japan illustrates how the matrix can be used to describe a company's operations strategy.

Seven-Eleven Japan

Economic stagnation and lack of consumer confidence in Japan during most of the 1990s hit its retail sector particularly hard. An exception was the convenience store sector of the consumer market, and dominant amongst the companies operating in this area was Seven-Eleven Japan (7-Eleven). A franchise convenience store chain, with over 7300 outlets in Japan and established in 1973, 7-Eleven has maintained its position in the industry by growing profits to a level almost unequalled in the Japanese retail industry. Its secret behind 24 years of consecutive growth has been its advanced inventory management system supported by sophisticated information technology.

Company legend has it that Toshifumi Suzuki, the Chairman and CEO of 7-Eleven, was inspired to devise his item-by-item control when he tried to buy a shirt at a retail shop. He did not find a suitable size because the shop had sold out, even though he was himself average sized. On

▶

inquiry, the shop assistant told him that they always ordered the same amount of stock in all sizes irrespective of demand.

7-Eleven determined never to run needless risks of this type with its customer loyalty. The latest generation of its Total Information System (TIS) integrates all information from its stores, head office operations, district offices, suppliers, combined distribution centres and its 650 field 'counsellors'. This system drives the company's inventory management and distribution/delivery systems. 7-Eleven has, over the years, encouraged its vendors to open common distribution centres where similar categories of goods, such as milk and dairy products, are combined for delivery to the stores on one truck. Thus, small deliveries are made on a regular basis which reduces the need for stock space in the stores but also guards against stock-outs. These common distribution centres also reduce the total number of deliveries a day to individual stores. In 1980 a typical store would receive over 30 deliveries per day; by 1999 this had shrunk to under 10. The company further refined this common distribution centre process by grouping items for each centre, not by type but rather by storage temperature, for example frozen foods, chilled foods, room temperature process foods, hot foods, etc. This grouping helps to maintain product quality. The Total Information System also allows the company to respond to changes in trends and customer demand. With an average floor space of just over 1000 square feet, 7-Eleven stores must make sure that every product sold is earning its shelf space. Networked cash registers and hand-held terminals allow sales staff to input details of the type of customer making each purchase. This is tracked, along with the time of day when the products are purchased, and analysed daily by product, customer type, and store. The aggregated results, as well as the data from individual stores, are used by 7-Eleven's field counsellors whose job it is to develop franchisees and 'help the stores to make more money'. By combining advanced information and distribution systems, 7-Eleven has been able to minimise the time between the receipt of orders from stores and the delivery of goods. This helps to ensure maximum shelf life for enhanced freshness and flavour.

7-Eleven's expansion has been carefully planned to ensure that it has a minimum presence of 50 stores in any area, thus reducing advertising and distribution costs. Franchisees are chosen partly by location and partly for their willingness to fit in with 7-Eleven procedures. To maintain the welfare of franchisees the company tries to ensure that skills and learning are shared between stores to continually enhance operations best practice. It seems to be paying off. Average daily sales per 7-Eleven store are more than 30 per cent higher than its main rival. Presumably this is why 7-Eleven's franchisees are prepared to pay relatively high royalty fees compared with its rivals.

The operations strategy matrix analysis for Seven-Eleven Japan

For a company like Seven-Eleven Japan, it is possible to find some kind of relationship between each performance objective and every decision area. However, in Figure 2.11, we have confined ourselves to some of the critical issues described in the box. This operations strategy matrix has been adapted slightly to combine speed and dependability under the single performance objective 'availability'. The relative degree of 'criticality' has also been indicated. Arguably, the pivotal intersection in this company's operations strategy matrix is that between its process technology, in the form of its Total Information System, and the flexibility which this gives it to understand and respond to both sales and suppliers' trends. Many of the other cells in the matrix derive from this particularly critical cell. Here process technology is enabling strategic action both in the development of the company's supply networks and in its general development and organisation strategy. Similarly, the enhanced flexibility, which the TIS gives, helps to reduce cost, increase availability and maintain quality.

As in most analyses of this type, it is the interrelationship between the intersections (cells) of the matrix which are as important to understand as the intersections

Figure 2.11 Operations strategy matrix for Seven-Eleven Japan

Resource development

	CAPACITY	SUPPLY NETWORK	PROCESS TECHNOLOGY	DEVELOPMENT AND ORGANISATION
QUALITY of products and services		Distribution centre grouping by temperature ******		Information sharing and parenting system spreads service ideas ******
Speed and dependability combined to indicate **AVAILABILITY**		Distribution centres and inventory management systems give fast stock replenishment ******		
FLEXIBILITY of response to sales and customers trends		TIS allows trends to be forecast and supply adjustments made *****	TIS gives comprehensive and sophisticated analysis of sales and supply patterns daily *******	
COST in terms of minimising: • operating cost • capital cost • working capital	Area dominance reduces distribution and advertising costs *****	Common distribution centres give small, frequent deliveries from fewer sources ******		Field counsellors with sales data help stores to minimise waste and increase sales ******
	• Location of stores • Size of stores	• Number and type of distribution centres • Order and stock replenishment	• The total Information System (TIS)	• Franchise relationships • New product/service development • Approach to operations improvement

*** very critical

** critical

* secondary

Market competitiveness

themselves. It is also worth noting that one column of issues (those concerned with supply networks) has all its cells filled in. Again, this is not unusual. In this case the reason lies in the purpose of this company. It is essentially a supply organisation. Its only reason for existence is to supply its franchise holders. Not surprising then that it should be particularly concerned with supply network issues.

The 'process' of operations strategy

The operations strategy matrix is an important concept because one needs to understand the 'nuts and bolts' of operations strategy. And it can be used during the process of formulating operations strategies. But it is not a complete process model as such. It may be a first step in understanding *how* reconciliation can be progressed, but in order to understand the activity of effecting reconciliation, we need to examine further issues.

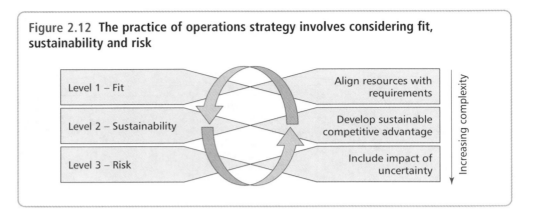

Figure 2.12 The practice of operations strategy involves considering fit, sustainability and risk

In Part 3 of this book we will take three different 'slices' through the practice of reconciliation, each exploring a potentially more complex level of analysis in the evolution of an operations strategy, namely, *fit, sustainability* and *risk* (see Figure 2.12). Here we simply introduce these ideas.

Level 1: Fit – aligning resources and requirements

Matching the performance of an operation's resources with the requirements of its markets may be the first, and most obvious, task of the reconciliation process, but this does not imply it is either trivial or straightforward. The uncertain, and sometimes fickle, nature of many markets makes it difficult to interpret their behaviour in such a way as to provide operations with clear and unambiguous objectives. Similarly, the capabilities and constraints of the operation's resources and processes may themselves be less than predictable, especially when they are being introduced into an existing operation. The process of achieving fit, therefore, is difficult even with internally coordinated communication between those parts of the firm responsible for market-facing activities and those responsible for internal resource-management activities. (Though in practice many of the problems of a lack of fit between market requirements and operations resources are the result of different parts of the firm pursuing different objectives, or pursuing the same objective in different ways.)

Figure 2.13 illustrates the concept of fit. The vertical dimension represents the nature of market requirements either because they reflect the intrinsic needs of customers or because their expectations have been shaped by the firm's marketing activity. This includes such factors as:

● strength of brand/reputation;

● degree of differentiation;

● extent of market promises.

Movement along the dimension indicates a broadly enhanced level of market 'performance'.

The horizontal scale represents the nature of the firm's operations resources and processes. This includes such things as:

● the performance of the operation in terms of its ability to achieve competitive objectives;

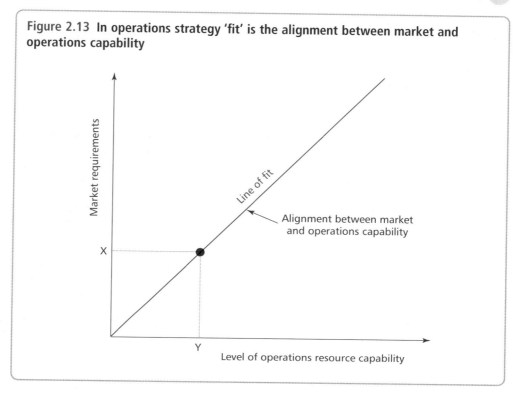

Figure 2.13 In operations strategy 'fit' is the alignment between market and operations capability

- the efficiency with which it uses its resources;
- the ability of the firm's resources to underpin its business processes.

Again, movement along the dimension indicates a broadly enhanced level of 'operations capability'.

The purpose of 'fit' is to achieve an approximate balance between 'market requirements' and 'operations capability'. So when fit is achieved, firms customers do not need, or expect, levels of operations performance which it is unable to supply. Nor does the firm have operations strengths which are either inappropriate for market needs or remain unexploited in the market. Chapter 13 will explore the practice of achieving fit in more detail.

Virgin Trains[8]

Under this single *banner brand* seemingly unrelated companies (drinks, airlines, music, wedding dresses etc.) have been brought together and become apparently successful. The Virgin brand stands above all for fun, style and fashionable efficiency. That is until Virgin bought part of the UK's newly privatised rail system. Realising that there was little 'fit' between an under-invested rail company and its innovative image, Virgin ran an ad. campaign promoting 'our platform' and 'our timetable'. It proclaimed that:

- *We believe the future of travel is the train.*
- *More frequent trains, more reliable trains.*

▶

● *Train journeys that are more entertaining.*

● *Trains that are cleaner, and much faster.*

● *It's what people want from trains.*

● *It's what we intend to provide.*

● *We're starting now!*

After which it laid out a timetable of investment up to 2005 to bring about its promises.

It was always going to be a difficult task to maintain Virgin Train's image during the interregnum between the time when they had to manage the resources which they bought and the time when they hoped to have their new resources developed in 2005. In reality it proved even more difficult than they realised. Virgin Rail became associated in the public's mind with train cancellations, delays, poor customer service, overcrowded carriages, and a continual stream of excuses.

In fact, much of the problem was outside Virgin's control. Railtrack, the track and station monopoly created by rail privatisation, had to deliver substantial track improvements to allow Virgin's investment in new trains to be realised. Only with an almost totally rebuilt track, together with advanced signalling systems, could Virgin's impressive new trains deliver their promised reduced journey times, together with a smooth and relaxing ride. Outsourcing its maintenance to the Anglo-French train maker Alstom has helped. They are now responsible, not only for maintaining the more problematic of the company's resources, but also for finding ways to improve the reliability of its locomotives. Ironically, these tend to be the newest in their fleet.

Nevertheless, the company's brand image looks less shiny. Reviewing the implications of this move the *Economist* magazine touched upon the risks associated with operational failure:

> Already, Mr Branson's rail businesses have suffered some reverses. The firm's West Coast and CrossCountry line did badly in a recent survey by rail regulators: each of its services had become less punctual. . . . Such difficulties are only to be expected when a firm enters a new business. However, they illustrate the greatest (threat) that Mr Branson faces . . . Virgin's brand, its most precious asset, may become associated with failure and strife.
>
> (*The Economist*, 21 February 1998)

Level 2: Sustainability – extending fit over time

So far, our analysis is essentially static – it looks at fit assuming no changes take place in either market requirements or operations resources. However, operations should do more than 'fit in' with current market requirements in a reactive manner. Rather they should (and are in a strong position to) actively support the creation of sustainable competitive advantage. They can do this in two ways. First, an operation should have the adroitness to develop the capabilities which allow it to move its performance in line with market changes. Second, it should be able to develop the capabilities which can be exploited by the company to make itself better and/or different in terms of its market performance. So, whether it is operations which are capable of moving in tandem with market changes, or operations capabilities which are capable of being exploited in the marketplace, there is a clear need for synchronicity between market and operations performance.

Figure 2.14 illustrates the idea of sustainability on the same axes we used to describe the concept of fit. Whereas fit means achieving a balance between market and operations performance, sustainability means extending or improving market and operations performance while simultaneously maintaining the balance. This is not just a matter of coordinating market and operations strategies. Notwithstanding

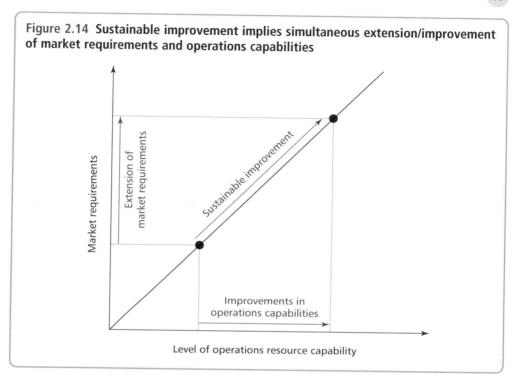

Figure 2.14 **Sustainable improvement implies simultaneous extension/improvement of market requirements and operations capabilities**

Market requirements (vertical axis)

Extension of market requirements

Sustainable improvement

Improvements in operations capabilities

Level of operations resource capability

a firm's intended strategies, some aspects of its marketing and operations *performance* can be shifted by events partially beyond its control. Marketing and operations may therefore lose alignment without any change in the firm's actions. For example, competitor action may radically change the expectations of customers by offering superior and/or different products and services. Similarly, an operations capability which may seem to be at the limits of achievable industry practice may look far less impressive with the introduction of new operations technologies or methodologies.

Thus sustainability not only implies progression along both market and operations performance axes, it also implies having the flexibility to cope with the axes themselves changing. Chapter 14 will explore sustainability in some more detail.

Nissan's fall from grace[9]

The Nissan Motor Company Limited has two of the most productive manufacturing operations in the automobile industry. The Smyrna factory, in Tennessee, makes its Altima Sentra and Frontier models, largely for the North American market, and has been ranked as one of North America's most efficient plants. Similarly, Nissan's plant in Sunderland, in the North East of England, shows in all the league tables as the most efficient automobile plant in Europe. Why then, by 1999, had the company become widely regarded as an industry basket-case, whose stock, according to Merrill Lynch, was only one notch above junk status?

Nissan's first automobile, the small-size Datsun passenger car, started rolling off the Yokohama plant's production lines in 1935. By 1960 Nissan was the first auto maker in Japan to receive the annual Deming prize for engineering excellence. Its Oppama and Zama plants, built in the 1960s, were widely regarded at the time as being state-of-the-art, while its Kyeushu plant, opened in

▶

1975, received the latest in advanced automation technology in 1992. Its engine technology also was, according to some experts, the best in the business.

Yet constantly enhancing its core manufacturing efficiencies proved insufficient to allow Nissan to sustain growth or profitability. Its factories may have been efficient, but by 2000 its products had been described as 'charismatically challenged' by some, and just plain 'dull' by others. The criticism most widely levelled at Nissan was that they had proved themselves incapable of understanding market changes, or responding to them when they became evident, without undermining the hard-won productivity gains in the factories. For example, throughout the 1990s, markets (especially in North America) moved towards the 4×4 sports utility and pick-up sector, collectively known as 'light trucks'. Nissan, nevertheless, stuck to its traditional passenger cars while its competitors manufactured the light trucks which could command higher prices. Even when an exciting new product did emerge, such as the Californian-designed 240Z, it emerged that Nissan's head office had almost blocked the development of prototypes. Perhaps most seriously, Nissan failed to develop common global platforms for its products. This allows automobile manufacturers to differentiate their vehicles in relatively small volumes, while achieving economies of scale through commonality of parts. The 10 per cent of the vehicle that is most visible can be configured to suit local tastes, while the remainder uses common components. So, for example, while Honda produced four clearly distinct vehicles and served nearly every global market with its Civic platform, in 1997 Nissan had approximately 30 platforms just for Japan alone, with things being made even more complex by the large variety of engines, transmissions, and trim levels.

By the spring of 1999 it had become clear that Nissan could no longer survive alone. The company was effectively taken over by Renault, the largest French automanufacturer. Renault brought a much-needed injection of design flair and innovation as well as cost-cutting expertise.

Level 3: Risk – market and operations performance out of balance

As firms struggle to maintain and extend their market performance and operations capabilities, their task is made more difficult by the uncertainties they face. Market requirements change, and, likewise, operations capabilities may change. Sometimes these changes may help a company to extend its market or operations performance. Market fashion may shift in a direction which allows a firm to exploit its operations capabilities more fully. Operations may find that they have scarce, or difficult to copy, resources. Often though, such changes expose a company to risks. And, just as the likelihood of unexpected market and resource changes has increased with the accelerating pace of operations technologies and turbulent markets, so the importance of risk as an aspect of operations strategy practice has increased. Indeed for many firms the effective and efficient management of operations strategy-related risk will become, or continue to be, one of their most important and problematic issues.

Many risks can be related to the uncertainty associated with both the development of an operational resource-base and shifting market requirements. Any operations strategy, therefore, must accommodate these risks. Figure 2.15 illustrates this idea, again using the axes of market requirements and operations capability. The inherent difficulty of synchronising market and operations improvement over time will almost certainly mean that a company will deviate from the line representing perfect 'fit'. Moving above the diagonal implies that market performance (that is, the requirements and/or the expectations of the market) are in advance of the operation's capability to satisfy it. The area below the diagonal implies that a firm has levels of competence or potential performance which are not being exploited in the marketplace. Both represent a risk (although different types of risk, as we shall see in Chapter 15).

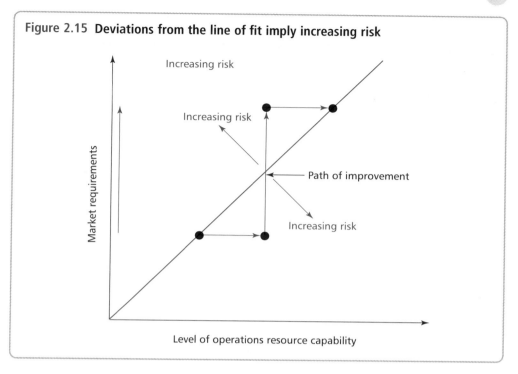

Figure 2.15 **Deviations from the line of fit imply increasing risk**

Virgin Trains vs. Nissan

Look back over the boxed examples of Virgin Trains and Nissan. The purpose of including these two companies' predicaments was not to criticise them as being irredeemably misguided or necessarily doomed. All companies go through bad patches. However, they do constitute examples of companies whose operations and market performance had become misaligned. But they were misaligned in different ways.

Figure 2.16 indicates the position of Virgin Trains and Nissan as they appear at the time of writing (early 2000). Virgin Trains carries the baggage of its own brand success with it in such a way as to highlight the inadequacy of its operations resources. It is in a position of operations risk, insomuch as the perceived failure of its operations resources is actively eroding the Virgin brand image. Hopefully, the expensive and long-term investments in its operations will move their performance up to a level that supports, and is in alignment with, all that is best in the Virgin brand.

Nissan has the opposite problem. Although parts of its operations resource base are excellent (the productivity of its core manufacturing plants), it has failed to leverage this potential advantage through its inadequate market performance. There is no point having efficient manufacturing operations if it is making intrinsically expensive products which the market doesn't want anyway. More customer focused design, based on a sound market strategy, could enable Nissan to exploit its operations strength. The 1999 investment of $5.2 billion by Renault, the French automaker, for 36.8 per cent of the company, signalled a more focused approach to new model development. Before the merger Nissan was planning to cut its vehicle platforms down to five while Renault was down to seven. The new merged operation envisaged ten platforms satisfying the needs of both brands.

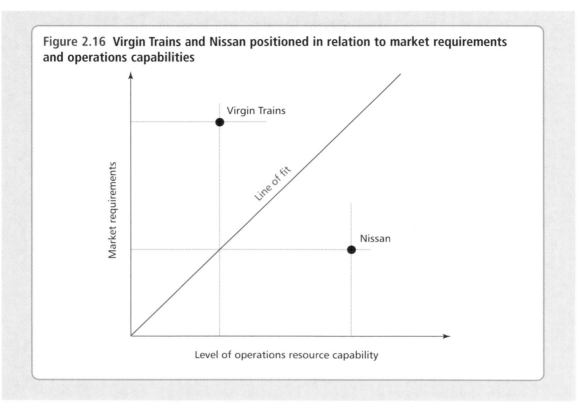

Figure 2.16 Virgin Trains and Nissan positioned in relation to market requirements and operations capabilities

SUMMARY ANSWERS TO KEY QUESTIONS

How do 'content' and 'process' contribute to the reconciliation process?

The reconciliation process is not a straightforward task. Neither markets nor resources are always easy to understand. Markets are uncertain and volatile whereas resource competences can be diffuse and difficult to pin down. Two sets of issues help to untangle this complexity. The first concerns the 'content' of operations strategy, that is, the building blocks from which any operations strategy will be formed. This includes the definition attached to individual performance objectives, together with a prioritisation of those performance objectives. It also includes an understanding of the structure and options available in the four decision areas of capacity, supply networks, process technology, and development and organisation. The second set of issues concern the 'process' of operations strategy, that is, how the reconciliation process takes place.

What are operations strategy performance objectives and what influences their relative priority?

Performance objectives are the general classifications under which we group competitive factors. Competitive factors are the dimensions of performance which define the company's intended market position. Here we use the five generic performance objectives of quality, speed, dependability, flexibility and cost. The exact definition of these five performance objectives will differ for individual operations. Nevertheless, the categories are broadly applicable in most circumstances. Each performance objective will have an effect both inside and outside the operation. The relative priorities of performance objectives will be influenced by customer importance and performance against competitors. The highest-priority objectives for operations are usually those that customers find important but where performance is relatively poor compared to competitors.

What are operations strategy decision areas and do they apply to all types of operation?

Operations strategy decision areas are grouping of decisions which shape the operation's resources. Here we use the four broad groupings of capacity, supply networks, process technology, and development and organisation. These four groupings are used partly because they relate to common operations strategy practice and partly because they all have a clear influence on an organisation's return on investment. Furthermore, they apply to all types of operation. The individual decisions within each group may vary, depending on the type of operation, but the groupings themselves are generic.

How do performance objectives relate to decision areas?

Performance objectives and decisions areas interact in a way that can be described by the operations strategy matrix. When devising an operations strategy it is important to ensure that, in terms of the matrix, the strategy is comprehensive (all obvious aspects are at least considered) and has the critical intersections identified.

What objectives should be pursued in the 'process' of operations strategy?

The most obvious objective of the 'process' of operations strategy is that there is some sort of *fit* between operations resources and market requirements. That is, there is alignment between the two. Alignment must also be achieved over time. That is, the strategy is *sustainable* in so much as it maintains and improves both operations resource performance and market performance. During the ongoing process of attempting to extend market and operations performance it is necessary to consider the *risks* deriving from the periodic and (hopefully) temporary misalignment between the two.

CASE EXERCISE – What would you do?

Dresding Medical

Since founding her company over ten years ago, Dr Laura Dresding had never been either so anxious or so enthusiastic about the future of Dresding Medical (DM). The company had enjoyed considerable success, both financial and in terms of market share, by designing, manufacturing and supplying a range of medical equipment to hospitals and clinics throughout Europe. Starting with cardiovascular devices, their range expanded to include neurological stimulators and monitoring diagnostic devices.

> 'Success has come largely from our research and development culture. Although around 50 per cent of our total manufacturing is done in-house, our core competence is an ability to understand the needs of clinicians and translate those into our products. We were among the first to expand the range and functionality of this type of equipment and integrate it with sophisticated diagnostics software. Admittedly our products tend to be relatively highly priced and we are coming under some cost pressures, but because of our technical excellence and our willingness to modify equipment to individual customer needs, we avoid too much pressure on our prices.'

DM's operations planning and control systems had been relatively informal. A team of specialist sales technicians discussed individual clinical needs with customers and wrote a 'product specification' for manufacturing to work to. Around 70 per cent of all orders involved some form of customisation from standard 'base models'. Manufacturing would normally take around three months from receiving the specification to completing assembly. This was not usually a problem for most customer; they were more interested in equipment being delivered on time rather than immediate availability. The manufacturing department was largely concerned with assembling, integrating and (most importantly) testing the equipment. Most components were made by suppliers who had been doing business with DM for some years and were capable of accommodating their strict quality requirements and their need to customise components. Laura Dresding knew the strengths and weaknesses of her manufacturing operations.

> 'Manufacturing is really a large laboratory. It is important to maintain that laboratory-like culture because it helps us to maintain our superiority in leading-edge product technology and our ability to customise products. It also means that we can call upon our technicians to pull out all the stops in order to maintain delivery promises. However, I'm not sure how manufacturing, or indeed the rest of the company, will deal with the new markets and products which we are getting into.'

Dr Dresding was referring to a new generation of 'small black box' products which the company had developed. These were significantly smaller and smarter devices which were sufficiently portable to be attached to patients, or even implanted; for example, a cardiac defibrillator which, when necessary, can jolt the heart into maintaining a healthy rhythm and diagnose how and why the heart has gone wrong. Other products included drug delivery systems and neurological implants. All these new products had two things in common. First, they took advantage of sophisticated solid state electronics and second, they could be promoted directly to consumers as well as to hospitals and clinics. Dr Dresding was under no illusions about the significance of these changes.

'On the market side we have to persuade health care and insurance companies to encourage these new devices. They may be expensive in the short term but they can save money in the long term. We are hoping that customer pressure will act in our favour. What is more problematic is our ability to cope with these new products and the new market they are addressing. We are moving towards being a consumer company, making and delivering a higher volume of more standardised products where the underlying technology is changing fast. We must become more agile in our product development. A new base model currently takes over three years to develop; we cannot afford to develop the new products in any more than 12 months. Also, for the first time, we need some kind of logistics capability. I'm not sure whether we should deliver products ourselves or subcontract this. Manufacturing faces a similar dilemma. On one hand it is important to maintain control over production to ensure high quality and reliability; on the other hand, investing in the process technology to make the products will be very expensive. There are subcontractors who could manufacture the products for us; they have experience in this kind of manufacturing but not in maintaining the levels of quality we will require. We will also have to develop a 'demand fulfilment' capability which will be able to deliver products at short notice. It is unlikely that customers would be willing to wait the three months our current customers tolerate. Nor are we sure of how demand might grow. I'm confident that growth will be fast but we will have to have sufficient capacity in place not to disappoint our new customers. We must develop a clear understanding of the new capabilities which we will have to develop if we are to take advantage of this wonderful market opportunity. Who knows, it could become the first step in transforming the whole company. I see no reason why, eventually, we should not move into running health management clinics ourselves. We are already developing technologies that could monitor patients at a distance. We can even re-programme implanted devices, without surgical intervention, based on our diagnostic systems.'

Further reading

Collis, D.J. and C.A. Montgomery (1997) *Corporate Strategy: Resources and the scope of the firm*, Urwin, Boston.

de Wit, B. and R. Meyer (1998) *Strategy: Process, Content, Context*, 2nd edn, International Thompson Business Press.

Hayes, R.H. and G. Pisano (1994) 'Beyond world class: the new manufacturing strategy', *Harvard Business Review*, Jan–Feb.

Hayes, R.H., G. Pisano and D.M. Upton (1996) *Strategic Operations: Competing through capabilities: text and cases*, The Free Press, New York.

Hill, T. (1993) *Manufacturing Strategy: The strategic management of the manufacturing function*, 2nd edn, MacMillan.

Stalk, G. and T. Hout (1990) *Competing Against Time*, The Free Press, New York.

Swink, M. and M.H. Way (1995) 'Manufacturing strategy: propositions, current research, renewed directions', *International Journal of Operations and Production Management*, Vol. 15, No. 7.

Upton, D.M. (1998) *Designing, Managing and Improving Operations*, Prentice Hall, NJ.

Voss, C.A. (1995) 'Alternative paradigms for manufacturing strategy', *International Journal of Operations and Production Management*, Vol. 15, No. 4.

White, G.P. (1996) 'A meta-analysis model of manufacturing capabilities', *Journal of Operations Management*, Vol. 14, No. 4.

Whittington, R. (1993) *What is strategy – and does it matter?*, Routledge, UK.

Notes on the chapter

1   Driver, C. and R. Johnston (2000) 'Understanding Service Customers: the value of hard and soft attributes', Warwick University Working Paper.

2   Sources: www.burgerking.com, Cebrzynski, G. (1999) 'BK's president looks to the future with a clarity of vision', *Nation's Restaurant News*, 13 Sept, NY; Tong, B. (2000) Private communication.

3   Hill, T. (1993) *Manufacturing Strategy*, MacMillan, UK.

4   Spring, M. and R. Bowden (1997) 'One more time: how do you win orders: a critical appraisal of the Hill manufacturing strategy framework', *International Journal of Operations and Production Management*, Vol. 17, No. 8.

5   An idea put forward by Eilan, S. and B. Gold (1978) *Productivity Measurement*, Pergamon Press, Oxford, UK.

6   *The Economist* (1991) 'When GM's robots ran amok', 10 August.

7   Cebrzynski, G. and B. Tong, op. cit.

8   Sources: Virgin advertising (1997); O'Connell, D. (1999) 'The toughest job in railways', *Sunday Business*, 13 June.

9   Sources: Gibney, F. Jnr (1999) 'Nissan calls for a two', *Time*, 1 March; *The Economist* (1998) 'Nissan on its knees', 16 March.

Time, trade-offs and targeting

Introduction

In this chapter we look at three related ideas which are fundamental to the process of reconciliation (Figure 3.1). We treat them at this stage because it is necessary to understand the way the 'mechanisms' of the reconciliation process work. The first idea is that the relative importance of the two perspectives of operations strategy, which we discussed in the previous chapters, are not always equally important. Sometimes market requirements dominate in such a way that reconciliation is achieved primarily by organising operations resources to fit whatever the market dictates. At other times the capabilities and constraints of operations resources will place a significant restriction on the organisation's choice of its target markets or, more positively, provide opportunities to move its market positioning. So, the relative importance of each side of the reconciliation equation is likely to change over time. The second idea is that, as the importance of each side of the reconciliation equation varies over time, operations may also wish to change the absolute and relative levels of its performance objectives. In most industries the increasing pressure to improve market position and resource capabilities means that operations are

Figure 3.1 Topics in operations strategy treated in this chapter

called on to enhance some specific aspects of their performance. The key issue is, do improvements in some aspects of performance necessarily mean a reduction in the performance of others? This is called the *trade-off* problem. The third idea is that operations may wish to exploit the trade-offs between objectives in order to be exceptionally good at one performance objective (or a very narrow set of them). By focusing on such limited objectives and sacrificing its ability to perform in the others, it may be able to target itself at a correspondingly narrow market to achieve a high degree of differentiation.

KEY QUESTIONS

- *Do the role and key performance objectives of operations stay constant, or vary over time?*
- *Are trade-offs between operations performance objectives inevitable, or can they be overcome?*
- *What type of trade-offs occur in operations?*
- *What are the pros and cons of focused operations?*

Operations strategy changes over time

Markets change over time. Customer demographics and needs are not a constant, so neither are market requirements. Nor are operations resource capabilities static. Fundamental to the concept of resource-based capabilities is that they develop over time. Not surprising then that the nature of the reconciliation process, and therefore the role of operations strategy, changes over time, though the stimulus for change may vary. At some times markets change fast. Competitors may be particularly aggressive, or novel products or services may redefine customer expectations. If so, the competitive agenda for the business will be influenced largely by how the organisation positions itself in its markets. The role of operations may be confined to providing support for, and implementing, market-driven decisions. For example, the popular music industry, not surprisingly, has been almost exclusively concerned with the market position of its 'products' (mainly recording artists). The CD manufacturing, distribution and retailing operations played a secondary role. (However, development in Internet-based forms of music distribution may influence this balance.)

At other times the focus for change may be within the resources and processes of the operation itself. New technologies may require a fundamental rethink of how operations resources can be used to provide competitive advantage. Internet-based technologies, for example, provided opportunities for many retail operations to shift, or enhance, market positioning. Other operations-based changes may be necessary, not to change, but merely to maintain a market position. They may even reflect opportunities revealed by the operations-based capabilities of competitors. For example, through the 1990s much of the focus of change in US and European automotive companies was within their operations processes, mainly because of the lower operations costs realised by their Japanese competitors. Again, this balance may change as niche markets become more distinctive. But this is the point. Although different industries may have a predisposition towards either market or operations concerns, the relative balance is likely to experience some kind of change over time.

Mapping operations strategies

To understand how an organisation's operations strategy changes over time is to understand how it views its markets, how it sees the role of its operations resources, and most of all, how it has attempted to achieve reconciliation between the two. It also illustrates how an organisation's understanding of its markets and resources evolves, often reacting to external pressures and internal possibilities. Of course, the minutiae of the thousands of decisions which constitute the mechanics of the reconciliation process over time are the key to understanding how the balance between markets and resources moves. Ideally we need to map the pattern and flow of each of these decisions, but this would be an immense task if our historical perspective is to be longer than a few years. Often, though, it is the nature of an organisation's products or services which one looks to to see how the internal reconciliation process resolved itself. Products and services are after all the outward manifestation of the reconciliation process. Within their design they embody the characteristics which the company hopes will satisfy the market and at the same time exploit its resource capabilities. Thus, to understand how a firm's operations strategy changes over time the three factors which we should trace are:

- changes in the market requirements of the firm's products or services;
- changes in its operations resources and processes;
- changes in the nature of how the firm attempts the reconciliation process, through its products and services.

VW – The first half century (plus)[1]

'Volkswagen has acquired symbolic stature for whole generations of people. Of all the motor vehicles that have been produced, the Beetle, the VW Bus, the Golf and the New Beetle are practically unparalleled in the extent of their identification with entire epochs of social history'. (Volkswagen Kommunikation).

For years Ferdinand Porsche had dreamt of designing a 'peoples' car'. Presenting his ideas to the Reich government in 1934, he found enthusiastic support for the idea. By 1936 the design of the people's car, or 'Volkswagen', had been developed and the first prototype models tested. By 1939 the factory was completed, although the Second World War meant that it was almost immediately turned over to the production of war vehicles. By the end of the War two-thirds of the factory had been destroyed, the local infrastructure was in ruins, and both material and labour were in desperately short supply. Yet the plant did produce some vehicles, mainly for the occupying British Army. Although attempts were made to sell the plant to various people, including the Ford Motor Company, no one seemed to want a ruined plant with its 'people's cars'. In 1948, the occupying authorities put in Heinrich Nordhoff, an engineer from the Opel Motor Company, to run the business. Nordhoff had faith in the basic concept of Porsche's design but added an emphasis on quality and engineering excellence, together with a concentrated export drive. Throughout the 1950s the company thrived. Overcoming the difficulties of manufacturing in a recovering economy, the company rapidly expanded both its manufacturing and its sales operations. The car

▶

itself, however, hardly changed at all. In fact, Nordhoff actively suppressed any change to the design. Nothing would be allowed to interfere with the core values of a simple, cheap, robust and standardised people's car. Yet the world was changing. Local economies were recovering fast from the devastation of war and customers were demanding more choice and some touches of luxury in their motor vehicles. Notwithstanding its earlier reluctance, eventually Volkswagen was forced to introduce a new model (the 1500) and increase its efforts to promote its products. In all essentials, however, the company strategy was unchanged. During the early part of the 1960s, the 1500 model helped to take some of the pressure off the company. But consumer tastes were still moving faster than the company's response. Although sales held up, increased costs, together with stiff price competition, were having a severe effect on the company's profitability. By the end of the 1960s the company had lost its glitter. Profits were declining and, in an attempt to find a new way forward, Volkswagen introduced several new products and acquired some smaller companies, most notably Auto Union GmbH from Daimler Benz, which later would form the nucleus of the Audi company.

Out of this somewhat rudderless period (Nordhoff had died in 1968), the company eventually started to find a coherent strategy. Although very different from the original Beetle, new models were formed around the designs emerging from Audi. More in tune with modern tastes, these models were front wheel drive, water cooled and held to be more stylish than the old Beetle. At the same time the company started to rationalise its operations to ensure some commonality between models and bring enhanced organisation to its (now global) manufacturing operations. All this took time and money but, in spite of large losses the year previously, the company resumed its profitability growth by the end of 1975. During the remainder of the 1970s and through the 1980s, Volkswagen continued to produce its successful Polo, Golf and Passat models. Production facilities continued to expand around the world, including the USA and Brazil. The last Volkswagen Beetle to be made in Germany rolled off the assembly line in 1980 but the model continued to be produced in other parts of the world for many years. But never again, Volkswagen vowed, would they be left behind consumer tastes. Design and product performance moved to the front of VW's strategy and all models were updated at regular intervals. The Spanish SEAT and Czech Skoda companies were also brought within the group. The next big challenge for the company came, not from the inadequacy of its models, but from its manufacturing facilities.

In the first half of the 1990s Volkswagen's models were still highly regarded and commercially successful, if not cheap to make. But its costs were significantly above both its local European rivals and its Japanese competitors. Add to this a slump in European car sales and, although by now it was by far the largest auto-maker in Europe, the prospects for VW looked bleak. Management structures at the company had become over-staffed and bureaucratic. Labour costs in Germany were 50 per cent above the European average and 35 per cent above those in the USA. One estimate had Volkswagen needing to operate at 95 per cent of capacity just to cover its costs. The break-even points of its rivals were significantly lower, at around 70 per cent. Productivity levels were also low. VW's Wolfberg plant produced 22 cars per employee compared with twice that in similar plants elsewhere in Europe. A fundamental cost-cutting exercise was seen by many commentators as the only thing that would save the company.

By the late 90s, once more things were looking brighter. The company had negotiated pay and flexibility deals with its employees, successfully cut the costs of buying parts from its supply base (at one point hiring the controversial José Ignacio López from General Motors) and was continuing to introduce its new models. The most eye-catching of these was the New Beetle, a design based on the old Beetle but with thoroughly modern parts under its skin. Just as significantly, the company worked on the commonality of its designs. Within the VW group several models, although looking different on the surface, were based on the same basic platform.

Understanding VW's operations strategy over time[2]

Few people would dispute that VW's strategy has changed over time. What is more important is to understand the nature of these changes and how, specifically, they affected the company's operations strategy. Figure 3.2 illustrates some of the more distinct phases in the company's history in terms of our definition of operations strategy. The requirements of the market have changed, not only in line with changing economic circumstances as world markets have grown, matured and become increasingly sophisticated over time, but also in response to how VW's competitors have behaved. Thus VW markets which were small, local and disrupted at the beginning of the period became increasingly large, international and subtle over time. But also the degree of competitive pressure changed. Competitor behaviour counted for little at the beginning of the period, but by the late 90s automobile markets had become fiercely competitive. Likewise with the nature of VW's operations resources and processes. The beginning of the period was marked by a desperate effort merely to obtain the resources required to satisfy even the most primitive of markets. Then, at various times through the next fifty years, VW's operations resources became more systematised, considerably larger, and far more complex. Its resources were reconfigured to manufacture different products, other car firms were acquired and, increasingly, the company's resources developed into an interconnected network of internationally located operations.

Notice how, in Figure 3.2, the reconciliation process is described in terms of the firm's product offerings. Often this is the most revealing way of illustrating the outcome of the reconciliation process. As we mentioned earlier, a firm's products or services are the outward manifestation of how it attempts to reconcile what it believes the market requires with what it is capable of producing. Thus, products and services are the visible embodiment of reconciliation. Embedded in the product or service is the package of performance characteristics which the firm is making available to the market. Within this package of performance characteristics are also to be found the prioritisation and trade-offs inherent within the firm's decision-making processes and behaviour. (We shall deal with trade-offs more fully later in the chapter.)

Figure 3.2 also shows the relative significance of market requirements and operations resources over time. This gives an indication of the relative degree of strategic activity within the firm's operations over time. It also gives us a clue as to the *role* of operations strategy over time. At some stages the role of operations strategy is relatively minor, often confined merely to implementing the company's market strategy. So, during the period 1959 to 1964 the firm's strategy was driven largely by a desire to change its market position slightly through the introduction of the 1500 model. The firm's operations strategy was limited to ensuring that the new model could be manufactured satisfactorily. Similarly, in the period 1976 to 1989, the firm's focus was mainly on how its markets could be segmented in order to achieve successful differentiation of its various products. At other times the strategy of the company not only relies on its operations capabilities but could be described as being driven by them. So, in the period 1946 to 1951 the company's strategy was dictated largely by the ability of its operations resources to produce the cars in sufficient quantity to satisfy its emerging market. Similarly, in the period 1990 to 1996, the firm's profitability, and even survival, depended on the ability of its operations resources to reduce its cost base significantly. In both these periods the company's

Figure 3.2 Market requirements, operations resources and strategic reconciliation at VW for half a century

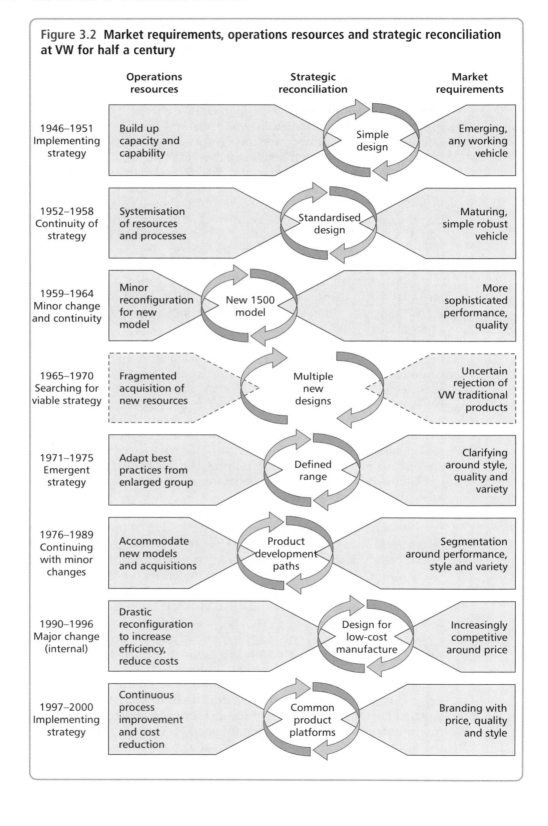

market activity was, to some extent, driven by its operations capabilities (or lack of them). At other times the relative roles of market and operations strategy are more balanced. (Even if, in the 1965 to 1970 period, they are balanced in terms of their mutual confusion.)

The key point here is not so much that the firm's operations strategy is at times better or worse than at other times. Rather it is that, over the long term, any firm can expect the role of its operations strategy to change as its circumstances change. However, one should not infer that the role of operations is entirely driven by uninfluencable environmental forces. Interwoven with the broad environmental factors which have influenced VW are a whole set of significant choices it has made. The company chose to suppress new designs in the 1950s, it chose to try out many designs in the late 60s and it chose to develop its common products platform strategy in the late 90s. The development of operations strategy over time is a combination of uncontrollable environmental forces and factors which can be more readily influenced. Above all, it is determined by choices about how operations resources are developed and the role we expect of the operations function within the firm. Notice how the two major crises for VW, in its loss of strategic direction in the late 60s and its loss of cost control in the early 90s, were preceded by a period where operations strategy had a relatively minor role within the company.

Note also that the process of strategic decision making is not always neat or necessarily even well thought out. At times Volkswagen, like any other company, were reacting to events in a manner which was more painful to them than if they had taken similar decisions earlier, before they became crises. The company's struggle to reduce its cost base during the 1990s is an example of this. At other times the company seemed to move towards a strategic position not so much through planning as through a slowly emerging consensus. These strategies are what we called in Chapter 1 *emergent strategies* and are discussed in the theory box. The concept of emergent strategies is an important one in operations strategy. Emergent strategies often emerge from the organisational resources which are the direct responsibility of operations.

Theory Box | **Emergent strategies**

Strategy is often characterised as the *pattern of decisions* made by organisations over time. The logic of this is that it is this pattern of decisions that reveals the underlying vision and intention of the organisation. However, what an organisation decides to do and what it actually does do are not necessarily the same thing. Sometimes strategic decisions are made which really are carried out with no discontinuity between intention and realisation. But not all intentions turn into realised action. Decisions may be made which are never fully implemented. The organisational will, which is necessary to drive the decision forward, may fade as its implications are fully understood. Or, the assumptions upon which the decision was based may come to be seen as false. Or, circumstances may change in unforeseen ways. There are many reasons why intended strategies may never be realised.

More significant for operations strategy, not all realised strategies were originally intended. That is, not every *pattern of actions* which describes the actual behaviour of an organisation is the result of a deliberate formal process of decision making. Some realised strategies *emerge* over time as being the best way forward. Mintzberg and Walters hold that strategies[3] often 'come about despite, or in the absence of, intentions'. They call these *emergent strategies*. These emergent strategies are often formed around several small, or limited, decisions which

▶

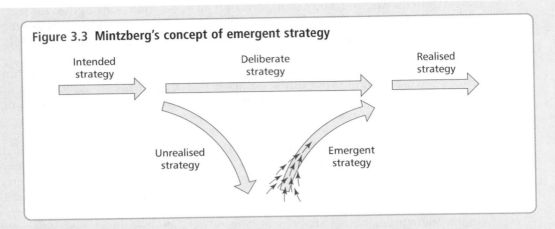

Figure 3.3 Mintzberg's concept of emergent strategy

are incremental in nature. Making these (not always related) incremental decisions may promote a consensus over future action as cumulative experience promotes a shared understanding of desired outcomes and activities. Emergent strategies are shaped over time through the learning which takes place within the operation's resources. They are not planned as such, but are a function of the experience gained as an organisation actually uses its resources. Emergent strategies derive from the way the organisation approaches the interaction between conceptualising issues and taking action. They may even derive from how the organisation exploits the circumstances with which it is presented.

So, when strategies are decided they may eventually become realised strategies through a *deliberative* process. If they do not make it through this process and remain *unrealised* they nevertheless contribute to the organisation's collective consciousness and experience. The *realised* strategies which do occur may derive from the deliberative process or may themselves emerge from that collective consciousness and experience. See Figure 3.3.

The law of limited objectives

In our analysis of the changing fortunes of the Volkswagen Company the role of the operations part of the business changed over time, but also their operations objectives changed. Different objectives became more or less important as the market circumstances of the company changed. In its early history, the very basic objective of making products available (a combination of *speed* and *dependability*) was pre-eminent in an environment where basic resources were difficult to obtain. Latterly, the company, by now far larger and more complex, was struggling with the task of reducing its *costs* while maintaining its performance in other areas. The issue here is, because of changing market requirements, *not all performance objectives are equally important*. But also, from a resource perspective, *operations cannot be exceptionally good at every single aspect of performance at the same time*. Volkswagen emphasised different aspects of performance at different points in time. And, in order to excel in some particular aspects of performance, they would, to some extent, sacrifice performance in others. This idea is usually referred to as the *trade-off concept* and is treated in the next section of this chapter.

Trade-offs

The trade-off concept is fundamental to our understanding of operations strategy, both in theory and practice, and is strongly related to the ongoing process of reconciliation. Perhaps most important, the idea of trade-offs is also at the heart of how operations seek to improve their performance over time. Of course there are many aspects to the subject of operations improvement and later we devote the whole of Chapter 11 to it. One of the many questions central to improvement efforts is, 'what do we want to be particularly good at?' Is there one particular aspect of performance which we wish to stress above everything else *('with us it is quality first, second and third')*?, or are we trying to achieve a balance between objectives *('we wish to offer the customer a wide range of services but not to the extent that costs get out of control')*? In order to answer these questions we need to understand the way performance objectives relate to each other. This is where trade-offs come in.

What is a trade-off?

All of us are familiar with the simple idea that (much as we would like) we cannot have everything. Most of us want some combination of health, wealth and happiness. But we also know that sometimes we must sacrifice one to get the others. Driving ourselves too hard at work may give us wealth but can have negative effects on both health and happiness. Of course we cannot let the wealth objective decrease too far or our poverty will undermine happiness and even health. We all instinctively understand that (a) the three objectives are related, (b) because some resource is finite (time, ability, etc.) we must, to some extent, trade off each objective against the others, (c) the trade-off relationship is not simple and linear (we do not decrease, or increase, our health by a fixed amount for every $1,000 earned), (d) the nature of the relationship will differ for each individual (some of us can derive great happiness *and* well-being from the process of making money) and perhaps most importantly, (e) none of us is always totally certain just how our own trade-offs operate (although some of us are better at knowing ourselves than others).

That these ideas also apply to operations was first articulated by a Professor Wickham Skinner at Harvard University. As ever in those days he was speaking of manufacturing operations, but broadly the same principles apply. He said,[4]

Few executives realise the existence of trade-offs. Yet most managers will readily admit that there are compromises or trade-offs to be made in designing an airplane or a truck. In the case of an airplane, trade-offs would involve matters such as cruising speed, take-off and landing distances, initial costs, maintenance, fuel consumption, passenger comfort, and cargo or passenger capacity. A given stage of technology defines limits of what can be accomplished in these respects. For instance, no one today can design a 500-passenger plane that can land on a carrier and also break the sonic barrier. Much the same thing is true of manufacturing. The variables of cost, time, quality, technological constraints, and customer satisfaction place limits on what management can do, force compromises, and demand an explicit recognition of a multitude of trade-offs and choices.

Theory Box | Paradoxes, dilemmas and trade-offs

The idea of trade-offs in operations can sometimes be confusing because there are several similar terms used to describe ideas that are close to that of the trade-off. Indeed the different views of trade-offs which we shall discuss in this section reflect a wider debate in business strategy concerning the extent to which businesses as a whole can achieve multiple strategic goals. Furthermore, there is no universally accepted distinction between terms such as trade-off, dilemma and paradox. However, there are differences in how the terms are used by writers on strategy.

A *paradox* is where two statements or descriptions of a problem are, or seem to be, mutually exclusive and yet each could be taken as 'truth'. There is no implication that any choice need be made between the two contradicting statements. Both operate simultaneously and are accepted as 'true' even though they are mutually exclusive. By definition a paradox cannot be solved. A choice need not be made. Paradoxes are sometimes related to *divergent problems*. These are:

> Problems that are not easily quantifiable or verifiable and that do not seem to have a single solution. The more rigorously and precisely they are studied, the more the solutions tend to diverge, or to become contradictory and opposite. For example, the problem of world peace seems to necessitate security and protection on the one hand, and reducing the threat of war by disarmament on the other. The education of children is a process of passing on past knowledge and culture . . . as well as a process of allowing freedom, autonomy, and self-development. . . . (Quinn, 1992)[5]

Thus a paradox is something we have to live with rather than solve, yet at the same time informs our decision-making processes.

A *dilemma* is a less disturbing and difficult concept to understand. A dilemma is where two or more aims seem to be contradictory and yet can (perhaps with difficulty) be reconciled. In fact 'dilemma theory' suggests that managers are not constantly making heroic decisions between alternative courses of action, rather they are constantly engaged in the process of reconciling seeming opposites. Usually dilemmas are stated as conflicts between broad aims rather than specific performance objectives. So, for example, there is a dilemma in choosing between organisational differentiation and integration, or between closeness to suppliers and the ability to strike a hard deal.

A *trade-off* is a more operational concept. A trade-off implies that there is a relationship between simultaneously desirable operations objectives. Furthermore, it implies that at least the broad form of this relationship is known. So, for example, '*We know that our costs will increase if we offer more choices of colour to our customers, and costs will increase even more dramatically if we also offer a choice of size*'. This statement identifies that costs will increase as variety increases and, furthermore, that costs will increase more rapidly for certain types of variety extension. Originally trade-offs were seen as relationships which were largely fixed and immutable. More recently trade-offs have been depicted as relationships between performance objectives which hold true for a given set of technological, organisational and attitudinal factors. By changing the nature of operations resources, so the nature of the trade-off relationship may also be changed.

Why are trade-offs important?

We judge the effectiveness of any operation by how well it performs. The call centre that can respond to our call and solve our problems within seconds, any time of the day or night, is superior to one that takes several minutes to answer our call and does not operate through the night. The plant that can deliver products in 24 hours is judged superior to one that takes 3 days, plants turning over their stock 25 times a year are superior to one which, operating under similar conditions, only manage to turn over stock 7 times a year, and so on. Yet in making our judgement we recognise two important characteristics of operations performance. The first is that all measures of performance will not have equal importance for an individual operation. Certain aspects of performance will outweigh others, their relative importance being determined by both the competitive characteristics of the market in which the operation is competing and, more importantly, the way in which the company chooses to position itself within that market. The second characteristic of performance which will shape our view of the operation is that we recognise that aspects of performance will, to some extent, trade off against each other. So for example, we are less impressed with the call centre that answers our calls quickly at all times of the day or night if its costs of running the operation make it necessary to charge us higher fees, or if the plant that delivers within 24 hours is achieving this only by investing in high levels of finished goods inventory. Though maybe we will be more indulgent towards the operation if we discover it has deliberately positioned itself in the market to compete primarily on instant response or fast delivery. Then the cost implications of high finished goods inventory may not matter so much. The operations have chosen to 'trade off' higher costs or high inventory to achieve fast response and fast delivery. However, we would be even more impressed with the call centre if it had 'overcome' the trade-off and was achieving both fast and 24-hour response *and* low cost levels. Similarly with the manufacturing plant, if it was achieving both fast delivery *and* low inventories. In both these examples we are using a broad understanding of the relationship between different performance objectives to judge the effectiveness of their operations management. But we are also implying that, in order to improve, these operations must overcome the trade-offs by changing the nature of the relationship between performance objectives.

Are trade-offs real or imagined?

Skinner's original idea of trade-offs was both straightforward and intuitively attractive. Essentially it formalised the notion that there is no such thing as a free lunch. Any operation, like any machine, is 'technologically constrained'.[6] It therefore cannot provide all things to all people. The trade-off relationships between competitive objectives (cost, quality, delivery, variety, inventory, capital investment, etc.) mean that excellence in one objective usually means poor performance in some or all of the others. Operations that attempt to be good at everything finish up by being mediocre at everything. Therefore the key issue of operations strategy is to *position* the competitive objectives of the operation to reflect the company's overall competitive strategy. Although Skinner has subsequently modified his original ideas, he maintains their essential validity: '*trade-offs . . . are as real as ever but they are alive and dynamic*'.[7]

The counter-view came from a new breed of more evangelical academics and consultants inspired by the perceived success of some (mainly Japanese) companies in overcoming, at least some, trade-offs, most notably that between cost and quality. They embraced the 'bottom up' improvement techniques of 'World Class' operations. Both trade-offs and positioning, they claimed, are illusions. Trade-offs are not real, therefore positioning is not necessary. Citing the success of many companies that achieved improvements in several aspects of performance *simultaneously*, they dismiss trade-offs as distractions to what should be the real imperative of operations, namely improvement. Making choices between alternative aspects of performance leads to 'merely good', as opposed to 'outstanding' achievements. This is what some called *'the tyranny of either/or'*. Rather than accepting the either/or approach, they recommend the more positive 'and/also' approach, which works towards 'having it all'. New forms of operations organisation and practice could overcome the 'technical constraints' of any operation, this being especially true if they are applied with a radical creativity hitherto unexpected in operations managers.

In spite of the appealing positive approach of this school, it could not fully explain away the intuitive appeal of the trade-off concept, and several attempts at an inclusive compromise which brings the two schools together were proposed. For example, it was suggested that some trade-offs did still, and would always, exist, while others had, for all practical purposes, been overcome by the new technologies and methodologies of manufacturing. Others suggested that while all trade-offs were real in the very short term, they could all be overcome in the long term. Most recent authors hold that 'trading-off' and 'overcoming trade-offs' are in fact distinct strategies, either of which may be adopted at different times by organisations. Neither are they mutually exclusive; operations may choose to trade off by repositing the balance of their performance, both as a response to changes in competitive strategy and to provide a better starting point for improvement. And key to overcoming trade-off constraints is the building of appropriate operating capabilities. Thus operations performance improvement is achieved by overcoming trade-offs, which, in turn, is achieved through enhanced operations capabilities.

The position taken in this book is close to the last school of thought. That is, that while there is a clear requirement for operations managers to position their operation such that they achieve the balance between performance objectives which are most appropriate for competitive advantage, there is also a longer-term imperative which involves finding ways of overcoming the intrinsic trade-offs caused by the constraints imposed by the operation's resources.

Houston, we have a problem[8]

On 3 December 1999 the Mars Polar Lander approached the outer layers of the Martian atmosphere. Its mission was to release two Deep Space 2 microprobes that would penetrate the plant's surface, analyse its soil and broadcast the results back to NASA. On entering the atmosphere the vehicle broke off contact. This was entirely as planned. It was then supposed to resume contact after landing. It never did. No one knows why. The best guess is that problems with its braking rockets caused it to crash disastrously into the surface of the planet. More embarrassing, this was the second Mars disaster. Only a few weeks earlier the Mars Climate Orbiter has probably burnt up in the Martian atmosphere. Both failures were later blamed on NASA's policy which it called *Faster, Better, Cheaper (FBC)*. Later this approach would be rechristened by critics, Faster, Cheaper . . . Splat!

FBC was a deliberate attempt to overcome what had always been seen in space exploration as a trade-off relationship. An old engineering proverb put it succinctly, 'Faster, better, cheaper – choose two of the above'. FBC challenged this and wanted all three. Critics of the FBC philosophy claimed that cutting budgets (cheaper) and going for ambitious project delivery dates (faster) had resulted in worse rather than better solutions. Certainly the panel set up to investigate the Mars programme failures concluded that the Mars projects were under-funded by as much as 30 per cent. Cost cutting had gone too far, especially in terms of getting rid of its more experienced engineers, who, being older and experienced, were expensive. In the previous five years more than 4500 scientists and engineers had left NASA, of whom only 1000 were younger than forty. The panel also pointed out that the Mars projects had been very tight on time. There is a relatively small launch window for missions to Mars which occurs only once every twenty-six months. The panel concluded that, with its budget cut and its launch date fixed, the only way for managers to operate when things started going wrong was to run an unacceptable degree of risk. Later NASA admitted that it had probably 'pushed the FBC philosophy too hard', and that it was 'time to rethink the approach'. Arguments still rage as to whether there is an absolute trade-off between speed, cost and quality in NASA projects, or whether the FCB philosophy is essentially the right approach that was just pushed too far.

A typology of trade-offs

Trade-offs are found in all types of operation and at all levels. Because trade-offs describe the relationships between different aspects of operations performance, any pair of performance measures potentially constitute a trade-off. Also, since they may represent a legitimate target for operations improvement, it is important to be able to identify an operation's trade-off relationships. Identifying trade-offs is best done by looking for them within specific categories. This requires a typology of trade-offs.

Our general list of generic performance objectives (quality, speed, dependability, flexibility and cost) provides a good starting point. For convenience we divide these

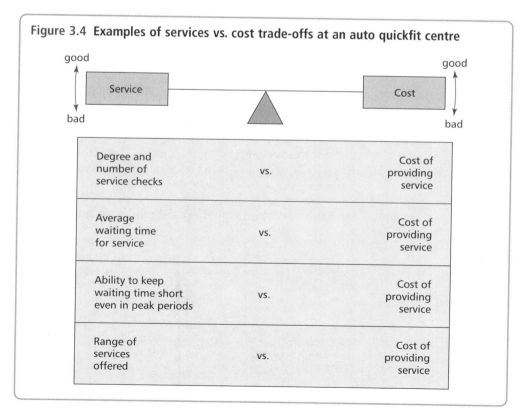

Figure 3.4 **Examples of services vs. cost trade-offs at an auto quickfit centre**

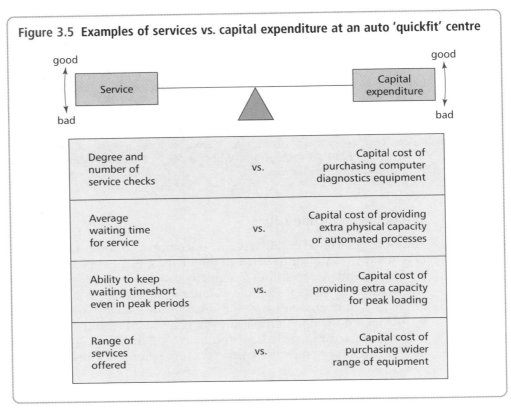

Figure 3.5 Examples of services vs. capital expenditure at an auto 'quickfit' centre

five generic performance objectives between, on one hand, the four which can be taken to constitute the *service* which an operation delivers to its customers, and, on the other hand, the *cost* of providing the service. Figure 3.4 illustrates this first category of trade-offs, between service and cost, for an operation which provides 'quickfit' services for automobile parts, tyres, etc. Various ways of enhancing the degree of service can be provided, but each of them may increase the cost of providing the service.

The level of service provided, and the operational cost of providing that service, are not the only two aspects of performance of interest within an operation's strat-

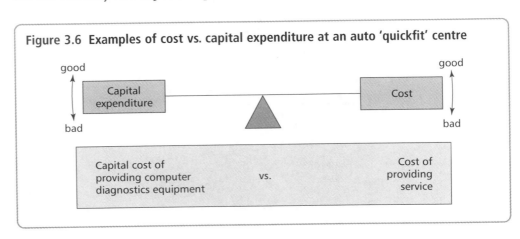

Figure 3.6 Examples of cost vs. capital expenditure at an auto 'quickfit' centre

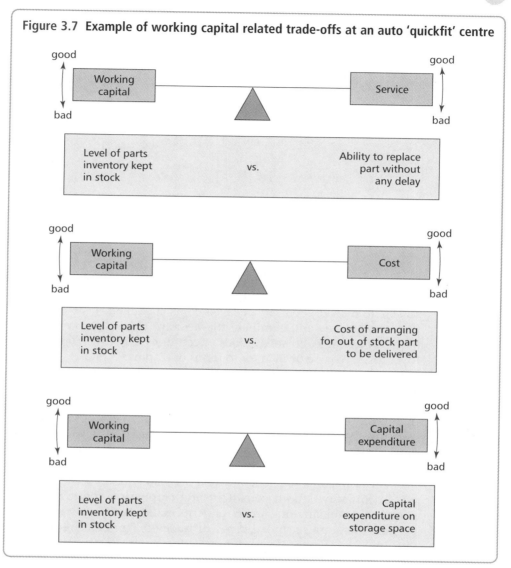

Figure 3.7 Example of working capital related trade-offs at an auto 'quickfit' centre

egy. Any operation may find it easy to provide superb service, even at relatively low operational cost, if it has an unlimited budget to spend on extra capacity or sophisticated process technology. It is important therefore to include capital expenditure as a performance category. Figure 3.5 gives some examples of how the automobile 'quickfit' centre may trade off between aspects of the service it delivers to its customers on one hand, and the degree to which it is willing to invest in capital expenditure in the operation.

In a similar way, the operation's cost of providing service can be improved if the business is prepared to invest capital expenditure, as is illustrated in Figure 3.6.

For many operations, especially those producing the more intangible services, these three categories of performance are sufficient to describe most trade-offs. However, for those operations where significant amounts of inventory occur, the

Figure 3.8 Trade-off categories

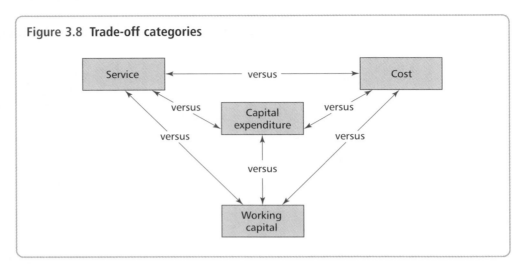

extent of investment in working capital must be included as a performance category. So, for example, a manufacturing, or any other materials processing, operation may be able to deliver good service levels to its customers, keep output rates (and therefore costs) steady and eliminate the need for extra capital expenditure on capacity by allowing large finished goods inventories. But this solution is not pain free. Inventories have to be paid for in terms of working capital. Figure 3.7 gives examples of how working capital is traded off with service, cost and capital expenditure at the automobile 'quickfit' centre.

Note that, as illustrated, the trade-offs shown in this, and other diagrams, show a high position as meaning good performance and a low position as meaning bad performance. When discussing service this is fine. High levels of service are taken as good and low levels generally regarded as bad. For cost, capital expenditure and working capital, however, the opposite holds true. High levels of any of these performance categories are generally taken as bad and low levels good. Depicting trade-offs in this way is both consistent and emphasises the major point of trade-offs, namely that making one aspect of performance better may make another worse.

Thus, there are six broad types of trade-off representing trade-offs between the four basic categories of operations performance. But there may also be trade-offs within each category of performance. The most obvious example is within the category of performance we have called 'service'. Service, as we have defined it, includes the generic performance objectives of quality, speed, dependability and flexibility. Each of these may trade off with each other. So, for example, at the automotive 'quickfit' centre, attempting to speed up the service time beyond the capabilities of the process may lead to a reduction in service quality. Similarly, broadening the range of service offered to customers may, by increasing the complexity of the operation, reduce its ability to dependably meet quoted service times. Figure 3.8 illustrates the overall trade-off typology.

Trade-offs in reconciliation

If trade-offs did not exist there would be no problem in reconciling market requirement with operations resources. Whatever the market demanded, operations resources could supply without excessive operational cost, capital expenditure or working capital. But trade-offs do exist. In fact they are the ultimate expression of why the reconciliation process is so problematic. Here we describe reconciliation in terms of the two elements in managing trade-offs within the operation:

- repositioning the balance between the different aspects of the trade-off, and
- overcoming the trade-off through improvement.

Reconciliation as repositioning trade-offs

While not the only way to manage trade-offs, repositioning clearly has a role in reconciling market requirements with operations resources. In fact at one time it was regarded as the only way of achieving reconciliation. An operation's relative achievement in each dimension of performance, it was argued, should be driven by the requirements of its markets. This would involve emphasising some aspects of performance and (inevitably) sacrificing others. Even when it was considered to be the sole route to reconciliation, repositioning the relative performance balance through trade-offs was never regarded as straightforward. Operations are bundles of complex organisational and technological systems. They cannot be simply repositioned by adjusting a set of simple controls. Two factors in particular complicate the repositioning process:

- There is a 'friction cost' of changing relative performance levels.
- The complexity of trade-off interrelationships can set in chain a set of other trade-offs.

As an example take a frozen food manufacturer. One of the trade-offs which its operations will have to manage is that between inventory levels of finished product and the ability to respond to unexpected demand, therefore giving better service to customers. The company has to choose between good customer service or good (i.e. low) working capital. In practice, changing the balance between these two dimensions of performance will itself involve some extra effort (and therefore cost) in order to decide exactly which products are to have their stock levels increased or reduced. More important, there is a degree of risk involved in making this choice. Get the decision wrong and both dimensions of performance could get worse. For example, suppose working capital is to be increased to give better customer service by investing in higher inventory levels in selected product lines. If the wrong products are chosen then working capital will increase while customer service levels could get worse. The company could finish up with high stock levels of the wrong products while failing to satisfy its customers in delivering the right ones. To some extent, changing the position of a trade-off involves moving to less well known operating conditions. This not only means extra planning effort but also extra risk. Factoring the extra planning with the increased risk together constitutes the *friction cost* of repositioning.

Even when the trade-off between working capital and customer service is executed well, in terms of making the correct stocking decisions, other relationships may complicate the issue. For example, increased inventory may give a better chance of responding to customer requirements, but it will also increase the average time products spend in finished goods storage. Given that this product has a limited life, quality may be compromised by extra time in storage and the 'shelf life' available to the customer may be reduced. So by repositioning the trade-off (between service level and working capital) in favour of service level, another trade-off (between service level on one hand and product quality and life on the other) has been affected. Repositioning trade-offs is rarely an isolated decision. In practice, attention cannot simply be focused on one, easily bounded, relationship. The *interrelationships between trade-offs* need to be considered.

British Airways trades off space utilisation for quality[9]

Until the mid-1980s, most airlines had traditionally operated a 'twin class' system – First Class and Economy Class. Then came Business Class, with service standards placed between First and Economy. Ideally designed for the burgeoning business travel market, it attracted customers from both the First and Economy Classes. British Airways' strategy was typical. On most non-European sectors, BA offered all three levels of cabin service to their customers, with First & Business Classes particularly popular on long haul flights, the transatlantic route being the single biggest market. By the mid-1990s the first class market seemed to be in terminal decline, with many airlines pulling out of the First Class product entirely and, instead, concentrating on offering superior service in Business Class.

British Airways, an airline proud of its service standards, as espoused in its slogan – *The World's Favourite Airline* – took a different view. They believed that the whole concept of First Class Travel needed to be redefined and in early 1994 they decided to refurbish their First Class cabins. Existing First Class cabins had 18 passenger seats, each with a 62 inch seat pitch, serviced by four cabin crew. BA's research using passenger focus groups showed that the most important factors associated with First Class Travel were, in fact, space related. The main challenge for BA was to create maximum passenger space within the existing area and simultaneously boost revenues from this segment. Their answer was a new design for their First Class cabins, the 'Bed in the Sky' – a private first class seat encased in a shell that could transform itself into a completely horizontal bed. With the help of in-cabin technology, all control facilities were accessible within an arm's length of the passenger seat – Audio/Video, Light Switches, Call Buttons, etc. However, the more spacious seats meant that cabin size, in terms of seating, was reduced to 14 passenger seats. BA was also able to complement the new cabin designs with improved standards of cabin service and cuisine.

This exercise, which was completed in mid-1996 with refitting all their 80 long-haul aircraft, succeeded in repositioning BA's First Class product. It now had a unique First Class offering with no comparable competition. But it also had higher fixed cost and fewer seats. Further, improved service quality meant greater running costs of the operation. This meant that BA had to increase its seat utilisation in order to generate higher revenues from its improved service. Results from BA show that by coming up with this differentiated product, it has been able to arrest the decline in first class travel, and increase its market share and revenues in the segment (estimates show that revenues have exceeded the business plan proposals by over 10 per cent). So successful was this exercise that in 2000 BA repeated the strategy in some of its Business Class products.

It is a mistake to dismiss repositioning as merely working within the existing constraints of an operation. Repositioning can result in sometimes substantial improvements in operations performance. For example, the box on British Airways' first class seat redesign shows that changing the balance between aspects of performance can result in superior performance overall. With its more luxurious seats, BA significantly raised the effective level of service it was offering its First Class passengers. However, this was at the expense of both the operational cost of providing that service (higher staff costs per passenger and space costs per passenger) and the degree of capital expenditure (replacing existing seats with more expensive seats). Yet the extra revenue it attracted with its higher quality product seems to have more than compensated for the extra operating and capital costs.

Reconciliation as overcoming trade-offs

Repositioning trade-offs was described earlier as moving the balance between dimensions of performance along an operation's 'natural frontier' (from X to Y in Figure 3.9). Using repositioning to achieve reconciliation between market requirements and operations resources is fine if market requirements lie within the natural frontier of the operation, as in area P in Figure 3.9. However, if market requirements are such that performance levels must fall within area Q then the only way to achieve reconciliation is either to abandon the target market which requires this combination of performance, or alternatively to *extend* the natural frontier of the operation so that its performance is improved to the extent that it can now satisfy market requirements – position Z in Figure 3.9.

For example, in many financial services firms that offer a 'direct call' service, one trade-off is that between the utilisation of staff in call centres and the time taken to respond to customer calls. If the company's human resource policies allow for a 'capacity cushion' of staff to be on duty they may not always be fully employed and therefore labour cost per transaction would be relatively high. However, because of the relative over-supply of staff, customers would only rarely have to wait more than a few rings before their call was answered. The company could therefore gain more business. Transaction costs may be high but so would be revenue. A *repositioning* approach would involve deciding on the balance between utilisation of staff (therefore transaction cost) and response time (therefore revenue) that would maximise profitability.

However, an *improvement* approach would seek to either:

- improve both dimensions of performance, or
- improve one dimension of performance while preventing or limiting any deterioration in the other.

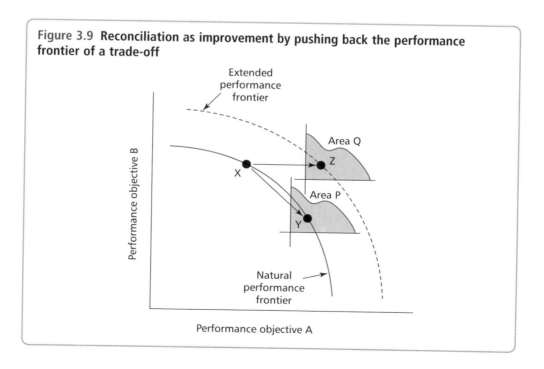

Figure 3.9 Reconciliation as improvement by pushing back the performance frontier of a trade-off

Both of these options would, in effect, push back the natural frontier of the operation's capabilities. In the case of the financial services company, with its trade-off between transaction cost and revenue, suppose the company decide to redesign their working time practices. Their new approach now involves paying a small premium to staff who live within a 20-minute journey time of their call centre. This premium would allow them to be 'on call' for certain periods when demand was relatively unpredictable. This allows each call centre to bring in staff at very short notice should their predictive systems indicate a higher than expected level of demand building up. Making such a change could materially affect the trade-off relationship between staff costs and customer response time by allowing better response time with only marginal increases in staff costs. The trade-off is still there, of course. Even with this new working time policy, staff utilisation and response time will trade off against each other. But now the trade-off is at a higher level – the operation's natural frontier has been pushed back.

Trade-off curves

In Figure 3.9 a convex curve represented the assumed relationship between any two aspects of performance. This means that the *rate* of deterioration in performance of one increases with increased performance in the other. In other words, there is an increasing rate of sacrifice in one aspect of performance if the operation wishes to extend its performance in the other; hence the convex nature of the curve. This seems to make sense for most operations. Even operating at its efficient 'natural frontier' an operation can make relatively small increases in one aspect of performance with only small sacrifice in the others. So, for example, an accounting firm can extend its client services to incorporate relatively small additions to accounting standards with only a small reduction in its staff productivity. But ask the operation to extend significantly beyond its normal operating practices and the effects are likely to be disproportionately greater. So, for example, if the accounting firm was asked by its multinational clients to incorporate dual standard accounting for both local and international standards, the effect on staff productivity would be very significant.

Three points need making about trade-off curves in general. The first is that an operation may not be operating at, or near, its 'natural frontier'. That is, its performance is not constrained by the level of development of its resources. If so, it can easily increase one aspect of performance with no reduction in another. In fact, the definition of the natural frontier is that the operation could not increase one aspect of performance without a reduction in another. So, if an operation finds it can move from A to B in Figure 3.10, the operation cannot be on its trade-off boundary. It can achieve any combination of (in this case) cost and variety within the limits required by its markets. In effect, the capability of the operation exceeds the requirements of its markets, at least in the short term. Second, the curve shown in Figure 3.10 is a *conceptual* representation of trade-off relationships. It is not, in practice, a smooth continuous curve but rather a series of discontinuities which, taken together, roughly follow the general convex relationship. Performance factors, such as variety, are not precisely measurable and a unit increase in variety may have little effect on cost, or it may have a significant impact. It will depend on the nature of how variety is increased. Furthermore, the exact effect on one aspect of performance of changing another is rarely known in advance, and is usually still open to interpret-

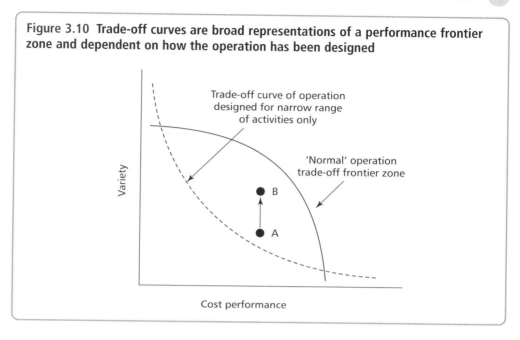

Figure 3.10 Trade-off curves are broad representations of a performance frontier zone and dependent on how the operation has been designed

Variety

Trade-off curve of operation designed for narrow range of activities only

'Normal' operation trade-off frontier zone

B

A

Cost performance

ation afterwards. The most useful way to think of the natural frontier is to see it as a 'frontier zone' rather than an clear boundary between what is possible and what is not.

Perhaps the most important point concerning trade-off curves is that their shape can depend on how an operation is organised. The convex shape which describes most relationships is that way because the resources and the deployment of resources in most operations are a compromise between different objectives. But operations can choose resources and deploy them in different ways. For example, suppose an operation was designed specifically to produce only a very narrow range of services or products with all its staff, process technology and infrastructure geared up to that aim only. Under these conditions considerable cost savings may be possible. For example, if an audit firm designed an operation to carry out *only* simple standard audits on small to medium-sized engineering manufacturing companies, it could develop processes and procedures specifically to meet the needs of such clients. It could devise expert systems to automate much of its decision making and it could train its staff with only the knowledge to carry out such audits. Focused and efficient, the operation could achieve exceptional productivity provided the demand could keep it fully employed. However, such an operation is something of a one-trick pony. Ask it to do anything else and it would have considerable difficulty. Increasing the variety placed on the operation outside its design specification would have an immediate and significant impact on its costs. In effect, designing the operation this way has made the relationship curve between variety and cost concave rather than convex. Asking the operation to move away from the performance objectives for which it was specifically designed brings an immediate penalty. Asking it to move even further away from its design specification also brings a cost, but not one to match that initial penalty. In effect, operations can 'trade off' trade-off curves. An operation can be designed to be reasonable in most aspects of performance under most conditions but in doing so one trades off its ability to have exceptional performance in a narrow range of objectives. Alternatively, one can design an operation to focus on a narrow range of objectives and achieve exceptional performance, but at the cost of a vulnerability to significant performance penalties should it be asked to do anything outside its design range. This is illustrated in the broken line in Figure 3.10 and is the basis of the concept of operations focus, discussed in the next section.

Targeting and operations focus

In this section we will review one of the most effective 'types' of operations strategy – using *focused* operations. This concept of focus is both powerful and proven because at its heart lies a very simple notion, that many operations are carrying out too many (often conflicting) tasks. The obvious result is that they are unable to perform them all with any real degree of success, whereas concentrating on one or two specific objectives, even at the expense of adopting a vulnerable 'concave' trade-off curve as discussed previously, can lead to substantially superior performance in those few objectives.

The concept of focus

Most of the early work on what was then called the 'focused factory' concept was carried out by Wickham Skinner of Harvard Business School. Based on his ideas of how trade-offs dominated operations decision making, he argued that one way of achieving an effective operations strategy is through the concept of factory focus. This meant that first a business should establish a consistent set of policies for the various elements of its operations, which will support, not only each other, but also marketing requirements. Second, because of the inherent trade-offs, one operation cannot provide peak performance in all performance objectives at the same time. In his article *The Focused Factory*,[10] Skinner based these arguments on his observations of a variety of US industries in the early 1970s. He found that most factories were trying to tackle too many tasks and therefore trying to achieve too many objectives. Because of this they were failing to perform well in any single objective. He concluded that a factory that was focused on a narrow range of products, and aimed at satisfying a particular section of the market, would outperform a plant that was attempting to satisfy a broader set of objectives. The equipment, systems and procedures that are necessary to achieve a more limited range of tasks for a smaller set of customers could also result in lower (especially overhead) costs. Focus, according to Skinner, can be expressed as dedicating each operation to a limited, concise, manageable set of products, technologies, volumes and markets, then structuring policies and support services so they focus on one *explicit* task, rather than on a variety of inconsistent, conflicting, *implicit* tasks.

Focus as operations segmentation

In Chapter 1 we briefly described how marketing managers attempt to understand their markets through the process of segmentation. Market segmentation breaks heterogeneous markets down into smaller, more homogeneous, markets. Within operations resources, what we have called 'focus' is very similar to the process of segmentation. In fact it can be regarded as operations segmentation. Operations, like markets, are complex. A whole range of different skills, process technologies, flow sequences, knowledge applications, individual decisions, and so on, come together to create a range of different products and/or services. Operations managers spend much of their time attempting to split up the tasks of managing these resources in order to simplify them and thereby manage them more effectively. In effect, they are segmenting their operations resources. And, just as in marketing there are continual debates around the best way to segment markets, so in operations there are similar debates as to the most sensible way to segment resources. Ideally, operations segmentation and market segmentation should correspond. That is, separate clusters of resources clearly and distinctively serve individual market segments; see Figure 3.11. The major problem with the whole idea of focus, however, is that what is a sensible basis for segmenting markets does not always map onto the ideal basis for segmenting operations resources. For example, an advertising agency may segment its market by the size of the promotional accounts of its clients. Ideally, it may wish to have different service offerings for large, medium and small accounts. Each of these offerings would have different mixes of services specialising in different types of communication, such as TV, posters, radio, press, etc. In this way they can position themselves as 'one-stop shops' that will produce entire marketing campaigns seamlessly for each market segment. However, from an operations viewpoint, the company's creative staff (its main resource) may retain their creativity more effectively if they work in teams focused on specific media. So, for example, one team specialising in TV advertising, another in press campaigns, and so on. So, what is ideal for the market (one-stop shops by size of promotional spend) does not match the ideal way of organising resources to maintain or improve their effectiveness (in this case, creativity).

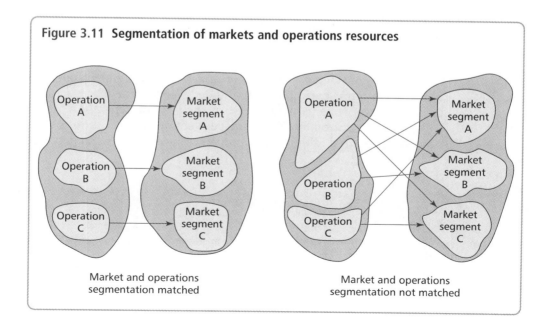

Figure 3.11 Segmentation of markets and operations resources

Market and operations
segmentation matched

Market and operations
segmentation not matched

Strategic focus

Although in this chapter we are dealing with the idea of focus as an operations concept, it is also at the centre of a lively debate within the corporate strategy area. The 1990s saw a reversal in the trend evident in the previous two decades of attempts to put together diversified corporations. Companies that try to extend their managerial capabilities across several diverse markets were generally punished by stock markets around the world. So, for example, in January 1997 the American giant PepsiCo announced that it would spin off its fast-food business. As well as making the fizzy drinks, for which it is famous, and snack foods, PepsiCo also owned Pizza Hut, Taco Bell and KFC (Kentucky Fried Chicken). Stock market analysts reacted favourably to news of the divestment. The previous structure had confused them. Analysts tend to assess restaurant businesses in terms of their cash flows, while packaged goods, such as drinks and snacks, are judged in terms of their earnings. PepsiCo's more focused rival Coca-Cola was far easier for the analyst to assess. But it is more than the imperfections of stock markets that has prompted companies like PepsiCo to focus on a narrower set of businesses. It is the failure of the diversified model.

Traditionally, diversified conglomerates were seen as having two main advantages. They allowed managers to take cash from stable and profitable parts of the total business and invest it in growth businesses which had long-term potential. And, with a well-chosen portfolio of businesses, when one business was at the low point in its business cycle others would be at the high point. The group as a whole, therefore, would maintain some kind of stability. But global capital markets now allow investors to make their own minds up where they want to invest, and business cycles are not as dramatic. So single-mindedness became the fashionable virtue. If corporate management's attention is unambiguously focused on one set of markets, it is argued, they are more likely to do what is right for those markets and businesses. This triumph of clarity and single-mindedness is exactly what focus, at a more operational level, is all about.

The 'operation-within-an-operation' concept

Any decision to focus an operation might appear to carry with it the need to set up completely new operations if further products/services are added to the range, and it is true that in some cases a failure to do this has undermined successful operations. However, it is not always feasible, necessary or desirable to do this and the 'operation-within-an-operation' (or 'plant-within-a-plant', or 'shop-within-a-shop') concept is a practical response that allows an organisation to accrue the benefits of focus without the considerable expense of setting up independent operations. A portion of the operation is partitioned off and dedicated to the manufacture of a particular product/delivery of a particular service. The physical separation of products/services will allow the introduction of independent workforces, control systems, quality standards, etc. In addition, this approach allows for easier supervision, motivation and accounting.

Low-cost airlines focus on ... low cost[11]

It all started with Southwest Airlines in the USA, which began operating back in 1971 and proved that, by organising its airline operations ruthlessly around providing a low-cost 'no frills' service, it could both grow its customer base and do so profitably. Around the world, and especially in Europe, Southwest's example inspired a number of imitators, who likewise focused on focus. In Europe the European Airlines Deregulation Act prompted the emergence of several low-cost airlines (LCAs). The larger airlines had been drawn towards longer-haul routes where their interconnecting network of services and their extended levels of service were a major attraction. So, even in Europe, which has a viable and popular rail network, several companies saw the opportunity to offer low-cost, short-haul services. Companies such as Virgin Express, Ryan Air and Easy Jet all adopted similar strategies for keeping costs down. To some extent these strategies included trading off levels of service for reduced costs. So complimentary in-flight service was kept to a minimum, secondary and sometimes less convenient airports were used, and one standard class of travel was offered. In other ways these companies attempted to overcome trade-offs by focusing their operations. For example, they focused on a standardised fleet of aircraft, thus keeping maintenance costs down. They focused on their key processes such as passenger handling while outsourcing more peripheral processes. They focused on direct sales to their customers, often pioneering low-cost channels such as the Internet. They also focused on those elements of the process which hinder the effective utilisation of their expensive resources, such as reducing aircraft turn-round time at the airports.

To keep focused, however, requires a clarity of vision. One European airline which was seen as an LCA, Debonair, attempt to break ranks with other LCAs by offering a slightly higher quality of service and a twin class of travel (including business class) and other such frills as a frequent flier programme and complimentary on-board services etc. Furthermore, the airline did not have the same uniform aircraft fleet as its competitors, operating instead with a variety of aircraft, most of which were of smaller capacity than its rivals. After less than three years of operation Debonair was forced by its liquidity problems to call in the receivers.

Types of focus

Just as there are many ways of segmenting markets, so there are several approaches to focusing operations. The organisation of process technologies staff and processes can be based on several criteria. Table 3.1 illustrates some of the more common approaches to focus. These can be placed on a spectrum from those that take market-related factors as being an appropriate way to segment operations resources, through to those that allow the resource characteristics themselves to dictate how operations are split up.

- *Performance objective focus* – The operation is set up solely to satisfy the performance requirements of a particular market or market segment. So all products or services produced in an operation have very similar characteristics in terms of generic performance objectives.

- *Product/service specification focus* – The operation is set up for a clearly defined product or service, or range of products or services, the implication being that each defined range of products or services is targeted at a clearly defined market segment.

- *Geographic focus* – Sometimes operations can be segmented in terms of the geographic market they serve. This may be because the characteristics of a company's different market segments are largely defined by their geographic location. Alternatively, it may mean that the nature of the service offered by an operation is geographically limited. Most high-contact operations, such as fast-food restaurants, would fall into this category.

- *Variety focus* – A company may wish to segment its operations in terms of the number of different activities (usually dictated by the number of different products or services) it is engaged in. So, for example, one site may concentrate on

relatively low variety or standardised products and services while another concentrates on high variety or customised products and services.

- *Volume focus* – High-volume operations, with their emphasis on standardisation
  and repetition, are likely to need different process technologies, labour skills and
  planning and control systems from those with lower volume. Volume focus
  extends this thinking to the creation of separate operations for different volume
  requirements.

- *Process requirements focus* – Here, a particular technology is the point of focus for
  the operation. This allows the organisation to concentrate on extending its
  knowledge and expertise about the process. Over the life cycle of a
  production/service system, the likely advantage to be gained from a process focus
  will change. As an operation starts up and moves into the growth phase, building
  process capability will be critical; however, as volumes stabilise the process itself

Table 3.1 Firms can use various criteria to 'focus' their operations

	Focus criteria	Ideal operations resource conditions	Ideal market requirements conditions
Operations segmentation based on market criteria	**Performance objectives** Cluster products/services by market requirements	Products and services with similar market requirements have similar processing requirements	Market segmentation is based clearly on customer requirements
	Product/service specification Limit number of products/ services in each part of the operation	Similar products and services require similar technologies, skills and processes	Products and services are targeted on specific market segments
	Geography Cluster products/services by the geographic market they serve	The geographic area where products and services are created has a significant impact on operations performance	Market segmentation can be based on geographic regions
	Variety Separately cluster high-variety products/services and low-variety products/ services together	The nature of technology, skills and processes is primarily determined by the variety with which products/services are created	Market segmentation can be based on the degree of product/service choice required by customers
	Volume Separately cluster high-volume products/services and low-volume products/ services together	The nature of technology, skills and processes is primarily determined by the volume at which products/services are created	Market segmentation can be summarised as 'mass markets' versus more 'specialised markets'
Operations segmentation based on resource criteria	**Process requirements** Cluster products/services with similar process requirements together	The process requirements (types of technology, skills, knowledge, etc.) of products/ services can be clearly distinguished	Products and services with similar processing requirements are targeted on specific market segments

will become more stable. A process focus can also become very significant as volumes decline and the organisation seeks to redirect its operations. However, many firms choose to close an operation rather than redirect it.

Theory Box | **Burning your bridges (or boats)[12]**

The nature of focus is that it is not ambiguous. Opting for excellence in a narrow set of objectives at the expense of the ability to be excellent at the others calls for a significant level of commitment to the objectives which have been chosen. The idea of commitment to a strategy has long been debated in business strategy and, before that, in military strategy.

A classic military illustration of commitment is shown in Figure 3.12. Two armies want to occupy an island, though neither is particularly keen to fight the other for it. Suppose Army 1 occupies the island pre-emptively and burns the bridge behind it. Army 2 then is likely to cede the island because it realises that Army 1 has no option other than to fight if Army 2 attacks. By restricting its own flexibility (to retreat) and ensuring its commitment, Army 1 has won the island without having to fight.

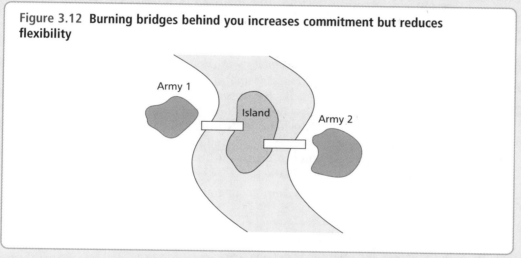

Figure 3.12 **Burning bridges behind you increases commitment but reduces flexibility**

An example of this is the action taken by the Spanish Conquistador Hernán Cortés. In 1518 he landed his twelve ships on the coast of Mexico and soon determined to strike inland to the Aztec capital to defeat the Emperor Montezuma. However, Montezuma's troops had such a fearsome reputation that Cortés' men were somewhat reluctant to face the far larger Aztec army, especially since they knew that capture would mean a horrible death. Discontent reached such a pitch that one group of men planned to steal a ship and sail back to their homes. Cortés' solution to this was to execute the chief conspirators and beach nine of his twelve ships. In the face of such focused commitment, his men had little option but to follow him.

Benefits and risks in focus

Different kinds of focus criteria carry different kinds of benefits and risk. However, usually the benefits and risks of focus can be summarised in the way illustrated in Figure 3.13.

Benefits include:

- *Clarity of performance objectives* – Clearly targeted markets imply at least some degree of discrimination between market segments. This in turn makes easier the task of prioritising those few performance objectives which are important for that market. This allows operations managers to be set relatively unambiguous and non-conflicting objectives to pursue in their day-to-day management of resources.

- *Developing appropriate resources* – A narrow set of focused resources allows those resources to be developed specifically to meet the relatively narrow set of performance objectives required by the market. Process technologies, skills and infrastructural resources can all be organised so as to trade off unimportant aspects of performance for those valued by the target market.

- *Enhanced learning and improvement* – A combination of clear objectives, together with resources organised to meet those objectives, can enhance an operation's ability to manage its learning and improvement of its processes. Certainly the opposite holds true. Broad and/or confused objectives, together with complex resource structures, make it difficult to build process knowledge, learn how to extend the capabilities of processes or thereby improve their performance.

The risks involved in focus include the following.

- *Significant shifts in the marketplace* – Although less common than 'scare stories' often suggest, it is clear that a dramatic shift in the overall competitive environment can undermine the effectiveness of a focus strategy. For example, in turn-of-the-twentieth-century New England, one firm dominated the market for domestic and commercial ice throughout North America. They had established an immensely successful and highly focused production and distribution system but they were powerless when a technical innovation – the domestic refrigerator – effectively removed their market.

- *Few economies of scale* – Within an operation, focusing often involves separating

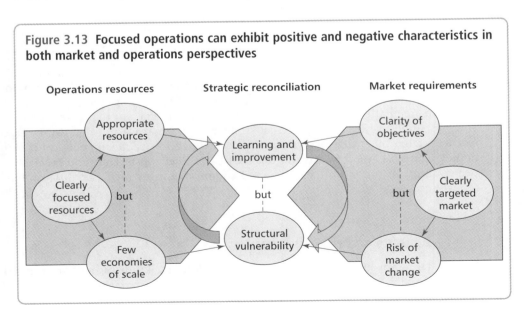

Figure 3.13 Focused operations can exhibit positive and negative characteristics in both market and operations perspectives

out resources which were once bundled together. This allows these resources to be developed appropriately for the market they serve but, because they no longer form part of a larger whole, they may not be able to achieve the same economies of scale as before. For example, a corporate purchasing department, buying goods and services for a whole corporation, may achieve economies of scale in the use of its resources and in its purchasing power. Splitting up such a department between businesses may allow them to enhance their capabilities in the type of purchasing necessary for each individual business but this may be gained at the expense of buying power and efficiency.

- *Structural vulnerability* – Combine the two risks above and any focused set of resources may be structurally vulnerable. Relatively minor changes in market requirements may destroy the benefits of being close to a market while, at the same time, there are few economies of scale to protect their viability.

Focus in insurance[13]

The insurance world is not known for great arguments regarding purpose and strategy. Yet one topic has pushed the world's largest insurance companies into opposing camps. The question is, *'Should composite insurance companies – those that underwrite both "life" policies and "property and casualty" policies – specialise in one or the other?'* On one side of the argument, Lincoln National, one of America's prominent insurance firms, sold its property business in 1998 in order to concentrate on life insurance. The same route has been taken by Prudential Insurance in the UK. In the other camp, AXA-UAP, the French-based insurance company, and American International Group, in the United States, are still in both businesses.

In many ways both parts of the insurance business look similar. Life insurance provides protection against the risks of dying prematurely (or living too long, in the case of annuities). Property and casualty (P and C) insurance provides protection against the risks of damage to cars, homes or other property, as well as other things such as business liability. Both are also similar operationally. Both act as investment trusts by collecting premiums up front and then investing the money in stocks and bonds in order to provide funds to pay out claims and provide profits. But it is not the similarities but the differences that make the case for focusing on one or the other.

Life insurance is a growth industry. In the developed world, ageing populations and a decline in the state provision of pensions is fuelling the growth. Life insurance products often include an element of saving as well as insurance against premature death. In some ways their main competitors are the providers of other long-term savings products such as banks. Risks are judged on an actuarial basis with one person's shorter-than-average life balancing another's longevity. This makes for a relatively stable investment environment. Assets need to be managed carefully in order to ensure a high return over the long term. Operational processes need to be able to keep a track on investments like those used by any other fund management operation.

Property and casualty insurance is very different. Premiums are paid against a specific risk, usually for a specific period, and disappear if the insured event does not happen. This is a mature industry where competition is largely centred around cost. Its key operations tasks are concerned with effective risk selection and the efficient handling of claims. Forecasting risk is usually far more difficult than with life insurance. Natural disasters are less predictable than death. This means that claims, and therefore profits, are more volatile. This in turn means that industry regulators will usually require P and C insurance companies to hold relatively large capital reserves to provide some stability against unexpected events. And although, like life insurance, premiums are invested in stock markets, the volatile nature of P and C insurance means that cash may be suddenly needed for large payouts. This means that investments must be relatively short-term and low risk.

▶

These differences between the two parts of the insurance business have led some British and American companies to focus on one side of the business or the other. But this is not happening in all regions. In Japan industry regulators have always kept P and C and life insurance totally separate but in other parts of the world industry structures work to keep them together. For example, the German insurance industry is very heavily regulated with little or no competition based on products or price differences. Customers, therefore, have no need of independent advice on which products to buy so insurers tend to have their own sales force or exclusive agents. In Britain and America most business is transacted through independent agents or brokers who identify the best deal for individual customers. With a dedicated and expensive sales channel already in place, however, German insurers are prone to use it to sell as many products as possible. This provides a considerable disincentive to reduce the total volume of sales by focusing on one side of the business or the other.

Drifting out of focus

Even when operations are set up to focus on one clearly specified set of objectives, they can, over time, drift out of focus. In fact some authorities would argue[14] that unfocused operations are often a result of a gradual, but insidious, drift away from a clear strategy. There can be several reasons for this.

- *New products and services* – Many companies, after developing new products or services, look to their existing operations to produce/deliver them. There is clearly a temptation to do this without examining the specific requirements of that particular product/service and evaluating the merits (and costs) of developing a new operation. Problematically, it is the firm's most successful operations that are perceived as being most able to cope with new products/services – even if their success is built upon focus.

- *Strategy drift* – In the absence of a clear competitive direction, managers often attempt to perform equally well against all of the many operations performance measures that exist. This (as discussed earlier) can lead to the dilution of the overall strategic impact of the firm.

- *Control by specialist* – Specialists in areas such as process technology, computer systems, inventory control, etc. will tend, in the absence of a more explicit operations strategy, to develop their own 'systems', which protect their own organisational position, or optimise their local objectives, at the expense of greater strategic objectives.

- *Company-wide solutions* – Looking for panaceas in the belief that one solution can cure all the problems of every operation, without sufficient regard for the need to tailor solutions to suit particular circumstances.

- *Business growth* – When operations have to stretch or be reconfigured to deal with larger volumes, this often leads to a loss of focus.

SUMMARY ANSWERS TO KEY QUESTIONS

Do the role and key performance objectives of operations stay constant or vary over time?

Both. Markets change, and the capabilities of operations resources develop over time. Therefore, not only does operations strategy change, the relative importance of its performance objectives will change. In fact, over the long term, the operations strategies of most enterprises can be seen to vary, either in response to deliberate attempts to change overall strategic direction, or in a more emergent sense where a consensus of the most appropriate strategic direction forms through accumulated operational experience.

Are trade-offs between operations performance objectives inevitable, or can they be overcome?

Both. Yes, trade-offs are always, to some extent, inevitable in that pushing an operation to extremes in one aspect of performance will inevitably mean some sacrifice in other aspects of performance. Yet trade-offs can, at the margin, be overcome. In fact the whole concept of operations performance improvement is, in effect, an attempt to overcome trade-offs. It is therefore the responsibility of all operations managers to seek ways of overcoming trade-offs.

What type of trade-offs occur in operations?

Any aspect of operations performance can trade off with any other. However, it is convenient to think of trade-offs between and within four sets of strategic performance measures: the *cost* of producing goods and services, the level of *service* that the operation can give to its customers, the *capital expenditure* the operation commits to its facilities, and the level of *working capital* (usually in the form of inventories) the operation works with.

What are the pros and cons of focused operations?

The benefits of focus include achieving a *clarity* of performance objectives which aids day-to-day decision making, developing resources in a manner *appropriate* to achieve a narrow set of objectives, and the enhanced *learning* and improvement that derives from concentrating on a narrow set of tasks. On the other hand, the problems with focus include the dangers inherent if there are significant *shifts in the marketplace* which may leave the operation 'stranded' with an inappropriate performance mix, the reduction in opportunities for *economies of scale* as operations are segmented internally, and some *structural vulnerability* because of the first two issues.

'Call-Us' Banking Services

'Call-Us' Banking Services (CUBS), a direct financial services company, offered a telephone-based banking service. Originally a regional Savings and Loan company with a small network of 'bricks and mortar' branches, they had expanded and developed into a direct banking operation that offered three types of financial product. The first and dominant product group was conventional *retail banking*. This service offered the normal range of savings and cheque accounts together with direct debit and payment facilities. The second product group was *loan services*. This was divided into *retail loans*, which offered a service to retailers wishing to provide their customers with credit facilities, and *personal loans*, where individual customers applied directly for loans. The third, and newest, product group was *insurance* offering both automobile and home contents insurance. This latter product group was branded differently from the other products and advertised its services separately.

The company's operations were centred around five call centres. Three of these were devoted to 'account management' for the retail banking services, one was devoted to loan products and one dealt exclusively with insurance products. All five call centres were in different locations within the region.

Account management activities for banking services consisted of simple debit and credit transactions which moved money between different accounts. Customers could phone in at any time of the day or night and conduct their transactions. Demand at any point in time was fairly predictable, especially during the daytime. Demand during the night hours was considerably lower than in the daytime and also less predictable.

> '*Most of the time we forecast demand pretty accurately and so we can schedule the correct number of employees to staff the work stations. There is still some risk of course. Scheduling too many staff at any point in time will waste money and increase our costs while scheduling too few will reduce the quality and response of the service we give.*' (Peter Fisher, Operations Director)

In the loan product call centre, the department that processes calls from retail customers was staffed only during normal retail opening hours. But during those hours it was important that sufficient capacity was provided to deal with retail customers' calls. Peter Fisher explained:

> '*This is a very competitive market. If a salesperson in a showroom phones in to arrange a loan for a customer and we don't answer within two or three rings, the salesperson will simply dial another company and we will have lost the business. Because of this we tend, if anything, to over-staff the department, especially during critical sales times such as Saturday morning.*'

Once contact was made by the retail store, the customer's details were keyed into the system which automatically checked them against a credit rating agency's database. Credit rating agencies are specialist suppliers of information who assess the credit worthiness of individual customers. Loan companies, such as this division of CUBS, purchased services from such agencies. Some agencies, for a higher fee, will guarantee faster and more detailed credit assessments. CUBS were currently considering whether to purchase this enhanced service. Other ways of improving service to 'retail' customers were being considered by Peter Fisher:

> 'Recently we have been experimenting with installing our own computers into retailers' showrooms. This would allow a salesperson to enter their customer's details and links directly and simultaneously to the credit agency and our own systems. It could provide a much faster service for retail customers and would tie them into our company, but it would take considerable investment to install such systems in all our customers' showrooms.'

The personal loans department in the loan call centre operated very much like the account management call centres. The service was provided 24 hours a day and provided services both to its own banking customers and anyone else who cared to apply for a loan. Similarly, the insurance products call centre operated round the clock and was proving very successful. Because it was a new service, all the technology and 'multi-function' information systems were designed specifically to support its operations.

> 'We had the advantage of not having to cope with different generations of information systems. Everything is new. This also means that our system response times are fast and we can devote more of our time to providing a more intimate service for the customer. We can also "cross-sell" car insurance to home contents insurance purchasers and vice versa.'

Peter was, overall, pleased with the way in which his operations had improved since the company 'went direct'. However, he felt that a more systematic approach could be taken to identifying improvement opportunities:

> 'I need to develop a logical approach to identifying how we can invest our time and money into improving the various aspects of operations performance. We need to both reduce our operating costs and maintain, and even improve, our customer service. At the same time the company, after investing huge sums into reshaping its operations, needs to be careful how it invests further in operations improvement.'

Further reading

Berry, W.L., C.C. Bozarth, T.J. Hill and J.E. Klompmaker (1991) 'Factory focus: segmenting marketing from an operations perspective', *Journal of Operations Management*, Vol. 10, No. 3.

Corbett, C. and L. van Wassenhope (1993) 'Trade-offs? What trade-offs? Competence and competitiveness in manufacturing strategy', *California Management Review*, Vol. 35, No. 4.

Hayes, R. and G.P. Pisano (1996) 'Manufacturing strategy: at the intersection of two paradigm shifts', *Production and Operations Management*, Vol. 5, No. 1.

Mintzberg, H. and J.A. Walters (1985) 'Of strategies: deliberate and emergent', *Strategic Management Journal*, July–Sept.

Rosenfield, D.B., R.D. Shapiro and R.E. Bohn (1985) 'Implications of cost–service trade-offs in industry logistics structures', *Interfaces*, Vol. 15, No. 6.

Schonberger, R.J. (1996) *World Class Manufacturing: The next decade*, The Free Press, New York, an example of the anti-trade-off view.

Skinner, W. (1992) 'Missing the links in manufacturing strategy', in Voss, C.A. (ed.) *Manufacturing Strategy – Process and Content*, Chapman & Hall, London.

Skinner, W. (1974) 'The focused factory', *Harvard Business Review*, May–June.

Skinner, W. (1969) 'Manufacturing – missing link in corporate strategy', *Harvard Business Review*, May–June.

Notes on the chapter

1 Based on information provided by Volkswagen Kommunikations, especially 'Volkswagen Writes History', 1998. Also 'VW: spinning its wheels?', *Business Week*, 22 November 1999; Culp, E. (1999) 'Costly VW faces bumpy ride', *Sunday Business*, 7 November; and Venuprasad, R. (1999) 'Volkswagen', Internal Document, Warwick Business School.

2 Mintzberg, in his classic paper, Mintzberg, H. (1978) 'Patterns of strategy formulation', *Management Science*, Vol. 24, No. 9, carried out an analysis of VW on which the first part of this analysis is based.

3 Mintzberg, H. and J.A. Walters, (1985) 'Of strategies: deliberate and emergent', *Strategic Management Journal*, July–Sept., pp. 257–272.

4 Skinner, W. (1969) 'Manufacturing – missing link in corporate strategy', *Harvard Business Review*, May–June, p. 136.

5 Quinn, J.B. (1992) *The Intelligent Enterprise*, The Free Press, New York.

6 Skinner, W. (1969) op. cit.

7 Skinner, W. (1992) 'Missing the links in manufacturing strategy', in Voss, C.A., *Manufacturing Strategy – Process and Content*, Chapman & Hall, London.

8 Sources: *The Economist* (1999) 'Faster, Cheaper . . . Splat', 11 December; Oberg, J. (2000) 'Houston we have a problem', *New Scientist*, 15 April.

9 Information taken from interviews given by British Airways staff to R. Venuprasad, Warwick Business School.

10 Skinner, W. (1974) 'The focused factory', *Harvard Business Review*, May–June, p. 113.

11 Venuprasad, R. (1999) 'The Low Cost Airline Industry', Internal report, Warwick Business School, and Doruille, M.G. (1999) 'The Southwest Airlines Story', Internal report, Warwick Business School.

12 For further discussion see Ghemawat, P. and Patricio del Sol (1998) 'Commitment versus flexibility?', *California Management Review*, Vol. 40, No. 4.

13 Source – 'Breaking Up Is Hard To Do', *The Economist*, 4 April 1998.

14 Hill, T. (1993) *Manufacturing Strategy*, Macmillan.

THE CONTENT OF OPERATIONS STRATEGY

Part 2 of this book examines the various 'decision areas' which together form the content (as opposed to the process) of operations strategy. Each of the four decision areas is treated first in a static and then in a more dynamic sense. The final decision area, 'Development and organisation', has an extra chapter dealing with the particularly important area of product and service development. However, remember that separating decisions in this way, although necessary for analysis, is artificial. In reality, most operations strategy 'content' decisions will have a significant impact on each other.

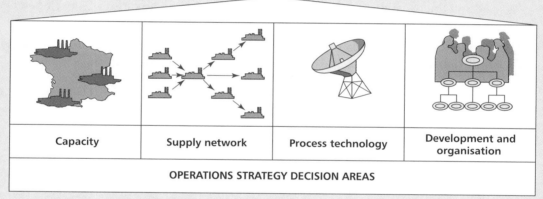

Resource usage

Capacity	Supply network	Process technology	Development and organisation

OPERATIONS STRATEGY DECISION AREAS

- Chapter 4 examines those decisions which shape the overall *capacity* of the operations resources, particularly the level of capacity and where the capacity should be located.

- Chapter 5 deals with the dynamics of the capacity decision by examining how capacity is changed over time in both its level and its location.

- Chapter 6 looks at supply networks, particularly the nature of the relationships which develop between the various operations in a network.

- Chapter 7 stands back and looks at the wider network, particularly in the advantages of taking a total network perspective, and how networks change over time.

- Chapter 8 characterises the various types of process technology which are at the heart of many operations; in particular, it looks at the effects of some newer types of technology on operations capabilities.

Continued overleaf

Continued from previous page

- Chapter 9 proposes some ideas which help operations to choose between different technologies and implement them once chosen.

- Chapter 10 examines the organisational structures within which operations resources are organised; in particular, it looks at the operations implications of adopting various types of organisational structure and the role operations can play within the organisation.

- Chapter 11 examines the way operations resources can be developed and improved within the organisation, especially how capabilities can be directed, developed and deployed in a cycle of improvement.

- Chapter 12 applies some of the issues covered in the previous chapters to the activities associated with product and service development and organisation.

Configuring operations capacity

Introduction

Capacity is the first of the operations strategy decision areas to be treated. This and the following chapter are devoted to different aspects of it. For operations managers there is something fundamental about the role of capacity-related decisions. The purpose of an operations function, at its most basic, is to provide and manage the means to supply demand – that is, to provide the *capacity* of the operation to supply. An operation's capacity dictates its potential level of productive activity. Capacity decisions, while clearly operations related, are decidedly strategic. They affect a large part of the business (indeed capacity decisions can *create* a large part of the business), are difficult to change in the short term and are framed in aggregated terms. And, as befits such fundamental decisions, the consequences of getting them wrong are almost always serious and sometimes fatal to a firm's competitive abilities. Too much capacity under-utilises resources and drives costs up. Too little capacity will limit the operation's ability to serve customers and therefore earn revenues. The risks inherent in getting capacity wrong lie both in having an inappropriately configured set of resources and in mismanaging the process of changing capacity over time. This chapter will look at the principles and ideas which shape how operations configure their capacity (Figure 4.1) while the next chapter will examine the nature of capacity reconfiguration.

Figure 4.1 Issues covered in this chapter

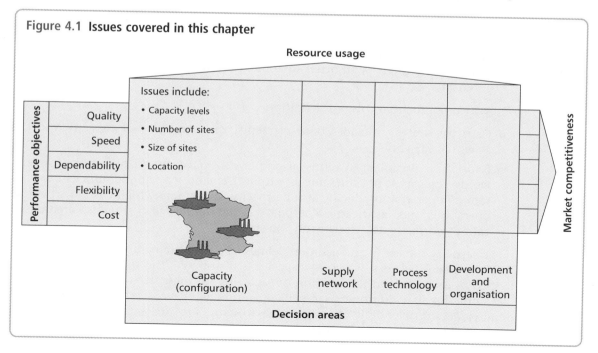

- *What individual decisions define the capacity strategy of a business?*
- *How do capacity decisions differ for different time-scales?*
- *What affects the size of an operation? i.e. how much capacity should it have?*
- *Between how many separate sites should an operation divide its capacity?*
- *Where should an operation locate its capacity?*

Capacity strategy

The most common use of the term 'capacity' is in the static, physical sense of the fixed *volume* of a container, or the space in a building. For example, a pharmaceutical manufacturer may invest in new 1000-litre capacity reactor vessels, a property company purchases a 50,000 square metre office block, and a cinema is built with ten screens and a total capacity of 2500 seats. These capacity measures describe the *scale* of these operations, but they do not necessarily reflect their *processing capacity*. This requires the incorporation of *time*. So the operations manager of the pharmaceutical company will be concerned with the level of output that can be achieved using the 1000-litre reactor vessel. If a batch of standard products can be produced every hour, the planned processing capacity could be as high as 24,000 litres per day. If the reaction takes four hours, and two hours are used for cleaning between batches, the vessel may only produce 4000 litres per day. So the capacity of an operation is:

> the maximum level of value-added activity over a period of time that the operation can achieve under normal conditions,

and the *capacity strategy* of an operation is:

> the pattern of decisions concerned with how operations configure and change their capacity in order to achieve a particular level of output potential.

Note two points from this last definition:

- Capacity strategy includes both elements, the *configuring* of capacity and the *change* of capacity.
- Capacity is described in terms of output *potential* from an operation. In other words, capacity is not the same as output. Demand may not be sufficient to warrant an operation producing at full capacity, and in many high customer contact operations, such as theatres, 'output' (i.e. the number of customers entertained) cannot normally exceed demand.

The capacity *strategy* of an operation defines its overall scale, the number and size of different sites between which its capacity is distributed, the specific activities allocated to each site and the location of each site. All these decisions are related. For example, an air conditioning servicing operation will have sites with relatively small individual capacity if it chooses to have many sites located no more than 30 minutes' travelling time from any customer. If it relaxed this 'response time' to 60

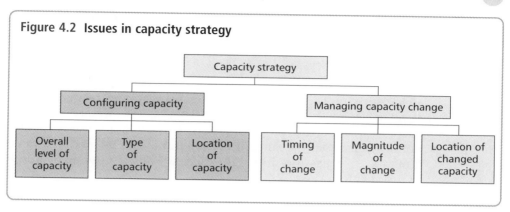

Figure 4.2 Issues in capacity strategy

minutes, it could have fewer, larger sites. Together these decisions determine the *configuration* of an operation's capacity, its overall shape, size and deployment. An appropriate configuration of capacity for one set of products or services, and pattern of demand, will not necessarily be appropriate for another. So when the nature of competition shifts in some way, companies often need to reconfigure their capacity. This process of changing (or reconfiguring) capacity is also part of capacity strategy. It usually involves deciding when capacity levels should be changed (up or down), how big each change step should be and overall how fast capacity levels should change. Figure 4.2 illustrates the strategic capacity decisions covered in this chapter.

Measuring capacity

Before treating the main issues concerning configuration, it is worth considering how capacity can be measured, since measurement is often a prerequisite for such decisions. In fact the complexity of most operations results in their capacity being dependent on many, sometimes ill-understood, factors. Only when an operation is highly standardised can its capacity be measured unambiguously. For example, a government office performing simple tax processing operations may have the capacity to perform 500,000 tax transactions per week, a soda bottling plant may be able to bottle 500,000 litres per week, and so on. In such standardised operations the output from the operation is the most appropriate measure of capacity. However, for most operations, especially those where a much wider range of outputs is produced, input measures are frequently used to define capacity. So, for example, the number of seat miles available per month for an airline, the number of beds available in a hospital, and so on.

Capacity and activity mix

Input measures of capacity are used usually because there is not a clear relationship between input and output. So, for example, in a hospital, the relationship between the number of beds available and the number of patients treated is not a constant. If all patients require relatively minor treatment, with relatively short stays in hospital, it may treat many people per week. Alternatively, if most of its patients require long and uncertain periods of treatment and recuperation, it will treat far fewer. The output from the hospital depends on the mix of activities in which it is engaged and, because many hospitals perform a wide variety of different activities, output is often difficult to predict. In fact, because very few operations have negligible variety, effective capacity will almost always be mix dependent.

Balancing capacity

The nature of the product/service, or the processes that produce them, will also affect capacity. For example, advances in treatment regimes and a better understanding of recovery procedures have increased the number of 'day cases' in many hospitals. A far higher proportion of patients do not stay overnight at all. This has not only increased the amount of output that can be produced from one factor of input (beds), it has also shifted the capacity constraint in many hospitals from beds to treatment processes.

Theory Box | **Utilisation and efficiency[1]**

The theoretical capacity of an operation is not the same as the output from that operation, nor is it the same as the effective capacity (that is, the realistic capacity) of the operation. It is, however, the combination of these three measures (theoretical or total capacity, effective capacity and output) which is used to calculate the two common measures of how an operation makes use of its capacity. These two measures are utilisation and efficiency.

$$\text{Utilisation} = \frac{\text{Actual output}}{\text{Total capacity}}$$

$$\text{Efficiency} = \frac{\text{Actual output}}{\text{Effective capacity}}$$

Generally, the difference between total and effective capacity is the capacity where useful output cannot be obtained through no fault of the operation itself. However, what constitutes unavoidable losses of capacity can be subject to some dispute. Firms usually make capacity allowances for demand fluctuations, maintenance losses, use of capacity for research and development, and so on, before attempting to measure the efficiency with which capacity is used.

Utilisation is used as one of the key measures of the performance of the operation. It is an indication of the proportion of the designed capacity that can be used to produce value-added goods or services. The justification for placing such importance on utilisation is usually that any lost production time could have been used to produce more outputs which would generate more profit (the 'opportunity cost' argument). Many organisations require high utilisation levels before they will authorise investment in additional capacity, arguing that this maximises the return on capital employed in the business. Utilisation may also be known by different names in different industries. For example:

- the 'room occupancy levels' in hotels;
- the 'load factor' for aircraft seats;
- 'uptime' in some manufacturing plants.

Utilisation can, however, be misleading. Low utilisation could result from many different issues, each with different implications, some concerned with market strategies, others with more operations-related causes. Nor is seeking high utilisation always desirable. High utilisation can adversely affect the customer if it reduces the speed and volume flexibility of the operation.

Table 4.1 Output and capacity loss data for the two divisions

	Ice Cream Division	Canned Foods Division
1 Total capacity	36,500 tonnes	117,200 pallets
(47 weeks × 7 days × 24 hrs)	(7896 hours)	(7896 hours)
2 No work scheduled (inadequate demand)	1477 hrs	805 hrs
3 Preventive maintenance	800 hrs	312 hrs
4 Research and development time	200 hrs	80 hrs
5 Shift changeover time allowance	165 hrs	165 hrs
6 Product changeover downtime	1120 hrs	1097 hrs
7 Breakdown maintenance	223 hrs	520 hrs
8 Quality failure downtime	163 hrs	195hrs
9 Material delay downtime	0 hrs	28 hrs
10 Labour shortage downtime	0 hrs	34 hrs
11 Other downtime	24 hrs	38 hrs
12 Actual output		
[Total capacity − (2+3+4+5+6+7+8+9+10+11)]	3724 hrs	4622 hrs
13 Planned loss ('unavoidable') (2+3+4+5+6)	3762 hrs	2459 hrs
14 Effective capacity (Total capacity − Planned loss)	4134 hrs	5437 hrs
15 Avoidable loss (Effective capacity − Actual output)	410 hrs	815 hrs
16 Utilisation (Actual output/Total capacity)	47.16%	58.54%
17 Efficiency (Actual output/Effective capacity)	90.08%	85.01%

Example

A food company has several divisions, two of which are its ice cream and its canned food divisions. In order to provide background information for its capital budgeting procedures, group operations executives have decided to monitor the utilisation and efficiency of each division's capacity usage. They require each division's management to report on output and also on the amount of time when the capacity is not being used. Table 4.1 shows the returns for the two divisions.

Lines 2 to 6 indicate losses which the company regards as outside the control of each division's operations management. Lines 7 to 11 indicate losses which, in the company's view, are avoidable.

As a mechanical exercise, the manipulation of data such as this is self-explanatory. What is more interesting are the questions it poses for the company:

- No work was scheduled for much of the available time. Is this because each division has too much capacity, or is it because of demand fluctuations over the year? Ice cream is a much more seasonal product than canned foods, which presumably accounts for the higher figure from this division.

- How should the group judge the different amounts of capacity lost to such 'unavoidable' activities as preventive maintenance, and research and development? Should the allocation of these times be left to the divisions or should an allowance be allocated based on market and operations factors? So, for example, presumably the ice cream division needs more preventive maintenance time because it is dealing with dairy products, which present health hazards unless equipment is cleaned regularly. It may also need more research and development

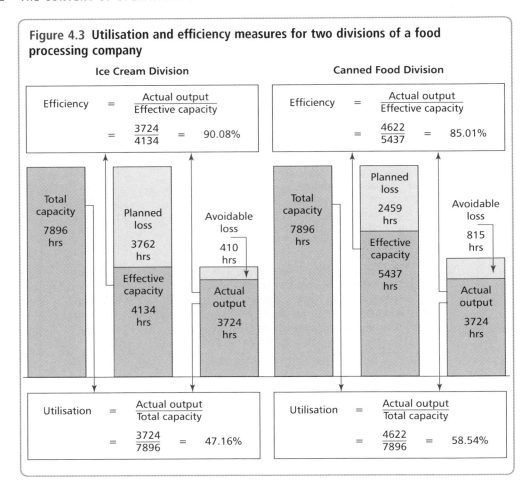

Figure 4.3 Utilisation and efficiency measures for two divisions of a food processing company

time because product innovation is more important in its markets than those of the canned food division.

● Why is the loss of capacity due to product changeovers counted as unavoidable? It is a significant loss of capacity and can be affected by the energy and expertise of each division's process engineers.

● Why does the canned food division have a better utilisation but worse efficiency? Is this because the ice cream market is such that meeting its seasonal demand will always mean a high degree of unavoidable losses? If so, does that account for the difference in utilisation? Does the ice cream division's higher efficiency mean that, once its market-related factors are discounted, it is better at exploiting the remaining capacity?

The important point here is not our inability to answer these questions because of our limited amount of information, rather it is that we ask the questions in the first place. Measuring utilisation and efficiency of capacity may be a difficult, and to some extent an arbitrary activity, but it does force an examination of how an operation is deploying its capacity related assets. Figure 4.3 illustrates.

Capacity at three levels

The provision of capacity is not just a strategic issue. It takes place in all operations minute by minute, day by day and month on month. Every time an operations manager moves a staff member from one part of the operation to another, he or she is adjusting capacity within the operation. Similarly, when setting shift patterns to determine working hours, effective capacity is being set. Neither of these decisions is strategic – they do not necessarily impact directly on the long-term physical scale of the operation. But shift patterns will be set within the constraints of the physical limits of the operation, and the minute-by-minute deployment of staff will take place within the constraints of the number and skills of the people present within the operation at any time. Thus, although capacity decisions are taken for different time-scales and spanning different areas of the operation, each level of capacity decision is made with the constraints of a higher level.

Table 4.2 illustrates this idea. Note, though, that the three levels of capacity decision used here are, to some extent, arbitrary and there is, in practice, overlap between the levels. Also, the actual time-scales of the three levels will vary between industries.

Table 4.2 Three levels of capacity decision

Level	Time-scale	Decisions concern provision of ...	Span of decisions	Starting point of decision	Key questions
Strategic capacity decisions	Years–Months	● Buildings and facilities ● Process technology	All parts of the business	● Probable markets to be served in the future ● Current capacity configuration	● How much capacity do we need in total? ● How should the capacity be distributed? ● Where should the capacity be located?
Medium-term capacity decisions	Months–Weeks	● Aggregate number of people ● Degree of subcontracted resources	Business – site	● Market forecasts ● Physical capacity constraints	● To what extent do we keep capacity level or fluctuate capacity levels? ● Should we change staffing levels as demand changes? ● Should we subcontract or off-load demand?
Short-term capacity decisions	Weeks–hours–minutes	● Individual staff within the operation ● Loading of individual facilities	Site Department	● Current demand ● Current available capacity	● Which resources are to be allocated to what tasks? ● When should activities be loaded on individual resources?

The overall level of operations capacity

The first capacity-related decision faced by any operation is 'How much capacity should we have?', or put simply, 'How big should we be?'. It sounds a straightforward question, but is in fact influenced by several factors particular to each operation and its competitive position. Each of the main factors which will influence the overall level of capacity will be discussed in this section. Figure 4.4 illustrates them. As usual, some of the factors are primarily related to the requirements of the market, while others are largely concerned with the nature of the operation's resources.

Forecast demand

Only rarely will a business decide to invest in a level of capacity which is exactly equal to its expectation of future demand. However, it is a starting point in trying to understand why operations finish up the size they are. So, for example, if a leisure business believes there is likely to be a demand for 500 rooms per night at a newly developed resort location, then it may build a 500-roomed hotel. If an insurance company's call centre is forecast to handle 500,000 calls per week and one operator can handle a call every 3 minutes, then it may build a 625-station call centre (operators have 40×60 minutes a week, so can receive $2400/3 = 800$ calls a week, so $500,000/800 = 625$ operators are needed). But capacity decisions are not always as simple as this. Although a 'single point' forecast of future demand for an operation's products and services will have a major influence on how big its operations will be, other considerations will affect the decision. It is these other factors, acting to modify a simple demand forecast, which reveal much about the strategic context of operations decisions.

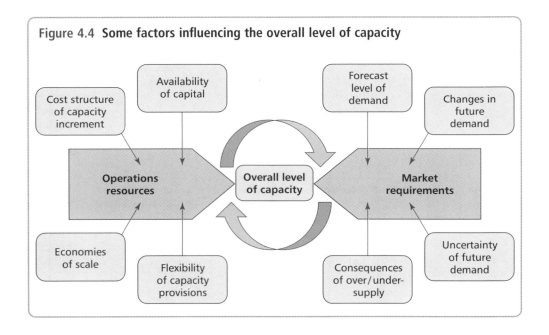

Figure 4.4 Some factors influencing the overall level of capacity

Category killers[2]

Sometimes capacity decisions can be made with the objective of influencing demand itself. The most obvious example of this is the 'category killer' in retailing. These are highly efficient distribution channels which sell a wide range of goods at discounted prices, often from low-cost edge-of-town superstores. The best-known category killer in retailing is the TOYS 'Я' US toy chain which started life in the United States but has now spread all over the world. The company's huge sites offer customers a wide selection of products at low prices. The sheer size of their operations gives customers the range of choice which attracts them in large numbers. The large numbers mean high throughput which, in turn, means not only that the company can build large capacity, low 'transaction cost' sites, but also that it can win substantial discounts from toy manufacturers, reducing costs even further (and attracting even more customers). Other sectors of the retail industry which have attracted category killer hopefuls include office suppliers (Office Depot), furniture (IKEA) and pet shops (Petsmart). Party City, an American chain of superstores devoted to selling party accessories such as plates, cups and Halloween masks, believes that the scale of its operations can effectively create demand that did not exist before. The size and variety of its stores generate consumer awareness, while retailing tricks, such as displaying matching balloons and lollipops next to basic cups and plates, can increase the average purchase per visit.

It is, however, possible to push the logic of category killers too far. In 1997 a judge at the Federal Trade Commission ruled that TOYS 'Я' US had illegally put pressure on their suppliers not to sell some of the most popular toys to warehouse-club discounters. Although the company appealed against the ruling, many in the industry were unsympathetic. As one commentator noted at the time, *'Killers make unconvincing victims'*.

Uncertainty of future demand

Even when the demand for an operation's products or services can be reasonably well forecast, the uncertainty inherent in all estimates of future demand may inhibit the operation from investing to meet the most likely level of demand. The economics of the operation may mean that, should the lower level of demand occur, the financial consequences would be unacceptable to the company.

Example

A company in the banking industry is planning to build a 'voucher processing' centre which will process cheques, credit card documents and so on for other retail financial services companies. Although demand is unsure, it is believed that it will be around 10 million documents per year. The capital cost of building the centre, together with document readers, automated sorting technology, sophisticated information technology, etc. will depend on the capacity of the centre. The higher the capacity of the centre, the bigger the building, the larger the capacity of the

Table 4.3 The three alternative capacity investments for the bank

Capacity of processing centre (documents/year)	Capital costs ($m)	Fixed costs per year ($m)	Variable cost per document ($)
5 million	2.2	0.28	0.01
10 million	4	0.6	0.01
15 million	5.5	0.8	0.01

computer systems and the more document readers will be needed. Table 4.3 gives details of the capital costs, fixed processing and variable processing costs and capacity, for three alternative investment options.

The retail banking customers pay, on average, $0.25 per document processed.

Given that the forecast for the centre's services are around 10 million documents per year, the company decides to build a centre with this capacity. Their (simplified) calculations are as follows.

Capital cost	=	$4 million
Operating cost per year	=	Fixed cost + (volume × variable cost)
	=	0.6m + (10m × 0.01)
	=	$0.7m
Revenue	=	10m × 0.25
	=	$2.5m
Profit	=	$2.5m − $0.7m
	=	$1.8m
Return	=	$1.8m/$4m
	=	45%

But to the company's great regret the forecasts turn out to be optimistic and annual demand is only 5 million documents per year.

This is how the simple return on investment figures now look.

Capital cost	=	$4m
Operating cost	=	$0.6m + (5m × $0.01)
	=	$0.65m
Revenue	=	5m × 0.25
	=	$1.25m
Profit	=	$1.25 − 0.65m
	=	$0.6m
Return	=	$0.6m/$4m
	=	15%

If the company had built a 5 million document capacity centre its return would have been acceptable, namely:

Capital cost	=	2.2m
Operating cost	=	$0.28m + (5m × $0.01)
	=	$0.33m
Revenue	=	5m × $0.25
	=	$1.25m
Profit	=	$1.25 − $0.33m
	=	$0.92m
Payback	=	$0.92m/$2.2m
	=	41.8%

Following a similar, but more comprehensive, analysis, the company could have explored the consequences of each of its three capacity options under a range of demand levels. It might even have refined its market research to the point where it felt able to assign probabilities to different levels of demand. Table 4.4 shows the crude payback figures for each capacity option at three levels of demand. It also shows probabilities of each level of demand actually occurring.

Table 4.4 Simple return on investment consequences of capacity investment for different demand levels

Capacity of processing centre (documents/year)	Annual demand (documents)		
	5 million probability = 0.3	10 million probability = 0.4	15 million probability = 0.3
5 million	41.8%	41.8%	41.8%
10 million	15.0%	45.0%	45.0%
15 million	7.3%	29.0%	51.0%

Using an expectation approach, the company can weigh each return on investment by the likelihood of it occurring. So,

If a 5 million capacity centre is built
Expected return   = $(0.3 \times 41.8) + (0.4 \times 41.8) + (0.3 \times 41.8)$
                        =   41.8%

If a 10 million capacity centre is built
Expected return   = $(0.3 \times 15) + (0.4 \times 45) + (0.3 \times 45)$
                        =   36%

If a 15 million capacity centre is built
Expected return   = $(0.3 \times 7.3) + (0.4 \times 29) + (0.3 \times 51)$
                        =   29.1%

So, the highest expected return is obtained when a centre with capacity only half of the expected demand is built. This is because of the basic financial consequences of failing to utilise a larger centre. Of course, there may be other market-related reasons why the company may not want to under-supply the market and so would build a larger centre. These will be discussed next. The purpose of this simplified example is that it demonstrates the magnitude of the effect that a mismatch between capacity and demand can have on the return on investment, or even the viability, of the company. The cost penalties of over-capacity can be very large compared, for example, with the cost savings normally obtained from routine improvement. Conversely the lost supply, revenue and profit opportunities of under-capacity can mean the difference between acquiring profitable market share and being consigned to be, at best, an industry follower.

Other consequences of over- and under-supply

Given that demand is uncertain, any operation will want to debate the consequences of over-supplying or under-supplying their markets in terms other than the short-term financial. There are obvious utilisation, and therefore resources, implications, as was implied in the previous example. These resource implications will also be dealt with in more detail later, when we consider break-even issues. But there may also be market-related implications of under- and over-capacity.

For example, the availability of excess capacity may give an operation the flexibility to respond to short-term surges in demand. This could be especially valuable when either demand needs to be satisfied in the short term, or when satisfying short-term demand can have long-term implications. The early stages of a product or service life cycle, especially when contested amongst several competitors, is a bad time not to be able to satisfy demand. Lost market share at this point may never be regained. By contrast, having less capacity than demand reduces an operation's ability to respond to market fluctuations. Paradoxically though, under-supplying a market may increase the value (and therefore price) of an operation's goods or services. Such a scarcity-based strategy, however, does rely on an appropriate market positioning and a confidence in the lack of competitor activity.

Changes in demand – long-term or short-term demand?

In addition to any uncertainty surrounding future demand, there is also the question of the time-scale over which demand is being forecast. For example, short-term expected demand may be higher than expected long-term sustainable demand. In which case, does an organisation plan to provide capacity to meet the short-term peak, or alternatively, plan to satisfy only longer-term sustainable levels of demand? Conversely, short-term demand may be relatively low compared to longer-term demand. Again, there is the same dilemma. Should the operation build capacity for the short or long term? Like many capacity strategy decisions, this is related to the economies of scale of individual operations and the ease with which they can add or subtract increments of capacity. The dynamics of changing capacity levels will be discussed further in the next chapter. Here we are concerned with the decision of where initially to pitch capacity levels.

Long-term demand lower than short-term demand

Suppose a confectionery company is launching a new product aimed at the children's market. From previous experience it realises that it must make an initial impact in the market with many sales based on the novelty of the product, in order to reach a lower but sustainable level of demand. It estimates that initial demand for the product will be around 500 tons per month. However, longer-term demand is more likely to settle down to a reasonably steady level of 300 tons per month.

A key issue here is whether the higher level of demand will sustain for long enough to recoup the extra capital cost of providing capacity to meet that high level. Furthermore, even if this is the case, can an operation with a nominal capacity of 500 tons per month operate sufficiently profitably when it is only producing 300 tons per month? If the answer to either of these questions is 'No', then a capacity-based analysis would tend to discourage investment at the higher level of capacity. The main problem with this approach is that it may prove to be self-fulfilling. Under-supplying the market may depress demand which would otherwise have grown to justify the 500 tons per month capacity level. More likely, competitors will take advantage of the company's inability to supply to increase their own share of the market. Of course, the company may wish to counteract any under-supply by adopting pricing and promotion strategies that minimise the effects of, or even exploit, product shortage. The lesson here is that setting the initial capacity level cannot be done in isolation from the company's market positioning strategy.

Short-term demand lower than long-term demand

Again, the issues here are partly concerned with economies of scale versus the costs of operating at levels below the operation's capacity. If the economies of scale of providing capacity at the higher level of demand mean that the profits generated in the long term are worth the costs associated with under-utilisation of capacity in the short term, then building capacity at the higher level may be justified. Once more though, the relationship between capacity provision, costs, and market positioning needs to be explored. Initial over-capacity may be exploited by producing at higher volume, therefore lower costs, and pricing in order to take market share or even stimulate the total market. Indeed, over-capacity may be deliberately provided in order to allow such aggressive market strategies.

The availability of capital

One obvious constraint on whether operations choose to meet demand fully is their ability to afford the capacity with which to do it. So, for example, a company may have developed a new product or service which they are convinced will be highly attractive in the marketplace. Sales forecasts are extremely bullish, with potential revenues being two or three times higher than the company's present revenue. Competitors will take some time to catch up with the company's technological lead and so they have the market to themselves for at least the next two years. All of this sounds very positive for the company; its products and services are innovative, the market appears to want them, forecasts are as firm as forecasts can be, and the company is in a position to make very healthy profits for at least the next two years. But consider what the company will have to do to its resource base. Irrespective of how novel or technologically difficult the new processing requirements are, there will certainly be a lot more of them. The company will need to increase its operations resources by two or three hundred per cent. The question must arise of whether it can afford to do this, or more accurately, whether it is prepared to face the consequences of doing this. Borrowing enough cash to double or triple the worth of the company may not be possible from conventional sources of lending. The owners may not wish to float the company at this stage. Other sources of finance, such as venture capitalists, may demand an equity stake.

Under these circumstances the company may forego the opportunity to meet forecast demand fully. Even though in pure accounting terms the return on any investment in operating capacity may be perfectly acceptable, the consequence in terms of ownership or vulnerability of the company to being taken over may not be worth risking. An alternative for the company may be to increase capacity only as fast as their currently feasible borrowing capability will allow. The risk then is that competitor companies will have the time to enter the market and reduce its longer-term potential for company.

Break-even points

One of the most basic, and yet most important, issues in capacity strategy is concerned with the relationship between the capacity of an operation, the volume of output which it is actually processing, and its profitability. Simple break-even analysis can illustrate the basics of this. Each additional unit of capacity results in a fixed-cost break. The fixed costs of a unit of capacity are those expenditures that have to be incurred irrespective of how much the capacity is actually being used. The variable costs of operating the capacity are those expenditures that rise proportionally to output. As volume increases for one operation, the additional capacity required

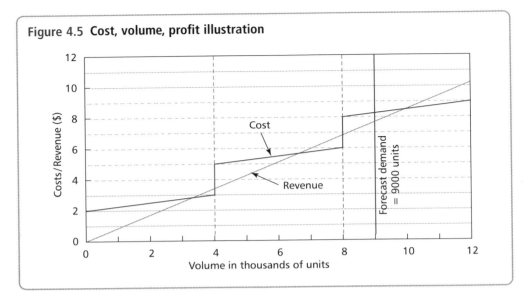

Figure 4.5 Cost, volume, profit illustration

can move an operation through its 'break-even' point from profitability to loss. Further additions to the capacity of the operation will be needed to cope with increased demand. Each addition brings a new set of fixed costs. Fixed-cost breaks may mean that there are levels of output within which a company might not wish to operate. This issue is particularly important when the fixed costs of operation are high compared with the variable costs.

Figure 4.5 shows how this might be in one operation. Each unit of capacity can process 4000 units of output per month. The fixed costs of operating this capacity are $2000 per month and the variable costs $0.25 per unit. The revenue from each unit processed to the operation is $0.9 per unit. Demand is forecast to be steady at around 9000 units per month. To meet this demand fully, three units of capacity would be needed, though the third unit would be much under-utilised. As Figure 4.5 shows, meeting demand fully, the company's total costs are higher than its total revenue. It would therefore be operating at a loss. Under these circumstances, the company might very well choose to process only 8000 units per month, not meeting demand but operating more profitably than if they were meeting demand.

Economies of scale

The relationship between the capacity of an operation, the volume at which it is operating and its profitability can be taken further. If the total cost of the output from an operation is its fixed costs plus its output multiplied by its variable costs per unit, then we can calculate the average cost per unit of output simply by dividing total costs by the output level.

So, for example, Figure 4.6(a) shows the unit cost for an increment of capacity of the operation described earlier. In reality though, the real average cost curve may be different from that shown in Figure 4.6(a) for a number of reasons.

● The real maximum capacity may be larger than the theoretical maximum capacity. For example, the theoretical capacity in Figure 4.6(a) was based on an assumption that the operation would be working 112 hours a week (14 shifts a week out of a possible 21 shifts a week) whereas the operation is theoretically available 168 hours a week. Utilising some of this unused time for production will help to spread further the fixed costs of the operation but may also incur extra costs. For example, overtime payments and shift premiums together with incrementally higher energy bills may be incurred after a certain level of output.

● There may also be less obvious costs of operating above nominal capacity levels. Long periods of overtime may reduce productivity levels, reduced or delayed maintenance time may increase the chances of breakdown, operating facilities and equipment at a higher rate or for longer periods may also expose problems which hitherto lay dormant. These 'diseconomies' of over-using capacity can have the effect of increasing unit costs above a certain level of output.

● All the fixed costs are not usually incurred at one time at the start of operations. Rather they occur at many points as volume increases. These points are called the fixed-cost 'breaks' of the volume–cost relationship. Furthermore, operations managers often have some discretion as to where these fixed-cost breaks will occur. So, for example, the manager of a delivery operation may know that at the level of demand forecast for next month a new delivery vehicle should be purchased. This extra vehicle (together with the extra fixed cost it brings) could be purchased now in order to improve service delivery next month, when it is technically needed, or delayed beyond next month. This last option may involve taking the risk that any vehicle breakdown would leave the operation dangerously short of capacity but may yet be preferred if the operations manager has little faith in next month's level of demand being sustained.

All these points taken together mean that, in practice, unit cost curves:

● are capable of being extended beyond nominal capacity;
● often show increases in cost beyond a certain level of volume;
● are best represented by a band of possible costs rather than a smooth, clean line.

This is illustrated in Figure 4.6(b).

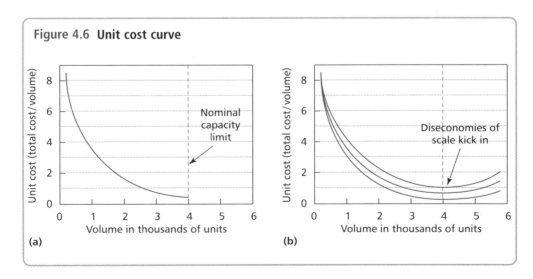

Figure 4.6 Unit cost curve

The factors that go together to reduce costs as volume increases are often called *economies of scale*. Those that work to increase unit costs for increased output beyond a certain volume are called *diseconomies of scale*. What we have described above are the economies and diseconomies of scale for a single increment of capacity within an operation. Yet the same logic can be applied for the whole operation. As more units of capacity are added, the total fixed costs per unit of potential output tend to decrease. So, for example, the number of people staffing support services such as maintenance, supervision, warehousing, etc. is unlikely to double when the capacity of the whole operation doubles.

What drives scale economies?[3]

Economies of scale are often thought of as being primarily an issue of reduced operational costs following from the ability to spread fixed costs over a larger volume of output. But the principle of scale allowing cost savings can penetrate into other corners of business activity. These are especially evident when firms merge. Here are some examples.

1 When Ford took over the car-making division of Sweden's Volvo for $6.45 billion in 1999, it made relatively little difference to Ford's overall size. Volvo's modest output of less than 400,000 cars per year was tiny by world standards. Yet the effect on Volvo's ability to compete was significant. Even in the short term, cost savings could come from tapping into Ford's logistics and purchasing functions. Ford's logistics network in the US could easily cope with Volvo's products and the United States was Volvo's biggest market. Similarly with purchasing: although Volvo had its own platform designs, even in the short term, it could substitute some of Ford's components which it bought from specialist suppliers. In the longer term, it could share basic automobile platforms with Ford. Jaguar, the UK luxury car company bought by Ford in the 1980s, was already doing this.

2 Size also matters in the pharmaceuticals market. One reason is the escalating cost of research and development. This led to mergers, such as that between Hoechst and Rhône-Poulenc. Combining these two European companies enabled them to attempt to compete with industry giants in the US, such as Merck, Pfizer, and Bristol-Myers Squibb. Largely because of expensive new technology for discovering disease mechanisms and potential drugs, even the largest companies could not hope to compete across every disease area. However, the bigger the company, the more areas can be covered. Similarly, the cost of marketing was growing, particularly in the US, where direct-to-consumer advertising, including pricey television campaigns, was fuelling profitable sales. Again though, only the largest companies could afford spending of this magnitude.

3 With sales of $16 billion and an output of 22.5 million tonnes, the merger between British Steel and Hoogovens of the Netherlands brought together two of the most efficient steel companies in Europe. It also created the third largest steel company in the world, just behind POSCO of South Korea and Nippon Steel of Japan. The merger was partly to capitalise on conventional economies of scale but it was also driven by another objective – it reduced the combined firm's currency risk. At the time of the merger British Steel (inside the European Union, but outside the Euro zone) had most of its plants in Britain but much of its sales in overseas markets. The British currency was also strong. In the year before the merger, currency changes had added about 12 per cent to British Steel's costs relative to those of its chief international competitors. Acquiring Hoogovens both diversified British Steel's sales portfolio and gave it the ability to switch production between the economic zones.

4 In the oil industry there is a saying that when the oil price is low, the cheapest place to drill is Wall Street. In other words, oil companies' stock prices, depressed as a result of a low oil price, make it cheaper to buy an oil company for its reserves than drill for new reserves yourself. Partly this motivated oil industry mergers such as those between BP and Amoco, Petrofina

and Total, and Exxon and Mobil. But even where exploration still makes sense, company size still helps. Bigger companies find it easier to pursue bold exploration policies, because the bigger the company, the bigger the gamble it can afford on discovering new oil fields. Of course, the more conventional reasons for merger still apply. BP Amoco reckoned that by applying its cost-cutting and drilling expertise across its expanded operation it could save up to $2 billion a year.

As the size of the operation increases it becomes possible eventually to replace the capacity which has been built up incrementally over time with new, larger and more integrated units. This may allow two further economies of scale. The first comes through the increases in operations efficiency which can be gained by integrating, or combining, the processes established separately over time. So, for example, each increase of capacity may have included a particular kind of machine which could be replaced by a larger, more efficient machine once total capacity exceeds a certain level. Second, the capital costs of building operations do not increase proportionally to their capacity. The reason for this is that whereas the capacities of many types of facilities and equipment which go into an operation are related to their volume (a cubic function), the capital cost of the facilities and equipment is related to its surface area (a square function). Generally the cost (C_y) of providing capacity in one increment of size y is given as follows:[4]

$$C_y = Ky^k$$

where K is a constant scale factor and k is a factor which indicates the degree of economies of scale for the technology involved. (Usually between 0.5 and 1.0.)

There may be, however, significant diseconomies of scale as the size of one site increases. The most significant of these are related to the complexity inherent in a large operation. As organisations grow larger they may become more unwieldy and need a greater degree of planning and coordination. More activities are needed just to keep the organisation operating and more staff are needed to manage the extra support processes. All this not only adds cost, it can make the whole operation incapable of responding to changes in customer demands. Very large operations find it difficult to be flexible because even if they can sense changes in the markets, they may not be able to respond to them. As operations grow communication also becomes more complex, which in turn provides more opportunities for mis-communication and errors.

Flexibility of capacity provision

Committing to an investment in a particular level of capacity may be managed in such a way as to facilitate later expansion. Effective capacity requires all the required resources and processes to be in place in order to produce goods and services. This may not necessarily imply that all resources and processes are put in place at the same time. It may be possible, for example, to construct the physical outer shell of an operation without investing in the direct and indirect process technologies which will convert it into productive capacity. There may, for example, be capital expendi-

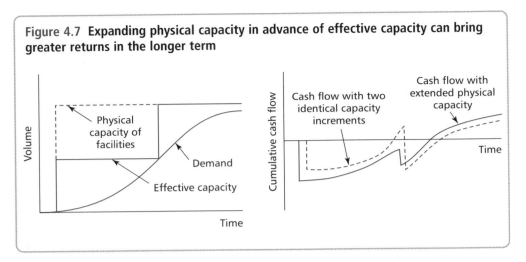

Figure 4.7 Expanding physical capacity in advance of effective capacity can bring greater returns in the longer term

ture efficiencies to be gained by constructing a larger building than is strictly necessary in the medium term, which can be fitted out with equipment when demand justifies it in the future. Clearly there is some risk involved in committing even part of the capital expenditure necessary before demand is certain. However, such a strategy is frequently employed in growing markets. Figure 4.7 illustrates how this kind of strategy may have benefits.

It shows alternative capacity strategies, and the resultant cash flow profiles, for an operation which is planning to expand its capacity to meet the forecast demand as shown in the figure. One option involves building the whole physical facility (with a larger net cash outflow) but only equipping it to half its potential physical capacity. Only when demand justifies it would expenditure be made to fully exploit this capacity. The alternative is to build a fully equipped facility of half the capacity. A further identical capacity increment would then be added as required. Although this latter strategy requires a lower initial cash outflow, it shows a lower cumulative cash flow in the longer term.

The number and size of sites

The decision of how many separate operational sites to have is concerned with where a business wants to be on the spectrum between many small sites on one hand and few large sites on the other. Once again, we can think of this decision as the reconciliation of market factors and resource factors. This is illustrated in Figure 4.8. Separating capacity into several small units may be necessary if demand for a business's products or services is widely distributed. This will be especially true if customers demand high absolute levels, or immediate service. Of course, dividing capacity into small units may also increase costs because of the difficulty of exploiting the economies of scale possible in larger units. A small number of larger units may also be less costly to supply with their input resources. There again, in material transformation operations, a single large unit will bear extra transportation costs in supplying its distributed market.

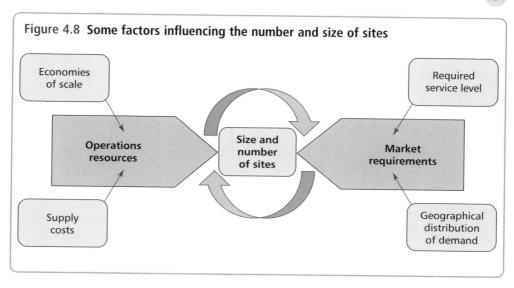

Figure 4.8 **Some factors influencing the number and size of sites**

Example 1 – Distribution operation

Suppose a company which stores and distributes books to book shops is considering its capacity strategy. Currently in its European market it has three distribution centres, one in the UK, one in France and one in Germany. The UK depot looks after the UK and Ireland, the French depot looks after France, Spain, Portugal and Belgium, and the German depot looks after the rest of Europe. The company is facing conflicting pressures. On one hand it wants to minimise the total operations cost of its distribution services, on the other hand it wishes to improve its level of service to its customers. In order to explore alternatives to its existing depots it engages a firm of consultants to evaluate two alternative proposals which had been discussed within the company. Option 1 would require the company to concentrate its operations in one central depot which would serve the whole of Europe. It is likely that this would be in the Netherlands, probably in Rotterdam. Option 2 would require the company to move in the opposite direction, in the sense that it envisages a depot to be located in each of its six sales regions in Western Europe. These regions are the Iberian Peninsula, the UK, France and the Benelux countries, Italy, Germany, and Scandinavia. The consultants decide to simulate the alternative operations in order to estimate (a) the cost of running the depots (this includes fixed costs such as rent and local taxes, heating, wages, security, and working capital charges for the inventory, etc.), (b) transportation costs of delivering the books to customers, and (c) the average delivery time in working days between customers requesting books and them being delivered. Table 4.5 shows the results of this simulation.

From Table 4.5 one can see that concentrating on one large site gives substantial economies of scale in terms of the costs of running the depot but increases transportation costs, and (because there is further, on average, to travel) increases the average delivery time. Conversely, moving to several smaller sites increases depot costs but reduces transportation costs as well as improving the average delivery time. The company is here in a dilemma. By moving to one large site it can save €9.1 million per year (the savings on depot costs easily outweighing the increase in transportation costs). Yet delivery times will increase on average by 1.4 days. Alternatively, moving to six smaller sites would increase costs by €9.3 million per year, yet gives what looks like a significant improvement in delivery time of 2.5 days. In theory the financial consequences of the different delivery times could be calcu-

Table 4.5 Analysis of existing operation and two options

Capacity configuration	Depot costs	Transport costs	Average delivery time (working days)
Current			6
three sites			
– Toulouse	€55.3m	€15.6m	6.3
– Birmingham			
– Hamburg			
One large site			
– Rotterdam	€41.1m	€20.7m	7.7
Six smaller sites			
– Madrid			
– Paris			
– Stockholm	€68.8m	€11.4m	3.8
– Milan			
– Berlin			
– Birmingham			

lated, combined with the capital costs of each option, and a financial return derived for each option. In practice, however, the decision is probably more sensibly approached by presenting a number of questions to the company's managers.

● Is an increase in average delivery time from 6.3 to 7.7 days likely to result in losses of business greater than the €9.1 million savings in moving to a large site?

● Is the increase in business which may be gained from a reduction in delivery time from 6.3 days to 3.8 days likely to compensate for the €9.3 million extra cost of moving to six smaller sites?

● Are either of these alternative positions likely to be superior to its existing profitability?

One final point. In evaluating the sizes and number of sites in any operation it is not just the increase in profitability which may result from a change in configuration that needs to be considered, it is whether that increase in profitability is worth the costs of making the change. Presumably either option will involve this company in not only capital expenditure, but a great deal of management effort and disruption to its existing business. It may be that these costs and risks outweigh any increase in profitability.

Example 2 – Retail operation

In the previous example, the main effects of changing the number of sites were cost related. The differences in service level given by the three options may have influenced demand, but that influence would have been indirect. This is not true in all types of operation. In high customer contact operations, such as retail or hotel operations, the effect of the number of sites (and their location, which we discuss next) on demand is usually far greater. This is the issue that faces one furniture retailer. It has to estimate how many potential customers would travel (say) 50 miles to visit its furniture stores. Some, for sure, depending on whether a reasonable alternative store was nearby and also depending on the perceived attractiveness of the store.

The range of products, quality of products and service, or prices may be worth a 50-mile drive. But how many of those customers who would be willing to drive 50 miles would drive 100 miles? Or 150 miles? Distance in high customer contact operations affects demand, and the number of individual sites the operation has affects distance. Fewer, larger sites generally mean longer distances for customers to travel in order to access the operation's services. However, each additional site, although attracting extra customers, will also attract some of the customers who would have visited the original single store. This effect is shown in the furniture retailer's calculations in Table 4.6. The first column indicates that with only one store the yearly gross margin earned by the company (gross margin is the difference between sales revenue and the amount paid by the store for the products it has sold) is estimated to be $10 million. If the company located two stores in the region its total gross margin would be $18 million. Indeed, for each additional store the marginal increase in total gross margin reduces. Table 4.6 also shows the total transaction costs of running the stores. This includes not only costs associated with each store such as rent, local taxes, security, etc. but also the cost of the distribution network which supplies the stores. Also included in the table are the capital costs of building the stores. The decreasing capital cost per store as the number of stores increases reflects both the economies of scale in construction (as design costs etc. are spread over more sites) and the reduced demand per store.

In this simple illustration, the best return on the investment in sites involves building two sites. However, it is more likely that the company would choose to maximise its gross earnings, provided that the return or payback on its investment was within its normally acceptable range. In this case the company can earn $5 million per year on a capital investment of $21 million by choosing to have three sites. Expanding to a fourth site would not appear to increase its gross earnings but would involve a further $5 million in investment. Unless there were other economies or market advantages to be gained by expanding its total volume of operation, it would be unlikely to invest in a fourth store.

Table 4.6 Costs and gross revenues for furniture store

Number of stores in the region	Total gross margin from all stores ($ million)	Total cost of running the stores (inc. distribution costs) ($ million)	Capital cost of stores ($ million)	Simple payback* (in years)
1	10	8	8	4
2	18	14	15	3.75
3	24	19	21	4.2
4	28	23	26	5.2

* Capital cost/(Total gross margin – Total cost of running the stores)

Location of capacity

Often the reason why operations are where they are is not always obvious. Sometimes historical reasons, now lost in the history of the operation, dictated location. Such operations are 'there because they're there'. Even more recent location decisions are not always logical. Entrepreneurial whim or lifestyle preference may overcome seeming locational disadvantages. In other cases the location decision is only reached after extensive thought and analysis.

The importance of location

The location decision is rarely unimportant but sometimes can be very important to the long-term health of an organisation. This is because the location decision can have a significant impact on both the investment in the operation's resources and in the market impact of the operation's resources. For example, locating a fire service station in the wrong place can both slow down the average time for the fire crew to respond to the call or increase the required investment to build the station, or both. Similarly, locating a manufacturing plant where it is difficult to attract labour with appropriate skills may affect the quality of its products (hence revenues), or the wages it has to pay to attract appropriate labour (hence costs).

Toyota moves to France[5]

The last 20 years have been marked by the expansion of many Japanese manufacturing companies abroad. Consumer electronics and automobile manufacturers, especially, have set up plants around the world in their major markets of South East Asia, Europe and the United States. In the contest to attract Japanese inward investment in Europe, the UK was the clear winner. Some large early arrivals, such as Nissan, were attracted to the UK by generous government-funded financial support and tax concessions in regional development areas. Most of these were areas of high unemployment, yet with a tradition of industrial activity. Later arrivals had much fewer direct financial incentives, but saw the other advantages gained by the early arrivals. In some areas a critical mass of Japanese companies had developed, creating a flow of good publicity back to Japan and encouraging further interest. This success was reinforced by a growth in support infrastructure, such as Japanese schools, social activities, and even food retailing, to help expatriate families feel at home. Add to this that the English language is the most likely to be any Japanese manager's second language, the language commonality between the UK and the USA, climate similarity between the UK and Japan, and even factors such as the availability of golf courses, and the UK became the clear favourite for inward investment.

In December 1997, then, it came as a shock when Toyota, which already had a successful UK plant, decided to build its new European plant in the French city of Valenciennes. Located in the depressed north-eastern part of the country, the French government was able to offer attractive direct and indirect aid. There was also speculation that the British government's reluctance to join the initial group of countries participating in Europe's new single currency had also affected the decision. Yet most industry commentators reckoned that the efficiency of Toyota's UK plant, together with the local infrastructure of suppliers it had built up, more than compensated for any currency risk.

What did become clear was that Toyota, in making its decision to move to France, was acknowledging the importance of making its products in the same market where they were being sold. Toyota had been disappointed with its relatively poor performance in selling its products in continental Europe. The French motor market was notoriously chauvinistic but there were also genuine concerns that Toyota's models were out of touch with French, and indeed general continental European, preferences. In the end Toyota felt that the new small car, which was to be made at Valenciennes, stood a better chance of succeeding in France if it was made in France.

In addition to its effects on investment, costs and revenue there is often a considerable disruption cost whenever an organisation chooses to change its location. The costs of physically moving the operation's resources may be high but the risks involved may be even more important. Complex arrangements involving changes to many parts of the operation's resources invariably increase the risk of something going wrong with the move. Delays can mean inconvenience to customers, interruption of supply and increased costs. All this adds a certain inertia to the location decision. Once made, a location decision is difficult to change, which is why few operations want to move frequently.

But organisations do move their location, and it is usually for one of two reasons. Either,

- there are changes in the demand for its goods and services, or
- there are changes in the supply of its input resources to the operation.

Where the stimulus for relocation is a change in demand it may be because of a change in the aggregated volume of demand. For example, if the demand for a clothing manufacturer's products is increasing beyond its capacity, the company could either expand at its existing site or, alternatively, if the site is not large enough, it could move to a larger site in another location. A third option would be to keep its existing site and find a second location for an additional plant. Two of these options involve a location decision. Similarly, a reduction in the aggregate volume of demand may mean the company under-utilising its site, selling or leasing part of the site, or moving to a smaller new site.

Some high customer contact operations do not have the choice of expanding on the same site to meet rising demand. For example, a fast-food restaurant chain competes, at least partially, by having locations close to its customers. As demand increases it may well respond by investing in more locations. There will come a time, however, when locating a new restaurant in between the areas covered by two existing ones will, to some extent, cannibalise demand. The other reason for relocation is some kind of change in the cost or availability of its supply of inputs. An oil company, for example, will need to relocate as the oil it is extracting becomes depleted. A manufacturing company might choose to relocate its operations to a part of the world where labour costs are low. In other words, the labour costs differential, in the context of its competitive position, has changed. Similarly, the value of the land it has occupied compared with an alternative location may become too great to forego the opportunity of releasing the value of the land.

Spatially variable factors

A prerequisite to making location decisions is understanding the spatial characteristics of costs, revenues and investment. 'Spatially variable' means that its value changes with geographical location. In not-for-profit organisations where revenue may not be a relevant objective, customer service may be used as a substitute. So, for example, the fire service may use average (or maximum) response time as its 'market phasing' objective. Figure 4.9 identifies some of the spatially variable factors which organisations may use in location decisions. Again, these are categorised as market requirements and operations resource factors.

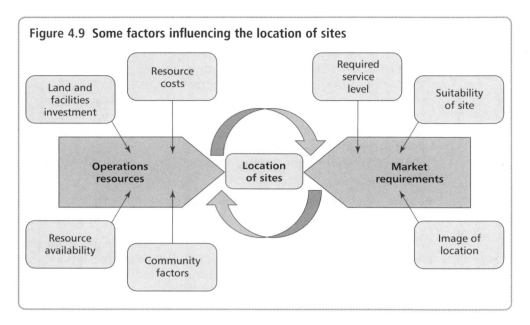

Figure 4.9 Some factors influencing the location of sites

Market requirement factors

The suitability of the site itself

The intrinsic characteristic of a location may affect an operation's ability to serve its customers and generate revenue. For example, locating a luxury business hotel in a high-prestige site close to the business district may be appropriate for the hotel's customers. Move it one or two kilometres away where it is surrounded by warehouses and it rapidly loses its attraction.

The image of the location

Some locations are firmly associated in customers' minds with a particular image. Suits made and sold in Saville Row, which is the centre of the up-market bespoke tailoring district in London, may be little better than high-quality suits made elsewhere. However, a location there will establish a tailor's reputation and possibly its revenue. The availability of appropriate local skills can also have an impact on how customers see the nature of an operation's products or services. For example, science parks are located close to universities because they hope to attract companies interested in using the skills available there. An entertainment production company may locate in Hollywood, partly, at least, because of the pool of talent on which it can draw to produce high-quality (or at least high revenue earning) projects.

Service level

For many operations this is by far the most important demand-side factor. Locating a general hospital, for example, in the middle of the countryside may have many advantages for its staff and even maybe for its costs, but clearly would be very inconvenient for its customers. Not only would those visiting the hospital need to travel long distances, but those being attended to in an emergency would have to wait longer than necessary to be brought in for admission. Because of this, hospitals are located close to centres of demand. Similarly, with other public services, location has a significant effect on the ability of an operation to serve its customers effectively. Likewise, other high customer contact operations such as restaurants, stores, banks, etc. have revenues which are directly affected by how easily customers can access the service.

Also, speed and dependability issues are becoming more important in many parts of manufacturing industry. Locating close to customers can be a competitive advantage or even a prerequisite for some customers. It is increasingly common for large manufacturers to demand that their suppliers build local plants, so as to ensure regular, fast and dependably supply. These may even be physically adjoining so that a supplier is able to deliver products through 'a hole in the wall' to its customer.

Operations resources factors

Land and facilities investment

If the operation is considering purchasing the land for its site this may be an important factor. If the operation is leasing the land then it is usually regarded as a supply-side cost factor. Certainly both land and rental costs vary between countries and cities. Figure 4.10 shows the costs of leasing office space in various cities around the world.[6] In the same way, investment in buildings can be a significant factor. Companies sometimes locate where they already have available land, or even unused buildings, in order to avoid the investment costs.

In some location decisions, investment in the infrastructure needed to support the main operations facility can be as significant, if not more so, than the investment in the operation itself. At a simple level, infrastructural investment may include such things as building access roads, improving waste disposal, or building power generation support. At a more extensive level, a company locating in an under-developed part of the world may need to invest in road, or even rail, links. It may even be necessary to invest significantly in the local supply industry, either providing sites

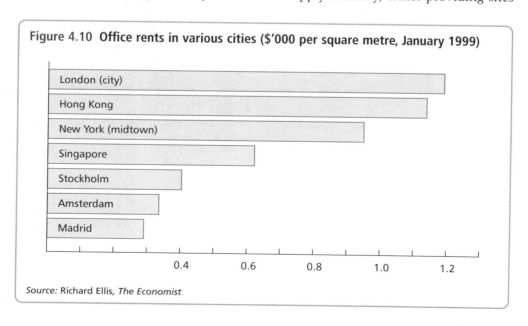

Figure 4.10 Office rents in various cities ($'000 per square metre, January 1999)

Source: Richard Ellis, *The Economist*

for suppliers or encouraging such things as producer cooperatives. Indeed, part of the deal which may be struck with the local government of the site may include a commitment to develop infrastructures.

Clustering for comfort[7]

Like-minded companies, with similar needs, seem to have an instinct to cluster together. Michigan is dominated by auto makers, northern Italy by knitted garment manufacturers, Connecticut by insurers, part of the English Midlands by racing cars, North Carolina has its furniture makers, and so on. The most famous cluster of all, though, is probably Silicon Valley in California. Microsoft may be based in Seattle, Compaq in Texas, and IBM operates out of New Jersey, but the centre of gravity for computer technology companies is, by common consent, the area south of San Francisco whose core is Santa Clara County.

But Silicon Valley is not an entirely recent creation. Back in 1938, Fred Terman, a professor at Stanford University, persuaded two of his students, Bill Hewlett and David Packard, to set up a company making electronic measuring equipment. In the 1950s Hewlett-Packard, together with several other companies, relocated to Stanford University's new industrial park. From that point, other companies became increasingly attracted to the area because of the skill of its labour pool, the spread of its network of suppliers and relatively easy access to venture capital. In many ways the catalyst for all this was the excellence of its research and education institutions such as Stanford, Berkeley and the Palo Alto research centre. It has been estimated that more than one thousand companies have emerged from Stanford University alone.

Just as important is the culture which has grown up in the area. This may even be more important than any conventional economic or technological factors. The Silicon Valley culture has been characterised as including the following.

- *A tolerance of failure* – companies go bankrupt, entrepreneurs learn what they did wrong and try again.

- *Mobility tolerance* – staff leave companies, the original company is upset but the staff start their own outfits.

- *People take risks* – at the forefront of technological advances, risk taking becomes a way of life. One estimate has it that out of twenty Silicon Valley companies, four will go bankrupt, six will stay in business but lose money, six will make only a modest return, three will do reasonably well, and one will do exceptionally well.

- *Enthusiasm for change* – fast-moving technology means that companies have to reinvent themselves continually.

- *Egalitarianism* – Silicon Valley is open to men and women of all nationalities. Youth and success are often prized more highly than age and seniority.

- *Sharing* – Silicon Valley is full of knowledge junkies whose chat sites, restaurants and social occasions are full of borrowed and shared ideas.

Resource costs – labour

Although wage and the other costs of employing people can vary between different areas in any country, it is more likely to be a significant factor when international comparisons are made. For example, Figure 4.11 shows the wage and non-wage costs of employment for a number of countries.[8] Here wage costs mean those costs to the organisation of paying wages directly to individual employees. Non-wage costs are the employment taxes, social security costs, holiday payments, and other welfare provisions which the organisation has to make in order to employ people. However,

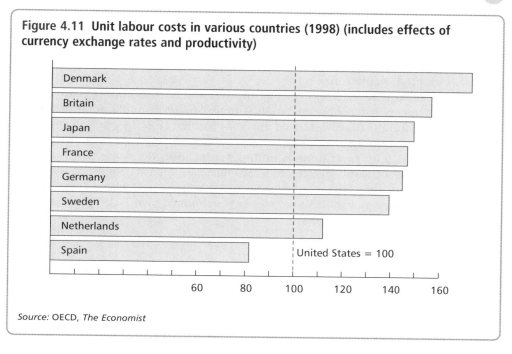

Figure 4.11 Unit labour costs in various countries (1998) (includes effects of currency exchange rates and productivity)

Source: OECD, *The Economist*

such labour costs should be treated with some caution. Two factors can influence them. The first is the productivity of labour. On an international level this is often inversely related to labour costs. This means that generally the average amount produced by each individual employed in a given unit of time is greater in countries with higher labour costs. This is at least partly because in countries with high labour costs there is more incentive to invest in productivity-enhancing technology. This effect goes some way in offsetting the large international variations in labour costs. The second factor is the rate of exchange of countries' currencies. Although in Figure 4.11 all costs are quoted in the same currency, exchange rates may swing considerably over time. This in turn changes relative labour costs. Yet in spite of these adjustments to the real value of relative labour costs, they may exert a major influence on the location decision, especially in industries such as clothing, where labour costs are a high proportion of total costs.

Resource costs – energy

Those operations which use large amounts of energy, for example aluminium smelting, may be influenced in their location decisions by the availability of relatively inexpensive energy. Low-cost energy sources may be direct, as in the availability of hydro-electric generation in an area, or indirect, for example a low-cost coal area which can be used to generate inexpensive electricity.

Resource costs – transportation

Transportation costs are clearly spatially variable because the operation's resources need to be transported (or transport themselves) from their point of origin to the operation itself. In many operations also, goods and services (or the people who perform the services) need to be transported from the operation to customers. Of course, not all goods and services are transported to customers. In operations such as hotels, retailers and hospitals, customers visit the operation to receive their services. In these cases we treat the ease with which customers access such services as a demand-side or revenue-influencing factor (or customer service factor in not-for-profit operations).

Proximity to sources of supply dominates location decisions where the cost of transporting input materials is high. So, for example, food processing or other agriculturally based activities are often located close to growing areas. Similarly, forestry and mining operations could only be located close to their sources of supply. Proximity to customers dominates location decisions where the transportation of products and services to customers is expensive or impossible. So, for example, many civil engineering projects are constructed where they are needed; similarly, accountancy audits take place at customers' own facilities because that is where the information resides.

Community factors

The general category of community factors are those influences on an operation's costs which derive from the social, political and economic environment of its location. These include:

- government financial or planning assistance;
- local tax rates;
- capital movement restrictions;
- political stability;
- language;
- local amenities (schools, theatres, shops, etc.);
- history of labour relations, absenteeism, productivity, etc.;
- environmental restrictions and waste disposal.

Community factors can be particularly influential on the location decision. Some issues obviously affect the profitability of the operation. For example, local tax rates can clearly affect the viability of a new location. Others are less obvious. For example, the European country which has had the most inward investment from Japanese companies is the UK. (See the box on Toyota's investment in France.) Some investments, especially the early ones, were influenced by the UK government's generous financial support and tax concessions. Other factors included a relatively cheap but well-educated workforce. Yet a less obvious, but equally important, factor was language. Many Japanese companies were accustomed to trading and producing in the USA. The English language is the first foreign language for most Japanese business people. Drawings of products and processes, for example, together with instruction sheets, computer programs, etc., were often immediately available for use without further translation for the UK. This means a lower risk of misunderstandings and mis-translation, smoothing communications between the new location and its Japanese head office.

The nature of location decisions

Although all location decisions will involve some, or all, of the market requirement

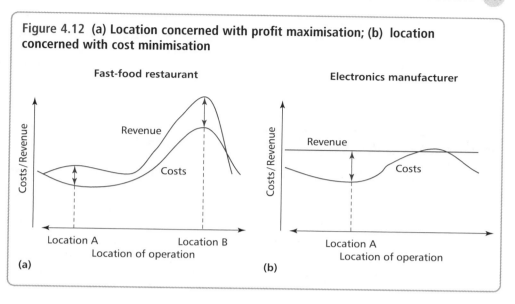

Figure 4.12 (a) Location concerned with profit maximisation; (b) location concerned with cost minimisation

and operations resource factors outlined above, the nature of the decision itself can vary significantly. Locating new fast-food restaurant franchises is a very different type of decision from locating a new electronics factory, for example. The differences between these two location decisions (or indeed any other location decisions) can be characterised on two dimensions. These are *the objectives of the location decision* and *the number of location options available.*

In many high contact operations, such as fast-food restaurants, retail shops and hotels, both costs and revenue are spatially variable. In other words, both the market and resource sides of the reconciliation process are significant. So, for example, locating a fast-food restaurant in an out-of-the-way location may allow it to operate with very low costs but its ability to attract customers (and therefore revenue) will be, likewise, very low. A more attractive location will undoubtedly be more expensive but would also attract higher custom. Figure 4.12(a) illustrates such a situation. Location B will maximise the gap between revenue and costs (and therefore operating profit); Location A has smaller profits but may be all that an operation could afford in ongoing costs. By contrast, an electronics manufacturer is unlikely to gain extra revenue just because of where it is located. Most low-contact operations have revenues which are relatively invariant to location. Costs, however, will vary with location. Thus, location is largely one of cost minimisation, this being an approximation for profit maximisation, see Figure 4.12(b).

The other major dimension of the location decision is concerned with the number of options between which a choice will be made. The electronics manufacturer may first all decide on a relatively large geographic region, such as the south-eastern states of the USA. Once that broad decision is made, the number of possible sites is very large indeed, in fact, for all practical purposes, infinite. The decision process involves narrowing the number of options down to a smaller representative number which can be systematically evaluated against a common set of criteria. Many high-contact operations, however, are not located in this way. More likely, a company will first of all decide on a relatively limited area. For example, '*We wish to locate one of our franchises in Charleston'*. Once this decision is made the search begins for a suitable site. The choice then is between any site which may be immediately available or, alternatively, waiting until a more attractive site becomes available. Each decision is, in effect, a yes/no decision of accepting a site or, alternatively, deferring a decision in the hope that a better one will become available.

SUMMARY ANSWERS TO KEY QUESTIONS

What individual decisions define the capacity strategy of a business?

Capacity strategy decisions can be divided into those that configure capacity and those concerned with changing the configuration of capacity. The former include defining the overall scale of an operation, the number and size of the sites between which capacity is distributed, the specific activities allocated to each site, and the location of each site. Reconfiguring capacity usually involves deciding when capacity levels should be changed, how big each step change should be, and, overall, how fast capacity levels should be changed.

How do capacity decisions differ for different time-scales?

Capacity-related decisions are conventionally divided into three time horizons – long-term strategic, medium-term, and short-term. Strategic decisions are those concerned with the provision of buildings, facilities and process technology, in all parts of the business, for at least months and probably years into the future. Medium-term decisions are concerned with how demand fluctuates over months and weeks and how an operation can supply its fluctuating demand within its physical capacity constraints. Short-term capacity decisions are concerned with the allocation of resources to tasks on a weekly, hourly, or minute-by-minute basis.

What affects the size of an operation? i.e. how much capacity should it have?

The starting point in determining the overall capacity level of any business will be its forecast for the future level of demand. However, actual capacity may not be the same as forecast demand. It may be modified to account for the relative certainty, or uncertainty, of demand, long-term changes in expected demand level and the consequences of over- or under-supply. Similarly, the nature of an operation's resources may also affect its size. The most obvious constraint will be the availability of capital needed to provide any level of capacity. The ratio of fixed to variable costs in any capacity increment, together with general economies of scale, will also have an influence. Finally, a company may choose to provide more of one kind of resource (for example, the size of the physical building) before demand warrants it. This may be in order to save capital costs in the long run.

Between how many separate sites should an operation divide its capacity?

The decision here concerns the choice between many small sites on one hand, or fewer larger sites on the other. The geographical distribution of demand, together with customers' required service level, will influence this decision, as will the economies of scale of the operation and the costs associated with supply. If demand is widely distributed between customers demanding high levels of service, and if there are no significant economies of scale or costs of supply, then the business is more likely to operate with many small sites.

Where should an operation locate its capacity?

Again, the required level of service from customers will influence this decision. Fast and regular supply implies location close to customer locations. Other market-related factors include the suitability of the site and the general image of its location. As far as operations resources are concerned, significant factors include the resource costs associated with the site, such as land and energy costs, the investment needed in land and facilities, the availability of any specialist resources required, and general community factors.

> **CASE EXERCISE – What would you do?**
>
> # Freeman Biotest Inc.[9]

Freeman Biotest was one of the largest independent companies supplying the food-processing industry. Its initial success had come with a food preservative, used mainly for meat-based products, and marketed under the name of 'FBXX'. Other products were subsequently developed in the food colouring and food container coating fields, so that now FBXX accounted for only 25 per cent of total company sales, which now were slightly over $100 million.

The decision

The problem over which there was such controversy related to the replacement of one of the process lines used to manufacture FBXX. Currently two such process lines were used; both had been designed and installed by Brayford Corp., a process equipment manufacturer. It was the older of the two Brayford lines that was giving trouble. High breakdown figures, with erratic quality levels, meant that output level requirements

Table 4.7 **A comparison of the two alternative process line configurations**

Process line configuration	Brayford	Bi-line 8
Capital cost	$5,900,000	$8,800,000
Processing costs	Fixed: $150,000/mth Variable: $750/kg	Fixed: $400,000/mth Variable: $600/kg
Design capacity	1050 kg/mth 98%±0.7% purity	1400 kg/mth 99.5%±0.2% purity
Quality	Manual testing	Automatic testing
Maintenance	Adequate but needs servicing	Not known – probably good
After-sales services	Very good	Not known – unlikely to be good
Delivery	Three months	Immediate

were only just being reached. The problem was: should the company replace the ageing Brayford line with a new Brayford line, or should it commission another process line, the 'Bi-line 8' line, which would be manufactured by a relatively new company, Bi-Line Inc.? The VP for Technology had drawn up a comparison of the two units, shown in Table 4.7.

The body considering the problem was the newly formed Management Committee. The committee consisted of the VP for Technology and the Marketing VP, who had been with the firm since its beginning, together with the VPs for Operations and Finance, both of whom had joined the company only six months before.

What follows is a condensed version of the information presented by each manager to the committee, together with their attitudes to the decision.

The Marketing Vice President

Currently the market for this type of preservative had reached a size of some $50 million, of which Freeman Biotest supplied approximately 48 per cent. There had, of late, been significant changes in the market – in particular, many of the users of preservatives were now able to buy products similar to FBXX. The result had been the evolution of a much more price-sensitive market than had previously been the case. Further market projections were somewhat uncertain. It was clear that the total market would not shrink (in volume terms) and best estimates suggested a market of perhaps $60 million within the next three or four years (at current prices).

Although the food preservative market had advanced by a series of technical innovations, 'real' changes in the basic product were now few and far between. FBXX was sold in either solid powder or liquid form, depending on the particular needs of the customer. Prices tended to be related to the weight of chemical used, however. Thus, for example, currently the average market price was approximately $1,050 per kg. There were, of course, wide variations depending on order size, etc.

> 'At the moment I am mainly interested in getting the right quantity and quality of FBXX each month. I'm worried that unless we get a reliable new process line quickly, we will have problems. The Bi-line 8 line could be working in a few weeks, giving better quality too. Furthermore, if demand does increase, the Bi-line 8 will give us the extra capacity.'

The Vice President for Technology

The major part of the VP for Technology's budget was devoted to modifying basic FBXX so that it could be used for more acidic food products such as fruit. This was not proving easy and as yet nothing had come of the research, although the Chief Chemist remained optimistic.

> 'If we succeed in modifying FBXX the market opportunities will be doubled overnight and we will need the extra capacity. I know we would be taking a risk by going for the Bi-line 8 machine, but our company has grown by gambling on our research findings, and we must continue to show faith. Also, the Bi-line 8 technology uses principles which will be in all similar technologies in the future. We have to start learning how to exploit them sooner or later.'

The Operations Vice President

The FBXX Division was self-contained as a production unit, located at the smaller of the company's two sites. Production requirements for FBXX were currently at a steady rate of around 1900 kg per month. The technicians who staffed the FBXX lines were the only technicians in Freeman Biotest who did all their own minor repairs and full quality control. The reason for this was largely historical: when the firm started, the product was experimental and qualified technicians were needed to operate the plant. Four of the six had been with the firm almost from its beginning.

'It's all right for some of my colleagues to talk about a big expansion of FBXX sales; they don't have to cope with all the problems if it doesn't happen. The fixed costs of the Bi-line 8 unit are nearly three times those of the Brayford. Just think what that will do to my budget at low volumes of output. As I understand it, there is absolutely no evidence to show a large upswing in FBXX. No, the whole idea (of the Bi-line 8 plant) is just too risky. Not only is there the risk. I don't think it is generally understood what the consequences of the Bi-line 8 would mean. We would need twice the variety of spares for a start. But what really worries me is the staff's reaction. As fully qualified technicians they regard themselves as the elite of the firm; so they should, they are paid practically the same as I am! If we get the Bi-line 8 plant all their most interesting work, like the testing and the maintenance, will disappear or be greatly reduced. They will finish up as highly paid process workers.'

The Finance Vice President

The company had financed nearly all its recent capital investment from its own retained profits, but would be taking out short-term loans next year for the first time for several years.

'At the moment, I don't think it wise to invest extra capital we can't afford in an attempt to give us extra capacity we don't need at the moment. This year will be an expensive one for the company. We are already committed to considerably increased expenditure on promotion of our other products and capital investment in other parts of the firm. I accept that there might eventually be an upsurge in FBXX demand but, if it does come, it probably won't be this year and it will be far bigger than the Bi-line 8 can cope with anyway, so we might as well have three Brayford plants at that time.'

Further reading

Brush, T.H., C.A. Maritan and A. Karnani (1999) 'The plant location decision in multinational manufacturing firms: an empirical analysis of international business and manufacturing strategy perspectives', *Production and Operations Management*, Vol. 8, No. 2.

Evans, P. and T.S. Wurster (2000) *Blown to Bits: How the new economics of information transforms strategy*, Harvard Business School Press.

Ferdows, K. (1989) 'Mapping international factory networks', in *Managing International Manufacturing*, K. Ferdows (ed.), Elsevier Science Publishers, Amsterdam.

Hayes, R.H. and S.C. Wheelwright (1984) *Restoring our Competitive Edge*, Wiley, New York.

Porter, M. (1990) *The Competitive Advantage of Nations*, The Free Press, New York.

Schmenner, R.W. (1982) *Making Business Location Decisions*, Prentice Hall, NJ.

Notes on the chapter

1 Source: Slack, N., S Chambers and R. Johnston (2001) *Operations Management*, 3rd edn, Financial Times–Prentice Hall, London.

2 Sources: Retail Research Report 39 (1993) Corporate Intelligence Research Publications, London; *The Economist* (1997) 'Trick or treat', 4 October.

3 Sources: *The Economist* (1999) 'Small, but perfect for reforming', 23 January; *The Economist*

(1999) 'Why big is still beautiful', 3 April; Griffiths, J. (1999) 'Volvo buy steps up scramble for size', *Financial Times*, 29 January.

4 Hayes, R.H. and S.C. Wheelwright (1984) *Restoring Our Competitive Edge*, Wiley, New York.

5 Source: *The Economist* (1997) 'Toyota learns French', 29 November.

6 *The Economist* (1999) 'Office rents', 13 March.

7 Source: *The Economist* (1997) 'A survey of Silicon Valley', 29 March.

8 *The Economist* (1999) 'Unit labour costs', 19 December.

9 Source: Based on Rochem Ltd, Slack, N., S. Chambers and R. Johnston (2001) *Operations Management*, 3rd edn, Financial Times-Prentice Hall, London.

Capacity dynamics

Introduction

In the previous chapter we looked at how capacity can be managed strategically from a relatively static perspective. Given our understanding of markets, costs and competitive objectives, we examined how we shape the configuration of our operations. In this chapter we look at some of the issues involved in 'reshaping' capacity, at least in the sense that capacity *levels* and *locations* will be changed over time. In the previous chapter it became clear that the level of likely demand was probably the most significant influence on capacity level. Demand, however, is rarely stable, so decisions need to be made as to how to change an organisation's resources to match the changes in the marketplace over time. In the short to medium term, there are many ways in which companies can deal with variations in demand. This chapter, however, considers the longer-term issues of matching the organisation's capacity to the longer-term needs of the market. Decisions in this area usually involve significant changes in capacity, like the purchase of new equipment, the opening of new facilities or the closure of sites. As such, long-term capacity planning involves major investment decisions, and the results of those decisions will define the scope of operations capability for some considerable time. Consequently, managing long-term capacity dynamics is a major component in an organisation's operations strategy. Figure 5.1 illustrates the place of capacity dynamics in the operations strategy matrix.

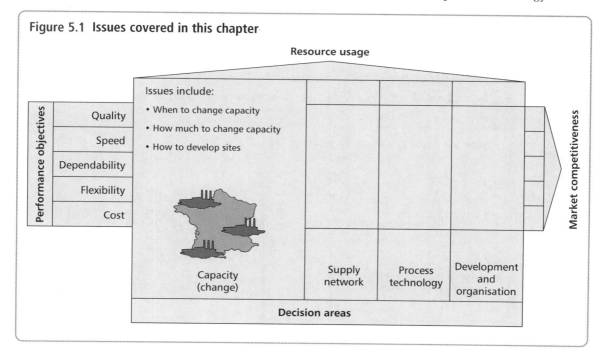

Figure 5.1 Issues covered in this chapter

Resource usage

Issues include:
- When to change capacity
- How much to change capacity
- How to develop sites

Performance objectives

Quality

Speed

Dependability

Flexibility

Cost

Market competitiveness

Capacity (change)

Supply network

Process technology

Development and organisation

Decision areas

- *How does the timing of capacity change influence the performance of the operation?*
- *How do operations choose between large or small increments of capacity change?*
- *What issues are important when changing the location of capacity?*

Capacity change

Planning changes in capacity levels would be easy if it were not for two characteristics of capacity – lead-time and economies of scale. If capacity could be introduced (or deleted) with zero delay between the decision to expand (or contract) and the capacity coming on (or off) stream, an operation could wait until demand clearly warranted the change. The fact that changing capacity takes time means that decisions need to be made before demand levels are known for sure. So deciding to change capacity inevitably involves some degree of risk. But so does delaying the decision, because delay may still mean that capacity is not appropriate to demand.

All this is made even more problematic because of economies of scale. In the previous chapter the 'economy of scale' effect was explained as the tendency for both capital and operating costs to reduce as the increment of capacity increases. This means that, when changing capacity levels, there is pressure to make the change big enough to exploit scale economies. Again though, this carries risks that demand will not be sufficient for the capacity to be utilised sufficiently for the scale economies to be realised. Conversely, changing capacity by too little may mean opportunity risks of tying the operation in to small, non-economic units of capacity. Put both long lead-times and significant economies of scale together and capacity change decisions become particularly risky.

In the rest of this chapter we will examine the management of capacity change, as indicated in Figure 5.2, by looking at three interrelated decisions, namely:

- The timing of any change in capacity.
- The magnitude of any change in capacity we may wish to make.

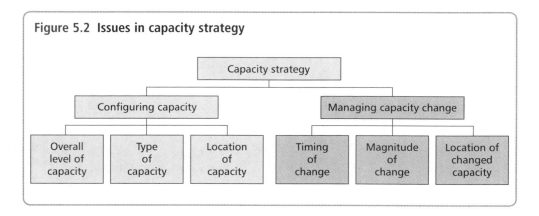

Figure 5.2 Issues in capacity strategy

- Taking timing and magnitude together, generally how fast might we want to expand? That is, what is the rate of change of capacity levels?

- If the capacity change involves some geographical redistribution of resources, what are the implications of changed or split-site locations?

Timing of capacity change

The first decision in changing capacity levels is *when* to make the change. As with so many capacity decisions, the forecast level of future demand will be a major influence on the timing of capacity change. Capacity will be increased, or decreased, when forecasts indicate that extra capacity is needed, or current capacity not needed. Forecasting though, especially with the long-term planning horizons necessary for capacity planning, is a very uncertain process. Therefore the degree of confidence an operation has in its forecasts will likewise influence the timing decision. So will the response of the market to under- or over-capacity. If competitive conditions dictate fast response times, then an operation might err on the side of timing capacity change to ensure over-capacity. Conversely, if customers are willing to wait, or if alternative supplies can be arranged, then there are fewer risks in under-capacity. Nor is the timing decision exclusively dictated by customers. Competitor activities and responses may also prompt capacity change. An operation may choose to invest in capacity even before demand warrants it just to pre-empt a competitor getting in first. The economics of the investment may even mean that whoever expands their capacity first renders capacity expansion by any other operation uneconomic. (This may be thought about in Game Theory terms, see box later.) Figure 5.3 includes these market-related influences on the timing decision, together with the operations resource-related influences of economy of scale and lead-time.

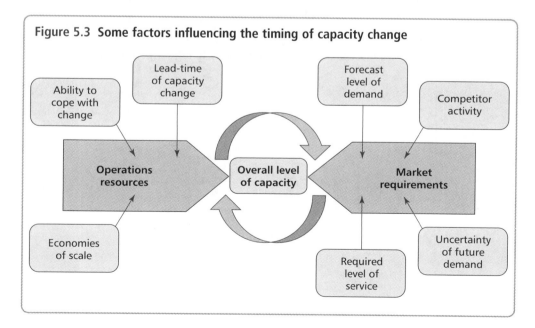

Figure 5.3 Some factors influencing the timing of capacity change

Generic timing strategies

Attempting to categorise capacity timing options is obviously difficult because of the, effectively infinite, number of times that could be chosen to expand or contract capacity in any number of steps. However, it is possible to identify three generic types of capacity timing. For example, Figure 5.4 shows the forecast demand for a new air conditioning unit. The company that manufactures it has decided to build 400-unit/week plants in order to meet the growth in demand for its new product. In deciding *when* the new plants are to be introduced, the company must choose a position somewhere between two extreme strategies.[1]

- *Capacity leads demand* – timing the introduction of capacity in such a way that there is always sufficient capacity to meet forecast demand.
- *Capacity lags demand* – timing the introduction of capacity so that demand is always equal to or greater than capacity.

Figure 5.4 shows these two extreme strategies, though, in practice, the company is likely to choose a position somewhere between the two extremes. Each strategy has its own advantages and disadvantages. These are shown in Table 5.1. The actual approach taken by any company will depend on how it views these advantages and disadvantages. For example, if the company's access to funds for capital expenditure is limited, it is likely to find the delayed capital expenditure requirement of the capacity-lagging strategy relatively attractive.

Smoothing with stocks

The strategy on the continuum between pure leading and pure lagging strategies can be implemented so that no inventories are accumulated. All demand in one period is satisfied (or not) by the activity of the operation in the same period. Indeed, for a customer-processing operation there is no alternative to this. An hotel cannot satisfy demand in one year by using rooms which were vacant the previous year. For some

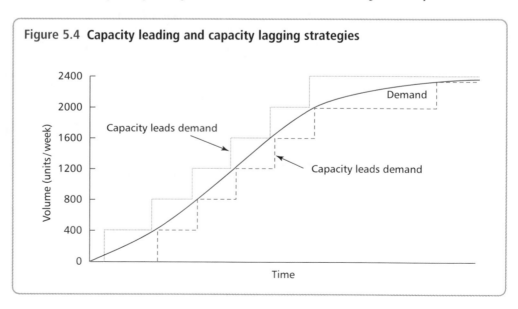

Figure 5.4 Capacity leading and capacity lagging strategies

Table 5.1 The advantages and disadvantages of pure leading and pure lagging strategies of capacity timing

	Advantages	Disadvantages
Capacity leading	Always sufficient capacity to meet demand, therefore revenue is maximised and customers satisfied.	Utilisation of the plants is always relatively high.
	Most of the time there is a 'capacity cushion' which can absorb extra demand if forecasts are pessimistic.	Risks of even greater (or even permanent) over-capacity if demand does not reach forecast levels.
	Any critical start-up problems with new plants are less likely to affect supply to customers.	Capital spending on plant early.
Capacity lagging	Always sufficient demand to keep the plants working at full capacity, therefore unit costs are minimised.	Insufficient capacity to meet demand fully, therefore reduced revenue and dissatisfied customers.
	Over-capacity problems are minimised if forecasts are optimistic.	No ability to exploit short-term increases in demand.
	Capital spending on the plants is delayed.	Under-supply position even worse if there are start-up problems with the new plants.

materials- and information-processing operations, however, the output from the operation that is not required in one period can be stored for use in the next period. Inventories can be used to obtain the advantages of both capacity leading and lagging. Figure 5.5 shows how this can be done. Here the plants, in the air conditioning manufacturer example, have been introduced such that over-capacity in one

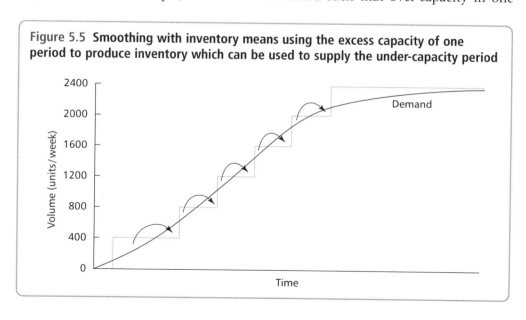

Figure 5.5 Smoothing with inventory means using the excess capacity of one period to produce inventory which can be used to supply the under-capacity period

Table 5.2 The advantages and disadvantages of the smoothing-with-inventories strategy

Advantages	Disadvantages
All demand is satisfied, therefore customers are satisfied and revenue maximised.	The cost of inventories in terms of working capital requirement can be high. This is especially serious at a time when the company requires funds for its capital expansion.
Utilisation of capacity is high and therefore costs are low.	Risks of product deterioration and obsolescence.
Very short-term surges in demand can be met from inventories.	

period is used to make air conditioning units for the following or subsequent periods. Capacity is introduced such that demand can always be met by a combination of production and inventories, and capacity is, with the occasional exception, fully utilised.

This may seem like an ideal state. Demand is always met and so revenue is maximised. Capacity is usually fully utilised and so costs are minimised. The profitability of the operation is therefore likely to be high. There is a price to pay, however, and that is the cost of carrying the inventories. Not only will these have to be funded, but the risks of obsolescence and deterioration of stock are introduced. Table 5.2 summarises the advantages and disadvantages of the 'smoothing-with-inventories' strategy.

Smoothing-with-stocks is essentially a compromise between leading and lagging but also involves some element of over-production during times of capacity leading, so that the surplus production can be used to fulfil market demand in periods of capacity lagging. Two points need to be made about this strategy:

● Obviously it can only be used where the output from an operation is storable. That is usually in make-to-stock manufacturing operations only.

● The working capital implications of any extensive use of this strategy could prove very expensive. Furthermore, the risk of product obsolescence or deterioration may make it difficult to implement in all but the most robust and commodity-like of products.

However, at the margin, some pre-stocking of output immediately prior to the disruption which is likely to be caused by new capacity introduction is not unknown.

Possible life-cycle effects

Whether operations choose predominantly leading, predominantly lagging, or (if they can) a smoothing-with-inventories stocks, will depend on their own circumstances. These will vary greatly, but some generalisations can be made, especially concerning how a company's position on the product/service life cycle can affect the choice of strategy.

At the product/service *introduction* stage of the life cycle, it is difficult to adopt any other than a *capacity-leading strategy*. Capacity must be available to produce the goods or deliver the services, otherwise customers will not have the ability to sample

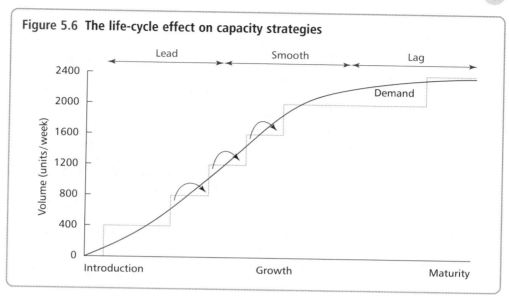

Figure 5.6 The life-cycle effect on capacity strategies

them and make a judgement of their acceptability. Furthermore, the main disadvantages of capacity-leading strategies, namely low utilisation and, therefore, high costs, are more likely to be tolerated at the introduction stage where competition might not be based on low prices.

During the *growth* phase of the life cycle, demand forecasting is particularly difficult because small changes in growth rates can result in very different levels of demand. With uncertain demand, the existence of high inventories might not seem as much of a disadvantage as when they are seen purely as a cost. Therefore *smoothing with inventory* might be preferred as a strategy where this is possible.

On reaching *maturity* the nature of competition usually emphasises low price more than in earlier stages. When price competition is tough, most companies will be more concerned with keeping their costs low. This will make the full utilisation of *capacity-lagging* strategies seem attractive. Figure 5.6 illustrates this.

Leading, lagging or smoothing

Which of these strategies is used and at what time is partly a matter of the company's competitive objectives at any point in time. Just as significant, though, is the effect these strategies have on the financial performance of the organisation. Both the capacity-leading strategy and the smoothing-with-stocks strategy will tend to increase the cash requirements of the company through earlier capital expenditure and higher working capital respectively. Sometimes companies may wish to time capacity introduction in order to have a particular effect on the balance of cash requirement and profitability. It may be that some strategies of capacity change improve profitability at the expense of long-term cash requirements, while others minimise longer-term cash requirements but do not yield as high a level of short-term profitability. Thus, capacity strategy may be influenced by the required financial performance of the organisation, which in turn may be a function of where the company is raising its finance, on the equity markets or from long-term loans.

Sparks from Flint[2]

Periods of capacity change, especially when capacity is being reduced, can be painful. On 5 June 1998, 3400 workers from the United Auto Workers (UAW) went on strike at General Motors' metal-stamping factory in Flint, Michigan. Within six days a components manufacturing plant within the group had followed suit. The dispute ended 54 days later. By that time 26 of GM's 29 North American plants had been affected and the company had lost $2.3 billion. What had started as a local dispute about investment at a metal-stamping plant had turned into the longest and costliest strike in the company's history. And the cause of all this? The company's difficulty in managing the reduction in its manufacturing capacity base.

Reducing levels of capacity is going to be difficult for any company when it involves taking away the livelihoods of individual workers. General Motors had a particularly difficult task in reconfiguring its capacity to compete with the high-tech, and often non-unionised, Japanese plants. At the time, GM was making almost $1 thousand less on each vehicle it sold than its arch-rival Ford. Much of this extra cost was because it had too many factories which were too small and too old-fashioned in their work processes. At the time GM had 14 stamping plants like Flint, when it probably needed fewer than 10. However, GM's real problems lay in the timing and manner of its capacity reduction plans. The UAW had negotiated its 'pattern' agreement with all the big three American car makers some time earlier. However, Ford and Chrysler had already done much of their slimming down when the agreement was struck. GM had to try to do the same under the more restrictive new agreement. Nor did GM's approach to the problem make their life any easier. Their relationship with the UAW had always been poor. At one point, early in the dispute, they secretly moved stamping dies out of the factory over a public holiday, an action the workers branded as underhand and sneaky. They were also accused, by union critics, of promising investment in exchange for better productivity and then reneging on the deal.

Capacity timing under conditions of uncertainty

Our treatment so far has assumed that both levels of demand and capacity plans are known and certain. Yet in any realistic capacity planning exercise there are two major types of uncertainty:

- the uncertainty of future demand, and
- the uncertainty in the timing of the new capacity's availability. Construction or delivery delays may push back the introduction of the new capacity; conversely, it may become available earlier than thought.

Figure 5.7 illustrates a capacity-leading strategy which is to be adopted by one company. Demand is forecast to rise (as all new products or service forecasts seem to) in a smooth S curve. Four increments of capacity are planned, as shown, to come on stream in such a way as always to fulfil demand. This may be the intended plan but, in reality, the likelihood of things happening like this are remote. Just take the introduction of capacity increment number 2 and examine what might happen if circumstances are not as forecast. This is illustrated in Figure 5.8(a).

Here we have the two uncertainties clearly illustrated. First of all, instead of a single line indicating forecast demand, the company have asked their forecasters to indicate what the likely maximum demand and minimum demand might be at any point. Secondly they have included uncertainty over the lead-time of the capacity increment. As illustrated, this means that they must start constructing the new

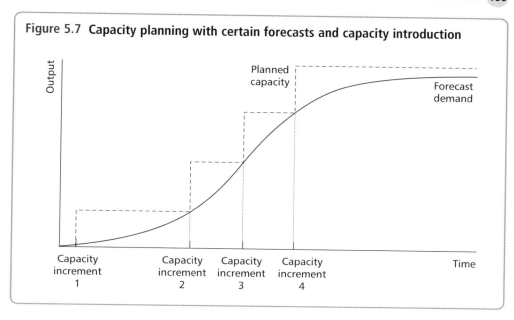

Figure 5.7 **Capacity planning with certain forecasts and capacity introduction**

capacity at time X in order for it to become available, as planned, at time Y. However, again (after discussions with their contractors and other people involved in the provision of the new capacity), they have come to the conclusion that the new capacity may come on stream early (at the 'earliest finish time') or late (at the 'latest finish time').

Let us look at what could happen at the extremes of demand and lead-time uncertainty. If the capacity becomes available at the earliest possible time the company's capacity will go up from point A to point D in Figure 5.8(b). However, if demand is at the lower limit of forecasts, demand will be at point C while capacity is three or four times greater at point D, a position of considerable over-capacity which must affect the company's costs of operation very significantly. Conversely, Figure 5.8(c) illustrates the situation where the capacity increment is delayed and does not add to total capacity until point B. Demand here is at the upper limit of the forecast range. Just before the moment of capacity expansion, the company will have less than half the capacity required to fulfil demand. This may lead to loss of business and market share to competitors. At the very least it would lead to a delay in sales revenue.

Because of considerations such as these, companies may wish to time capacity expansion to avoid either under-capacity or over-capacity, depending which is regarded as the most damaging.

Because of considerations such as these, capacity planning often has to include contingencies to allow for demand and capacity lead-time uncertainties. This obviously adds extra costs to any capacity provision plan, or alternatively, threatens a firm's ability to capture revenue. Firms also may seek to reduce the level of uncertainty by adopting more flexible approaches to the provision of capacity. Where the capacity lead-time is long and demand difficult to forecast, these issues come to the forefront of capacity planning.

The airline industry exhibits both these characteristics. Orders need to be placed with aircraft manufacturers often several years in advance of their delivery. These

Figure 5.8 (a) Demand and lead-time uncertainties; (b) capacity on stream early but demand on lower boundary of forecast; (c) capacity on stream late and demand on upper boundary of forecast

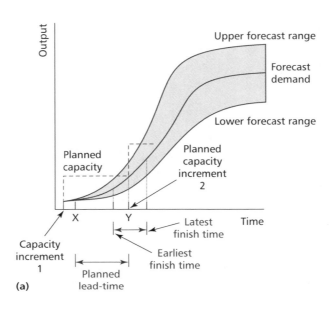

(a)

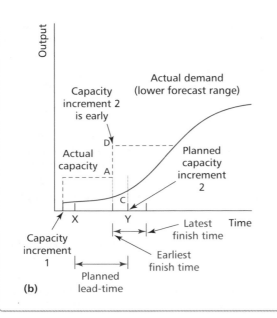

(b)

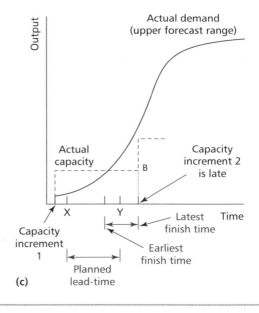

(c)

orders will be based on the airline's best estimate of the demand for its services in several years' time. But the airline industry is both cyclical and subject to disruption by unexpected international events. For example, the Gulf War in the early 1990s had a catastrophic effect on demand for flights, especially out of the United States. Similarly, the economic crises which faced nations in Asia in the mid-1990s reduced demand in an important and (hitherto) fast-growing part of the market. Similarly, the lead-time for aircraft manufacture is influenced by the balance between demand and capacity at the aircraft manufacturers (in the passenger aircraft industry, now consolidated to two major manufacturers, Boeing and Airbus). Like any other business, airlines do not like operating where demand is lower than capacity. (Utilisation in the airline industry is called 'load factor'.) Low load factors translates into high unit costs and low margins, given that most costs for servicing a route are fixed by the number and length of flights rather than the number of passengers on the aircraft. On the other hand, too high a load factor can prevent airlines from obtaining highly profitable last-minute bookings and can affect the ability of customers to rearrange their itinerary. However, airlines do not like to forego growth when the potential is there. Historically there has been a tendency for airlines to be optimistic when ordering aircraft during an economic upswing in anticipation of high growth in the future. Unfortunately, given the lags in receiving the aircraft, they are often delivered at the start of the next cyclical downturn. Given that aircraft manufacturers charge relatively high prices for cancellation of options on their aircraft, capacity planning in this industry can be extremely risky. This is why many airlines lease much of their capacity, either from other airlines or from leasing companies (which may be owned by the aircraft manufacturers themselves). The airline will own its own 'core' fleet of aircraft and lease the balance on relatively flexible terms. By expanding its core fleet only gradually, and timing its leasing periods with those times it wants to retain the option of making permanent additions to its core fleet, the airline tries to reduce its exposure to capacity risks.

Theory Box   Decision trees

One method of illustrating decisions made under uncertainty, such as the capacity timing decision, is to use a decision tree. Decision trees are a formalisation of any decision that has a number of options, the outcomes from which will be affected by future and uncertain events. Once drawn, they can be used to organise the use of simple expectation probability theory, so as to choose the option with the best expected outcome (although other decision criteria may be used, such as avoiding the worst outcomes).

Figure 5.9 shows a simple decision-tree representation of a capacity timing decision. Here a firm needs to choose between expanding this year or not. Expanding its capacity will cost it $8 million. However, it faces uncertain future demand. If demand does grow in the coming year, it is likely to do so to a level that would fill the new unit of capacity. If demand does not grow, it is likely to stay level and be roughly in balance with the company's existing capacity. Forecasts indicate that there is a 50–50 chance of demand growing or remaining level. Profits from the operation will depend on whether capacity has been expanded and on the subsequent level of demand.

▶

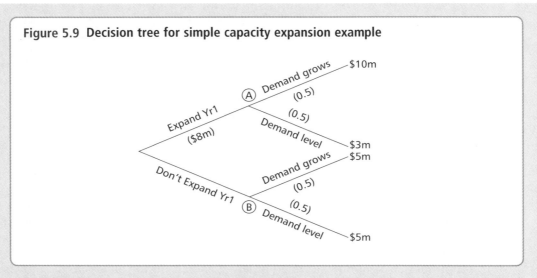

Figure 5.9 Decision tree for simple capacity expansion example

If the company decides to expand its capacity:

There is a 0.5 chance of demand growing, earning the company $12m in profits.

There is a 0.5 chance of demand being level, earning the company $5m in profits.

So *expected* profits = (0.5 × 10) + (0.5 × 3)
                      = $6.5m

But the company would have paid out $8m to expand its capacity.

If the company does not expand its capacity:

The company will earn $5m in profits whatever happens to demand.

Given these outcomes, the company decides that it does not wish to spend $8m to have expected profits of $6.5m when it can be sure of $5m without any capital outlay (especially when there is a 50 per cent chance that it will earn $2m *less* than it would do without any investment).

Sequential capacity decisions

Decision trees are a useful, but very simplified, framework by which to structure capacity timing decisions. They are used, usually, as a 'first-level analysis'. However, they are at their most useful when used to model sequential investment decisions. For example, suppose the company introduced in the theory box on decision trees extended its analysis to include the possibility of also expanding in year 2. The decision tree now looks more complex (see Figure 5.10) but it does enable a more useful analysis. The decision tree again indicates the profits earned for each set of decision options, this time over the two-year period. It also indicates that the probabilities of demand growing in the second year depend on whether it has grown in the first year.

To analyse this tree we need to take a perspective of how the second-year decision would be made, depending on what had happened in the first year. These are points C to F in Figure 5.10.

Figure 5.10 Decision tree for two-year analysis

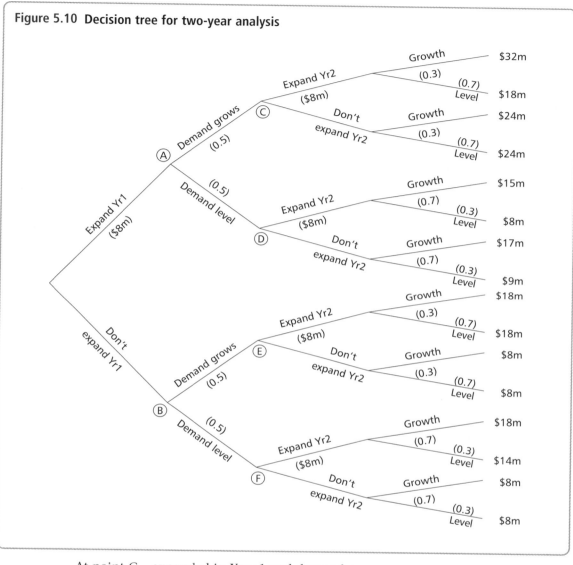

At point C – expanded in Year 1 and demand grew.

If company expands in Year 2, expected profits $\quad= (0.3 \times 32) + (0.7 \times 18)$

$$= \$22.2\text{m}$$

If company doesn't expand in Year 2, expected profits $\quad= \$24\text{m}$

The company would not choose to expand because expected profits would be lower and $8m investment is needed.

At point D – expanded in Year 1 and demand was level.

If company expands in Year 2, expected profits $\quad= (0.7 \times 15) + (0.3 \times 8)$

$$= \$12.9\text{m}$$

If company doesn't expand in Year 2, expected profits = $(0.7 \times 17) + (0.3 \times 9)$

= $14.6m

Again the company would choose not to expand because expected profits would be lower and $8m investment is needed.

At point E – did not expand in Year 1 and demand grew.

If company expands in Year 2, expected profits = $18m

If company doesn't expand in Year 2, expected profits = $8m

The company would expand because, even with $8m expenditure, the cash flow is higher than not expanding.

At point F – did not expand in Year 1 and demand was level.

If company expands in Year 2, expected profits = $(0.7 \times 18) + (0.3 \times 14)$

= $16.8m

If company doesn't expand in Year 2, expected profits = $8m

The company would expand, again cash flow would be higher even with investment in extra capacity.

Working back to points A and B.

At point A there is a 0.5 chance of $24m profit.

and a 0.5 chance of $14.6m profit

(i.e. there would be no further expansion no matter what happened to demand).

So expected profit at point A = $(0.5 \times 24) + (0.5 \times 14.6)$

= $19.3m

At point B there is a 0.5 chance of $10m profit (after expenditure of $8m on the expansion).

and a 0.5 chance of $8.8m profit (after expenditure of $8m on the expansion).

So expected profit at point B = $(0.5 \times 10) + (0.5 \times 8.8)$

= $9.4m

The company should therefore expand in Year 1 because its expected cash flow (after the $8m for expansion) would be $19.3 - 8 = $11.3m, higher than the expected profit of not expanding in Year 1.

Then, if demand in Year 1 does grow (point C), or remains level (point D), no further expansion is justified.

Note that extending the analysis for the further year has changed the original decision described in the theory box. Horizon time is an important issue in all capacity change decisions.

The chip cycle[3]

One particular problem in managing capacity investment is illustrated by the semiconductor industry. It is a highly unstable industry, amongst other reasons because the demand for chips can change rapidly, new fabrication plants (fabs) can take more than a year to build and, when built, have very high fixed costs. The long lead-times mean that it is difficult to adjust capacity smoothly as prices change or demand fluctuates. Most operations turn down their output when demand and prices are falling. But, if the investment decision to build a new fab plant was taken before demand started falling, it could come on stream just as prices are slumping. This in turn depresses prices even further. All this is made even worse by the huge cost of new fabs. Driven to make a return on its investments before their technology gets out of date (perhaps in as little as three to five years' time), the chip-making operation will want to run the plant as near to full capacity as possible. It may be reluctant to cut production even when demand levels are falling. The resulting surplus production can push prices even lower. Of course, the opposite can happen. When demand rises the long lead-times mean that there is no instant extra capacity and prices soar in the resulting shortage. Not surprisingly, capacity planning in the semiconductor industry is not regarded as an easy job.

Figure 5.11 Cyclical growth in the microchip industry

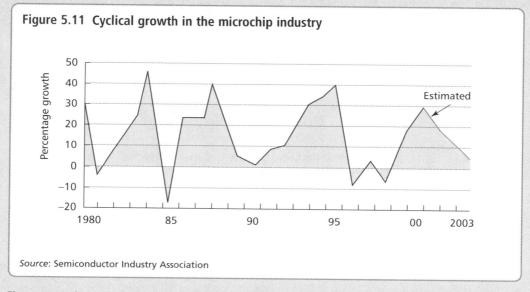

Source: Semiconductor Industry Association

Figure 5.11 shows how growth in the semiconductor industry has varied over the past 20 years. That some sort of cycle will continue is not disputed. The exact timing of the next downturn or upswing, however, is always the cause of fevered speculation amongst industry analysts. As one industry chief put it: *'Sometime during the next economic cycle the supply of micro chips and the demand for them will exactly match ... for half an hour.'*

Competitor activity

Earlier we used a simple decision-tree format to structure a capacity timing decision. In such a model, the environment in which the decision is being made is assumed to be independent of the decision itself. So the chances of the market growing or remaining level were not affected by the company's decision to expand or not.

However, in most markets, rival firms will watch each other closely and shape their own actions on the basis of what their competitors are doing. Thus the environment is not only related to the decision itself, but the relationship is rarely benign, or even neutral. In other words, there are significant issues in the competitive environment which are controlled by competitors who will act partly in response to our decisions and usually against our interests. So, for example, a decision to expand or contract capacity at a particular point in time may be affected by how we believe a competitor might react. (See the theory box on game theory.)

Theory Box **Game theory**

Game theory is a study of the strategic behaviour of rational 'players', each of whom has a set of possible actions, or strategies, available to them. The outcomes of choosing a strategy depend on the action of the other players. Although studied by economists for more than 50 years, game theory has revolutionised some branches of economics over the past 20 years. Its power lies in modelling the choices available to companies in oligopoly markets. An oligopoly is the area between being a monopoly and having perfect competition. Thus, most organisations compete in an oligopoly, that is, there is a finite number of known competitors, who take decisions in the light of how they believe the others will act. So, for example, when McDonald's increased its prices alongside the introduction of its new Arch Deluxe sandwich in May 1996, its rival, Burger King, cut its prices by 5 per cent. By doing so Burger King increased its market share (of the US market), as did Wendy's, both at the expense of McDonald's. This is a typical decision which game theory is designed to model. Burger King's price reductions were prompted, at least partly, by McDonald's strategy.

Figure 5.12 illustrates a typical game theory formulation for a capacity decision. Our own

Figure 5.12 Game theory formulation for capacity expansion decision where outcomes depend on the actions of competitors

	Competitor	
	Increase capacity	Don't increase capacity

Us — Increase capacity

Over-capacity

	Us	Competitor
Demand =	75,000	75,000
Price =	85	85
Cost =	55	55
Unit profit =	30	30
Total profit =	2,250,000	2,250,000

Balance

	Us	Competitor
Demand =	100,000	50,000
Price =	90	90
Cost =	40	50
Unit profit =	50	40
Total profit =	5,000,000	2,000,000

Us — Don't increase capacity

Balance

	Us	Competitor
Demand =	50,000	100,000
Price =	90	90
Cost =	50	40
Unit profit =	40	50
Total profit =	2,000,000	5,000,000

Under-capacity

	Us	Competitor
Demand =	50,000	50,000
Price =	120	120
Cost =	50	50
Unit profit =	70	70
Total profit =	3,500,000	3,500,000

company and a competitor are the two major players in a particular market. We are both deciding whether to increase capacity. Currently the total demand of 100,000 units is shared equally between the two of us and we each have a capacity of 50,000 units. The market price for our products is 100 and our costs are 50 per unit. Thus we each make 50,000 × 50 = 2,500,000 profit.

Demand in the next period is forecast to increase by 50,000 to 150,000. If we decide to increase our capacity by the standard increment of 50,000 units, our profits will depend on whether our competitor does the same. Similarly, if we decide not to increase capacity, again, our profits will depend on our competitor's action. Figure 5.12 shows our forecasts for the outcome, both to ourselves and our competitor, depending on what we and the competitor decide to do.

Arguably, the best outcome for us jointly would be for neither to increase capacity. This would result in under-capacity in the market, the same level of demand but higher prices. In fact, this will not happen. If we believe our competitor will increase their capacity, the profit to us will be 2,250,000 if we also increase capacity, or 2,000,000 if we do not. We would therefore increase capacity. If we believe that our competitors will not increase their capacity, increasing our own capacity would result in a profit to us of 5,000,000. Not increasing our capacity would result in a profit to us of 3,500,000. We would therefore increase our capacity. Thus, in this case, unless we cooperate with the competitor, it is always in our interests to increase our capacity. Furthermore, looking at it from the competitor's point of view, it is always in their interests to increase their capacity. In fact, this is not an unusual situation. It can be added to the list of reasons of why over-capacity exists in so many industries discussed in the box on 'Over-reaching to over-capacity'.

The magnitude of capacity change

The previous chapter examined some of the advantages of large capacity increments (economies of scale, category killer effects, etc.). Large units of capacity also have some disadvantages when the capacity of the operation is being changed to match changing demand. If an operation where forecast demand is increasing seeks to satisfy all demand by increasing capacity using large capacity increments, it will have substantial amounts of over-capacity for much of the period when demand is increasing, which results in higher unit costs. However, if the company uses smaller increments, although there will still be some over-capacity it will be less than that using large capacity increments. This results in higher capacity utilisation and therefore lower costs. Remember, though, that the larger increments of capacity can be intrinsically more efficient (because of economies of scale) when they are well utilised.

For example, suppose that the air conditioning unit manufacturer forecasts demand increase over the next three years, as shown in Figure 5.13, to level off at around 2400 units a week. If the company seeks to satisfy all demand by building three plants, each of 800 units capacity, the company will have substantial amounts of over-capacity for much of the period when demand is increasing. Over-capacity means low capacity utilisation, which in turn means higher unit costs. If the company

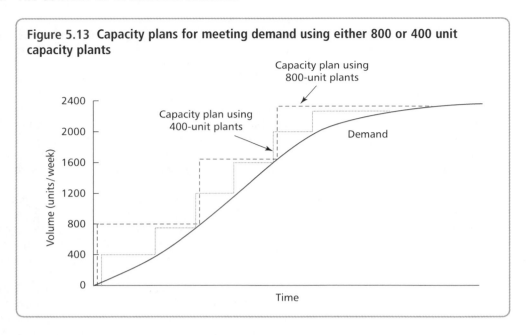

Figure 5.13 Capacity plans for meeting demand using either 800 or 400 unit capacity plans

builds smaller plants, say 400-unit plants, there will still be over-capacity but to a lesser extent, which means higher capacity utilisation and possible lower costs.

Risks of over-capacity with large capacity increments

The inherent risks of changing capacity using large increments can also be high. For example, if the rate of change demand unexpectedly slows, the capacity will be only

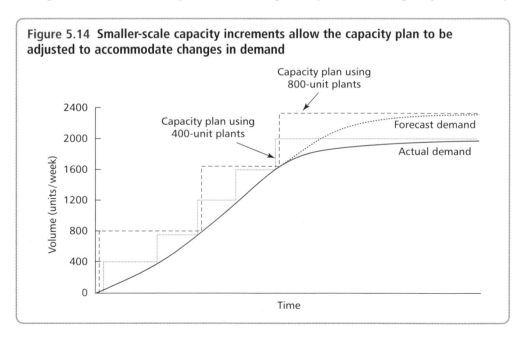

Figure 5.14 Smaller-scale capacity increments allow the capacity plan to be adjusted to accommodate changes in demand

partly utilised. However, if smaller units of capacity are used the likelihood is that the forecast error would have been detected in time to delay or cancel the capacity adjustment, leaving demand and capacity in balance.

For example, if demand does not reach 2400 units a week but levels off at 2000 units a week, the final 800-unit plant will only be 50 per cent utilised. However, if 400-unit plants are used the likelihood is that the over-optimistic forecast would have been detected in time. Figure 5.14 shows the financial consequences of adopting each of the two strategies in this case.

Over-reaching to over-capacity[4]

There are few industries where the total demand for products and services matches the cumulative capacity of all the firms in the industry. In many industries capacity far exceeds demand. The automotive, computer chips, steel, chemicals, oil and hotel industries all have significant over-capacity because of over-investment and/or a collapse in demand. Take the automobile industry for example. One estimate claimed that the industry worldwide was wasting $70 billion a year because of over-capacity. By 2000 around 30 per cent of all car-making capacity was unused. The lost profit amounted to around $2000 per car, which is more than the combined industry profits worldwide. This is partly bad news for those firms with the higher level of over-capacity because most car plants can only make significant profits when operating at over 80 per cent of capacity.

The same problem affects silicon chip manufacturing. (See previous box.) Here the problem is the inherent uncertainty of market demand for individual types of chip, the long lead-time needed to construct a plant and the $2 billion or so needed to fund some types of plant. The result, in the late 1990s, was a collapse in the market price, especially for the relatively low-technology D-Ram memory chips.

However, over-capacity may not be viewed with too much alarm. Many of the well-known Western hotel chains in Asia, such as Westin and Sheraton, do not own the property itself, but confine themselves to managing it. The owner may be a local property developer or business person who invested for prestige or tax purposes. Many of the management contracts of this type, put together in the booming 1980s and 90s, included fees based on a percentage of total revenue as well as a percentage of gross operating profits. So, even with no profit, the management company could make healthy returns. By contrast, other hotel chains, such as Shangri-La Asia, Mandarin-Oriental and Peninsular Hotels, both owned and managed their hotels. Because of this they were far more exposed to the consequences of over-capacity because it hit profits directly.

So why do companies invest, even when there is a high risk of industry over-capacity and thus under-utilised operations? One reason, of course, is optimistic forecasting. The risks of mis-forecasting are high, especially when there is a long gap between deciding to build extra capacity and the capacity coming on stream. A second reason is that all capacity is not the same. Newer operations are generally more efficient and may have other operations advantages compared to older operations using less state-of-the-art technologies. Thus, there is always the chance that a new operation coming on stream will attract business at the expense of older capacity. A third reason is that investment decisions are usually made by individual firms, whereas industry over-capacity is a result of all their decisions taken together. So a firm might be able to reduce its costs by investing in new capacity but the prices it receives for its products and services are partly determined by the cumulative decisions of its competitors. This also explains why it is not always easy to reduce over-capacity in an industry. Often it is in nobody's interest to be the first mover to shut down capacity. The costs of closing down capacity are paid by its owner. The benefits, however, in terms of higher prices and margins, are spread across the industry as a whole. So every firm wants capacity to be reduced as long as it is not its own capacity.

Capacity cushions

A related concept to the 'magnitude of capacity change' decision is that of the 'capacity cushion'. This is the amount of planned capacity which is above the forecast level of demand in a period. Companies may deliberately plan for a capacity cushion so that they can cope with aggregated demand even if it turns out to be greater than forecast. Alternatively, they might judge that extra capacity might be needed to absorb the inefficiencies caused by an unplanned mix of demands on the operation, even if the aggregated level of demand is as expected.

The magnitude of any capacity cushion is likely to reflect the relative costs to the organisation of having either over- or under-capacity. The costs of over-capacity relate to the financing of the capital and human resources which are not being used to produce revenue. The cost of under-capacity is either the opportunity cost of not supplying demand or the extra cost of supplying demand by unplanned means such as overtime or subcontracting. One suggested approach to quantifying this concept is to make the size of any capacity cushion proportional to the following ratio:[5]

$$(C_s - C_x)/C_s$$

where C_s = the unit cost of shortage and C_x = the unit cost of excess capacity.

It is suggested that if this ratio is greater than 0.5 then a capacity cushion is appropriate; if it is less than 0.5 a 'negative cushion' is appropriate. So when C_x is large (as in capital-intensive industries), capacity cushions, if they are justified at all, will tend to be small, whereas in industries where C_s is large (because of large profit margins) and C_x is small (because of low capital intensity), a relatively large capacity cushion may be justified.

Taken together, decisions of timing and magnitude dictate the rate of capacity change. But organisations may see a limit to the rate they want to expand (or indeed contract) under certain circumstances.

Balancing capacity change

One of the complicating factors in planning for capacity change is that the capacity of a whole chain of operations will be limited by the lowest capacity or *'bottleneck'* part of the chain. For example, if the 800-unit capacity air conditioning plant, introduced earlier, not only assembles products but also manufactures the parts from which they are made, then any change in the assembly plant must be matched by changes in the ability to supply it with parts. Similarly, further down the chain, operations such as warehousing and distribution may also have to change their capacity. For the chain to operate efficiently, all its stages must have more or less the same capacity. This is not too much of an issue if the economic increment of capacity is roughly the same for each stage in the chain. However, if the most cost-effective increment in each stage is very different, changing the capacity of one stage may have a significant effect on the economics of operation of the others. For example, Figure 5.15 illustrates the air conditioning plant example. Currently the capacity of each stage is not balanced. This could be the result of many different factors involving historical demand and capacity changes. The bottleneck stage is the warehouse, which has a weekly capacity of 900 units. If the company wants to increase output from its total operations to 1800 units a week, all four stages will require extra capacity. The economy of scale graphs for each stage are illustrated.

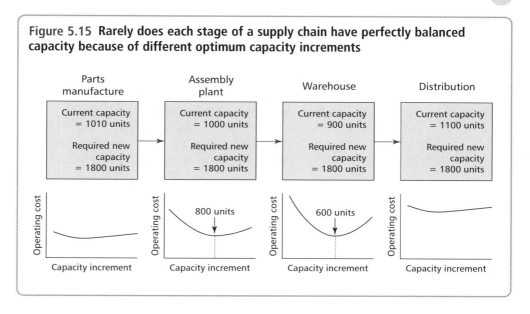

Figure 5.15 Rarely does each stage of a supply chain have perfectly balanced capacity because of different optimum capacity increments

They indicate that for the parts manufacturing plant and the distribution operation, operating cost is relatively invariant to the size of capacity increment chosen. Presumably this is because individual trucks and/or machines can be added within the existing infrastructure. However, for both the assembly plant and the warehouse, operating costs *will* be dependent on the size of capacity increment chosen. In the case of the assembly plant the decision is relatively straightforward. A single addition to the operation of 800 units will both minimise its individual operating costs and achieve the required new capacity. The warehouse has more of a problem. It requires an additional capacity of 900 units. This would involve either building units of sub-optimum capacity or building two units of optimal capacity and under-utilising them with its own cost penalties.

The same issues apply on a wider scale when independent operations are affected by imbalance in the whole chain. Air travel is a classic example of this. Three of the most important elements in the chain of operations that provides air travel are the terminals which provide passenger facilities at airports, the runways from which aircraft take off and land, and the aircraft themselves operating on all the various sectors, which include the airport. Each of these stages, in planning their capacity, is subject to different pressures. Building new terminals is not only expensive in terms of the capital required, but also subject to environmental considerations and other issues of public concern. Similarly, runways, which govern the number of 'slots' (opportunities to take off and land), are usually the subject of public interest. The individual aircraft that use these facilities are both far smaller units of capacity in themselves and form an element in the capacity chain which is subject to normal business commercial pressures. Different sizes of aircraft will be used for different routes depending on the 'density' (volume of demand) of the route. Because they represent relatively small units of capacity, the number of aircraft using an airport can change relatively smoothly over time. Runways and terminals, however, represent large increments of capacity and therefore change less frequently. Also, within each part of the chain the effective capacity may improve because of technical changes. Terminals are becoming more efficient in the way they can handle large amounts of baggage or even tag customers with micro-chipped tickets so that they can be traced and organised more effectively. All of which can, to some extent, increase the capacity of a terminal without making it any larger. Likewise, runways can accommodate more aircraft landing by providing more 'turn-offs' which allow aircraft to clear the main runway very soon after landing in order to let the next aircraft land. On high-density routes the aircraft themselves are getting larger. When the number of slots available to an airline is limited, and if route density warrants it, very large aircraft can increase the number of passengers carried per landing or take-off slot. However, these changes in effective capacity at each stage in the chain may affect the other stages. For example, very large aircraft have to be designed so as to keep the air turbulence they cause to a minimum so that it does not affect the time between landing slots. Also, very large aircraft may need different terminal equipment such as the air bridges which load and unload passengers.

SIMEX[6]

The capacity of the Singapore International Monetary Exchange (SIMEX) expanded rapidly in the early 1990s. Trading volume in 1994 alone rose by 53 per cent and SIMEX was gaining business rapidly in the booming South East Asian financial market. For example, it obtained the Nikkei futures contract to deal in Japanese stock markets futures operations. It won the business largely because SIMEX was both efficient and lightly regulated compared to the less flexible and higher-cost Osaka Securities Exchange (OSE). Almost as many Nikkei – 225 – futures contractors traded in Singapore as on the OSE.

The Singapore government was well aware of the dangers of such rapid growth in financial trading organisations and was determined that SIMEX would not outgrow its ability to regulate itself satisfactorily. *'We don't want to promote markets faster than we can adequately supervise them . . . given our aversion to market failures in the financial sector. . .'* (Richard Hu, Singapore's Finance Minister, speaking in early 1995). Yet only weeks later Mr Hu may have wished that he had been even more careful when he announced that a new panel would be set up to advise on rule changes at the future exchange. This was in response to the collapse of Barings, the British investment bank. It had suffered huge losses on the SIMEX through the activities of the 'rogue trader' Nick Leeson.

The lesson of all this? Capacity change is not just about putting in (or taking out) the physical aspects of capacity. It also means making sure that physical capacity changes are balanced with infrastructural changes to ensure that the operation can continue maintaining its levels of safety and quality notwithstanding the increase in volume and the disruption that such increases bring with it.

Changing location

If a company is small, notwithstanding any other advantages it may have, it is unlikely to enjoy many economies of scale. As it grows it will presumably configure itself internally so as to capture the scale economies that come from its increased level of activity. This may mean adopting higher-volume technologies and gearing up their infrastructure to allow indirect resources to be used more effectively. As growth continues, eventually the level of activity in the operation will be such that any losses of scale economies from splitting the operation into two or more parts are relatively small. This is when total capacity decisions must also include location decisions. The argument for or against operating across a few relatively large, or many relatively small, sites was treated in the previous chapter. Here we extend the debate to include the issue of how the *role* of sites may vary or develop over time, especially when a company's expansion includes overseas sites.

Configuration and coordination

Decisions relating to how organisations choose to locate their operations, and especially change the location of their operations, often distinguish between configuration decisions and coordination decisions.[7] Configuration is broadly what we discussed in our treatment of location in the previous chapter. It means exactly where facilities are located and what resources are allocated to each location. Coordination refers to questions of how to integrate the activities of each site so as to achieve the organisation's overall strategic objectives. In many ways coordination is more of an infrastructural decision and indeed we shall refer to it in later chapters when we discuss the development and organisation of operations resources. The reason for raising it at this point is that both configuration and coordination issues come into play when companies change their locations as a result of broad capacity dynamics.

Example

A company which manufactures and markets breakfast cereals is entering a new regional market in a part of the world in which it has not operated before. Volume forecasts indicate that, after a slow start while its brands establish themselves, volume will grow relatively quickly. The technology employed to manufacture breakfast cereals is of three types, 'flaking', 'puff' and 'extrusion'. These technologies are mutually exclusive. Products that depend on flaking technology cannot be made on equipment designed for extrusion. Forecasts indicate that for the first year of operation the company will need three production lines, one of each technology. After the first year the company is likely to require several more of each technology. The dilemma for the company is whether they should start with one manufacturing location in which they could house the three different production lines, or alternatively, whether they should start with three locations, each devoted to a separate technology. The advantage of developing one mixed technology site is that, even in the first year of operation, the site is working with three lines which can share some general infrastructural costs such as supervision, planning and maintenance. The disadvantage is that after two or three years of growth, the site will be both large and complex because of the slightly different requirements of the three technologies. Developing three sites from the start would mean that in the long term each site could focus solely on the needs of one of the technologies and could therefore gain the improvements from specialising in a single technology. This is likely to mean higher degrees of process knowledge and better manufacturing performance in the long term. However, in the short term each of the three sites will be significantly under-utilised, only having one line in each, yet still require a certain degree of infrastructural services.

In this example we have two sets of conflicting pressures. First, there is a conflict between the short-term needs of the organisation and its long-term needs. Having initially only one manufacturing site would minimise production costs in the short run but would be an inferior configuration in terms of the long-run development of its operations. This is because focused plants devoted to single technologies are easier to coordinate internally, which in turn can lead to long-term superior performance. The other conflict is between the familiar 'market requirements' and 'operations resource' needs. It may be that, in the long term, a number of sites, all of which use mixed technologies, may be better at serving different areas of the market, each area having an 'all-purpose' site which can serve all its needs. But, as we have just argued, more focused single technology sites may develop the operation's resources more effectively.

The final choice for this company will depend upon its own assessments of market requirements, cost pressures and the potential for process improvement. The key point, however, is not so much what is best for this company but rather that the location decision has involved *both* configuration and coordination issues.

The role of sites

A further example of how the dynamic nature of location decisions can affect the more infrastructural side of operations strategy comes when the role, or contribution, of each site within an organisation is considered. Professor Kasra Ferdows calls this the 'strategic role' of sites.[8] To identify these roles he distinguishes between two variables:

● The main motive for establishing the site – for example to gain access to low-cost inputs such as labour or raw materials, to use local technological resources such as specific software development skills, or to provide proximity to a market, such as the breakfast cereal example mentioned previously.

● The extent of the capabilities, or 'technical activities', at the site – is the site limited to simply carrying out activities under the complete control of a distant headquarters, or at the other extreme, is it responsible for the technological development of its products and services, processes planning, procurement, distribution, etc.?

Bringing these two various sets of variables together, he identified six generic roles for sites (in fact, in developing these ideas Professor Ferdows is talking about manu-

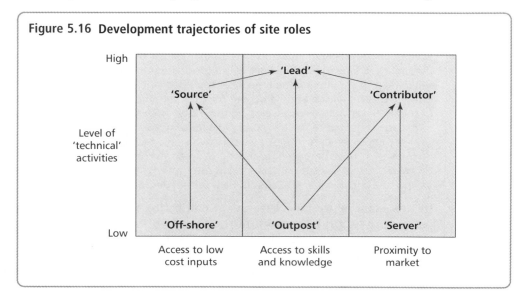

Figure 5.16 Development trajectories of site roles

facturing sites in an international context, but the ideas can be used more generally). See Figure 5.16.

In this manufacturing context the six roles for a factory which Ferdows identifies are as follows.

- *Off-shore factory* – its role is limited to producing specific items at low cost. Local management have relatively little discretion as to how production is organised and most, if not all, product and process technology is likely to be dictated by head office.

- *Source factory* – although again established primarily for low-cost production, managers in this kind of plant are allowed more discretion over how to exploit the opportunities they have to reduce costs. They may also have discretion on how best to distribute this knowledge to other plants.

- *Server factory* – this type of plant is likely to be set up in order to serve specific regional markets, perhaps to reduce distribution costs or overcome tariff barriers. The way in which it produces its products, however, is likely to be dictated largely by its headquarters.

- *Contributor factory* – although primarily serving a regional market, this type of factory may be expected to develop original ways of serving its market and test out new products which are later rolled out in other markets.

- *Outpost factory* – these factories are set up in order to exploit some local factor which is unavailable elsewhere. As such, they are expected to supply information to other factories.

- *Lead factory* – although set up originally to exploit local factors, a lead factory's contribution has progressed to the point where it can educate other plants in some aspect of the firm's business. It is a centre of innovation to which other parts of the organisation look for the development of unique capabilities.

Ferdows' main point is that organisations can gain advantage by developing the role of their locations from that where they represent a relatively passive unit of production capacity, through to a role where they are expected to develop and deploy unique capabilities which can be transferred to other parts of the organisation. These trajectories of development generally move from a low level of discretion and capabilities through to increasing levels of 'technical' or knowledge-creating activity. Sites may also change their primary purpose. For example, those set up as outposts in order to gain local skills and knowledge may develop this in such a way as to reduce costs and therefore become 'source' plants, or develop new markets and thus become 'contributor' plants. This in turn may lead to development of unique levels of knowledge which qualify them as 'lead' plants.

Lincoln Electric's foreign adventure[9]

Lincoln Electric was one of the leading and most successful manufacturers of arc-welding products in the world. Founded in 1895, the Cleveland, Ohio, company also made industrial electric motors, though arc-welding products accounted for almost 90 per cent of sales. As well as its plants in the States, the company also had marketing and manufacturing operations in Australia, Canada and France. But its big expansion outside the USA came in the mid-1980s when one of its Swedish competitors, ESAB, bought two of Lincoln's smaller American rivals. Because of anti-trust

▶

laws, Lincoln could not buy any of its domestic competitors and so accelerated its programme of overseas acquisitions. Plants were bought in the United Kingdom, Norway, Germany, the Netherlands, Spain and Mexico. In addition, three new plants were built in Japan, Venezuela and Brazil. Unfortunately though, many of these plants were bought at the peak of their market cycles, when the cost of acquisition was at its highest. The five years following its overseas expansion saw many of its new markets slip into recession. For example, Lincoln's largest acquisition, the German Messer Griesheim company, suffered from the recession that followed the high cost of German reunification in the early 1990s.

Nor was the picture any brighter in terms of manufacturing costs. Lincoln had prided themselves on their operations expertise. They had considerable experience in reducing costs through advanced manufacturing methods and their own particular incentive scheme, with its heavy emphasis on bonuses and piecework. They assumed that their production methods and their incentive schemes would be just as effective in their new foreign plants. They were not. The different approach to work and cultural expectations, particularly in their European plants, were not fully understood by Lincoln's management.

> 'Our corporate management lacked sufficient international expertise and had little experience running a complex, dispersed organisation. Our managers didn't know how to run foreign operations; nor did they understand foreign cultures. Consequently we had to rely on people in our foreign companies – people we didn't know and who didn't know us.'
> (Donald Hastings, Chairman Lincoln Electric Company)

When their European acquisitions started to haemorrhage money in 1992, the American management needed to go over to Europe to see what the problems were. It was then that they found that their chief financial officer didn't even have a passport. But making the trips to Europe opened the eyes of Lincoln's management. It became clear that with plants operating at less than 50 per cent of capacity, costs could never be competitive. Furthermore, many of the company's European managers did not believe that American-made products could be satisfactorily imported into their own markets. If this was the case, then the company was doomed to run uneconomic plants in markets where otherwise they would not be able to sell their products.

In fact Lincoln found that they could sell American-made products in Europe. Furthermore, they found that they could boost sales through direct encouragement from headquarters rather than leaving each country's sales force to do their own thing, though they found it necessary to scale down much of their European capacity considerably, and indeed shut down the whole Messer operation. They even had to close the newly built plants in Brazil, Venezuela and Japan.

After two very difficult years Lincoln's overseas operations were back making profits. The company, though, had come close to disaster. It had also learned two valuable lessons. First, don't try to expand capacity overseas without accepting that the management team overseeing the expansion needs international experience. Second, operations practices that have been successful in one context do not necessarily guarantee success under different cultural and market conditions.

SUMMARY ANSWERS TO KEY QUESTIONS

How does the timing of capacity change influence the performance of the operation?

Capacity can be introduced to either lead or lag demand. Lead demand strategies involve early capital expenditure and under-utilisation of capacity but ensure that the operation is likely to be able to meet demand. Lagging capacity strategies involve later capital expenditure and full utilisation of the capacity but fail to fulfil forecast demand. If inventories are carried over so as to smooth the effects of introducing capacity increments, it may be possible to achieve both high sales and high utilisation of resources, therefore low costs. However, working capital requirements will be higher because the inventory needs to be funded. Coming together with high levels of capital expenditure, this may provide cash flow problems for an operation.

How do operations choose between large or small increments of capacity change?

Changing capacity in large increments can minimise the costs of changing capacity (closure costs if demand is decreasing and capital expenditure if demand is increasing) but can also mean a significant mismatch between capacity and demand at many points in time. Conversely, changing by using small increments of capacity will match demand and capacity more exactly but require more frequent changes. Especially when increasing capacity, these changes (i.e. small extension to capacity) can be expensive in capital cost and disruption terms. Often it is the risks of making too large a change in capacity that weigh heavily with operations, especially when forecasts of future demand are uncertain. Generally, the more uncertain is future demand, the more likely operations are to choose relatively small increments of capacity change. Notwithstanding this, there is a general pressure in many industries towards building new capacity even when over-capacity exists in the industry. This is partly because individual businesses operate on a different level of analysis than the industry as a whole. Partly it is because new capacity is usually technologically more advanced and therefore less likely to be under-utilised than the old capacity which it is seeking to replace.

What issues are important when changing the location of capacity?

Changing the absolute level of capacity in a business and changing the location of sites are rarely independent decisions. For example, expansion may mean automatically having to choose a further location if the current location has insufficient room for expansion. Two issues tend to be considered in location change decisions. These are the configuration of what facilities are located where, and the coordination between those resources. Although coordination is more of an infrastructural issue, it is affected by the configuration of sites. Spanning both these issues is the role which is expected of individual sites. Some authorities recommend that individual sites should be expected to develop enhanced capabilities which can benefit other sites.

Delta Synthetic Fibres[10]

'When you are a small player in this business you really do need to develop your own approach to doing business. We are not in the same game as the BASFs or ICIs of this world. Our key objectives are three things – niche markets, focused production and innovative products.' (Paul Mayer – CEO, Delta Synthetic Fibres)

DSF was a small but technically successful company in the synthetic fibre industry. The company was heavily dependent on the sales of one product, Britlene, which they had developed themselves in the late 1980s and which by 1996 accounted for some 97 per cent of total revenue (the other 3 per cent came from the sale of licences). In fact, since its foundation the company had specialised in producing a single product at one time (although packed and shipped in different ways). The original product, 'Teklon', had been replaced by 'Deklon', which had in turn been replaced by 'Britlene'. None of these product changes had required substantial changes to the company's processes.

From Britlene to Britlon

Britlene was used mainly as a 'blend fibre' in heavy-duty clothing, although smaller quantities were used to produce industrial goods such as tyre cord, flexible industrial drives and insulating sleeves. Its main properties were very high wear resistance, together with high thermal and electrical insulation. Sales of Britlene, especially in the United States, had started to fall off in 1996 as competitor products eroded DSF's traditional markets. These products rarely matched the technical specification of Britlene but were significantly less expensive. In 1996 the company had developed a new product, Britlon. Britlon had all the properties of Britlene but was superior in its strength, heat-resistant qualities and electrical insulation. It was hoped that these additional properties would open up new clothing uses (e.g. a substitute for mineral wool) as well as allow entry into the far larger markets associated with thermal and electrical insulation. By late 1996 the major technical and engineering problems associated with bulk production of Britlon seemed to have been solved.

Synthetic fibre manufacture

The basic production method of Britlene and Britlon was similar to that of most man-made fibres. To make a man-made fibre, an oil-based organic chemical is polymerised (a process of joining several molecules into a long chain) in conditions of intense pressure and heat, often by the addition of a suitable catalyst. This polymerisation takes place in large autoclaves (an industrial pressure-cooker). The polymer is then extruded (forced through a nozzle like the rose of a garden watering-can), rapidly cooled and then either spun on to cones or collected in bales. After this, a variety of different conversion processes were used to add value before the product was shipped to the customer.

Production processes were relatively flexible in that they could be used to process most types of fibre with little modification. However, the polymerisation process was usually designed for one type of polymer and might need substantial modification before a different polymer could be made.

Current facilities

Britlene was produced at the company's three factories, Teesside in the UK, Hamburg in Germany and Chicago in the USA. The largest site was Teesside with three lines. There was one line at each of the other two sites. All five production lines had a nominal design capacity of 5.5 million kg per year of Britlene. However, after allowing for maintenance and holidays, expected output was 5 million kg per year. Each plant operated on a 24 hours per day, 7 days per week basis.

The cost of raw materials was more or less the same at each location, but labour costs, general employment costs, local taxation and energy costs did vary. The Hamburg plant had the highest production costs, followed by the Chicago plant, with the Teesside plant having the lowest cost per kilogram produced (at full utilisation). However, the cost differences between the plants were less than the differences in the input costs. Partly this was because of higher productivity at both the Hamburg and Chicago plants, and partly because all three Teesside lines were relatively old and prone to breakdown.

DSF's markets

The largest single market for Britlene was still the UK, although the percentage of sales to UK customers had declined from over 60 per cent in 1990 to around 41 per cent in 1996. The potential for volume growth was greatest in the Far East markets, especially Japan and South Korea, and least in the UK. Earnings growth potential, however, was likely to be greatest in continental Europe and the USA. In terms of market sector, both industrial and domestic clothing were growing only slowly, while general industrial markets had grown from practically nothing in 1990 to around 13 per cent of sales in 1996 and were likely to grow further in the next five years, especially in the USA. Thermal and electrical insulation markets, after fast growth in the early 1990s, had grown only slowly over the last two years.

> 'We are trading in two quite different types of market. Clothing, both industrial and domestic, is relatively predictable, and we are established suppliers with a relatively large share of a very small market. The industrial and insulation markets, however, are far larger in themselves and we have only a tiny share. In the clothing markets we are competing, usually on price, against very similar products. In the other markets we are competing against a whole range of different materials, usually on product performance and supply flexibility.' (Tim Williams, Vice President Marketing)

Exhibit 1 shows market volumes for 1996.

Tim Williams also saw the new product changing the sales profile of the company.

> 'Britlon is a technically superior material which is also likely to be marginally less expensive to produce. We should be able to, at least, maintain our share of the clothing market and possibly stop the margin erosion we have suffered in this sector over the last few years. But the real benefits are going to show in the insulation and, to only a slightly less extent, in the industrial markets. The improved strength and insulation properties of Britlon should let us capture a greater share of a larger and more profitable market.'

Exhibit 2 shows the aggregated volume and price forecasts for both products for 1997 through to 2002.

Creating a Britlon capability

Britlon's production process was very similar to that used for Britlene; however, a totally new type of polymerisation unit would be needed prior to the extrusion stage. Also, the

Exhibit 1 Market volumes by product and region 1996 (millions of kg)

Market sectors	UK	Continental Europe	USA	Far East
Clothing – industrial	8.04	3.74	1.69	1.84
Clothing – domestic	1.22	0.09	N.A.	N.A.
Industrial – general	0.52	1.02	1.10	0.73
Thermal insulation	0.41	0.39	1.01	N.A.
Electrical insulation	0.18	0.64	1.10	0.98
Total	10.37	5.88	4.90	3.55

Exhibit 2 Forecasts for Britlene and Britlon

	Potential sales	
	Britlene	*Britlon*
	millions of kg p.a.	*millions of kg p.a.*
1996 (Actual)	24.7	–
1997	22	–
1998	20	–
1999	17	3 assuming availability
2000	13	16
2001	11	27
2002	10	29

	Price forecast (p. per kg)	
	Britlene	*Britlon*
1997	98	–
1998	98	–
1999	95	125
2000	90	120
2001	85	120
2002	85	120

technologies for polymerisation were mutually exclusive. Britlon and Britlene could not be produced on the same line. Early in the development of Britlon, DSF had approached Alpen GmbH, an international chemical plant construction company, for help on a large-scale plant design of the new unit. Together they produced and tested an acceptable design for the new line and had explored different construction methods. Essentially there were two ways of acquiring Britlon capacity. DSF could convert the old Britlene lines, or they could construct entirely new lines.

For a conversion, a new polymer unit would need to be constructed alongside the old line (without interfering with production). When complete, it would be connected to the extrusion unit which would itself require only minor conversion. Alpen were quoting a lead-time of two years for either the construction of a new Britlon line or to convert an old Britlene plant to Britlon production.

Exhibit 3 Estimated Britlon capital costs

The table below gives estimated costs and stage payments required by Alpen for Britlon polymer line and extrusion unit construction.

Type of order	Cost – (£ million)	Timing	
Whole *new* 'Britlon' line including polymer and extrusion units	4.8	Begin	6 months from order
		On stream	2 years from order
Conversion of 'Britlene' line to 'Britlon' line	3.0	Begin	6 months from order
		On stream	2 years from order

The cost of a new plant is payable in three 6-monthly instalments – £1,000,000 being due one year after ordering, £1,000,000 due 6 months later and the balance on completion.

The cost of a conversion is payable in three 6-monthly instalments of £1,000,000, 1 year and 18 months from the order and on completion.

> 'The long lead-times which are being quoted for constructing this type of process are partly a result of a high level of demand for Alpen's services because of their reputation for providing sound technical solutions in process design. Also, I guess they are a bit cautious because of the technical novelty of this process.'
> (Liam Flaherty, Vice President Operations)

Although the lead-time for building a new line was the same as for a conversion, the capital cost of the latter was lower. Exhibit 3 shows the capital estimates for both conversion and new lines. Economies of scale were such that, whether converted or built new, the capacity of Britlon plants would be around 5 million kg per year.

The capacity working group

In the fall of 1996 Paul Mayer set up the capacity working group to consider the introduction of the new product. However, he did place some limits on what the company would do.

> 'The creation of an entirely new site would increase the complexities of multi-site operation to an unacceptable level. Conversely, the complete closure of one of the three existing sites is, I consider, a waste of the human and physical resources that we have invested in that location. I believe expansion could take place at one, two or all of the existing sites.' (Paul Mayer)

Further reading

DeToni, A., R. Filippini and C. Forza (1992) 'Manufacturing strategy in global market: an operations management model', *International Journal of Operations and Production Management*, Vol. 12, No. 4.

DuBois, F.L., B. Toyne and M.D. Oliff (1993) 'International manufacturing strategies of US multinationals: a conceptual framework based on a four industry study', *Journal of International Business Studies*, Vol. 24, No. 2.

Hayes, R.H. and S.C. Wheelwright, (1984) *Restoring our Competitive Edge*, Wiley, Chapter 3.

Hayes, R.H., S.C. Wheelwright and K. Clark (1988) *Dynamic Manufacturing*, The Free Press, New York.

Porter, M.E. (1989) 'Changing patterns of international competition', *California Management Review*, Vol. 28, No. 2.

Tombak, M.M. (1995) 'Multinational plant location as a game of timing', *European Journal of Operational Research*, Vol. 86, No. 4.

Notes on the chapter

1 Hayes, R.H. and S.C. Wheelwright (1984) *Restoring our Competitive Edge*, Wiley, New York.

2 Sources: *The Economist* (1998) 'Can GM and the unions take each other on trust?' 1 August; *The Independent* (1998) 'How bosses and workers pranged GM', 10 August; *The Economist* (1998) 'A man of flint', 20 June.

3 Sources: *The Independent* (2000) 'No doom soon for microchips', 18 October; *Financial Times* (1999) 'When the chips are up', 16 July; *The Economist* (1996) 'Saving chips from market dips', 20 January; *The Economist* (1997) 'Chips on their shoulders', 1 November.

4 Sources: *The Economist* (1999) 'Double parked', 9 January; *The Economist* (1999) 'Empty rooms? So what?', 5 June; *The Economist* (1997) 'Europe's great car war', 8 March; *The Economist* (1995) 'Over-refined Europeans', 15 July; Jowit, J. (1999) 'Overcapacity costing car sector $130 billion', *Financial Times*, 19 January.

5 Hayes, R.H. and S.C. Wheelwright (1984) op.cit.

6 Source: *The Straits Times* (1995) 'SIMEX expands', 13 October.

7 Porter, M.E. (1986) 'Changing patterns of international competition', *California Management Review*, Vol. 28, No. 2.

8 Ferdows, K. (1997) 'Making the most of foreign factories', *Harvard Business Review*, March–April.

9 Hastings, D.F. (1999) 'Lincoln Electric's harsh lessons from international expansion', *Harvard Business Review*, May–June.

10 This case was written by Professor Nigel Slack of Warwick Business School. It is based on an original example from Peter Jones of Sheffield Business School.

Supply network relationships

Introduction

All businesses are both customers for some other businesses' products and services, *and* suppliers of products and services to their own customers (often other businesses). No operation therefore, or part of an operation, can be seen as existing in isolation. All are part of an interconnected network of not only their own customers and suppliers, but their customers' customers and suppliers' suppliers. Viewed one way, this network is the market context in which an organisation's operations strategy is developed. If we include government agencies, labour markets and other similar bodies as customers, suppliers or both, a company's network becomes its total business environment. Thus the supply network is the ultimate expression of an operation's market. But, the network also contains the resources and processes which together produce products and services. So, in considering how an operation fits into the supply network, we are at the crossroads of market positioning and resource development. Fundamental to the strategic design of any operation's resources are network-related questions such as, should we carry out this activity or get it done for us by another company?, which of our current suppliers (if any) do we want to buy and incorporate into our current operation?, and, how should we develop trading relationships with suppliers and customers? We will treat the strategic development of supply networks in two chapters. This chapter defines what we mean by a supply network and looks at alternative forms of the individual relationships with immediate customers and suppliers (Figure 6.1). The following chapter treats supply networks as whole entities and examines their dynamic behaviour.

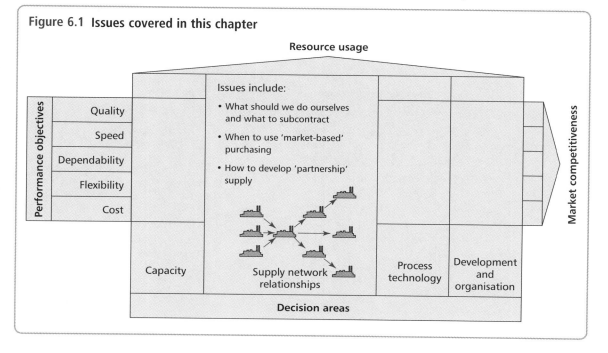

Figure 6.1 Issues covered in this chapter

Resource usage

Performance objectives

| Quality |
| Speed |
| Dependability |
| Flexibility |
| Cost |

Issues include:
- What should we do ourselves and what to subcontract
- When to use 'market-based' purchasing
- How to develop 'partnership' supply

Capacity   Supply network relationships   Process technology   Development and organisation

Decision areas

Market competitiveness

Supply network strategy

The broad subject of supply networks ('supply chain management', 'demand chains', 'strategic purchasing', 'supplier development', 'efficient consumer response', etc. – there are many sub-categories and different perspectives) has been one of the most fashionable elements within operations strategy over the past few years. Indeed, there is an argument that operations strategy is too limiting and that, as a subject, it should be subsumed within the broader perspective of 'supply strategy'.[1] Here we examine supply networks from the viewpoint of the individual businesses that operate within them. In order to do this we must first clarify the nature of supply networks and the terminology used to describe them. Following which, it is necessary to explore the types of relationships that can form, or be developed, between pairs of operations in a network (called *dyads* in supply network speak). Both these issues will be covered in this chapter. Having developed an understanding of the scope and form of network relationships, we can explore how larger parts of a network behave over time and Chapter 7 will cover the dynamic behaviour of networks. Figure 6.2 illustrates the topics we shall cover in this and the next chapter.

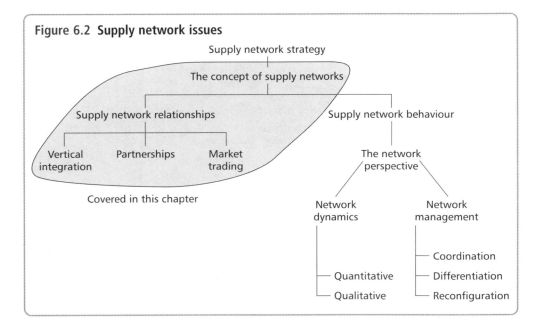

Figure 6.2 Supply network issues

What are supply networks?

Although the idea of supply networks, or supply chains (the difference between the two will be explained later), has received considerable attention over the past few years, many aspects of the concept are not new. After all, at the heart of the supply network concept is the idea of buyer–supplier relationships, and buyer–supplier trading relationships have always been at the heart of all business. Yet in other ways, the idea of standing back and seeing each separate operation as part of a large, inter-connected, and often complex network of relationships is relatively new, or at least has come to be seen as having important new implications. In our terms:

> **a supply network is an interconnection of organisations which relate to each other through upstream and downstream linkages between the different processes and activities that produce value in the form of products and services to the ultimate consumer.**[2]

Figure 6.3 Supply networks are the interconnections of relationships between operations

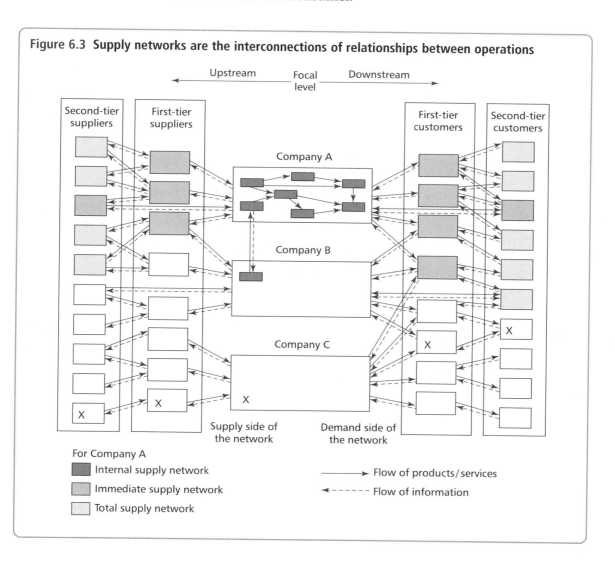

Figure 6.3 illustrates a supply network. It may look complex, though in fact it is considerably simpler than most real supply networks. However, let us use it to make some general points about the nature of supply networks.

- The three main companies in this network (Companies A, B and C) are at the centre of the network. This is because, in this case, the network has been drawn by Company A. Companies B and C could be its direct competitors or firms with which it cooperates. Company A is called the 'focal' company of the network and together with Companies B and C forms the 'focal level' of the network. In other words, the network is drawn from Company A's perspective. Company A's suppliers, together with its suppliers' suppliers and so on, form the *upstream* or *supply side* of the network, while its customers and customers' customers etc. form the *downstream* or *demand side* of the network. What is upstream and what is downstream is therefore defined only in terms of from whose perspective the network is being drawn.

- Upstream and downstream here imply that the dominant flow in the network is from left to right. This is the flow of products and services which are being exchanged for money. Note, however, that flow occurs in both directions, products and/or services one way and the information that triggers the supply of the products and services the other way. Of course, the products or services themselves may be defined in terms of information (being supplied with consultancy advice or market information, for example) but in Figure 6.3 the dotted lines are used to indicate the information *that is the stimulus for supply*. In practical terms, much of modern supply network management is concerned as much with managing the flow of information upstream as it is with managing the flow of products and services downstream.

- At the most intimate level we could visualise the various micro-operations within Company A as forming their own *internal supply network*. Moving outside its boundaries, Company A will have direct contact with a number of suppliers and a number of customers; this forms the *immediate supply network* for Company A. The linkages of suppliers to Company A's suppliers, and customers to Company A's customers, form its *total supply network*.

- The boundary between what is part of the internal network and what is part of the immediate network can change. Company A may choose to cease engaging in one type of activity currently performed internally and instead buy in those services from a supplier. Conversely, it may choose to engage internally in an activity previously bought in from a supplier. Similarly, it may choose to expand or contract its organisational boundaries downstream to its customers. This issue is conventionally referred to as the degree of *vertical integration* within Company A.

- Companies that are predominantly part of the focal level's immediate supply network are often called *first-tier* suppliers or *first-tier* customers. The companies one level beyond this are often called *second-tier* suppliers and customers, and so on. This does not mean that focal companies can trade only with first-tier customers and suppliers. In Figure 6.3 both Company A and Company B deal directly with a second-tier supplier and a second-tier customer.

- Focal companies may trade, or even cooperate on a longer-term basis, between themselves. In this example it would appear that Company A occasionally sub-contracts work to Company B. This may be because Company B has surplus capacity or because Company B can perform certain activities that Company A cannot. This may be an arrangement that suits both companies on the other hand it may be a long-term threat to Company A which has to rely on the abilities of Company B to satisfy its own customers.

- The relationships between companies within the network are not always exclusive. Company A may purchase exactly the same products or services from a number of different suppliers, who in turn may 'multi-source' from several second-tier suppliers. Indeed the degree of exclusivity of supply is one of the important supply network decisions which all companies have to make. In this example Company C seems (by accident or design) to engage in more *single sourcing* and *exclusive supply* relationships than either Companies A or B.

- The focal company's networks all involve several parallel relationships, each having several first-tier suppliers and several first-tier customers, which themselves may have more than one second-tier supplier or customer. But within these parallel relationships there are several *supply chains*. These are the sequential linkages of operations which intersect at the focal company. So, for example, the operations marked with an X form one of the supply chains passing through Company C.

Inter-operations relationships in supply networks

Drawing the physical shape of a supply network reveals only part of the picture. To understand the nature of any operation's supply network we also need to assess more qualitative issues. How does an operation relate to other players in its network? Does it have a close and intimate knowledge of its immediate supply network? And does it make sure that its immediate supply network also has an intimate understanding of its own operations? Does it rely on other players only for trivial activities, or trust some important parts of the value-adding activities to other operations?

Types of relationship

Writers on supply network management have offered several ways of categorising the relationships between players in supply networks. Here we again distinguish between the market and resource perspectives of relationship,[3] see Figure 6.4.

In terms of the resources relationships with suppliers:

- the degree to which activities are performed in-house – from performing all activities within the operation at one extreme, to totally outsourcing all activities at the other extreme;

- the importance of the activities performed within the operation – from outsourcing only trivial activities at one extreme, to outsourcing even strategically important or significant activities at the other extreme.

In terms of the market relationship:

- the structure of market relationships in terms of the number of supply relationships used by an operation – from using many suppliers for the same set of activities at one extreme, through to a few or even one supplier for each set of activities at the other extreme;

Figure 6.4 The market and resource dimensions of supply networks

	Extent of activity (quantitative)	Nature of activity (qualitative)
Market relationships	'Structure' Number of relationships	'Posture' Closeness of relationships
Resource scope	Degree of activity performed 'in-house'	Importance of activity performed 'in-house'

- the 'posture' of market relationships in terms of the closeness of those relationships – from transactional or 'arm's length' relationships at one extreme, through to close and intimate relationships at the other extreme.

In practice, the extent and the nature of both market relationships and resource scope are related. So, for example, in terms of resource scope, if an operation attempts to do everything in-house it is by definition doing both important and relatively unimportant activities within the operation. Conversely, if it does nothing in-house, both important and unimportant activities are outsourced. Organisations are unlikely to outsource their important activities before the relatively unimportant ones. Therefore, a mid-point on the resource dimension would be where an operation outsources relatively trivial activities while keeping in-house those it regards as strategically important.

Aspects of market relationship may also be related. So, for example, by definition a transactional approach to sourcing implies little or no loyalty to any one supplier. It is likely therefore that an operation indulging in transactional market relationships will, over time, have brief relationships with many different suppliers, usually whoever is cheapest at any point in time. On the other hand, close and intimate relationships involve often considerable effort in building and maintaining an appropriate style of contact between an operation and its suppliers, again requiring considerable effort. It is unlikely therefore that an operation dedicated to developing close relationships could maintain such relationships with more than a few key suppliers for each activity. Indeed it may not be possible to develop the required degree of closeness and trust with suppliers unless they are free of direct or indirect short-term competition with other operations vying to supply the same products or services.

Figure 6.5 illustrates this. Different types of supply network relationship can be positioned in terms of their implied resource scope and market relationships. At an extreme on both dimensions is the vertically integrated operation. This type of operation performs everything (or almost everything) within the organisation's boundaries. Little or nothing is subcontracted to other players in the network. Almost by definition therefore, each part of the operation will receive supply from another part, or parts, of the same macro operation. Unless the organisation has chosen to perform the same activity in many different parts of its operations there will be few (probably one) internal suppliers. This allows the potential for very close relation-

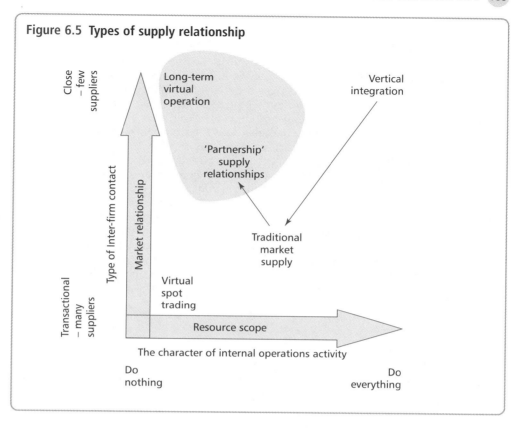

Figure 6.5 Types of supply relationship

ships. At least there is no commercial confidentiality barrier to an open and intimate relationship between internal suppliers and internal customers.

At the other extreme an operation may choose to do nothing in-house and buy in all its requirements. This is the so-called virtual company. The essence of virtuality in supply relationships is that the legal entity of the company retains relatively few physical resources. Rather its network is one of information and contacts with other players in the network who can supply all it requires to satisfy its own customers. (See box on Hollywood.) When the nature of these supply relationships is impermanent, market-based and transactional, this type of network relationship could be called virtual spot trading. Spot trading means that at any point in time an organisation looks at the spot price, or spot terms of supply, and makes a choice independently of what its previous or future choices might be.

Virtually like Hollywood[4]

As far as supply network management is concerned, could that most ephemeral of all industries, Hollywood's film-making business, hold messages for even the most sober of operations? It is an industry whose complexity most of us do not fully appreciate. The American writer Scott Fitzgerald said, 'You can take Hollywood for granted like I did, or you can dismiss it with the contempt we reserve for what we don't understand . . . not half a dozen men have ever been able to keep the whole equation of [making] pictures in their heads.' The 'equation' involves balancing

▶

the artistic creativity and fashion awareness, necessary to create a market for its products, with the efficiency and tight operations practices which get films made and distributed on time. But although the form of the equation remains the same, the way its elements relate to each other has changed profoundly. The typical Hollywood studio once did everything itself. It employed everyone from the carpenters, who made the stage, through to the film stars. Cary Grant was as much of an employee as the chauffeur who drove him to the studio, though his contract was probably more restrictive. The finished products were rolls of celluloid which had to be mass produced and physically distributed to the cinemas of the world. No longer. Studios now deal almost exclusively in ideas. They buy and sell concepts, they arrange finance, they cut marketing deals and, above all, they manage the virtual network of creative and not so creative talent that go into a film's production. A key skill is the ability to put together teams of self-employed film stars and the small, technical specialist operations that provide technical support. It is a world that is less easy for the studios to control. The players in this virtual network, from film stars to electricians, have taken the opportunity to raise their fees to the point where, in spite of an increase in cinema attendance, returns are lower than at many times in the past. This opens opportunities for the smaller, independent studies. One way to keep costs low is by using inexpensive, new talent. Some of the most profitable films have been those that didn't cost a fortune to produce. Technology could also help this process. Digital processes allow easier customisation of the 'product' and also mean that movies can be downloaded direct to cinemas (and direct to individual consumers' homes).

Not all virtual operations need be based on transactional market relationships. On the contrary, when almost all its activities are outsourced an organisation may seek to compensate for its lack of control over suppliers by attempting to build long-term and close relationships with a relatively few suppliers. This could be termed the long-term virtual operation.

Figure 6.5 also illustrates some of the trends in the nature of supply network relationships. Broadly speaking, these are as follows.

- An increase in the proportion of goods and services outsourced – generally companies are performing fewer activities in-house. The idea of 'core capability' is important here. The discrimination between what is a core capability to the long-term competitiveness of the organisation and what is less strategically important has often provided the basis for outsourcing, the argument being that a company can achieve both better efficiency and more operational effectiveness by concentrating on a few important activities and outsourcing the rest. Especially for companies that deal in a number of specialised technologies, it has proved almost impossible to maintain expertise in everything. Subcontracting at least some of these activities to other parts of the network allows access to technological innovations while reducing the risk of being stuck with outdated resources.

- Organisations are reducing the number of their suppliers – for activities of any reasonable complexity there is a transaction cost of buying in products and services. Specification and quality levels must be agreed, delivery times organised and prices agreed. Reducing the number of supply contacts will potentially reduce these transaction costs. Just as important, the time saved managing a large number of suppliers can be invested into improving the quality of fewer, more secure and potentially more valuable relationships.

- Generally organisations are attempting to develop 'partnerships' with suppliers and customers. This may take the form of some combination of long-term contractual agreements, co-location of resources, transparency of cost information, integrated systems and procedures, automated electronic financial communication, and so forth.

Not all these changes happened at the same time. Generally, companies started to reduce the scope of their activities before understanding the importance of developing their relationships with customers and suppliers. Thus, many companies moved from the classical vertically integrated operation through to what is now sometimes called traditional supply management. This reduced the scope of what an organisation chose to do internally but relied on simple market mechanisms to determine which suppliers should provide the goods and services hitherto produced in-house and which customers should be given priority in terms of service and supply. Although the trend towards outsourcing activities has continued, the parallel trend towards closer relationships with fewer suppliers has moved supply network relationships into what has been called 'partnership' supply. The remainder of this chapter will examine the advantages and disadvantages of both vertical integration and traditional market-based supply as well as describe how partnership ideas have developed.

Sky·Chefs[5]

Most airlines used to cook food for their passengers. It seemed sensible; they could keep control over its quality while coordinating its manufacture with the requirements of their aircraft. But catering can hardly be classed as a core activity for an airline. This is why many airlines now contract out food preparation to specialist suppliers. Sky Chefs, one of the six firms that control around two-thirds of the $9.5 billion market, is largely owned by the German airline Lufthansa. With over one-fifth of the world market, it claims significant economies of scale over airlines' in-house operations. For example, Sky Chef's kitchen at JFK Airport in New York coordinates 7000 pieces of food each hour. Every day 400 pounds of beef and 100 pounds of shrimp, together with many other ingredients, go into the 7500 meals it prepares. The kitchen itself is organised in production cells just like a factory. It takes, on average, one and half minutes to 'construct' each meal. New production methods, involving chilling partly cooked food, improved the quality of the food, while throughput time for the food (what is known as 'crate to plate' time) halved to just 30 hours. Most significantly, one estimate places the average cost of a meal on a domestic flight in America at $4.13 per passenger, compared with $5.62 per passenger previously.

Vertical integration

Vertical integration is the extent to which an organisation owns the network of which it is a part. At a strategic level it involves an organisation assessing the wisdom of acquiring suppliers or customers. At the level of individual products or services it means the operation deciding whether to make a particular component or to perform a particular service itself, or alternatively buy it in from a supplier.

An organisation's vertical integration strategy can be defined in terms of:[6]

- the *direction* of integration;
- the *extent* of the span of integration;

● the *balance* among the vertically integrated stages.

Figure 6.6 illustrates these three aspects of vertical integration.

The direction of vertical integration

If a company decides that it should control more of its network, should it expand by buying one of its suppliers or should it expand by buying one of its customers? The strategy of expanding on the supply side of the network is sometimes called *backward* or *'upstream' vertical integration* and expanding on the demand side is sometimes called *forward* or *'downstream' vertical integration*. Backward vertical integration, by allowing an organisation to take control of its suppliers, is often used either to gain cost advantages or to prevent competitors gaining control of important suppliers. This is why backward vertical integration is sometimes considered a strategically *defensive* move. Forward vertical integration, on the other hand, takes an organisation closer to its markets and allows more freedom for it to make contact directly with its customers. For this reason, forward vertical integration is sometimes considered an *offensive* strategic move.

The extent of vertical integration

Some organisations deliberately choose not to integrate far, if at all, from their original part of the network. Alternatively, some organisations choose to become very vertically integrated. Take many large international oil companies, such as Exxon, for example. Exxon is involved with exploration and extraction as well as the refining of the crude oil into a consumable product – gasoline. It also has operations which distribute and retail the gasoline (and many other products) to the final customer. This path (one of several for its different products) has moved the material through the total network of processes, all of which are owned (wholly or partly) by the one company.

The balance among stages

The final vertical integration decision is not strictly about the ownership of the network; it concerns the capacity and, to some extent, the operating behaviour of each stage in the network which is owned by the organisation. The *balance* of the part of the network owned by an organisation is the amount of the capacity at each stage in the network which is devoted to supplying the next stage. So a totally balanced network relationship is one where one stage produces only for the next stage in the

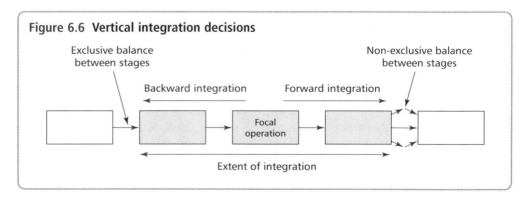

Figure 6.6 Vertical integration decisions

network and totally satisfies its requirements. Less than full balance in the stages allows each stage to sell its output to other companies or buy in some of its supplies from other companies. Fully balanced networks have the virtue of simplicity and also allow each stage to focus on the requirements of the next stage along in the network. Having to supply other organisations, perhaps with slightly different requirements, might serve to distract from what is needed by their (owned) primary customers.

The perceived advantages of vertical integration

Although extensive vertical integration is no longer as popular as it once was, there are still companies that find it advantageous to own several sequential stages of their supply network. Indeed very few companies are anywhere close to 'virtual', with no vertical integration of stages whatsoever. What then are the reasons why companies still choose to integrate vertically? Most justifications for vertical integration fall under four categories:

- It secures dependable delivery of input goods and services.
- It may reduce costs.
- It may help to improve product or service quality.
- It helps in understanding other activities in the supply network.

Securing dependable delivery

The most fundamental reason for engaging in some process in-house rather than outsourcing it is that it can't satisfactorily be outsourced. Supply may be unstable and subject to long-term gluts or shortages. One reason why the oil companies, which sell gasoline, are also engaged in extracting it, is to ensure long-term supply. In some cases there may not even be sufficient capacity in the supply market to satisfy the company. It therefore has little alternative but to supply itself. For example, some specialist electronic components are manufactured in-house by equipment manufacturers until potential suppliers have developed the capacity and knowledge to supply from outside.

Reducing costs

This reason sounds straightforward but isn't. The most common argument here is that 'We can do it cheaper than our supplier's price'. Such statements are often made by comparing the marginal direct cost incurred by a company in doing something itself against the price it is paying to buy the product or service from a supplier. Sometimes this is a good reason for moving some activity in-house. But in addition to direct costs there must be some allocation of indirect costs. If there really is no allocation of indirect costs it means that the company is inefficiently run anyway (which is an argument for improving the operating practices of the company rather than vertically integrating any new process into its activities). Cost saving through integration is also dependent on the assumption that start-up and learning costs will be relatively trivial, and that the cost savings will be such as to maintain, or even improve, the return on assets of the company, allowing for any increase in investment necessary to perform the activity in-house. A more straightforward case can be made when there are technical advantages of integration through performing an activity in-house. For example, the companies that roll kitchen foil will first of all roll it to the required gauge (thickness) in giant rolls up to two metres wide. They will then 'slit' these rolls into the widths we buy in the supermarket. Two activities which could be performed by two different companies in the supply network. Yet if it is technically feasible and convenient to slit the foil in line with the rolling process, it saves the loading and unloading activity in between rolling and slitting as well as any transportation necessary. This argument can be taken further to include not only the direct technical activities but also the indirect activities such as quality control, human resource management or financial management. Putting two sequential processes together may genuinely reduce costs (or even improve the effectiveness) of such ancillary processes. However, perhaps the most frequently deployed cost argument in favour of vertical integration is that it reduces the *transaction costs* of dealing with suppliers and customers (see the Theory Box on transaction costs).

Theory Box Transaction cost economics[7]

Transaction costs are expenses, other than price, which are incurred in the process of buying and selling. For example, transaction costs may include such things as searching the market for the best combination of price, quality and delivery, ensuring that legal contractual arrangements are in place, setting up monitoring arrangements for quality, delivery, etc., time spent in negotiating and re-negotiating contracts, and effecting sanctions if the terms of the agreement are not adhered to. Similarly, there will be a set of costs incurred by suppliers to ensure that the transaction is beneficial for them. The idea of transaction costs has been used traditionally by economists to explain why pure markets 'fail'. If the price for buying a product or service in the marketplace, plus the transaction cost of arranging the purchase, is greater than the internal cost of producing the product or service, then it would seem to make sense to produce the product or service in-house. However, if transaction costs can be lowered to the point where the external purchase price plus transaction costs is less than the internal cost, there is little justification for the vertical integration of the activity. In this way transaction costs are seen, first of all, as being a key issue in deciding whether vertical integration is a better alternative than purchasing the products and services in the open market. But also transaction costs are seen as a central issue in justifying partnership relationships. If partnership can reduce transaction costs below the point where vertical integration is sensible, then it is worth exploring how the partnership can be developed.

This leads on to the question of what are the main drivers of transaction cost. Four conditions are often quoted which lead to high transaction costs:

- *Opportunism* – the cost of transacting business with a firm that is likely to seek only its own short-term best interests will be higher than dealing with a firm that will work in the joint interest. Extra contracts may be needed, prices may be raised to compensate for the risk, relatively little effort may be put in to ensure the best service, and so on.

- *Asset specificity* (see Theory Box on asset specificity later) – if a specific investment has to be made, or is made, for one stream of transactions, whoever made the investment is vulnerable to exploitation by the other. This may be compounded by the fact that a small number (perhaps only one) of suppliers are willing to make such an investment. This in turn may increase the chances of opportunistic behaviour.

- *Uncertainty* – one way of avoiding opportunistic behaviour by the firms is to insist on a comprehensive contract. However, since most transactions take place under conditions of uncertainty, it is not possible to include every possible occurrence within the contract. The higher the level of uncertainty, the more difficult it is to develop a satisfactory contract and therefore the higher the transaction costs.

● *Frequency* – if transactions occur frequently each one may be subject to complex and costly re-negotiations.

Note how all four drivers of transaction cost are themselves a function of the trust that exists in the relationship between two firms. With total trust all four drivers of transaction cost are reduced almost to zero.

Improvement to product and service quality

Sometimes vertical integration can be used to secure specialist or technological advantage by preventing product and service knowledge getting into the hands of competitors. The exact specialist advantage may be anything from the 'secret ingredient' in fizzy drinks through to a complex technological process. In either case the argument is the same. 'This process gives us the key identifying factor for our products and services. If anyone but ourselves performs this activity we cannot keep it to ourselves for any length of time. Vertical integration therefore is necessary to the survival of product or service uniqueness.'

Learning by owning

Some companies, even those famous for their rejection of traditional vertical integration, do choose to own some parts of the supply network other than what they regard as core. So, for example, Benetton, the Italian fashion garment manufacturer, although subcontracting the majority of their manufacturing processes, still do some work in-house. Some of this in-house work is devoted to core processes such as fabric dyeing (a core process which defines their products). But some of the processes will merely perform activities which are also outsourced. One reason for this is that outsourcing the whole of one activity may result in the company getting out of touch with improvements in that process and failing to learn new techniques. Similarly, McDonald's, the restaurant chain, although largely franchising its retail operations, does own some retail outlets. How else, it argues, could it understand its retail operations so well?

The disadvantages of vertical integration

The arguments against vertical integration tend to cluster around a number of observed disadvantages of those companies that have practised vertical integration extensively. These are:

● It creates an internal monopoly.
● You can't exploit economies of scale.
● It results in loss of flexibility.
● It cuts you off from innovation.
● It distracts you from core activities.

It creates an internal monopoly

At the core of this argument is the assumption that external market mechanisms are more efficient at keeping operations close to market requirements than are any internally devised planning mechanisms. Operations, it is argued, will only change when they see a pressing need to do so. If the consequences of not maintaining or exceeding the levels of service and efficiency required by the market is that the operation goes out of business, then the motivation to remain competitive is a powerful one. Furthermore, market forces are relatively transparent. If the operation does not produce services and goods of sufficient quality, or takes too long in delivering them, or fails to keep its delivery promises, or will not change to suit customers' requirements, or cannot profitably meet competitors' prices, then it loses business. Customers stop placing orders, everyone can see the lack of activity, suppliers feel less sure of their future business and owners and shareholders demand to know what is happening. Either the company improves its performance to match what is available elsewhere in the market or, alternatively, ceases to trade and the business goes to those operations that can satisfy their customers. Such incentives and sanctions do not apply if the supplying operation is part of the same company.

You can't exploit economies of scale

Any activity which is vertically integrated within an organisation is probably also carried out elsewhere in the industry. Unless an operation has a unique process or, alternatively, is the overwhelmingly dominant player in the industry, the effort it puts into any process will be a relatively small part of the sum total of that activity within the industry. Specialist suppliers that can serve more than one customer are likely to have volumes (sometimes substantially) larger than any of their customers could achieve doing things for themselves. This allows specialist suppliers to reap some of the cost benefits of economies of scale, the benefits of which can be passed on in terms of lower prices to their customers.

It results in loss of volume flexibility

Heavily vertically integrated companies by definition do most things themselves and buy in relatively few products and services. This means that a high proportion of their costs will be fixed costs. They have, after all, invested heavily in the capacity which allows them to do most things in-house. A high level of fixed costs relative to variable costs means that any reduction in the total volume of activity can easily move the economics of the operation close to, or below, its break-even point. Conversely, low fixed costs (even with high variable costs) mean that the fluctuations in volume of demand have far less impact on the profitability of the operation.

It cuts you off from innovation

Depending on how it is defined, a second type of flexibility may be impaired by vertical integration: new product and service flexibility – in fact innovation generally. Vertical integration means investing in the processes and technologies necessary to produce products and services. As soon as that investment is made the company has an inherent interest in maintaining the appropriateness of that technology. No one likes to invest in processes which are soon overtaken by superior technologies. Abandoning such investments can be both economically and emotionally difficult.

The temptation is always to wait until any new technology is clearly established before admitting that one's own is obsolete. This may lead to a tendency to lag in the adoption of new technologies and ideas. Nor is it only the new technologies and ideas available in the free market to which a low vertically integrated company has access. It is also the ideas sparked off through the company's dialogue with customers and suppliers. There is a considerable body of evidence to suggest that customers and suppliers are a major (if not the major) source of innovation.[8] The ongoing information exchange between customers and suppliers who have mutual self-interest in each other's success is in many ways the ideal breeding ground for innovation. However, isolate a process from the rest of the market by integrating it within the total organisation and it is cut off from its potentially richest sources of ideas.

It distracts you from core activities

The final, and arguably most powerful, argument against vertical integration concerns any organisation's ability to be technically competent at a very wide range of activities. The argument goes something like this. Any organisation will have a set of things which it needs to be good at. The reason that customers do not do these things themselves is that a supplier can do them better. Over the years it has learned how to do the difficult things associated with the supply. If it was not doing something difficult then other companies would have moved in to do it themselves and the activity would no longer be profitable. So, if most companies are earning their profits by being good at something that others find difficult, then it is in their interests to maintain that expertise which other people do not have. One of the worst things they can do is attempt to be equally good at many other things. They can be profitable by being very good indeed at a narrow range of activities, but they find it far more difficult to be profitable by being merely reasonably good at a very wide range of activities. 'Reasonably' good is not sufficient protection against some other company entering the market in order to be even better.

When vertical integration is appropriate

Although vertical integration is clearly an important issue, and although many research studies have been published in the area, don't expect too much unambiguous guidance on whether vertical integration is a good thing or a bad thing. However, notwithstanding the fact that there seems to be at least some evidence to support almost every view on vertical integration, some points have emerged which command some degree of consensus.

- Vertical integration is not fashionable. Far more organisations over the past twenty years have tended to de-integrate rather than integrate. Companies most frequently justify this in terms of 'sticking to the business that they know best'.

- Vertical integration is easier to justify when the total of all costs incurred by all the processes integrated are reduced. (At times vertical integration has been justified by looking at savings in one part of the network only.) This is most clearly demonstrated when there are technical cost savings of integration (such as the in-line slitting mentioned earlier).

- Vertical integration is generally regarded as a high-risk strategy since it means high levels of investment. If the environment in which the vertically integrated company is operating is relatively stable then the risk may be worthwhile. However, if the market is likely to undergo significant changes in its levels of activity or types of products or service produced, then vertical integration exposes the company's lack of flexibility.

● Generally vertical integration makes its difficult for a company to access the innovations which become available in the supply market. This is especially true when those innovations are autonomous (that is, they do not depend on other innovations for their contribution to a company's competitiveness). The case for vertical integration is stronger when innovations are systemic (that is, an innovation in one part of the network requires innovations in other parts of the network to exploit its full contribution to competitiveness).

● Most (but not all) practical studies of the performance of companies with different degrees of vertical integration come up with one of two findings. Either they show that cost or profitability performance (measured, for example, in terms of return on sales or return on assets) reduces with increasing vertical integration, or they show that there is a V-shape relationship where companies with medium levels of vertical integration perform worse than those with either high levels or low levels of vertical integration.

Traditional market-based supply

At the very opposite extreme from vertical integration is the idea that both customer and supplier relationships are defined by 'pure' market forces. In fact in many ways the justifications for market-based supply relationships are the mirror image of those used to justify vertical integration. Namely:

● Competition between alternative suppliers promotes best value.
● Suppliers gain natural economies of scale.
● Customers can exploit the inherent flexibility of outsourced supply.
● It enables the exploitation of innovations no matter where they originate.
● It helps businesses to concentrate on their core activities.

There is little point in rehearsing these arguments again but it is worth noting that the case in favour of market-based relationships is usually made on the first of the above points. The free market, with suppliers vying against each other for a customers' business, is the best long-term guarantee of low costs. No prospective supplier will survive under conditions of competitive markets, it is argued, unless they are providing something very close to what the customers want. Certainly the dynamics of the market relationship can be exploited to keep the cost of outsourced goods and services at a minimum. Since outsourced goods and services are at least 50 per cent of most organisations' total costs this is important. Relatively small reductions in the price paid for outsourced goods and services can have a major effect on profits. For example, consider the following simple example.

Total sales	=	£10,000,000
Purchased goods and services	=	£7,000,000
Other costs	=	£2,500,000
Therefore, profit	=	£500,000

Profits can be doubled to £1,000,000 by any of the following:

- increasing sales revenue by 100 per cent;
- decreasing 'other costs', such as salaries, by 20 per cent;
- decreasing the cost of purchased goods and services by 7.1 per cent.

A doubling of sales revenue can occur in some fast-growing markets, but is by any standard an ambitious target for any marketing manager. Decreasing other costs by 20 per cent, especially if the majority of these are salaries, is again possible but difficult. However, reducing the cost of purchased goods and services by 7.1 per cent, although a challenging objective, does seem the most realistic option. This is why cost reduction is genuinely important to many companies' supply strategy. Because outsourcing costs are such a large proportion of total costs, relatively small changes in the price paid for outsourced goods and services will have a large impact on profits, and the higher the proportion of total costs devoted to outsourced goods and services, the more pronounced this effect is.

Problems with relying on market mechanisms

Although market forces are the most important long-term influence on most business relationships, there are in practice some considerable problems in relying exclusively on market mechanisms. We shall group these problems under three headings:

- coping with buyer–supplier uncertainties;
- the cost of making purchase decisions;
- strategic risks.

Coping with buyer–supplier uncertainties

Relatively few purchasing decisions are made around a single unambiguous factor. Theoretically, if all companies in the market are offering exactly the same product with exactly the same conditions of delivery and quality, the purchasing company could make the decision of which company to use exclusively on the basis of price. However, there again, there may be issues of payment terms, long-term security of supply, ability to buy other goods and services in a one-stop-shop transaction, and so on, to take into account. Single-dimension purchasing decision making is unusual. It is found most frequently at the extreme upstream ends of supply networks where commodity-like products (and sometimes services) are being traded. For most purchase decisions several dimensions will need to be considered, and sometimes traded off. In order to make these trade-offs between cost, quality, delivery, product performance, flexibility and so on, the purchasing company needs to understand and evaluate all the options it faces. That is, all the prospective suppliers who could provide whatever is being purchased. This is no mean task. There may be a large number of suppliers with subtly different product and service offerings which may themselves change in the near future. Thus there is 'market uncertainty' caused by a lack of perfect information. Managers are forced to decide under conditions of what is sometimes called 'bounded rationality'.

Even if it were possible to identify and evaluate all the real and potential offerings which the market could provide, it is sometimes difficult to get the required clarity of information *internally*. There may be some difficulty within a purchasing organis-ation of knowing exactly what is needed. Especially when technologies are newly emerging or complex, it is difficult to set down a precisely defined specification on which to evaluate purchasing opportunities. This is sometimes called 'need uncer-tainty'. There is also uncertainty concerning the degree of confidence the purchas-ing organisation has in its potential suppliers. Although a supplying company may be clear in saying what it will do, unless there is a history of proven reliable supply, how does the purchasing company know it can trust its supplier? This is called 'transaction uncertainty'.

Obviously purchasing companies will seek to minimise all these uncertainties. There is even a market value in helping purchasing companies to do this. Some industry associations provide data on their members to prospective purchasers of their members' services. In a similar way with consumer products, many of us buy automobile or hi-fi magazines which list these available products together with their performance and price details. At other times companies seek to limit the effort that goes into reducing uncertainty. Some companies have a list of preferred suppliers which contains details of companies supplying particular services from which alternative providers will be chosen on a transaction-by-transaction basis. Other methods of coping with uncertainty include working with internal designers to reduce any ambiguity around how products and services are specified internally. Likewise, transaction uncertainty can be reduced by seeking 'references' from other customers of potential suppliers.

The cost of making purchase decisions – transaction costs

Whatever mechanisms are used to reduce buyer–supplier uncertainties it is evident that some considerable effort is involved. This brings us to the second problem with relying on market mechanisms – they can be expensive to manage. Finding out information from suppliers, looking into the history and track record of potential suppliers, working with internal staff to understand exactly what is required, and so on, all needs resourcing in some way. Decisions need to be made on sifting through the potential suppliers in order to choose one (or sometimes more). Furthermore, these decisions need to be reviewed periodically to check whether the chosen sup-pliers are still the cheapest and best or whether there are now better suppliers in the market. All this is the traditional role of the purchasing function within businesses, and the purchasing function has always been faced with the 'perfect decision dilemma'. Put simply, this is that, in a free market, in order to reach the very best decisions as to which are the best set of suppliers to choose, you need a very large purchasing resource to make the 'best' decision. Again, in practice, companies will accept something less than a perfect decision in order to limit the resources needed to make the choice. It will do this by a number of common-sense mechanisms such as identifying the most important suppliers in terms of value of purchases, or in terms of long-term strategic impact, and concentrating on them. Nevertheless, the transaction cost which goes into the purchase decision when using free-market mechanisms is an important issue for companies adopting this approach.

Strategic risks

This final problem, with an over-reliance on market mechanisms, has been much debated. It is simply that if companies choose to outsource some of their activities to the 'best' suppliers, the market mechanisms that made those suppliers the 'best' could result in the suppliers becoming more profitable and more powerful than the purchasing company. The purchasing company then is 'hollowed out'. It is left with few activities of long-term value or importance. Here the issue comes down to the fact that, if an operation is going to outsource some of its activities to the market, it should be very careful that it does not choose the wrong things to outsource. It may have to be made in a dynamic environment, with competitors actively pursuing similar developments and markets developing in a fast and unpredictable manner. For example, when IBM started manufacturing personal computers the industry was in a state of flux. Although clearly a significant development, few visionaries could see exactly how the market might develop. Because PCs were different from its current mainframe-type products, IBM set up a separate business to design, produce and sell these new products. Unable to perform every single activity necessary to the development of such products, IBM made (with hindsight) two critically important outsourcing decisions. It outsourced the design of its micro processor to one of the several alternative suppliers at that time, namely Intel. Second, it outsourced the development of its operating system to a small but dynamic supplier called Microsoft.

Samsung's subcontracted success[9]

One of the best-known cautionary tales which illustrates the inherent dangers involved in sub-contracting is that of General Electric's microwave oven experiences. Although the microwave industry at the beginning of the 1980s was dominated by Japanese domestic appliance manufacturers, such as Matsushita and Sanyo, General Electric was enjoying reasonable success in the US market with its purpose-designed microwave oven plant in Maryland. However, it soon came under price pressures from its Japanese competitors. What seemed an obvious solution was to subcontract the manufacture of some of its more basic models, where margins were relatively small. GE explored the idea of subcontracting these models to one of its main rivals, Matsushita, even though giving one of its main competitors such an advantage was considered risky. GE also found a small, but go-getting, Korean company that was already selling very simple (and very cheap) models in the US. After much consideration GE decided to continue making the top of the range models itself, subcontract its cheaper models to Matsushita, but also place a small order of 15,000 units of its cheaper models with the Korean company, partly to see whether they could cope with the order. Of course it also made sense for GE to send their own engineers to help the Korean company transfer knowledge and ensure that quality standards would be maintained. The GE engineers found that, although the Korean company had little knowledge, they were very willing to learn. Eventually the Korean's production line started producing reasonable quality products, still at very low prices. Over time, the Korean company were given more and more orders by GE, who found that they were making more margin on the Korean sourced products than those coming out of their Maryland plant. This became particularly important as the market continued to mature and costs came under increased pressure. The Maryland plant attempted to cut its own costs but this proved especially difficult with so much of its volume now subcontracted to the Korean company. In the end the Maryland plant was closed and GE withdrew entirely from the microwave oven (indeed the whole domestic appliance) market. And the Korean company? It was called Samsung, and within 10 years of starting to make them it became the world's largest manufacturer of microwave ovens.

Using market mechanisms

Some authorities argue that two factors are particularly important in determining whether market mechanisms are appropriate in shaping buyer–seller relationships and in determining exactly how market mechanisms are used:[10]

- the number of alternative suppliers in the market, and
- the resource cost to the buyer of changing suppliers.

Figure 6.7 illustrates how the market and the resource dimensions influence the use of market mechanisms. The bottom-right and top-left parts of the matrix are relatively straightforward. When the cost to the buyer of making a change in supplier is very high and anyway there are few alternative suppliers to switch to, it is unlikely that buyers would want to use pure market mechanisms. The buyer's hand is relatively weak whereas the supplier has relatively high short-term security. Under these circumstances it is likely that some kind of partnership agreement may be appropriate (we shall deal with partnership relationships next). Conversely, in the top left-hand part of the matrix, buyers have many alternative suppliers and, furthermore, the costs of moving between suppliers are low. It could be argued that under these circumstances, leveraging the free market is the best way for a buyer to keep the performance of their suppliers competitive.

Between these parts of the matrix the issue is less straightforward. The issue is as much *how* to use market mechanisms as it is *whether* to use market mechanisms. A key factor here is what we earlier called market uncertainties (we aren't entirely sure

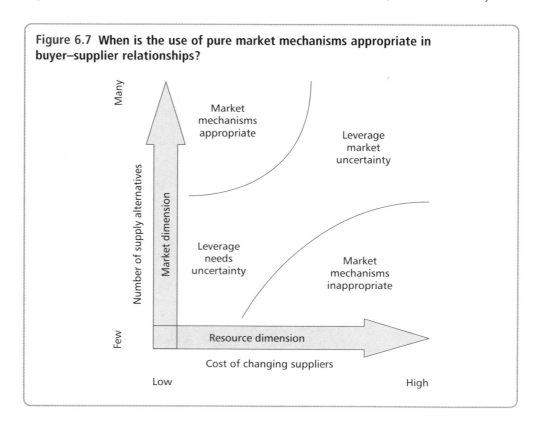

Figure 6.7 When is the use of pure market mechanisms appropriate in buyer–supplier relationships?

what is available out in the supplier market) and needs uncertainties (we aren't entirely sure what we need from the supplier market). In the bottom left-hand part of the matrix buyers have little market uncertainty. There are few alternative suppliers and it is not difficult to negotiate with them all over the subtleties and trade-offs of what and how they supply. They are willing to enter into this type of negotiation because they know that you could switch to an alternative supplier relatively easily. However, both of you know that you cannot be constantly switching suppliers. Because there are few alternative suppliers, your promiscuous behaviour soon would make you an unattractive customer. Under these circumstances needs uncertainty becomes a key issue. From the buyer's point of view a sensible question to ask existing suppliers would be, *'Given that you and other alternative suppliers are relatively close in what you can offer, how can your company offer some combination of supply performance to me which helps me solve my problems?'* The top right-hand part of the matrix is very different. Here there are many alternative suppliers. No buyer can have perfect knowledge of all of them so there is high market uncertainty. Also, because there are many alternative suppliers, the chances are that there is a wide range of alternative deals and supply performance levels available. Although buyers can easily find an alternative supplier, they will only do so if the gap between existing suppliers' performance and prospective new suppliers' performance is sufficiently high to recoup the high cost of switching. Existing suppliers know that buyers will be reluctant to switch unless the performance gap is large. Therefore negotiation is likely to centre around exploiting market uncertainty. The buyers stance could be, *'I can easily find a better supplier but will not switch to them if you can promise to come close to matching their performance.'*

An army marches on its services[11]

The most surprising things can be outsourced. Even activities that are fundamental to the interests of a State may be better bought in than done by the State itself. The very defence of the State involves a whole collection of activities, only some of which directly prevent aggression or keep the peace. There is a broad trend towards privatising these non-direct workings of defence forces. In Australia, for example, private companies maintain its military aircraft and bases. In Britain private firms run various parts of the military infrastructure such as some naval dockyard activities. The boss of the American Halliburton Company claimed during the Balkan crisis that *'The first person to greet our soldiers as they arrive in the Balkans, and the last one to wave good-bye, is one of our employees'*. During that campaign his company was involved in doing the laundry, setting up tents and temporary toilet facilities, and other essential, but peripheral activities. Its five-year contract in the Balkans brought it around $1 billion in revenue. In a world where governments are expecting greater value for money from their defence forces, outsourcing offers two major advantages – cheapness and flexibility. Partly this is because the companies can hire local staff on short-term contracts. Some military experts, however, also see outsourcing as carrying risks. Relying on local staff might compromise security, especially when a conflict involves warring ethnic groups. Non-service personnel may also be, not unreasonably, reluctant to maintain their devotion to service under the threat of heavy fire.

Partnership supply

The development of partnership relationships between customers and suppliers in supply networks is sometimes seen as a compromise between the 'extremes' of vertical integration and market trading. To some extent this is true. It certainly attempts to achieve some of the closeness and coordination efficiencies of vertical integration without the necessity for customers to own the assets that supply them. It also attempts to achieve the sharpness of service and the incentive to continually improve, which is often seen as the benefit of traditional market trading, without the transaction costs of managing supply channels. Yet partnership is not just a mixture of vertical integration and market trading. It is a relatively new concept of how relationships in supply networks can be formed, such that the relationship itself, and especially the trust that is engendered within it, effectively substitute for the ownership of assets.

The remainder of this chapter will be largely devoted to examining some of the elements which, together, characterise partnership relationships. The interaction between these elements is complex and subject to much academic debate. However, there is a general agreement that at the heart of partnership lies the issue of the *closeness* of the relationship. We have identified some of the major issues which contribute to closeness and divided them into those which are primarily related to the *attitude* with which the customer and supplier approach the relationship, and those which relate to the *actions* undertaken by both parties. See Figure 6.8.

Essentially, partnership relationships between suppliers and customers can be viewed as strategic alliances. These have been defined as

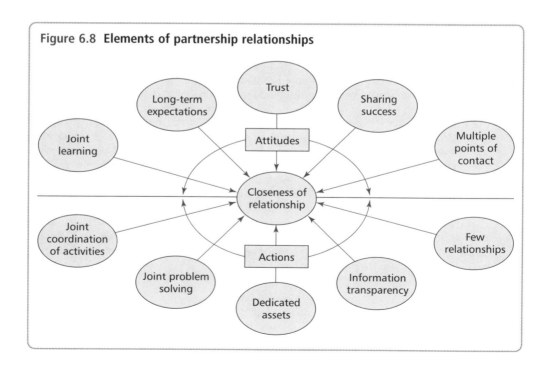

Figure 6.8 Elements of partnership relationships

relatively enduring inter-firm cooperative arrangements, involving flows and linkages that use resources and/or governance structures from autonomous organisations, for the joint accomplishment of individual goals linked to the corporate mission of each sponsoring firm.[12]

In such an alliance partners are expected to cooperate, even to the extent of sharing skills and resources, to achieve joint benefits beyond those they could achieve by acting alone.

Closeness

Closeness refers to the degree of intimacy, understanding and mutual support which exists between partners in a network. It also reflects the degree of interdependence of the partners. An analogy is often drawn between the concept of closeness and intimacy in business relations and how the word is used in personal relations. Interpersonal intimacy relies on the attitude with which individuals approach the relationship with their partner/friend, and is also affected by an accumulation of individual actions. Both are important. Intimacy relies on each partner's belief in the other's attitude and motivation in maintaining the relationship. It is that belief that helps dispel any doubt that we can rely on supportive actions from our partner. But it is also those actions which, over time, deepen and enhance the positive beliefs and attitudes concerning the relationship itself. In this way, closeness can be seen as both the result of, and the objective of, the interplay between attitudes towards the relationship and the ongoing activities which are the day-to-day manifestations of the relationship.

Trust

In this context trust means

the willingness of one party to relate with another in the belief that the other's actions will be beneficial rather than detrimental to the first party, even though this cannot be guaranteed.[13]

In other words, it means that suppliers or customers are willing to take a risk that they might be treated (in their view) badly by their partner because they believe that their partner will not in fact do so. So, closely aligned with the concept of trust is that of willingness to take risks in a relationship. The greater the degree of trust, the greater is the willingness to make oneself vulnerable to the actions of the other, even though this vulnerability is not as keenly felt because of the existence of trust. If there were no risk involved in a relationship there would be no need for trust, and without some degree of trust there is little justification for taking risks with a partner. Although most organisations are aware of different degrees of trust in their relationships with suppliers or customers, they do not always see trust as an issue to be managed explicitly. Sometimes this is the result of a broad philosophical view of the issue ('*in the end suppliers will always look after their own interests, it's foolish to believe otherwise*'). At other times it may be that managers do not believe such a nebulous concept can be either analysed or indeed managed ('*trust is one of those things which is either there or it isn't, you can't account for it like profit and loss*'). However, almost all research in the area of supplier–customer relationships highlights the role of trust in determining the scope and limits to the relationship. Furthermore, it is at the heart of any understanding of partnership relationships.

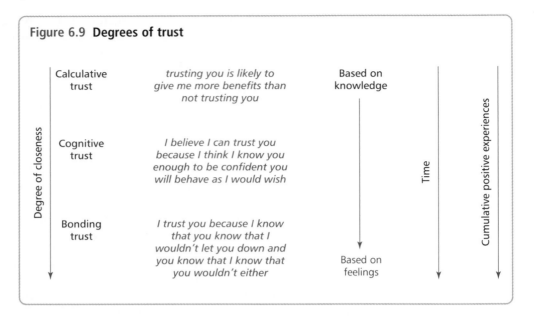

Figure 6.9 Degrees of trust

It is useful to think of trust in three stages.[14] At the most basic, *calculative trust* is the trust that arises because one of the parties calculates that trusting the partner is likely to lead to a better outcome than not trusting them. Underlying this is often the belief that the benefits from maintaining trust are greater than those from breaking it. Beyond this is what is known as *cognitive trust*, trust which is based on a sharing of each partner's cognitions or understandings of aspects concerned with the relationship. By knowing how each other sees the world, each partner is able to predict how the other will react. In other words, the other partner's behaviour can be anticipated; it therefore comes as no surprise and, therefore, will not threaten the relationship. Even deeper is the idea of *bonding trust*. This is based on partners holding common values, moral codes and a sense of what obligations are due to each other. The partners identify with each other at an emotional level beyond the mere mechanics of the day-to-day transactions which occur. Trust is based on the belief that each party feels as well as thinks the same. Figure 6.9 illustrates. Progression through these states of trust is often associated with time and the accumulation of positive, relationship-building experiences.

Sharing success

An attitude of shared success means that both partners recognise that they have more to gain through the success of the other partner than they have individually, or by exploiting the other partner. Put simply, it means that both customers and suppliers are less interested in manoeuvring in order to get a bigger slice of the pie and are more interested in increasing the size of the pie. It is this belief that helps to prevent individual partners from acting against the interests of the other in order to gain immediate advantage, what economists call *opportunistic behaviour*. However, in order to make opportunistic behaviour unprofitable, it must be clear that the size of pie will indeed be larger if both partners cooperate. It also is important to have an agreement as to how the larger pie will be divided up. Game theory provides a useful insight into this issue (see Theory Box on game theory).

Theory Box Game theory (again)

Back in Chapter 5 we introduced the idea of game theory and used it to examine capacity change decisions. Game theory is also used to illustrate some of the examples of cooperation in supply networks. Take what is a classic game theory problem known as the 'Prisoner's Dilemma'. It involves two thieves, Mr Orange and Mr White, who, having been arrested, are being questioned by the police. The evidence being circumstantial, the police need a confession to ensure a full conviction. Mr Orange and Mr White are kept in separate cells with no communication between them, and each is told that if he confesses he will be set free but the other will receive a ten-year sentence. If both of them confess, both will get a five-year sentence. However, if neither confesses, each knows that a lesser charge will result in them both receiving a three-year sentence. Figure 6.10 illustrates this.

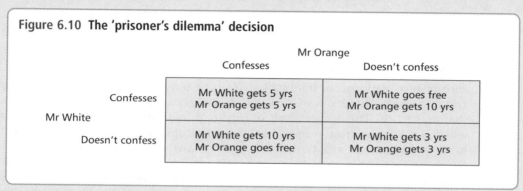

Figure 6.10 **The 'prisoner's dilemma' decision**

Given these circumstances, the risk of not confessing (a cooperative strategy) is very high. For example, if Mr Orange does not confess and Mr White does then Mr Orange will receive the worst possible outcome, perhaps made worse by the knowledge that Mr White will go free. Rationally, neither thief would keep quiet (i.e. cooperate), both would confess and each get a five-year sentence. Note a number of points from this simple problem.

- It is what is known as a non-zero-sum game. That is, one player's gain is not always at the expense of the other. The total years served if both cooperate (don't confess) is less than any of the other outcomes.

- What we described as the 'rational' strategy of confessing (non-cooperation) holds true only if we have insufficient trust in the other player to act cooperatively.

- The assumption is that this is a one-off game. That is, there will be no future plays such as one thief exacting a dreadful revenge on the other in some future 'game'.

- If the game was repeated several times each player would be influenced by the previous behaviour of the other. Trust between the two could grow with increasing evidence of cooperative behaviour. Conversely, any trust might quickly be destroyed after only one episode of non cooperative behaviour.

In an interesting experiment, Axelrod[15] invited several contestants to devise different strategies which would be tested out in repeated playings of the prisoner's dilemma game. The winning strategy was in fact one of the simplest. Derived by Anatol Rapoport, it was called the tit-for-tat strategy. Its only rules were:

- Cooperate on the first encounter of the game.

- After that, do whatever your opponent did in the previous round.

According to Axelrod, this strategy works because,

- It is 'nice' – it never starts a non-cooperative move itself.
- It is provocable – it retaliates against non-cooperative play quickly.
- It is forgiving – it does not bear any grudges and the retaliation lasts only as long as the opponent continues not to cooperate.

'Tit-for-tat won the tournaments not by beating the other player, but by eliciting behaviour from the other player that allowed both to do well. . . . In a non-zero sum world, you do not have to do better than the other player to do well for yourself. This is especially true when you are interacting with many different players. . . . The other's success is virtually a prerequisite for doing well yourself.'[16]

Long-term expectations

Partnership relationships imply relatively long-term relationships between suppliers and customers. This fits in with our previous comments on both the role of trust and sharing success. The deeper levels of trust require time to develop and game theory tells us that cooperation is more likely when games are repeated. Furthermore, there is no need to incur the transaction costs of frequent changes of partner, always assuming that the partner behaves in the best interests of the other. All of which points to long-term relationships – *but not necessarily permanent ones*. At the heart of the partnership concept is that either party could end the partnership. That is (partly) what keeps each motivated to do the best for the other. Maintaining the relationship is an affirmation that each partner has more to gain from the relationship than from ending it.

Multiple points of contact

By 'multiple points of contact' we mean that communication between partners is complex and involves many links between many individuals in both organisations. This sounds, at first, as though it is an action rather than an attitude – 'go and establish many points of contact'. In fact, it is best thought of as an attitude which allows, and indeed encourages, multiple person-to-person relationships. It implies that both partners are sufficiently relaxed in their mutual dealings not to feel they have to control every discussion and development. Over time, this may lead to a complex web of agreements and understandings being formed, perhaps not in the legal contractual sense of a single 'all embracing' agreement, but as a multi-stranded, intertwined 'velcro-connected' binding of the two partners.

Joint learning

Again, this sounds like an action – 'go out and learn from each other'. In reality, though, it is more of an attitude – 'let us approach this relationship in a sense of mutual learning'. Presumably, a partner has been selected on the basis that, if a supplier, the partner has something to contribute beyond what the customer can do themselves. That is, they have expertise and experience which the customer finds valuable. While the customer would not necessarily wish to gain technical knowledge of these core processes (they have, after all, decided not to do these things themselves), it may be able to learn much about the application of whatever is supplied. For example, suppose a retail bank has a partnership agreement with a credit agency which gives credit risk assessments of the bank's customers who are applying for loans. Whereas the bank would not wish to carry all the information which would enable it to judge the loan applicants themselves, it can do more than merely wait until the credit agency pronounces on the applicants' credit worthiness. In discussions with the credit agency it may be able to improve the questions it asks of applicants, and it may also be able to screen out certain applicants at an earlier stage of the application process. It is therefore learning how to deploy the credit agency's services (preferably) to both their advantages. Similarly, the credit agency might wish to further refine its decision-making processes in consultation with the bank's experiences of which customers were indeed credit worthy. In this way the partners learn from each other to their joint advantage.

Few relationships

Partnership relationships do not necessarily imply single sourcing by customers (obtaining all of one type of supply from a single supplier), nor does it imply exclusivity by suppliers (a supplier agreeing not to supply a customer's competitors). However, even if the relationships are not monogamous, they are not promiscuous. Partnerships inevitably involve a limit (sometimes a severe limit) on the number of other partnerships, if for no other reason that a single organisation cannot maintain intimacy in a large number of relationships. Furthermore, it also implies that the other partner has some say in the other's relationships. Generally, partners agree the extent to which they might form other relationships which may involve some longer-term threat to their partner. Sometimes customers are obliged to source products or services from more than one supplier. A single supplier may not be able to fulfil volume, location, or variety requirements. Similarly, a single customer, no matter how close, may not be able to take sufficient volume to make exclusive relationships economic. However, it is worth stressing that the recent general move towards having fewer suppliers is related to the general desire to develop closer relationships with those which remain.

Joint coordination of activities

Partly because there are fewer individual customers and/or suppliers with whom to coordinate, the quantity, type and timing of product and service deliveries are usually subject to a greater degree of mutual agreement in a partnership relationship. However, notwithstanding the mutuality of interest, it is usually the customer side of a partnership which has a far greater say in the coordination of activities than the supplier. Customers, after all, are closer to the demand-driven end of a supply chain and thus subject to a greater degree of demand pull. Coordination becomes particularly important if the customer end of the partnership is interested in just-in-time delivery. Just-in-time reduces the buffers between customer and supplier which were there partly to compensate for a lack of supply coordination. A customer's increased involvement in a supplier's day-to-day planning and control (combined with a degree of trust) allows these buffers to be reduced, or even eliminated.

Information transparency

Open and efficient information exchange is a key element in partnership as well as the natural consequence of the various attitudinal factors discussed earlier. It means that each partner is open, honest, thorough and timely in the way they communicate with each other. Such information exchange is both a product of mutual trust, and therefore closeness, and a way of further establishing them. As a way of encouraging appropriate decisions to be made by each party, and as a way of preventing misunderstanding between the parties, efficient information exchange and dissemination is vital. However, there is a downside. As closeness is extended, the nature of the information exchanged by the partners may become increasingly sensitive. This may mean that it would be embarrassing to one party if it leaked beyond the partnership. More seriously, it may mean that, if the information is commercially valuable, leakage could mean one partner being placed at a commercial and/or strategic disadvantage.

Joint problem solving

Partnerships do not always run smoothly. In fact, the degree of closeness between partners would be severely limited if they did. When problems arise, either minor problems concerned with the day-to-day flow of products and services, or more fundamental issues concerned with the nature of the relationship itself, they will need to be addressed, by one or both partners. The way in which such problems are addressed is widely seen as being central to how the partnership itself develops. In fact it can be argued that it is only when problems arise that the opportunity exists to explore fully many of the issues we have been discussing regarding trust, shared success, long-term expectations, and so on. Furthermore, successful problem solving requires a degree of joint coordination, information transparency, and cannot happen unless there are relatively few relationships (and therefore problems).

Dedicated assets

One of the more evident ways of demonstrating a commitment to partnership, and one of the most risky, is by one partner (usually the supplier) investing in resources which will be dedicated to a single customer. For example, suppose a 'translation services' company has a partnership with a major customer for whom it translates technical documents. Because the customer's needs are very specific (perhaps requiring the translation of obscure technical terms), the partners decide to set up a specialist 'cell' within the customer's technical department. This cell will contain specialist translators together with specially developed translation software, which is used to facilitate the process. In this case both parties are making some kind of investment. The customer is allocating space for the translation cell, though the supplier is making the greater investment of both human resources and technology. Obviously, the translation company will only do this if it is convinced that the partnership will be long-term, that advantages can be gained by both parties and that the customer will not exploit the investment in order to bargain the price down below what was originally agreed. This last point, regarding the vulnerability of firms that make investments in dedicated assets, is one much debated by economists. (See the Theory Box on asset specificity.)

Theory Box | **Asset specificity[17]**

Economists call an asset 'specific' if it has a high value only when it is used to perform certain tasks, and has relatively little value doing other things. If a supplier invests in specific assets it is increasing the risks that if the relationship ends its investment in the assets will be wasted. Furthermore, it may also increase the risk of a breakdown occurring. This is sometimes called 'the hold-up problem'. There are various types of asset specificity. Location specificity is when suppliers, or customers, locate their resources close to, or inside, the other's location, usually in order to minimise communication or inventory costs. Physical assets specificity is where customers, or suppliers, invest in process technology that is specifically designed for a narrow range of tasks associated with the relationship. Human resource specificity is when employees of customers, or suppliers, develop skills that are specific to the partnership.

Originally, some economists argued that the risk of asset specificity was largely on the customer's side. After a supplier has made an investment in specific assets, the customer has too much to lose by attempting to obtain supply from elsewhere. However, in practice, asset specificity holds the risks of hold-up both ways. The supplier is usually required to make the greater investment and thus has much to lose if its customer goes elsewhere.

Which type of relationship?

Although there is no simple formula for choosing what form of relationship to develop with all individual suppliers and customers, it is worth attempting to identify some of the more important factors which can sway the decision. Before doing so, however, it is worthwhile reminding ourselves that firms do not make an overall policy decision to adopt one of the three forms of relationship we have described here. Rather they make a whole set of decisions for each one of their activities, ranging from performing the activity themselves (vertical integration) through to outsourcing using the pure market mechanism, and all forms of partnerships in between. Thus, most firms have a portfolio of widely differing relationships with their suppliers and customers. Each of these decisions will have been influenced by a whole set of factors which, as usual, we describe in terms of market and resource factors (see Figure 6.11).

From a market perspective, the most obvious issue will be how the firm intends to differentiate itself through its *market positioning*. If a firm is competing primarily on price then the relationship could be dictated by minimising transaction costs (see the Theory Box on transaction cost economics). If it is competing primarily on product or service innovation, then it may well wish to form a collaborative alliance with a partner with whom it can work closely. Unless, that is, the market from which innovations derive is turbulent and fast growing (as with many software and Internet-based industries), in which case it might wish to retain the freedom to change partners quickly through the market mechanism. However, in such turbulent markets, a firm might wish to develop relationships that *reduce its risks*. One way to do this is to form relationships with many different potential long-term customers and suppliers, until the nature of the market stabilises. Opportunities to develop relationships, however, may be limited by the *structure of the market* itself. If the number of potential suppliers, or customers, is small, then it would probably be sensible to attempt to develop a close relationship with at least one customer or sup-

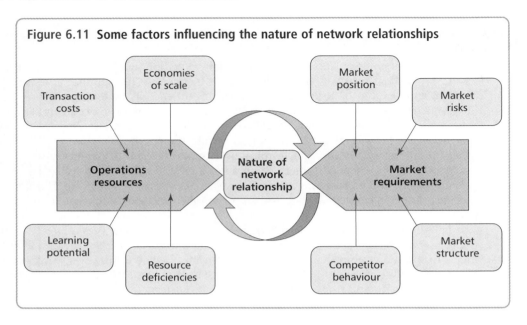

Figure 6.11 Some factors influencing the nature of network relationships

plier. Opportunities to play off customers and suppliers against each other may be limited. Firms will also be influenced by likely *competitor behaviour*. For example, close partnership, or even vertical integration, may be seen as a defensive move against a competitor acquiring a major supplier or customer.

From an operations resource perspective, *economies of scale* are important if the total requirement for a given product or service falls below the optimum level of efficiency. A low level of output is one of the main factors that prevents firms doing things in-house. A related issue is the level of *transaction costs* involved in outsourcing (see the Theory Box on transaction cost economics). Low intrinsic transaction costs might favour market-based relationships, while the possibility of jointly reducing transaction costs makes partnership an attractive option. Partnership also becomes attractive when there is the *potential for learning* from a partner. An absence of any potential learning suggests a more market-based relationship. Finally, although obvious, it is worthwhile pointing out that any sort of outsourcing, whether partnership or market-based, may be as a response to some sort of *resource deficiency*. That is, a firm will go outside for products and services if it does not have the resources to create them itself.

SUMMARY ANSWERS TO KEY QUESTIONS

What are supply networks?

A supply network is an interconnection of organisations which relate to each other through upstream and downstream linkages between the different processes and activities that produce value in the form of products and services to the ultimate consumer. In the most limited sense this means the customers and suppliers with whom an operation has direct contact. In its broadest sense it can mean the whole complex interconnection of companies that make up the industry within which the operation works.

How can operations organise the task of performing activities in-house?

Deciding on the extent of vertical integration means that an operation draws the boundaries of its organisation in terms of the direction of integration, the extent, or span, of integration, and the balance between its vertically integrated stages. In doing so, an organisation is primarily trying to leverage the advantages of coordination, and cost reduction, as well as trying to secure product and process learning. However, the disadvantages of vertical integration can be significant. The internal monopoly effect is often held to inhibit improvement. In addition, vertical integration is said to limit economies of scale, reduce flexibility, insulate a firm from innovation, and be distracting from what should be the core activities of the firm.

How can operations use traditional market relationships to organise out-of-house activities?

At the opposite extreme from vertical integration is the use of market trading to buy in products and services. Because in most organisations a substantial part of costs are expended on bought-in products and services, this is an important issue. The advantages are largely concerned with overcoming the disadvantages of vertical integration. Primarily, that it gives an operation the flexibility to seek out the best deal in terms of cost innovation etc. However, the uncertainties, risks and, above all, transaction costs associated with pure market trading may also be significant.

How do partnership relationships seek to gain the best of both worlds?

Long-term partnerships with a relatively small number of strategic partners have been put forward as a way of maintaining the coordination and low transaction cost effects of vertical integration, while at the same time avoiding the internal monopoly effect on operations improvement. The major problem with partnerships, however, is the difficulty of maintaining the attitudes and activities which bolster the high degree of trust which is necessary for them to work effectively.

Aztec Component Supplies

The senior management team at Aztec Component Supplies knew that they were facing a decision crucial to the future of the company. A plastic injection mouldings manufacturer, they had for the past 20 years specialised in providing industrial mouldings for domestic appliance manufacturers. They were especially adept at moulding relatively large components, such as the outer casing for carpet cleaners. Large components were difficult to make to the high levels of tolerance and finish that customers demanded. Because of this ability they had increasingly focused on the few large customers who were willing to pay their prices. Five years ago twelve customers accounted for around 80 per cent of Aztec's sales, now three customers accounted for over 90 per cent of sales.

The decision concerned an approach which had been made to them by their largest customer, the Desron Corporation. One part of Desron was already their largest customer with around 65 per cent of their output. Desron now wanted Aztec to become a sole supplier for a wider range of their larger components. It would, in the first instance, be a three-year deal whereby Aztec would devote manufacturing cells for each component type exclusively to supply Desron. Although Aztec would not be prevented from dealing with other customers, the amount of business Desron were promising would initially be 5 per cent more than their current total sales and (according to Desron) could double within five years. Because Aztec would be manufacturing parts currently made by other suppliers, the total variety of parts would increase by around 40 per cent. Prices would be held at current levels in the first year but then would be reduced by 5 per cent per year.

Aztec would be responsible for reducing costs in line with price reductions (average cost savings at Aztec had averaged between 2 and 3 per cent per year in the past few years). If Aztec accepted the deal it would also mean them purchasing some new larger machinery to cope with the increased proportion of physically large parts. David Lopez, Aztec's CEO, did not see this as a problem.

'We need to replace many of our machines anyway. This provides us with the stimulus to do it and our calculations indicate that the deal would give us a good return on the investment. Investment isn't the problem, it's the risks of doing the deal that worry me. How do we know that we can cope with the increased variety? We will need to increase the flexibility of our manufacturing operations to cope with this variety, while at the same time reducing costs and maintaining quality levels. And can we achieve a minimum of 5 per cent annual cost reduction? It's higher than we've ever done before. They will help us by providing their own engineers to reconfigure our production system but that will mean exposing ourselves to their scrutiny. I'm nervous about that, the next thing they will be wanting is to examine our financial accounts. Also, what if they ditch us after three years? If we accept this deal we cannot keep much of our other business. Just coping with the Desron business will mean us expanding by 5 per cent. Once we have dropped our other customers I doubt if we could get them back easily. Most of all, are we prepared to act as a servant to such a large corporation? Are we ready to put up with so much interference in our business? They are talking about putting their own quality people and production planning people in offices in our plant! As part of the deal they are also insisting that we abandon our MRP (Material

Requirement Planning) system and use the more modern ERP (Enterprise Resource Planning) system they use. They are also insisting that we lease the ERP system from an applications service provider.'

(Applications service providers (ASPs) hold computer applications such as ERP systems, together with dedicated databases, on their own servers which their clients access using Internet-type technologies.)

Alice Chang, the Purchasing Vice-President of Desron, was particularly keen that 'single source' suppliers, such as Aztec might be, outsourced their planning and control effort using ASPs:

'Getting our suppliers to use ASPs is particularly important for us. It encapsulates what we are trying to do with sole suppliers. First, we want them to use compatible systems to ensure seamless coordination of material flows between their plants and ours. Second, we don't want to get into negotiations every time we update our systems. We can do a deal with the ASPs for suppliers to update their own systems at relatively low cost at the same time as we update. Third, there needs to be far more transparency around planning decisions with our suppliers. We don't want to get into plastic injection moulding ourselves, that isn't our business, but we want to ensure as smooth a supply of parts as if their operation was an integral part of our plants.

It is difficult to understand why they are hesitating in accepting this deal. We both agree that, providing they can keep reducing costs, they will be overall more profitable and get better return on assets under the new deal. Also they will have a chance to participate in, and directly influence, our success on which they themselves ultimately depend. For example, they will be expected to take an active part in new product development so they can contribute their expertise in moulding for our mutual benefit. We are not even preventing them from dealing with other companies. I would prefer that they didn't, of course. Just coping with our increased business will be a tough job for them. But they have to understand that unless they make up their minds soon, and fully commit to the deal, we will lose patience. They are not a particularly large supplier, accounting for less than 10 per cent of our purchased parts expenditure. The Desron Group are fifty times bigger than they are, can't they see we are in a position to help them?'

Further reading

Brandenburgr, A.M. and B.J. Nalebuff (1996) *Co-opetition*, Doubleday, New York.

Child, J. and D. Faulkner (1998) *Strategies of Co-operation: Managing Alliances, Networks and Joint Ventures*, Oxford University Press, Oxford.

Evans, P. and T.S. Wurster (2000) *Blown to Bits*, Harvard Business School Press, Boston.

Ford, D.L. (1998) *Managing Business Relationships*, Wiley.

Grayson, K. and T. Ambler (1999) 'The dark side of long-term relationships in marketing services', *Journal of Marketing Research*, Vol. XXXVI, February.

Jarillo, J.C. (1993) *Strategic Networks: Creating the Borderless Organisation*, Butterworth Heinemann, Oxford.

Kaku, R. (1997) 'The path of Kyosei', *Harvard Business Review*, July–August.

Lamming, R. (1993) *Beyond Partnership: Strategies for Innovation and Lean Supply*, Prentice Hall International, UK.

Macbeth, D.K. and N. Ferguson (1994) *Partnership Sourcing: A Integrated Supply Chain Approach*, Financial Times Publishing, London.

Stuart, I., P. Deckert, D. McCutcheon and R. Kunst (1998) 'A leveraged learning network', *Sloan Management Review*, Summer.

Wood, C.H., A. Caufman and M. Merenda (1996) 'How Hadco became a problem-solving supplier', *Sloan Management Review*, Winter.

Notes on the chapter

1 Harland, C.M., R.C. Lamming and P. Cousins (1999) 'Developing the concept of supply strategy', *International Journal of Operations and Production Management*, Vol. 19, No. 7.

2 Christopher, M. (1992) *Logistics and Supply Chain Management*, Financial Times, London.

3 For example, see Ford, D.L. (1998) *Managing Business Relationships*, Wiley.

4 Sources – 'Hollywood's Fading Charms', *The Economist*, 22 March 1997; 'When companies connect', *The Economist*, 26 June 1999; Wolf, M., *The Entertainment Economy*, Penguin Books, London, 1998.

5 'A pressurised environment', *The Economist*, 13 March 1999.

6 Hayes, R. and S.C. Wheelwright (1984) *Restoring our Competitive Edge: Competing through manufacturing*, Wiley.

7 Transaction cost literature goes back to Coase, R.H. (1937) 'The nature of the firm', *Economica*, Vol. 4, pp. 386–405. More recently, it has been examined by, amongst others, Williamson, O.E. (1997) 'Transaction Cost Economics; the governance of contractual relations', *Journal of Law and Economics*, Vol. 22, pp. 233–261.

8 Von Hippel, E. (1988) *The Sources of Innovation*, Oxford University Press, New York.

9 Magaziner, I.C. and M. Patinkin (1989) 'Fast heat: how Korea won the microwave war', *Harvard Business Review*, January–February.

10 Kapoor, V. and A. Gupta (1997) 'Aggressive sourcing – a free-market approach', *Sloan Management Review*, Fall.

11 *The Economist*, 'War and peace work', 10 July 1999.

12 Parkhe, A. (1993) 'Strategic Alliance Structuring: a game theoretic and transaction cost examination of interfirm co-operation', *Academy of Management Journal*, Vol. 36, pp. 794–829.

13 Child, J. and D. Faulkner (1998) *Strategies of co-operation: Managing alliances, networks and joint ventures*, Oxford University Press, Oxford.

14 Lane, C. and R. Backmann (eds) (1998) *Trust Within and Between Organisations*, Oxford University Press, Oxford.

15 Axelrod, R. (1984) *The Evolution of Co-operation*, Basic Books, New York.

16 Axelrod, R. op. cit.

17 Several economists have discussed asset specificity. The best known is Williamson, O.E. (1985) *The Economic Institutions of Capitalism*, The Free Press, New York.

Supply network behaviour

Introduction

Having described the idea of a supply network in the last chapter, we then focused in on the types of relationship that could exist between pairs of operations in the network. In this chapter we metaphorically stand back from individual customer–supplier pairings and look at the way larger parts of a network (such as a supply 'chain' of several sequential operations) change, or are changed, over time. In doing so we will distinguish between short-term and longer-term network changes. We also need to distinguish between the behaviour of networks when acted upon by forces outside a single operation's direct control and how operations, acting alone or together with others in the network, attempt to 'manage' network behaviour. Figure 7.1 illustrates the coverage of this chapter.

Figure 7.1 Issues covered in this chapter

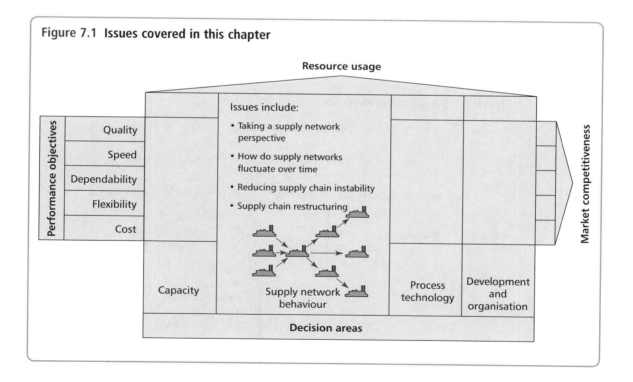

- *What are the advantages of taking a 'total supply network' perspective?*
- *Are there 'natural' dynamic behaviours which supply networks exhibit?*
- *In what way do companies try to change the nature of the supply network of which they are a part?*

Network behaviour

The essence of supply network management is that operations can derive some advantage from examining, understanding and influencing the other operations in the network of which they are a part. It is the last objective – 'influence' – that poses the greatest debate. The degree of influence that managers have over the resources that create their products and services is, to some extent, a function of how close the resources are. If they are located, say, in another division of the business, they will be managed (partly) in the interests of that division, which may not totally coincide with other parts of the business. If the resources are in a supplier's or customer's business, influencing the resources is even more difficult. The resources in customers' customers and suppliers' suppliers are several degrees more difficult to influence. Yet, if the other operations in the network are to be influenced, an essential prerequisite is that we understand the way in which they influence, and are influenced by, the

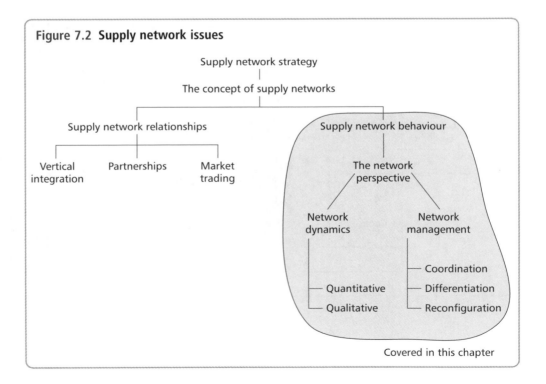

Figure 7.2 Supply network issues

dynamics of the network. And, before any understanding of network dynamics can be undertaken, it is necessary to establish the benefits of taking a perspective that takes in all (or a significant part of) the network.

All of which poses three questions.

- What are the benefits of taking a supply network perspective?
- If we cannot directly superintend the behaviour of other parts of the network, how can we understand the way they are likely to behave?
- Once we understand their likely behaviour, how can we deploy whatever influence we do have, so as to better 'manage' the behaviour of the network?

The remainder of this chapter will examine these three questions. See Figure 7.2.

A supply network perspective

We started the last chapter by taking a 'supply network perspective'. So, how does a 'perspective' help to give competitive (or general strategic) advantage to an operation? A 'perspective' does not change anything in reality. No resources are reconfigured. No markets are changed. Taking a 'network perspective' is not a decision as such, it is merely a way of seeing operations in the context of the other operations with which they interact. Yet the network perspective can be the starting point for some particularly profound and significant decisions which shape the operation, its resources and its competitive objectives. This largely explains why the topic (usually called by its supply *chain* management form) has been the focus of such management attention in recent years. The supply network perspective encourages six particularly significant aspects of operations strategy thinking which were previously under-emphasised. These are:

- It enhances understanding of competitive forces.
- It enhances understanding of cooperative forces.
- It identifies the particularly significant relationships.
- It promotes a focus on long-term issues.
- It confronts the operation with its strategic resource design options.
- It highlights the 'operation to operation' nature of business relationships.

It enhances understanding of competitive forces

Although immediate customers and immediate suppliers are the main concern for most companies, there are advantages in looking beyond these immediate contacts. When a business sees itself in the context of the whole network it may help it to understand why its customers and suppliers act as they do. Any operation has only two options if it wants to understand its ultimate customers at the end of the network. Either it can rely on all the intermediate customers and customers' customers, etc., which form the links in the network between the company and its end customers, to transmit the end customer needs efficiently back up the network, or it can take the responsibility on itself for understanding how customer–supplier relationships transmit competitive requirements through the network. Increasingly, organisations are taking the latter course. Relying exclusively on one's immediate network is seen as putting too much faith in someone else's judgement of things which are central to an organisation's own competitive health.

It enhances understanding of cooperative forces

A supply network perspective leads naturally to considering suppliers and customers, upstream and downstream respectively in the network. Because both customers and suppliers may have dealings with competitor companies, it also leads naturally to considering the role of competitors. But the perspective of identifying the role of customers, suppliers and competitors misses out a further category of companies in the supply network – 'complementors'. (The Theory Box on co-opetition takes this idea further.) Most businesses would find their lives more difficult if it were not for other businesses providing complementary services and products. For example, Internet-based B2C (business to consumer) retailers depend on 'order fulfilment' delivery companies, DVD player manufacturers depend on pre-recorded movies sold and rented in DVD format, vehicle manufacturers depend on financial service companies to make the loans which allow customers to buy their cars, hot-dog manufacturers depend on mustard makers, and so on. Without making efforts to ensure complementary companies in the supply network, a company may find it difficult to thrive, or even fail completely. The much quoted example of this is the Sony Betamax video cassette recorder which, although in many ways better than the VHS system which won out in the marketplace, was handicapped partly by the lack of rental movies in the Betamax format.

Theory Box | **Co-opetition and the value net[1]**

In the previous chapter we demonstrated how game theory can be used to understand some aspects of the relationships between players in a supply network. Professors Brandenburger and Nalebuff also take a game theory approach to understanding business networks, concentrating on the nature of the players in the network 'game', the way they add value, and the rules, tactics and scope of such games. From an operations strategy view, it is their view of network players and their roles that is of interest. Figure 7.3 illustrates what they call the 'value net' for a company. It sees any company as being surrounded by four types of players: suppliers, customers, competitors and complementors.

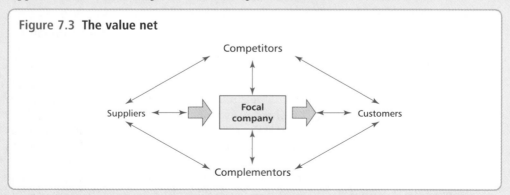

Figure 7.3 The value net

They make a number of points about the role and relationships of these players.

- Complementors enable customers to value your product or service more when they have their product and service as opposed to when they have yours alone. Competitors are the opposite, they make customers value your product or service less when they can have their product or service, rather than yours alone.

- Competitors can also be complementors and vice versa. For example, adjacent restaurants may see themselves as competitors for customers' business. A customer standing outside and wanting a meal will choose between the two of them. Yet in another way they are complementors. Would that customer have come to this part of town unless there was more than one restaurant for him or her to choose between? Restaurants, theatres, art galleries, tourist attractions generally, all cluster together in a form of cooperation to increase the total size of their joint market. It is important to distinguish between the way companies cooperate in increasing the total size of a market and the way in which they then compete for a share of that market.

- Customers and suppliers have 'symmetric' roles. Historically, insufficient emphasis has been put on the role of the supplier. Harnessing the value of suppliers is just as important as listening to the needs of customers. Destroying value in a supplier in order to create it in a customer does not increase the value of the network as a whole. For example, pressurising suppliers because customers are pressurising you will not add long-term value. In the long term it creates value for the total network to find ways of increasing value for suppliers as well as customers.

- All the players in the network, whether they be customers, suppliers, competitors or complementors, can be both friends and enemies at different times. This is not 'unusual' or 'aberrant' behaviour. It is the way things are. The term that Brandenburger and Nalebuff use to capture this idea is 'co-opetition'.

It identifies the particularly significant relationships

The key to understanding supply networks lies in identifying the parts of the network that contribute to those performance objectives valued by end customers. Any analysis of networks must start therefore with an understanding of what constitutes competitive performance at the 'downstream' end of the network. This helps to identify the parts of the network that contribute most to satisfy end customer requirements. This analysis will probably show that (the various) links in the network will contribute something; but not all contributions will be equally significant. Even if each part of the network understands what is important, not every part of the network is necessarily in a position to do something about it. For example, the important end customers for some types of automotive are the installers and service companies who deal directly with end consumers. They are supplied by 'stockholders' whose competitive success relies on a combination of price, range and, above all, a high availability of supply. That means having all parts in stock and delivering them fast. Suppliers of parts to the stockholders can best contribute to their customers' competitiveness partly by offering a short delivery lead-time but mainly through dependable delivery. The key players here are the stockholders. Without effective service levels and competitive prices from them, the end customers will not be as likely to buy the products of the parts manufacturer. The best way of winning end-customer business is by helping the key players in the network, in this case by giving them prompt delivery which helps keep costs down while providing high availability of parts.

It promotes a focus on long-term issues

There are times when circumstances make some parts of a supply network weaker than their adjacent links. A major plant breakdown, for example, or a labour dispute, might disrupt an operation. How then should its immediate customers and suppliers react? Should they exploit the weakness as a legitimate move to enhance their own competitive position or should they ignore the opportunity, tolerate the problems, and hope the customer or supplier will eventually recover? Sometimes short-term adversarial opportunities seem too good to miss, and short-term issues too pressing to give thought to how the total supply network is being affected. However, a longer-term view would be to weigh the relative advantages to be gained from assisting or replacing the weak link. Similarly, when considering investment decisions, an operation will look at its current, and likely future, levels of demand. When the operation's 'vision' is restricted to its immediate customers, the overall industry dynamics shaping demand may not be obvious. Extending the operation's vision to include its total supply network will sensitise the operation to trends in parts of the network which may take time to work through to its own level in the industry. A routinely established habit of considering all external relationships as part of the total supply network is not a guarantee of long-term self-interest or an antidote to short-termism, but it does help.

Dell's perishable products[2]

It has become a famous story. Michael Dell, a biology student at the University of Texas at Austin, had a side-line in buying up unused stock of PCs from local dealers, adding components, and re-selling the now higher-specification machines to local businesses. The side-line grew to over $50,000 per month. He quit university and founded a computer company which was to revolutionise the industry's supply network management. Entering the personal computer market in 1984, Dell realised that there was little point in trying to develop all the components for his computers himself. It was too expensive and too cumbersome a business. Better to make good contacts with specialist component manufacturers and take the best of what was available in the market. Dell says that his commitment to outsourcing was always done for the most positive of reasons. '*Outsourcing, at least in the IT world, is almost always a way to get rid of a problem a company hasn't been able to solve itself . . . that's not what we're doing at all. We focus on how we can coordinate our activities to create the most value for customers.*' While Dell insist that their suppliers maintain a quality, price and innovation edge, they do see them as partners (see partnership relationship described in the previous chapter), a point emphasised by Michael Dell: '*When we launch a new product, their engineers are stationed right in our plants. If a customer calls up with a problem, we'll stop shipping product while they fix design flaws in real time.*' With a neat symmetry, the technology that Dell produces has enhanced the economic incentive to collaborate with suppliers. They can share design and performance databases with suppliers, enabling them to shorten product development times.

In Dell's early days this kind of thinking was revolutionary in the computer industry. But Dell also applied it to the demand side of their business. Seeking ways to undercut their rivals, Dell started to sell its computers direct to its customers, bypassing retailers. This allowed the company to cut out the retailer's (often considerable) margin, which in turn allowed Dell to offer lower prices. However, the move was controversial. Computers are complex purchases, it was argued, customers need to have their hands held while they are making up their minds, they won't buy a product they can't see and touch. Time, though, was on Dell's side. Corporate customers (Dell's main market) were becoming more sophisticated and needed less of the type of support that compensated for their own lack of product familiarity. Even domestic consumers needed less hand holding. But cutting out the link in the supply network between them and the customer also had two other huge benefits. First, it offered an opportunity for Dell to get to know their customers' needs far more intimately. At the simplest level, this allows them to forecast based on the thousands of customer contact calls they receive every hour. In a longer-term sense, it allows them to talk with customers about what they really want from their machines. In this way design decisions are made in an environment of realistic customer awareness. The second advantage of Dell's direct sales model is that it cuts the time taken for components to move from suppliers through the supply chain to the end customer; this reduced Dell's level of inventory to under 10 days' worth, as opposed to over 80 days for some competitors. Preventing its computers from languishing on shelves waiting to be sold is particularly important when 80 per cent of the cost of the computer is in its components, and those components are falling in price by around 30 per cent a year. In effect, the product is perishable. Its value is deteriorating over time. But because Dell is shifting its computers through the supply chain faster than its rivals, less value is lost. This gives Dell a significant cost advantage. In 1996, when the price of memory chips (about 20 per cent of a PC's cost) dropped by three-quarters, Dell is reckoned to have achieved almost a 10 per cent cost saving.

It confronts the operation with its strategic resource options

A supply network perspective illustrates to any operation exactly where it is positioned in its network. It also, therefore, highlights where it is **not**. That is, it clearly delineates between the activities which are being performed by itself and those which are being performed by other operations in the network. This prompts the question of why the operations boundaries are exactly where they are. Should the operation extend its direct control over a greater part of the network through vertical integration? Alternatively (and more likely in the past few years), should it outsource some of its activities to specialist suppliers? Furthermore, should it encourage particular patterns of relationships in other parts of the network? Again, it is the network perspective that raises the questions: and sometimes helps to answer them. For example, Dell's (see box) consideration of its options helped it to develop its superior supply network configuration.

It highlights the 'operation to operation' nature of business relationships

Finally we come to what may be the most far-reaching implication of a supply network perspective. It concerns the nature of the relationships between the various businesses in the network. Traditionally these relationships have been seen as 'customer–supplier' relationships. There is clearly little new in studying customer–supplier relationships. Organisations have always been concerned to do profitable business with their customers and ensure effective supply from their suppliers. What is new in the way supply networks are now treated is that rather than conceptualising the relationship as 'doing business' with customers and suppliers, we are concerned with the 'flow of goods and services' between operations. That is, the analysis is brought to the level of exactly *what* is flowing between operations and *how* the flow is managed. Look at any supply network and the vast majority of businesses represented in it have other businesses as their customers rather than end customers. Not that the end customer is unimportant. On the contrary, end customers are the *raison d'être* of the whole network. But behind each business serving the end customer is a whole network of other businesses. Each of these businesses has an operation which depends for its effectiveness on the supply of goods and services from other operations. In other words, to the end customer, it is the chain of operations lying behind the one they can see that is important. For that chain of operations the important questions are not 'How can I sell to my customer?' and 'How can I get supplies from my supplier?' Rather the questions should be 'How can my operation help my customer's operation to be more effective?' and 'How can my supplier's operation help my operation to be more effective?'

The implications of this are important. For the whole supply chain to operate effectively, the chain of operations must interface effectively with each other. For that to happen each operation in the network must understand the nature of their suppliers' and their customers' *operations*. After all, how can any company sell goods and services to a customer when it doesn't fully understand how it can make that customer's life easier? Similarly, how can any operation help its suppliers to supply more effectively if it doesn't understand the nature of its supplier's operations? This implies a very significant reorientation in the mindsets of the people in the organisation who have not traditionally seen themselves as requiring operations management knowledge.

Network dynamics

Supply chains are often referred to as pipelines of product (and sometimes service) flow. The image of a pipeline, though, is somewhat misleading. Pipelines are supposed to carry liquid at a reasonably ordered and constant rate. Supply chains rarely do, even when they are supposed to. This is because supply chains have their own dynamic behaviour patterns which tend to distort the smooth flow of information up the chain and product moving down the chain. In practice, flow in supply chains can be turbulent, with the activity levels in each part of the chain differing significantly and the flow of products, services and information varying, even when demand at the end of the chain is relatively stable. Small changes in one part of the chain can cause seemingly erratic behaviour in other parts. This phenomenon is known as 'supply chain amplification', 'supply chain distortion', 'the Forrester effect'[3] (after the person who first modelled it), or most descriptively 'the bull whip effect'. Whatever it is called, it is important to understand it, for although it is essentially a short-term phenomenon, the measures that operations try to put in place in order to deal with it have more strategic implications.

For convenience we shall examine the underlying causes of supply chain behaviour in terms of their

● quantitative behaviour, and
● qualitative behaviour.

Quantitative supply chain behaviour

Often the flow of goods and services between operations in a supply network is managed by having physical inventories of items at points in the network to absorb short-term imbalance between supply and demand. That is the purpose of inventories. If demand and supply between adjacent operations in a network were perfectly synchronised in terms of specification and timing, goods and services would

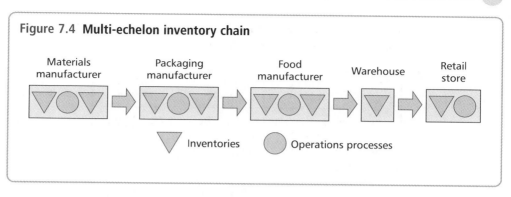

Figure 7.4 **Multi-echelon inventory chain**

flow smoothly through the network, pausing only to receive value-adding processing. Inventories help supply networks to overcome the lack of such perfect synchronicity. Figure 7.4 illustrates a chain of operations in a network where the focal company is a food manufacturer, showing all the main inventories (but not the several in-process inventories within the manufacturing operations). Even in this simple illustration there are eight interconnected inventory systems. The second-tier supplier's (material producer's) inventories will feed the first-tier supplier's (packaging producer's) inventories, who will in turn supply the main operation. After the products have been manufactured they are distributed to local warehouses from where they are shipped to the retail stores. Such networks are said to have *multi-echelon inventory systems*. They are common, particularly in consumer goods networks.

Supply chain dynamics

Multi-echelon supply chains do have an 'uncoupling' effect on the operations they connect, which has some advantages for each individual operation's efficiency. Unfortunately, they also introduce an 'elasticity' into the chain which often dramatically limits the effectiveness of the chain as a whole. This is largely because of the errors and distortions which are introduced to decision making in the chain. Not that the managers of each individual operation are acting irrationally. On the contrary, in fact the main cause is a perfectly understandable and rational desire by the different links in the supply chain to manage their product rates and inventory levels sensibly. To demonstrate this, examine the production rate and stock levels for the supply chain shown in Figure 7.5. This is a four-stage supply chain where an original equipment manufacturer (OEM) is served by three tiers of suppliers. The demand from the OEM's market has been running at a rate of 100 items per period, but in period 2 demand reduces to 95 items per period. All stages in the supply chain work on the principle that they will keep in stock one period's demand. This is a simplification but not a gross one. Many operations gear their inventory levels to their demand rate. The column headed 'stock' for each level of supply shows the starting stock at the beginning of the period and the finished stock at the end of the period. At the beginning of period 2 the OEM has 100 units in stock (that being the rate of demand up to period 2). Demand in period 2 is 95 and so the OEM knows that it would need to produce sufficient items to finish up at the end of the period with 95 in stock (this being the new demand rate). To do this it only needs manufacture 90 items; this, together with five items taken out of the starting stock, will supply demand and leave a finished stock of 95 items. The beginning of period 3 finds the

Figure 7.5 Fluctuations of production levels along supply chain in response to small change in end-customer demand

Period	Third-tier supplier		Second-tier supplier		First-tier supplier		Original equipment mfg.		Demand
	Prodn.	Stock	Prodn.	Stock	Prodn.	Stock	Prodn.	Stock	
1	100	100 100	100	100 100	100	100 100	100	100 100	100
2	20	100 60	60	100 80	80	100 90	90	100 95	95
3	180	60 120	120	80 100	100	90 95	95	95 95	95
4	60	120 90	90	100 95	95	95 95	95	95 95	95
5	100	90 95	95	95 95	95	95 95	95	95 95	95
6	95	95 95	95	95 95	95	95 95	95	95 95	95

Orders   Orders   Orders   Orders

[3]   [2]   [1]   [OEM]   ✶ Market ✶

Items   Items   Items   Items

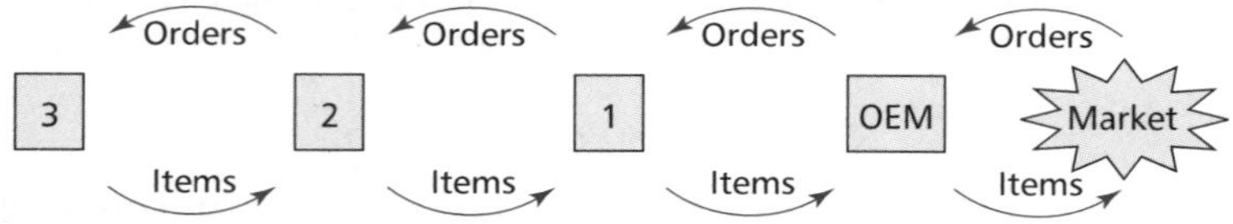

(Note – all operations keep one period's inventory)
Source: Reproduced from Slack *et al.* (2001) *Operations Management,* 3rd edn, Financial Times-Prentice Hall.

OEM with 95 items in stock. Demand is also 95 items and therefore its production rate to maintain a stock level of 95 will be 95 items per period. The OEM now operates at a steady rate of producing 95 items per period. Note, however, that a change in demand of only five items has produced a fluctuation of ten items in the OEM's production rate.

Now carry the same logic through to the first-tier supplier. At the beginning of period 2 the second-tier supplier has 100 items in stock. The demand which it has to supply in period 2 is derived from the production rate of the OEM. This has dropped down to 90 in period 2. The first-tier supplier, therefore, has to produce sufficient to supply the demand of 90 items (or the equivalent) and leave one month's demand (now 90 items) as its finished stock. A production rate of 80 items per month will achieve this. It will therefore start period 3 with an opening stock of 90 items but the demand from the OEM has now risen to 95 items. It therefore has to produce sufficient to fulfil this demand of 95 items and leave 95 items in stock. To do this it must produce 100 items in period 3. After period 3 the first-tier supplier then resumes a steady state, producing 95 items per month. Note again, however, that the fluctuation has been even higher than that in the OEM's production rate, decreasing to 80 items per period, increasing to 100 items per period, and then achieving a steady rate of 95 items per period.

This logic can be extended right back to the third-tier supplier. If you do this you will notice that the further back up the supply chain an operation is placed the more drastic are the fluctuations caused by the relatively small change in demand from the final customer. In this simple case the decision of how much to produce each month was governed by the following relationship:

Total available for sale in any period = Total required in the same period

Starting stock + production rate = Demand + closing stock

Starting stock + production rate = 2 × demand (because closing stock must be equal to demand)

Production rate = 2 × demand − starting stock

Music to customers' ears

The idea of the impresario has always been prominent in the music industry. Seeing an opportunity, bringing artists together, and managing the whole into a saleable package is the business that lies behind all live musical performance. But perhaps the greater impresarios are the giant record companies, such as Warner, Sony, Polygram and EMI. Like the live music impresarios, their job is to understand the nature of commercial opportunity and encourage and bring together the various elements that make a commercially successful recorded product. Song writers, singers, the backing instrumentalists, other artists, the engineers and producers who mix the final sound, are all essential parts of the mix. At one time the recording companies employed all of these people on a salary or contract basis. Now most work freelance, with the exception of the major headline artists themselves, who usually have exclusive recording contracts with one company. But the nature of this 'supply side' to the record business has changed over time. Most obviously, many of the individual elements in the mix have merged. Singer/songwriters accompanying themselves are now the norm, although it would have been very unusual in the early days of the recording business. Artists, especially those with firm views on artistic control, then became involved in the producing and engineering of their own recordings. This has been considerably facilitated by reductions in the size and cost of recording equipment, the 'process technology' of the music business. More recently it is the engineers and producers themselves who dominate the supply side. Using samples, almost as commodity supplies, they create the final track.

The changes on the demand side of the business, however, are likely to be more dramatic and will certainly happen faster. After a recording had been made, the recording company would use a 'master' to manufacture a physical product: discs or tapes. They may, or may not, own the factories that actually made the products, but they certainly would manage the process of physically distributing the products through to the retail stores where the products were eventually sold to consumers. Then came the Internet. Using fast connections and the MP3 (Mpeg 1 layer 3) software program, music, often pirated, could be downloaded onto consumers' computers to a quality level almost as good as that of CDs. This development terrified the music industry and started a debate which pitched the intellectual property rights of artists, and the profits of record companies, against what many saw as the democratisation of music. No one knew how much impact the Internet would have on the music business. It made the ordering of conventional CDs more convenient in the same way that Amazon.com had in the book industry. This, however, was a threat to record stores. It also made it easier to allow the customisation of individual CDs, which could then be sent to consumers. This was a threat to the companies that distribute standard products as well as the stores that sold them. If copyright and profits could be protected, record companies could perhaps allow customers to pay for and download their music directly, but this was a threat to the disc manufacturers. With the advent of small, but sophisticated, recording technology it allowed artists to record their own music and sell it directly over the net. Could this wipe out the whole business?

Qualitative supply chain behaviour

The example in Figure 7.5 limited itself to one aspect of the quantitative effect of supply chain dynamics. But the causes of supply chain fluctuation are also caused by more qualitative issues. These are concerned with how links within their chain perceive each other's requirements and behaviour. At each link in the supply chain, there is the potential for misunderstandings and misinterpretation both of what each operation wants and how each is seen to be performing. If a supplier does not have full understanding of its customer's needs it is unlikely to be serving that customer satisfactorily. Furthermore, it may not be able to make the logical association between how it should be serving its customers and, therefore, what demands it should be placing on its own suppliers. There are three logical links which have to be correctly executed:

- understanding customer's needs correctly;
- understanding the association between what an operation's customers need and therefore what its suppliers should be providing;
- ensuring that suppliers really do understand what is required.

These three links represent the information specifying market requirements flowing back up the supply chain. For the chain to be working effectively it is also necessary to ensure that the performance of each part of the chain is monitored. Again, any operation in the chain can identify three logical links which must be in place for effective supply chain performance monitoring:

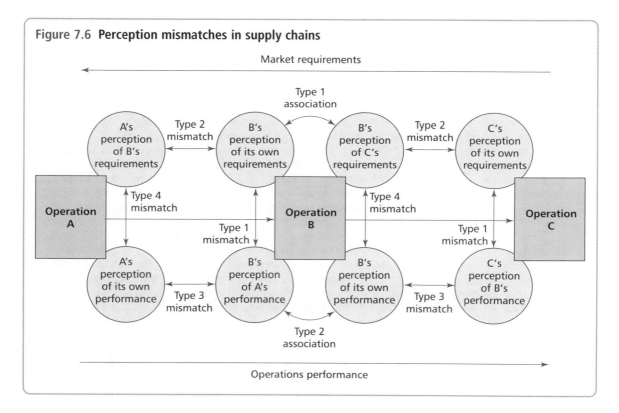

Figure 7.6 Perception mismatches in supply chains

- Suppliers understand how they are performing.
- The operation itself understands the association between its supplier's performance and its ability to serve its own customers.
- The operation is correctly interpreting its customer's view of its own performance.

In a research study, which tracked the perceptions of supply chains providing spare parts, Harland[4] investigated this issue and identified four types of mismatch which can occur between and within each stage in a supply chain. Figure 7.6 shows these mismatches based on Harland's terminology.

- A Type 1 mismatch is that between what a customer believes its needs to be and what it sees itself as getting from its supplier. This is the most serious of the potential mismatches if the customer's perception of its supplier's performance falls below what it believes its own requirements to be.
- A Type 2 mismatch is essentially a gap between the perception of what a supplier believes its customer wants and what its customer really does believe it wants. It is a market positioning mismatch, which could occur because of a lack of understanding between A's sales and marketing function and B's purchasing function.
- A Type 3 mismatch is the gap between a supplier's view of its own performance and how its customer views its performance. A may believe that it is performing well enough while B, in reality, is either wanting different things from its supplier or, alternatively, has different standards against which it is assessing A's performance.
- A Type 4 mismatch shows how a supplier rates its own performance against what it believes its customer to want. Significant gaps here should be driving the supplier's own operations improvement programmes.

When extended to a supply chain, as shown in Figure 7.6, as opposed to a simple customer–supplier pairing, two further linkages are worth considering. These are shown on the diagram as a Type 1 association and Type 2 association.

- A Type 1 association is the link an operation makes between how it is served by its supplier and what it believes its customer wants. A strong association means that the supply relationship significantly affects an operation's ability to serve its customers. It is a measure of the degree of fit between its supply strategy and its overall operations strategy.
- A Type 2 association is the link between how an operation is, in reality, served by its supplier and how it is capable of serving its own customer. It is a measure of the extent to which an operation's competitive success or failure can be explained by its supplier's performance. It also dictates the approach an operation could take to developing its supply strategy.

Table 7.1 pursues the analysis from the viewpoint of operation B – the focal operation. Of course, one could extend it to look further into suppliers and customers. So, for example, it may be useful to understand the Type 1 mismatch in the customer's operation. That, after all, will be shaping their view of us as a supplier. Similarly, one might investigate the Type 4 mismatch in a supplier. This would tell us the extent to which problems with supply are a result of their operation's failure rather than requirement or performance misunderstandings.

This type of analysis highlights some obvious questions with which an operation

Table 7.1 Understanding the qualitative dynamics of supply chains

Gaps	Definition	What it indicates	Questions to ask
Type 1 **Association** *Supply strategy*	The association between what an operation believes its customer wants and what it believes it needs from its supplier.	The significance of a supply relationship for competitive success.	What are the key competitive factors for our customers? Which of these rely on our supplier's performance?
Type 2 **Association** *Supply development*	The association between how an operation views its own performance and how it views the performance of its suppliers.	The effectiveness of a supplier relationship on competitive success.	What have been our competitive successes and failures? To what extent were our competitive successes and failures the result of supplier performance?
Type 1 **Mismatch** *The supplier improvement gap*	The gap between our view of our own requirements and our view of our supplier's performance.	Prioritisation for supplier development.	What do we need from our suppliers? What are we getting from our suppliers? What are the main gaps?
Type 2 **Mismatch** *The market positioning gap*	The gap between what we believe we need from our suppliers and what they think we need.	The perceived differences in requirements between customers and suppliers.	Can we be sure that our assumptions concerning our customer's needs and priorities are correct? Can we be sure that our suppliers have the correct assumptions regarding our needs and priorities?
Type 3 **Mismatch** *The operations performance gap*	The gap between how we see our supplier's performance and how they see their own performance.	The differences in perception of operations performance between customers and suppliers (objective performance could be different from both).	Can we be sure that our customers see our performance in the same way that we do? Can we be sure that our suppliers judge their own performance in the same way that we do?
Type 4 **Mismatch** *The operations improvement gap*	The gap between our perception of what our customers want and our perception of our own performance.	The differences between an internal perception of performance and an internal perception of customers' requirements.	Even assuming our perception of customers' needs and their view of our performance are correct, are we meeting our customers' requirements?

can assess its own supply chain performance. Here it is enough to point out that, even in the simple three-stage supply chain shown in Figure 7.4, there are ample opportunities for gaps to exist between market requirements and operations performance within the chain. And every time there is a gap between the perceptions of customers and suppliers, and every time there is a failure within an operation to understand the associations between its supply-side and demand-side requirements and performance, information is distorted. This distortion can lead to operations developing their resources inappropriately. Investments may be made, systems and processes designed, and operations strategies formed which inhibit the effective integration of the operation within its network. In fact one can view the cumulative effect of these gaps up and down a supply chain as being the qualitative equivalent of the bullwhip effect discussed earlier. Mistaken perceptions in any part of the chain can become amplified as they are further distorted by the mis-communications and perception gaps between other operations in the chain.

Supply chain instability

Put together these qualitative 'perception dynamics' of Figure 7.6 with the quantitative dynamics shown in Figure 7.5 and it is easy to understand why supply chains are rarely stable. Figure 7.7 shows the fluctuations in orders over time in a typical consumer goods chain. One can see that fluctuations in order levels (the demand at the preceding operation) increase in scale and unpredictability the further back an

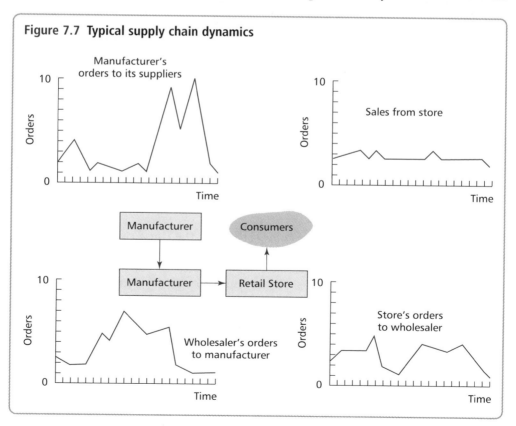

Figure 7.7 Typical supply chain dynamics

operation is in the chain. Relatively small changes in consumer demand can, if not checked, cause wild and disruptive activity swings at the first-tier supplier. While Figure 7.7 only shows the quantitative fluctuations in each stage of the chain, these can be caused by both conventional 'bullwhip' distortions and qualitative perceptual distortions. For example, if a perception gap causes an incorrect or mis-timed order to be delivered, the supplying operation may have to step up its rate of activity to compensate for its incorrect delivery. This will have knock-on effects both up and down the chain.

Aluminium can[5]

Aluminium is the most plentiful metal in the world. It is also strong and light. This makes it ideal for applications from jumbo jet bodies to drink cans and from high-speed trains to high-speed ferries. But aluminium faces two big problems in its battle with other materials, whether they be conventional steel or high-tech polymers. First, it is expensive. Aluminium is difficult to extract and requires large amounts of energy. Electricity can make up 30 per cent of the production costs for aluminium. However, because it is lighter than steel, less is needed. Aluminium prices have also been falling to the point where it becomes attractive even for car bodies. The automobile industry is the prize market for aluminium companies. That is where serious volumes could be generated. This leads to the second problem with aluminium – its price fluctuates, sometimes wildly, on the commodity markets. This causes instability in aluminium supply chains. For the aluminium producers at the upstream end of the supply chain, where the fluctuations are at their wildest, this is serious. It led to what the industry hopes will be a ground-breaking 10-year supply agreement between Alcan (the second largest aluminium company) and General Motors. The multi-billion-dollar agreement guarantees General Motors a fixed supply and (most important) stable price for its aluminium, in effect hedging the risk of price fluctuations over the period. In a further bid to ensure stability, Alcan also finalised an innovative 'operational stability' agreement with its unions which promised no strikes for 18 years.

Causes of supply chain instability

Again, bringing both quantitative and qualitative effects together, four major causes of this type of supply chain behaviour can be identified.[6] These are demand forecast updating, order batching, price fluctuation, and rationing and shortage gaming. The common element in all these causes of supply chain dynamics is that the nature, or quantity, of the orders placed on a supplier does not, in reality, reflect the nature and quantity of demand.

- *Demand forecast updating* – this was the cause of the dynamics which were illustrated in Figure 7.5. The order sent to the previous operation in the chain is a function of the demand it receives from its own customers, plus the amount needed to replenish its inventory levels. Inventory levels are, in turn, partly a function of that period's demand. In effect, the view an operation holds about future demand is being changed every decision period.

- *Order batching* – every time a supermarket sells a box of breakfast cereal it does not order a replacement from its suppliers. Rather it waits until it needs to order a sufficient quantity to make the order administration, transport, etc. economic. This batching effect may be exaggerated further when many customers batch their orders simultaneously. For example, many computer-based stock systems place orders at the beginning or at the end of each month. The effect on the supplier may be that although consumption of the products it supplies to consumers may be steady, the orders it receives are all concentrated at the end/beginning of the month.

● *Price fluctuation* – businesses often use the price mechanism in the short term to increase sales. Special offers 'for a limited time only' are not confined to the retail end of a chain. The same thing happens among manufacturers and distributors. Wherever it occurs, the result of price promotions is the same: customers place orders for quantities of goods that do not correspond to their immediate needs. They will 'forward buy' while the price is cheap and then order nothing in the immediate aftermath of the promotion. Artificially inducing distortions into the supply chain in this way has been called the 'dumbest marketing ploy ever' in a now famous *Fortune* magazine article.[7]

● *Rationing and shortage gaming* – this cause of supply chain distortion occurs when demand exceeds supply. Under such circumstances, a supplier may ration supplies to its customers. For example, it might allocate a fixed proportion of each customer's orders for delivery to them. Of course, if the customer is aware that this is happening, it is in their interests to place a larger order in the hope that they will still get what they need, even after the order has been rationed down. This has the effect of killing the supplying operation's marketing information. It can no longer distinguish between what its customers really need and what they are ordering in order to obtain supplies. If the supplier's planning is then based on these exaggerated orders, it will find itself moving from shortage to glut as soon as short-term demand is satisfied. This effect can be observed in the toy industry after almost every Christmas season. Whatever had been the 'hot' toy, and consequently difficult to get hold of before Christmas, is in embarrassing over-supply by the end of January – which makes it less desirable anyway.

Network management

Operations spend most of their supply chain effort in trying to overcome the worst effects of the supply chain dynamics described in the last section. While the first step in doing this is clearly to understand the nature of these dynamics, there are several, more proactive, actions which operations take. Here we classify these as follows.

● *Coordination activities* – efforts to synchronise supply chain behaviour and improve its throughput efficiency.

● *Differentiation activities* – efforts to ensure that supply chain policies are appropriate for the way different products and services are competing.

● *Reconfiguration activities* – changing the stages in a supply network or the relationship between them.

Coordination

Efforts to coordinate supply chain activity have been described as falling into three categories.[8]

● *Information sharing* – demand information, not just from immediate customers, is transmitted up the chain so that all the operations can monitor true demand, free of the normal distortions. Information regarding supply problems, or shortages, may also be transmitted down the line so that downstream customers can modify their schedules and sales plans accordingly.

- *Channel alignment* – this is the adjustment of scheduling, material movements, pricing and other sales strategies, and stock levels to bring them into line with each other.

- *Operational efficiency* – each operation in the chain can reduce the complexity of its operations, reduce costs and increase throughput time. The cumulative effect of these individual activities is to simplify throughput in the whole chain.

Table 7.2 illustrates some of the individual activities which address the four causes of supply chain instability discussed earlier.

Table 7.2 Coordinating mechanisms for reducing supply chain dynamic instability[10]

Causes of supply chain instability	Supply chain coordination activities		
	Information sharing	Channel alignment	Operational efficiency
Demand forecast update	• Understanding system dynamics • Use of point-of-sale (POS) data • Electronic data interchange (EDI) • Internet • Computer-assisted ordering (CAO)	• Vendor-managed inventory (VMI) • Discount for information sharing • Consumer direct	• Lead-time reduction • Echelon-based inventory control
Order batching	• EDI • Internet ordering	• Discount for truck-load assortment • Delivery appointments • Consolidation • Logistics out-sourcing	• Reduction in fixed cost of ordering by EDI or electronic commerce • CAO
Price fluctuations		• Continuous replenishment programme (CPR) • Everyday low cost (EDLC)	• Everyday low price (EDLP) • Activity-based costing (ABC)
Shortage gaming	• Sharing sales, capacity, and inventory data	• Allocation based on past sales	

(Adapted from Lee, H.L. *et al.* (1997) 'The Bullwhip Effect in Supply Chains', *Sloan Management Review,* Spring.)

Automotive system suppliers[9]

Take a look at the front part of a car. Just the very front part, that is. The bit with the bumper, radiator grill, fog lights, side-lights, badge and so on. At one time each of these components came from different specialist suppliers. Now the whole of this 'module' is likely to come from one 'system supplier'. Traditional car makers are getting smaller and are relying on system suppliers such as TRW in the US, Bosch in Germany and Magna in Canada to provide them with whole chunks of car. Some of these system suppliers are global players that rival the car makers themselves in scope and reach. Typical is Magna. Based in Canada, it has more than 40,000 employees throughout the US, Canada, Mexico, Brazil and China, making everything from bumper/grill sub-assemblies for Honda, GM and DaimlerChrysler, instrument panels for the Jaguar XK8 and metal-body exteriors for the BMW Z3 sports car. Magna, like the other system suppliers, has benefited from this shift in car maker supply strategy, which was accelerated during the recession of the early 1990s. Cost pressures forced car makers to let their suppliers take more responsibility for engineering and pre-assembly. It also meant them working with fewer suppliers. In Ford's European operations, their Escort model took parts from around 700 direct suppliers, while the newer Focus model used only 210. Future models may have under 100 direct suppliers. A smaller number of direct suppliers also makes joint development easier. For example, Volvo, which places a heavy emphasis on safety, paired up with Autoliv to develop safety systems incorporating side airbags. In return for their support Volvo got exclusive rights to use the systems for the first year. A smaller number of system suppliers also makes it easier to update components. While a car maker may not find it economic to change its seating systems more than once every seven or eight years, a specialist supplier could have several alternative types of seat in parallel development at any one time.

Differentiation

The concept of 'fit', meaning strategic alignment, is one of the fundamental principles of operations strategy, as we described in Chapter 2. It applies to supply networks as much as it does to the individual operations within them. In its supply network (or more accurately in this case, supply chain) context the principle of fit means differentiating between different market requirements in the way that they are served by the operation's resources within the supply chain. Put simply, supply chains, just like operations, need to ask, 'How do we compete?'. If the answer turns out to be, 'We compete in different ways in different parts of the market', then the supply chains serving those markets need to be organised in different ways. By contrast, if a supply chain is organised in a standardised manner, notwithstanding the different market needs it is serving, there will be considerable scope for the quantitative and (especially) qualitative distortions described previously. Here we will take an approach articulated by Marshall Fisher of Wharton Business School,[11] who makes a connection between different types of market requirements and different objectives for operations resources.

Different market requirements

A fundamental point, made in Part I of this book, was that market requirements differ. Even operations producing one set of products and services may find themselves serving markets with different needs. For example, Volvo GM Heavy Truck Corporation, which sells commercial trucks and spare parts throughout the United States, found itself with a combination of poor service levels, caused through stock-outs of critical parts, at the same time as its inventory levels were growing at an unacceptable rate. Market analysis revealed that spare parts were being used in two very different situations. Scheduled maintenance was predictable to the extent that spare parts were ordered well ahead of time. Emergency repairs, however, were far more difficult to predict and needed spare parts instantly. The fact that the parts are identical is irrelevant. The issue is that they are serving two different markets with different characteristics. It is a simple idea and it applies in many industries. Chocolate manufacturers have their stable lines but also produce 'media related' specials which may last only a matter of months. Garment manufacturers produce classics, which change little over the years, as well as fashions that last only one or two seasons. In both cases the demand for the former is relatively stable and predictable, whereas the demand for the latter is far less predictable. Furthermore, the price (and the margin) commanded by the innovative fashion product is likely to be higher than the more functional product. However, the innovative product may have to be heavily discounted once it becomes less attractive in the market. The important issue here, however, is that the different types of markets will need serving in different ways by their supply chains.

Different resource objectives

The design and management of supply chains involves attempting to satisfy two broad objectives – speed and cost. Speed means being responsive to customer demand within the chain. Its virtue lies in the ability it gives the chain to keep customer service high even under conditions of fluctuating or unpredictable demand. Of course, speed also contributes to keeping costs down. Fast throughput in the supply chain means that products do not hang around in stock and, therefore, the chain consumes little working capital. Other contributors to keeping costs down include keeping the processes, especially manufacturing processes, well utilised.

Figure 7.8 illustrates two supply networks, structurally identical, but organised in different ways. The top network is designed for low cost. Inventories are kept low, especially in the downstream parts of the network, so as to maintain fast throughput and low working capital. The inventory in the network is concentrated primarily in the manufacturing operation, where it can help to keep utilisation high and manufacturing costs low. The predominant flow of products and information occurs up and down the chain. Information must flow quickly from the outlets to the manufacturer and supplier so that their schedules can be given the maximum amount of time to adjust efficiently. Products then flow as quickly as possible down the chain to replenish what little stocks are kept in the downstream outlets.

By contrast, the lower network is organised for high service levels and responsive supply to the end customer. The inventory in the network is deployed as close to the customer as possible, so as to cope with what may be dramatic changes in customer demand. Of course, fast throughput from the upstream parts of the network is still needed to replenish the downstream stocks, but it would not be sufficient in itself to give a high enough level of end customer availability. Again, although products and information will flow up and down the network, it is also important to ensure flow across the downstream part of the network. So, for example, if stock-outs occur in one of the outlets it may be faster to transfer product from other outlets to where it is needed. This is why some retail stores invest in information systems which allow them to check whether one location has a product in stock which another location has temporarily run out of.

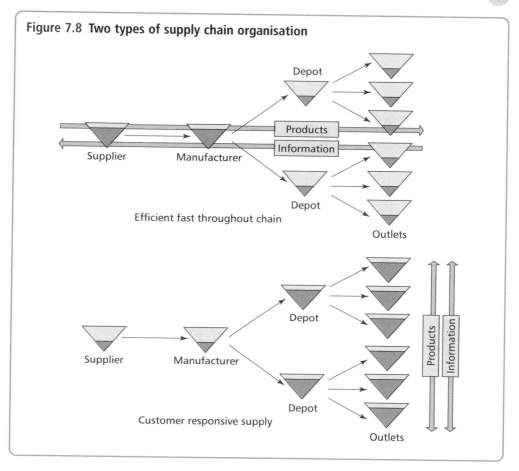

Figure 7.8 Two types of supply chain organisation

Efficient fast throughout chain

Customer responsive supply

Achieving fit between market requirements and supply chain resource policies

Professor Marshall Fisher's advice to companies reviewing their own supply chain policies is, first, to determine whether their products are functional or innovative, second, to decide whether their supply chain is efficient or responsive, and third, to plot the position of the nature of their demand and their supply chain priorities on a matrix similar to that shown in Figure 7.9. Ideally, the company's supply chain policies should match with its dominant market requirements.

Useful though this kind of analysis is, it does pose two questions.

● Does it imply that market requirements are either predominantly functional or predominantly innovative? That is, they are not two ends of a continuum but rather represent a fundamental dichotomy. Similarly, can supply chains be organised to mix responsiveness and efficiency in different proportions, or again, should they be designed to be one or the other?

● Whatever the answer to the first question, what if a company has a mix of products, some of which are functional and others innovative? Can both of these products be moved down the same supply chain? If so, is that supply chain a com-

Figure 7.9 Matching the operations resources in the supply chain with market requirements

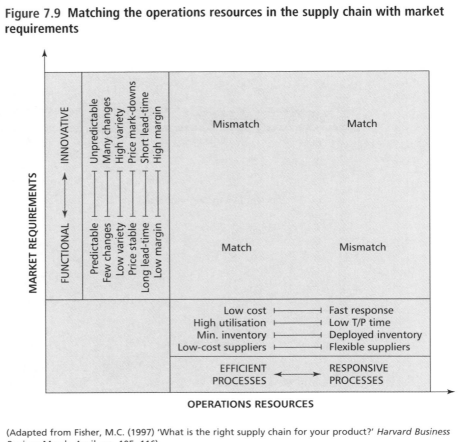

(Adapted from Fisher, M.C. (1997) 'What is the right supply chain for your product?' *Harvard Business Review*, March–April, pp. 105–116)

promise between responsiveness and efficiency, or does one give different products different priorities? Alternatively, does it imply that separate supply chains are necessary for different types of product?

Under the surface[12]

Behind some of the best-known brand names in electronics, such as Hewlett-Packard and IBM, lie companies that few outside of the industry have ever heard of. These companies, such as SCI Systems and Solectron, are the companies that make the circuit boards that go into their better known customers' products. Some of these companies, in what is known in the industry as 'contract manufacturing', are growing at up to three times faster than their customers in computer, communications and instrument electronics. But it didn't always used to be like this. Just as Ford used to make almost everything that went into its cars, down to the steel and the glass, electronics companies, such as IBM, produced everything from handles to hard drives and silicon to software. Now they specialise more in the downstream assembly, applications and marketing, and, of course, the overall design of their products.

So what made the difference? The underlying issue, as it often is, is the economy of scale which contract manufacturers could bring to component-making activity. It is a specialist job where dedicated expertise and high utilisation of process technology are important. The trigger to the change, though, was down to the changes in the process technology itself. This was the move from manual assembly of components onto boards to 'surface-mount' technology. Surface-mounting positions the tiny components directly onto the circuit board. This gives the degree of precision and the reduction in product size which is central to products such as palm-top computers, cell-phones and video cameras. Unfortunately, this process technology is so expensive it needs to be run at high levels of utilisation as well as needing complex set-up and maintenance support. Far better to leave such a complex activity to the specialists. Once mastered, the technology can deliver lower costs, higher flexibility (if a product doesn't sell it's the contract manufacturer that carries the can), faster time-to-market for new products, as well as the level of know-how and advice that enables the development of even better products.

Reconfiguration

The most fundamental approach to managing network behaviour is to reconfigure the network so as to change the scope of the activities performed in each operation and the nature of the relationships between them. This could mean changing the trading relationships between operations in the network. It could also mean merging or consolidating the activities currently performed in two or more separate operations into a single operation. Alternatively, it could mean bypassing a stage in a current supply network and dealing directly with a current supplier's supplier, or customer's customer.

Changing network linkages

As an example of how the linkages in a supply network could be changed, consider Figure 7.10. A manufacturing operation which has three plants is supplying eight customers. In the arrangement in Figure 7.10(a) each plant supplies each customer. This means that in total there are four routes (24 links between each pair of plant and customer). Each plant must have separate lines of communication with all eight customers and each customer will need to communicate directly with each of three plants.

Now consider the second arrangement in Figure 7.10(b). Two regional warehouses have been imposed between the plants and the customers. The three plants now distribute their products to the two regional warehouses from which their local customers are supplied. There are still 24 routes but simplified by using only six plant–warehouse and eight warehouse–customer links. More significantly, each plant now has to deal directly with only two immediate demand-side links for its products instead of the previous eight. Similarly, each customer now has to deal with only one supplier (its local warehouse) instead of three as previously. Figure 7.10(c) simplifies the linkages even further, but it does this by transferring complexity to the plants themselves. Whereas, in the previous two network structures, each plant concentrated on one set of activities, this final design requires each plant to widen the scope of its activities so as to be able to serve the total needs of its customers.

Merging the activities of operations

Reconfiguring a supply network often involves parts of the operation being merged – not necessarily in the sense of the change of ownership of any physical assets, but

Figure 7.10 Reconfiguring supply networks shifts complexity

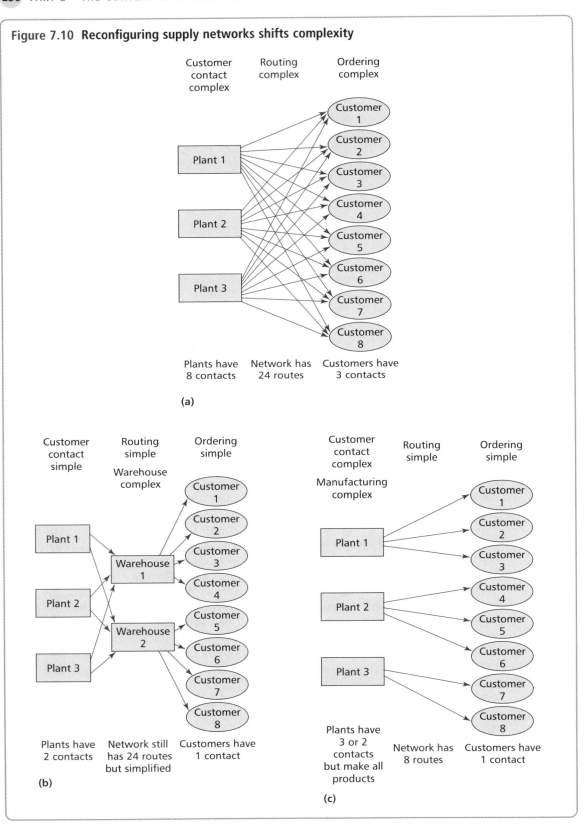

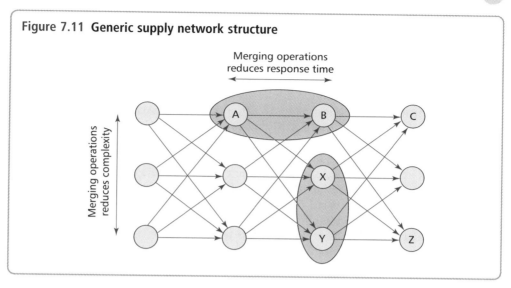

Figure 7.11 Generic supply network structure

Merging operations reduces response time

Merging operations reduces complexity

rather in the redeployment of the responsibility for carrying out activities. Generically, activities can be merged along the network or across it. Figure 7.11 illustrates a generic supply network structure with both types of merger indicated. Merging activities along the chain is often done to speed up throughput time. So, for example, operation C in Figure 7.11 may require its supplier B to incorporate the activities once performed by operation A. From C's viewpoint it can then negotiate response times with B alone, rather than having to second-guess B's dependence on A's response times. By contrast, operation Z is encouraging the merger of the activities of operations X and Y. This will have the effect of reducing complexity for operation Z. Rather than deal with two supplier operations, it now has one that can perform both tasks. The box on automotive supply describes mergers of both these types, but predominantly mergers across the network.

Of course, there are downsides to both along and across network mergers. Merging activities along the network may reduce the potential for suppliers achieving economies of scale. The box on electronic contract manufacture, 'Under the surface', illustrates this. Mergers across the network are sometimes criticised as being attempts by customers merely to transfer their problems back to their suppliers, although, broadly speaking, in the automotive sector, across the network mergers are seen by first-tier system suppliers as creating an opportunity to add value.

Disintermediation

Disintermediation is the rather clumsy term used to mean one or more operations being bypassed in a supply chain. This need not mean that those bypassed operations become totally redundant, it just means that for some final customers they are not used. So, for example, more than a hundred years ago companies started selling goods to consumers through catalogues. This 'disintermediated' the retail stores. Yet retail stores still exist, indeed catalogue selling was started by retailers. It became an alternative channel for providing service to customers.

Disintermediation is becoming a particularly significant issue because of the potential of technology to bypass traditional elements in supply chains. The box on Dell Computers earlier in this chapter provides a good example of disintermediation. Initially through their telephone ordering service, and latterly through their far more sophisticated Internet presence, Dell have disintermediated both the specialist stores which provide advice as well as products to consumers, and the direct sales teams which sell directly to other businesses. Again, it is not that computer retailing operations will necessarily disappear, even if the Dell-type supply chain is likely to become the orthodox way of selling in the industry. A very similar thing happened in corporate banking. Originally corporate banks serving medium or large business clients borrowed money on the capital markets at one rate of interest and lent it to their corporate clients at a higher rate of interest. This 'spread' between the two interest rates was how they earned their revenue. Other services which may have been provided to clients were used to justify, or even increase, this spread. Now large corporations have direct access to those same capital markets, partly because information technology makes it easy for them to do so. Corporate banking now makes its revenue by guiding and facilitating this process, advising clients on the best way to exploit capital markets. Corporate banks charge fees for these services. Disintermediation has caused the whole business model of corporate banking to change.

Internet-based technologies are having a particularly interesting effect on how supply chains are becoming disintermediated. Internet retailers such as Amazon.com could profoundly affect the nature of conventional retailing. The box on changes in the music business, earlier in the chapter, was a good illustration of this. Figure 7.12 illustrates just how far these changes may go in the music business. The top network illustrates the traditional structure of the recorded music business, though there have been changes as discussed in the box. The lower supply chain offers a fundamentally different way of serving the customer.

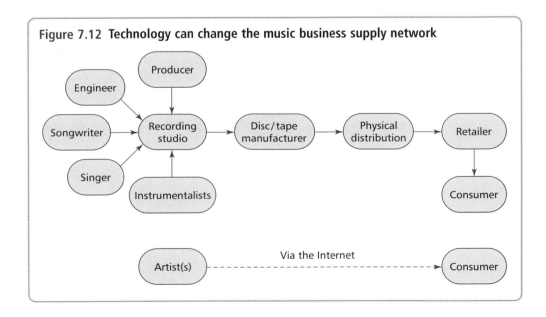

Figure 7.12 Technology can change the music business supply network

What happens when the supply chain manages you?

An implicit assumption running through our discussion of supply chain management (and one that is almost universal in all writings on supply networks) is that the customer holds the balance of power in the buyer–supplier relationship. This power is assumed to be held unilaterally, and allows the customer to influence suppliers who will be willing to conform to their requirements. Yet, in reality this is not always the case, for example when a customer is significantly smaller than a supplier and when the business represents a small proportion of the supplier's sales, but a large proportion of the customer's costs. What then is the likelihood that a customer can 'manage' their immediate suppliers? The balance of power is firmly with the supplier and the company may be more managed by, than managing, its supply chain. Some small companies, especially those making low-tech, highly standardised products, may never find themselves in a position of having much leverage with their large suppliers. Their only option, maybe, is to multi-source because in such scenarios, supplier loyalty cannot be guaranteed. However, many small companies have unrealised sources of strength. They may be able to trade with something other than money. They may have process or market knowledge which itself is valuable to their suppliers. By developing and deploying core competencies such as technological or market know-how, powerful suppliers may be willing to invest in the relationship, even when it is not a large proportion of their sales.

Example

Company X manufactures assay and analysis machines for the examination of soil samples. These machines almost always involve the use of radioactive sources. These radioactive sources are the key component of most of the company's products and are bought from two or three large companies. Although small, Company X is a typical customer for the radioactive source suppliers who, despite having some large customers, sell more than 75 per cent of their products to small customers not much larger than Company X. Frustrated by the difficulty in gaining their radioactive source suppliers' attention, Company X launched two initiatives. The first involved exploring ways in which the radioactive sources could be used more effectively within their own product designs. The second involved surveying their own customers (mainly mineral exploration companies and laboratories) in order to determine likely future trends in their market. The results from both of these initiatives were made available to the most receptive of their radioactive source suppliers.

> 'In effect we said to them, look, we can offer you two invaluable pieces of knowledge. First, we can tell you how you could modify your products to be better for your small customers, especially those in similar fields to ours. Of course there was a risk in that for us, but we figured that, even though our competitors might get this knowledge, we could always keep ahead of them in terms of how that knowledge could be deployed. Second, we said to them, your business depends on your customers' customers. They are our immediate customers. We have taken the trouble to get to know them very well indeed. Therefore we can jointly develop a model of how the industry could develop in the future. We offered ourselves up as valuable "knowledge partners" to them in developing our joint business. We were saying to them, hey, you can get real competitive advantage by working in partnership with us.'

SUMMARY ANSWERS TO KEY QUESTIONS

What are the advantages of taking a 'total supply network' perspective?

Although a 'perspective' does not necessarily change anything in reality, it can change the way an operation views its role and its relationships with other operations in the supply network. In particular a supply network perspective helps to:

- enhance understanding of competitive forces;
- enhance understanding of cooperative forces;
- identify the particularly significant relationships in the network;
- promote a focus on long-term issues;
- confront the operation with its strategic resource design options;
- highlight the 'operation-to-operation' nature of business relationships.

Are there 'natural' dynamic behaviours which supply networks exhibit?

Yes. Because supply networks are interrelationships of independent operations, the way in which each operation relates to the others in the network provides an opportunity for supply network distortions. These distortions can be considered in both a quantitative and a qualitative sense. Quantitative distortions are caused by the necessity to manage the inventories between operations in the supply network. This can lead to short-term imbalance between supply and demand, the overall effect of which is to amplify the level of activity fluctuations back up the supply chain. So, relatively small changes in ultimate demand can cause very large changes in the output levels of operations upstream in the supply chain. Qualitative distortions can occur through misperceptions in the way market requirements are transmitted up a supply chain and the way in which operations performance is viewed down the supply chain. It can also be caused by mismatches between what is perceived as required by customers and suppliers and the performance which is perceived as being given to customers.

In what way do companies try to change the nature of the supply network of which they are a part?

Operations attempt to overcome the worst effects of distortions in the supply chain, usually by one of three methods, coordination, differentiation and reconfiguration. Coordination attempts to line up the activities of operations in a supply chain through information sharing, channel alignment and changes in operational efficiency. Differentiation involves adopting different supply chain management strategies for different types of market. Reconfiguration involves changing the scope and shape of a supply chain. This may mean attempting to merge or reorder the activities in a supply chain, so as to reduce complexity or response times in the network. Increasingly, technology is having the effect of disintermediating, or cutting out, operations in supply chains.

> ## CASE EXERCISE – What would you do?

Zentrill

Zentrill were a medium-sized chain of fashion women's apparel retailers with 120 stores, typically relatively small units, in premier High Street locations and shopping malls around the country. Their clothes were stylish without being at the extremes of fashion and aimed at relatively affluent customers between the ages of 30 and 60. Gross margins (the difference between what Zentrill pay for clothes and what they sell them for) were undisclosed but, as is common in this part of the fashion market, were very high. Typically an outdoor coat retailing at $1,000 would cost the company less than $200. Zentrill's designs were exclusive and styled by both in-house design staff and outside consultant designers. All Zentrill's tailored garments (everything apart from knitwear and accessories) were manufactured by Lopez Industries, a small but high-quality garment manufacturer in Mexico. Traditionally the fashion retail industry in the northern hemisphere has two seasons; January to July is the Spring/Summer season and August to December is the Autumn/Winter season. Both break-points between seasons have traditionally been marked by 'sales' where surplus product is marked down for clearance. The proportion of items sold in these sales, or sold through intermediaries (with the Zentrill label removed), could be very high. Typically at Zentrill only around 50 per cent of items were sold at full price. This caused anxiety to Zentrill's merchandising vice president, Mary Zueski:

> 'Achieving only 50 per cent full-price sales is obviously an issue to us. Although no worse than most of our competitors, reducing the proportion of discounted sales is the best way to increase our profitability. Sometimes we are left with surplus items because our designers have just got it wrong that season. We can never predict exactly what will sell. However, usually we are quite good at knowing our market. What is more annoying is when a customer walks out of a store because an item which we could have sold to her is not in stock or is not available at that store in her size. Every time this happens, hundreds of dollars are walking out of the store with her. Ideally we would like to be able to promise such a customer that we could deliver the item to her within 24 or 48 hours. Even if we can't do that, it is important that we sense how sales of different lines are going and flex our order quantities from our manufacturer during the season. Although Lopez is a great supplier in many ways, they do not seem to be very good at being able to change their production plans at short notice. Otherwise our relationship with them is very good. Our designers like them because they can make almost anything we choose to design and their quality is excellent, as it should be in our part of the market.'

Manuel Lopez, the CEO of Lopez Industries, was fully aware of Zentrill's views.

> 'I know that they are happy with our ability to make even the most complex designs to an exceptionally high level of quality. I also know that they would like us to be more flexible in changing our volumes and delivery schedules. We obviously could not deliver within two days. The problem of the customer walking out because a size or style is not available in a particular store is caused by the way they manage their own inventory. But I admit that we could be more flexible within the season on a week-by-week basis. Partly, I am reluctant to do this because we have to buy in cloth at the

beginning of the season based on the line-by-line forecast volumes which Zentrill pro-vide for us. Even if we could change our production schedules, we could not get extra deliveries of cloth, nor can we return any surplus cloth to the cloth manufacturers. The problem is that we only deal with high-quality and innovative European cloth manu-facturers, usually German or Italian. They provide the type of cloth that Zentrill's designers like to work with. Also, it can give us a competitive advantage because much of the cloth is either lightweight or stretches or has some other characteristic that makes it difficult to machine. Over the years we have developed considerable skill in machining this type of cloth to high-quality standards. Not many garment manufac-turers can do that on a mass production basis. Sometimes I think we know more about the characteristics of these cloths than the manufacturers do. Unfortunately most of our cloth suppliers are very large compared to us, so we do not represent much busi-ness for them. Perhaps we should persuade Zentrill to let us use smaller cloth suppliers who would be more flexible?'

Typical of the cloth suppliers to Lopez Industries was Schweabsten, a German company which both manufactured cloth and tailored men's and women's wear under is own label. Felix Mayer was Schweabsten's marketing vice president:

'We compete primarily on quality and innovation. Designing cloth is as much of a fashion business as designing the clothes into which it is made. Around a third of our output of cloth goes to make our own-labelled garments. We do not manufacture these, of course, that is done by a whole collection of subcontract manufacturers. In fact that is our main problem, finding subcontract manufacturers for our own-label products who can cope with high-fashion cloths and designs while still maintaining quality. The other two-thirds of our output goes to tens of thousands of customers around the world. These vary considerably in their requirements, but presumably all of them value our quality and innovation.'

Further reading

Barney, J.B. (1999) 'How a firm's capabilities affect its boundary decisions', *Sloan Management Review*, Spring.

Brandenburger, A.M. and B.J. Nalebuff (1996) *Co-opetition*, Doubleday, New York.

Caplan, S. and M. Sawhney (2000) 'E-hubs: the new B2B market places', *Harvard Business Review*, May–June.

Child, J. and D. Faulkner (1998) *Strategies of Co-operation: Managing Alliances, Networks and Joint Ventures*, Oxford University Press, Oxford.

Evans, P. and T.S. Wurster (2000) *Blown To Bits: How the new economics of information trans-forms strategy*, Harvard Business School Press, Boston.

Lorange, P. (1996) 'Interactive strategies – alliances and partnerships', *Long Range Planning*, Vol. 2, No. 4.

Sinha, I. (2000) 'Cost tranparency: the net's real threat to prices and brands', *Harvard Business Review*, March–April.

Notes on the chapter

1   Brandenburger, A.M. and B.J. Nalebuff (1996) *Co-opetition*, Doubleday, New York.

2   Sources – Dell, M. (1998) *Direct From Dell: Strategies that revolutionised an industry*, Harper Business, New York; 'Selling PCs like bananas', *The Economist*, 5 October 1996; Magretta, J.

(1998) 'The power of virtual integration: an interview with Dell Computer's Michael Dell', *Harvard Business Review*, March–April; Ross, S.A. (1999) 'Dell Computer Corporation', Internal Report, Warwick Business School.

3 Forrester, J.W. (1961) *Industrial Dynamics*, MIT Press, Boston.

4 Harland, C.M. (1996) 'Supply chain management: relationships, chains and networks', *British Journal of Management*, Vol. 1, No. 7.

5 Mortished, C. (1999) 'Aluminium producers bid for safety', *The Times*, 13 August; 'Aluminium can – but will it?', *The Economist*, 14 November 1998.

6 Lee, H.L., V. Padmanabhan and S. Whang (1997) 'The bull whip effect in supply chains', *Sloan Management Review*, Spring, pp. 93–102.

7 Sellers, P. (1992) 'The dumbest marketing ploy', *Fortune*, Vol. 126, No. 5, pp. 88–93.

8 Lee, H.L. *et al.*, op. cit.

9 Zwick, S. (1999) 'World cars', *Time Magazine*, 22 February 1999.

10 Based on Lee, H.L. *et al.*, op. cit.

11 Fisher, M.L. (1997) 'What is the right supply chain for your product?', *Harvard Business Review*, March–April, pp. 105–116.

12 'Make it up', *The Economist*, 27 January 1996.

Process technology – definition and characteristics

Introduction

Technology has had, and will continue to have, a profound impact on all organisations. Yet despite a widespread acceptance of its significance, strategic analyses too often treat this resource category as a generic 'black box' that only technical experts understand. However, for operations strategy, such ignorance is not a realistic option because nearly every 'world-class' service or manufacturing operation will be exploiting technology in building competitive advantage. To help structure our review of the nature and impact of technology as it applies to operations processes, we will focus in this chapter on clarifying *what* is meant by the term process technology (Figure 8.1). We begin by distinguishing between process and product/service technology and then further refine our discussions by classifying two types of process technology. The first contributes 'directly' to the production of goods and services, for example robots welding body panels or sorting machines processing mail. The second type of process technology (one receiving increasingly significant investment) is the 'indirect' or 'infrastructural' technology that acts to support core transformation processes, for example Enterprise Resource Planning (ERP) systems and the scheduling systems that plan transport routes and staff rostering for mail

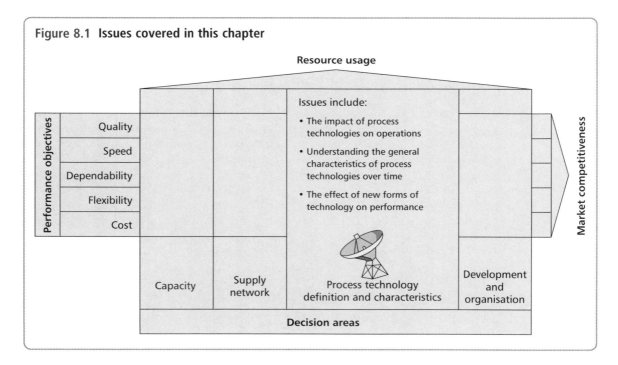

Figure 8.1 Issues covered in this chapter

delivery. The chapter introduces a series of analytical dimensions for identifying the technical, managerial and 'operations strategy' characteristics of both types of technology. It then concludes with a discussion of the profound impact of IT and revises the technology characteristics accordingly. In Chapter 9 we turn our attention to asking 'why' operations make process technology investments and explore 'how' managers can make such investments work in practice.

KEY QUESTIONS

- *What is 'process' technology?*
- *What are suitable dimensions for characterising process technology?*
- *How do market volume and variety influence process technology?*
- *How are newer technologies affecting these dimensions?*

Although the word 'technology' is frequently used in managerial conversation, what does this term actually mean? If we are to get to grips with the specific impact of technologies upon operations strategy, then a more precise definition will be needed. To this end, we employ a generic definition for technology similar to that used as a corporate slogan by white goods manufacturer Zanussi (a division of Electrolux). In their advertisements they talk about their products being the result of the *appliance of science*.

What is process technology?

This chapter and the next focus upon *process* technology as distinct from *product or service* technology. In manufacturing operations, it is a relatively simple matter to separate the two. For example, the product technology of a video cassette recorder (VCR) is embodied in the way it converts TV signals into a form which can be recorded on a tape, the way it controls the movement of the tape, the way it reads information recorded on the tape and converts it into television pictures etc. On the other hand, the process technology that manufactured the VCR is nothing like that. It consists of machine tools making metal components, machines mounting electronic components on to printed circuit boards, machines shaping and bending the casing and robots assembling all the different components.

In service operations, however, it can be far more difficult to distinguish process from product/service technology. For example, large theme parks like Disney World use flight simulator type technologies in some of their rides. These are large rooms mounted on a moveable hydraulic platform and when combined with wide-screen TV projection they can give a realistic experience of, say, space flight. Using technology in this way is just one of many achievements from what Disney calls its 'Imagineers', but is it product/service or process technology? It clearly 'processes' and adds value to Disney's customers – they literally enter one side and emerge (hopefully) happier for the experience at the other. But the technology is also part of the product. In fact customers go there especially to 'experience' specific forms of technology. It is an integral part of what they are paying their entrance fees for. In cases like this, product/service and process technologies are, in effect, the same thing.

Theory Box **The product/process innovation life cycle**

The idea that the life cycles of product and process technologies differ is based on research from the 1970s that investigated the competitive dynamics of a number of different manufacturing industries.[1] These 'life cycles' indicated the relative importance of product or process technology over time. Both are related to important market, organisation and competitive concerns. For instance, an innovative new product enters (almost by definition) a fragmented market and, as such, will tend not to be mass manufactured because of initially low and uncertain volumes. However, the innovative nature of the product implies some considerable effort having been devoted to the product's technology. Over time as the product becomes established, dominant designs emerge and competitors force products to become increasingly commodity like. In this context, cost minimisation becomes critical and the role of process innovation becomes more significant. Product and process innovation cycles are shown in Figure 8.2 (a).

Even within this generic manufacturing model, however, there are clear distinctions between types of product. Across many industries the distinction between product technology and the process technology that it controls is also blurring. For example, there is no real conceptual insight to be gained by Motorola in separating the development of a new generation of processor from their ability to actually manufacture it. Equally, most chemical and pharmaceutical manufacturers drive new products from the development of new production processes. The original research (conducted largely in the auto industry) described assembled products, whereas the non-assembled product/process life cycle (i.e. petrochemicals and pharmaceuticals) has a number of different features. In particular these include a greater and earlier emphasis on process innovation and a tendency towards less 'breakthrough' innovation and more incremental improvement (Figure 8.2(b)).

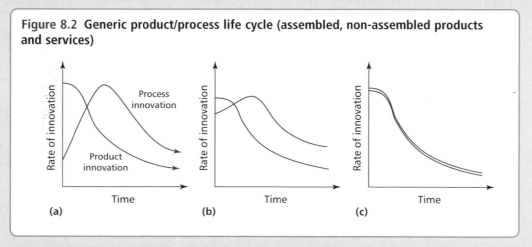

Figure 8.2 Generic product/process life cycle (assembled, non-assembled products and services)

For many service businesses the product/process distinction is even more difficult to conceptualise. The key technological considerations are inevitably those that relate to process because the process is itself the service; these 'product' and process life cycles become the same thing (see Figure 8.2(c)).

Notwithstanding the conceptual problems of separating product/service and process technology in some operations, in this chapter we shall be examining how process technologies add value in the creation of products and services. Therefore, bearing the potential overlap in mind and combining the Zanussi slogan with our transformation process view of operations, we can say that

> process technology is the 'appliance of science to any operations process'.

Of course, even with such a definition it is still difficult to make practical generalisations about process technologies. They have their roots in a range of physical, chemical and, increasingly, biological and information sciences. They can be used to transform a wide variety of different inputs: a computer processes information, medical equipment processes patients, a petroleum refinery processes crude oil, and so on. Different process technologies also have different roles within the organisation. The role of some technology is to produce products and services directly, while other process technology provides support for the production of products and services.

So, if a critical part of any operations strategy is the analysis of and shaping of its approach to process technology, we must first be able to describe the key characteristics of such technology in order to be able to identify the issues that influence its development. In this chapter this means making distinctions between different types of process technology, more specifically between:

- direct or indirect process technology, and
- material, information or customer processing technology.

Direct or indirect process technology

Above we defined process technology as the 'appliance of science to operations processes'. This definition brings images of *manufacturing* operations readily to mind: heavy-duty rollers flattening ingots of red-hot steel in an integrated steel plant, or an injection-moulding machine creating plastic toys, or even a coating machine spreading a precise amount of chocolate over a candy bar. Here the process technology physically transforms resources and, in many ways, helps to define the very nature of the operation. But, although less obvious, the same also applies to *service* operations. Regardless of whether it is the ferry transporting passengers between Manhattan and Liberty Island or the document scanning and processing systems used to transform customer application information into a life insurance policy, they are also forms of process technology.

These examples also have something else in common – the process technology described acts *directly* on inputs to their respective product/service transformation processes. In other words, the overall purpose of this direct process technology is to produce products and services for an operation's external customers. With this in mind we can further refine our general definition of process technology such that

> direct process technology is the 'appliance of science to those processes which directly contribute to the production and delivery of products and services'.

Although both manufacturing and service operations are (increasingly) reliant upon different forms of technology in a wide range of different value-adding transformation processes, even a superficial review of capital investment in most organisations reveals that information and interconnection technologies are often where the most significant investments are being made. This is having a major impact on operations. It is clear that we need to consider infrastructural IT investments as forms of process technology. In mass services like retailing, for example, stock control systems employ integrated hardware and software to link specific customer requirements into complex and extensive supply chains. Intelligent yield planning and pricing systems provide airlines with the cornerstone of their competitive strategies and many professional service firms (consultants, accountants, engineers, etc.) utilise information databases in order to retain experience despite high staff turnover rates. So modifying our core definition once more,

> indirect (or supporting) process technology is the 'appliance of science to the processes which provide or support the infrastructure for those processes which directly contribute to the production and delivery of products and services'.

Figure 8.3 illustrates these two types of process technology.

The overlap between direct and indirect technologies

In a similar manner to our earlier discussion of product/service and process technology, many operations may find this distinction between direct and indirect difficult to conceptualise. Once again some overlap between direct and indirect process technology is evident. For example, the functional capabilities of an insurance company's IT system will define the types of product that the firm can offer. If the IT system can cope with flexible payments, this can be offered to make the product more attractive to customers. The same IT system may also have the capability to support the insurance company's call centre which allows it to offer its products 24 hours a day and give a fast response to its customers. Here again, the IT system is acting as *direct* process technology in the sense that it is defining the company's products. But *the same IT system* may also forecast demand, schedule call centre staff

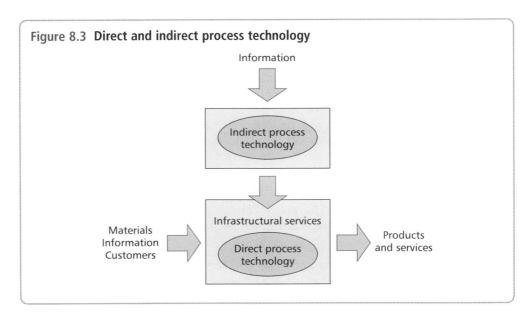

Figure 8.3 **Direct and indirect process technology**

to meet demand and issue billing details. In performing these activities the system is acting as *indirect* process technology. In fact indirect process technology can impact on activities normally associated with direct technology in two ways:

1 By allowing types of product or service that are not possible without it – the 24-hour availability with fast response is, in effect, a new product for the insurance company.

2 By making it economically feasible to offer certain types of product or service – the call centre may only be worthwhile if it can be managed efficiently.

Material, information or customer processing?

In Chapter 1 we classified operations by distinguishing between those which *predominantly* processed materials, information or customers. Process technologies can be similarly classified. They can be either materials processing (as in manufacturing operations), information processing (as in financial services, for example), or

Table 8.1 Some process technologies classified by their primary inputs and purpose

Description of the nature of the transformation	Material processing technologies	Information processing technologies	Customer processing technologies
Physical properties transformed	Flexible manufacturing systems (FMS) Weaving machines Baking ovens		Surgical equipment Milking machines
Informational properties transformed		Optical character recognition machines Management information systems Global positioning systems	Medical diagnostic equipment Body scanners
Possession properties transformed	Automatic vending machines	Search engines on the Internet Online financial information systems	
Location properties transformed	Container handling equipment Trucks Automated guided vehicles (AGVs)	Telecommunication technologies	Aircraft Mass Rapid Transport (MRT) systems
Storage/ accommodation transformed	Automatic warehouse facilities Low temperature warehouses	Archive storage systems	
Physiological state transformed			Renal dialysis systems
Psychological state transformed			Cinema digital projection Computer games Theme park rides

customer processing (as in retail, medical, hotel, transport operations, etc.). Table 8.1 shows some common process technologies of each type. It also indicates the nature of the change for which the technologies are being used. Note the range of both technologies and purposes for which they are used. Note also that most of these technologies, although placed under one category, often have secondary, though important, elements in other categories. For example, many material processing technologies used in manufacturing, while predominantly being engaged in processing steel, plastic or some other physical material, may also be processing information. This information will relate to the physical dimensions, or some other property, of what is being processed. The machine, while processing materials, may also be deciding whether tooling needs changing because of excessive wear, whether to slow the rate of processing because the material's temperature is rising too fast, noting small variations in physical dimensions to plot on process control charts, and so on. In effect an important aspect of the technology's capability is to *integrate* materials and information processing. Similarly, the Internet-based technologies used by online book retailers may be handling information associated with a specific order but are also integrating this information with characteristics of what you, as a customer, have purchased previously, in order to suggest further items you may wish to buy. Sometimes technologies integrate across all three types of technology. The systems used at the check-in gate of airports is integrating the processing of airline passengers (customers), details of their flight, destination and seating preference (information) and the number and nature of their items of luggage (materials).

Taken historically, process technology changes more in some periods than others. Since the 1980s most types of operation have, arguably, seen a noticeable increase in the rate of innovation in their process technology. In practice, most of the newer technologies are different from those they have replaced because of their information processing capabilities. Radical changes in telecommunications and Internet-based technology, the totally automated 'factory of the future', and large and/or faster aircraft are just some of the process technologies which will have a dramatic impact on operations. Behind almost all of these technological advances is one dominant factor: the availability of commercially available, low-cost micro-processing. The ubiquitous 'micro-chip' does not do much that was not achievable 30 years ago but it can do it in ways that are several orders of magnitude faster, smaller and cheaper. It is this that is having such an impact in so many process technologies.

Characterising process technology [1]

Most operations managers cannot avoid involvement with process technologies. They need to be able to manage them on a day-by-day basis and also articulate how technology can improve operational effectiveness. Other functional areas will, of course, also be involved. Engineering/technical functions analyse and generate available technological alternatives, accountancy and other control functions analyse the costs and returns to be gained from investment in the technology, and human resources need to understand the impact on the organisation's staff. Yet it is often the operations manager who must act as an impresario for the contributions from other functional areas and who is likely to take responsibility for the process technology's implementation. Moreover, process technology is expensive and the associated capital investment and cash flow requirements on their own will render this 'decision area' particularly significant. But in addition to its balance sheet implications, process technology also offers a number of specific technical and managerial challenges.

The technical and managerial challenge of process technology

A key responsibility of operations managers, if they are to carry out their 'impresario role' within the organisation, is to have a grasp of the technical nature of process technologies. This does not necessarily mean that operations managers need to be experts in engineering, computing, biology, electronics, or whatever is the core science on which the technology is based. It does mean, however, that they need to know enough about the principles behind the technology to be comfortable in evaluating some technical information, capable of dealing with experts in the technology and confident enough to ask relevant questions. The following example illustrates some of these challenges. It describes the role that process technology plays in the extremely competitive world of theme park rides, where operations seek to develop newer, faster, higher and ever more frightening rides.

Into Oblivion[2]

After more than a year of secret development, the summer of 1998 saw Alton Towers Theme Park in Staffordshire, England (owned by Tussaud's Group) unveil what had become known throughout the industry as their Secret Weapon 4 (SW4). This ride – called *Oblivion* – was the world's first vertical drop roller coaster. The ride was designed and manufactured in Switzerland by the specialist roller-coaster design firm, Bolliger and Mabillard. The firm from Monthey, Switzerland, was founded in 1988 and has a reputation for innovation. In 1992, for example, they invented – at the Six Flags Great America park in Gurnee, Illinois – the world's first suspended coaster where people's feet actually hang down below them during the ride. SW4 was demonstrated initially to journalists and ride enthusiasts (who, on the Web, had been speculating for a long time about what SW4 might be). This level of speculation was actively encouraged and, before launch day, *Oblivion* was the subject of an intensive marketing campaign that sought to tease customers about the exact nature of the 'entertainment' that awaited them.

> *'Taking the plunge in a way never experienced before are passengers test-riding the world's first roller coaster with a vertical drop. Passengers on the 160-second ride endure a four-second pause dangling face-first over a dark tunnel before dropping 200 ft into it at 70 mph ... moving rapidly from light to dark will induce the same sort of disorientation as jet pilots experience. By the end of the ride, passengers' pulse rates will have soared to about 180 beats per minute – the equivalent of a hard workout.'*

The ride has proved to be extremely successful. Alton Towers is open for only 8 months of the year, yet *Oblivion* manages to throughput approximately 3.5 million passengers in that time. Despite the relatively short length of the ride, this popularity inevitably created major queuing issues. Therefore, in addition to the physical processing technology challenges of the ride, there was also a need to develop active queue entertainment systems. There are different themed stages – the four stages of *Oblivion* – to the process, each involving a different video presentation. In stage one, participants are told about the physical effects the ride may have on their bodies, including a suggestion that it may make your skull rattle! Stage two encourages people to consider whether they can cope, and stage three links messages such as 'is this really entertainment?' with answers like 'it's just a ride'. As the riders are strapped in to the train, they hear the fourth-stage message, 'Welcome to Oblivion, there is no reason, there is no rationale'. Pragmatically, the Alton Towers marketing manager explains it thus:

> *'It's basically to get people excited in the queue ... we really want to make the entertainment last longer than the ride.'*

If we consider the above example it illustrates many of the challenges that process technology created for all types of operations. For instance, the Alton Towers management had to answer a series of technical questions, such as:

- *What does the technology do which is different from other similar technologies? Does the technology provide capabilities that have hitherto been difficult to obtain?* In the theme park market, most customers will make only one visit per year (a typical ticket costing upwards of $50) and they have an increasing variety of choices. Widely acknowledged 'uniqueness' is therefore a very valuable competitive attribute. Oblivion was the first vertical drop ride and comprised a number of unique technical elements. For instance, the nature of the ride necessitated a very complex lifting system, using four separate conveyor systems.

- *How does it do it? That is, what particular characteristics of the technology are used to perform its function?* Looking at the lifting system, for instance, the first vertical conveyor is the lift mechanism which (much stronger than a normal coaster chain) lifts the train to the apex of the track; a horizontal conveyor then takes the train to the drop point where it engages with the drop conveyor. This vertical conveyor takes the train slightly over the edge of the drop crown and puts it into a holding position that helps to maximise the passenger's ride sensation. After a suitably 'tantalising' period, this conveyor accelerates away and effectively allows the train 'to drop'. The final horizontal conveyor picks up the train after its braking run and takes it to the loading/unloading station's control systems.

- *What constraint does using the technology place on the operation?* Very few firms manufacture their own process technology and often they have little input to the design process beyond the setting of the original concept. The management of the supply-chain aspect of process technology development has a major influence upon eventual technical and competitive success or failure. Although there were one or two delays in the development of the ride, in this case the relationship with Bolliger and Mabillard seems to have been successful. Ultimately, however, rivals can now hire the firm to create something equivalent (or more likely, even better) for themselves.

- *What skills will be required from the operations staff in order to install, operate and maintain the technology?* Although the physical manifestation of the technology may be its metal frame, hydraulic devices, rotating mechanisms, etc., often this does not represent its most critical or complex aspect. For *Oblivion*, there is a software system that links together all the different elements and controls their interactions. The ride operator has a very different role, therefore (not like a classic fairground operator who physically spins the carriage on a ride). He or she is a monitor of system performance whose intervention is rarely, if ever, needed.

- *What capacity does each unit of technology have? There may be a choice between employing several small units of process technology, or one large-scale unit of technology.* The unique nature of the technology means that it has a 'natural scale' defined largely by the technical characteristics of the ride (its vertical drop, track and car size, etc.), and therefore effective capacity management (i.e. high utilisation of a single unit) was a key challenge for Oblivion. In order to maximise the throughput of riders on the roller coaster (1950 per hour in this case) multiple trains were required to be on the track at any one time. However, given that this ride is much shorter than a traditional one, this requirement necessitated yet further innovative process solutions. The ride's designer explained how they achieved this by 'loading and unloading two trains at once . . . one train will be on the lift hill, and another ready to drop. One train will be at the start of the brakes. The other two will be sitting outside the station waiting to come in and unload'.

● *What is the expected useful lifetime of the technology? Will its technical performance deteriorate over time? How easy will it be for the technology to be upgraded in line with future technological developments?* In a competitive market, 'uniqueness' is clearly an invaluable competitive attribute but it is one that is very difficult to sustain, especially as rivals can quickly observe the technology or in this case commission the same firm of design engineers who created the original. The functionality of the technology will not deteriorate in the short term (although health and safety requirements will necessitate regular maintenance and eventual refit) but as vertical rides become commonplace and other parks offer longer and scarier drops, the relative performance of the technology will diminish. The combined effect of the competitive dynamic, the one-off nature of the ride and the service context it operates in means that little, if any, consideration was given to potential upgrades for the technology as it dates over time.

The above questions illustrate some of the critical 'technical' questions that need to be answered when considering the actual and potential role for process technologies. In line with our generic model of operations strategy, process technology poses challenges both in terms of how it might help the operation to address the requirements of specific markets and how it might also underpin operations resource capabilities. In the next chapter we shall turn in more detail to the specific challenge of choosing and implementing process technologies. But before embarking on this discussion we can begin to translate the above list of questions into a more generic set of critical process technology characteristics. The following three dimensions provide a backdrop for exploring the overall significance of process technology within operations strategy and later in this chapter allow us to identify some trends which have been prompted by newer forms of (information) technology. These dimensions are:

● the scale of the process technology;
● the degree of automation of the process technology;
● the nature of the integration of the process technology.

By adopting these three dimensions we do not wish to imply that they are all equally relevant for all types of technology. Rather, they are general descriptive categories under which we can categorise a wide range of alternative process technology options.

Scale – the capacity of each unit of technology

Scale is an important issue in almost all process technologies. It is also closely related to the discussion in Chapters 4 and 5 dealing with capacity strategy. Then we treated the overall scale of an operation and the scale of capacity increments in relation to market demand and forecast changes in demand. Here we delve inside 'capacity' to explore how individual units of process technology go to make up the overall capacity of an operation. For example, consider a small regional airline serving just one main route between two cities. It has an overall capacity of 2000 seats per day

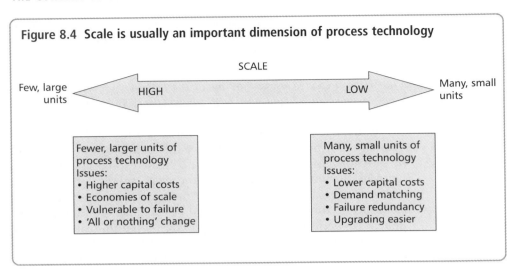

Figure 8.4 Scale is usually an important dimension of process technology

in either direction on its route. This capacity is 'defined' by its two 200-seater aircraft making five return journeys each day between the two cities. An alternative plan would be to replace its two identical 200-seat aircraft with one 250-seater and one 150-seater. This gives the company more flexibility in how it can meet varying demand levels throughout the day. It also may give more options in how its aircraft are deployed should it take on another route and buy additional aircraft. Of course, costs will be affected by the company's mix of aircraft. Generally, at full utilisation larger aircraft offer superior cost performance per passenger mile than smaller aircraft. The important point here is that by adopting units of process technology (aircraft) with different scale characteristics, the airline could significantly affect its operation's performance.

Those process technologies deployed in commodity industries like steel or petrochemicals often benefit from scale and therefore tend to come in large capacity increments. Other technologies have a 'natural scale' that is much smaller. The Oblivion theme-park ride described earlier in the chapter is an example – making the cars any bigger would be technically difficult because of the nature of the vertical drop, especially given that the ride already has some of the largest-diameter track ever used on a roller coaster. Similarly, many rapid prototyping technologies appear to offer almost science-fiction-like capabilities. In some machines a laser is moved through a tank of photosensitive liquid plastic, thus materialising a prototype model almost 'out of the air'. However, because of the science used in this type of technology, they cannot economically be used to make full-scale car models. There are a wide range of factors that influence the scale of process technology used within an operation, some of which are noted in Figure 8.4.

● *What is the capital cost of the technology?* Broadly speaking, the larger the unit of technology the more is its capital cost but the less its capital cost *per unit of capacity*. Similarly, the costs of installing and supporting the technology are likely to be lower per unit of output. Likewise, operating (as opposed to capital) costs per unit are often lower on larger machines, the fixed costs of operating the plant being spread over a higher volume.

● *Can the process technology match demand over time?* As discussed in Chapters 4 and 5, there is a traditional trade-off between large increments of capacity exploiting economies of scale but potentially resulting in a mismatch between capacity and demand, and smaller increments of capacity with a closer match between capacity and demand but fewer economies of scale. The same argument clearly applies to the units of process technology that make up that capacity. Also, larger increments of capacity (and therefore large units of process technology) are difficult to stream on and off if demand is uncertain or dynamic. Small units of process technology with the same or similar processing costs as larger pieces of equipment would reduce the potential risks of investing in the process technology. This is why efficient but smaller-scale technologies are being developed in many industries. Even in industries where received wisdom has always been that large scale is economic (i.e. steel and electricity generation), smaller, more flexible operations are increasingly amongst the most profitable (see the box on electricity-generating technology).

● *How vulnerable is the operation?* Building an operation around a single large machine introduces greater exposure to the risk of failure. Suppose that the choice is between setting up a mail sorting operation with ten smaller or one very large machine. If there is a single machine failure, then the operation with ten machines is more robust, as 90 per cent of the mail can still be sorted. In the large-scale machine operation – no mail can be sorted.

● *What scope exists for exploiting new technological developments?* Many forms of process technology are advancing at a rapid rate. This poses a threat to the useful life of large units of technology. If an operation commits substantial investment to a few large pieces of equipment, it changes them only infrequently and the opportunities for trying out new ideas are somewhat limited. Having a broader range of different technological options (albeit each of a smaller scale) makes it easier to take advantage of new developments – providing the operation can cope with potential inconsistencies.

Micro-power[3]

Big is no longer beautiful in the world of power generation. Traditionally, economies of scale have ruled in the construction of power stations. Generating electricity meant burning fossil fuels to drive giant turbines which produced electricity. Not many years ago, giant plants burnt coal and produced 2000 MW (megawatts) of electricity. Even smaller nuclear plants were built to produce 1000 MW. But technological development, market pressures and environmental concerns have acted together to change the whole outlook of the industry. Now a plant producing only 100 MW is seen as too expensive, too risky and needing too long to construct. In June 2000, ABB (the global technology company) launched its 'Alternative Energy Solutions' programme. The company, which had recently sold its business making large-scale power plants, had begun to concentrate on making small 10 MW systems, the consumption of a fairly large factory.

Behind this move was a belief by ABB that there would be a general move from large centralised power plants, whose energy was distributed through grids around a large region, to 'virtual utilities' which can link small-scale power plants serving individual operations. The future of electricity generation could be one involving large numbers of individual operations. Offices, or even houses, could each generate small amounts of electricity, perhaps using new technologies such as fuel cells housed in units no larger than an average domestic heating boiler. 'Net meter-

▶

ing' would allow any surplus energy generated to be sold into the electricity grid, with electricity being taken off the grid in the conventional way when local consumption exceeded generation capacity. In effect, the electricity meter would run backwards or forwards depending on whether electricity was being bought or sold. Ironically, the first person to have this vision was Thomas Edison. More than a hundred years ago, he imagined a world of connected, flexible and decentralised power plants in all large homes and offices.

Degree of automation – what can the machine do?

No technology (as yet) operates continually, totally and completely in isolation, without some degree of human intervention ever. This may be the almost continual and direct control over a bus given to its driver, or the occasional intervention of a control engineer in a pharmaceutical manufacturing plant. The relative balance between human and technological effort in a unit of technology is usually referred to as its capital intensity or degree of automation. We shall use the latter term.

The earliest applications of automation to physical (material) transformation processes revolved around relatively simple and regularly repeated tasks. This was because technology could not compete with human dexterity or analytical power. Technology is 'dumber' than humans; it cannot match people in many delicate tasks or those requiring complex (and especially intuitive) thought processes. But technology can repeat tasks endlessly and is capable of repeating these tasks with precision, speed, power and many other qualities. The strong drive towards greater automation in both manufacturing and service operations is largely related to this desire to operate faster and/or deliver reduced direct labour costs. However, the true impact of automation needs to be assessed in broader terms. There are a number of different competitive factors that need to be considered before automating; see Figure 8.5. These might include:

● *What degree of support is required?* In many cases there have not been overall savings associated with automation, especially if a complex system requires regular and expensive maintenance. It is common for a shift towards greater capital intensity to necessitate the employment (either directly or contractually) of more engineers, programmers, etc. who normally come with a much higher price tag than the direct labour that was replaced.

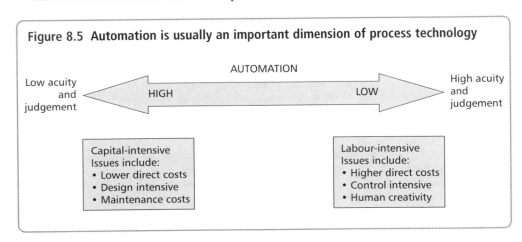

Figure 8.5 Automation is usually an important dimension of process technology

AUTOMATION

Low acuity and judgement — HIGH — LOW — High acuity and judgement

Capital-intensive
Issues include:
• Lower direct costs
• Design intensive
• Maintenance costs

Labour-intensive
Issues include:
• Higher direct costs
• Control intensive
• Human creativity

- *What scope exists for future, further improvements?* Once a process has been automated, it is usually less capable of performing a wide range of activities. This may restrict future improvement through redesigning the process.

- *How much improvement creativity is needed?* There is always an ongoing cost associated with employing people, but this needs to be weighed against the potential source of creativity they constitute. Is it worth getting rid of human potential along with its cost?

- *How flexible is the process?* If customer requirements change, how easy will it be to modify the technology? Can it cope with either new product possibilities or major volume shifts? Labour intensive technologies can usually be changed more readily by controlling them in a different way. Capital-intensive technologies may have designed rigidities.

- *How dependable is the process?* Although highly automated technology might require fewer people and have greater capability, it can be less robust than a combination of basic technology and less fragile than humans. Making changes to the technology can become longer and more difficult, subtle changes to input resources can have a huge impact, and so on. Tried and tested technology may appear to offer fewer differentiated benefits but it is often more robust.

Degree of coupling – how much is joined together?

In manufacturing, a great deal of emphasis has been placed upon implementing advanced manufacturing technologies (AMTs) as a response to competitive cost and quality pressures. Much of the 'advance' in these technologies has come from the 'coupling' or integration of activities that were previously separated into separate units of process technology. Coupling could consist of physical links between pieces of equipment, for example a robot removing a piece of plastic from an injection moulder and locating it in a machine tool for finishing. Alternatively, it could mean merging the formerly managerial tasks of scheduling and controlling these machines with their physical activities to form a synchronised whole.

Many of the direct benefits (and likewise the risks and costs) associated with

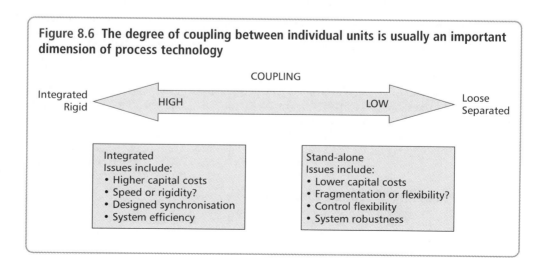

Figure 8.6 The degree of coupling between individual units is usually an important dimension of process technology

increased coupling (Figure 8.6), echo those described with respect to automation and scale (see Figure 8.4). For example:

- The integration of separate processes often involves high capital costs. The automatic movement of materials between processes, for example, may involve additional materials-handling technology.

- At its simplest, increasing coupling removes much of the fragmentation caused by physical or organisational separation. So, for example, a 'speed' revolution has taken place in many financial services; a mortgage application is now usually accepted provisionally over the phone, whereas once it took three weeks of paperwork. This change can be directly attributed to the increased coupling of technology in financial services whereby individuals or teams can manage all aspects of a service delivery process.

- Closer coupling between units of process technology can lead to a greater degree of synchronisation. For any materials-processing technology this can increase throughput speed by reducing delays between tasks, thereby reducing work-in-process (WIP) and costs. As the many advocates of just-in-time production systems have argued, reducing WIP, in effect, increases coupling, speeds up throughput and improves process discipline because such systems require each part of the coupled system to be working effectively.

- Closer integration can increase exposure (with positive and negative effects) if there is a failure at any stage. The failure of a single stage in an integrated production line will probably stop the whole system. Less coupling can mean more system robustness if work can be re-routed to bypass failed stages.

Ditching the pipes[4]

Look at any processing plant in the chemical industry and you will see miles of pipes: pipes that move chemicals from one process to another, pipes that carry away excess heat from the processes, and pipes that connect pumps, valves, centrifuges and so on. In fact, over 75 per cent of the capital cost of a conventional process plant goes into the structural work and plumbing which connect what are known as 'unit operations' together. These unit operations are the separate processes such as filtration, distillation and evaporation which are the building blocks of most chemical processing. Recently though, a new philosophy has intruded into the conventional world of process plant design. This is called process intensification (PI). Although the idea has been around for more than 20 years, it is now having an impact in the design of process technology in the chemical industry. It attempts to make plants dramatically smaller and harder-working by designing equipment which will increase coupling by performing two or more hitherto separate activities in the same unit of technology. Using PI condensation, distillation and reboiling can all happen in the same piece of equipment, a reactor can also act as a heat exchanger, and so on. It all has the effect of making process technology smaller and reducing overall costs. In this way chemical plants, always regarded as being tightly coupled, have extended their integration to the extent that once-separate processes are now fully merged together.

Linking the three dimensions

The automation, scale and coupling dimensions are all strongly related. For example, the larger the unit of capacity, the more likely it is to be capital rather than labour intensive; this gives more opportunity for high coupling between its various

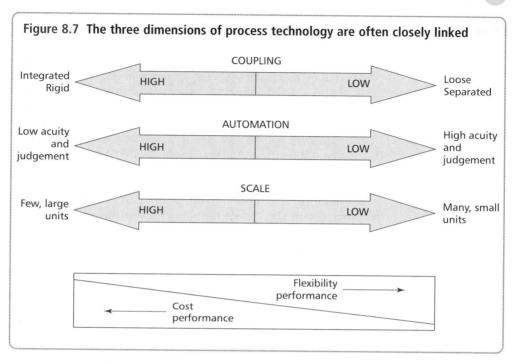

Figure 8.7 **The three dimensions of process technology are often closely linked**

parts. Conversely, small-scale technologies, combined with highly skilled staff, tend to be more flexible than large-scale, capital-intensive, closely coupled systems. As a result, these systems can cope with a high degree of product variety or service customisation ('bespoke' tailors and 'boutique' strategy consulting firms are examples of this). Conversely, where flexibility is of little importance (with standardised, low-cost products such as industrial fastenings, or a mass transaction service such as letter sorting) but achieving dependable high volumes and low unit costs is critical, these inflexible systems come into their own. Figure 8.7 illustrates the interrelationship of these three dimensions of scale, automation and coupling. At one extreme are the relatively small-scale, loosely coupled technologies which, together with the humans who operate them, exhibit a high level of acuity and judgement. The characterising feature of these types of technology is their flexibility. At the other extreme are the process technologies which are large, rigidly integrated and, because they are attempting to incorporate some of the activities normally done by human beings, have relatively low acuity and judgement compared to the human beings they replace. These types of technology are usually characterised by having very low operating costs compared to those at the other end of the scale.

Remember though, although the three dimensions of process technology do often go together in this way, they do not always match perfectly. In fact the whole relationship between where units of process technology may lie on these scales on the one hand, and the balance between cost and flexibility on the other, is changing. However, first we will examine how these dimensions of process technology are conventionally linked to market requirements. Later we will explore how newer forms of technology are changing this linkage.

Relating technology characteristics to market requirements

Our convention for describing market requirements is to use the five generic performance objectives of quality, speed, dependability, flexibility and cost. As we pointed out in the above discussion, process technology has a particularly significant impact on two of these – flexibility and cost. Several authors on operations strategy have made a further link to the volume and variety requirements of the market. The logic goes something like this. Companies serving high-volume, and therefore usually low-variety, markets usually have a competitive position which values low prices, therefore low-cost operations are important, therefore process technologies need to be large, automated and integrated. Conversely, low-volume, high-variety operations need the flexibility that comes with small-scale, loosely coupled technologies with significant human intervention.

The product–process matrix

The product–process matrix was first described by Robert Hayes and Stephen Wheelwright (both of Harvard Business School). Although they used it to link the volume and variety requirements of the market with process design in general, here we use it to draw a link between volume and variety on the one hand and the three

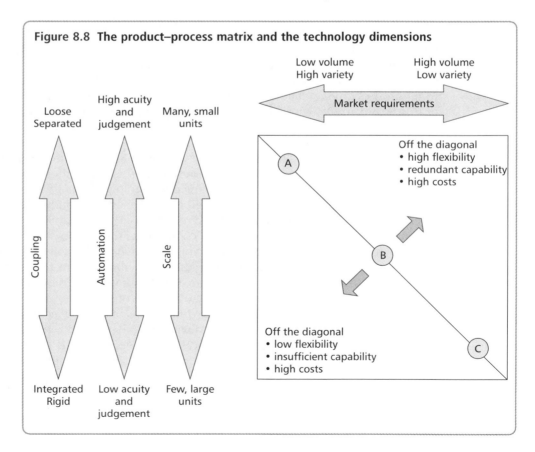

Figure 8.8 The product–process matrix and the technology dimensions

dimensions of process technology on the other. This is shown in Figure 8.8. The relationship between the volume/variety and process technology dimensions suggests that there is a 'natural' diagonal fit and that deviating from the 'diagonal' will therefore have predictable consequences for the operation.

Operations to the right of the diagonal have more capability to deal with their requisite variety than is necessary. Such surplus capability will normally be associated with excess operating costs. Similarly, operations to the left of the diagonal have insufficient flexibility to cope with their requisite variety. This may result in substantial opportunity costs (being unable to fulfil orders economically), not to mention the competitive impact of having insufficient capability. Remember, though, that the matrix cannot prescribe the 'correct' process technology. It can, however, give a general idea of how an operation's process technology profile will need to be adapted as its market context changes.

Moving down the diagonal

Operations will change their position in the matrix. For example, a 'home-made' luxury ice-cream product, selling a few litres in a farm shop, might begin life by being manufactured in a farmer's own kitchen using domestic equipment (position A in Figure 8.8). Growth in sales (and health and safety legislation) would necessitate investment in a small production facility, although, because of the different varieties, the production unit will still need some flexibility (position B in Figure 8.8). Ultimately, if projected demand for some flavours and sizes reaches mass-market levels, major continuous-flow process investment will be necessary (position C in Figure 8.8). Equally, at this stage the product might become attractive to a large established manufacturer because the volume and variety of demand would match its existing integrated production facilities.

The natural trajectory of movement 'down' the product/process matrix can be observed in many different operational contexts. Many financial service firms, for instance, have been able to make major reductions in their back-office operations by reducing clerical and administrative staffing and cost levels through investment in large-scale, integrated, automated process technology. The following example illustrates this in more detail.

Voucher processing in retail banking

Many large retail banking groups have successfully applied the volume/variety logic to their voucher processing operations. Although, throughout the financial services sector, volumes of paper-based transactions employing vouchers, such as cheques, are declining in absolute terms, the total volumes remain substantial. As a result, there remain substantial costs associated with the 'clearing' process (receiving paper transactions, checking data, updating accounts, transporting paper to other financial institutions). During most of the last 30 or 40 years banks in most developed countries have been merging and therefore getting larger. Simultaneously, they have attempted to standardise products and procedures within their own operations.

Generally this has led to a lower variety of distinct activities being carried out in higher volume across a bank's network of operations. This is illustrated by the move from position [1] to [2] in Figure 8.9. Traditionally, every branch had its own 'desktop' voucher processing technology, and customer service staff would have to spend a proportion of every day operating this system. Clearly, performing identical activities in a fragmented manner across hundreds or thousands of separate operations results in each individual back-office operation at each branch operating well

▶

below economic capacity levels. In the past ten years, most retail banks have substantially redesigned their operations as indicated in the move from [2] to [3] in Figure 8.9.

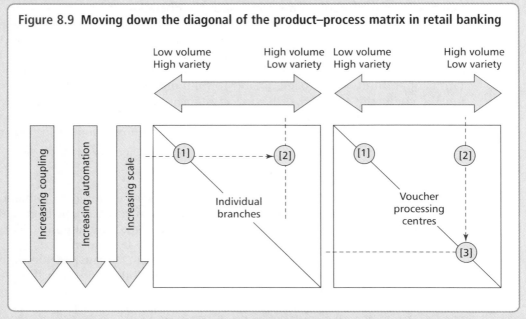

Figure 8.9 Moving down the diagonal of the product–process matrix in retail banking

Most banking businesses now have a small number of large, automated voucher processing centres with high-volume, integrated, processing lines. Individual branches send their unprocessed cheques to these centres, where optical character recognition technology reads thousands of cheques per minute and processes all the requisite data.

Moving on the diagonal has its challenges

We can use the above box on how process technology has developed in retail banking to illustrate some general points about how operations change their position on the product/process matrix:

- A traditional branch dealt with nearly all the variety (services, products, etc.) that the bank offered, but equally dealt with relatively small volumes. While the branch network operated as a series of autonomous units, therefore, the small-scale, labour-intensive and stand-alone process technology appeared to be completely appropriate.

- When one begins to consider the entirety of the branch network, the absolute level of variety does not change; however, the total volume is far greater. This suggests that there was perhaps too much flexibility in the network as a whole and that there was substantial scope for simplification and redesign that might exploit larger-scale (lower unit cost) technology. Interestingly, one of the most significant challenges associated with the transition to stage 3 in Figure 8.9 was developing the (now critical) integrating systems that allowed relatively small volumes of vouchers to be moved from branch to centre and back again.

● After establishing their VPC networks (often overcoming a number of innovative technology implementation difficulties), many banks have substantially reduced the transaction unit costs associated with voucher processing. There is recognition that such systems are less flexible than before and more vulnerable to failure (as discussed earlier in this chapter). However, the risk was felt to be more than justified by the cost savings.

● Moving to a position on the diagonal towards the bottom of the matrix often requires a greater degree of standardisation and control in associated operations. In banking, for example, while voucher processing was performed at branches, small variation in procedure could be tolerated and even small errors rectified relatively easily. When vouchers were shipped to regional VPCs, branch procedures had to be totally standardised and any errors made by the branch could cause major disruption in the high-volume environment of the VPCs.

● An operation's whole approach to managing its technology, together with its organisational culture, will usually have to change as an operation's position on the diagonal changes. Many banks encountered unexpected problems when they moved over to large VPCs. Some of these were the result of having to cope with unfamiliar new technology. Most banks had anticipated that. What they had not anticipated was the change in managerial approach that was required. The people staffing the new VPCs were often long-standing bank employees. They had never before worked in high-volume operations. They had to learn how to be 'factory managers' rather than 'bank managers'. Some retail banks called their operations function 'Manufacturing' to emphasise this point.

Moving from one point to another on the diagonal cannot always be done without moving off the diagonal at some point. Some banks made the move to very large VPCs in two steps. First, they assigned area voucher processing responsibility to a number of the larger branches. Each day they would take in vouchers from the surrounding ten or fifteen smaller branches and act as a mini VPC. Because they were still relatively small they could cope with some variation in their satellite branches' operating procedures. Unfortunately, when the move to full regional VPCs was made this tolerance of variety in branch operating procedures proved problematic for the (now inflexible) technology until all branches could be brought into using standardised procedures.

Learning from being 'off the diagonal'

Moving away from the 'natural' diagonal usually proves costly, but can also provide learning opportunities for any operation having to cope with the resulting problems. Consider the following story about a traditional manufacturer of hand tools, for example. The firm received repeated requests from their main customers (out-of-town DIY superstores) for a rationalisation of their product offering. This led them to revise their screwdriver range, replacing some 50 separate types with a newly designed (and better branded) set of 9.

1 The original range was manufactured in batches in a number of stand-alone processes which cropped steel bar, forged the end, trimmed, heat treated, ground, sometimes plated, marked and inserted the blades into the handles. A set of process technologies that were small scale, fairly manual, not integrated and very flexible.

2 The narrow product range prompted the company's production engineers to draw up plans for a new production system that integrated several of the operations in the original process sequence. This involved investing in rotary forging, large bed grinders and induction coil heat treatment – as well as materials-handling technology. There would be more capital equipment, fewer people, larger machines and less changeover flexibility.

3 However, a delay in gaining approval for the capital cost resulted in the new product range being made on the old, flexible but inefficient process. Initially this seemed as if it meant redundant flexibility and high costs. The operation had not moved down the technology dimensions, yet the product profile had moved to the right.

4 But rather than accept cost disadvantages as an inevitable consequence of having inappropriate technology, the company actively tried to exploit the advantages that their position gave them. For example, the old flexible technology could manufacture smaller batches than seemed to be warranted. But by issuing forecasts weekly rather than monthly as before, production schedules could be accommodated which matched demand much more closely and gave lower finished goods inventory. The old system was being exploited to improve responsiveness and thus reduce working capital requirements. Admittedly, total manufacturing costs were higher than would have been the case with the new technology, but not as high as they would have been without the changes to the forecasting and scheduling procedures.

5 Eventually, the new technology superseded the old, but not quite as originally conceived. The company had become impressed with the benefits of a flexible, responsive operation. They were unwilling to sacrifice their changeover flexibility for a more automated, higher production rate, process. Consequently, several changes were built into the new integrated system to allow the same responsiveness as before. In some ways the new system was still less flexible than the old (9 types instead of 50), but not where it mattered.

There are clear lessons here. Although the product–process matrix can give us a general indication of how process technology should/will differ for different product profiles, it does not prescribe a 'correct' technology. It gives a general idea of how technology will need to be adapted as product profiles change, but this does not preclude breaking the connection between the dimensions of technology so as to get some of the best of all worlds. Any company finding itself off the diagonal could usefully ask how it can exploit the benefits which its position gives it, and what it must do to overcome the negative effects of its position.

Market pressures on the flexibility/cost trade-off?

The traditional *flexibility/cost* trade-off inherent in the scale, automation and integration dimensions of process technology (and the product/process matrix for that matter) is coming under increasing pressure from more challenging and demanding markets. In many sectors, increased market fragmentation and the demand for more customisation is reducing absolute volumes of any one type of product or service. Simultaneously, shortening product/service life cycles can mean periodic step changes in the requirements placed on an operation and its process technology. This can severely reduce the potential for applying large-scale and relatively inflexible,

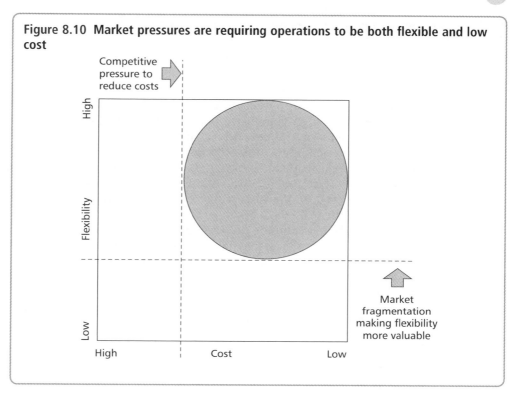

Figure 8.10 Market pressures are requiring operations to be both flexible and low cost

though traditionally low-cost, technologies. Yet at the same time, there is increasing pressure to compete on cost which is driving ongoing reductions in direct labour and placing increased emphasis on automation. In fact, for many traditionally labour-intensive sectors such as the banking industry referred to earlier, absence of sufficient technological investment (and the corresponding presence of 'too many staff') has a significant impact on analyst and shareholder confidence and therefore share price. Both these pressures are placing conventional process technology solutions under strain. See Figure 8.10.

Of course, this competitive challenge has proved to be simply too much for many operations but, interestingly, many of those that have survived and prospered have not abandoned technology in their operations strategies. Rather, many operations have more fully embraced process technology, albeit in new IT-rich forms. Indeed it is increasingly difficult to overstate the impact that information technology is having upon organisational life. There is almost no sphere of operations where computing technology in one form or another has not had a substantial impact. The evidence for this quantum shift is not hard to uncover. For instance, in the US – where one might argue that the digital revolution has been most profound – between 1978 and 1985 the proportion of capital equipment stock tripled from 1.8 to 7.8 per cent. By 1988, investments in hardware alone had reached $35.7 billion (and IT in general accounted for 42 per cent of total business expenditure) and by 1998, this had reached $95.7 billion.

Characterising process technology [2]

Originally, IT exhibited similar characteristics to other types of process technology. For example, 20 years ago a mass service utilising what was at the time 'cutting-edge' IT could carry out complex 'batches' of parallel transactions. This might have been a large retailer monitoring sales and inventory levels or a bank reconciling counter transactions. The high-volume, low-variety characteristics of these transactions justified investment in the expensive, large-scale mainframe computers needed to undertake these activities. Today's IT, however, exhibits very different characteristics. Rapid technological advances have meant that the relative power of computers has increased almost exponentially. This is perhaps unsurprising given the potential benefits; however, at the same time the relative cost of this power has reduced almost as rapidly.

These two factors combine not only to make the widespread application of computing to operations almost inevitable but also to alter the traditional cost versus flexibility trade-off. So while many of today's IT applications can cope with both volume and variety, this (often redundant) capability appears not to have resulted in extra costs. In order to capture the impact of this dramatic change we can modify our original dimensions (scale, automation and integration) more accurately to reflect the characteristics of IT-rich process technology. These dimensions now become:

- the *scalability* of the technology;
- the degree of *analytical content* embodied in the technology;
- the *connectivity* of the technology.

As we stressed before, these three dimensions may not all be equally relevant for all types of IT-rich process technology. Rather, they are general descriptive categories under which we can categorise 'new' technology options.

From 'scale' to 'scalability'

One of the key challenges for information processing is still to judge how much computing capacity is required. This is especially true if the process technology is customer facing and in a dynamic marketplace (such as e-commerce) where demand uncertainty and variability are common. As many business-to-consumer Web companies have discovered, too little capacity means that the technology (web site server etc.) can quickly become swamped and lead to extreme customer dissatisfaction. (It is worth reflecting at this point on your own experience of trying to connect to and use a very busy web site.) Conversely, too much technology means excess invested capital to service too few customers.

But information is transmitted far more easily between units of technology than either materials or customers. As we indicated earlier, information technology also has the capability of overcoming traditional links between volume and variety. Both of these factors mean that information technology processes can be linked relatively easily to combine their total processing capacity. Because of this, in many new technologies, the dynamic capacity challenges relate less to *absolute scale* and more to *scalability*. By scalability we mean the ability to shift to a different level of useful capacity quickly, cost-effectively and flexibly. There are a number of critical drivers underpinning scalability; see Figure 8.11. These include:

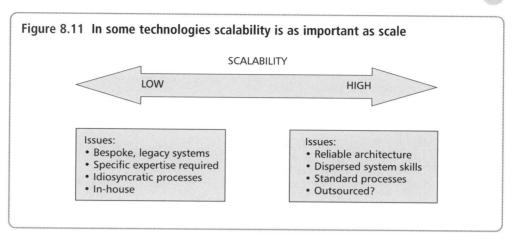

Figure 8.11 In some technologies scalability is as important as scale

- *The system architecture* – Upgrading the functionality of an IT system (i.e. what it can do) is usually a matter of evolution rather than revolution. Because such technology changes quickly it is frequently being upgraded. Sometimes totally separate and only partially connected systems are installed alongside existing ones. So, because of upgrading, some systems finish up with patched and inconsistent system architectures. This does not mean that they are in themselves inefficient. However, it does make them difficult to scale up because they do not fit conveniently with other units of technology. Thus the underlying consistency and stability of an IT platform's architecture is an important determinant of its scalability. Also, a more stable platform often will have support staff who have developed a greater depth of expertise.

- *Underlying process standardisation* – Often linked to stable system architectures are standardised processes. If the IT is stable, one of the possible reasons for changing a process is removed. On the other hand, processes which have been adapted to match system changes over time can become hugely idiosyncratic. So, a combination of processes which have developed independently of each other and 'legacy' IT systems (outdated but expensive to replace) can make scaling such operations difficult. It is partly because of these issues that many organisations have adopted 'off-the-shelf' internal business process management systems such as enterprise resource planning (ERP). Indeed, many adopters of ERP systems have chosen to change their business processes to match the IT rather than the other way around.

From 'automation' to 'analytical content'

Even when considering automation of the most sophisticated forms of material and customer processing technology there is usually an underlying strategic choice to be made about the balance between people and technology. The choice is often between emphasising the power, speed and general physical abilities of automation against the flexible, intuitive and analytical abilities of human beings. However, an increasing number of purely information transformation processes are entirely automated (including most processing technology in the financial services sector,

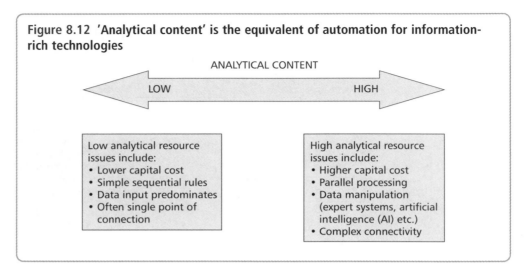

Figure 8.12 'Analytical content' is the equivalent of automation for information-rich technologies

ANALYTICAL CONTENT

LOW   HIGH

Low analytical resource
issues include:
• Lower capital cost
• Simple sequential rules
• Data input predominates
• Often single point of
  connection

High analytical resource
issues include:
• Higher capital cost
• Parallel processing
• Data manipulation
  (expert systems, artificial
  intelligence (AI) etc.)
• Complex connectivity

for instance). We need a different metric to differentiate between different information processing technologies which are 100 per cent 'automated' , or very close to it.

Consider the range of new information-based technologies. Sophisticated data management and decision-making systems are being used to enhance existing processes. These might include adding automatic measurement and process control to manufacturing technology or the use of expert systems to help authorise financial transactions. For example, American Express has its 'Authorizer's Assistant' system to help authorise transactions. This form of automation is very different from, say, that used to read bar-codes in a retail outlet. Both process information but the former tackles far greater underlying task complexity. The characterising dimension for technology that can cope with the increasingly complex tasks is the degree of analytical resource or *analytical content* that the system can bring to bear on a task. Once again there are a number of different drivers that influence the analytical content of the technology (see Figure 8.12). These include:

● *The amount of parallel processing required* – One of the real operational attractions of IT is that it can transform sequential tasks into ones that can be carried out in parallel. This parallel processing could be in a complex multinational design process, such as that used by Ford for their global product development platform or more simply in IT 'work-flow' applications for compiling an insurance policy. In order to do this, and regardless of the precise tasks, the IT requires internal scheduling and data management protocols that are inherently more analytical than those employed in a straightforward sequential process.

● *The level of customer interaction* – The greater the degree of customer interaction, often the greater the information 'richness' that must be input, processed and output. This can be directly related to the underlying task complexity with which the technology has to cope. Although using the keypad on your telephone to order cinema seats with a credit card is a valuable automated and interactive service, such a system is really only a virtual vending machine. The system has a finite (and relatively small) number of options (just like the limited range of snack foods in a vending machine). The analytical content of the system, such as checking seat availability and verifying the credit card, is relatively low (using the vending machine analogy again, it is like checking if a particular candy bar has run out and then verifying that coins are correct).

From 'coupling' to 'connectivity'

Traditionally, coupling for material processing technology (e.g. flexible manufacturing systems) and information processing technology (e.g. electronic data interchange systems) has meant physically 'hard wiring' together disparate process elements and, as a result, has been economically viable only at higher volumes and has lacked the flexibility to cope with very high variety. However, over the past decade the critical trend in information processing has been a move towards *platform independence*. This means allowing communication between computing devices regardless of their specification. In certain applications this has indeed allowed greater integration to occur. Increasingly, it is not just interconnection within the organisation that is important but also integration across organisational boundaries. For example, supermarkets have dramatically altered the way they manage their buying process. Connected IT systems allow many suppliers access to a common data 'warehouse' that gives them real-time information about how each of their products is selling in all stores. Such systems enable the supply companies to modify their production schedules in order to meet demand more precisely and ensure fewer stock-outs. The defining technological characteristic associated with platform independence is not coupling in the classic sense of integration, but rather a greater degree of *connectivity*. There have been two key drivers that have allowed 'connectivity' (and the corresponding networks such as the Internet) to develop at such a phenomenal rate (see Figure 8.13).

● *Hardware development* – Client/server systems have, for the past decade, been seen as the future of computing. These systems were initially promoted as a less costly replacement for mainframe technology. Yet their real advantage has been their ability to permit the separation of the user interface, the processing application and data sources. This has encouraged the development of interconnection tech-

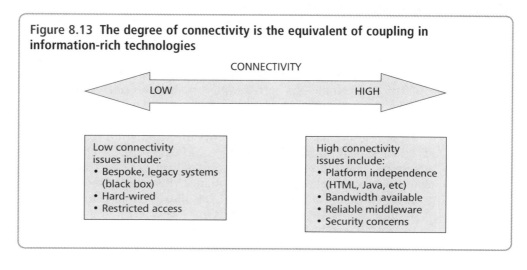

Figure 8.13 **The degree of connectivity is the equivalent of coupling in information-rich technologies**

CONNECTIVITY

LOW   HIGH

Low connectivity
issues include:
• Bespoke, legacy systems
  (black box)
• Hard-wired
• Restricted access

High connectivity
issues include:
• Platform independence
  (HTML, Java, etc)
• Bandwidth available
• Reliable middleware
• Security concerns

nology, including software protocols and connection technology (such as bandwidth enhancement).

● *Software development* – Arguably, *the* distinguishing feature of the development of the World Wide Web has been the adoption of a universal browser interface, which has considerably expanded the potential for connectivity. The protocol known as HTML (HyperText Mark-up Language) tells *any* web browser the layout and functionality of any web page. Other developments, such as the equally platform-independent Java programming language (an object-oriented language developed by Sun Microsystems), can enhance content interaction and give more attractive web pages, but also allow for greater functional interconnectivity.

The issues connected with connectivity are similar to those concerned with scalability and analytical content. Low connectivity is often associated with idiosyncratically designed, bespoke and 'legacy' IT systems. Often such systems come with restricted opportunities for the access which is a prerequisite to connectivity. High-connectivity technologies, on the other hand, are usually based on the platform independence discussed above and have the bandwidth capacity to enable rich communications. Sometimes, however, their very openness and easy access can give security concerns. Much new technology, although offering wonderful levels of connectivity, creates new opportunities for fraud, 'denial of service' attacks, and so on.

Linking the three dimensions

After describing the automation, scale and coupling dimensions we stressed how all three are strongly related. The same is true of these three extended dimensions of process technology (scalability, analytical content and connectivity). For instance, effective scalability is generally predicated upon connectivity (hence the emphasis upon standardisation in systems architecture and underlying operating processes). The analytical functionality that is so central to complex task automation is normally built upon a collection of different applications and data sources and therefore the greater the connectivity, the greater the analytical power etc.

Including process technology trends

So, markets seem to be demanding both greater flexibility and lower costs simultaneously from process technology. To the traditional mindset, which we illustrated in Figure 8.7, this seems to be difficult, bordering on impossible. Yet remember our discussions on trade-offs between performance objectives back in Chapter 3. There we saw the development and improvement of operations (including process technology) as being a process of overcoming trade-offs.

Now we must include developments in information technology, especially their effect of shifting traditional balances and trade-offs. In effect we have argued that emerging scalability, analytical content and connectivity characteristics have enabled process technologies to enhance their flexibility while still retaining reasonable efficiency and vice versa. This is illustrated in Figure 8.14.

In other words, these recent trends in process technology are having the net effect of overcoming some of the traditional trade-offs inherent within the dimensions of process technology. This has, for some industries, changed the nature of the prod-

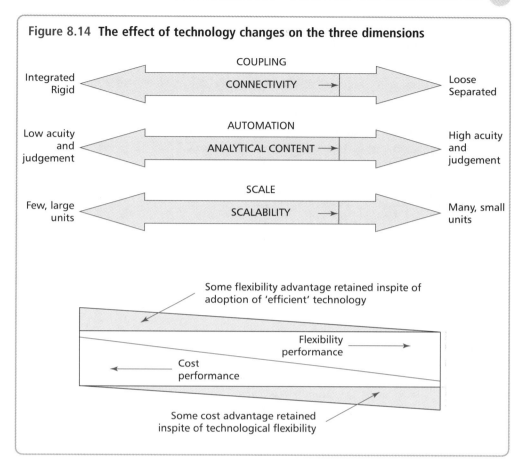

Figure 8.14 **The effect of technology changes on the three dimensions**

uct–process matrix, which we discussed earlier. Figure 8.15 shows how three separate but connected ideas have come together.

- The three dimensions of process technology – scale, automation and coupling – are related to the volume/variety characteristics of the market. In traditional process technologies, especially those with relatively little IT element, large, automated and tightly coupled technologies were capable of processing at low cost but had relatively little flexibility. This made them suitable for high-volume, low-variety processes. If process requirements were for high variety but low volume, process technology is likely to consist of smaller separated units with relatively little automation.

- Trends in the development of each dimension of process technology, especially those related to their increasing richness in information processing, are overcoming some of the traditional trade-offs within each dimension. In particular, technology with high levels of scalability can give the advantages of flexible, small-scale technology and yet be quickly expanded if demand warranted it. Similarly, even high-volume information processing technology can still display the relatively high analytical content at one time reserved for more manual

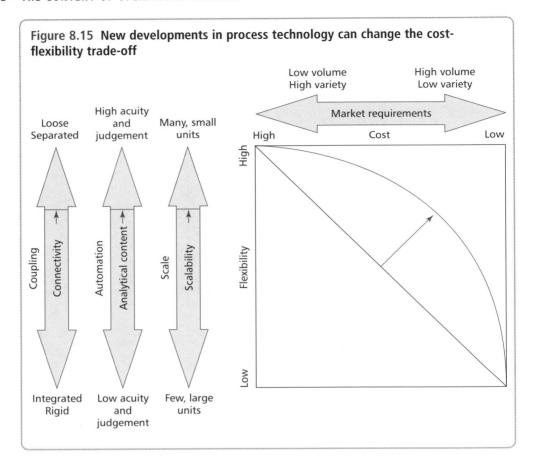

Figure 8.15 New developments in process technology can change the cost-flexibility trade-off

processes. Finally, technology with high connectivity can integrate processes without the rigidity once associated with high coupling.

● Market trends are themselves calling for simultaneously high performance in both cost and flexibility. No longer is it acceptable to suffer high costs if flexibility is demanded by the market, nor operations rigidity if costs need to be kept low. As far as market requirements are concerned, the ideal area in the traditional product–process matrix is one that delivers both low cost and high flexibility.

This is why information processing technology has had such an impact in so many industries. In effect it has partially overcome some of the traditional trade-offs in choosing process technology. But note the words 'partially' and 'some'. There are still trade-offs within technology choice even if they are not as obvious as they were once. Moreover, information processing and computing power has undoubtedly had a major impact on almost all technologies but there are still limits to what computers can do (see the box). In the next chapter we will turn our attention to the more practical 'why' and 'how' challenges associated with process technology.

What computers can't do[5]

It is an image that has been around in popular culture for years – that computers will eventually take over from human beings, either benignly in order to make our lives easier, or more worryingly, in some Terminator-type struggle for dominance. Even within the more mundane world of business, there is an underlying assumption that the limits to advances in process technology are governed by the limits to computing power, and the limits to computing power will take only a combination of time, money and effort to overcome. But computers cannot, and probably will never be able to, perform certain tasks. Some problems are inherently non-computable. It can be mathematically proven that some tasks cannot be solved by computer, such as figuring out whether it is possible to cover an infinitely large plane with a given set of different tiles. This is not because computers are not powerful enough as such, it is just that a computer's logic cannot tackle such problems. Another class of problems which are puzzling to computers are those known as 'intractable' problems. For example, working out whether there is a guaranteed winning strategy for an arbitrary chess position cannot be solved, even with parallel processing, in less than many trillions of years. Another category of tasks which puzzles computers are known as 'NP-complete' problems. Working out the shortest route around several cities or putting together a typical school timetable are examples of this kind of problem. Perhaps the most problematic types of task are those that require creativity and/or intuition. Although computers can bring much-needed discipline to such problems, they still need the human touch. Just as significant, computers cannot hold a decent conversation, and as customers we still feel more secure dealing with human beings, at least some of the time.

SUMMARY ANSWERS TO KEY QUESTIONS

What is 'process' technology?

Getting beyond a view of technology as a 'black box' is critical for any operations strategy. To help structure our review of technology we defined it in generic terms as the practical 'appliance of science'. Process technology is technology as applied to operational processes and is traditionally treated as separate from product/service technology. This distinction is inevitably less clear in many service operations where the product is the process. We can further classify two types of process technology. The first is that contributing 'directly' to the production of goods and services. The second type is the 'indirect' or 'infrastructure' technology that acts to support core transformation processes.

What are suitable dimensions for characterising process technology?

Although generic dimensions will always fail to capture completely the rich detail of any individual piece of process technology, it is normally useful to describe scale (capacity of each technology unit), automation (what the machine can do) and coupling (how much is or can be joined together) characteristics. Although these three dimensions are unlikely to be equally relevant for all types of technology, they do offer a useful categorisation for comparing a range of process technology options.

How do market volume and variety influence process technology?

There is often a 'natural' diagonal fit relationship between the volume/variety and process technology dimensions. For example, the larger the unit of capacity, the more likely that it is capital rather than labour intensive, which gives more opportunity for high coupling between its various parts. Where flexibility is unimportant but achieving dependable high volumes and low unit costs is critical, such inflexible systems come into their own. Conversely, small-scale technologies, combined with skilled staff, tend to be more flexible than large-scale, capital-intensive, closely coupled systems. As a result, these systems can cope with a high degree of variety.

How are newer technologies affecting these dimensions?

We can modify our original dimensions (scale, automation and integration) to more accurately reflect the characteristics of IT-rich process technology. More suitable characteristics are therefore scalability, analytical content and connectivity. We argued that these new characteristics were overcoming the traditional flexibility/cost trade-off and that new process technologies were able to enhance operational flexibility while still retaining reasonable underlying efficiency and vice versa.

CASE EXERCISE – What would you do?

Bonkers Chocolate Factory

Chocolate making starts with a series of primary processes to convert milk, sugar and cocoa into thick viscous liquid chocolate. The conching process is a critical element of the primary process, taking fatty powders and, through a shearing action between large contra-rotating rollers which releases fats and disperses solids, producing liquid chocolate with various controllable physical properties, such as temperature and viscosity. This chocolate is then used at secondary processes: to mould solid bars, to coat biscuits and assortments, and to make speciality products such as Easter eggs. Late in 1996, at a meeting of the Bonkers Chocolate Management Committee, discussion centred on the purchase of additional equipment for the Chocolate Department. The Engineering Director was proposing the implementation of a new in-house conching technology, whereas the Manufacturing Director wanted his €3 million capital application for a fifth conventional conch machine (to provide an additional 25 per cent capacity) approved.

> 'I believe that we cannot survive and grow without this type of leading-edge development. In my view, the old technology is often barely able to achieve the demands placed on it by the complex new products being dreamed up by our Development Department. There are at least six advantages of this technology, not all of which can be evaluated financially: (1) Trials indicate that for 50 per cent of recipes, fat content can be reduced by up to 1 per cent without significant changes to flavour or texture. As cocoa butter is expensive, this could give significant savings for some products. (2) The new process gives much greater control over viscosity, allowing more precise coating, potentially reducing reject levels on all coated products. (3) Conventional conches take hours to clear for a recipe change, during which time the output is a mixture of two recipes, which can, therefore, only be used on the lower quality specification product (usually selling at a lower price). The new conch, in comparison, fully clears all

material in less than half an hour, reducing the cost of materials. (4) The new conch-ing process will allow a much wider range of chocolates to be produced, as it can pro-duce to a higher viscosity and to tighter tolerances. (5) We believe that the technology will work at any size from one-tenth to double the size of conventional conches. They can be custom-built for our specific needs. (6) The new conch occupies 150 m^2 on one level, whereas a similar-sized, conventional machine occupies 200 m^2 on three levels (total 600 m^2). These modern and efficient process technologies will be critical in our future developments; Mars and Nestlé are certainly investing heavily in their factories.'
(Engineering Director)

'If we cannot approve the purchase of another conch machine, we won't meet forecast demand growth for 1997/8, and will be forced to cut back on expansion plans. We already experience frequent capacity problems in the chocolate plant ... it is nearly impossible to plan an efficient sequence of production to satisfy the needs of all the secondary user departments. We should purchase another (identical) conventional conch machine to be installed in under 6 months and we would have considerable flexibility ... to move staff around the different conches, to plan for any type of choco-late on any conch, and to hold standard spare parts. The new technology conch could take 12 to 15 months to develop, would require different skills in production and maintenance and different planning rules. All this would be too disruptive, just when we need to concentrate on output and new product development.'
(Manufacturing Director)

'I support the purchase of another conventional conch so we get into production by mid-1997; the new technology conch would not be into production until at least 6 months later. But, even more importantly, while we know that the small trial machine has made chocolate which the tasting panel cannot distinguish from our standard product, there is no guarantee that would be the case for a machine ten times larger. We know that conching is critical in creating our unique Bonkers Best flavour and tex-ture, so we should take no risks and stick with the process we have been using for at least 80 years. The extra capacity will allow us to go ahead with trials and product launches, which are already being disrupted by capacity and planning constraints.'
(Sales Director)

'We will have to defend existing volume brands by maintaining price competitiveness and quality (taste). The factories must be able to support this by delivering cost reduc-tions but we must also launch new, high-quality, high-margin products at a faster rate than ever before. I know there are plenty of eager competitors out there ready to erode our shelf space in the corner shops and supermarkets. Realistically, not all of these new products will be a success and few will ever reach even 10 per cent of the weight of sales of core products. Taken together, however, they will be very profitable and provide most of our projected growth. I think you can see why I favour the con-ventional conch technology. It minimises the fixed-cost burden of extra capacity and ensures low-cost production without any risks associated with new processes.'
(Marketing Director)

The Director of Engineering had been expecting resistance from Sales and Marketing but had made attempts to convince manufacturing of the advantages of the new conch tech-nology. The Finance Director also objected, on the grounds that providing the same level of capacity in the new process would cost about €4 million rather than €3 million. It appeared that two years of research and trials had been for nothing – but he sprang to the defence of his proposal.

'I understand your worries but trials of the one-tenth-scale conch have been success-

fully used on our full product range and the tasting panel reports no detectable changes in taste, texture or aroma. I also accept that the new conch could delay capacity by around 6 months and cost a little bit more. The relative annual cost saving of the new technology conch (compared to a conventional conch) in the primary processes would be around €280,000: the labour saving is only small, perhaps half a person or around €20,000. Space savings are estimated by Finance to be worth around €40,000 in opportunity cost. Improved control of cocoa fat content will save the department around €60,000 based on our trials on the prototype machine. The biggest saving is reduced material wastage at changeovers: we expect a €160,000 reduction here. But the big benefits will be seen in the secondary departments, where there will be much more control of coating thickness and fewer quality and productivity problems. Unfortunately, these savings are much more difficult to predict! Our conventional capital expenditures applications have always had to demonstrate clear departmental cost savings such as reductions in direct labour and associated overheads which result from automation technologies. The opportunities for further automation of high-volume production processes are diminishing as the variety of our products is expanding.'

The Chairman was alarmed to find that there was no agreed strategy for the purchase of conching capacity but recognised that the decision had to be made quickly and appropriately.

Further reading

Bensaou, M. and M. Earl (1998) 'The right mind-set for managing information technology', *Harvard Business Review*, September–October, pp. 119–128.

Davenport, T.H. (1993) *Process Innovation*, HBS Press, Boston, MA.

Kwon, T.H. and R.W. Zmud (1987) 'Unifying the fragmented models of information systems implementation', in Boland and Hirscheim (eds) *Critical Issues in Information Systems Research*, Wiley.

Mills, P.K. and D.J. Moberg (1990) 'Strategic implications of service technologies', Chapter 5 in D.E. Bowen *et al.* (eds) *Service Management Effectiveness*, Jossey Bass, pp. 97–125.

Taninecz, G. (1996) 'What's the ROI?' *IW Electronics and Technology*, October, pp. 45–48.

Hayes, R.H. and S.C. Wheelwright (1984) *Restoring our Competitive Edge*, Wiley, New York, pp. 212–227.

Notes on the chapter

1 Abanathy, W.J. and J. Utterback (1975) 'Dynamic model of product and process innovation', *Omega*, Vol. 3, No. 6.

2 Source: *The Times*, 6 March 1998.

3 Sources: Boyle, S. and C. Henderson (2000) 'Small scale is beautiful', *Financial Times*, 10 August; *The Economist* (2000) 'The Dawn of micro-power', 5 August.

4 Source: Swan, R. (2000) 'Engineers face new challenges and tough contracts', *Financial Times*, 3 July.

5 Source: Harel, D. (2000) *Computers Ltd: What they really can't do*, Oxford University Press.

Process technology – choice and implementation

Introduction

In the previous chapter we concentrated on the 'what' of process technology by identifying the dimensions that characterise it and discussing some of the directions in which process technology is developing. In this chapter we deal with the 'why' and 'how' questions (Figure 9.1). Why should companies invest in process technology? And, once committed, how can they ensure that their investments are implemented so as not to waste the potential of the process technology? Given the substantial amount of capital that is invested in new technology, it is important to clarify the strategic drivers associated with process technology selection, after which the chapter will review the benefits and risks associated with such systems. The risks are particularly important given the number of high-profile failures and claims of waste that seem to go hand-in-hand with such investments. Ultimately, even the most strategically appropriate and well-designed process technology needs to be implemented. Regardless of the context, there are a number of recurrent themes associated with implementation success and failure that require further investigation. The chapter will conclude with an examination of the specific challenges posed by 'indirect' process technology.

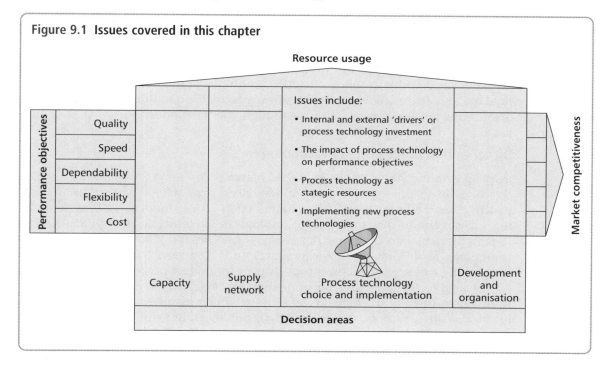

Figure 9.1 Issues covered in this chapter

Resource usage

Issues include:

- Internal and external 'drivers' or process technology investment
- The impact of process technology on performance objectives
- Process technology as stategic resources
- Implementing new process technologies

Performance objectives

- Quality
- Speed
- Dependability
- Flexibility
- Cost

Capacity

Supply network

Process technology choice and implementation

Development and organisation

Market competitiveness

Decision areas

Why invest in process technology?

So, why do organisations choose to invest in possibly expensive, and often risky, process technology? Henry Ford, a man whose legacy remains a major influence on modern operations practice, reveals part of the answer in his memoirs, when he describes how the competitive benefits associated with mass manufacturing operations are directly related to process technology:

> Our foundry used to be much like other foundries. When we cast the first "Model T" cylinders in 1910, everything in the place was done by hand; shovels and wheel-barrows abounded. The work was then either skilled or unskilled; we had moulders and we had labourers. Now we have about five percent of thoroughly skilled moulders and core setters, but the remaining 95 percent are unskilled, or to put it more accurately, must be skilled in exactly one operation which the most stupid man can learn within two days. The moulding is all done by machinery.[1]

Ford's view highlights one of the major drivers (and sources of controversy) for capital investment in 'direct' process technology – technology helps to de-skill work and thereby a firm is able to reduce wage rates, reduce training requirements, increase labour flexibility and reduce its overall costs. This is not a surprising objective. Cost reduction remains the most universal of the generic operational performance objectives. Crucially, this de-skilling process did not just deliver cost benefits, it also enabled Ford's fledgling operation to hire large numbers of people (agricultural workers etc.) without the craft skills necessary for traditional car making, thus overcoming a major capacity obstacle to high-volume production.

Direct and indirect process technology

In the previous chapter we distinguished between *direct* process technology, which acts directly to produce produces and services, and *indirect* process technology, which helps to manage the activity of production. Understanding the basis for judging investment in direct process technology is, in principle, not difficult (even though the actual decision may not be easy). The benefits of any new direct process technology apply directly to the products and/or services it produces. However, establishing a clear motivation for investment in indirect process technologies that do not act directly upon core transformation processes is sometimes less straightforward. Often there is an ambiguity of purpose which represents one of the greatest practical challenges associated with such technologies. But while there are potential difficulties with judging the financial benefits of investments that impact right across an operation, we can still highlight a number of specific motivations for indirect process technology investment. As an illustration of just how significant the impact of such forms of process technology can actually be, it is instructive to look at Cisco Systems (see box).

Cisco Systems[2]

Cisco Systems sells nearly 80 per cent of the routers and other networking technology that underpins the Internet (and corporate intranets). During the 1990s, in providing data networks to large corporations, it was the dominant player in a market growing at almost 25 per cent a year! Earlier, however, Cisco had most of the growing pains that face many young technology companies. Their market appeared to offer unlimited opportunities, but in getting bigger they faced operational bottleneck after operational bottleneck. Perhaps unsurprisingly, given the nature of the products they sell, it was Internet applications that enabled them to overcome most of these problems. For example:

● In a rapidly growing technological environment, customer orders can be vague or impossible to fulfil. When every month sees the introduction of new products or derivatives, updating the firm's catalogues is a real challenge. Whatever the reason, for Cisco this meant that one in three orders were inaccurate. Today, approximately 8 per cent of Cisco's sales come from the Web, where customers selecting from an online catalogue are helped to get their order exactly right (and can track its progress). The whole process of ordering, contract manufacturing, fulfilment and payment is automated.

● As well as providing an ordering portal for the firm, the Web has also changed the nature of supply chain management. Cisco's suppliers know exactly what materials and components they need to ship to the factory because they can access their stock replenishment software via a web browser.

● Network equipment is expensive, highly customised, each application requires careful configuration and, as a result, clients expect continuous support. Unfortunately, the highly trained engineers who can deal with a full range of technical problems are hard to find (and very expensive). Cisco decided therefore to put as much information as possible online, leaving customers to resolve many problems on their own. This is 'externally' successful (customers go to the site to get information, they use it to share their experiences and in turn have created an even more valuable resource) and has also freed up 'internal' capacity by obviating the need to respond to a huge volume of relatively trivial questions. Freeing these staff has allowed more than 80 per cent of queries to be answered online and, although sales are over six times their 1994 level, technical support staff numbers have only doubled.

Larry Carter, chief financial officer of Cisco Systems (previously at Motorola), claims that 55 per cent of orders pass through Cisco's system without being touched by anyone and believes that Cisco is saving well over $500m a year by using the Web. If the application of 'virtual' processing technology allowed Cisco to become what it is today, the information architecture it adopted continues to provide it with strategic benefits. Although the firm currently employs 14,500 staff, its intranet allows senior managers to find out instantly (from a desktop PC) about purchasing, recruitment, and general financial activity (including an instant read-out of the net revenue effect of every order). Specific examples of the positive impact of this infrastructural technology include:

● Closing the quarterly accounts would take up to ten days. Today, although it is down to two days and has halved the cost of finance to 1 per cent of sales, the goal is to be able to obtain 'close' information within a day on any day in the quarter. Such knowledge, in addition to allowing rapid competitive response, also frees the 600 people who used to spend ten days a quarter tracking transactions to be more usefully employed on things such as mining data (see later) for business intelligence.

▶

● Travel and expenses are dealt with entirely on the Web, with reimbursement within two days. Employees needing to communicate can find each other wherever they are in the world. As mentioned above, procurement and recruiting are all web based but so are employee benefits. So, for instance, selling shares in the company (all employees are shareholders) simply takes a mouse and a couple of seconds.

During this period Cisco Systems appear to have applied and leveraged indirect process technology in a seamless fashion across their business. The possibilities that exist for applying technology to support direct transformation processes fall into a wide variety of categories. The Cisco example illustrates a number of them.

Improving information management

Cisco's intranet and Internet systems provide their managers with access to a huge range of financial data. This offers them a range of functionality, from accurate and timely revenue information to the rapid placement of orders and the ability to automate payments. More generally, by collating information from transactions and improving the ability to manipulate information, any firm can move much closer to its chosen marketplace. Cisco's technology, for instance, allows information on customer requirements to be reviewed and potential opportunities explored. In cases like their online product support systems, the customers actually input critical competitive information themselves. In other areas, like the preparation of quarterly reports, the time-saving aspects of the support technology free key staff to turn the vast array of data into useful knowledge.

In another example, American Airlines gained several years' worth of competitive advantage by tracking its customers' flying patterns more closely than its competitors. Similarly, for a retailer, the use of loyalty cards and sophisticated EPOS technology allows them to capture information on their customers. However, without some further manipulation this data is worth little. Ever since Wal-Mart discovered that putting beer and nappies next to one another on the same aisle would increase sales, so-called 'data mining' has become a source of competitive advantage. Analysing sales data showed that men with small children often bought nappies and beer at the same time (we will leave it to the individual reader to establish a plausible sociological explanation for this phenomenon!). The managerial response to this finding was to co-locate the two items, thus hoping that even more men would get the same idea and beer sales would increase – an assertion that turned out to be true. Today, most retailers invest in support systems that allow non-technical users to 'drill down' into data stores and extract unexpected patterns from stores of data. The basic concept of applying statistical techniques to sets of data is not new, but it is only with investment in the underlying process technology that it can be a feasible tool.

Integrating information

When a process needs to draw upon data that is stored in many different locations, it represents a barrier to both data manipulation and overall productivity improvement. A critical factor when considering the relative success of Cisco in exploiting technology applications was its relative lack of history. How many of these advantages would Cisco have been able to realise if it had been 50 rather than 15 years old? In 1999, their Chief Financial Officer argued that the absence of 'baggage' (such as legacy systems, resource dependencies, existing routines, etc.) was crucial. Cisco's competitors in the converging market for data networking and telecom equipment were companies such as Lucent Technologies (formerly AT&T), Nortel Networks and Alcatel with lots of history to deal with. The costs associated with maintaining fragmented legacy systems with old code, hardware, etc. should not be underestimated. In addition to the removal of legacy maintenance costs, eliminating multiple data sources should remove the need for multiple keying of data and allow for staff reduction and/or relocation. Possessing a common, integrated IT infrastructure can overcome fragmentation and provide a beneficial degree of organisational consolidation. At the simplest level, this can be illustrated by the connection of desktop PCs in an organisation via a common e-mail system. This begins to transform what were little more than glorified typewriters and calculators into an integrated communications network. Such integration can then help to improve operational performance by supporting decision making. For example, J.C. Penney, the US department store, put in place a video link infrastructure to permit all 1500 of its store managers to be actively involved in the central purchasing decision. Similarly, Harvard Professor Shoshana Zuboff describes how computer-based 'integrating' technologies allow operators in a paper mill to capture information about resource and energy utilisation and then use it to try to optimise overall consumption levels.

Disintermediating stages in the supply chain

Human intermediaries can be relatively inefficient and expensive for passing information, whereas information processing technologies, especially those predicated upon common information protocols, can be particularly good at connecting, say, buyers and sellers and helping them to exchange information about a transaction. So, for example, if suppliers can directly access a firm's production management systems this can remove the need for much of a purchasing department's traditional activity. At Cisco Systems all information on various aspects of core transformation processes (like manufacturing and assembly) is integrated to allow managers and suppliers to improve performance by removing traditional barriers. The Cisco 'dynamic replenishment' system allows suppliers to bypass traditional inventory control, production scheduling, purchasing, and order placement activities.

More fundamentally, once such an infrastructure is in place the potential exists for the complete bypassing (or disintermediation) of certain activities. This kind of disintermediation can result in a radical change to the core transformation process. For instance, although an online brokerage system still completes the same profile of tasks as a traditional one, the IT infrastructure allows customers to directly access market information, execute trades and so on. Likewise, the entire 'B2C' Internet phenomenon was driven by an aspiration on the part of large players in various supply chains to bypass specific stages (such as fast-moving consumer goods (FMCG) manufacturers seeking to avoid retailers). Like Cisco, another celebrated example of the advantages of disintermediation comes from Dell computers, one of the first to encourage customers to log onto their web site and place orders directly, thereby not having to coordinate or negotiate a share of the value with retailers.

Overcoming geographical constraints

Given the scale and scope of Cisco's global operations, their systems are crucial in allowing them to facilitate the management (including the recruitment, remuneration, training and development, etc.) of a widely dispersed workforce. In a similar vein, many global businesses are able to operate effectively only because of the advent of a robust technological infrastructure. The Ford Motor Company uses information technology to connect its disparate regional and national design processes into an integrated global product development system. Similarly, in global banking and trading, global integration gives a 24-hour network capability because as Tokyo shuts London opens, as London shuts New York opens. In such markets the rapid dissemination of market information from one country to another has become a prerequisite for competitive success.

Of course, the removal of such operating obstacles also brings some disadvantages. For example, once specific geographical locations are no longer needed in the resource base of, say, high street retail operations (such as booksellers and banks) then one of the largest barriers to entry for those markets is removed (or at least diminished). The result can be a range of new entrants and the need for radical shifts in the strategies of established players. In the UK, for instance, new financial service channels (technology enabled) have contributed directly to the closure of 50 per cent of high street branches over a ten-year period.

Other drivers of process technology investment

While it is important to emphasise the positive 'internal' drivers of investment in direct and indirect process technology, it is also critical that we highlight other 'external' drivers. We can split these into (albeit often overlapping) 'demand side' and 'supply side' factors. This generic model is shown in Figure 9.2 and in order to illustrate its implications we have populated it with a few examples that we shall explore further.

Demand-side drivers of process technology

Demand-side drivers exert a powerful external influence upon a firm's motivation to invest in its operations, and new process technology is no exception. The most obvious form for these demand-side drivers to take is that of customer requirements. In other words, process technology deployed in order to respond to specific customer

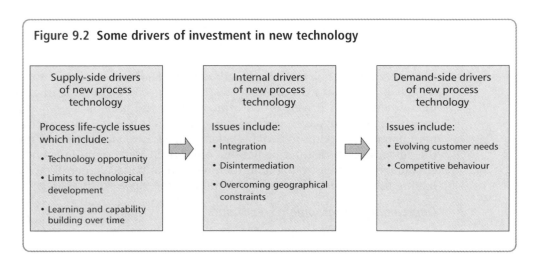

Figure 9.2 Some drivers of investment in new technology

Supply-side drivers of new process technology	Internal drivers of new process technology	Demand-side drivers of new process technology
Process life-cycle issues which include:	Issues include:	Issues include:
• Technology opportunity	• Integration	• Evolving customer needs
• Limits to technological development	• Disintermediation	• Competitive behaviour
• Learning and capability building over time	• Overcoming geographical constraints	

needs, regardless of whether this is a requirement for enhanced product functionality or service features. In addition to specific customer concerns, however, there are equally significant competitive drivers that we also need to consider.

Meeting evolving customer needs

The obvious driver of a firm's motivation to invest in new process technology is that there has been some kind of change in customer needs. So, for example, in the food industry, regardless of whether requirements emerge for particular recipes (i.e. following media-led food fashions), alternative formats (i.e. more biscuits in a 'family' packet) or new packaging types (i.e. individually wrapped for snacking), each change requires manufacturers to modify their process technology. Some changes derive from specific requirements whereas others are part of longer-term trends. As a specific example, several new processing technologies, such as the in-packet pasteurisation of fresh pasta, have developed as the result of a general trend in customer preference for processed foods with high 'perceived' freshness (this is not necessarily the same as actual freshness).

Other market changes can have a more profound impact. For instance, changes in consumer attitudes towards fat (especially saturated fat) have led many manufacturers, including global margarine producers like Procter and Gamble, to invest huge sums in developing and adopting technologies which could process reduced fat and reduced cholesterol-bearing products.

In a similar fashion, as more and more organisations come to use and rely upon third-party global logistics, this has driven up the customer and competitive pressures upon providers like DHL, Federal Express, United Parcel Services, TNT, etc. As a result of these increased customer requirements, many logistics processes have been enhanced by indirect process technology that receives data about a package and then monitors its progress, noting precisely when it reaches its intended destination. Of course, such a parcel tracking system cannot by itself alter aircraft capabilities and make it any quicker to fly, say, from Los Angeles to Singapore. However, it can help to improve the dependability of core logistics transformation processes because accurate process information can reduce errors, help identify areas for improvement and, more importantly, create an enhanced service proposition. Couriers therefore began to allow customers to access (via a phone or web site) their tracking systems and find out the exact location of their package – thus greatly increasing the perceived quality of the service.

Responding to competitor behaviour

Customer requirements, however, are not the only influence on process technology from the demand side of the operation. Rational or not, process technology is as subject to trends and fashions as any other marketplace. Regardless of the sector, managers in many organisations spend much of their time thinking about their rivals (the popularity of benchmarking provides strong evidence of this). The adoption of a new technology by a rival is of great interest, especially in those markets where firms compete head-to-head. If the technology is available on the open market, simply copying the investment may not bring competitive advantage, but it is unlikely to bring disadvantage either. Many years ago, for example, all serious users of IT had a mainframe system. At the time there was a widespread business cliché stating that 'no one got fired for buying IBM'. In other words, the safe thing to do was to adopt the same technology as everyone else. In a similar fashion, ERP systems were rapidly adopted by entire sectors (e.g. petrochemicals) and although this technology addressed fundamental business needs, competitor adoption certainly played a significant part in many decisions to invest. Some insights into how competitive processes can modify individual incentives and thereby drive technological investments can be afforded by the 'entrapment' game. (See the Theory Box 'Technological races'.)

Theory Box **Technological races**[3]

The 'entrapment' game is essentially an auction 'with a twist'. The auctioneer announces to the players that she is going to auction off a £20 note to the highest bidder. After someone opens the bidding, each following bid must exceed the previous one by at least 50p. The 'sting in the tail' is that once the bidding stops, not only the highest but also the second-highest bidder must give their bids to the auctioneer. The highest bidder gets the £20 note and the second highest gets nothing! Regardless of the type of player, the pattern of bidding remains very similar. Following the opening bid, offers quickly proceed to £10, or half the amount being auctioned. There is then a pause, as the players digest the fact that, with the next bid, the total of the two highest bids will exceed £20 and push the auctioneer into profit. Imagine yourself as the second-highest bidder at this point, considering what your options actually are. You can give up and take a certain loss of £9.50 or you can risk a little more and possibly win £9.50. At this point in the game, it is common for all but the top two bidders to drop out.

If we return to our auction, as the bidding approaches £20, there is a second pause as the bidders appear to be pondering the fact that even the highest bidder is likely to lose money. Again, consider the alternative: dropping out means definitely losing £19.50. Once the £20 threshold has been crossed, the bidding quickens again, and from then on it is a battle of nerves. And if you are thinking to yourself that you would never be so silly as to get involved in a game that so strongly favoured cost escalation, reflect on the following. A psychology professor claims that over ten years he won more than $17,000 auctioning $20 bills to his MBA students at the Kellogg Graduate School of Management – one of the best US business schools!

Players in the entrapment game 'auction with a twist' face similar drivers to those firms considering investments in new performance-enhancing technologies. If there are any kinds of 'winner takes all' factors at play (i.e. first-mover advantage) then investing just a little more than a rival can shift the results in one's favour. At the same time, these factors also mean that very often the second-placed player faces minimal returns on his or her investment, if not actual losses and (of at least equal significance) the potential for appearing foolish.

Supply-side drivers of process technology

In the previous chapter we defined process technology as the 'appliance of science' to operational processes. Therefore it seems clear that any advances in the underlying scientific base of different process technologies can and will prompt development in the technologies themselves. Since few organisations carry out such fundamental research and development activities themselves, this provides us with an indication of the importance of 'supply side' drivers of process technology.

Technological opportunities and the process life cycle

For every progressive organisation that effectively exploits its technological opportunities, there are many more that seem incapable of capitalising on new ideas and developments. But also, conversely, because scientific developments often occur independently of specific market dynamics, companies may be faced with a potential process technology in search of a sensible market application. Raytheon, for example, the US engineering conglomerate, lost over $5 million with their first microwave oven by marketing it to industrial users and emphasising the technical performance of the underlying technology, rather than marketing it to catering operations and demonstrating the rapid cooking of popcorn. In the previous chapter we discussed some of the difficulties associated with separating product/service and process life cycles. Despite these practical and theoretical concerns, the notion that a process technology has a specific life span is still a powerful one – especially when discussing whether to exploit a specific technological opportunity.

In this application, the S-curve is a graph of the relationship between research effort (investment) put into improving a process technology over time and the performance outcome that is achieved as a result. The S-curve shape is as it is because of a number of factors. Initially, returns from any innovative process technology are low but as the technology is more widely adopted and its basic performance is improved, returns grow rapidly. Finally as a technology matures, it becomes increasingly difficult to gain further technological progress no matter how much money is thrown at it. Several authors[4] have used this curve to argue that as organisations reach the upper limits of a technology (point A in Figure 9.3), further investment is better spent on an entirely new S-curve that represents a new technology and a host of new opportunities (position B). Celebrated examples of a lack of awareness of the S-curve abound. For example, none of the top ten manufacturers of vacuum tubes (in the 1950s) was quick enough to see the impact of semiconductor technology and none of them was in this new top ten.

Although the model is conceptually attractive, it should not be taken as offering simple prescriptions for operations strategy. It is useful, however, in forcing organisations to consider some critical questions:

● *How do we really know that a technology has reached its limit?*

● *How can we be sure that customers will value investment in a new process*

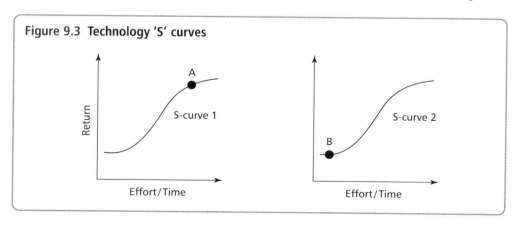

Figure 9.3 Technology 'S' curves

technology? What about past investments and the underlying capability base we have developed?

● *Will we be able to replicate the same level of capability?*

In an early academic contribution to the resource-based view of the firm (see Chapter 1), a bathtub metaphor was used to represent an organisation.[5] Adapting this for the context of this chapter, the water in the bath represents the 'stock' of technological resources (tangible and intangible) at a particular point in time. Current capital investment is represented by the water 'flowing' in through the tap and the strategic depreciation of the technological base (through substitution, imitation, etc.) is represented by the flow of water leaking through the drain. Crucially, the metaphor illustrates that while capital investment in technology can be immediately altered, underlying resource stocks cannot – thus suggesting that time and timing play a central role in the development of process technology-led advantage.

Evaluating process technology

Evaluating process technology quite literally means determining its value or worth. It involves exploring, understanding and describing the strategic consequences of adopting alternatives. Although there can be no 'all-purpose' list of attributes to be evaluated, indeed the precise nature of the attributes to be included in any evaluation should depend on the nature of the technology itself, it is useful to consider three generic classes of evaluation criteria:

1 the *feasibility* of the process technology;

2 the *acceptability* of the process technology;

3 the *vulnerability* associated with the process technology.

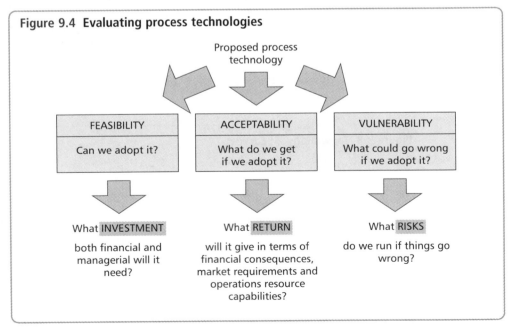

Figure 9.4 Evaluating process technologies

The 'feasibility' of technology indicates the degree of difficulty in adopting it, and should assess the investment of time, effort and money that will be needed. The 'acceptability' of technology is how much it takes a firm towards its strategic objectives. It is the return the firm gets for choosing it. The 'vulnerability' of technology indicates the extent to which the firm is exposed if things go wrong. It is the risk that is run by choosing the technology (see Figure 9.4).

We will begin our review of these criteria by looking at the basic feasibility of any process technology proposition. After all, if a project is not feasible given all the practical constraints that exist, then the acceptability of any potential return or ongoing vulnerabilities is essentially irrelevant!

Evaluating feasibility

All process technology decisions have resource implications – even the decision to do nothing liberates resources that would otherwise be used. In this context we are not just talking about financial resources which, although critical, are no help if, say, the technical skills necessary to design and implement a technology are not available. Therefore, if the resources required to implement technology are greater than those that are either available or can be obtained, the technology is not feasible. So evaluating the feasibility of an option means finding out how the various types of resource that the option might need match up to what is available. Four broad questions are applicable:

1 *What technical or human skills are required to implement the technology?* Every process technology will need a set of skills to be present within the organisation, so that it can be successfully implemented. If new technology is very similar to that existing in the organisation, it is likely that the necessary skills will already be present. If, however, the technology is completely novel, it is necessary to identify the required skills and to match these against those existing in the organisation.

2 *What 'quantity' or 'amount' of resources is required to implement the technology?* Determining the quantity of resources (people, facilities, space, time, etc.) required for the implementation of a technology is an important stage in assessing feasibility because it is time dependent. Rarely will a lack of sufficient, say, process engineers, rule out a particular process technology, but it could restrict when it is adopted. So, a firm may deliberately choose to delay some of its process technology decisions because it knows that its current commitments will not allow it. In order to assess this type of feasibility a company may compare the aggregate workload associated with its implementation over time with its existing capacity.

3 *What are the funding or cash requirements?* The previous two questions can be difficult to answer in a meaningful way but this does not diminish their significance. However, in any real investment evaluation one 'feasibility' factor will inevitably come to dominate all other considerations – do we have enough money? Because of this significance we will spend a little more time reviewing some of the many approaches that have been developed to aid managers in their analysis of cash flow and funding requirements over the lifetime of an investment project.

Assessing financial requirements

In most process technology decisions the most important feasibility question is, 'How much financial investment will the technology require, and can we afford it?' At its simplest, this could mean simply examining the one-off cost of the purchase price of the technology. Usually, though, an examination of the effect of the cash requirements on the whole organisation is necessary. If so, it is often necessary to simulate the organisation's cash flow over a period of time. Computing the total inflow of cash over time as it occurs, and subtracting from it the total outflow of cash as it occurs, leaves the net funding requirement for the option. For example, Figure 9.5 shows the net cash inflows likely to be earned if a proposed technology is adopted and the cash outflows associated with its purchase and implementation.

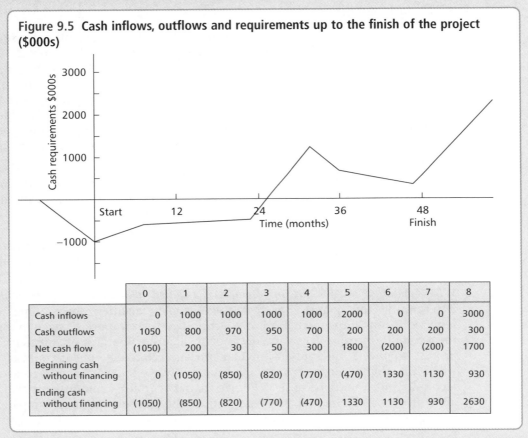

Figure 9.5 Cash inflows, outflows and requirements up to the finish of the project ($000s)

	0	1	2	3	4	5	6	7	8
Cash inflows	0	1000	1000	1000	1000	2000	0	0	3000
Cash outflows	1050	800	970	950	700	200	200	200	300
Net cash flow	(1050)	200	30	50	300	1800	(200)	(200)	1700
Beginning cash without financing	0	(1050)	(850)	(820)	(770)	(470)	1330	1130	930
Ending cash without financing	(1050)	(850)	(820)	(770)	(470)	1330	1130	930	2630

The resulting cash requirements show that a maximum funding requirement of $1,050,000 occurs within the first eight months of the project, and diminishes only slowly for two years. After that, the project enjoys a large net inflow of cash. Of course, this analysis does not include the effects of interest payments on cash borrowed. When it is decided how the cash is to be raised (i.e. borrowed from a bank or private investor, raised from the equity markets) this can be included.

4 *Can the operation cope with the degree of change in resource requirements?* We have assessed feasibility in terms of the skills, the quantity of resources required and funding necessary. Any one of these could render the investment infeasible. Yet even if all these resource requirements can quite feasibly be obtained individually by the organisation, the degree of change in the total resource position of the company might itself be regarded as infeasible. Consider, for instance, a bespoke manufacturer of road-racing bicycles being encouraged to leverage its reputation for high quality into the 'top end' of the mass cycle market (i.e. much higher volumes). This would require the firm to make substantial investment in automated tube welding equipment. The firm is confident that it will be able to obtain all the different categories of resource required for the project. It believes that it can recruit the appropriate expertise in sufficient quantity from the labour market. Furthermore, it believes that it could fund the project until it broke even. Yet in the final analysis, the company regards the investment as infeasible. It decides that absorbing such a radical new process technology in a relatively short time frame would put too great a strain on its own capacity for self-organisation. Thus sometimes it is not the absolute level but rather the rate of change in resource requirements that renders a project infeasible.

Evaluating acceptability

By the 'acceptability' of a process technology, we mean the benefit it is expected to bring to an operation. Unsurprisingly, the greater the benefits, the greater the overall acceptability. Evaluating acceptability can be done from many technical and managerial perspectives. Here we limit our discussion to cover the financial

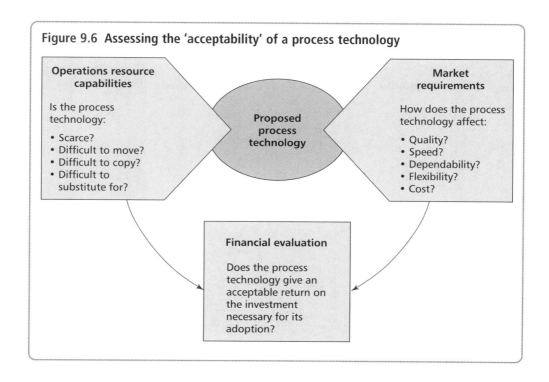

Figure 9.6 Assessing the 'acceptability' of a process technology

Operations resource capabilities

Is the process technology:

• Scarce?
• Difficult to move?
• Difficult to copy?
• Difficult to substitute for?

Proposed process technology

Market requirements

How does the process technology affect:

• Quality?
• Speed?
• Dependability?
• Flexibility?
• Cost?

Financial evaluation

Does the process technology give an acceptable return on the investment necessary for its adoption?

perspective on evaluation and the 'market requirements' and 'operations resource' perspectives. Figure 9.6 summarises the different elements of our analysis.

Acceptability in financial terms

Financial evaluation involves predicting and analysing the financial costs to which an option would commit the organisation, and the financial benefits that might accrue from acquiring the process technology. However, 'cost' is not always a straightforward concept.

Acquisition and opportunity costs

An accountant has a different view of 'cost' to that of an economist. The account-ant's view is that the cost of something is whatever you had to pay to acquire it orig-inally. The economist, on the other hand, is more likely to define costs in terms of the benefits forgone by not investing elsewhere: that is, the opportunity cost of the technology. Thus, to the economist, the cost of investing in a process technology is whatever could be gained by investing an equivalent sum in the best feasible alternative investment. While opportunity costing has obvious intuitive attractions, and is particularly useful in process technology investments where alternative tech-nologies may bring very different benefits, it does depend on what we define as the best feasible alternative use of our resources. The accountant's model of acquisition cost is at least stable – if we paid $1,000 for something, then its value is $1,000, irres-pective of whatever alternative use we might dream up for the money.

The life-cycle cost

The concept of life-cycle costing is useful in process technology evaluation. It involves accounting for all costs over the life of the investment which are influenced directly by the decision. For example, suppose a company is evaluating alternative integrated warehousing systems. One system is significantly less expensive and

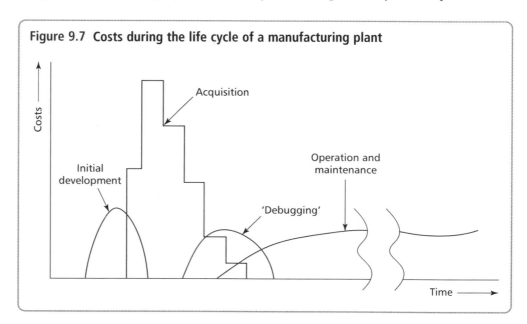

Figure 9.7 Costs during the life cycle of a manufacturing plant

seems at first sight to be the least costly. But what other costs should the company consider apart from the acquisition cost? Each system would require some initial development to remedy outstanding technical problems before installation. The systems would also have to be 'debugged' before operation, but, more importantly, during its years of life the plant will incur operation and maintenance costs which will in part be determined by the original choice of system. Finally, if the company wants to look so far ahead, the disposal value of the plant could also be significant. Figure 9.7 shows how these costs might occur over the life of the system. In fact, total life-cycle costing is impossible in any absolute sense. The effects of any significant investment ripple out like waves in a pond, impinging on and influencing many other decisions. Yet it is sensible to include more than the immediate and obvious costs involved in a decision, and a life-cycle approach proves a useful reminder of this.

The time value of money: net present value (NPV)

One of the most important questions to be answered in establishing the 'real' value of either costs or benefits is determining *when* they are incurred or realised. This dynamic is important because money in your hand today is worth more to you than the same money would be worth in a year's time. Conversely, paying out a sum in one year's time is preferable to paying it out now. The reason for this has to do with the opportunity cost of money. If we receive money now and invest it (in a bank account or in another project giving a positive return), then in one year's time we will have our original investment plus whatever interest has been paid for the year. Thus, to compare the alternative merits of receiving $100 now and receiving $100 in one year's time, we should compare $100 with $100 plus one year's interest. Alternatively, we can reverse the process and ask ourselves how much would have to be invested now, in order for that investment to pay $100 in one year's time. This amount (lower than $100) is called the *present value* of receiving $100 in one year's time.

For example, suppose current interest rates are 10 per cent per annum. The amount we would have to invest to receive $100 in one years' time is:

$$\$100 \times \frac{1}{1.10} = \$90.91$$

$$\$100 \times \frac{1}{(1.10)} \frac{1}{(1.10)} = \$100 \times \frac{1}{(1.10)^2} = \$82.65$$

The rate of interest assumed (10 per cent in our case) is known as the *discount rate*. More generally, the present value of x in n years' time, at a discount rate of r per cent is:

$$\frac{x}{(1 + r/100)^n}$$

Limitations of conventional financial evaluation

Conventional financial evaluation has come under criticism for its inability to include enough relevant factors to give a true picture of complex investments. Nowhere is this more evident than in the case of justifying investment in process technologies comprising a significant IT element. Here costs and benefits are both uncertain, intangible and often dispersed throughout an organisation. Indeed, with all the talk about there being a 'new economy', the myriad discussions about computers removing cost (labour) from operational processes, or the impact of the creation of knowledge and information-based markets, you could be forgiven for thinking that the computer age was an unambiguously positive thing for business. Until recently, however, there has been little actual evidence that for all the IT investment that firms have made, there has been any real impact upon overall productivity.

Theory Box | **The IT productivity dilemma**

Despite the huge IT investments that the US service sector made during the 1980s, its productivity remained static while that of manufacturing grew by 2 per cent (and this limited growth was the subject of major hand-wringing from policy observers). Just before the end of the century, however, US productivity finally began to grow, leading many observers to talk about an economic miracle. Ultimately, whatever the overall economic impact, the long lag between substantial IT investment beginning (hundreds of billions of dollars in the US service sector during the 1980s) and productivity improvements becoming measurable raises a number of interesting managerial issues. Curiously, these productivity problems had an interesting precedent. A study by Paul Davis of Stanford University found that it took industry two decades to reap competitive benefits from investment in electricity. Initial investment in electric motor technology began at the turn of the nineteenth century but it wasn't until 1920 that productivity began to improve. So perhaps the answer is simple. It takes time and actual competitive pressure for managers to recognise that technology by itself will not automatically deliver benefits – rather they and their staff have to be organised in such a way as to exploit its advantages and ignore the attractions of its inherent newness where appropriate.

Of course, in the face of these conceptual and analytical difficulties we are not suggesting that we should (even if we ever could!) abandon such forms of evaluation completely but rather recognise their limitations and make sensible modification to conventional techniques where possible. US performance measurement guru Professor Kaplan[6] makes a number of suggestions as to how such financial evaluation techniques can be used in a manner sensitive to the attributes of recent process technology. These include:

● Not setting discount rates too high. Some companies set rates too high in the belief that this makes for high-return projects rather than recognising the huge contribution that innovation can make to operational performance and overall competitiveness.

● Not simply evaluating technologies against current competitive conditions, but rather including assumptions about competitors investing in similar technologies.

● Including all support and development costs in any appraisal. The total cost of many new process technologies is often significantly larger than their basic 'purchase price'.

● Including all benefits deriving from the technology which can be measured in some way. For example, include stock inventory reductions, reduced floor space and increased quality. Likewise, it is important to take account of intangible benefits such as increased flexibility, shorter manufacturing times and increased learning. This might not necessarily mean estimating the financial benefits directly, but asking what the cash flows from these intangible benefits would have to be in order to make the investment attractive, and then judging whether such cash flows could reasonably occur. For example, suppose we calculate that the amount of cash flow to bring the NPV of an investment up to zero is $300,000 per year for the next five years. The question then becomes, 'Do we believe that increased flexibility and other benefits which are difficult to measure will give us an extra cash flow of $300,000 per year for the next five years?' If the answer is 'Yes', the investment may be worthwhile.

Acceptability in terms of impact on market requirements

Extending the idea of considering all competitive benefits from an investment, we have argued elsewhere in this chapter that process technology can impact *all* of the generic operational performance objectives: quality, speed, dependability, flexibility *and* cost. The questions listed in Table 9.1 can help provide a framework for assessing the impact of any proposed investment on each of them. In order to illustrate this we have applied them to a generic analysis of the effect of process technology on the airline industry.

Although the examples in Table 9.1 were set in the airline industry, we could have done the same for any industry. The most important point to emerge from any similar analysis in any sector is that the market opportunities associated with process technology are far greater than the traditional narrow focus on cost reduction. Any sensible evaluation of process technology *must* include all the effects impacting on quality, speed, dependability, flexibility *and* cost. As we stressed in Part 1 of the book, the generic performance objectives are very rarely equally important for all types of operation. Their relative importance will reflect the actual and intended market position of the organisation. The implication of this for evaluating process technology is straightforward. Any evaluation must reflect the impact of process technology on each performance objective relative to their importance to achieving a particular market position. Often there will be trade-offs involved in adopting a new process technology. Reverting to our airline examples earlier, one advantage of having a fleet of mixed aircraft is the flexibility it provides to match aircraft to routes as the demand on different routes changes. Yet different types of aircraft require different spare parts, different maintenance procedures, different interfaces with ground technology and so on. This may add more cost and complexity to the total airline operations than is gained through the benefits of flexibility. For example, Airbus Industrie, the European airline consortium and great rival to the US aerospace giant Boeing, claims that its strategy of common cockpit and flight control systems across its range of planes saves considerable cost. Commonality in such systems allows pilots and ground crews to deal with similar systems with 120-seater to 400-seater aircraft.

Acceptability in terms of impact on operational resources

Using the generic performance objectives can help us to characterise the potential contribution that process technology can make to market requirements. For instance, if we consider Cisco Systems again, their early and complete exploitation

Table 9.1 Evaluating the acceptability of process technology investment on market criteria

	Generic questions	*Example*
Quality	Does the process technology improve the specification of the product or service? That is, does it provide something better or different which customers value?	An airline investing in in-flight entertainment technology to enhance the specification of its flight services.
	Does the process technology reduce unwanted variability within the operation? Even if absolute specification quality is unaffected by process technology, it may contribute to conformance quality by reducing variability.	An airline investing in maintenance equipment which keeps the performance of its aircraft and ancillary systems within very tight tolerances. This reduces the risk of failure in equipment as well as increasing the internal predictability of the airline's processes.
Speed	Does the process technology enable a faster response to customers? Does it shorten the time between a customer making a request and having it confirmed (or a product delivered etc.)?	The check-in technology used by airlines at airport gates and lounges in effect allows customers' requests for seating or dietary requirements to be explored quickly, and if possible confirmed.
	Does the process technology speed the throughput of internal processes? Even if customers do not benefit directly from faster process throughput within an operation, technology increasing 'clock speed' can benefit the operation by, for instance, reducing costs.	The technology which allows the fast loading of customers' bags and in-flight catering supplies, allows fuel to be loaded and engines to be checked etc. all reduces the time the aircraft spends on the ground. This allows the aircraft to be used more intensively.
Dependability	Does the process technology enable products and/or services to be delivered more dependably? Although many of the causes of poor dependability may appear to be outside the control of an operation, technology may help to bring some of the factors within its control.	Specialist navigation equipment installed in aircraft can allow them to land in conditions of poor visibility, thus reducing the possibility of delays due to bad weather. Customers benefit directly from such an increase in dependability.
	Does the process technology enhance the dependability of processes within the operation? Again, even when customers see no direct result of more dependable technology, it can provide benefits for the operation itself.	Airlines invest in advanced aircraft communications technology. Efficient communication between aircraft and control centres reduces the possibility of miscommunication, which, even when presenting no danger, can waste time and cause confusion. Indeed, an oft-cited concern of many airlines is that airports around the world do not always match their investment in communications technology – preventing maximum productivity gains from their equipment.

	Generic questions	*Example*
Flexibility	Does the process technology allow the operation to change in response to changes in customer demand? Such changes may be in either the level or nature of demand.	When an airline considers the mix of aircraft types to include in its fleet, it does so partly to retain sufficient flexibility to respond to such things as timetable change or unexpected demand.
	Does the process technology allow for adjustments to the internal workings of the operations processes?	Some aircraft (notably the Boeing 777) permit the precise configuration of cabins and seating to be changed. While this may not happen very frequently, it offers airlines the flexibility to provide a different mix of services without having different types of aircraft.
Cost	Does the process technology process materials, information or customers more efficiently? As we mentioned previously, this is by far the most common basis for justifying new process technology, even if it is not always the most important. It is never unimportant, however.	A major driver for airlines to invest in new aircraft is the greater efficiency ($/passenger mile flown) of each new generation of aircraft that derives from the overall design of the aircraft and, most especially, the engines powering them.
	Does the process technology enable a greater effectiveness of the operations processes? Even if straightforward efficiency is unaffected, process technology can aid the deployment of the operations capabilities to increase profitability or general effectiveness.	The 'yield management' decision support systems used by airlines enable them to maximise the revenue from flights by adjusting capacity and pricing strategies to match demand patterns.

of reliable 'virtual' processing technology was not only the source of their market advantage but also a critical factor in allowing the firm to grow its operations so rapidly. It had a direct impact on the operation's generic performance objectives, lowering costs on product support, giving better quality product support, faster order processing, more dependable deliveries, more flexible stock management, and so on. At the same time, however, it is important to build up a picture of the contribution that process technology can make to the longer-term capability 'endowment' of the operation. We can use the dimensions described in Chapter 1 as being 'strategic' according to the resource-based view of the firm. As a reminder, these four dimensions are:

- the *scarcity* of resources;
- how difficult the resources are to *move*;
- how difficult the resources are to *copy*;
- how difficult the resources are to *substitute for*.

These four dimensions provide us with a 'first cut' mechanism for assessing the impact that a specific technological resource will have upon sustainable competitive

Table 9.2 The four dimensions of 'strategic' operations resources

	Generic questions	*Example*
Scarcity	Does the technology represent any kind of first-mover advantage? In other words, how much of the developed technology (or perhaps its underlying R&D) is not possessed by competitors?	Such resources might include bespoke production facilities in industries like petrochemicals and pharmaceuticals, where first-mover advantage often generates superior returns.
	Does the technology help create or exploit proprietary product/service knowledge, perhaps in the tangible form of a database?	Capturing customer data over time and then exploiting this information has long been a core element of airline competitive strategies – such information is extremely scarce.
Difficult to move	How much of the process technology was developed in-house? If a process technology is unique and, moreover, it was developed 'in-house', then such resources cannot easily be accessed without purchasing the firm.	The value of resource immobility helps to explain the increased emphasis being placed upon infrastructure development in the management consulting sector – to facilitate the retention of skills, knowledge and experience.
	How many of the critical technological resources 'don't walk on legs'? In other words, highlight those resources that are more than contractually tied into the operation.	Mobility concerns in, say, the IT sector explain the emergence of more complicated contracts (constraining subsequent employment etc.) and wage inflation for certain key staff.
Difficult to copy	How far down the 'learning curve' is the process technology?	Experiences such as those documented in high-volume processes, like Intel and semiconductors, can create competitive performance barriers.
	How strong is your legal protection? Patents offer some protection, even though the process is long, often expensive and may attract greater competitive risk than simply having better site security.	In the competitive confectionery market, for instance, there is almost pathological secrecy associated with proprietary production processes but very little recourse to the filing of patents.
Difficult to create a substitute	What, if any, market mechanisms exist to prevent process technology simply becoming irrelevant through the introduction of a substitute?	Traditional EDI-type connections integrate supply chains but can also help to establish de-facto standards and introduce switching costs. They can therefore prevent rivals offering substitute services.

advantage. Cisco Systems' technology investment, for instance, developed their underlying capability profile by creating widespread internal access to unique market and product information, supported inimitable supplier relationships, and established first-mover customer links and a reputation for innovation that was difficult for rivals to substitute for. Table 9.2 develops these four dimensions with examples.

Tangible and intangible resources

It is important to recall that in our discussion in Chapter 1 on the importance of operations resources and process we were careful to distinguish between tangible and intangible resources. Tangible resources are the actual physical assets which the company possesses. In process technology terms these will be the machines, computers, materials handling equipment, and so on, used within the operation. Intangible resources are not necessarily directly observable but nevertheless have value for the company. Things such as relationship and brand strength, supplier relationships, process knowledge, and so on are all real but not always directly tangible. This concept of intangible resources is important when considering process technology. A unit of technology may not be any different physically from the technology used by competitors. However, its use may add to the company's reputation, skills, knowledge and experience. Thus, depending on how the process technology is used, the value of the intangible aspect of a process technology may be greater than its physical worth. If the usefulness of process technology also depends on the software it employs, then this also must be evaluated. Again, although software may be bought off the shelf and is therefore available to competitors, if it is deployed in imaginative and creative ways its real value can be enhanced.

In order to look at how these dimensions can be used in practice it is instructive to apply them to different examples of manufacturing and service process technology. To begin we will look at the creation of an additional Web-based service for an already well-established and successful US retailer, Payless ShoeSource.

Creating www.payless.com for Payless ShoeSource, USA

Although now operating in other countries (over 200 stores in Canada, some in Puerto Rico etc.), Payless ShoeSource remains a largely US-based operation. The original Payless operation opened in 1956 in Topeka, Kansas with an extremely simple yet revolutionary service concept – instead of being guided by an employee towards their footwear purchase, customers browse independently in a self-service environment. This simple, yet appealing, concept gave, and continues to give, their operations a basic efficiency that allows them to sell their shoes at low prices (today most of their products sell for less than $15 a pair). In 1996, Payless ShoeSource Inc. was spun off from its by then more diversified parent and became an independently traded company on the New York Stock Exchange (trading as PSS). Like most successful garment manufacturers, the business exploits a global network of factories and agents. Although somewhat late compared with other retail sectors and other competitors, in 1999 the firm launched its new online retail business. The synergy with their established self-service retail concept seemed to be strong. Adopting a relatively cautious approach to the new operation, PSS deployed an 'off-the-shelf' web front-end and order receipt system created by the Internet division of IBM. The 'back office' order processing was completed using the pre-existing (and completely tried and tested) systems developed to support hundreds of individual retail outlets across North America.

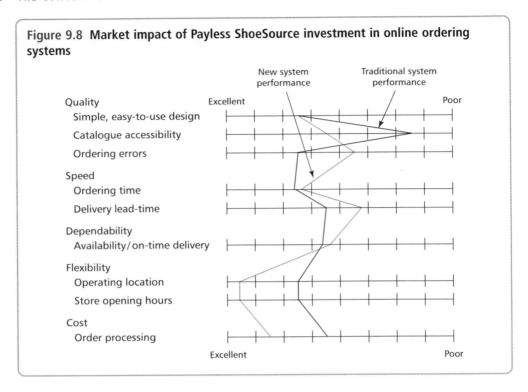

Figure 9.8 Market impact of Payless ShoeSource investment in online ordering systems

We will apply the market requirements and resource-based analyses described above. The complete analyses are also summarised in Figures 9.8 and 9.9.

- *Quality* – The online ordering system is essentially an extension, or new front-end, on the inventory and order management systems used to support the existing Payless stores. However, the simple-to-use web site (following the tradition of their self-service stores) does offer some additional features such as a permanently available up-to-date catalogue and corporate information for the firm's investors. The likelihood of ordering errors, though, could be greater if customers do not follow the site instructions.

- *Speed* – Although customers can now place orders from home, the physical distribution of shoes etc. exploits the same back-office delivery systems as before. Therefore the overall speed of delivery can even be, if a customer has to wait for a courier to deliver their goods, actually slower than visiting a store with the product in stock.

- *Dependability* – Because the underlying processes are the same, just as they are no faster, they are no more dependable in terms of product availability (although actual stock is more visible) and on-time delivery.

- *Flexibility* – The introduction of a complementary web-based service effectively extends the scale of their retail operations. The number of potential customers is no longer restricted to those within a reasonable travel distance from a store and likewise the ordering process is now available 24 hours a day, 365 days a year.

- *Cost* – Online transaction costs are a fraction of those associated with the traditional store-ordering process which could involve considerable amounts of staff

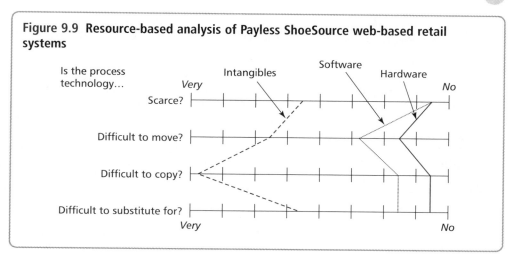

Figure 9.9 Resource-based analysis of Payless ShoeSource web-based retail systems

time. Unlike a start-up web retailer, Payless' exploitation of established processes massively reduced their initial costs and, by increasing total volumes, reduced overall unit transaction costs.

We can analyse the resource profile of the technology in a similar fashion. Interestingly, most of the hardware and software elements deployed by Payless were 'off-the-shelf' items: from the standard network servers to IBM's Internet store solution. Figure 9.9 charts this resource profile and distinguishes between hardware, software and the intangible aspects of the technology.

● *Scarce?* Although Payless created a fairly standard retail web site, more crucially it enables the company to leverage their existing brand and thereby reinforce/protect it.

● *Difficult to move?* It would be very difficult for another retailer to rapidly grow the same web presence independently of the already established retail brand and customer relationships (including sales data, customer preferences, etc.) that underpin it.

● *Difficult to copy?* With the exception of specific logos and graphical elements, the basic functionality of any web 'store front' can easily be copied (especially one bought off the shelf from a global supplier). To a lesser extent this is also true for any back-office processes (recognising how far down the learning curve Payless are after decades in business). However the firm's reputation – and the trust this creates – is inimitable.

● *Difficult to create a substitute for?* Interestingly, on the S-curve, one could argue that the Internet is the twenty-first-century substitute retail technology. However, there is nothing that renders the technology itself intrinsically difficult to substitutes. Most crucially for Payless, a web presence extends their market position (more than 4000 stores), allowing them to exploit and defend their already significant incumbent's advantage.

We will now apply exactly the same analytical process to an example of manufacturing process technology. Hewlett-Packard's Medical Products Group in the USA makes a range of products, including ultrasound equipment for medical imaging.

Hewlett-Packard, Medical Products, USA[7]

A global corporation with a reputation for technological innovation and excellence, Hewlett-Packard (HP) operates in a large number of different marketplaces. One of their operations serves the healthcare sector, producing a range of different monitoring and therapeutic equipment to hospitals and clinics around the world. In 1996, their US business took the decision to invest in a form of manufacturing technology that, while widespread in other sectors, was not prevalent in healthcare products. This was surface mount technology (SMT) which uses high speed and accurate placement mechanisms to assemble electronic components onto their printed circuit boards (PCBs). The decision to adopt SMT for the construction of electronic devices reflected an awareness of the improved performance characteristics that such process technology would bring. These included greater complexity and packing of micro-components onto a single assembly, thus allowing for increased functionality and at the same time reducing the size and weight of products. However, the technology was difficult to justify on simple cost-payback terms alone.

SMT replaced the old method of placing the components into pre-drilled holes in the PCBs. This old process was difficult, costly and relatively slow, and also contributed to quality problems, especially in the post-insertion soldering process. Additionally, because the new technology was able to provide accurate and continuous data on processes, it allowed the division to move from a total inspection approach to quality to the introduction of statistical process control.

In selecting a specific supplier of SMT equipment, HP Medical was able to draw on the expertise of the rest of the corporation and, working in collaboration with the machinery vendors, invested sufficient capital to be able to purchase the best technology available at that time. Temporary personnel with specific SMT skills and experience were hired to ease the transition to the new technology.

Again, let us analyse the market and resource impacts of HP's new process technology. This is summarised in Figures 9.10 and 9.11.

- *Quality* – Surface mount technology (SMT) is designed to offer 'better' control (allowing SPC to be applied) and quality than the 'old' insertion process – it removes the need for process stages that introduced major sources of product failure. Moreover, HP was in a position to critically appraise different suppliers and had the capital available to purchase the very best equipment.

- *Speed* – Again, the nature of the SMT process allows manufacturing to work reliably at a faster throughput rate than the old process. HP combined the introduction of new technology with a process redesign to allow faster materials flow through factory.

- *Dependability* – Overall, no real change because previously they had used comprehensive inspection, but SMT's better quality, fewer failures and faster throughput meant dependability at less cost.

- *Flexibility* – HP largely justified their investment because it gave them the capability not only to make their existing products more effectively and efficiently but, more importantly, to allow them to design and manufacture a new, extended product range.

- *Cost* – In addition to all the above benefits, they were also able to lower unit costs, especially as an associated corporate redesign gave greater volumes to a single SMT process site.

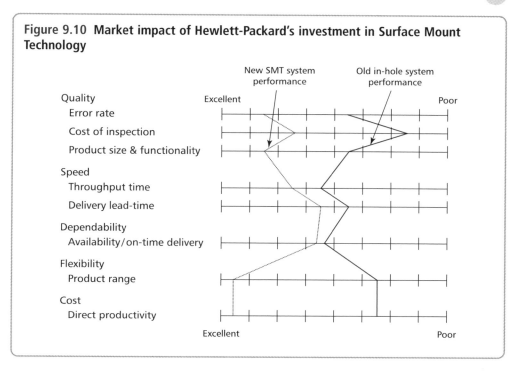

Figure 9.10 Market impact of Hewlett-Packard's investment in Surface Mount Technology

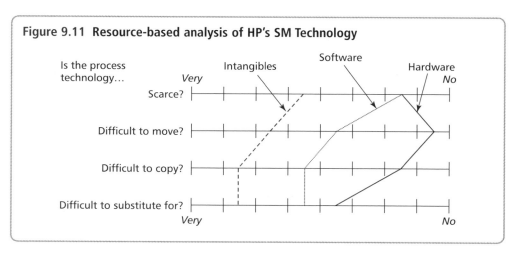

Figure 9.11 Resource-based analysis of HP's SM Technology

Shifting our attention to the investment's technological resources, it is noticeable that most elements were bought in from external vendors. The SMT machines themselves, the process control software and hardware, SPC systems and even the temporary specialists deployed during the start-up phase were all bought in. However, although the hardware was off-the-shelf, the software and intangible aspects of the process technology provide more strategic capabilities.

● *Scarce?* While expensive and not exactly ubiquitous (in the same way that web portals are, for instance), SMT is still an off-the-shelf technology that has become established as an industry standard. However, HP worked with specific suppliers to access best-in-class machines that were modified for their own specific requirements.

- *Difficult to move?* Markets exist for both SMT machines and implementation skills. However, the infrastructure changes and process control systems that were developed around the technology are not as readily 'tradable' since they comprise a large element of in-house effort and trial and error implementation.

- *Difficult to copy?* As stated above, the more infrastructural elements that allowed the SMT implementation to be economically and organisationally successful (i.e. the structure adopted, the process control and product manufacturing data generated) are difficult to imitate.

- *Difficult to substitute for?* SMT substitutes for in-house technology and, given the industry dynamic, it is almost inevitable that another substitute will be developed eventually.

Perhaps unsurprisingly, cost and quality benefits are important in both of the cases. It is interesting to note, however, that although both investments aimed to reduce unit costs, in neither case is there any argument for a corresponding reduction in labour as a result of the investment. The resource analysis of the examples also reinforces an issue that we have touched upon several times already in this book. Namely, that much of the strategic benefit from, in this case, the process technology does not necessarily come from tangible 'pieces of equipment' but rather from the intangible 'skills, knowledge and experience', inter-organisational 'relationships' and reputation they underpin, promote and create.

A 'not for profit' example

In the introduction to the book we argued that many, if not most, of the ideas to be discussed would be equally interesting for 'not for profit' or public sector operations. It is therefore interesting to look at the role of process technology in this kind of organisation.

Consider, for instance, a Windows-based data management system for a police force to help manage their crime laboratory. The lab is where samples from a range of crime scenes are tested in a large variety of different processes (DNA testing, fingerprint analysis, etc.) that vary widely in their sophistication and complexity. Although speed is often of the essence in the lab, accuracy and dependability are equally critical, as is their legal requirement to store and access information over extended periods of time (for legal appeals, long-term investigations, etc.). While this operation does not have a market position as such, it still has a set of social and legal priorities which are its direct equivalent. Figure 9.12 illustrates this by adding a further line to the profile which indicates what the laboratory's performance targets are. Although the new process technology does not improve operations performance in all aspects of the crime lab's 'market' requirements, it does improve some specific areas of performance and does not appear to have any negative effects.

It is when we turn our attention to the resource profile of the technology that the relevance for 'not for profit' operations of dimensions derived from a competitive marketplace needs to be more closely examined. Although we might see the usefulness of a unique and difficult-to-copy crime database in the 'war against crime', the positive advantage of having resources which rank highly on the RBV dimensions is not clear for an accountable public sector operation. Figure 9.13 illustrates.

Figure 9.12 Performance of laboratory analysis and data-based systems

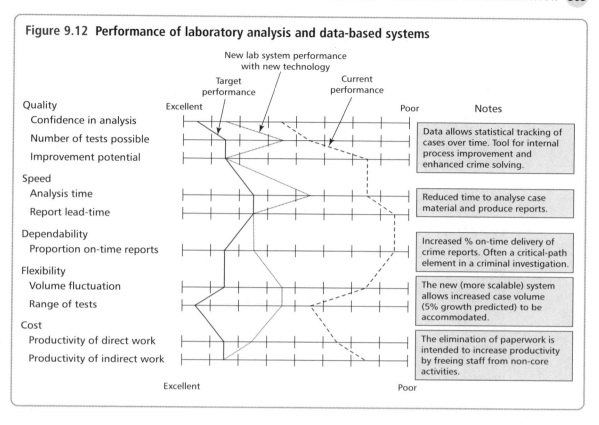

Figure 9.13 Resource-based performance of laboratory analysis and database systems

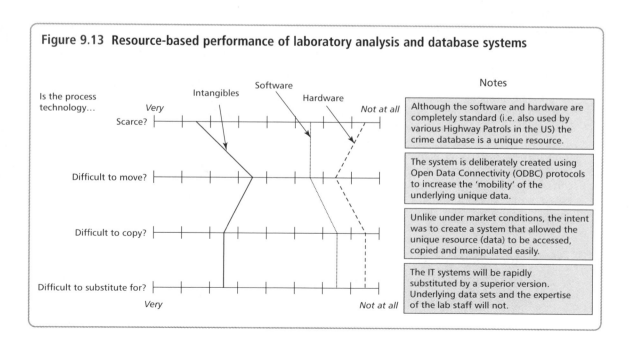

In other words, if a resource (like knowledge or experience) is difficult to move or copy this can contribute to sustainable advantage in a competitive marketplace. However, such characteristics can act against critical public sector objectives such as effective information transfer or even accountability over performance. In this type of application, therefore, it is necessary to see the resource characteristics as useful in a different way. So, for instance, imagine that the staff experience associated with analysing particular types of DNA evidence is crucial for the crime lab but very difficult to copy and therefore shared both within and between labs. The operations strategy response might therefore be to diminish (rather than embrace) this 'imitability' characteristic by developing systems and procedures that seek to codify (i.e. papers, technical diaries, open databases) and encourage regular sharing of experience (i.e. seminars, staff exchanges, apprenticeships).

Evaluating vulnerability

There have been some spectacular and very public failures associated with the introduction of new process technology (see the box 'When second is best'). Yet presumably all of these process technology 'failures' were at one time determined to be both feasible and acceptable to the operation. Their subsequent failure highlights one further important issue to explore – vulnerability. That is, what exposure is the firm accepting if something goes wrong with the technology once the decision to invest is made? We will return to a more formal discussion of risk in Chapter 15 but at this stage it is worth highlighting some common sources of vulnerability associated with process technology.

When second is best

For the past 20 years the airports of the world have used what are known as 'tug cart and conveyor belt' systems to move baggage on and off aircraft and around the airport. Denver International Airport (DIA) was going to be the pioneer in a new type of system where bags would be individually handled on automatic carts or 'destination-coded vehicles'. But at DIA it all went wrong. The system proved unreliable and difficult to make work properly. Instead of the original $185 million, the eventual cost was over $300 million for only a partially operating system. The airport, which was due to open in 1993, was delayed three times and eventually a further $70 million had to be spent installing a conventional conveyor belt system. This highly publicised failure caused Oslo's Gardermoen Airport to think twice before adopting its own new baggage-handling technology. However, Oslo learned from Denver's mistakes. Their own system, the Dutch-manufactured Bagtrax system, is up to four times quicker than the conventional belt system, requires less maintenance and is cheaper to operate. But unlike Denver's system, it is less complicated and less prone to breakdown. In effect, it allows the airport to tailor baggage delivery to requirements. A single bag can be sent to a single destination without having to start up a whole conventional belt system.

Adjustment costs

Calculating the true costs of implementing any technology is notoriously difficult. This is particularly true because more often than not, Murphy's Law seems to prevail. This law is usually stated as *if anything can go wrong, it will*. This means that most implementations of process technology will incur 'adjustment costs' before the tech-

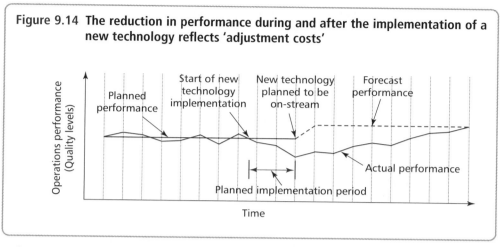

Figure 9.14 The reduction in performance during and after the implementation of a new technology reflects 'adjustment costs'

nology works as expected. This basic effect has been identified empirically in a range of manufacturing operations. It has also been estimated that during the 1980s, managers in the US service sector spent a large proportion of the nearly $200 billion expended on hardware and software on making their initial investments work. Bruce Chew of Massachusetts Institute of Technology argues that adjustment costs stem from unforeseen mismatches between the new technology's capabilities and needs and the existing operation. New technology rarely behaves as planned and as changes are made, their impact ripples throughout the organisation. Figure 9.14 is an example of what Chew calls a Murphy Curve. It shows a typical pattern of performance reduction (in this case, quality) as a new process technology is introduced.

Technologists, having demonstrated that a new process technology is both a feasible and acceptable investment, predict a particular level of performance improvement. In the earlier Hewlett-Packard SMT illustration, for example, a decrease in throughput time or an increase in right-first-time production was forecast. It is recognised that implementation may take some time, therefore allowances are made for the length and cost of a 'ramp-up' period. However, as the plant prepares for the installation, the distraction causes performance actually to deteriorate. Even after the start of the implementation this downward trend continues and it is only weeks, indeed maybe months later that the old performance level is reached. The area of the dip indicates the magnitude of the adjustment costs, and therefore the level of vulnerability faced by the operation. In the following section we turn our attention to processes for overcoming or at least minimising these adjustment costs.

Vulnerability because of changed resource dependencies

All process technologies depend for their effective operation on support services. Specific skills are needed if the technology is to be installed, maintained, upgraded and controlled effectively. In other words, the technology has a set of 'resource dependencies'. Changing to a different process technology often means changing this set of resource dependencies. This may have a positive aspect. The skills, knowledge and experience necessary to implement and operate the technology can be scarce and difficult to copy and hence provide a platform for sustainable advantage. But there can also be a downside to a changed set of resources dependencies. For example, the specific skills needed to implement or operate a new process technology, because they are scarce, could become particularly valuable in the labour market. The company is vulnerable to the risk of the staff who have these skills leaving in order to leverage their value. This was a particular problem when many organisations were implementing enterprise resource planning (ERP) systems. The extensive training programmes necessary to give staff the skills to implement ERP systems shifted the 'knowledge power' to staff to the extent that it made staff retention difficult.

Issues of trust and power also influence the vulnerability created by dependence upon external organisations such as suppliers and customers. If there is a high degree of trust between a firm and its technology supplier, it can be entirely appropriate to become dependent for the installation, maintenance and upgrading of process technology upon a particular external provider. Dependence can also work the other way. Customers may ask for a particular piece of technology to be dedicated to their business. Again, this can be entirely legitimate if the operation trusts its customer to continue generating work for them over a suitable period. However, such exclusive relationships inevitably introduce vulnerabilities. For example, suppose an operation is choosing between alternative suppliers of software. One supplier seems to be particularly price competitive, very service-oriented and has developed a particularly effective leading-edge application. Unfortunately, this supplier is also smaller than the alternative suppliers. Although its products and service may be superior, it is itself more vulnerable to business pressures. If it went out of business the company would be left with unsupported infrastructure. Under these circumstances the company may decide that choosing this supplier would expose it to unacceptable levels of vulnerability.

Why high-tech *Hamlet* failed to do his turn[8]

In August 1996, Canadian Robert Lepage planned to bring his critically acclaimed one-man reworking of Shakespeare's *Hamlet* to the Edinburgh festival. When it was cancelled on its opening night almost 3000 tickets had already been sold for its run at the King's Theatre. His production of *Elsinore*, which *The Times* described as 'a show of beguiling originality', relied heavily upon a range of complex multimedia effects. When interviewed, the actor-director admitted that the show's (described as 'a remarkable synthesis of dazzling theatre technology and cinematic convention') complete reliance upon high-tech equipment was 'a bit too risky'.

Everything had been tested during the rehearsal period and all the systems appeared to be working well, as indeed they had during the past six months of the show's international tour. However, on the day of the opening, one of the four motors which turned the revolve, upon which were mounted the production's large and elaborate sets, completely failed. Initially an electrical problem within the theatre was suspected but closer investigation revealed that a motor part was at fault. Unfortunately, no spare parts were available anywhere in the UK and as a result the show had to be cancelled. Brian McMaster, director of the festival, argued that 'working in the theatre today you have to take an incomparable number of risks. Some of those risks don't come off.'

Assessing future flexibility[9]

The risk inherent in process technology choice can also be viewed as how it constrains the range of options or 'room for manoeuvre' in future decisions. For example, if a construction firm purchases a special piece of equipment which is

Figure 9.15 Machine requirements for five alternative demand patterns

Demand scenario	Machine requirements
1	C A E I
2	A E C D G H
3	D G J I H E C
4	C G H E B
5	A F G C J B N

Number of times machine mentioned:
A = 3
B = 2
C = 5
D = 2
E = 4
F = 1
G = 4
H = 3
I = 2
J = 2

capable of doing one currently important and frequent task (but few other tasks) with great efficiency, the ability of the operation to cope with a totally different mix of tasks will be seriously impaired. This does not mean that the decision to buy the special-purpose equipment was necessarily the wrong one, but it does limit one's future options. If there is an alternative option which does not limit what can be done in the future (especially if uncertainty is high), then trading off short-term efficiency for long-term flexibility may be considered.

Suppose a specialist machining company is considering replacing ten of its oldest machines. The market for its products, however, is likely to change quite drastically in the next few years, so it is not entirely clear whether all the machines will be needed. Since the company does not want to renew machines which are unlikely to be useful in the future, it engages in an exercise to try to determine the five most likely 'product-mix scenarios', and to decide which machines would be needed under these five possible futures. The machines to be replaced are labelled A–J, and the requirements for these machines are shown for each alternative scenario in Figure 9.15.

Machine C is mentioned five times, and so will be needed no matter which of the alternative scenarios materialises. At the other end of the scale, machine F is mentioned only once. So, if we choose to replace machine C as our first decision, we are not constraining our future actions, whereas if we choose machine F, it would inevitably have an effect on our future decisions. To maintain maximum future flexibility, machine C should be renewed first. Note that, if we choose machine F, it does not mean to say that we have 'damned' ourselves if scenario 5 does not occur. We can generally undo our decision – but at a cost. Note also that we are not taking into account factors such as the likelihood of each scenario to occur, the cost of each machine replacement, or the capacity needs of the company. Beware of too great an emphasis on future flexibility. It can lead to a reluctance to take any decision at all, on the grounds that delay will not commit us to any future that might not occur – the vacillator's ideal excuse! It is therefore critical to assess future flexibility in situations either:

● where uncertainty is very high, and therefore putting probabilities on future events becomes very difficult or meaningless, or

● where the cost of redressing a 'wrong' decision is high, and so the total cost of a series of decisions is very sensitive to the initial decisions in the series.

Given its inherent and increasing complexity, it is little wonder that most operations experience practical difficulties with process technology. Some of the reasons for these problems will be evaluation failures. No amount of clever project management will rescue a process technology implementation if the strategic criteria by which it was selected were inappropriate. However, as Murphy's Law suggests, even armed with the most robust rationale in the world, operations can still fail to make their technology work for them. The following section explores some of the challenges faced when trying to implement new process technology.

Implementing process technology

The demonstrable existence of Murphy's Law (discussed earlier) in many process technology projects suggests that there are systemic characteristics associated with such implementations which need to be understood. It is argued[10] that the greatest 'adjustment' costs derive from a mismatch between the process technology and the operations processes that receive it. This 'gap' exists, first, because new process technology rarely behaves exactly as expected and, second, the impact it will have on existing and complex operations processes can never be completely predicted. In some ways this argument is an inversion of the classic saying, *what you don't know can't hurt you*. From an implementation point of view it seems more likely that, *what you don't know can, and indeed probably will, hurt you!*

Resource and process 'distance'

The degree of difficulty in implementing process technologies within an existing operation will depend on the degree of novelty of the process technology itself *and* the changes required in the operation's processes. The less that a process technology resource is understood (influenced perhaps by the degree of innovation or the level of involvement of external suppliers), the greater its 'distance' from the current resource base of the operation. Similarly, the extent to which an implementation requires an operation to modify its existing processes, the greater the 'process distance' (see Figure 9.16).

The greater these organisational 'distances' or the greater the mismatch between the technology and operation, the more difficult any implementation is likely to be. This is because such distance makes it difficult to adopt a systematic approach to analysing change and learning from mistakes. In fact the learning which can be gained from an implementation is a key issue, not only in managing that particular technology implementation but also in managing those in the future. Those implementations which involve relatively little process or resource 'distance' provide an ideal opportunity for organisational learning. As in any classic scientific experiment,

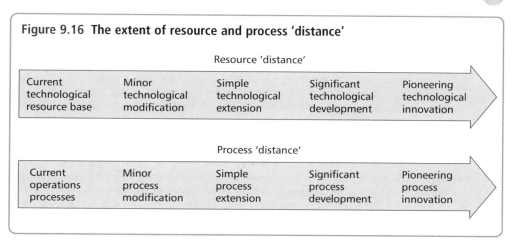

Figure 9.16 The extent of resource and process 'distance'

the more variables that are held constant, the more confidence you have in determining cause and effect. Conversely, in an implementation where the technology and process 'distance' means that nearly everything is 'up for grabs', it becomes difficult to know what has worked and what has not. More importantly, it becomes difficult to know why. Such a model of change has a great deal of common-sense validity but also reflects theoretical findings in the academic literature. For example, most innovation research argues that opportunities for successful product/service development will tend to exist close to an organisation's current stock of capabilities (resources and processes) because what a firm currently does strongly influences the firm's 'learning range'. Figure 9.17 combines the resource and process distance ideas to illustrate further this concept of learning range.

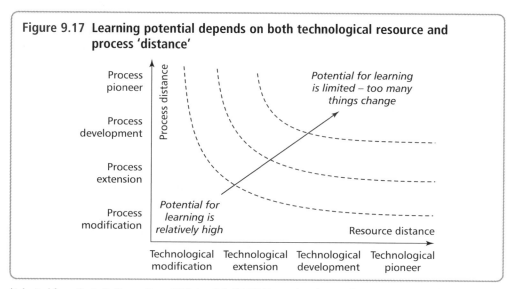

Figure 9.17 Learning potential depends on both technological resource and process 'distance'

(Adapted from Dosi, G., Teece, D. and Winter, S.G. (1992) 'Towards a theory of corporate coherence', in Dosi, G., Giametti, R. and Toninelli, P.A. (eds) *Technology and Enterprise in a Historical Perspective*, Oxford University Press)

ERP systems

In recent years, Enterprise resource planning (ERP) systems have become extremely popular[11] with a range of different manufacturing and service operations. The vendors are very good at articulating the potential benefits of closer integration – including better coordinated logistics, faster response times and closer operational control – of a wide range of real-time business processes under common software architecture. In the case of the market-leading SAP R/3 system, for example, there are nearly 100 modules that can be integrated, covering most key management functions. The intent is that all transaction information is entered into the system at its source and done only once. Consider, for instance, a manufacturing firm receiving an order for a product. The transaction is entered (manually or through electronic data interchange (EDI)) into the system and the data is then sent to the master database, which accesses and updates the other business processes. For example, the finance process is instructed to raise an invoice, the sales and marketing processes are advised of sales and customer information, the production process triggers the manufacturing etc. If the system does not have its own scheduling software, it can (to varying degrees) be integrated with pre-existing packages.

Weighed against such potential benefits, however, are the 'adjustment costs' associated with many of the implementations. ERP systems quickly developed a reputation for being very expensive, with 200/300 per cent cost and time overruns being commonly cited for reasonably sized installations. Given that such systems are predicated on both substantial IT development **and** process redesign work (i.e. resource and process distance), it should not be surprising that costs and time-frames are proving to be larger and longer than predicted.

In order to make any implementation work, all operations need to be able to learn 'as they go along'. The newer the technology and the more radical the change to the underlying processes, the harder an operation will have to work in order to learn effectively. A frequently cited example is enterprise resource planning (see box), the implementation of which usually implies considerable resource and process 'distance'. In such implementations top management support is needed to ensure that a cross-functional approach is taken and cross-functional problems are overcome. Such implementations also require adequate resources – money, time and people. A number of new technology installations have suffered because of management efforts to compress the available time unrealistically or 'over-control' other resources. So, for example, senior technical staff may be reassigned to their next project before the implementation is complete. In particular, top management can support efforts to overcome resource and process distance.

Overcoming resource distance

The newer the technology, the less an operation is likely to know about it and the more technical problems there are likely to be. Because of this, technologies may be treated by managers as an art form, rather than a science. Many information technology-rich implementations fall into this category and organisations may become over-dependent upon key individuals and suppliers. Successful implementers, on the other hand, tend to build close relationships with both internal and external suppliers that are characterised by a two-way flow of information, rather than an 'eyes shut', off-the-shelf purchase. At the very least, this requires operations managers to be able to converse in a common technological language as a basis for meaningful communication.

Effective project management and pilot operations

Although obvious, it is worth stressing that process technology implementation needs to be effectively project managed. This is a specialist subject in itself. Techniques such as Project Evaluation and Review Technique (PERT) and Gantt charts are used to plan and control projects so as to meet cost and time goals. Organisational structures including strong project managers are used to ensure unambiguous lines of responsibility. While conventional project management remains a necessary condition for effective implementation, it is not by itself sufficient to achieve strategically successful implementation. A more 'thoughtful' model of project management is needed to cope with the technology 'distance' involved in most implementations. Such models of project management need to consider the potential for failure and recognise that not only will failures happen but that they can be viewed as an increased opportunity for learning. One very clear manifestation of a company's commitment to learning can be seen in the role of pilot or trial operations. The idea of running a complete 'experiment' of a new technology is a very powerful one. But in many organisations, delays combine with managerial cost pressures to turn a pilot into a 'first-off' without giving any time to reflect upon the lessons learnt. However, problems that arise should not only be solved, they should also be seen as a source of learning. This allows knowledge to be gained which can improve the process and prevent future problems. The positive role of failure has to be recognised. In the context of technology implementation (especially if the overall resource change is significant), adopting a strategy of 'intelligent failure' is critical. Failure can occur without necessarily triggering organisational blame and recrimination.

Jackson Hewitt Tax Services[12]

Jackson Hewitt Tax Services is the second-largest tax preparation business in the United States (the largest is H&R Block). They had undergone rapid growth during the 1990s by adopting a classic franchising strategy (growing from 49 offices in 1988 to 1342 offices in 1996) and adapting more successfully than their rivals to a major shift in their business environment. In 1986, the US Inland Revenue Service (IRS) started testing electronic filing. This allowed tax preparation firms to transmit individual income tax returns directly to the IRS. The scheme, intended to save the IRS from a huge volume of paper processing, went nation-wide in 1990. The system has reduced the level of errors (2 per cent on an electronic submission compared with closer to 15 per cent on a paper one) and proved to be very popular (in 1990, 4.19 million returns were filed electronically; by 1996, this had risen to 14.85 million). Jackson Hewitt had been using an electronic system since 1982 and, unlike many of their rivals (including H&R Block), the introduction of electronic filing did not necessitate the addition of an extra process step. They promoted it extensively, offering it as a free or very low-cost option. The technology infrastructure that they require has to support the delivery of a number of specific operational requirements:

- As a critical element in their competitive advantage, the firm did not want to find itself lagging behind in technology. It needed to expand as quickly as possible in order to maximise its first-mover advantage.

- The tax business is very seasonal, with 20 per cent of business transactions completed in one week (4 per cent of annual business is done on a single day) and this inevitably places a great deal of emphasis on their process technology being dependable.

- Like most franchises, the organisation is geographically dispersed but, given the nature of the

▶

business, rapid and reliable communications are critical. Management reports need to be created and distributed almost immediately to all franchisees and management.

● With rapid and substantial growth, systems could not effectively be redesigned and rebuilt every year.

Given these challenges, the implementation process was conducted as a staged process over 12 months, allowing people time to become used to the systems and suggest changes and improvements where necessary.

● *Internal test* – The software and systems were largely bought in but the corporate staff tested the whole system to check that key features operated as promised. The user manuals and other documentation were also double-checked.

● *Field test* – Selected franchisees tested the system to provide a more objective evaluation than that provided by the staff who ordered/commissioned the software and systems.

● *Blast test* – Given the demands of a seasonal service, approximately 30 franchisees send pre-packaged tax returns into the corporate network at a pre-determined time in order to simulate peak volumes and expose possible difficulties.

● *Production test* – Two weeks before the start of the tax season, selected offices prepared sample returns and transmitted them for processing. The corporate office processed these returns, generated simulated IRS acknowledgements and sent the results back.

The final challenge was to get the franchisees to agree to upgrade their equipment when the corporate centre deemed it necessary. Their ability to manage the costs was increased by providing a rolling year ahead equipment profile (which described the minimum requirements for this year, the recommended requirements and the minimum for next year).

Upgrading over time

One of the great problems with proprietary technological solutions has always been that their functionality rapidly falls behind that available on the broader market. Therefore an issue of major importance in closing the resource distance is to consider the upgrade path that a technology permits. Even those organisations that adopt entirely open systems and protocols, who employ off-the-shelf software and buy only from large, well-established companies, still face the challenge of upgrading from one generation of technology to another. The box on Jackson Hewitt Tax Services provides some illustrations of how an organisation can not only successfully implement a technology infrastructure effectively but also plan for future upgrades.

A key issue at Jackson Hewitt was the flexibility inherent in their hardware and software. In order to cope with volume growth, the hardware and software was selected to be as scalable as possible. Unix was selected as the operating system because of its scalability characteristics and therefore a database management system that operated on virtually every Unix platform was also chosen. It was felt that Intel processors (available through a range of different vendors) had a long history of increasing performance at a decreasing cost – offering an economical hardware upgrade path. The real value of this approach was proven when the company bought a new multiprocessor Unix machine in 1994. The initial transition to this architecture had taken place in phases over two years. The '94 upgrade to a more powerful machine was completed in less that two weeks with minimal changes to the system software.

Overcoming process distance

As technologies change more and more rapidly, one of the key issues facing management is how to keep up to date and to know if the technologies will work in the particular environment of the organisation. It has been suggested[13] that in many US firms, the company's technical staff have an undue influence over process technology choice. Technologists can lack a detailed view of what the operation and its markets require and this can contribute to poor-quality decision making. Successful companies make it their business actively to seek out such information and expect both their managers and technical staff to spend substantial time visiting suppliers and other operations. With any new technology, managers must anticipate potential problems that change may bring. These include obvious problems such as job losses or more subtle implications such as changing job roles and responsibilities. New technologies are increasingly characterised by their cross-functional impact and by the significant involvement of IT systems development and software programming. Successful implementation is therefore unlikely to occur if the relevant skills are missing from the implementation team. All new technologies and applications require the acquisition of new skills and experience. Implementation must therefore include sufficient resources and time for recruitment and/or training.

It is more than 50 years since Coch and French[14] argued that a key mechanism for overcoming resistance to change was to include the people *to whom* the change would happen in the process, and allow them to influence *what* changes would take place. After all, by including people in the decision process, they are more likely to 'buy in' to the change. Also, involving users in the design of the processes affected by technology implementation allows designers to access their detailed knowledge and experience. This is especially important because much process technology is often developed, at least partially, by external contractors and consultants. Although they may understand the details of the technology, they often lack sufficient practical understanding of the tasks that the system will be required to perform.

Involving users

Professor Dorothy Leonard of Harvard Business School argues that the term 'user involvement' is insufficiently precise because it covers a multitude of different approaches to interaction, each with its own advantages and disadvantages. She proposes a model of four different modes of user involvement, each of which offers a progressively greater degree of descriptive and prescriptive value.

- *Delivery mode* – When users (and managers for that matter) have very little knowledge of the underlying technology, it is relatively easy for external system vendors or internal developers to treat an infrastructure project like a product to be finished and then delivered to the client. This 'over the wall' mode of development requires almost no interaction with users and, where interaction exists, the feedback may have little impact beyond possibly improving the next generation of technology. The critical strategic question is whether such a one-way flow of information is sufficient to help develop underlying operational resources and capabilities.

- *Consultancy mode* – The next mode, requiring slightly more user interaction, is closer to a classic consultancy project. Designers/vendors recognise that there are established patterns of work (routines etc.) in the processes that they are helping to automate and invest time asking questions of experienced users. Again, although this accesses more of the firm's operational resources, it does not necessarily contribute to their development because the flow of information remains largely one-way.

- *Co-development mode* – Here, a mode that is much closer to a form of partnership is involved. This approach can be very effective when levels of uncertainty are higher (either the developers' uncertainty about the existing system or users' uncertainty about the technology) because in this situation there is less pre-existing knowledge to be captured and worked with.

- *Apprenticeship mode* – Users wanting a greater degree of independence from vendors often seek a mode of implementation whereby lead users are almost apprenticed to the developer. This radically changes the nature of the implementation process, moving it much closer to what we described in an earlier section as 'learning'. Such an approach is normally more time and money intensive but from a capability-building perspective it is very attractive.

Most project management texts commit a great deal of time and space to discussions of project team composition. However, the choice of which users to involve in a process technology implementation project is a slightly different issue that justifies further discussion. Although the criteria used for selection in 'real' projects will be varied, Dorothy Leonard suggests three useful dimensions for thinking about different types of users:

- *Form of expertise* – Certain users might be the best operatives in the organisation but this does not guarantee that they are capable of articulating what it is they do. Equally, they may well lack the critical skills to question a system development process.

- *Representativeness* – Earlier we discussed the value of adopting a pilot approach to implementation. Doing so poses a problem common in all scientific experiments. Namely, 'is it representative of a broader sample or did something atypical occur during the experiment?' This is an issue that needs to be considered when selecting user participants for any systems implementation project. Are their skills and experience of the specific type of technology, or computers in general, representative?

- *Willingness* – A basic question perhaps, but some studies[15] have shown that levels of user satisfaction amongst development participants are related to the level of involvement they originally wanted in the process, compared with the involvement they actually had. Anyone who is forced to spend more time than they believe reasonable on a project may resent it, regardless of the outcome.

Increasing the level of user involvement is, of course, not unambiguously positive. Truly radical solutions do not always emerge from discussions limited to current experience. Such a limited range of experience can also lead to the development of processes that address today's rather than tomorrow's difficulties. Despite such concerns, the benefits of increased user involvement in overcoming process 'distance' are usually regarded as significant.

SUMMARY ANSWERS TO KEY QUESTIONS

Why invest in 'process' technology?

Although process technology was traditionally a point of distinction between manufacturing and service operations, there are very few, if any, of today's high- or medium-volume services that would be competitive without exploiting direct process technology. Leaving aside competitor and customer drivers for investment, process technology can deliver quality, speed, dependability, flexibility, and cost advantages. Of course, it can be more difficult to attribute specific financial or competitive benefits to some process technology investments – especially those like IT infrastructures that impact broadly across an operation. Such technologies can provide a range of benefits such as improving the management of information, disintermediating process stages, and overcoming constraints to global operating. Additionally, process technology investments make critical contributions that can add to the longer-term capability 'endowment' of the operation.

How can process technology be evaluated?

Evaluating process technology quite literally means determining its value or worth. It involves exploring, understanding and describing the strategic consequences of adopting alternatives. We outlined three possible dimensions: (1) The 'feasibility' of technology indicates the degree of difficulty in adopting it, and should assess the investment of time, effort and money that will be needed. (2) The 'acceptability' of technology is how much it takes a firm towards its strategic objectives. This includes contribution in terms of cost, quality, speed, etc. as well as the development of strategic resources. In general terms it is about establishing the return (defined in a very broad manner) the operation gets for choosing a process technology. (3) The 'vulnerability' of technology indicates the extent to which the firm is exposed if things go wrong. It is the risk that is run by choosing that specific technology.

What factors drive successful implementation of process technology?

In general implementation terms, the less that a process technology resource is understood (influenced perhaps by the degree of innovation or the level of involvement of external suppliers), the greater its 'distance' from the current resource base of the operation. Similarly, the extent to which an implementation requires an operation to modify its existing processes, the greater the 'process distance'. In other words, from an implementation point of view it seems more likely that what you don't know can, and indeed probably will, hurt you! Mechanisms for improving the likelihood of implementation success therefore need to help operations to bridge these resource and process gaps. These include pilot operations, tolerating intelligent failure and comprehensive involvement of users.

Ontario Facilities Equity Management (OFEM)

Facilities management now is a multi-billion-dollar business in most developed economies. Facilities management companies offer a range of property management services, including basic maintenance, cleaning, fitting and supplying office equipment, heating and environmental services, 'disaster recovery' services and, increasingly, information technology equipment hosting and leasing.

> 'Facilities management is the basic housekeeping of business. It may not be glamorous but it is vital. It has always been done, of course, usually in-house by people who often had other responsibilities. As buildings and services became more sophisticated, the provision of even standard office services required more cash and more expertise. Most large companies soon found that companies like OFEM could provide these services better and cheaper. That is what we have to keep in mind as we move into providing more (and more varied) services – we have to be better and cheaper than our customers could do it themselves. If we ever forget that we will be in trouble.'
> (Guy Presson, CEO OFEM)

The Security Division

Within OFEM, the Security Division looked after the development and installation of security equipment and systems in clients' property. These included alarm and intrusion systems, security enclosures (safes), surveillance and monitoring systems, and entry security systems. In fact, entry security systems were becoming particularly important for the company. Many firms were becoming increasingly security conscious. As companies became more information based, they felt themselves vulnerable to industrial espionage or threats from individuals and groups dedicated to causing disruption, either for its own sake or to pursue political ends. Entry security systems had the purpose of permitting entry into various parts of a building only for those individuals who were authorised to be there. Traditionally, this had been done using swipe cards or various kinds of security PIN numbers and codes.

> 'Entry security systems are now in routine use. There are very few of our clients who do not want some kind of personnel security system, and they expect us to be able to provide it. Financial services companies have been in the forefront of our customers demanding increasingly tight security. More recently it has been IT-based companies who have made the running in demanding security. Some of our most demanding clients now are those with large web-hosting operations. They demand several levels of security, as a minimum at the 'building', 'department' and 'machine' levels. In other words, individuals need to be checked for access authorisation as they enter the building, when they enter a particular part of the building, and before they can use an individual terminal to access computer systems. Machine-level security has traditionally been provided using encrypted security passwords. However, passwords are particularly problematic because they are either forgotten, written down or even shared. In fact it is not difficult to guess many people's passwords.'
> (Mirella Freni, Head of Security Division)

Technological developments

The Security Division was facing a period of technological change in so much as several new developments in security technology were starting to emerge. These were affecting both what was known as 'front-end' and 'back-end' elements of security systems.

Back-end technologies were the systems which record, analyse and interpret the data from front-end technology such as swipe cards etc. These systems enabled companies to know exactly who was where, and when. In addition to the use of such information for security purposes, it could also be used for monitoring employee working hours and so on. Systems were now becoming available which could detect 'abnormal' behaviour in staff. For example, if the same swipe card was used to enter a building within minutes of it being used to leave the building, this could prompt an investigation to check that it had not been lost and picked up by an unauthorised individual. OFEM were considering adopting this type of technology. It would mean working closely with systems developers to provide a generic system which could be customised to the needs of individual clients. This would be expensive but the company felt that they could probably charge clients for the extra services this technology would provide. The systems themselves were very similar to those used by credit card companies to detect unusual behaviour but would need some modification. It was estimated that OFEM would need to invest between C\$2.5 million and C\$3 million over the next two years to have these systems up and running. The revenues from such an enhanced service were difficult to estimate but had been put as high as C\$1 to C\$1.5 million per year.

It was the recent 'front-end' technological developments that were even more intriguing. These involved the application of *biometrics* – using human features for unique identification. This technology was becoming available commercially for the routine identification of individuals through features such as eye characteristics, fingerprints, voice recognition and even body odour. In particular, fingerprint recognition and iris (the central part of the eye) recognition looked promising. Fingerprint identification was in many ways the simpler of the two.

'One advantage of using fingerprints for unique identification is that the same system can be used at all levels of security. Fingerprints can allow access to buildings, departments, and can also allow access to an individual machine. Panasonic has already produced some laptops for one life insurance company with a fingerprint reader built in. This means that the security risks of losing a laptop or having it stolen are virtually eliminated. Such technology can also be used for mobile phone security. But fingerprint recognition is not perfect. It can be affected by machine malfunction or changes and damage to an individuals' skin.' (Mirella Freni, Head of Security Division)

More exciting in the long run was the prospect of extensive use of iris recognition. An individual's iris is one of the most uniquely identifiable characteristics and one that does not change over time. Surprisingly, it also works well if the person is wearing spectacles, contact lenses or even sunglasses.

'This is probably the real technology of the future; it is already being used by some ATM manufacturers to prevent cash machine fraud and there have been trials at several high-security establishments. Again, we can use the same technology at building, departmental and machine levels. In fact, machines will become even easier to use. There will no more need for passwords, no necessity to repeatedly enter the same data such as personnel details, and it will even be easier to share computers without losing the advantages of security. Cameras can be built into the screens of computers which will enable them to discriminate between different users with different levels of security clearance.' (Mirella Freni, Head of Security Division)

There were, however, some drawbacks to using iris recognition. Even though it was more reliable than using fingerprints, the general problem of reliability remained an issue. The problem of falsely accepting someone who was not authorised to use a system was not an issue, rather it was the problem of falsely rejecting genuine users. Anything other than a tiny proportion of false rejections would be very irritating to any clients' staff. Second, the technology, although likely to be widely used in the future, was relatively new to the company. There was the risk that there may be disadvantages which had not yet been thought of. Fingerprinting was a better understood technology. Third, in some companies some staff had proved reluctant to subject themselves to this security. There was still the impression that the technology involved 'laser scanning' the eye. This sounds dangerous to most people, though in fact the system did not use lasers but rather simple digital camera-like technologies. Finally, some groups were worried that the technology could be used intrusively to monitor employees' use of systems, or even levels of staff attention as they worked at the screen.

Costs and benefits

Both fingerprinting and iris recognition systems would be expensive to develop. It had been estimated that at least C$1 million a year would be needed for the next three years, probably a little more than this for the iris recognition systems. In the Security Division's overall budget of C£15 million this was not necessarily a prohibitive sum; the real problem lay with the uncertainty of any revenue coming from such an investment.

> 'Whereas investing in more sophisticated back-end systems will mean extra revenue for us, it is unlikely that we could charge much, if anything, extra for improved front-end security. There is no real extra service even though there is a higher level of security. I'm not sure that customers would be willing to pay significantly more for this. OK, some of our real security-minded customers may do so, but most won't. Yet this is the way technology is moving. Certainly our competitors are considering adopting such technologies, and if they are doing it we should be considering it. Also, it we master iris recognition in particular, other business may be open to us, such as the maintenance of ATMs and so on. At the moment the critical decision for us is where to invest our money. Back-end? Front-end? Or both? And if we go for new front-end technology, should it be fingerprint based or iris recognition?'

(Mirella Freni, Head of Security Division)

Further reading

Zuboff, S. (1988) *In the Age of the Smart Machine*, Basic Books, New York.

Remenyi, D., A. Money and A. Twite (1993) *Measuring and Managing IT Benefits*, 2nd edn, Blackwell.

Leonard, D. (1995) *Wellsprings of Knowledge*, Harvard Business School Press.

Fichman, R.G. and S.A. Moses (1999) 'An incremental process for software implementation', *Sloan Management Review*, Winter, pp. 39–52.

Davenport, T.H. (1993) *Process Innovation*, HBS Press, Boston, MA.

Bensaou, M. and M. Earl (1998) 'The right mind-set for managing information technology', *Harvard Business Review*, September–October, pp. 119–128.

Andreu, R. and C. Ciborra (1996) 'Core capabilities and information technology: an organizational learning approach', in B. Moingeon and A. Edmonson (eds) *Organizational Learning and Competitive Advantage*, Sage.

Notes on the chapter

1 Ford, H. (with Crowther, S.) (1924) *My Life and Work* (Revised edition), Heinemann.
2 Information drawn from Corporate website (www.cisco.com) and *The Economist*, 3 October 1998 and 26 June 1999.
3 Adapted from Frank, R.H. and P.J. Cook (1995) *The Winner Takes All Society*, Penguin.
4 Foster, R.N. (1986) *Innovation: The Attacker's Advantage*, Summit Books, New York.
5 Dierickx, I. and K. Cool (1989) 'Asset Stock Accumulation and Sustainability of Competitive Advantage', *Management Science*, December, pp. 1504–1511.
6 Kaplan, R. and D. Norton (1993) 'Putting the Balanced Scorecard to Work', *Harvard Business Review*, Vol. 71, pp. 134–147.
7 This HP example is taken from an Australian government-sponsored study, *International Best Practice in the Adoption and Management of New Technology*, Norma Harrison and Danny Sampson (1997), ISBN 0 642 27443.
8 From an article by Dalya Alberge, *The Times*, 15 August 1996.
9 Rosenhead, J. (1980) 'Planning Under Uncertainty', *Journal of the Operational Research Society*, Vol. 31, pp. 331–341.
10 Chew, W.B., D. Leonard-Barton and R.E. Bohn (1991) 'Beating Murphy's Law', *Sloan Management Review*, Spring, pp. 5–16.
11 As with any form of new technology, one must be very wary about quoting relative popularity.
12 Grunberg, D.B. (1998) 'Information technology at Jackson Hewitt Tax Service', *Journal of Consumer Marketing*, Vol. 15 (3), pp. 282–289.
13 Hayes, R.J. and S.C. Wheelwright (1984) *Restoring our Competitive Edge*, Wiley, New York.
14 Coch, L. and French, J. P. R. Jr. (1948) 'Overcoming resistance to change', *Human Relations*, No. 1, pp. 512–532.
15 Doll, W. J. and Torkzaden, G. (1989) 'A discrepancy model of end-user computing involvement', *Management Science*, Vol. 35, (10), pp. 1151–1171.

Operations organisation and role

Introduction

Successful operations depend not only on the nature and attributes of the resources contained within the firm but also on how those resources are organised, supported and developed. This and the following two chapters are devoted to these tasks which we group under the general heading of 'development and organisation'. This chapter examines how resources are distributed, together with the responsibility relationships between clusters of resources – the *organisational structure* of the company. We take an operations perspective on organisations by exploring how some of the alternative organisational structures found in practice cope with the twin pressures of reconciling market requirements and developing operations resource capabilities. We then go on to explore the position of the operations function within the organisation. The following chapter will examine operations development and improvement, the organisational mechanisms and procedures for developing operations resources over time. Then, in Chapter 12, we shall look at a particularly important issue of development and organisation – how operations are organised to develop new products and services.

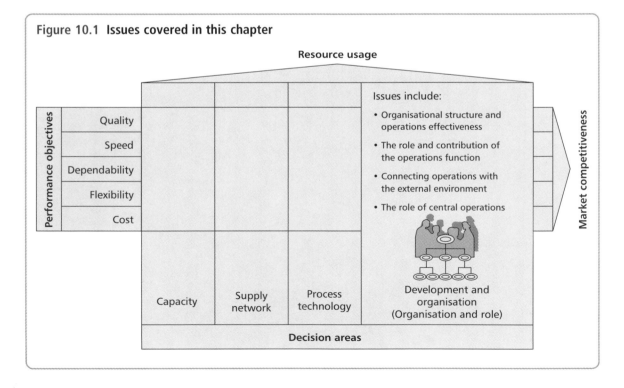

Figure 10.1 Issues covered in this chapter

- *How does a firm's organisational structure impact on the two objectives of operations strategy – fulfilling market requirements and developing operations resource capabilities?*

- *How does the operations function position itself within the organisation, especially with respect to its interaction with the external environment?*

- *What can the relationship be between the central operations function and the business operations functions?*

Almost all operations have organisational structures – clusters of resources bound together by sets of shared responsibility with recognised relationships between the clusters. The way organisations design their structure has a very special role within the range of operations strategy decisions. As a 'pattern of decisions' which shape the internal organisation of resources, 'organisational structure' is clearly a fundamental 'output' of operations strategy. Yet the organisation's structure also provides the mechanics by which strategy is formed and, as such, is an 'input' to operations strategy. Managing this paradox presents a particular challenge, both to those who attempt to devise operations strategies and those who implement them. In order to do so it is important to understand the nature of alternative forms of organisational structure and the role which operations, as a distinct function, plays within the structure.

Organisational structure

Organisational structure is integral to operations strategy

It is a mistake to think that the relationship between organisational design and operations management is limited just to understanding the implications for operations management of the way organisations are designed. The two topics are far more intimately entwined. Just look at the reasons why organisational designs have been changing and are likely to change further. They are shifting their structure in response to the dual, and often conflicting, pressures of serving turbulent markets, whose requirements are continually changing, while at the same time preserving, and even extending, the essential capabilities that enable them to differentiate themselves from competitors. The organisation's structure is therefore not just the context of the reconciliation process, it also represents the corporate memory of how strategy has shifted and accommodated to these pressures over time. It embodies the company's attitude to trade-offs and improvements, and it is the ultimate operationalisation of any attempt at focusing appropriate resources on target markets. All these issues are central to the reconciliation process. The location and level of capacity, and the firm's efforts to change them, define and redefine its organisational structure. The demise of vertical integration in many industries, the reliance on outsourced partnerships, and the relationship skills which this implies, are all reflected in a firm's organisational structure (and change the balance of power within it). Likewise, technology has, in many industries, totally redefined the role of individuals within their organisational context. It has set constraints on their actions, and yet often provides the potential to exploit as yet unthought of opportunities. One cannot disentangle the decisions and concerns of operations strategy from those of organisational design.

In fact we are here at the heart of the deeper debate. One side of the debate holds that the organisational structure of a firm should be regarded as part of the deliberative decision processes of operations strategy, in that it reflects what is important to the operation, in terms of satisfying market requirements. Alternatively, others hold that the structure of an organisation has a life of its own. It reflects the informal as well as the formal relationships, such as the longer-term politics and deeply rooted views of the organisation. If so, maybe there is a limit to the malleability of any organisation's structure. It is, above all, a creation of the firm's history. Even if formal organisation structures are changed, informal behaviour may follow the pattern established over the long term. To some extent, maybe even the view an organisation holds of its markets, together with its preferred market position, is itself a reflection of the assumptions and values embedded within its organisational structure. Once again, we are back to a familiar debate. Does (and should) some element of operations strategy reflect the firm's desired market position, or does (should) it reflect the way its resources have developed over time?

As ever, it is the balance between these two views which is the key practical issue in operations strategy. What is important is to understand how market requirements and operations resource characteristics each act to exert influence over the eventual design of the firm's organisational structure.

What is organisational structure?

So, what do we mean by 'organisation structure'? There are many different ways of defining the term. Here we take the relatively conventional view that it means the way in which tasks and responsibilities are divided into distinct groupings, and how the responsibility and coordination relationships between the groupings are defined. It is important to accept, though, that to understand any organisation's structure we must include the informal relationships which build up between groups as well as their more formal relationships, as defined in the firm's articulated structure. The implication of this is that explicit decisions, intended to shape an organisation's structure, should be made with the understanding that they can promote or inhibit the development of informal relationships. Indeed, it is these informal relationships which do much to define the effectiveness of different organisational structures in different circumstances.

Theory Box   **Perspectives on organisations[1]**

How we illustrate organisations says much about our underlying assumptions of what an 'organisation' is and how it is supposed to work. For example, our illustration of an organisation as a conventional 'organogram', as in Figure 10.3, implies that organisations are neat and controllable with unambiguous lines of accountability. Even a little experience in any organisation demonstrates that rarely, if ever, is this the case. Nor does it take much more experience to question whether such a mechanistic view is even appropriate, or desirable. In fact, seeing an organisation as though it was unambiguously machine-like is just one of several metaphors commonly used to understand the realities of organisational life. One well-known analysis by Gareth Morgan proposes a number of 'images' or 'metaphors' which can be used to understand organisations:

- *Organisations are machines* – the resources within organisations can be seen as 'components' in a mechanism whose purpose is clearly understood. Relations within the organisation are clearly defined and orderly, processes and procedures that should occur usually do occur, and the flow of information through the organisation is predictable. Such mechanical metaphors are popular because they appear to impose clarity on what is usually seen as deviant, messy behaviour within the organisation. Indeed, where it is important to impose clarity (as in much operations strategy analysis) such a metaphor can be useful. It is, however, a particularly limiting way of thinking about organisations. Flexibility and creativity are not emphasised, nor is independence of thought or action.

- *Organisations are organisms* – organisations are also living entities. Their behaviour is dictated by the behaviour of the individual humans within them. Individuals, and therefore the organisation, adapt to circumstances just as different species adapt to the environmental conditions in which they need to survive. The organism image helps us to understand how organisations interact with their environment, work through their life cycle and relate to other 'species' of organisation. This is a particularly useful way of looking at organisations if parts of the environment (such as the needs of the market) change radically. The survival of the organisation depends on its ability to exhibit sufficient flexibility to respond to its environment. However, the natural environments in which real organisms live are reasonably well understood, and are independent of the views of the organism itself. The social and political environment in which organisations exist is partly a function both of how they act and how they choose to see the environment. Organisations, even in the same industry, may see the opportunities and threats in very different ways.

- *Organisations are brains* – organisations process information and make decisions. No machine, or perhaps even organism, comes close to the degrees of sophistication of which a human brain is capable. Organisations, like brains, make decisions. They balance conflicting criteria, weigh up risks and decide when an outcome is acceptable. They are also capable of learning, changing their model of the world in the light of experience. This emphasis on decision making, accumulating experience and learning from that experience is important in understanding organisations. Brains, like organisations, are capable of developing and of organising themselves. However, organisations are clearly not unitary entities like brains. They consist of conflicting groups where power and control are key issues.

- *Organisations are cultures* – an organisation's culture is usually taken to mean its shared values, ideology, pattern of thinking and day-to-day ritual. Different organisations will have different cultures stemming from their circumstances and their history. Because an organisation's internal structure and view of itself are influenced by its culture, we can think of an organisation as an expression of its culture. A major strength of seeing organisations as cultures is that it draws attention to their shared 'enactment of reality'. Within this the symbolism present in processes and procedures is seen to be important. Looking for the symbols and shared realities within an organisation allows us to see beyond whatever that organisation may formally say about itself. Unfortunately 'culture' has, in many organisations, come to be seen as something that can be changed at whim. Although managers can influence the evolution of culture, they cannot control it as if it were an air conditioning unit.

▶

- *Organisations are political systems* – organisations, like communities, are governed. The system of government is rarely democratic, but nor is it usually a dictatorship. Within the mechanisms of government in an organisation are usually ways of understanding alternative philosophies, ways of seeking consensus (or at least reconciliation) and sometimes ways of legitimising opposition. Individuals and groups seek to pursue their aims through the detailed politics of the organisation. They form alliances, accommodate power relationships and manage conflict. Formal structures of authority may not always reflect the reality of influence and power. Such a view is useful in helping organisations to legitimise politics as an inevitable aspect of organisational life. However, seeing organisations exclusively as political systems can lead to cynicism or the pursuit of organisational power for its own sake.

The objectives of organisational design

The way in which any business organises its resources will have an effect on its ability to develop those resources and serve its markets. The link between the design of an organisational structure and the effectiveness of that organisational structure is less clear than most operations strategy decisions. Designing an organisation to achieve specific objectives will never guarantee that those objectives are achieved. Rather the task of organisational design is to create the setting which encourages the desired performance. As usual, we can examine the objectives of organisational design both from a market and a resource perspective (see Figure 10.2).

From a market requirements viewpoint, the key issues frequently relate to the conflict between efficient organisations and responsive organisations. For example, in some industries with very large amounts of investment sunk into processes which have significant economies of scale, an organisational structure may be based largely around these production units in order to ensure their *efficient* usage. Conversely, if a company's markets are particularly uncertain, prone, say, to radical changes in the

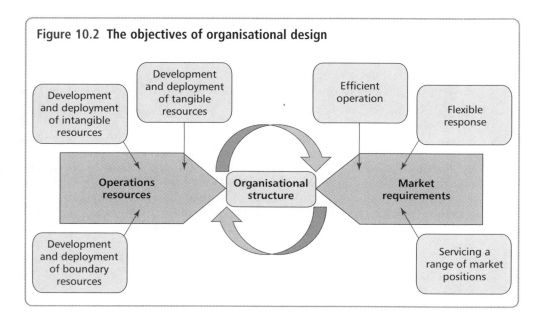

Figure 10.2 The objectives of organisational design

nature or level of demand, its structure may sacrifice some efficiency in order to increase its ability to respond *flexibly* to market changes. In addition to efficiency and flexibility, some companies may be faced with very different market needs in each of the markets it serves. Here organisational structure must service a *range* of different market positions. So, from a market-requirements perspective, any organisation structure can therefore be evaluated in terms of its:

- efficiency and costs;
- flexibility to respond to market changes;
- ability to service a range of market requirements.

The structure of the organisation can also be seen as the medium for the development of an operation's capabilities. In particular, organisational structures can influence the development (or acquisition) of resource capabilities as well as their deployment. For example, the organisation referred to above, which organised itself round its expensive process investments in order to gain economies of scale, may also wish to do so in order to bring together similar *tangible* resources in order to develop their capability. Tangible assets grouped together can also promote learning and cross-fertilisation between essentially similar resources. In other organisations, for example in creative industries, a major attraction to talented (and therefore scarce) staff may be the opportunity to work with, and learn from, like-minded specialists. An organisational structure which exploited the intrinsic attraction of working with talented peers while encouraging the learning and development which is possible for such a critical mass of expertise could have a significant impact on a company's ability to compete in the longer term. If such *intangible* resources were spread around the organisation such that they became disconnected from their natural base of expertise, they might not be able to develop to their full potential. Worse still, because their intrinsic need for self-development is neglected, they might exercise their essential mobility and leave. Other companies may inhabit a more fluid environment where they form alliances with other companies in order to assemble an appropriate bundle of resources perhaps only for a short time. Many media companies, for example, operate in this way. Here organisational structure needs to reflect the need to form both internal and external *networks*. Such networks may not be very long term in nature. The organisation therefore has to be capable of bundling together appropriate resources, even if it is for a short time, and yet not lose the learning which accumulates as it moves from alliance to alliance. So, from an operations resource perspective, organisational structures can be evaluated in terms of their:

- ability to manage tangible resources;
- ability to manage intangible resources;
- ability to network across conventional organisational boundaries.[2]

So, for any organisation's structure, an operations strategy analysis should address two basic questions. First, is the organisational structure likely to deliver the required performance objectives which will satisfy market requirements? Second, does the organisational structure encourage the development and deployment of strategic operations resources? Organisational design decisions are often an attempt to achieve an appropriate balance within and between these two questions. The problem here is that (as with so many other operations strategy decision areas) what the market may require often conflicts with what is best for resource development. And as ever, the reconciliation process is not always straightforward. However, three points need to be borne in mind as we examine some of the issues associated with alternative organisational structures. The first is that organisational structure and that organisation's operations strategy need to be connected in some way. The second is that the connection between the two will rarely be perfect. There is no ideal organisation for any particular set of circumstances. Handling the compromises and trade-offs is at the core of organisational design. Third, any particular organisational design does not guarantee a predictable set of behaviours within the organisation. An organisation may be designed so that people can behave in a particular way, but whether they will, even with an organisational structure which encourages the behaviour, is another matter.

Types of organisational design

Although there are many alternative approaches to organisational design, most, in practice, are attempting to divide an organisation into discrete parts which are given some degree of authority to make decisions within their part of the organisation. All but the very smallest of organisations needs to delegate decision making in this way if for no other reason than that it prevents decision-making overload. More positively, it allows specialisation in so much as decisions can be taken by the people who are the most familiar with the relevant part of the organisation. This in turn is likely to have an impact on the motivation of staff. Those allowed to exploit their local expertise to influence the resources in their own part of the organisation will probably be more committed than when decisions are made elsewhere. The main point at issue in organisational design is what dimension of specialisation should be used when grouping parts of the organisation together. There are three basic approaches to this:

- Group resources together according to their *functional purpose* – so, for example, sales, marketing, operations, research and development, finance, etc. could form the main groupings in the organisation. Some of these would have further subdivisions. So different sales teams would be set up for different markets, different research and development teams for different developments, and so on.

- Group resources together by the *characteristics of the resources themselves* – this may be done, for example, by clustering similar technologies together (extrusion technology, rolling, casting, etc.). Alternatively, it may be done by clustering similar skills together (audit, mergers and acquisitions, tax, etc.). It may also be done according to the resources required for particular products or services (chilled food, frozen food, canned food, etc.).

- Group resources together by the *markets* which the resources are intended to serve – again this may be done in various ways. Markets may be defined by location, with distinct geographical boundaries (North America, South America, Europe and Middle East, South East Asia, etc.). Alternatively, markets may be defined by the type of customer (small firms, large national firms, large multinational firms, etc.).

Within a single organisation, resources can be grouped in several different ways. Moreover, the lines of responsibility and direct communication linking the resource clusters can also be configured in different ways. There are an infinite number of possible organisational structures. However, some pure types of organisation have emerged. These types are useful in illustrating different approaches to organisational design, even if, in their pure form, they are rarely found.

The U-form organisation

The unitary form, or U-form, organisation clusters its resources primarily according to their functional purpose. Figure 10.3 shows a typical U-form organisation with a pyramid management structure, each level reporting to the managerial level above.

At the apex of the pyramid the chief executive controls the activities of the various functions, coordinates their joint activities and arbitrates in any disputes. This form of organisational structure derives from the advent of the rise of 'professional' management which emerged, especially in the large single-product firms such as steel and oil, around a century ago. The problem with the U-form organisation is that as companies become both larger and more complex, it becomes increasingly difficult for managers to retain effective control. Either the number of people reporting to each manager has to increase or more managerial levels are needed. In the former case, managers quickly reach the limit of their information processing ability. In the latter case, senior managers quickly become too removed from day-to-day decisions. However, for relatively simple and/or small organisations the U-form can be efficient, at least in a bureaucratic sense. But efficiency is not the same as effectiveness. Functionally based structures can prize narrow process efficiency above both customer service and the ability to adapt to changing market circumstances. The classic disease of such bureaucratic structures is that efficiency becomes an end in itself, while the broader set of organisational goals count for little when compared to narrow cost objectives. Worse, functions may become primarily concerned with their own survival, power and security. Even so, if the tendency to excessive bureaucratisation is avoided, the U-form has one clear advantage – it keeps together intangible expertise within the function. This can promote a climate in which technical knowledge is created and shared amongst a community of functional experts. The

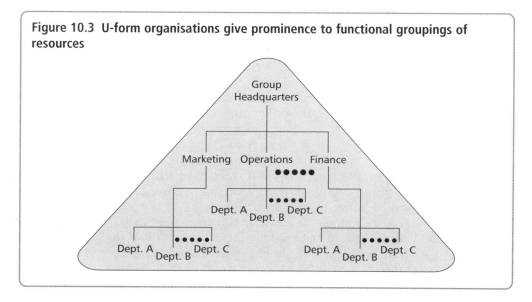

Figure 10.3 U-form organisations give prominence to functional groupings of resources

problem then with the U-form organisation is not so much the development of capabilities but with the flexibility of their deployment.

Theory Box | **Organic and mechanistic structures[3]**

One of the most influential organisational studies, although now 40 years old, is that by Burns and Stalker. They studied firms in several industries, including man-made fibres, engineering, and, most especially, the electronics industry, while it was undergoing rapid market and technological change. Their purpose was to look at the relationship between what was a particularly competitive and uncertain environment and the way in which the different firms chose to organise themselves. Burns and Stalker's main idea was that it was possible to identify a range of organisational forms from pure mechanistic to pure organic. The forms closer to the organic end of the spectrum are more adept at surviving under conditions of environmental turbulence. Whereas the mechanistic structure was classically bureaucratic, with a heavy emphasis on functional groupings, recognised chains of authority and an emphasis on internal efficiency, organic structures were more flexible. They also emphasised less rigid divisions of responsibility, informality of decision making and shared responsibility. This combined to give a uniform sense of company strategic direction, as well as a common sense of purpose. Burns and Stalker were keen to point out that, although organic structures were better in uncertain environments, they were not recommending such a structure for all companies. Informal communication and decision making can also be less efficient than a more bureaucratic form and so may not be appropriate for companies competing primarily on cost in relatively stable environments.

The M-form organisation

This form of organisational structure emerged as it became clear that the functionally based structure of the U-form was cumbersome when companies became large, produced many diverse products and services and served several, often complex, markets. It groups together either the resources needed for each product or service group, or alternatively, those needed to serve a particular geographical market, in separate divisions. Within each division, resources may be organised using the conventional functional U-form. The separate functions such as operations, for example, will therefore be distributed throughout the different divisions (see Figure 10.4). This can reduce economies of scale and thus the operating efficiency of the structure. However, it does allow each individual division to focus on the specific needs of its markets, thus enabling it to tailor the nature and extent of its services to what each market requires. Similarly, some forms of flexibility can be enhanced. For example, if a new product, service or market emerges, rather than expect an existing division to cope with its specialised needs, a new division can be formed to service the new market's need without interfering with the rest of the organisation. Also, the M-form's ability to specialise around specific technologies gives it a similar advantage as the U-form when managing its tangible resources. However, the dispersal of its 'knowledge based' intangible resources may reduce its ability to develop a creative mass of skilled individuals in each division. To compensate for this dispersal of expertise, M-form organisations may develop enhanced networking skills, so that they can obtain expertise from other divisions (or from outside the organisation's boundaries).

Figure 10.4 The M-form separates the organisation's resources into separate divisions

Matrix forms

Matrix structures are a hybrid, usually combining the M-form with the U-form. In effect, the organisation has simultaneously two different structures (see Figure 10.5). In a matrix structure each resource cluster has at least two lines of authority, for example both to the division and to the functional groups. So an operations manager may be directly responsible to his or her division head, while at the same time having a (sometimes weaker) reporting responsibility to the head of the operations function for the whole company. Sometimes reporting relationships may be even more complex. For example, a team of accountants in a large accountancy firm could be responsible to the head of their technical specialism (for example, audit or

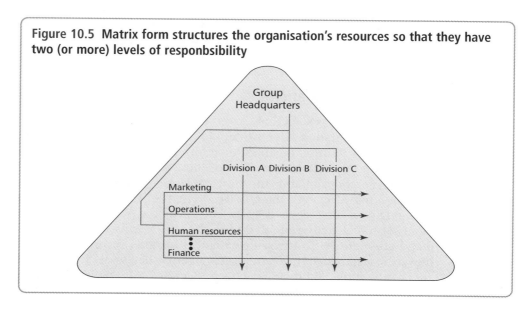

Figure 10.5 Matrix form structures the organisation's resources so that they have two (or more) levels of responbsibility

taxation), the industry sector specialism (e.g. construction, financial services, etc.) and their regional market (United States, Europe, Far East, etc.).

While a matrix organisation ensures the representation of all interests within the company, its obvious drawbacks are its complexity, its cost and the potential it creates for considerable role ambiguity. However, not only does it retain the high levels of market-focused service from the M-form organisation, if well managed it can also be relatively flexible as market conditions change. Furthermore, its ability to coordinate and share knowledge across several organisational dimensions means it can be effective in developing and deploying tangible, intangible and network resources. Matrix organisations are seen by some as 'yesterday's fashion'. However, while they are no longer a novel form of design, they do appear still to be both popular and effective.

Dow's history of the matrix

Dow Chemicals was one of the pioneers of matrix management in the 1960s. Since then, they have been almost continually refining their matrix ideas. Early on, they found that what seemed an ideal organisational structure on paper, in practice generated miles of red tape, scores of committees and a labyrinthine bureaucracy. Multiple reporting channels led to confusion and conflict. Overlapping responsibilities resulted in both battles over organisational territory and ambiguity in decision making. Dow blames its original matrix structure for several poor decisions. In bulk chemicals, for example, economies of scale should dictate a small number of large plants. Yet in spite of this, too many plants were built, largely because of each geographic area's insistence that it needed its 'own plant'.

Rather than ditching the whole idea, Dow decided to adapt its original matrix structure to make it flexible enough to handle different priorities within a single management system. To do this a small team at headquarters sets the business priorities for each type of business. Only after this is the decision taken over which of the three elements of the matrix – product, function, or geographical area – will carry most weight in decision making. This varies according to the type of decision and the type of market.

Dow credits its flexible matrix structure with piloting the company through a number of successful innovations. For example, making its European division the first to buy its oil-derived feedstocks on the spot market, which most chemical companies now do. It also redesigned some of its plants to change over from naptha to liquefied gas feedstocks inside 24 hours. Competitors could take several days to change.

The N-form organisation

The 'N' in N-form is sometimes taken to stand for 'new' or 'novelty' but more often now is taken to stand for 'network'. In N-form organisations, resources are clustered into groups as in other organisational forms, but with more delegation of responsibility for the strategic management of those resources. N-forms have relatively little hierarchical reporting and control. Each cluster of resources is linked to the others to form a network, with the relative strength of the relationships between clusters changing over time, depending on circumstances (see Figure 10.6). Senior management set broad goals and attempt to develop a unifying culture but do not 'command and control' to the same extent as in other organisation forms. They may, however, act to encourage any developments they see as beneficial to the organisation as a whole. N-forms have been described as organisations *'where information about the whole is stored in each part of the organisation. This means that strategy, guid-*

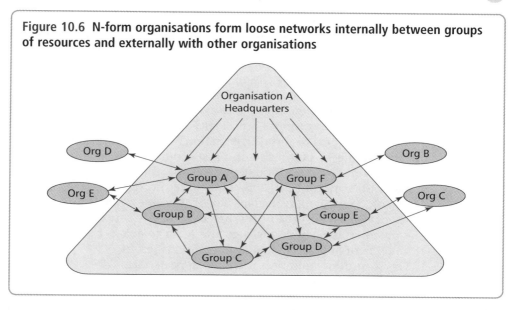

Figure 10.6 N-form organisations form loose networks internally between groups of resources and externally with other organisations

ing principles of behaviour, and access to detailed information are widely shared in the organisation. It implies a "firm as a brain" model of action rather than a "brain of a firm" model – the entire firm is supposed to think and act directly on thinking'.[4]

The concept of the network organisation is also sometimes taken to describe the relationship a company has with other separate companies. The company as a whole, as well as comprising a network of resource clusters internally, also sees itself primarily as a part of a larger network of separate companies. The boundaries of the organisation are thus less well defined than in other organisational forms. Relationships and alliances may form between companies to meet the market needs of the time, with the alliances changing as market needs change. Within the organisation, individual resource clusters, acting independently, may even make their own alliances with outside firms. To some extent these loose, and sometimes fuzzy, networks imply that each resource cluster is developing expertise in a very specific range of skills. It is the network itself that links these skills to form resource sets capable of satisfying widely differing and dynamic market requirements. Thus the market emphasis of N-forms is on flexibility, while the resource emphasis is on networking competencies. Nor should customer service or efficiency suffer if those networking skills are well deployed. Likewise, specialisation should help the development and deployment of both tangible and intangible assets. All of which sounds ideal; however, it should be stressed that real examples of N-form organisations are not easy to find. Rather than a well-defined organisational type, it may be better to take the N-form as a set of ideas which can influence other structures, most notably the matrix form.

Comparing the forms

Table 10.1 summarises the market requirement and operations resource characteristics of each of the organisational forms described above. Remember, though, that this table uses pure types of organisational form. In reality most companies are hybrids. Because of this, Table 10.1 should not be considered as evaluating distinct organisational options. It does, however, give a general indication of the implications inherent in moving an organisational form towards any of the pure types. As usual, when taking an operation strategy perspective on this, trade-offs and reconciliations figure prominently in the analysis. So the advantages of the traditional functional U-form organisation lie in its ability to develop and foster intangible assets, especially knowledge-based assets. But this is gained at the cost of bureaucracy and rigidity as well as a difficulty in managing across organisational or functional boundaries. M-form organisations can be exceptionally effective at serving the specific needs of a range of markets but their fragmented nature restricts their potential for developing and deploying operations resource capabilities. The N-form organisation, by contrast, appears to suffer no significant disadvantages. Because it is organic in nature it can adapt flexibly to serve a range of markets with reasonable efficiency. Likewise, because it is based on loosely coupled clusters of resources, it has the potential to share knowledge and learn to adapt, both of which encourage the development and deployment of operations resources.

The N-form organisation therefore appears ideal. However, it is easy to slip into an argument whose logic quickly becomes circular. N-form organisations are defined as loose clusters of resources whose relationships are formed in order to provide high levels of market service flexibility and efficiency while developing tangible, intangible and network resources. It is not surprising, therefore, that in our simple analysis the N-form rates highly in these criteria. The difficulty lies in actually maintaining the stability of resources clustered in this way. Relying on an overall 'vision' or 'organisational culture' to manage potential internal conflicts is not something that can be created overnight. Nevertheless the ideas behind the N-form organisation are both interesting and have profound implications for the operations functions within any organisation. In order to understand these implications it is necessary to examine the overall role of the operations function within the organisational structure.

Table 10.1 Comparing the pure types of organisational form

	Ability to meet market requirements			Ability to develop and deploy operations resources		
	Service (Quality, Speed, Dependability)	*Flexibility* (Flexibility)	*Efficiency* (Cost)	*Tangible* (Capacity, Process Technology)	*Intangible* (Development and organisation)	*Network* (Supply networks)
U-form organisation	Low (for all but small companies)	Low	Medium (for simple markets)	Medium/High (for simple markets)	High	Low
M-form organisation	High	Medium/High	Medium	Medium	Medium	Medium
Matrix organisation	High	Medium/High	Medium	Medium/High	Medium/High	Medium/High
N-form organisation	High	High	High	High/Medium	High/Medium	High

The organisational position and role of operations

The overall structure of an organisation clearly has an impact on its operations function. Managing 'operations' when it is a single coherent functional authority poses very different challenges to managing a loose and fluid collection of resources in a network-based organisation. But also, within the context of different organisational structures, the operations function may choose to define its position differently, especially in terms of how it relates to its outside environment. Nor is the organisational position and role of the operations function independent of how effectively it has contributed to strategy. Successful operations functions are likely to be looked on to fill a more demanding role than ones which have been less effective. So three important questions are:

- How do different organisational forms affect the nature of operations management?
- How should the operations function interface with the outside environment?
- What roles can the operations function occupy within the organisation?

Organisational structure and operations role

In the conventional U-form structure, 'operations' is usually a fully defined functional hierarchy with (hopefully) significant board-level representation and a direct line of responsibility running from senior decision makers through to operational-level operations managers. M-form structures may dilute the strength and coherence of the operations function, but often not by much. After all, divisionalisation is often a response to increasing size. The operations function in a single division of a large company may be larger than that of a U-form medium-sized company. Even so, more than a single division implies at least the possibility of an increase in the complexity of functional relationships. The matrix form takes this a whole step further with operations expertise both more dispersed and with more 'dotted line' relationships. Network forms bring further degrees of intricacy. Added to complexity is a degree of transience and ambiguity as relationships develop within operations itself, between operations and other functions and between separate enterprises.

Table 10.2 summarises some of the implications of the various organisational forms for the operations function. The *degree of specialisation* within operations is usually high in U-form organisations. Specialist departments devoted to each area of

Table 10.2 The operations function in different organisational forms

Organisational form	Degree of 'technical specialisation'	Degree of centralisation	Degree of delegated authority	Relationship with other functions	Relationship with external environment
U-form	High	High	Low	Formal	Formal/limited
M-form	Medium	Medium	Medium	Formal and Informal	
Matrix form	Medium/Low	Medium/Low	Medium/High	Informal and Formal	
N-form	Low	Low	High	Informal	Informal/many points of contact

quality, planning and control, process design, purchasing and so on, can flourish because of the economies of scale and scope within the function. Operations departments may have to become more generalist in M-form, matrix structures, and especially N-form organisations. Similarly, the *degree of centralisation* is, by definition, high in the U-form structure and reduces as operations resources are dispersed in M-, matrix and N-forms. However, as resources become less centralised, control becomes both more difficult and less appropriate, so the *degree of discretion* which operations managers have to make decisions independently must increase. Also, along with more decentralisation and more independence comes an increasing *complexity of communications* as organisation structure moves from simple U-forms to less straightforward N-forms. When the communication is between operations and other functions, U-form organisations tend to rely on the relatively formal channels implied by its hierarchical nature, likewise the M-form. However, matrix organisations, with their several 'dotted line' relationships, need substantial informal as well as formal relationships to make them work. N-form organisations are, again by definition, relationship based, and these sometimes fluid and flexible relationships necessarily build more informal than formal lines of communication.

Interfacing with the external environment

Of all the implications for the operations function implied by Table 10.2, perhaps the most important is that of how operations relates to its external environment. Partly this is because, as we have mentioned before, environmental conditions can change quickly, requiring a fast response from the operation, and partly also because

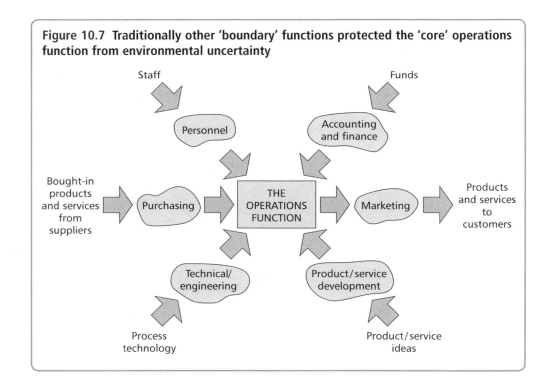

Figure 10.7 Traditionally other 'boundary' functions protected the 'core' operations function from environmental uncertainty

the conventional wisdom as to how operations *should* interface with its environment has changed.

Classical organisational theory saw the operations function as a 'core' function, pursuing its purpose deep within the organisation and protected from the outside environment by 'boundary' functions. Indeed, in many organisations the responsibility for acquiring the inputs to the operation and distributing its outputs to customers is not given to the operations function. For example, the people who staff the operation are recruited and trained by the personnel function; the process technology for the operation is probably selected and commissioned by a technical function; the materials, parts, services and other bought-in resources are acquired through a purchasing function; and the orders from customers which trigger the operation into activity will come through the marketing function. The other functions of the organisation are, in effect, forming a barrier or buffer between the uncertainties of the environment and the operations function (see Figure 10.7).

These relationships have developed partly for stability, important because it allows the operation to organise itself for maximum efficiency. Organisational buffering may also allow the other functions to specialise in their own particular tasks and leave the operations function to get on with the job of producing goods and services. However, the concept of buffering the operations function is increasingly seen as having a number of drawbacks:

● The time lag of communicating between the 'boundary' function and the operations function makes change difficult. By the time the operations function has responded, the insulating function may have 'moved on to the next problem'.

● Operations never develops the understanding of the environment (e.g. labour or technological markets) which would help it exploit new developments.

● Operations is never required to take responsibility for its actions. There is always another function to blame and unhelpful conflict may arise between functions.

● In many businesses the operations function can be only partially insulated from its external environment because of the nature of the business itself. Customers in many type of service physically enter the operation; they are part of the input to the operations processes.

The 'visibility' of the operations function

The degree of 'visibility' of an operation is the extent to which its customers have some presence while the operation's resources are adding value for them. It is also referred to as 'customer contact'.[5] It means how much of the operation's activities are exposed by its customers, or alternatively, how much the operation is 'exposed' to its customers. Obviously 'customer processing' operations, such as hotels, have more of their activities visible to their customers than most material processing operations, such as a steel plant. But even customer processing operations exercise some choice as to how visible they wish their operations to be.

For example, in clothes retailing, an organisation could decide to operate as a chain of conventional bricks and mortar shops. Alternatively, it could decide not to have any shops at all but rather to run an Internet-based operation. The 'bricks and mortar' shop operation is a high-visibility operation. Customers will have a relatively short waiting tolerance, and will judge the operation by their perceptions of it rather than always by objective criteria. So high-visibility operations require staff with good customer contact skills. Customers are free to request goods which clearly would not be sold in such a shop, so 'received variety' is high. Nor can customer arrivals be perfectly predicted. All of which does not make it easy for high-visibility operations to achieve high productivity of resources. Contrast this with the Internet-based retailer. It is not 'zero visibility'; it still has to communicate with its customers through its web site. It may even be interactive in quoting real-time availability of items. As with the 'bricks and mortar' shop, customers will react badly to slow, poorly designed or faulty sites. But overall the operation has far lower visibility. Most of the process is more 'factory like'. This allows the tasks of finding the items, packing and dispatching them to be standardised by organising staff, who need no customer contact skills, so as to achieve high staff utilisation. The Internet-based organisation can also centralise its operation on one (physical) site, whereas the 'bricks and mortar' organisation, because of its high-visibility nature, necessarily needs many shops close to centres of demand. For all these reasons the Internet operation will have lower costs than the physical shop chain.

Implications of high 'visibility'

The implications of high visibility for the operations function are threefold. First, the nature of the skills needed by operations managers will be different to low-visibility operations. Increased exposure to the environment requires faster response and more discretion at an operational level. No store manager can refer to higher managerial levels before reacting to spurts in demand, supply interruptions or natural disasters. Furthermore, the skills which will need to be fostered within the operations are likely to include as much emphasis on 'customer handling' as on core 'technical' skills. Second, the activities which make up the operations function will be geographically distributed around the company's sites. This makes it difficult to put together a critical mass of operations expertise to consolidate learning, debate strategic direction, and so on. It also means that operations managers often have divided lines of authority. So, in the clothes retailer, a store manager may have a 'dotted line' relationship with a central merchandising function (part of what we would class as 'operations') as well as a direct reporting line into a regional manager. Third, in high-visibility operations the term *operations* is less likely to be used. More important, what we call operations (the production and delivery of products and services) is likely to be difficult to disentangle from other functions such as marketing. Consequently, individual managers may carry responsibility for activities which cross conventional functional boundaries.

Visibility as a dimension of organisational design

This last point is particularly important because it influences how managers see themselves and therefore how an organisation structure will work in practice. For example, Figure 10.8 represents the degree of overlap between three areas of managerial activity which are often organised into separate functions. In a defence electronics company it is feasible (if not always desirable) for Operations, Marketing and New Product Development to be organised completely separately. The technical expertise needed to design complex electronic products is probably collected together in a large and separate department or maybe on a separate site. Similarly, the marketing task in defence electronics is partly an exercise in foreign policy, the economics of aid and understanding local defence politics. Nor may the defence

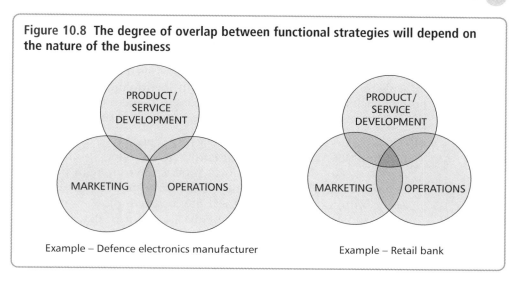

Figure 10.8 The degree of overlap between functional strategies will depend on the nature of the business

Example – Defence electronics manufacturer

Example – Retail bank

electronics marketers have much contact with its manufacturing operations function beyond an understanding of delivery lead-times. This is not the ideal way of organising interfunctional interfaces maybe, but it is a feasible model (and close to the truth in some companies of this type).

Contrast this with the retail division of a bank. Although parts of the bank will have low-visibility 'back-office' operations managers who look after 'information factories', the high-visibility branch operations will present a less clear picture of functional separation. A branch manager is clearly responsible for the production and delivery of services and is therefore part of the overall 'operations' activity of the bank, but also he or she is both directly selling the bank's services and is in a unique position to understand customer behaviour and preferences. Notwithstanding the almost certain existence of a central sales and marketing function, the branch manager is the main operational agent of the sales effort. Similarly, many new services cannot be designed without some input from those delivering them. And, given the sometimes loose specifications of some financial services, the branch operation will effectively determine the effective service specification. By necessity, in the bank branch, all the functions have a significant degree of overlap.

This idea of functional overlap (and here we focus on the overlap between operations and other functions) is becoming a key issue in defining the organisational position and role of operations. It can be summarised in the question, 'To what extent should the operations function deliberately expose itself to outside contact with its business environment?' Once it was a relatively easy decision. Manufacturing operations functions were 'back office'. Service operations were predominantly 'front office', with some of the more routine tasks performed away from the customer in a back office. Now more options are open to most types of operation. Service operations are making a clearer organisational delineation between their front and back offices. Conversely, some manufacturing operations are positioning themselves as 'service factories' with explicit responsibilities for looking after customer needs. Many manufacturing operations functions are also taking responsibility for supply-side development such as the 'supplier development' teams which help suppliers to improve their operations performance for the benefit of both supplier and customer.

Service factories

The idea that low-visibility factories can shift towards seeing themselves as high-visibility providers of service is sometimes known as the *service factory* concept. Professors Chase and Garvin propose that, while a total change of mindset may be difficult to achieve in one go, it is worth identifying a clear service model that is both explicit and transparent and can convey the idea of what needs to be done and why. They propose four models, although they admit there may be many more.[6]

● *The laboratory* – In this model the factory is encouraged to think of itself as a testing ground for new products and processes. In effect it is using its technical skills to provide advice, both to its own product development people and maybe also to outside customers. Potential or actual customers for new products are presented with, not just the physical product, but a longer and earlier relationship which allows them to witness the development of that product. They therefore develop confidence in such things as product performance, quality data, and so on.

● *The consultant* – The factory may also be able to provide services to customers after they have taken possession of the products. Staff from manufacturing operations could contribute to customer training in how to use the products, quality control procedures which best fit with the product, or even troubleshooting if the product fails to perform up to customer expectations. Chase and Garvin quote the example of Tektronix, a manufacturer of electronic equipment, who encourage customers who buy their oscilloscopes to phone a freephone number if they have any problems. This connects them directly to the shop floor where the product was made.

● *The showroom* – Factories can also be used to act as a working demonstration of a company's products. For example, one would expect a software producer to be able to demonstrate the full potential of its own software in its own organisation. Not only does this show that an organisation has full confidence in its products and services, it also provides it with the opportunity to experience how they work in practice. If the 'showroom' concept is used in this way, it also has elements of the 'laboratory' model.

● *The dispatcher* – After-sales support may include the provision of additional product accessories and spare parts. These would normally be ordered from a separate warehouse or service facility. However, the factory itself can be organised to provide customers with extra, or replacement, parts. The factory thus becomes involved in part of the customer-facing logistics activity.

In all these examples customers are being encouraged to see the factory as their 'source of service', the customer being impressed as much by the way the products are made as by the products themselves. All of which extends the expectations which the company will have of its operations managers. As the walls of manufacturing operation become increasingly transparent, they need the skills appropriate to managing high-visibility operations, where customers see at least part of the value being added to their products. Operations managers in supermarkets or hotels know that customers judge the operation by both its 'products' *and* its processes. So it follows that effort should be put into customers' perception of the operation as well as into the product itself. This may extend to managing the 'ambience' of a factory, however far fetched that might seem in some industries.

Yamazaki Mazak

The overseas plants of Yamazaki Mazak, the Japanese machine tool manufacturer, provide an ideal example of how to use a factory as a showroom (and as a schoolroom). The first thing that strikes the visitor (and there have been thousands; the company have never been slow to see the benefits of 'high customer contact' manufacturing) is the look and style of the place. 'Bonsai trees and Japanese ornaments adorn airy conference rooms, and a formal Japanese garden overlooks the foyer in this sylvan factory', as one enthusiastic visitor wrote of Yamazaki Mazak's UK plant. The ostensible motive from Yamazaki's open door policy is to show off their own products. What better way to convince customers to buy machine tools than to show them making other machine tools? But it goes deeper than that. The plant is clean and patently well ordered. The products are displayed in a state-of-the-art configuration. The company's managers will not hesitate to explain how quality and now productivity match their Japanese plants. The underlying message is 'Our products are good because we are good at making them'.

Manufacturing in services

At the same time as some manufacturing operations are becoming more visible to their customers, some service operations are getting less so. Not that, in general, service operations are reducing their level of visibility, rather many are splitting their high-visibility operations away from those that do not need to be seen by customers. Traditionally this has been known as the back-office–front-office separation. This enables the high-visibility (front-office) part of an operation to organise itself to meet customers' immediate needs. At the same time the back office can focus on the more 'manufacturing like' performance measures such as efficiency, without being distracted by having to deal directly with customers. For many service businesses it is this back-office–front-office split which is the dominating factor in organisational design.

Changes in operations organisation in retail banking

In Chapter 8 we touched on some of the process technology changes which have taken place in retail banking. These were only part of a more fundamental change in the way banking operations were organised. Although not all banks have reorganised in this way, many of the larger ones have.

Before reorganisation

The High Street bank branch was an important part of many communities. Bank managers, often pillars of local society, ran multifaceted and (in larger branches) complex businesses. Each branch had tellers who cashed cheques and received the money to be paid in. Enquiry clerks answered customer queries. The manager and assistant managers interviewed customers if they wanted a loan or to arrange insurance or to transact other business such as the buying and selling of stocks and shares. Each branch also had a back-office operation. This would include records clerks processing requests for new accounts or the payment of standing orders, and a 'machine room' which encoded cheques and paying-in slips. This involved using electronic ink to print codes on to the documents prior to them being sent to a central clearing department where they were read by machine. Individual branches would also print cheque books for their customers, establish securities for any loans that customers wished to take out, arrange for the purchase of stocks and shares with stockbrokers, often kept share certificates in the branch, and so on. In this way by far the majority of banks' operations effort was concentrated at the branches, even though much of it

▶

was 'back office' within the branch. Only a limited number of activities such as 'cheque clearing' or the physical transportation of cash were organised centrally by the bank's headquarters.

After reorganisation
Branches are primarily sales operations. Most branches still have tellers, although some only have enquiry clerks, other transactions being performed by automatic teller machines (ATMs). ATMs can now also deal with simple requests such as account information. Branches continue to have managers but with far less individual discretion. Their job is to sell the bank's services as efficiently as possible. Almost all of what used to be performed as branch-based back-office operations is now entirely centralised. Central 'account management centres' open accounts and set up standing orders, 'voucher processing centres' take in cheques and credits prior to encoding and sending to clearing, 'printing departments' manufacture cheque books (on a largely automated process where individual customer replenishment orders are triggered by the use of a specially coded cheque). All of these centres are almost zero-visibility operations; information factories whose job is to operate accurately, efficiently and dependably. Other centres do have some limited visibility. 'Lending centres' deal with telephone requests for loans and monitor loan accounts. Most of the monitoring is done automatically by computer systems with only very few exceptions ever being looked at by the bank's staff. 'Securities centres' arrange for securities for loans, again with some limited contact with customers. Other centres have higher visibility. For example, 'relationship management centres' deal with higher 'net worth' customers, sometimes by phone but often visiting them in their homes. 'Mortgage centres' and general call centres deal with telephone enquiries and then pass on requests to the low-visibility centres.

Two effects are particularly important here. First, there is the large-scale separation and centralisation of low-visibility, and even some higher-visibility, activities into central operations which can achieve far greater economies of scale than a system based on distributed branches. Second, there is the change in our own behaviour as customers. Many of the banking transactions once we would have expected to visit a branch to transact, then we were more willing to mail our requests to a branch, then to telephone a call centre with the request and now, increasingly, use the Internet. While not everyone sees this as progress, most banks gained considerable cost savings from this type of reorganisation.

The role of the operations function

By the 'role' of the operations function we mean something beyond its obvious responsibilities and tasks in the company's organisational structure. We mean the underlying rationale of the function – the reason that the function exists. After all, why should any business go to the bother of having an operations function? As we discussed in Chapter 6, most companies have the option of contracting out the production of their services and goods. They could simply pay some other business to provide what their operations function currently does for them. This then prompts the further question, 'What does the operations function have to do in order to justify its continued existence within the business?' In these terms, three roles are particularly important for the operations function:[7]

- as the *implementer* of business strategy;
- as a *support* to business strategy;
- as the *driver* of business strategy.

Implementing business strategy

A basic role of operations, certainly from a top-down perspective, is to implement strategy. Most companies who make deliberative efforts to formulate strategy rely on the operation to put it into practice. You cannot, after all, touch a strategy; you cannot even see it; all you can see is how the operation behaves in practice. So when a strategy is decided upon, the first role of any operations function is to see that it happens – to *operationalise* the strategy. If a utility decides to expand its customer enquiry service, for example, its operations function must make sure that its call centres have adequate levels of capacity and support systems to cope with the changed demand. The implication of this role for the operations function is very significant. Without the ability to implement even this role, the most original and creative strategy can be rendered totally ineffective.

Supporting business strategy

More positive than the rather reactive role of 'implementing' is operations' role of 'supporting' strategy.[8] This implies that operations management can develop its resources in a more general sense in order to provide the capabilities which are needed to allow the organisation to achieve its strategic goals. For example, if a manufacturer of computer peripherals has decided to compete by being the first in the market with every available new product innovation, then its operations function needs to be capable of coping with the changes that constant innovation will bring. It must develop or purchase processes which are flexible enough to manufacture novel parts and products. It must organise and train its staff to understand the way products are changing and put in place the necessary changes to the operation. It must develop relationships with its suppliers which help them respond quickly when supplying new parts. Although it cannot precisely forecast the exact nature of future innovations, the better the operation is at doing these things, the more support it is giving to the company's general strategy of 'being innovative'. This role for operations is different from that of implementing strategy. Here operations is developing general capabilities which are appropriate to a general strategic direction. The specific operations activities which will become necessary as the strategy is implemented are not yet known. But implementation will presumably be easier because these supporting capabilities have been developed.

Driving business strategy

A third role for operations is in 'driving' strategy by developing unique capabilities to the point where they provide a long-term competitive advantage for the organisation. Of course, all functions of the business can develop such capabilities. Different parts of the business have different effects on a company's ability to prosper. In our view, operations has a particularly important long-term role. For example, if the finance function does not control cash flow accurately, the business could run out of cash and go out of business almost immediately. If Marketing fails to understand the nature of the company's markets, and how it should position itself, the company will find it difficult to thrive. Poor marketing management will hamper the company in the medium term. No amount of excellent financial management or clever market positioning, however, can compensate for lack of operations capability in the long term. Sloppy service, badly made products, slow delivery, broken promises, too little choice of products or services, or an operations cost base which is too high will eventually sink any company. Conversely, any business which makes its product and/or services better, faster, on time, in greater variety and less expensively than its competition has a special long-term advantage. The important point here is that many of the things that promote long-term success come directly or indirectly from the operations function. It is the operations part of the business that is the ultimate custodian of competitiveness.

'World class' operations (WCO)

The role of the operations function, its position inside and outside the organisation and its responsibility to be an important 'driver' of an organisation's strategy are all concerns of the 'world class' operations (WCO) concept. Indeed, the WCO approach elevates the role of managing operations resources in a similar way to the 'reconciling market requirements and operations resources' approach we have taken throughout this book. Both concepts have a common theme,

> that excellence in managing the resources and processes which are internal to an enterprise will change its positioning in its external environment.

There is, however, an important distinction between these two concepts. Although both articulate a more proactive and central role for operations, the 'reconciliation' concept does not prescribe a single model of exactly what role operations should take, nor does it advocate any specific strategies. The 'reconciliation' concept takes a 'contingency' approach to how the operations function should contribute to overall strategic aims. That is, different organisations with different strategic objectives are likely to need different operations strategies with different decisions taken regarding capacity technology infrastructure, and so on. By contrast, the (WCO) concept tends to be far more prescriptive as to what 'solutions' are best in all (or most) circumstances. These prescriptions include most of the 'three-letter acronyms' which have proliferated since the early 1980s, such as JIT, TQM and BPR. Some authors who support this view try to encapsulate the idea in one all-embracing concept. For example, the 'lean thinking' approach taken by Womack and Jones extends their JIT-based ideas first popularised in their book *The Machine That Changed the World*. They propose a set of ideas which are claimed to improve the performance of any operation. Typical is their prescription for airlines (*all* airlines, that is, regardless of their circumstances):

> Why aren't airlines like Northwest (and its global partner KLM) and airframe builders like Boeing and Airbus working on low-cost, point-to-point services using smaller jets instead of developing ever-larger aircraft? And why aren't they developing quick turnaround systems for small jets at small airports instead of constructing Taj Mahal terminals at the absurd 'hubs' created in America after airline deregulation – and long present in Europe and East Asia due to the politically motivated practice of routing most flights of state-controlled airlines through national capitals? (One hour of the seven hours spent on the trip just cited was taxiing time in the Detroit hub and a second was occupied with self-sortation inside the terminal).[9]

The difference between WCO and other approaches is this emphasis on specific solutions rather than the process of operations strategy formulation. In other words, *what* you do rather than *how* you do it. Such a 'one size fits all' approach has been criticised as being overly simplistic, but it does have the advantage of clarity and enthusiasm. The original operations strategy concepts, as espoused by Skinner,[10] departed from the 'one best way' assumption by introducing the idea that operations strategy decisions should be contingent on overall strategy. The WCO concept is more proactive (sometimes evangelical) in tone but still holds a single set of prescriptions.

The role of 'central operations'

Operations managers are increasingly expected to contribute to strategy formulation, both directly by representing the constraints and capabilities of operations resources, and indirectly by interpreting strategy into its operational implications. This is a relatively new responsibility for managers, increasing the emphasis on the strategic development of the operation as opposed to its day-to-day management. In some, especially larger, companies this has led to separating the development task from the routine management of the operation.

Operations 'staff' and 'line'

The first set of people occupy classic 'staff' positions. They have a monitoring, planning and shaping role. They are the ones who are charged with building up the company's operations capability. They may look forward to the way markets are likely to be moving, judge the best way to develop each part of the operation, and keep an eye on competitor behaviour. All of which are tasks which need close liaison with marketing planners, product and service development and finance. They are also tasks which need some organisational 'space' to be performed effectively. They are certainly not tasks which coexist readily with the hectic and immediate concerns of running an operation. These people constitute what could be termed 'central operations'. The second set of people, those who run the day-to-day operations, have a very different set of tasks. Theirs is partly a reactive role, one which involves finding ways round unexpected problems: reallocating labour, adjusting processes, solving quality problems, and so on. They need to look ahead only enough to make sure that resources are available to meet targets. Theirs is the necessary routine. Knowing where the operation is heading, keeping it on budget and pulling it back on course when the unexpected occurs: no less valuable a task than the developer's but very different.

While these descriptions are clearly stereotypes, they do represent two types of operations task. The issue, for organisational design, is whether it is wise to separate them organisationally. It may cause more problems than it solves. Although it allows each to concentrate on their different jobs, it also can keep apart the two sets of people who have most to gain by working together. Here is the paradox: the development function does need freedom from the immediate pressures of day-to-day management but it is crucial that it understands the exact nature of these pressures. What makes the operation distinctive? Where do the problems occur? What improvements would make most difference to the performance of the operation? Questions only answered by living with the operation, not cloistered away from it. Similarly, the day-to-day operations manager has to interpret the workings of the operation, collect data, explain constraints, and educate developers. Without the trust and cooperation of each, neither set of managers can be effective. Separating them into two 'camps' is not necessarily the best way to promote either trust or cooperation. Most important, Operations will have to take a leading part in the implementation of whatever changes are devised by central operations; a process not made easier by organisation separation.

Headquarters as parent

Where there is a separation, the relationship between headquarters staff generally and the individual businesses within a corporation is sometimes termed 'parenting' in the field of corporate strategy. It is an interesting metaphor which we can use as a starting point in examining the role of 'central operations'.[11] Headquarters in their role as parent can wield significant influence over the performance of individual businesses and therefore the group as a whole. They can create value through their guidance, implementation of performance measures, specialist help and so on. On the other hand, they can destroy value by excessive bureaucratic planning, burdening the businesses with excessive overheads, or giving misguided advice. A key question, therefore, is, 'What can individual businesses, or the group as a whole, gain from having a central operations function?' Unless the costs and distractions of central operations are outweighed by the benefits within the organisation, there is little sense in doing anything other than making individual businesses exclusively responsible for their own operations development.

Although the parenting metaphor is not universally recognised and is seen as being over-hierarchical by some authorities, it clearly has power. This is what Goold, Campbell and Alexander[12] have to say about it

> There are different roles within the family for the parent and the businesses (children) . . . the parent needs to balance advice and encouragement with control and discipline. It also needs to recognise that the businesses (children) change and mature over time, and that a relationship that may have worked well in their early years will probably need to change as they grow. Businesses (children) like to know where they stand with their parents, including what will be regarded as good and bad behaviour. While businesses (children) can learn an enormous amount from each other, they also tend to compete with each other, as well as against the outside world; the parent has an important role in creating a family environment in which friendly relationships between businesses (children) are fostered and mutual aggression is diffused. Parents that smother their businesses (children) with close attention may end up being rejected as interfering bores, while parents that let their businesses (children) go entirely their own way are abdicating their responsibility to attempt to help them maximise their true potential.

Figure 10.9 illustrates four ways in which the headquarters parent can create value for its businesses. *Stand-alone* influence involves providing a minimum framework which will encourage the individual businesses to thrive unaided in their own markets. This usually involves such minimum control interventions as setting and monitoring performance targets, approving major items of capital expenditure and selecting the very top managers for each business. *Linkage* influence involves headquarters in attempting to exploit the linkages between different business units in a way that would not happen if those business units were independent. This is usually an attempt to achieve 'synergy', that is, making the group of operations worth more than the sum of the parts. This may be achieved through setting transfer prices between individual divisions, encouraging inter-business trading relationships and encouraging product or service development which will benefit other businesses within the group. *Central functions and services* influence involves the parent developing a range of service functions within its headquarters which will provide specialist and cost-effective service to its businesses. These services can both exploit the economies of scale which result from centralisation and develop knowledge which will be of value to the group as a whole. *Corporate development* activities relate

Figure 10.9 Four ways in which corporate head office can add value

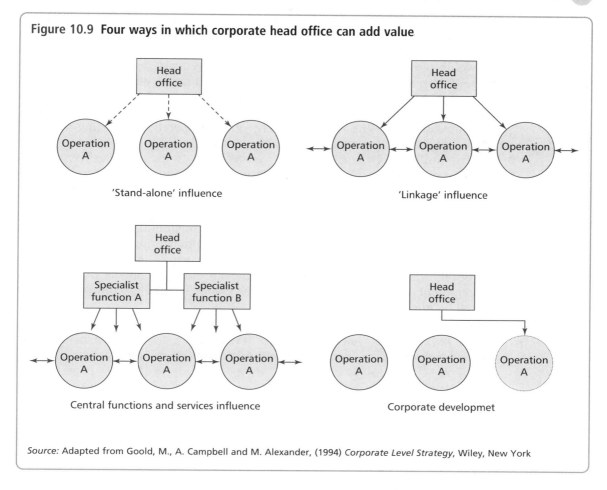

'Stand-alone' influence

'Linkage' influence

Central functions and services influence

Corporate developmet

Source: Adapted from Goold, M., A. Campbell and M. Alexander, (1994) *Corporate Level Strategy*, Wiley, New York

to the influence which headquarters will have on shaping the portfolio of businesses within the group. In other words, the way in which it buys, sells and develops individual businesses.

These different ways in which headquarters can create value are not mutually exclusive. A headquarters organisation can emphasise some or all of them. However, the more responsibilities which are taken by corporate headquarters, the greater number of people will be needed at the headquarters and the higher the costs will be. Also, different responsibilities imply different levels of headquarters staffing. Classic conglomerates, which thrived in the 1970s and 80s, such as Hanson, provided minimum 'stand-alone influence' with a very small corporate headquarters staff. Conversely, those companies with large central functions and services, a classic example of which is the 3Ms Corporation, will necessarily have a relatively large headquarters staff.

Four types of central operations function

Here we are particularly concerned with how headquarters *operations* staff can act to create value for their company and its individual operations. Central operations could be involved in any of the four headquarters parenting responsibilities. Particularly though, they tend to become involved in the provision of central functional services, in its broadest sense. This includes the provision of central resources which could provide technical advice, information systems capabilities, laboratory testing services, improvement teams, quality procedures, environmental services, and so on. It also could be taken to mean the general coordination of all operations activity in the different parts of the company. This may include the compilation of performance statistics, the encouragement of inter-operations learning, and the development of broad operations strategies.

Within this, how central operations exercises its responsibilities very much depends on the view it has of operations strategy and development. For example, we can use the dimensions which define the perspectives on operations strategy described in Chapter 1.

- *Top-down or bottom-up?* – If central operations has a predominantly top-down view of the world, it is likely to take a programmatic approach to its activities, emphasising the implementation of overall company strategy. Conversely, if it takes a bottom-up view, it is more likely to favour an emergent model of operations development where individual business operations together contribute to the overall building of operations expertise.

- *Market requirements or operations resource focus?* – If central operations takes a market requirements view of operations development, it is likely to focus on the explicit performance achieved by each business operation and how far that per-

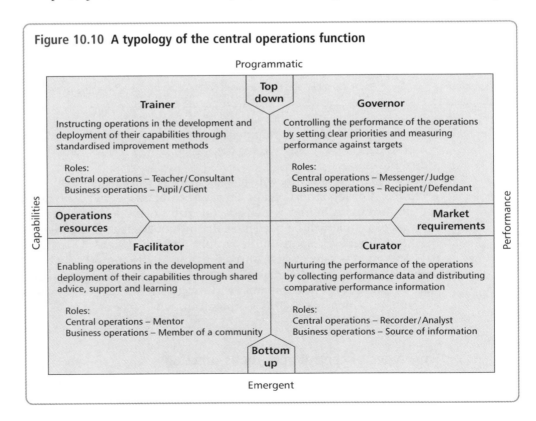

Figure 10.10 A typology of the central operations function

formance serves to satisfy the operation's customers. An operations resource focus, on the other hand, emphasises the way in which each business operation develops its competences and successfully deploys them in its marketplaces.

We can use these two dimensions to define a typology of the central operations function as shown in Figure 10.10. It classifies central operations into four pure types called governors, curators, trainers and facilitators, a typology based on Merali and McGee's work.[13] Although, in practice, the central operations function of most businesses is a combination of these pure types, usually one type predominates.

Central operations as governor

Here we use the term 'governor' to describe the role of central operations first in its imperial sense. The ancient Roman Empire ruled its provinces by appointing governors whose job it was to impose the will of the Emperor and Senate on its possessions. They acted as the agent of a central authority, interpreting the Imperial will and arbitrating over any disputes within the framework of central rule. The word governor, however, is also used in mechanics to denote the mechanism which prevents an engine running out of control and damaging itself. Central operations of this type interpret strategy in terms of market performance, set clear goals for each business operation, judge their performance and, if performance is not to target, want to know the reason why. They are likely to have a set of predetermined responses to 'fix' operations that do not perform up to requirements and tend to expect results to improve in the short term.

Central operations as curator

Central operations can be concerned primarily with performance against market requirements without being top-down. They may take a more emergent view by acting as the repository of performance data and ideas regarding operations practice for the company as a whole. We use the term 'curator' to capture this idea. Curators collect information and examples so that all can be educated by examining them. Central operations therefore will be concerned with collecting performance information, examples of best practice, and so on. They will also be concerned with disseminating this information so that operations managers in different parts of the business can benchmark themselves against their colleagues and, where appropriate, adopt best practice from elsewhere. The term curator can also be taken to mean more than a collector. It can also imply someone who nurtures and cares for the exhibits. So central operations acting as curators may also analyse and explain the performance data and examples of operations practice they collect. In this way they educate business operations and encourage debate around operations practice.

Central operations as trainer

Moving from the market requirements to the operations resources emphasis shifts the focus more to the development of internal capabilities. If the mindset of central operations is top-down their role becomes one of a 'trainer'. Trainers go to some effort to develop clear objectives, usually derived from overall company strategy, and devise effect methods of instructing their 'pupils'. Because the specific needs of individual operations may differ, 'trainer' central operations may devise improvement methodologies which can, to some extent, be customised to each business operation's specific needs. However, their approach is likely to be common with a relatively coherent and centralised view of operations development. Even if individual business operations do initiate contact with central operations, they do so in the role of clients seeking advice on central policy from 'consultants' who bring a standardised approach. These internal consultants can, however, accumulate considerable experience and knowledge.

Central operations as facilitator

In some ways this final type of central operations is the most difficult to operate effectively. Central operations are again concerned with the development of operations capabilities but do so by acting as facilitators of change rather than instructors. Their role is to advise, support and generally aid the development and deployment of capabilities through a process of mentoring business operations. They share responsibility with the business operations in forming a community of operations practice. The development of the relationships between central operations and business operations is crucial in encouraging shared learning. The value placed on these relationships themselves becomes the prime, though somewhat diffused, mechanism for control of the improvement process. Implicit in this type of central operations is the acceptance of a relatively long-term approach to operations development.

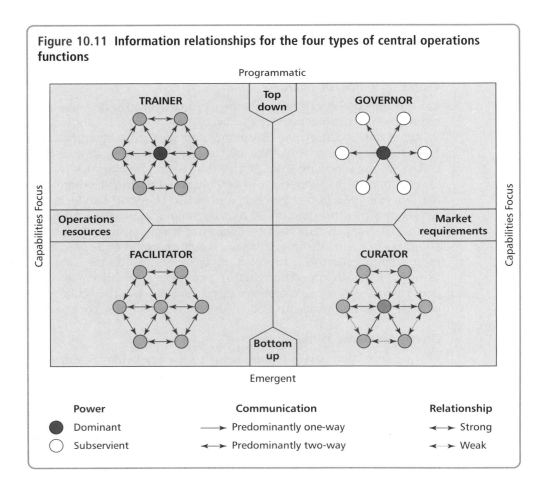

Figure 10.11 Information relationships for the four types of central operations functions

Central operations and information networks

The different types of central operations will play different roles within the information network which connects business operations to central operations and to each other. Figure 10.11 illustrates the likely nature of these information networks. In both the governor and trainer types, central operations is the dominant power player. Their vision of what the individual business operations should be doing dominates the rest of the network. When the emphasis is on individual business operations performance, as in the governor type, there is relatively little, if any, communication between the businesses. Because operations resource competences are more diffuse than hard performance measures, the trainer type will have to accommodate the needs and views of business operations to some extent and also rely on individual business operations having some, albeit weak, sharing of operations practice. Central operations which adopt a more emergent approach implicitly accept a two-way relationship between themselves and the business operations; only in this way can central operations be aware of emergent practice. The curator type, by publishing comparative performance data, is, to some extent, encouraging some communication between the individual business operations. The facilitator type of central operations, however, is entirely dependent on regular, strong and two-way communication between themselves and the community of business operations which they guide.

SUMMARY ANSWERS TO KEY QUESTIONS

How does a firm's organisational structure impact the two objectives of operations strategy – fulfilling market requirements and developing operations resource capabilities?

An organisation's structure refers to the way in which it clusters its resources together and designs the communication relationships between the clusters of resources. Although, in practice, there are an infinite number of possible organisational structures, some 'types' have emerged. These range from the functionally dominated U-form at one extreme, through multi-divisional M-form and matrix forms, to N-form network organisation structures. All these structures can be evaluated against their ability to meet market requirements and their ability to develop and deploy operations resource capabilities. Broadly speaking, traditional U-form organisations can be effective at developing internal capabilities but are poor at deploying them into the market. M-form and matrix organisations seek compromises between market and resource effectiveness, while N-form organisational structures claim to be effective both in terms of market focus and resource capability development and deployment. However, although network forms have clearly influenced many organisations structures, examples of its pure form are relatively unusual.

How does the operations function position itself within the organisation, especially with respect to its interaction with the external environment?

The position and role of operations will take different forms depending on the overall organisational structure. U-forms tend to have operations functions which are specialised, centralised and formal. At the other extreme, N-forms tend to have operations functions which have less technical specialisation and centralisation but are decentralised and informal. Operations' relationship with its external environment varies from formal and limited with U-forms through to informal with many points of contact for N-form. However, the external 'visibility' of the operations function is tending to become greater in most organisations. Indeed, although traditionally the operations function has been seen as needing protection from environmental change, it is now recognised that there may be advantages in exposing the function to external contacts, especially customers. This has led to the concept of 'service factories' in manufacturing.

What can the relationship be between the central operations function and the business operations functions?

In large organisations there is often a separation between 'staff' operations managers who provide support and develop strategy for the function and 'line' operations managers who are directly responsible for producing and delivering products and services. While this separation between staff and line is not always regarded as a positive move, if such a separation exists, the relationship between the two must be defined. One method of doing this is to distinguish between top-down and bottom-up approaches to the relationship, and the market requirements or operations resource focus. This leads to a four-way classification which implies different roles for central operations.

CASE EXERCISE – What would you do?

The Thought Space Partnership

We need radical change ...

'It was a total shambles. Thought Space is supposed to be one of the leading creative companies in this part of the world. Yet we manage to come over as being indecisive and inefficient. We always used to boast that we had the three Cs – creativity, commercialism and competence. We had some of the best minds who were capable of the most creative solutions, we understood the commercial priorities of our clients and we always delivered on time, and on budget. Not in this case. The Cityscope project has been dogged by confusion and problems from the beginning; we ought to rename the three Cs as confusion, criticism and chaos. Nor have we ever had such bad publicity. OK, so it was not an easy assignment. The overall purpose and objectives were never that clear and there was political interference from the start. The city council approved the money but against such opposition that it was always going to be controversial. Also, the sponsors were being leaned on, politically. Some didn't really want to contribute at all. On top of that, the whole project was managed by committee. Some of them thought it was a kind of theme park, others that it should be a museum, for some it was a performance space, for others an Expo.*

Yet we can't blame them entirely. We should have known what kind of project it was. The real point is that we might have been able to offer a leadership role if it wasn't for our inability to recognise the project for what it was. The different perceptions of each department in the Partnership reflected the differences within the project itself. "Events" saw it as a cross between an exposition and a performance. "3D design" saw it as some kind of gallery or museum. "Technical Solutions" thought of it more as a theme park. "Graphics" just saw it as a nuisance. None of them ever really worked together. They may be experts in their field but this type of project called for some creative collaboration. It also called for some fast footwork as ideas developed and as the political processes within our client group began to be evident. Relying on a single project coordinator was crazy. Even an experienced guy like Gordon could not get everyone to pull together.

The real point is that large complex projects like this will soon become our main business. Depending on how you define our assignments, around a third of our business is already heavily cross-functional; we can't afford to have Tech Solutions pleasing themselves what they develop, Events always seeking high-profile business irrespective of the internal chaos it causes, 3D design seeing themselves as the real creative ones and Graphics virtually declaring independence. No, I would scrap the whole functional organisation. We need to form dedicated but temporary teams for each assignment. These could then both integrate the various skills we have and understand the exact nature of the task we are being set. They could respond flexibly and appropriately to each assignment. When not engaged on a particular assignment, staff could carry out some of the more routine departmentally based work. We are supposed to be one of the most creative partnerships in the business. Why can't we be creative with our own organisation?'
(Caroline Hesketh – Creative Partner)

One mistake doesn't mean it's broke . . .

'Look, I know we didn't cover ourselves in glory with the Cityscope project but let's not over-react. Admittedly it was not a well-executed piece of work but it's made to seem worse by the fact that a couple of journalists decided to make a story out of us. In reality we were no worse than any of the other creative agencies who were used on the project. It's just that our zone attracted more controversy. We were unlucky as much as we were incompetent. It is certainly no reason for totally shaking up the whole organisation.

The existing groups work well together. One of the ways we get such creativity out of our people is by hiring very capable minds, letting them mix with other equally challenging individuals and expecting them to hone their skills in the commercial reality of their clients' projects. It's the interplay of ambitious, challenging individuals with shared skills which makes for creativity. Most of our clients are still wanting the services of one, or at the most two, of our groups. Graphics and Events work largely alone. Tech Solutions and 3D design do work together more than any two other groups, but only about 30 per cent of their work is collaborative. Breaking up the departments would be both profoundly unpopular with most of our staff and risk destroying our experience base. I cannot see why we cannot continue to use the Project Manager idea for the larger cross-functional projects. If Cityscope was a failure it was a failure of project management. It's the cross-functional project management skills that we need to develop. I know Gordon is experienced but no one could have foreseen the can of worms which this project was to become. Perhaps the real lesson from this is not that we need a new organisation, rather it is that we should be more careful about the kind of assignment we take on, and we need more project management experience. That's what we need to buy in. There is plenty of work about which can be done under our existing structure. Why try to fix something that ain't broke?'
(Jeff Siddon – Creative Partner)

Further reading

Morgan, G. (1996) *Images of Organisation: New Edition*, Sage, Thousand Oaks, CA.

Miles, R.E. and C.C. Snow (1995) 'The new network firm: a spherical structure based on a human investment philosophy', *Organisational Dynamics*, Vol. 23, pp. 5–18.

Nelson, R.R. (1991) 'Why do firms differ, and how does it matter?' *Strategic Management Journal*, Vol. 12, pp. 61–74.

Chandler, A.D. Jnr. (1991) 'The functions of the HQ unit in the multibusiness firm'. *Strategic Management Journal,* Vol. 12, pp. 31–50.

Volberda, H.W. (1998) *Building the Flexible Firm: How to Remain Competitive*, Oxford University Press.

Mohaman, S. A., J.R. Galbraith, E.E. Lawler 3rd, and Associates (1998) *Tomorrow's Organisation: Crafting Winning Capabilities in a Dynamic World*, Jossey-Bass, San Fransico.

Notes on the chapter

1 Morgan describes these and other metaphors in Gareth Morgan (1986) *Images of Organisation*, Sage.

2 Nanda, A. (1996) 'Resources, capabilities and competencies', in Moingeon, B. and A. Edmundson (eds) *Organisational learning and Competitive Advantage*, Sage.

3 Burns, T. and G.M. Stalker (1966) *The Management of Innovation*, Tavistock Publications.

4 Sölvell, O. and I. Zander (1995) 'Organisation of the Dynamic Multi-national Enterprise', *International Studies of Management and Organisation*, Vol. 24, pp. 17–38.

5 Chase, R.B. (1981) 'The customer contact approach to services', *Operations Research*, Vol. 21, No. 4.

6 Chase, R.B. and D.A. Garvin (1989) 'The service factory', *Harvard Business Review*, July–August.

7 Slack, N. (1991) *The Manufacturing Advantage*, Business Books 2000, London.

8 Another idea first proposed by Wickham Skinner; see Skinner, W. (1985) *Manufacturing: the formidable competitive weapon*, Wiley, New York.

9 Womack, J.P. and D.T. Jones (1996) *Lean Thinking*, Simon and Schuster, New York.

10 Skinner, W. (1978) *Manufacturing in the Corporate Strategy*, Wiley, New York.

11 Goold, M., A. Campbell and M. Alexander (1994) *Corporate-level Strategy,* Wiley, New York.

12 Goold, M., A. Campbell and M. Alexander (1994) op.cit.

13 Merali, Y. and J. McGee (1998) 'Information competences and knowledge creation at the corporate centre', in Hamel, G., C.K. Prahalad, H. Thomas, and D. O'Neal (1998) *Strategic Flexibility*, Wiley, New York. Here we use somewhat different terminology.

Operations development and improvement

Introduction

A large body of work has grown around how operations can be developed, enhanced and generally improved. Some of this work focuses on specific techniques and pre-scriptions. Other work looks at the underlying philosophy of improvement. Of course, all of operations strategy is concerned with improving operations. Our treat-ment of the other 'content' decision areas in operations strategy, such as capacity, supply networks and technology, is all based on the implicit assumption that we take decisions in these areas in order to improve the operation. Also, in the next part of this book we devote three chapters to the practice of operations strategy. These chap-ters will look at how operations strategy can be formulated by taking these operations strategy content decisions as the 'raw material' of the formulation activity. However, most organisations review their overall operations strategy relatively infrequently, and they do not expect the operation to 'freeze itself' between each major strategic review. Rather, organisations also aspire to develop and improve their operations on a more routine basis. In this chapter we are concerned, not with strategy formulation on the grand scale, but with the more general issues of how companies can shape the routines which encourage the ongoing development of their operations (Figure 11.1).

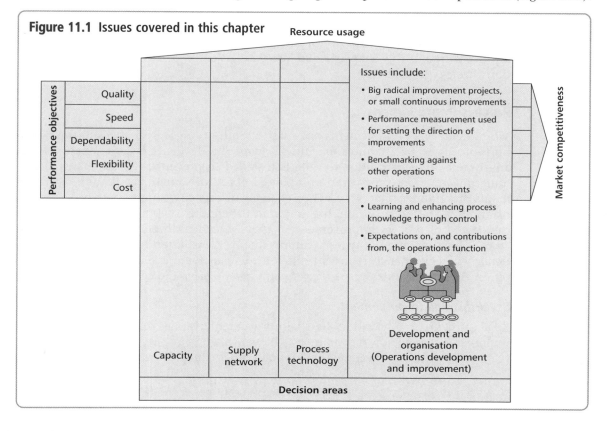

Figure 11.1 Issues covered in this chapter

Resource usage

Performance objectives: Quality, Speed, Dependability, Flexibility, Cost

Market competitiveness

Issues include:

- Big radical improvement projects, or small continuous improvements
- Performance measurement used for setting the direction of improvements
- Benchmarking against other operations
- Prioritising improvements
- Learning and enhancing process knowledge through control
- Expectations on, and contributions from, the operations function

Decision areas: Capacity, Supply network, Process technology, Development and organisation (Operations development and improvement)

KEY QUESTIONS

- *What are the differences between managing large 'breakthrough' improvement and managing continuous improvement?*
- *How do the needs of the market direct the ongoing development of operations processes?*
- *How can the ongoing management and control of operations be harnessed to develop their capabilities?*
- *What can operations do to deploy their capabilities into the market?*

Development and improvement

In this chapter we examine the *development* of operations resources and processes, that is, the way in which operations build their capabilities and by doing so *improve* their performance. Many authorities stress the importance of how organisations manage their development and improvement efforts. For example, *'The companies that are able to turn their . . . organisations into sources of competitive advantage are those that can harness various improvement programs . . . in the service of a broader [operations] strategy that emphasises the selection and growth of unique operating [capabilities].'*[1] But as with the previous chapter, we must accept some ambiguity as to the role of the development and improvement activity within operations strategy. On one hand it is a *content* decision area in the sense that there are decisions to be taken about how the operation thinks about and organises its own development. On the other hand, because we are dealing with the way in which improvement decisions are made, the topics covered in this chapter could also be considered part of the *process* of operations strategy formulation.

Process improvement

Most operations improvements are relatively minor ongoing changes to the operations processes. Every time a machine is adapted to facilitate faster changeover and any time a software failsafe routine is installed to prevent the mis-keying of customer information, the operation is being improved. Sometimes, though, improvements are grander, involving major changes in capacity, supply networks, process technology and organisation. It is important therefore to apply some calibration to the degree of process improvement so that we can distinguish between different ways of treating different types of improvement. We will start by examining two particular strategies which represent different, and to some extent opposing, philosophies. These two strategies are *breakthrough improvement* and *continuous improvement*.

Breakthrough improvement

Breakthrough, or 'innovation'-based, improvement assumes that the main vehicle of improvement is major and dramatic change in the way the operation works, the total redesign of a computer-based hotel reservation system, for example. The impact of these improvements is relatively sudden, abrupt and represents a step change in practice (and hopefully performance). Such improvements are rarely inexpensive, usually calling for high investment, often disrupting the ongoing workings of the operation, and frequently involving changes in the product/service or process technology. Moreover, a frequent criticism of the breakthrough approach to improvement is that such major improvement are, in practice, difficult to realise quickly.

| Theory Box | **Business process re-engineering** |

Typical of radical 'breakthrough' improvement is 'business process re-engineering' (BPR). BPR is a blend of a number of ideas which have been current in operations management for some time. Just-in-time concepts, process flow charting, critical examination in method study, operations network management and customer-focused operations all contribute to the BPR concept. It was the potential of information technologies to enable the fundamental redesign of processes, however, which acted as the catalyst in bringing these ideas together. BPR has been defined as:

> **the fundamental rethinking and radical redesign of business processes to achieve dramatic improvement in critical, contemporary measures of performance, such as cost, quality, service and speed.**[2]

Underlying the BPR approach is the belief that operations should be organised around the total process which adds value for customers, rather than the functions or activities which perform the various stages of the value-adding activity. The core of BPR is a redefinition of the micro organisations within a total operation, to reflect the business processes which satisfy customer needs. And even if BPR is not an entirely original idea, it can be seen as a useful collection of principles which embody the 'breakthrough' approach. The main principles of BPR have been summarised as follows:[3]

- Rethink business processes in a cross-functional manner which organises work around the natural flow of information (or materials or customers). This means organising around outcomes of a process rather than the tasks which go into it.

- Strive for dramatic improvements in the performance by radically rethinking and redesigning the process.

- Have those who use the output from a process perform the process. Check to see if all internal customers can be their own supplier rather than depending on another function in the business to supply them (which takes longer and separates out the stages in the process).

- Put decision points where the work is performed. Do not separate those who do the work from those who control and manage the work. Control and action are just one more type of supplier–customer relationship which can be merged.

The whole BPR approach is not without its critics. Three criticisms in particular are levelled which could be used also as arguments against high-profile 'breakthrough' approaches more generally:

- BPR is often treated as a cure-all for every problem. It is like, say the critics, attempting major surgery on every ailment, even those that would cure themselves naturally with some simple physiotherapy.

- BPR is merely an excuse for doing something more contentious, usually getting rid of staff.

Companies that wish to 'downsize' (that is, reduce numbers of staff within an operation) are using BPR as an excuse. This puts the short-term interests of the shareholders of the company above either their longer-term interests or the interests of the company's employees.

- BPR does not address the essential capabilities of the operation. A combination of radical redesign together with downsizing can mean that the core of experience is lost. This leaves the operation vulnerable to any environmental changes since it no longer has the knowledge and experience of how to cope with unexpected changes.

Continuous improvement

Continuous improvement, as the name implies, adopts an approach to improving performance which assumes more and smaller incremental improvement steps, for example simplifying the question sequence when taking a hotel reservation. While there is no guarantee that such a small step towards better performance will be followed by other steps, the whole philosophy of continuous improvement attempts to ensure that they will be. Continuous improvement is not concerned with promoting small improvements *per se* but it does see small improvements as having one significant advantage over large ones – they can be followed relatively painlessly by other small improvements. Thus continuous improvement becomes embedded as the 'natural' way of working within the operation. So, in continuous improvement it is not the *rate* of improvement that is important, it is the *momentum* of improvement. It does not matter if successive improvements are small; what does matter is that every month (or week, or quarter, or whatever period is appropriate) some kind of improvement has actually taken place.

The differences between breakthrough and continuous improvement

One analogy which helps to understand the difference between breakthrough and

Table 11.1 Some features of breakthrough and continuous improvement (based on Imai)[4]

	Breakthrough improvement	Continuous improvement
Effect	Short-term but dramatic	Long-term and long-lasting but undramatic
Pace	Big steps	Small steps
Time-frame	Intermittent and non-incremental	Continuous and incremental
Change	Abrupt and volatile	Gradual and constant
Involvement	Select a few 'champions'	Everybody
Approach	Individualism, individual ideas and efforts	Collectivism, group efforts, systems approach
Stimulus	Technological breakthroughs, new inventions, new theories	Conventional know-how and state of the art
Risks	Concentrated – 'all eggs in one basket'	Spread – many projects simultaneously
Practical requirements	Requires large investment but little effort to maintain it	Requires little investment but great effort to maintain it
Effort orientation	Technology	People
Evaluation criteria	Results for profit	Process and efforts for better results

continuous improvement is that of the sprint and the marathon. Breakthrough improvement is a series of explosive and impressive sprints. Continuous improvement, like marathon running, does not require the expertise and prowess required for sprinting; but it does require that the runner (or operations manager) keeps on going. Table 11.1 lists some of the differences between the two approaches. But, notwithstanding the fundamental differences between the two approaches, it is possible to combine the two, albeit at different times. Large and dramatic improvements can be implemented as and when they seem to promise significant improvement steps, but between such occasions the operation can continue making its quiet and less spectacular kaizen improvements.

The degree of process change

While continuous improvement implies relatively small changes to operations processes (but carried out frequently, in fact continually), breakthrough improvement implies substantially greater changes to processes. However, this dichotomy is a simplification used to highlight differences in improvement philosophy. The scale of improvement is a continuum. The scale shown in Table 11.2 characterises process change as being, in order of increasing degree of change, concerned with 'modification', 'extension', 'development' and 'pioneer' levels of change. Table 11.2 also illustrates what these degrees of process change could mean in two types of process.

Table 11.2 The degree of process change can be characterised by changes in the arrangement and nature of process activities

	Degree of process change			
	Modification	Extension	Development	Pioneer
Arrangement of activities (what is done)	Minor rearrangement of activities	Redesign of sequence or routing between activities	Redefinition of purpose or role activities	Novel/radical change
Nature of activities (how it is done)	No or little change to nature of activities	Minor change in nature of activities	Some change in core methodology / technology process	Novel/radical change
Example: Thin film precision coating process	New reel-change unit, allows faster changeovers	Clean-room filtering technology introduced which reduces contamination	High-energy drying allowing shorter drying path and energy savings	High-capacity machine with 'fluid electron' vacuum coating gives exceptional quality and low costs
Example: Health monitoring / diagnostics process	Patient completes pre-check-up questionnaire and brings it to regular check-up	Nurse performs initial checks at clinic, including new combined heart and respiration testing	Internet-based pre-visit routine allows test programme to be customised for each patient plus after-visit monitoring of patient health routine	Total remote testing/ monitoring service using 'body shirts' which download via Internet

Modifications to existing processes are relatively small changes where the nature of the activities within a process remain largely the same even if there are some minor rearrangements in the details of the sequence or arrangement of the activities within the process. At the other extreme, 'pioneer' change implies adopting radically different, or at least novel to the operation, types of change both to what is done in the process and how it is done. What we have termed extension and development lie in between these extremes. Continuous improvement is usually taken to mean degrees of process change limited to 'modification' or 'extension' changes to the process. Breakthrough improvement is usually assumed to mean what we have termed 'development' or 'pioneer' process change. For example, illustrations of business process re-engineering described in the press tend to be at this end of the scale, although some examples of BPR are relatively minor, what we have called 'extension' change.

The most important issues here are, first, that the greater the degree of process change the more difficult that change is to manage successfully, and second, that many small changes need managing in a different way from few, relatively large changes.

Improvement cycles

A recurring theme in operations process development is the idea that continuous improvement is cyclical in nature – a literally never-ending cycle of repeatedly questioning and adjusting the detailed workings of processes. There are many improvement cycles which attempt to provide a prescription for continuous improvement, some of them proposed by academics, others devised by consultancy firms. And although most of these cycles are not 'strategic', the concept of improvement as a cycle can be translated to mean an ongoing readjustment of strategic understandings, objectives and performance. In fact the model of operations strategy and reconciliation between market requirements and operations resources itself implies ongoing cyclical readjustment. Market potential responds to the capabilities which the operations function is capable of *deploying*. Conversely, the operation adjusts its resources and processes in response to the *direction* set by the company's intended market position. Also, within the operations function, operations capabilities are continually *developed* or evolved by learning how to use operations resources and processes more effectively. Similarly, within the marketing function, the company's intended market position may be refined and adjusted at least partly by the potential market positionings made possible because of operations capabilities.

Direct, develop and deploy

Figure 11.2 illustrates the strategic improvement cycle we shall use to structure this chapter. It employs the three 'operations strategy' elements of direct, develop and deploy described above, plus a market strategy element.

● *Direct* – A company's intended market position is a major influence on how the operations function builds up its resources and processes. Some authorities argue that the most important feature of any improvement path is that of selecting a direction. In other words, even micro-level, employee-driven improvement efforts must reflect the intended strategic direction of the firm.

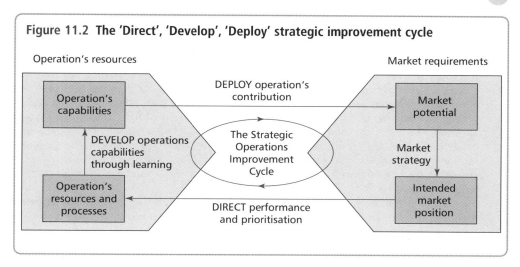

Figure 11.2 The 'Direct', 'Develop', 'Deploy' strategic improvement cycle

- *Develop* – Within the operations function those resources and processes are increasingly understood and developed over time so as to establish the capabilities of the operation. Essentially this is a process of learning.

- *Deploy* – Operations capabilities need to be leveraged into the company's markets. These capabilities, in effect, define the range of potential market positions which the company may wish to adopt. But this will depend on how effectively operations capabilities are articulated and promoted within the organisation.

- *Market strategy* – The potential market positions which are made possible by an operations capabilities are not always adopted. An important element in any company's market strategy is to decide which of many alternative market positions it wishes to adopt. Strictly, this lies outside the concerns of operations strategy. In this chapter we shall restrict ourselves to examining the direct, develop and deploy elements.

In reality, the improvement process is never so straightforward, sequential or simple. This cyclical model is not prescriptive. Rather, it merely identifies the types of activity which together contribute to operations improvement at a strategic level. Moreover, no organisation would execute each link in the cycle in a rigorous sequential manner. The activities of directing the overall shape of the operations resources and processes, developing their capabilities through learning, deploying the operations contribution and deciding on market strategy, all should occur continually and simultaneously.

ABB develops its Web capabilities[5]

ABB is one of the world's three biggest electrical engineering companies. Of Swiss-Swedish origin, it is an international company although it has been run from the top by largely Swedish management. In 1997 Göran Lindahl took over from Percy Barnevik as the boss of the company. While its history is based on electrical engineering, the company has moved towards higher-tech engineering products while selling its more traditional businesses such as the manufacture of railway rolling-stock. Most of its customers remain other industrial businesses rather than consumers.

The overall development of the company's operations has been strongly influenced by the *direction* given from its customers, especially in the way it has moved away from heavy engineering towards industrial control and automation and, in particular, the Internet. Increasingly, its customers wanted more than straightforward products. They also wanted the company's skills in the form of consultancy as well as other services. The experience of Sune Karlsson, head of the company's transmission and distribution division, was typical. '*Customers,*' he says, ' *prefer to talk about solutions, not products.*' Because of this, the use of web sites emerged as an ideal way of satisfying their customers' broader and more sophisticated needs. Customers such as Lindt and Sprüngli, the Swiss chocolate company, started to use ABB web sites to check out how other companies organised preventive maintenance. Another customer, DuPont, the US chemical giant, interacted with secure ABB web sites to learn about new kinds of control software. It became clear that ABB could customise web sites to help tailor-make solutions for their customers' problems.

Developing the company's capabilities in using web sites for knowledge-management became a priority for the company. These capabilities were *developed* partly through their dealings with customers but also in the way they used their internal intranet system (called 'Pipe') to coordinate knowledge within the company. This intranet system carries details of hundreds of company research projects to thousands of managers worldwide. It helped individual parts of the company to share their experiences with sister companies on the other side of the world. It has also helped the company to speed up the commercialisation of technology, reduced the chances of 'reinventing the wheel', and saved substantial amounts of money. Just as important, it added to the company's accumulated understanding of how to run such web sites.

This understanding allowed them to *deploy* their capabilities for the benefits of their external customers. Their ambitions were established as harnessing the Internet to be the major communications path to contribute the company's technological expertise to its corporate customers. Of course, it also helped them to understand their customers' ideas and to pick up sales opportunities. ABB's relationship with its customers, always treasured by the company as one of its major assets, had been enriched by the company's capability to do what Mr Lindahl called '*linking customers to ABB's brain power – the knowledge tucked away in the minds of its employees*'.

This cycle of development and improvement within any company invariably meant new ideas, new skills, and sometimes new people. In October 2000, Göran Lindahl announced his resignation as boss of the company. Although generally well regarded, he felt that the changes he had brought about in the company now required someone more attuned to an IT-based, Internet-enabled future.

Setting the direction

An important element in the improvement process is the influence a company's intended market position has on the way it manages its resources and processes. In the view of many, it is the only important element. According to this view, operations improvement is a constant search for better ways of supporting the company's markets. And although the model of operations development used here (and our view of operations strategy generally) also takes into account the influence of operations capabilities on market position, the 'direction' to improvement provided by market requirements is clearly an important element. At its simplest, it involves translating the intended market position of the organisation into performance goals or targets for the operation. In fact, just as the whole improvement task can be seen as a cycle, so can each stage. In this case the cycle involves the ongoing refinement of these targets. For example, a company may decide that its customers place reasonable importance on its products being delivered on time. It therefore sets a target

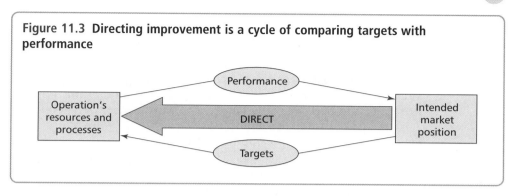

Figure 11.3 Directing improvement is a cycle of comparing targets with performance

on-time delivery performance of 99.5 per cent. However, it finds that some customer requirements are so complex that manufacturing time is difficult to forecast and therefore delivery dates cannot be met. Because of this, its overall delivery performance is only 97 per cent. However, it emerges during discussions with those customers that they understand the inherent difficulty in forecasting delivery times. What is important to them is not that the original delivery date is met, but that they are given at least two weeks' notice of what the delivery date will actually be. Thus the failure of the operation's performance to match its target prompts the targets to be changed to reflect customers' real requirements more exactly. It is the cycle of setting targets and attempting to meet them that can lead to a more accurate interpretation of the real requirements of the market. In this section of the chapter we will briefly examine three approach as to managing this cycle: performance measurement systems, benchmarking, and 'importance-performance' comparisons (see Figure 11.3).

Performance measurement

At a day-to-day level the direction of improvement will be determined partly by whether the current performance of an operation is judged to be good, bad or indifferent, so some kind of *performance measurement* is a prerequisite for directing improvement. Traditionally, performance measurement has been seen as a means of quantifying the efficiency and effectiveness of action.[6]

Performance measurement, as we are treating it in this chapter, concerns four generic issues:

- What factors to include as performance targets?
- Which are the most important?
- How to measure them?
- On what basis to compare actual against target performance?

What factors to include as performance targets?

In operations performance measurement there has been a steady broadening in the scope of what is measured. First, it was a matter of persuading the business that because the operations function was responsible for more than cost and productivity, it should therefore measure more than cost and productivity. For example, '*A ... major cause of companies getting into trouble with manufacturing is the tendency for many managements to accept simplistic notions in evaluating performance of their manu-facturing facilities . . . the general tendency in many companies is to evaluate manufactur-ing primarily on the basis of cost and efficiency. There are many more criteria to judge performance'.*[7] After this, it was a matter of broadening out the scope of measurement to include external as well as internal, long-term as well as short-term, and 'soft' as well as 'hard' measures. The best-known manifestation of this trend is the 'Balanced Scorecard' approach taken by Kaplan and Norton (see the Theory Box).

The degree of aggregation of performance targets

From an operations perspective, an obvious starting point for deciding which per-formance targets to adopt is to use the five generic performance objectives, quality, speed, dependability, flexibility and cost. Of course, these can be broken down fur-ther into more detailed performance targets since each performance objective, as we have mentioned before, is in reality a cluster of separate aspects of performance. Conversely, they can be aggregated with composite performance targets. Broad aspects of performance such as 'customer satisfaction', 'operations agility' or 'pro-ductivity' can give a higher-level picture of both what is required by the market and what performance the operation is achieving. These broad targets may be further aggregated into even broader aims such as 'achieve market objectives' or 'achieve financial objectives', or even 'achieve overall strategic objectives'. This idea is illus-trated in Figure 11.4. The more aggregated performance targets have greater strategic relevance in so much as they help to draw a picture of the overall performance of the business, although by doing so they necessarily include many influences outside those that operations strategy would normally address. The more detailed perform-ance targets are usually monitored more closely and more often, and although they provide only a very limited view of an operation's performance, they provide in

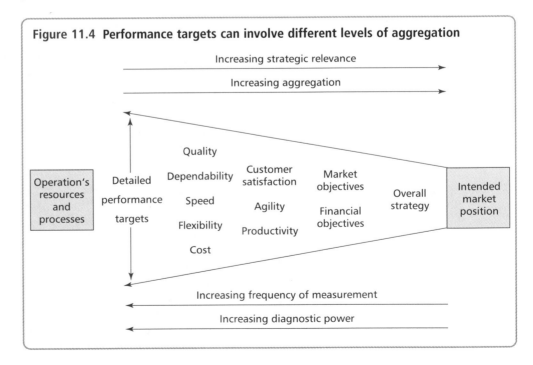

Figure 11.4 Performance targets can involve different levels of aggregation

many ways a more descriptive and complete picture of what should be and what is happening within the operation. In practice, most organisations will choose to use performance targets from throughout the range.

Theory Box   ## The balanced scorecard approach[8]

Dissatisfaction with traditional performance and control systems, often designed and managed by accounting specialists, led to the development of the Balanced Scorecard Approach. As well as focusing almost exclusively on financial measures of performance, traditional performance measurement systems did not provide the important information that is required to allow the overall strategy of an organisation to be reflected adequately in specific performance measures. Although the balanced scorecard approach does include financial measures of performance, it also includes more operational measures of customer satisfaction, internal processes, innovation and other improvement activities. In doing so it measures the factors behind financial performance which are seen as the key drivers of future financial success. In particular, it is argued that a balanced range of measures enables managers to address the following questions:

- How do we look to our shareholders (financial perspective)?
- What must we excel at (internal business perspective)?
- How do our customers see us (the customer perspective)?
- How can we continue to improve and create value (innovation and learning perspective)?

The approach attempts to bring together many disparate elements which reflect an organisation's strategic position. These may include product or service quality measures, product and service development times, customer complaints, labour productivity, and so on. At the same time it attempts to avoid performance reporting becoming unwieldy by restricting the number of measures and focusing especially on those seen to be essential. The advantages of the approach are that it presents an overall picture of the organisation's performance in a single report and by being comprehensive in the measures of performance it uses, encouraging companies to take decisions in the interests of the whole organisation rather than sub-optimising around narrow measures. Developing a balanced scorecard is a complex process and is now the subject of considerable debate. One of the key questions that has to be considered during this process is how should specific measures of performance be designed? It is recognised that inadequately designed performance measures can result in dysfunctional behaviour, so teams of managers are often used to develop a scorecard which reflects their organisation's specific needs.

Which are the most important performance targets?

One of the problems of devising a useful performance measurement system is trying to achieve some balance between having a few key measures on the one hand (straightforward and simple, but may not reflect the full range of organisational objectives), and, on the other, having many detailed measures (complex and difficult to manage, but capable of conveying many nuances of performance). Broadly, a compromise is reached by making sure that there is a clear link between competitive strategy, the key performance indicators (KPIs) which reflect the main performance objectives, and the bundle of detailed measures which are used to 'flesh out' each key performance indicator. Obviously, unless competitive strategy is well defined (not only in terms of what the organisation intends to do but also in terms of what the organisation will not attempt to do), it is difficult to focus on a narrow range of key performance indicators. So, for example, an international company which responds to oil exploration companies problems during drilling by offering technical expertise and advice might interpret the five operations performance objectives as follows:

- *Quality* – Operations quality is usually measured in terms of the environmental impact during the period when advice is being given (oil spillage etc.) and the long-term stability of any solution implemented.
- *Speed* – The speed of response is measured from the time the oil exploration company decide that they need help to the time when the drilling starts safely again.
- *Dependability* – is largely a matter of keeping promises on delivering after-the-event checks and reports.
- *Flexibility* – is a matter of being able to resource (sometimes several) jobs around the world simultaneously, i.e. volume flexibility.
- *Cost* – The total cost of keeping and using the resources (specialist labour and specialist equipment) to perform the emergency consultations.

The company's competitive strategy is clear. It intends to be the most responsive company at getting installations safely back to normal working, while also providing long-term effectiveness of technical solutions offered with minimum environmental impact. It is not competing on cost. The company therefore decide that speed and quality are the two performance objectives key to competitive success. This it translates into three key performance indicators (KPIs):

- the time from drilling stopping to it starting safely again;
- the long-term stability of the technical solution offered;
- the environmental impact of the technical solution offered.

From these KPIs several detailed performance measures were derived. For example, some of those which related to the first KPI (the time from drilling stopping to it starting again) were as follows:

- the time from drilling stopping to the company being formally notified that its services were needed;
- the time from formal notification to getting a team on site;
- on-site time to drilling commence time;
- time between first arrival on customers site to getting full technical resources on site;
- etc.

How to measure performance targets?

The five performance objectives – quality, speed, dependability, flexibility and cost – are really composites of many smaller measures. For example, an operation's cost is derived from many factors which could include the purchasing efficiency of the operation, the efficiency with which it converts materials, the productivity of its staff, the ratio of direct to indirect staff, and so on. All of these factors individually give a partial view of the operation's cost performance, and many of them overlap in terms of the information they include. Each of them does give a perspective on the cost performance of an operation, however, which could be useful either to identify areas for improvement or to monitor the extent of improvement. If an

Table 11.3 Some typical partial measure of performance

Performance objective	Some typical measures
Quality	Number of defects per unit
	Level of customer complaints
	Scrap level
	Warranty claims
	Mean time between failures
	Customer satisfaction score
Speed	Customer query time
	Order lead time
	Frequency of delivery
	Actual *versus* theoretical throughput time
	Cycle time
Dependability	Percentage of orders delivered late
	Average lateness of orders
	Proportion of products in stock
	Mean deviation from promised arrival
	Schedule adherence
Flexibility	Time needed to develop new products/services
	Range of products/services
	Machine change-over time
	Average batch size
	Time to increase activity rate
	Average capacity/maximum capacity
	Time to change schedules
Cost	Minimum delivery time/average delivery time
	Variance against budget
	Utilisation of resources
	Labour productivity
	Added value
	Efficiency
	Cost per operation hour

organisation regards its 'cost' performance as unsatisfactory, therefore, disaggregating it into 'purchasing efficiency', 'operations efficiency', 'staff productivity', etc. might explain the root cause of the poor performance.

Table 11.3 shows some of the partial measures which can be used to judge an operation's performance.

On what basis to compare actual against target performance?

Whatever the individual measures of performance which we extract from an operation, the meaning we derive from them will depend on how we compare them against some kind of standard. So, for example, in Figure 11.5, one of the company's performance measures is delivery performance (in this case defined as the proportion of orders delivered on time, where 'on time' means on the promised day). The actual figure this month has been measured at 83 per cent. However, by itself it does

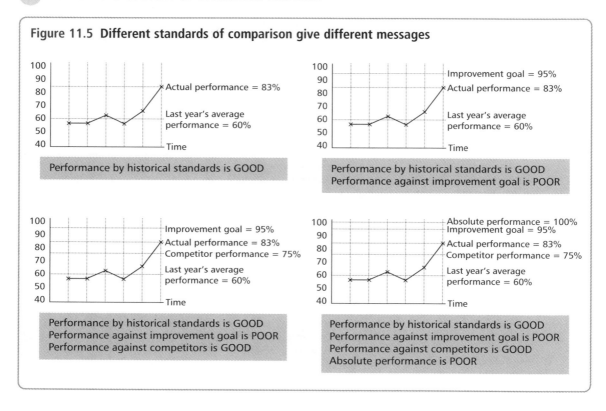

Figure 11.5 Different standards of comparison give different messages

not mean much. Yet as Figure 11.5 shows, any judgement regarding performance is very dependent on the basis of comparing performance against targets.

An obvious basis for comparison involves using an *historical* standard. The second graph in Figure 11.5 shows that, when compared to last year's performance of 60 per cent, this months' performance of 83 per cent is good. But there again, with an average performance last year of 69 per cent, the company is likely to have some kind of *improvement goal* in mind which represents what is regarded as a reasonable level of improvement. So, if the improvement goal was 95 per cent, the actual performance of 83 per cent looks decidedly poor. The company may also be concerned with how they perform against *competitors*' performance. If competitors are currently averaging delivery performances of around 75 per cent, the company's performance looks rather good. Finally, the more ambitious managers within the company may wish at least to try to seek perfection. Why not, they argue, use an *absolute* performance standard of 100 per cent delivery on time? Against this standard the company's actual 83 per cent again looks disappointing.

Benchmarking

Another very popular, although less 'day-to-day' method for senior managers to drive organisational improvement is to establish operational *benchmarks*. By highlighting how key operational elements 'shape up' against 'best in class' competitors, key areas for focused improvement can be identified. Originally, the term 'benchmark' derives from land surveying where a mark, cut in the rock, would act as a reference point. In 1979 the Xerox Corporation, the document and copying company, used the term 'competitive benchmarking' to describe a process *used by the manufacturing function to revitalise itself by comparing the features, assemblies and components of its products with those of competitors'.*[9]

Since that time, the term benchmarking has widened its meaning in a number of ways.[10]

- It is no longer confined only to manufacturing organisations but is commonly used in services such as hospitals and banks.

- It is no longer practised only by experts and consultants but can involve all staff in the organisation.

- The term 'competitive' has been widened to mean more than just the direct comparison with competitors. It is now taken to mean benchmarking to gain competitive advantage (perhaps by comparison with, and learning from, non-competitive organisations).

Types of benchmarking

There are many different types of benchmarking (which are not necessarily mutually exclusive), some of which are listed below:

- *Non-competitive benchmarking* is benchmarking against external organisations which do not compete directly in the same markets.

- *Competitive benchmarking* is a comparison directly between competitors in the same, or similar, markets.

- *Performance benchmarking* is a comparison between the levels of achieved performance in different operations. For example, an operation might compare its own performance in terms of some or all of our performance objectives – quality, speed, dependability, flexibility and cost – against other organisations' performance in the same dimensions.

- *Practice benchmarking* is a comparison between an organisation's operations practices, or way of doing things, and those adopted by another operation.

The objectives of benchmarking

Benchmarking is partly concerned with being able to judge how well an operation is doing. It can be seen, therefore, as one approach to setting realistic performance standards. It is also concerned with searching out new ideas and practices which might be able to be copied or adapted. For example, a bank might learn some things from a supermarket about how it could cope with demand fluctuations during the day. The success of benchmarking, however, is largely due to more than its ability to set performance standards and enable organisations to copy one another. Benchmarking is essentially about stimulating creativity and providing a stimulus which enables operations better to understand how they should be serving their customers. Many organisations find that it is the process itself of looking at different parts of their own company, or looking at external companies, that allows them to understand the connection between the external market needs which an operation is trying to satisfy and the internal operations practices it is using to try to satisfy them. In other words, benchmarking can help to reinforce the idea of the direct contribution which an operation has to the competitiveness of its organisation.

Importance–performance mapping[11]

Importance–performance mapping is a particularly useful approach to directing operations improvement because it explicitly includes both of the major influences on the generic performance objectives which define market requirements:

- the needs and importance preferences of customers, and
- the performance and activities of competitors.

Both importance and performance have to be brought together before any judgement can be made as to the relative priorities for improvement. Because something is particularly important to its customers does not mean that an operation should give it immediate priority for improvement. The operation may already be considerably better than its competitors in this respect. Similarly, because an operation is not very good at something when compared with its competitors' performance does not necessarily mean that it should be immediately improved. Customers may not particularly value this aspect of performance. Both importance and performance need to be viewed together to judge improvement priority.

Yet, although we have associated importance with the view of customers and performance with the activities of competitors, the approach may be adapted to deviate from this. For example, a company may choose to give importance to some aspect of operations activity even when customers do not find it important. If a company is working towards providing customised products or services in the near future, it may regard flexibility as being more important than do its customers who are, as yet, unaware of the change in the company's market stance. Neither is performance always judged against competitors. Although it may be an obvious benchmark, it does presuppose the existence of competitors. Many not-for-profit

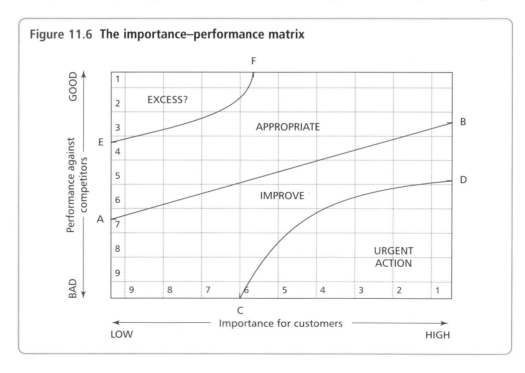

Figure 11.6 The importance–performance matrix

organisations may not see themselves as having competitors as such. They could, however, assess their performance against other similar organisations. Alternatively, they could measure performance against customer perception or customer expectations.

The importance–performance matrix

The priority for improvement which each competitive factor should be given can be assessed from a comparison of their importance and performance. This can be shown on an importance–performance matrix which, as its name implies, positions each competitive factor according to its score or ratings on these criteria. Figure 11.6 shows an importance–performance matrix where both importance and performance are judged using (in this case) a simple 9-point scale and where the matrix is divided into zones of improvement priority.

The first zone boundary is the 'lower boundary of acceptability' shown as line AB in Figure 11.6. This is the boundary between acceptable and unacceptable performance. When a competitive factor is rated as relatively unimportant (8 or 9 on the importance scale) this boundary will in practice be low. Most operations are prepared to tolerate performance levels which are 'in the same ballpark' as their competitors (even at the bottom end of the rating) for unimportant competitive factors. They only become concerned when performance levels are clearly below those of their competitors. Conversely, when judging competitive factors which are rated highly (1 or 2 on the importance scale) they will be markedly less sanguine at poor or mediocre levels of performance. Minimum levels of acceptability for these competitive factors will usually be at the lower end of the 'better than competitors' class. Below this minimum bound of acceptability (AB) there is clearly a need for improvement, above this line there is no immediate urgency for any improvement. However, not all competitive factors falling below the minimum line will be seen as having the same degree of improvement priority. A boundary approximately represented by line CD represents a distinction between an urgent priority zone and a less urgent improvement zone. Similarly, above the line AB, not all competitive factors were regarded as having the same priority. The line EF can be seen as the approximate boundary between performance levels which were regarded as 'good' or 'appropriate' on one hand and those regarded as 'too good' or 'excess' on the other. Segregating the matrix in this way results in four zones which imply very different priorities:

- *The 'appropriate' zone* – This zone is bounded on its lower edge by the 'lower bound of acceptability', that is, the level of performance below which the company, in the medium term, would not wish the operation to fall. Moving performance up to, or above, this boundary is likely to be the first-stage objective for any improvement programme. Competitive factors which fall in this area should be considered satisfactory, at least in the short to medium term. In the long term, however, most organisations will wish to edge performance towards the upper boundary of the zone.

- *The 'improve' zone* – Any competitive factor which lies below the lower bound of the 'appropriate' zone will be a candidate for improvement. Those lying either just below the bound or in the bottom left-hand corner of the matrix (where performance is poor but it matters less) are likely to be viewed as non-urgent cases. Certainly they need improving, but probably not as a first priority.

● *The 'urgent-action' zone* – More critical will be any competitive factor which lies in the 'urgent-action' zone. These are aspects of operations performance where achievement is so far below what it ought to be, given its importance to the customer, that business is probably being lost directly as a result. Short-term objectives must be, therefore, to raise the performance of any competitive factors lying in this zone at least up to the 'improve' zone. In the medium term they would need to be improved beyond the lower bound of the 'appropriate' zone.

● *The 'excess?' zone* – The question mark is important. If any competitive factors lie in this area their achieved performance is far better than would seem to be warranted. This does not necessarily mean that too many resources are being used to achieve such a level, but it may do. It is only sensible therefore to check if any resources which have been used to achieve such a performance could be diverted to a more needy factor – anything which falls in the 'urgent-action' area, for example.

Example: TAG Transport

TAG Transport is a successful logistics company which is reviewing one of its fastest-growing services – an overnight, temperature-controlled, delivery service for chilled food. It is particularly keen to improve the level of service which it gives to its customers. As a first stage in the improvement process it has devised a list of the various aspects of its operations performance:

● Price/cost – the price (including discounts etc.) which it can realise from its customers and the real internal cost of providing the service.
● Distribution quality – the ability to deliver goods in an undamaged state and its customers' perceptions of the appearance of its vehicles and drivers.
● Order/dispatch quality – the courtesy and effectiveness of its customer-facing call centre staff.
● Enquiry lead-time – the elapsed time between an enquiry from a new customer and providing a fully specified proposal.
● Drop time – the earliest time each morning when delivery can be made.
● 'Window' quote – the guaranteed time window around the drop time within which delivery should be made.
● Delivery performance – the proportion of actual deliveries made within the quoted 'window'.
● Delivery flexibility – the ability to change delivery destination.
● Volume flexibility – the ability to provide extra capacity at short notice.
● Documentation service – the reliability of documents such as temperature control charts supplied with each delivery.

Based on its discussions with customers, the laboratory manages to assign a score to each of these factors on the 1 to 9 scale. A score of 1 for 'importance' means that the factor is extremely important to customers and 9 means that it has no importance. For *performance* a score of 1 means that TAG is considerably and consistently better than any of its competitors; a score of 9 means that it is very much worse than any competitor. TAG plotted the importance and performance rating they had given to each aspect of performance on an importance–performance matrix. This is shown in Figure 11.7. It shows that the most important issue, delivery performance, is also where the company performs well against its competitors. Several issues need improving, however, three urgently. Enquiry lead-time, order/dispatch quality and delivery flexibility are all relatively important yet the company scores poorly against its competitors.

Figure 11.7 The importance–performance matrix for TAG's 'overnight temperature-controlled' service

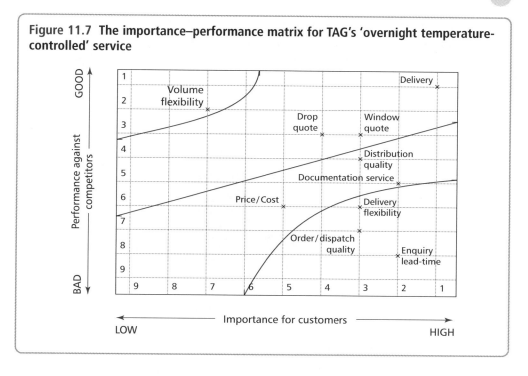

The sandcone theory

Techniques such as the importance–performance matrix assume that the improvement priority given to various aspects of operations performance is contingent upon the specific circumstances of an organisation's market position. But some authorities believe that there is also a generic 'best' sequence in which operations performance should be improved. The best-known theory of this type is sometimes called the *sandcone theory*. Although there are slightly different versions of this, the best known is that originally proposed by Arnoud de Meyer and Kasra Ferdows.[12] In fact, the sandcone model incorporates two ideas. The first is that there is a best sequence in which to improve operations performance, the second is that effort expended in improving each aspect of performance must be cumulative. In other words, moving on to the second priority for improvement does not mean dropping the first, and so on.

According to the sandcone theory; the first priority should be *quality*, since this is a precondition to all lasting improvement. Only when the operation has reached a minimally acceptable level in quality should it then tackle the next issue, that of internal *dependability*. Importantly though, moving on to include dependability in the improvement process should not stop the operation making further improvements in quality. Indeed improvement in dependability will actually require further improvement in quality. Once a critical level of dependability is reached, enough to provide some stability to the operation, the next stage is to turn attention to the *speed* of internal throughput, but again only while continuing to improve quality and dependability further. Soon it will become evident that the most effective way to improve speed is through improvements in response *flexibility*, that is, changing things within the operation faster; for example, reacting to new customer requirements quickly, changing production volumes rapidly and introducing new products faster. Again, including flexibility in the improvement process should not divert attention from continuing to work further on quality, dependability and speed. Only now, according to the sandcone theory, should *cost* be tackled head on.

▶

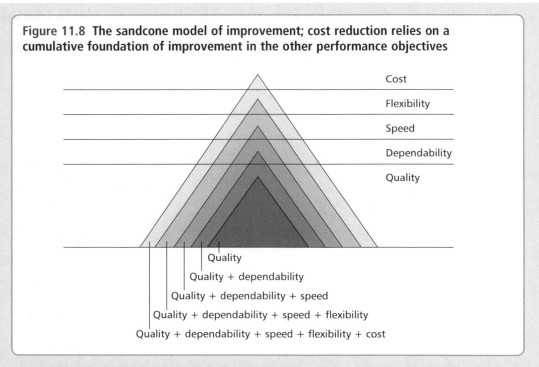

Figure 11.8 The sandcone model of improvement; cost reduction relies on a cumulative foundation of improvement in the other performance objectives

The 'sandcone model' is so called because the sand is analogous to management effort and resources. To build a stable sandcone a stable foundation of quality improvement must be created. Upon such a foundation one can build layers of dependability, speed, flexibility and cost – but only by widening up the lower parts of the sandcone as it is built up (see Figure 11.8). Building up improvement is thus a cumulative process, not a sequential one.

Developing operations capabilities

Underlying the whole concept of continuous improvement is a simple yet far-reaching idea – small changes, continuously applied, bring big benefits. Small changes are relatively minor adjustments to those resources and processes *and the way they are used*. In other words, it is the interaction between resources, processes and the staff who manage and operate them wherein lies the potential inherent in continuous improvement. It is the way in which humans learn to use and work with their operations resources and processes that is the basis of capability development. Learning, therefore, is a fundamental part of operations improvement. Here we examine two views of how operations learn. The first is the concept of the *learning curve*, a largely descriptive device which attempts to quantify the rate of operational improvement over time. Then we look at how operations learning is driven by the cyclical relationship between *process control* and *process knowledge*.

The learning/experience curve

The relationship between the time taken to perform a task and the accumulated learning or experience was first formulated in the aircraft production industry in the 1930s. The learning curve argues that the reduction in unit labour hours will be proportional to the cumulative number of units produced. Further, that every time the *cumulative* output doubles, the hours reduce by a fixed percentage. For example, in much labour-intensive manufacturing (e.g. clothing manufacture) a reduction in hours per unit of 20 per cent is found every time cumulative production has doubled. This is called an 80 per cent learning curve. When plotted on log-log paper, such a curve will appear as a straight line – making extrapolations (and strategic planning) more straightforward. Such 'learning' curves are still used in the aerospace, electronics and defence industries.

The patterns that exist in labour hours have also been found when costs are examined. They have been found not only in individual product costs but also in operation and industry-wide costs. When used to describe cost behaviour, the term 'experience curve' rather than learning curve is used. Where costs are not available, price has often been found to be a suitable proxy. An example of an experience curve is shown in Figure 11.9. It charts the progress of a 'voucher processing operation' in a bank. Voucher processing operations sort, read (using optical character recognition) and process the information from the paper documents generated by the branch operations of the bank. This figure shows how the average cost of processing a voucher reduced over time. To begin with, the operation had not used the type of large machines used in these processes, nor had it organised itself to receive the hundreds of thousands of vouchers from the branches it serviced. Over time it learned how to organise itself and to use the machines effectively. Although the data in Figure 11.9 stops at a point in time, future learning can be extrapolated from the operation's 'learning history'. This enabled the bank to establish its capacity requirements for the future, work out the cost savings from using such large processing operations and provide improvement targets for this and other similar operations.

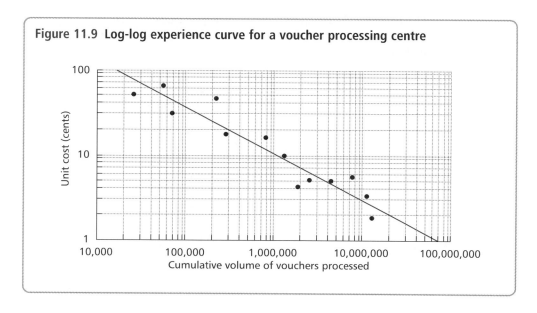

Figure 11.9 Log-log experience curve for a voucher processing centre

Limits to experience-curve-based strategies

There are clearly risks associated with any strategy that is based exclusively on one form of analysis. In this instance, basing the long-term competitive viability of a firm solely on the potential for ongoing cost reduction is open to a number of serious criticisms:

● Attributing specific costs is notoriously difficult and overhead costs are often arbitrarily allocated. In addition, units may perform poorly because they have the oldest capital equipment and their volume–variety mix may be inappropriate, factors which the experience may not capture.

● The product or service may be superseded. Innovation from within or (even less predictably) from outside of an industry can shift the competitive 'rules of the game'.

● Relentless pursuit of cost reduction (to the detriment of all the other key performance measures) can lead to operational inflexibility. Although traditional trade-off models are questioned in the 'world-class operations' paradigm, there remains an inevitable link between cost and flexibility.

● The control of cost is not the only way that an operation can contribute to the competitive position of the firm. Competing on quality, service, speed, etc. are all equally viable strategic options.

Process knowledge and process control

A more recent perspective on how learning enhances process capability emphasises the link between process control and process knowledge. In attempting to control operations processes, it is argued, managers are constantly enriching their process knowledge through a learnt understanding of the detailed characteristics of process behaviour. Or, arguing the point the other way round, processes which are not in control cannot be well understood. And if they are not well understood, how can

---

Figure 11.10 Developing operations capabilities is encouraged by a cycle of attempting to control processes which enhances process knowledge which, in turn, makes control easier

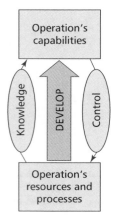

their capability be fully developed? Once again, this part of the overall strategic improvement cycle is itself a cycle. Indeed it is the whole interrelated cycle of increased process control driving the learning that enriches process knowledge, which in turn enables greater process control etc., which is the 'engine' of operations capability development. Let us therefore look further into these two issues of process control and process knowledge and examine how they influence capability development (see Figure 11.10).

Process control

Processes are dynamic. Demands upon them change *over time,* as does their performance. This is why the performance of processes is often charted over time. Figure 11.11 shows a typical process performance chart. Some aspect of process performance (usually an important one) is measured periodically, either as a single measurement or as a small sample of measurements. These are then plotted on a simple time-scale. Very few operations do not do this in some way, charting customer complaints, output and so on. There are clear advantages in doing so. The first is to check that the performance of the process is, in itself, acceptable. Figure 11.11 has the upper and lower bounds of acceptability in process performance marked. In this case the actual process performance is well within this margin of acceptability. The second reason is to check if process performance is changing over time. The natural variation inherent in all processes means that no single figure can be used to answer this question, but charting can reveal if there is a trend over time. At first glance there is a suspicion of a downward trend in the chart shown in Figure 11.11. The third reason is to check on the extent of the variation in process performance. Figure 11.11 shows the upper and lower bounds of variation of process performance so far. This band indicates the limits of how performance has varied, at least for the period being studied. Because the variation band is clearly narrower than the band of acceptability there does not seem much chance of the process's performance becoming unacceptable unless there is some distinct change in process behaviour.

A key question for all processes is, why does their performance vary? Some variation is there simply because no process is perfect in an imperfect world. Our understanding of physics and chemistry, let alone human behaviour, is insufficient to

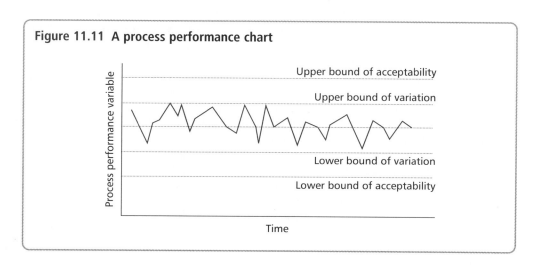

Figure 11.11 A process performance chart

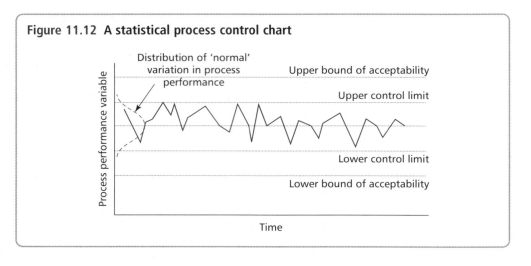

Figure 11.12 A statistical process control chart

create perfectly predictable systems of any sort. All processes therefore have a degree of *normal* variation which is an intrinsic characteristic of the process itself. But some variation may be caused by an identifiable interference with the 'normal' working of the system. A blocked pipe, defective materials or information, demotivated staff or a disintegrating gearbox will also cause the process to vary. These causes are *abnormal* in the sense that they are due to assignable causes outside the intrinsic variation of the process. A classic use of process charting is to look for process performance readings which are outside an expected band of variation, identify what has caused the abnormal performance reading, and 'problem solve' to prevent that cause happening again. Thus, unexpected performance readings act as a stimulus for identifying and removing problems in the process. But to do this effectively it is necessary to have a more systematic approach to defining what is 'abnormal' performance. Usually this is done by setting *control limits* statistically. Figure 11.12 illustrates how the expected band of variation is defined by upper and lower control limits set at ± 3 standard deviations of a normal distribution which describes 'normal' process variation. It is not within the scope of this book to dwell on the statistics that underlie this but it is important to understand that drawing control limits on a statistical basis allows the 'normality' of the system's behaviour to be identified at a known level of confidence.

It is not just abnormal variation which is important to process improvement. Normal variation also poses a problem. The obvious one is that wide, but normal, variation increases the chance of the process's performance going outside the acceptable band. A more subtle point is that wide variation masks changing in process behaviour. Figure 11.13 shows the performance of two processes both of which are subjected to a change in their process behaviour at the same time. The process on the left has such wide natural variation that without the centre lines and control limits it would be difficult to identify that a change had taken place until some time after the change had occurred.

Conversely, the process on the right has a far narrower band of natural variation. Because of this, the same change in average performance is more easily noticed (both visually and statistically). So, the narrower the natural variation of a process, the more obvious are changes in the behaviour of that process. And the more obvi-

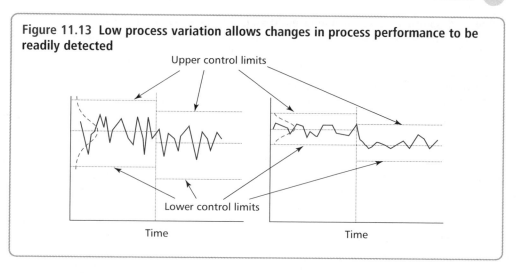

Figure 11.13 Low process variation allows changes in process performance to be readily detected

ous are process changes, the easier it is to understand how and why the process is behaving in a particular way, that is, the greater is our knowledge of the process. Accepting variation in any process is accepting some degree of ignorance as to how the process works. Perfect knowledge can give perfect control and zero variation. No process will ever reach that point, of course; the important issue is the close connection between process control and process knowledge.

Process knowledge

No process will ever reach the point of absolutely perfect knowledge – but most processes can benefit from attempting to move towards it. Moreover, few if any processes operate under conditions of total ignorance. Most operations have at least some idea as to why the processes behave in a particular way. Between these two extremes lies the path of process improvement along which operations managers attempt to journey. It is useful to identify some of the points along this path. One approach to this has been put forward by Roger Bohn.[13] He described an eight-stage scale ranging from 'total ignorance' to 'complete knowledge' of the process (see Table 11.4).

- *Stage 1, Complete ignorance* – There is no knowledge of what is significant in processes. Outputs appear to be totally random and unconnected with any phenomena that can be recognised.

- *Stage 2, Awareness* – There is an awareness that certain phenomena exist and that they are probably relevant to the process, but there is no formal measurement or understanding of how they affect the process. Managing the process is far more of an art than a science, and control relies on tacit knowledge (that is, unarticulated knowledge within the individuals managing the system).

- *Stage 3, Measurement* – There is an awareness of significant variables that seem to affect the process with some measurement, but the variables cannot be controlled as such. The best that managers could do would be to alter the process in response to changes in the variables.

- *Stage 4, Control of the mean* – There is some idea of how to control the significant

Table 11.4 Characteristics of Bohn's eight stages of process knowledge[14]

Stage Term	Indication	Operations activity	Process learning	Process knowledge	To maintain	To move up
1 Complete ignorance	Pure chance	Expertise-based	Artistic	In people's heads		Tinkering
2 Awareness	Art				Professionalism	Develop standards and systematic measures
3 Measurement	Measure good output				Preserve standards	Eliminate causes of large disturbance to process
4 Control of mean	Mean made stable				Observe and correct deviations from limits	Eliminate causes of important variance, identify new sources of variability
5 Process capability	Transitions between products and processes are known		Natural experiments	Written and oral	Eliminate new causes of variability	Stabilise process transitions and differences in process conditions for different parts
6 Process characterisation	Transitions between products and processes are known				Monitor process parameters and transitions and eliminate causes of new variability	Scientific experimentation and theory building on important variables for new product introduction
7 Know why	Science about all key variables	Procedure-based	Controlled experiments and simulations	Databases and software	Science enquiry and debate	Scientific experimentation and theory building on all variables
8 Complete knowledge	Know all variable and relationships for products now and in the future					

variables which affect the process, even if the control is not precise. Managers can control the average level of variables in the process even if they cannot control the variation around the average. Once processes have reached this level of knowledge, managers can start to carry out experiments and quantify the impact of the variables on the process.

- *Stage 5, Process capability* – The knowledge exists to control both the average and the variation in significant process variables. This enables the way in which processes can be managed and controlled to be written down in some detail. This in turn means that managers do not have to 'reinvent the wheel' when repeating activities.

- *Stage 6, Know how* – By now the degree of control has enabled managers to know how the variables affect the output of the process. They can begin to fine-tune and optimise the process.

- *Stage 7, Know why* – The level of knowledge about the processes is now at the 'scientific' level with a full model of the process predicting behaviour over a wide range of conditions. At this stage of knowledge, control can be performed automatically, probably by microprocessors. The model of the process allows the automatic control mechanisms to optimise processing across all previously experienced products and conditions.

- *Stage 8, Complete knowledge* – In practice, this stage is never reached because it means that the effects of every conceivable variable and condition are known and understood, even when those variables and conditions have not even been considered before. Stage 8 therefore might be best considered as moving towards this hypothetically complete knowledge.

From operational to strategic

Our previous discussions regarding process control and knowledge may seem surprisingly operational for a book about the more strategic aspects of managing operations. Yet the strategic management of any operation cannot be separated from how resources and processes are managed at a detailed and day-to-day level. The process knowledge, process control cycle of capability development is one of the best illustrations of this. As an operation increases its process knowledge it has a better understanding of what its processes can do at the limits of their capability even though those limits are continually expanding. This allows them to develop better products and services not only because of the enhanced process capability but also because of the operation's confidence in that capability. Similarly, as process knowledge increases, some of the more obvious operations trade-offs can be overcome. Often processes become more flexible in terms of widening their range of capabilities, without excessive additional cost. This in turn allows the operation to produce a wider range of products and services. At the same time, fewer process errors means better conformance quality and (usually) happier customers. Most staff too will prefer to work in a process that is under control. Certainly, process *uncertainty* can undermine staff morale. Retaining good staff within chaotic processes is not easy in the long term. Well-controlled processes will also have fewer errors and waste, therefore high efficiency and therefore low cost. It can even affect relationship with suppliers. High levels of process knowledge imply an understanding of how input will affect the process. Armed with this knowledge, relationships with suppliers can develop on a more professional basis. There can be many other benefits of tight process control leading to enhanced process knowledge, the ones described above are illustrated in Figure 11.14. The important point here is that whereas grappling with the details of process control may seem operational, its benefits are not. The increased revenue opportunities of better products and services, a wide product range and customer loyalty, together with better supply relationships, good staff and lower costs, are unquestionably strategic.

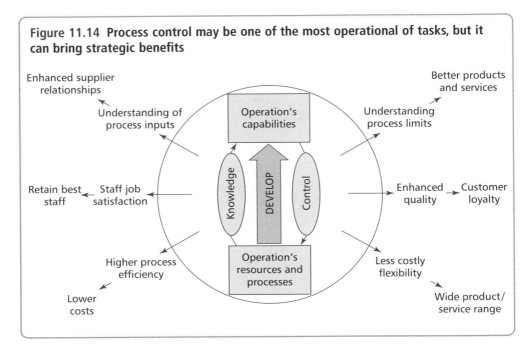

Figure 11.14 Process control may be one of the most operational of tasks, but it can bring strategic benefits

Turnround at Rexam's Portland Plant[15]

Sometimes the improvement which grows out of process control can have dramatic consequences. For the Portland Plant of Rexam Graphics, the international packaging group, it saved the plant from closure. One of Rexam's smaller sites, located in Portland, Oregon, the plant made coated imaging products, most notably the coated papers for inkjet printers. 'Coating lines' deposit a precision layer of specialised chemical onto rolls of high-quality paper, after which the rolls are slit and the paper cut into its finished size. Through the early 1990s the performance of the plant had not been good. Often it had been running at a loss and its major customers, including large companies such as Hewlett-Packard, were sometimes less than enthusiastic about its quality levels. At the time, this caused some consternation in the plant, as Tom Bickford, then the boss of the plant, explained: *'the perception was that we were always making to specification and the culture was that if it is within specification then it is OK. We didn't fully understand how close we were to not being able to make the product properly. Sophisticated customers like Hewlett-Packard insisted on receiving process chart data along with the product, so they knew how little control we had over our processes'*. Eventually customer dissatisfaction forced the company to start addressing its quality problems in terms of process control. This involved a number of initiatives, including the following:

- Clear 'shut-down' rules were devised with the plant's process operators. These formalised the conditions under which the process would be stopped if there was any suspicion that it was not in control. No production was to be made if there was reason to believe that it might not be acceptable.

- Training in statistical process control (SPC) was given to all operators and SPC charts became the main vehicle of communication concerning quality and productivity issues. Daily reviews of control chart data were held, including both plant management and workers.

- Once a month the whole plant was shut down and all three shifts were brought together to discuss quality and process control issues.

● A common problem-solving methodology was adopted by the plant. This was a proprietary 'problem-solving cycle', which provided a common language for all personnel in the plant with which to tackle and discuss quality problems.

Unfortunately, before the effects of all these actions had worked through to bottom-line performance, Rexam told the plant's senior management that the decision had been taken to close the plant down. *'It was no surprise'*, said Tom Bickford, *'We had a few months of grace but as far as the Group were concerned we were a lost cause. The real irony was that we knew that we had already turned the corner. We were convinced that we had the plant back in control. That is why we refused to give up even then.'*

Notwithstanding the closure decisions and bolstered by their newfound confidence in their ability to control the plant's processes, the management pushed even further with tightening process control limits. Eventually the new mood in the plant began to be evident in its financial performance. Productivity improved as the confusion sown by making substandard product was eliminated. Customers began to be impressed with the dramatic improvement in product and process quality levels. More significantly, the Groups North American President started to take notice. The closure decision was reversed and the plant went on to become an example for the whole Group of how process control can provide the ultimate in strategic benefits ... survival.

Deploying capabilities in the market

Operations capabilities are of little benefit if not used. Indeed, it could be argued that operations capabilities do not really exist unless they are used. They remain nothing more than unrealised potential. A vital element in strategic operations improvement, therefore, is the ability to leverage developed operations capabilities into the market. Not that operations capabilities will necessarily exclusively define a company's market position. We are not suggesting that because a company's operations has a particular capability it should *always* attempt to exploit it in the market. But the deployment of capability does create potential in the market. How this potential is realised (or not) and how organisations target market segments is beyond the scope of this book. However, what is very much important to operations strategy is how the operation can deploy its capabilities to provide the *potential* for the organisation to inhabit profitable market segments.

Again, we use the idea of a cycle within the overall strategic improvement cycle. This is illustrated in Figure 11.15. Operations capabilities must provide a *contribution* to what the organisation regards as being its range of potential market positions, but how the operation can contribute to this potential is influenced strongly by the *expectations* which the rest of the organisation has for its operations.

The four-stage model

The ability of any operation to contribute to opening up market potential for the organisation and the organisational aims, expectations and aspirations of the operations function has been captured in a model developed by Professors Hayes and Wheelwright of Harvard University.[16] With later contributions from Professor Chase of the University of Southern California,[17] they developed what they call the 'Four-Stage Model' which is ideal for evaluating the effectiveness of the contribution/expectation cycle. The model traces the progression of the operations

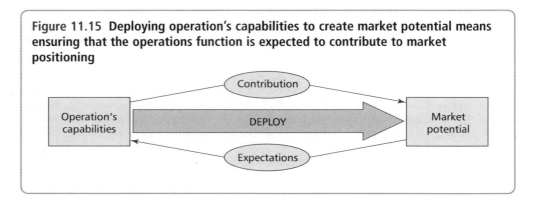

Figure 11.15 Deploying operation's capabilities to create market potential means ensuring that the operations function is expected to contribute to market positioning

function from what is the largely negative role of Stage 1 operations to it becoming the central element of competitive strategy in excellent Stage 4 operations.

Stage 1 – Internal neutrality

This is the very poorest level of contribution by the operations function. In a Stage 1 organisation, the operation is considered a 'necessary evil'. The other functions in the organisation regard it as holding them back from competing effectively. The operations function, they would say, is inward-looking and at best reactive. It certainly has very little positive to contribute towards competitive success. The best that can be expected from the operations function is to cure the most obvious problems. Certainly the rest of the organisation would not look to operations as the source of any originality, flair or competitive drive. The expectations on it are to be 'internally neutral', a position it attempts to achieve not by anything positive but by avoiding the bigger mistakes.

Stage 2 – External neutrality

The first step of breaking out of Stage 1 is for the operations function to begin comparing itself with similar companies or organisations in the outside market. A Stage 2 operation has achieved a sufficient level of capability to cease holding the company back, even if it may not yet be particularly creative in its contribution to competitiveness. It is expected, at least, to adopt 'best practice' and the best ideas and norms of performance from the rest of its industry. It is expected to be 'externally neutral' with operations capabilities similar to its competitors. This may not give the organisation any competitive advantage but neither is operations the source of competitive disadvantage.

Stage 3 – Internally supportive

Stage 3 operations may not be better than their competitors on every aspect of operations performance but they are broadly up with the best. Nevertheless, good as they may be, Stage 3 operations aspire to be clearly and unambiguously the very best in the market. They try to achieve this level of contribution by a clear understanding of the company's competitive or strategic goals. Then they organise and develop their operations resources to excel in the things in which the company needs to compete effectively. The expectation on the operations function is to be 'internally supportive' by providing credible support to operations strategy.

Stage 4 – Externally supportive

At one time, Stage 3 was taken as the limit of the operations function's contribution. Yet Hayes and Wheelwright capture the emerging sense of the growing importance of operations management by suggesting a further stage – Stage 4. The difference between Stage 3 and Stage 4 is admitted by Hayes and Wheelwright to be subtle, but nevertheless important. A Stage 4 company is one that sees the operations function as providing the foundation for its future competitive success because it is able to deploy unique competencies which provide the company with the performance to compete in future market conditions. In effect, the contribution of the operations function becomes central to strategy making. Stage 4 operations are creative and proactive. They are likely to organise their resources in ways which are innovative and capable of adaptation as markets change. Essentially they are expected to be 'one step ahead' of competitors – what Hayes and Wheelwright call being 'externally supportive'.

Figure 11.16 brings together the two concepts of *role* and the *contribution* of the operations function. Moving from Stage 1 to Stage 2 requires operations to overcome its problems of implementing existing strategies. The move from Stage 2 to Stage 3 requires operations actively to develop its resources so that they are appropriate for long-term strategy. Moving up to Stage 4 requires operations to be driving strategy through its contribution to competitive superiority. Notice also how moving up from Stage 1 to Stage 4 requires operations progressively to adapt the *roles* of the operations function discussed in the previous chapter, *implementer, supporter and driver,* as shown in Figure 11.16.

Two points are important in understanding the power of the four-stage 1 to 4 model. First, it is linked to the company's aspirations (at least their operations management aspirations). In other words, there is an active desire (some might say even

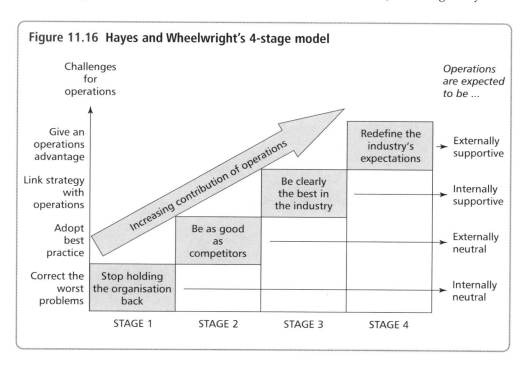

Figure 11.16 Hayes and Wheelwright's 4-stage model

an evangelical desire) to improve the operation. Second, it is the endpoint of progression which emphasises the increasing importance and centrality of operations strategy to overall competitive advantage. The idea of a proactive and inventive 'Stage 4' operations function, described by Hayes and Wheelwright, foreshadows the somewhat later concept of 'world-class operations'. That is, the idea that companies should aspire not only to have performance levels equal to, or better than, any other similar business *in the world,* but should achieve this superiority *because* of their operations ability.

SUMMARY ANSWERS TO KEY QUESTIONS

What are the differences between managing large 'breakthrough' improvement and managing continuous improvement?

Although it is common to distinguish between major 'leaps forward' in terms of operations improvement on the one hand, and more continuous incremental improvement on the other, these are really two points on a spectrum describing the degree of operations change, the main point being that different degrees of change require managing in different ways. Major improvement initiatives (such as most business process re-engineering) are dramatic and radical changes in the way operations resources and processes are organised. Such changes are intermittent and non-incremental 'projects'. They therefore need to be managed as projects with 'champions' and project managers being given responsibility to coordinate the individual ideas and efforts of the staff involved in the change. The risks of such projects tend to be high because failure can affect the whole project. Also, the degree of change implies relatively large investment of time, effort and probably capital. Continuous improvement, on the other hand, is less dramatic and longer term, involving small incremental steps. Change is gradual and constant and involves most or all staff. Here it is the collective motivation and culture which is important in maintaining the momentum of the improvement. Coordination becomes important because there will probably be many different small projects happening simultaneously. Although little capital is usually required, managerial time can cumulatively be greater than in breakthrough improvement. Continuous improvement is often described as a 'never-ending cycle'. In fact the concept of the cycle can also be used to put in place the routines and procedures which help to embed continuous improvement at a more strategic level. One such cycle uses the stages 'direct', 'develop', and 'deploy' to link market position to market potential.

How do the needs of the market direct the ongoing development of operations processes?

Usually market needs make their impact on how operations improve themselves through formal mechanisms such as performance measurement systems and benchmarking efforts, although these formal mechanisms are themselves cycles, in so much as they involve continually seeking gaps between the formal targets for the operation set by what the market requires and the actual performance of the operation. Designing performance measurement systems includes four generic issues. First, what factors to include as performance targets? Clearly such factors must adequately describe performance and be reasonably comprehensive. It is likely that performance measures at different levels of aggregation will be needed. Approaches such as the 'balanced scorecard' approach have tried to encourage a broader view of performance measurement. The second question is, what are the most important performance targets? These are the aspects of performance which reflect the particular market strategy adopted by an organisation. Often these are contained in a small number of key performance indicators (KPIs). The third question is, how to measure the performance targets? Usually a number of measures are needed to describe broader or more aggregated performance measures adequately. The final question concerns the basis on which to compare actual against target performance. Different bases of performance can affect how we judge performance. Typically, bases for comparison are against historical standards, against improvement goals, against competitors or against some idea of absolute perfection. Benchmarking is also used to direct improvement within operations. Benchmarking studies, however, tend to be carried out less frequently than ongoing performance measurement. One particular type of benchmarking is importance–performance mapping. This involves formally assessing the relative importance and performance of different aspects of the operation and plotting them on a matrix.

How can the ongoing management and control of operations be harnessed to develop their capabilities?

As operations gain experience they improve. In some ways this improvement is predictable and can be plotted over time using learning or experience curves. Of more immediate concern in operations strategy, however, is how operations can improve by building their capabilities over time. An important mechanism of capability building is the way in which operations increase their knowledge of their processes through attempting to control them. Process control (especially using approaches such as statistical process control) attempts to reduce the variation within a process. This will usually involve examining deviations from expected performance and 'problem solving' out the root causes of such variation. This in itself improves the process and makes it more predictable. Because it is more predictable it becomes easier to control, and so on. And although such control may be very operational in nature, the results of the improvement it brings can result in important strategic benefits.

What can operations do to deploy their capabilities into the market?

The extent to which an operation deploys its capabilities to create the potential for the organisation to operate in profitable parts of the market is shaped partly by the expectations placed on the operations function. The greater the expectations on the operations function, the more it will attempt to make a significant strategic contribution. The greater the contribution it makes, the higher the expectations of the rest of the organisation will be, and so on. One, relatively well known, model for assessing contribution is the Hayes and Wheelwright four-stage model. This model traces the progression of the operations function from the largely negative role of stage 1, to becoming the central element in competitive strategy in so-called stage 4 operations.

Customer Service at Kaston Pyral

'One of the trends in our business has been the increasing internationalisation of call centres. Companies have realised that they do not necessarily have to be physically represented in the country whose market they are serving. Decreasing telecommunications costs have made us all aware that we can get unheard-of economies of scale by focusing on large and sophisticated call centres which can serve a whole continent, or even the whole world.' (Lisa Jackson, Customer Service Vice President, Kaston Pyral US)

Kaston Pyral Group (KPG) is an international manufacturer and installer of heating, air conditioning, environmental control and condition monitoring systems. While the company's products still included electromechanical devices and (mainly) gas burning heating devices, heat exchangers, etc., increasingly they provided the sophisticated software which controlled and monitored both their own, and competitors', systems. These control systems could be updated independently of the hardware. They could also be integrated with other building and environmental management systems to provide 'total monitoring and maintenance' control. This could include remote diagnostics capabilities which allowed KPG's engineers to spot potential problems even before the customer had noticed. The customer service division of KPG provided customers with a range of services, including spare parts supply, maintenance and technical support. Technical support was becoming particularly important because the integration of new KPG systems with 'legacy' control systems could cause unforeseen problems. In most markets around the world the division had their own service centres but also used contract service engineers. Until recently the division also operated call centres in each country in which it operated. The call centres would take orders for spare parts and arrange delivery, investigate billing queries, arrange for regular or emergency repair and maintenance visits and provide technical support for installed hardware and control software.

Merging the call centres

The customer service division had recently decided to merge its individual country-based call centres into three regional call centres which would cover its three regional markets worldwide. Last year the call centre in Antwerp, the Netherlands, had expanded its capacity by five times and had taken over responsibility for all European customer service. A single centre in Kuala Lumpur, Malaysia, was planned to serve the Asian market. Lisa Jackson's responsibility was to oversee the merger of the North American call centres (previously in New Jersey, Montreal and Mexico City) into a new centre located in Atlanta, Georgia. The changeover to the new centre was planned to be phased over 20 weeks. Lisa was ten weeks into the changeover. Things were going well, as Lisa explained.

'Our current concerns are centred around managing the changeover smoothly. Atlanta is a greenfield site and most of our staff are relatively inexperienced, but we have put a lot of effort into training and we have managed so far without any real disaster, although it's been a steep learning curve for all of us. We are currently operating at 75 per cent of our planned final volume and can already see how concentrating all activities on one site will allow us to achieve economies of scale compared to having separ-

ate country-based centres. We have invested in the latest telecommunications technology and call handling systems which allow us to route calls to associates (call centres operators) with the appropriate technical and language skills. The larger scale also allows us to cope with the 'natural' uncertainty in the volume and type of calls which come in. Around 40 per cent of our staff are bilingual and 5 per cent trilingual which gives us the flexibility to cope with fluctuating demand between English-, Spanish- and French-speaking customers. In fact, because all our customers are businesses, most of them can speak English; however, we always try to use the appropriate language. It is a matter of courtesy and it also helps to build relationships with our customers.'

The customer survey

Prior to the changeover period the New Jersey centre had carried out an extensive survey of its US customers. The summary results are shown in Figure 11.17. Lisa was pleased to have this data.

'The New Jersey centre's survey provides us with a good benchmark. In the short term we have to make sure that we at least match this level of performance and in the long

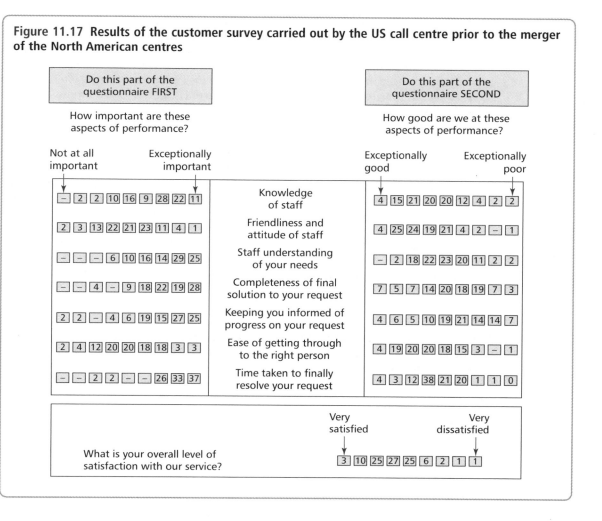

Figure 11.17 Results of the customer survey carried out by the US call centre prior to the merger of the North American centres

Table 11.5 Atlanta call centre performance measures during the first ten weeks of changeover period

Week of Changeover	Volume of calls taken	Number of associates (full-time equivalents)	Calls per associate hour	Average call time (mins)	Average wait time (mins)	Abandoned calls (%)
1	2,650	104	0.64	28.6	5.3	0.08
2	7,800	185	1.06	25.4	8.9	0.06
3	10,600	260	1.04	19.8	8.8	0.04
4	19,900	280	1.75	14.2	5.5	0.05
5	42,200	285	3.70	11.6	5.4	0.03
6	56,000	311	4.61	11.4	3.9	0.03
7	60,000	312	5.01	8.8	4.4	0.03
8	59,400	325	4.98	8.6	2.1	0.03
9	64,800	325	5.30	9.0	4.7	0.02
10	64,400	325	5.29	8.2	4.9	0.03

term we must improve on it. Certainly the overall level of satisfaction score is not good enough. Our challenge is to achieve excellence in all aspects of service. But customer service is not the only thing we have to monitor. It is vital that we get some financial payback for the investment in the new centre. That is why we also intend to monitor productivity-based measures closely. In fact, since the new centre started we have been recording our progress closely on four key measures (Table 11.5 shows these measures for the first ten weeks of the centre's operation). These are the measures that we have decided will be the key performance indicators for the centre. "Calls per associate hour" is the best measure we have of our associates' productivity and the "average call time" is a related measure which indicates how efficient the associates are at dealing with customer queries. As we get better at routing calls to the right associate quickly and efficiently and as our associates get to know the business better, the average call time should shrink to below eight minutes. "Average wait time" and the "percentage of abandoned calls" give us an indication of how well we are matching our capacity to demand throughout the day. We have already started to experiment with using control charting procedures to monitor some of these performance measures, specifically, average call time, average wait time, and the percentage of abandoned calls. It is by using this type of technique that we aim to develop one of the most efficient call centres of its type.'

The future

The progress of the call centre reorganisation in the customer service division was being watched closely by Kaston Pyral's group management. The European reorganisation had gone reasonably well and the US centre seemed to be on track. Eddie Karowski, KPG's CEO, was keeping a close watch on the new call centre strategy because he believed that customer service would become the way the company could differentiate itself.

'Our business is getting more competitive every year. We already have a range of products which is (we believe) the best in the world. Surveys show that the functionality and reliability of our equipment is outstanding compared to our competitors. But they are catching up fast. To stay ahead we need to do three things really well. First, we must be more innovative in the new products and services we introduce, especially now that new technology such as the control and diagnostics power of new software can be *integrated into our systems; the potential for exciting new offerings is vast. No one really knows what customers want in this area. I suspect they all want slightly different things from their hardware, control software and the services we offer, but whatever emerges we must be in a position to supply it. Second, whatever we finish up doing, we have to give impeccable service. Excellent customer service builds relationships and is the best way of establishing customer loyalty. Third, we have to make sure that we are always in a position to keep the customers updated with the new product and service offerings which could benefit them in order to make the best of sales opportunities. Our call centre operations have the potential to help us in all of these areas. The question which we have to answer is how best to make sure that the three new consolidated call centres become the power house for keeping us ahead of the competition.'*

Further reading

Bessant, J. and S. Caffyn (1997) 'High involvement innovation', *International Journal of Technology Management*, Vol. 14, No. 1.

Davenport, T. and L. Prusak (1998) *Working Knowledge: How organisations manage what they know*, Harvard Business School Press, Boston, MA.

DeToni, A. and S. Tonchia (1996) 'Lean organisation management by process and performance measurement', *International Journal of Operations and Production Management*, Vol. 16, No. 2.

Hammer, M. and J. Champy (1993) *Reengineering the Corporation*, Nicholas Brearley Publishing.

Kaplan, R. and D. Norton (1996) 'Using the balanced scorecard as a strategic management system', *Harvard Business Review*, Jan–Feb.

Lebfried, K.H.J. and C.J. McNair (1992) *Benchmarking: A tool for continuous improvement*, Harper Collins.

Leonard-Barton, D. (1992) 'The factory as a learning laboratory', *Sloan Management Review*, Fall.

Leonard-Bart, D. (1995) *Wellsprings of Knowledge: Building and sustaining the sources of innovation*, Harvard Business School Press, Boston, MA.

Nevis, E.C., A.J. DiBella and J.M. Gould (1995) 'Understanding organisations as learning systems', *Sloan Management Review*, Winter.

Pisano, G.P. (1994) 'Knowledge, integration and the locus of learning: an empirical analysis of process development', *Strategic Management Journal*, Vol. 15, pp. 85–100.

Upton, D. (1996) 'Mechanisms for building and sustaining operations improvement', *European Management Journal*, Vol. 14, No. 3.

Notes on the chapter

1 Hayes, R.H. and G.P. Pisano (1996) 'Manufacturing strategy: at the intersection of two paradigm shifts', *Production and Operations Management*, Vol. 5, No. 1.

2 Hammer, M. and J. Champy (1993) *Re-engineering the Corporation*, Nicholas Brearley Publishing.

3 Hammer, M. (1990) 'Re-engineering work: don't automate, obliterate', *Harvard Business Review*, Vol. 68, No. 4.

4 Imai, M. (1986) *Kaizen – the key to Japan's competitive success*, McGraw-Hill.

5 Source: Marsh, P. (2000) 'Welding metal to the Internet', *Financial Times*, 30 October.

6 Neely, A.D. (1998) *Measuring Business Performance*, Economist Books, London.

7 Skinner, W. (1974) 'The focused factory', *Harvard Business Review*, May–June.

8 See Kaplan, R.S. and D.P. Norton (1996) *The Balanced Scorecard*, Harvard Business School Press, Boston, MA.

9 Camp, C. (1989) 'Benchmarking: the search for best practices which lead to superior performance', *Quality Progress*, Jan–May.

10 Pickering, I.M. and S. Chambers (1991) 'Competitive benchmarking: progress and future development', *Computer Integrated Manufacturing Systems*, Vol. 4, No. 2.

11 This section is based on Slack, N. *et al.* (1997) *Operations Management*, 2nd edn, Financial Times-Prentice Hall, UK.

12 Ferdows, K. and A. de Meyer (1990) 'Lasting Improvement in Manufacturing', *Journal of Operations Management*, Vol. 9, No. 2.

13 Bohn, R.E. (1994) 'Measuring and managing technical knowledge', *Sloan Management Review*, Fall.

14 Adapted from Bohn (1994) op.cit.

15 Source: Discussions with company staff.

16 Hayes R.J. and S.C. Wheelwright (1984) *Restoring our Competitive Edge*, Wiley, New York.

17 Chase, R.B. and R.J. Hayes (1991) 'Beefing up operations in service firms', *Sloan Management Review*, Fall, pp. 15–16.

Product and service development and organisation

Introduction

Even in less pressured times, product and services development was important. The products and services produced by an operation are, after all, its 'public face' in so much as they are what markets judge a company on: good products and services equals good company. Because of this, it has always made sense to devote time and effort to how new products and services are developed. Moreover, it has long been accepted that there is a connection between how companies go about developing products and services and how successful those products and services are in the marketplace. Being good at it really does make a difference. What has changed over the past few years is both the speed and scale of market and technology changes and our understanding of just how closely connected are the processes by which products and services are developed and the outcomes from those processes. Given that product and service development is a core issue for operations strategy, it is appropriate that it is treated here (Figure 12.1). And, even though it is a subject in its own right, it can still benefit from an operations strategy analysis.

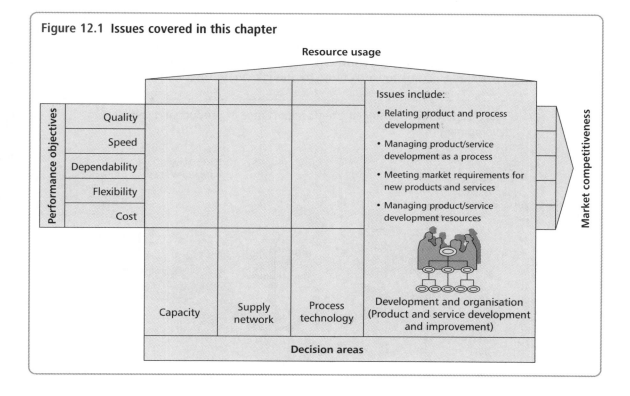

Figure 12.1 Issues covered in this chapter

KEY QUESTIONS

- *Why is the way in which companies develop their products and services so important?*
- *What process do companies use to develop products and services?*
- *How should the effectiveness of the product and service development process be judged in terms of fulfilling market requirements?*
- *What operations resource-based decisions define a company's product and service development strategy?*

The strategic importance of product and service development

Figure 12.2 illustrates some of the more important reasons why product and service development is seen as increasingly strategically important. From a market perspective, international competition has become increasingly intense. In many markets there are a number of competitors bunched together in terms of their product and service performance. Even small advantages in product and service specifications can have a significant impact on competitiveness. This has made customers both more sophisticated in exercising their choice and often more demanding in terms of wanting products and services that fit their specific needs. Also, markets are becoming more fragmented. Unless companies choose to follow relatively narrow niche markets, they are faced with developing products and services capable of being adapted in different ways to different markets. If this were not enough, product and service life cycles have become shorter. An obvious way to try to gain advantage over competitors is to introduce updated products and services. Competitors respond by doing the same and the situation escalates. While not every industry has such short life cycles as, say, the entertainment or fashion garment industries, the trend, even in industrial markets, is towards more frequent new product and service introductions.

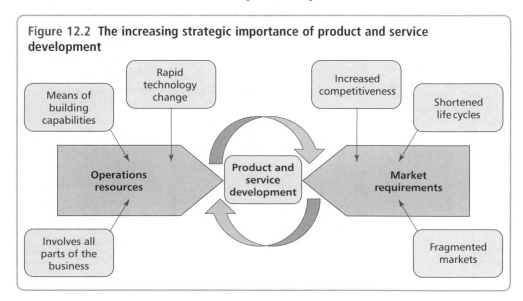

Figure 12.2 The increasing strategic importance of product and service development

A different, but equally important, set of pressures affect the operations resources which have to develop and deliver new products and services. Perhaps most importantly, rapid technology changes have affected most industries. New material technologies open up new possibilities in automobile manufacture. New (and smaller and cheaper) electronic technologies have transformed the world of consumer electronics and computing. New biotechnologies have opened up unexpected possibilities in pharmaceuticals. And, arguably the most widespread in its effects, Internet-based technologies have introduced startlingly new possibilities (and uncertainties) for almost all products and services in all industries. Partly because of the scale and pace of such technological developments, it has become increasingly obvious that effective product and service development places responsibilities on every part of the business. Marketing, purchasing, accounting, operations, are all, like it or not, an integral part of any organisation's ability to develop products and services effectively and efficiently. Every part of the business is now faced with the question, 'How can we deploy our competencies and skills towards developing better or different products and services?' This last point is particularly important. New product and service development is now seen as the mechanism by which all parts of the business, but especially operations, leverages their capabilities into the marketplace.

Developing products and services and developing processes

For convenience and for ease of explanation we often treat the design of products and services on the one hand, and the design of the processes which produce them on the other, as though they were totally separate activities. In many organisations the two developments are organised separately. But this does not imply that they necessarily *should* be treated or organised separately, and they are clearly interrelated. It would be foolish to develop any product or service without taking into consideration the constraints and capabilities of the processes that will produce it. Similarly, developing processes to take advantage of new technologies or process methods will have implications for the development of products and services in the future. Successful developments often have a history of both product/service and process development (see the box on the development of the ballpoint pen).

Introducing the ballpoint pen[1]

In 1938, two Hungarian brothers, Ladislao and Georg Biro, patented a design for a revolutionary ballpoint pen. By 1944 the brothers had managed to develop a manufacturing process and started to produce their first commercial products. Distribution rights for the US market were bought by a fountain pen manufacturer called Eversharp. However, a Chicago businessman, Milton Reynolds, had seen the biro pen while travelling in Europe, had liked what he saw and had a copy product on sale in a New York department store before Eversharp received their first delivery. Not surprisingly, Eversharp sued in the courts and in the legal wrangling which followed it emerged that in fact there had been an earlier patent for a ball-writing pen as far back as 1888. Meanwhile, both Eversharp and Reynolds enjoyed some success with their ballpoint pens, Reynolds developing the first product enhancement when they introduced a retractable point which clicked in and out of the pen barrel.

However, although the design was revolutionary, it was far from perfect. The pens were prone to blotting and leaking, and sales dropped severely as the public lost patience with such unreliable products. Eventually both Eversharp and Reynolds were forced out of business because of the

▶

problems. Another established pen company, Parker, then stepped into the market but with a product redesigned to overcome its reliability problems. In fact Parker enjoyed many years of commercial success with their improved product. This success encouraged other companies to enter the market, perhaps the most innovative being Bic, a French manufacturing company. Bic's success lay in developing the manufacturing process to a level that enabled them to produce pens which could sell at around a tenth of their competitor products. This revolutionised the market. The ballpoint's competitor, the fountain pen, became a low-volume niche product and the ballpoint became a consumer disposable.

The degree of product change is important

Just as it was important in the previous chapter to understand the degree of process change expected of the development process, so here it is important to understand the degree of product or service change. Again, we can construct a conceptual scale which helps to give some degree of discrimination between different levels of change. Also again, we can calibrate this scale from relatively minor modifications to a product or service at one extreme, through to the novel and/or radical changes exhibited by a 'pioneer' product or service. In the previous chapter we distinguished between *what* is done in a process and *how* it is done. The equivalent here is the distinction between what is seen externally to have changed in the product or service and how the product or service performs its function through its internal mechan-

Table 12.1 The degree of product/service change can affect both its external appearance and its internal methodology/technology

| | Degree of product/service change | | | |
	Modification	Extension	Development	Pioneer
External customer awareness (what is seen)	Little/None	More functionality	'Next generation' progression	Novel/radical change
Internal methodology/ technology (how it is done)	Minor/isolated	Some changes to original methodology / technology	Extensive redesign of original method / technology	Novel/radical change
Example: Exercise machines	Minor engineering change to component parts	Extra options on control/display of computer	Aesthetic redesign and changes to internal resistance mechanism	'Total health monitoring' concept with intelligent machines' response to body monitoring and full automatic analysis
Example: Bank card services	Minor changes to back-office procedures	Improvement of monthly statement with analysis of expenditure	Incorporation of smart-card technology	Ultimately flexible 'one card' concept with advanced smart-card capability and links with other financial services.

isms. Table 12.1 describes four levels of change, 'modification', 'extension', 'development' and 'pioneer', in terms of the product or services external and internal characteristics. It also shows two illustrative examples, one based on a company that manufactures exercise machines, the other a financial service company that runs a bank card service. Remember, though, that the level of change implied by these categories of development to products and services is approximate. What is important is to recognise that the nature of the product and service development process is likely to be different depending on the degree of product/service change.

Relatively small 'modification' changes, such as those described in the two examples in Table 12.1, are likely to be relatively frequent and will probably be made using routine procedures. Most companies have standard procedures such as 'engineering change orders' (ECOs), where small changes are proposed in one part of the organisation and approved by other relevant departments. But although these small modifications may be incorporated into standard procedures, they may still require organisation-wide exposure, especially if the part of the product or service being modified has high 'connectivity'. Connectivity is the degree to which changes in one part of a product or service impacts on other parts. It is a concept which can also apply at an organisational level and is important in understanding why, as the degree of product or service change moves thorough 'extension' and 'development' to 'pioneer', the changes become more difficult and more risky. Fundamental changes to products and service almost always involve the whole organisation. So, in addition to the obvious difficulties of market acceptability and resource capability inherent in high degrees of product and service change, the coordination between functional strategies must be well managed.

Dyson's pioneering vacuum cleaners[2]

On 3 October 2000 James Dyson, the inventor of the bagless vacuum cleaner, walked victorious from the British High Court. He had been suing Hoover over the infringement of his 1980 patent of his 'double cyclone' vacuum cleaner mechanism, an invention which, in the words of the judge, had 'turned the industry on its head'.

His idea had emerged over 20 years earlier when, sweeping the carpet at his home, he had been struck by the inefficiency of conventional vacuum cleaners which used filter bags. A professional designer by background, he was working on a 20 ft tall industrial cyclone used to capture unwanted dust at a powder coating plant. Although this technology was well known in the ventilation industry, Dyson wondered why no one had used cyclones in vacuum cleaners. To make the technology applicable to vacuum cleaners he invented the double cyclone, one of which separates out the larger items such as pieces of paper or dog hairs, the other catching the smaller particles. Four years and 5127 prototypes later, he had a workable model. The problem was, none of the existing vacuum cleaner manufacturers were interested. Hoover, Electrolux, Philips and Black and Decker were all approached. They all had two problems. The first was that the dual-cyclone technology was just too different from existing technology. The degree of change was too great for them to take the risk of adopting it. Second, existing vacuum cleaner manufacturers made handsome profits from selling the disposable filter bags. Dyson had to go into business for himself in order to bring his idea to market. After the trial, when asked whether he would now license his design to Hoover, he was dismissive: 'They had 20 years when they could have done that.'

Product and process change should be considered together

We can put together the degree of process change scale from the previous chapter with the scale indicating the degree of product/service change described in Table 12.1. This is done in Figure 12.3. Advanced or 'blue sky' research and development lies beyond both of these scales, but it is from this direction that most radical innovation emerges. The dotted lines indicate the degree of difficulty encountered in the development process. Put simply, product/service change is easier when the underlying processes which produce them are not being changed at the same time, and vice versa. Figure 12.3 also shows three service/process developments at a bank. Making changes to the services offered in a bank branch involves relatively minor 'product' and process changes compared with the redesign of both product and process involved in a major new call centre. This, in turn, is less than the development of a totally new Internet banking service.

Managing the overlap between product and process development

Because it is often difficult to untangle a service 'product' from the process that produces it, operations developing new services know they have to develop new processes concurrently. But manufacturing operations are different. It is often both possible to develop products independently of the processes that make them and also common practice for many companies. Yet, because product development and process development are not the same thing, it does not mean that they *should* not overlap. In fact one of the more important trends in product design has been the considerable effort which recently has been put into managing the overlap. There

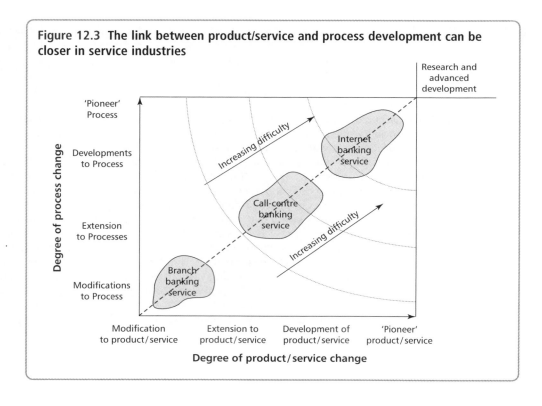

Figure 12.3 The link between product/service and process development can be closer in service industries

are probably two reasons for this. First, there is a growing recognition that the design of products has a major effect on the cost of making them. Many decisions taken during the development of products such as the choice of material, or the way components are fastened together, will all define much of the cost of making the product. It clearly make sense, therefore, to build into the development process the need to evaluate product design choices in terms of their effect on manufacturing processes as well as the functionality of the product itself. Second, the way overlap is managed between product and process development has a significant effect on the effectiveness and efficiency of the development process itself. This is particularly true for the time between the initial product or service concept and its eventual delivery into the market, and the overall cost of the total development effort. We shall deal with this issue later in the chapter.

Theory Box Modular design and mass customisation

Two separate, but related ideas – *modularity* in product and service design and *mass customisation* – have made an impact on product and service development. We will consider them separately and then bring the two ideas together.

- *Modularity* – is a strategy for organising complex products (and services) and processes efficiently. A modular system is composed of units (or modules) that are designed independently but still function as an integrated whole.[3] So rather than designing a product and service as a totally integrated and indivisible whole, the design is divided into modules which can be put together in various ways. Putting different modules together will result in products or services with different functionality. Yet because the modules themselves are standardised, they can be produced in a standardised low-cost manner. The most obvious examples of modular design are in the computer industry where relatively complex products can be built up using smaller subsystems. Customers who have different requirements can simply choose which modules they require within the overall product. Provided the overall architecture of the design (the way modules fit together and the functions they perform) and the interfaces between the modules allow for easy connection and communication, then modularity can offer considerable advantages. For example, innovative ideas can be tried out in one module without it necessarily interfering with the design of the product or service as a whole. So, suppose a medical centre offers a range of different health check-up services. If it designs its processes and systems to separate its different clinical procedures, it could introduce new tests in one area while leaving the others undisturbed. Of course, it would have to ensure that the interfaces between the improved test area and the other parts of its services processes (records, diagnostics, follow-up appointments, and so on) could handle any new information generated.

- *Mass customisation* – is the ability to provide customers with high levels of variety and customisation through flexible and responsive processes and flexible product and service designs.[4] The vision of mass customisation is to reduce radically the effect of the assumed trade-off between variety and cost. Some authorities see it as an inevitable successor to mass production, while others argue that there is little essentially new in the idea, rather it pushes existing ideas such as flexibility and agility to their logical conclusion.[5] The mass customisation concept includes the ideas that, as far as market requirements are concerned, markets are becoming increasingly fragmented, while as far as operations resources are concerned, new forms of organisation and technology are allowing greater degrees of flexibility and responsiveness. Thus, it is possible to 'mass produce' a basic family of products or services which can still be customised to the needs of individual customers. The major management task, therefore, is to understand the implications of market and operations developments and harness them by embracing an attitude which stresses sensitivity to customers' individual needs and a willingness to supply

▶

them with customised offerings. This means changes in the way the operation produces its products and services and the way it markets them. But, of particular relevance here, it also implies a different approach to *designing* products and services. Predominantly this involves the standardisation and modularisation of components (see above) to increase variety while reducing production costs.

One much-quoted example of how modular design contributed to mass customisation is the way Black and Decker, the hand tool manufacturer, produced a wide range of well over one hundred basic hand tools, each with their own variants, from a relatively small set of modular and standardised components. The first consequence of this modular approach was more effective and efficient design. *'Much of the work in design and tooling was eliminated because of the standardisation of motors, bearings, switches, ... etc. New designs could be developed using components already standardised for manufacturing ability. The product did not have to start with a blank sheet of paper and be designed from scratch'.*[6] The second was drastically reduced production costs because standardised parts enabled standardised production processes.

Product and service development as a process

There are two views of how to characterise product and service development. One sees it as essentially a creative process where a technical understanding of the mechanisms involved in the service or product is brought together with ingenuity and flair. The emphasis should be on creativity, novelty and innovation. For all this to happen the people involved must be given the space and time to be creative. Of course, the activity has to be managed but not to the point where it interferes with originality. Typically this view of product and service development sees the activity as a collection of, sometimes interdependent, projects. And although some aspects of project management may be relevant in guiding the activity, it cannot be regarded as a 'process'. Processes are what create products and services on a routine basis, whereas product and service development is the creation of original one-offs. Furthermore, the raw material of this knowledge is a substance which is difficult to define and even more difficult to identify. Product and service development, therefore, must focus on its *outcome* and not worry too much about how that outcome is achieved.

The counter-argument contends that, as with everything, output depends on process. Great ideas for products and services emerge from a process that makes them great. Therefore, of course, one should examine the process of product and service development. While no two development projects are exactly alike, there is sufficient commonality in all such projects to be able to model the process and work on improving its overall performance. The normal generic performance objectives which apply to any operations process, quality, speed, dependability, flexibility and cost, all have relevance to product and service development. Most companies would willingly adopt an approach which gave them higher-quality designs for new products and services, delivered faster and more dependably while maintaining sufficient flexibility to incorporate new ideas which are produced at lower cost. It makes sense, therefore, to apply similar approaches to improving product and service development processes as one would to any other process. Define the steps in the process, examine the characteristics of how prospective product and service designs flow through the resources which act upon them, look for bottlenecks and attempt to smooth them out, identify critical points in the flow and guard against quality failures at these points, and so on. This is the approach we shall take. Product and service development is a process, and *needs to be managed strategically.*

Product/service development – an operations strategy analysis

Product and service development can be treated as a coherent operation in its own right. We include it here as a part of the development and organisation decision area because developing products and services is clearly vital to any organisation's strategic development. However, the topic could be treated as an entirely separate function (which it is in many organisations). Indeed for professional design consultancies, for example, it is their whole reason for existing. We include the topic within operations strategy not because we believe product and service development should be always an integral part of the operations function organisationally. Rather, it is because of the difficulty in untangling the process of producing and delivering

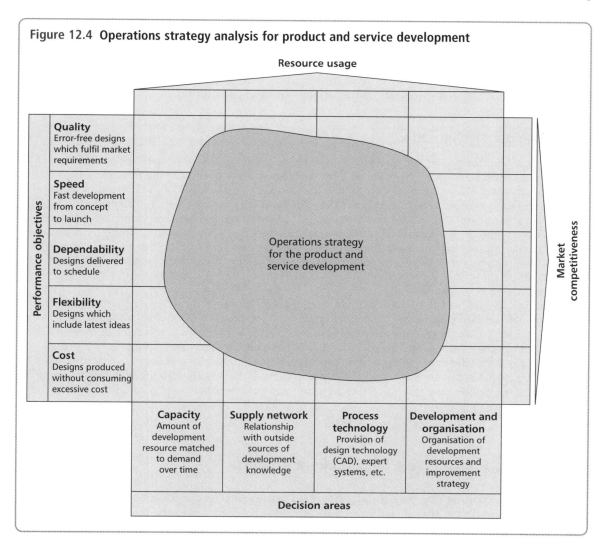

Figure 12.4 Operations strategy analysis for product and service development

products and services and that of developing those products and services in the first place. Also, because we treat the topic as an integral part of operations strategy does not mean that no benefit can be derived from analysing product and service development as a distinct operations strategy in its own right.

For example, Figure 12.4 illustrates how an operations strategy matrix (discussed in Chapter 2) can be constructed for product and service development operations. The generic performance objectives of quality, speed, dependability, flexibility and cost can be used to describe the impact of new or modified products and services in the marketplace. In order to achieve competitive 'production' of product and service designs, the resources and processes which are used to develop them will themselves need organising along the lines of any other operation. The company's design *capacity* will have to be matched to the demand placed on it over time, relationships with an external *supply network* for design and development knowledge will have to be established, *process technologies* such as computer aided design (CAD) systems, expert systems, simulations, and so on may be needed, also the resources technology and processes used to develop products and services will need *organising* and themselves *developing* over time. All decision areas are of some relevance to most companies' development efforts.

The remainder of this chapter will first examine the nature of the product and service development process and then use the operations strategy approach to illustrate the requirements of the market and the capabilities of development resources.

Boulanger or baguettier[7]

The end result of design and development efforts is often influenced by external and environmental factors as much as the result of internal decision making. Look at the traditional French loaf – the baguette. All over the world it is the image of French tradition. Sold as much for its 'Frenchness' as for its taste, the origins of its stick-like shape have become the subject of many romantic (but false) stories. One says the baguette was invented by Napoleon's troops during the Russian campaign. Because their traditional round loaves took up too much space, it is said, Napoleon ordered that the new shape of bread should be designed so it could be carried down soldiers' trouser-legs. In fact French bakers are called boulanger because they make boules (balls), and did so up until the 1920s. By that time most French bakeries had adopted the new steam ovens which could caramelise the starch on the outside of a loaf, giving it its golden crisp crust. Also, the slaughter of the First World War had resulted in a severe manpower shortage which made it difficult to prepare the traditional boule from sour dough – a lengthy and labour-intensive process. Finally, in 1920 the French government passed a law which prevented baking before 4 o'clock in the morning. This meant they did not have time to bake boules fresh for the breakfast table. Baguettes took far less time to prepare, and, being sweeter and softer than traditional sour dough boules, were a hit with the customers. Thus, the French 'traditional' baguette was shaped by social change, technological innovation and government legislation.

The product and service development process

Describing the way in which organisations develop products and services is problematic because different organisations will adopt different processes. Furthermore, what companies specify as a formal product or service development procedure, and what happens in reality, can be very different things. Yet three ideas do seem to have found wide acceptance:

- The development process moves through a series of stages. Sometimes stages are missed out and sometimes the process recycles back through stages. Also, different authors define the stages in different ways. But, somewhere towards the beginning of the process, there are stages concerned with collecting ideas and generating product and service concepts, and towards the end of the process, there are stages concerned with specifying the detail of the product or service.

- As the development process moves through these stages, the number of alternative design options reduces until one final design remains. The process often includes decision points which screen out options deemed to be unsatisfactory.

- As these possible design options are reduced there is a move from a state of uncertainty regarding the final design to a state of increasing certainty. One consequence of this is that the ability to change the design gets increasingly limited. Making changes at the end of the process can be considerably more expensive than making them at the beginning.

Stages of development

Different authors present different stage models which attempt to describe product and service development. These vary in the number and type of stages they include but are broadly similar. Figure 12.5 illustrates a typical stage model. Remember, though, that even if we assume that these stages are not sequential, it is a somewhat simplistic approach to describing what really happens in product and service development. The reality of bringing products and services from concept to market introduction is in reality both complex and messy.

Figure 12.5 A typical 'stage model' of the product and service development process

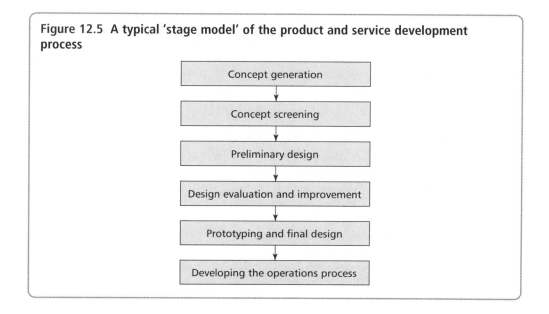

Concept generation

Ideas for new product or service concepts may be generated from sources outside the organisation, such as expressed customers' needs or competitor activity, or from sources within the organisation such as sales staff and front-of-house operations staff, or, more formally, from the R&D department. There are many market research tools for gathering data in a formal and structured way from customers, including questionnaires and interviews. These techniques, however, usually tend to be structured in such a way as only to test out ideas or check products or services against predetermined criteria.

Concept screening

Not all concepts, or variants within a concept, have the potential to be developed through to market launch. The purpose of the concept-screening stage is to take the flow of concepts emerging from the development process and evaluate them. Concepts may have to pass through many different screens, and several functions might be involved, each using different criteria to screen the proposals. Screening may be divided into three sets of criteria related to market positioning, operations/technical implications and financial evaluation:

● Does the proposed product or service occupy a market position which is both attractive in its own right and consistent with the organisation's overall marketing strategy?

● Does the proposed product or service exploit existing operations resource capabilities or help the operation to develop attractive new capabilities?

● Is the investment in the proposed product or service feasible, and is the return from this investment acceptable?

Preliminary design

This stage represents the beginning of detailed work on the product or service design. It includes defining what will go into the product or service. This will require the collection of information about such things as the *constituent component parts* which make up the product or service package, *the product/service structure,* that is, the order in which the component parts of the package have to be put together, and the *bill of materials* (BOM), that is, the quantities of each component part required to make up the total package. This stage also may include specifying *how* the various components are put together to create the final product or service.

Design evaluation and improvement

This stage takes the preliminary design and attempts to improve it before the prototype product or services are tested in the market. There are a number of techniques that can be employed at this stage to evaluate and improve the preliminary design. Some of these techniques are concerned with costing the proposed product or service and identifying areas for cost improvement. Some are concerned with fully exploring the technical characteristics of the product or service in an effort to improve its overall value. Most are based on an approach which emphasises systematic questioning of exactly what each part of the product or service is intended to contribute to its overall value, why it is being done in a particular way and how it might be done differently. It is not the purpose of this book to explore any of these techniques in detail; however, one particular approach is worth mentioning because of its similarity to our overall approach to operations strategy. This is quality function deployment (QFD) and is described in the theory box.

Theory Box Quality function deployment[8]

Quality function deployment (QFD) is a technique that was developed in Japan at Mitsubishi's Kobe shipyard and used extensively by Toyota, the motor vehicle manufacturer, and its suppliers. It is also known as the 'house of quality' (because of its shape) and the 'voice of the customer' (because of its purpose). The technique tries to capture *what* the customer needs and *how* it might be achieved.

Figure 12.6 shows an example of quality function deployment being used in the design of a new information system product.

- The WHATs, or 'customer requirements', are the list of competitive factors which customers find significant. Their relative importance is scored, in this case, on a 10-point scale.

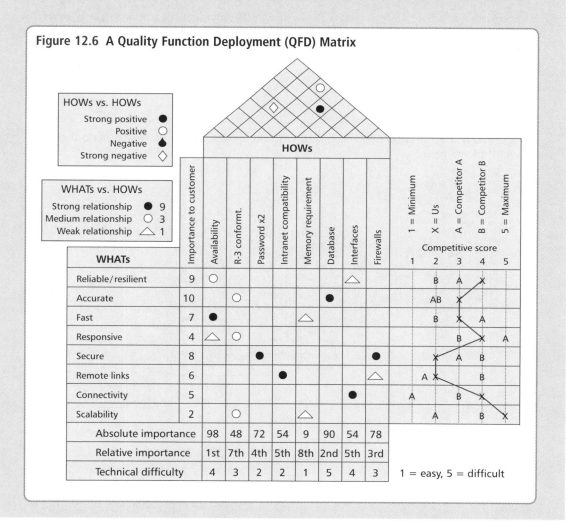

Figure 12.6 A Quality Function Deployment (QFD) Matrix

- The competitive scores, which indicate the relative performance of the product, in this case on a 1 to 5 scale. Also indicated are the performances of two competitor products.

- The HOWs, or 'design characteristics' of the product. These are the various 'dimensions' of the design which will operationalise customer requirements within the product or service.

- The central matrix (sometimes called the relationship matrix) represents a view of the interrelationship between the WHATs and the HOWs. This is often based on value judgements made by designers.

- The bottom box of the matrix is a technical assessment of the product. This contains the absolute importance of each design characteristic. (For example, the design characteristic 'interfaces' has a relative importance of $(9 \times 5) 1(1 \times 9) = 54$). This is also translated into a ranked relative importance. In addition, the degree of technical difficulty to achieve high levels of performance in each design characteristic is indicated on a 1 to 5 scale.

- The triangular 'roof' of the 'house' captures any information the team has about the correlations (positive or negative) between the various design characteristics.

Although the details of QFD may vary between its different variants, the principle is generally common, namely to identify the customer requirements for a product or service (together with their relative importance) and relate them to the design characteristics which translate customer requirements into practice. In fact this principle can be continued by making the HOWs from one stage become the WHATs of the next, as in Figure 12.7. Some experienced users of QFD have up to four linked matrices in this way.

Figure 12.7 QFD matrices can be linked with the 'hows' of one matrix forming the 'what' of the next

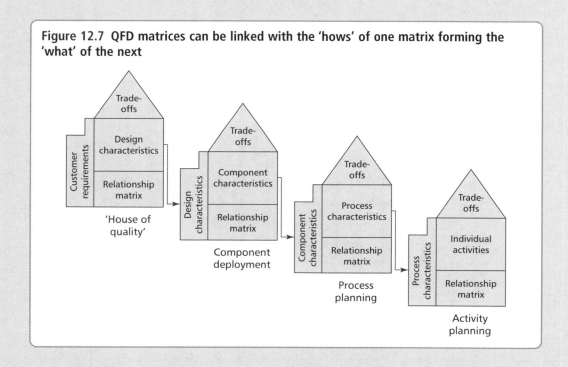

Prototyping and final design

Often 'close to final' designs are 'prototyped'. Partly the next stage in the design activity is to turn the improved design into a prototype so that it can be tested. This may be to learn more about the nature of the proposed product or service but often it is also to reduce the risk inherent in going straight to market. Product prototypes may include clay models of car designs and computer simulations, for example. Computer simulations can be used as service prototypes but also can include the actual implementation of the service on a pilot basis. Many retailing organisations pilot new products and services in a small number of stores in order to test customers' reaction to them.

Developing the operations process

Most models of product and service development assume that the final stage will involve developing the operations processes which will eventually produce the designed product or service. Although we dealt with process development in the previous chapter, it is important to stress again that, in practice, produce/service development on the one hand and process development on the other are inexorably linked. Placing this stage at the end of the development process, however, does reinforce the idea that, generally speaking, if the development process is intended to design products and services which will fulfil a market need, then process decisions can only take place after some product or service characteristics have been decided.

Product and service development as a funnel

Although stage models such as we illustrated in Figure 12.5 are useful in identifying the activities which must at some time take place within the overall development activity, they do not form a strict set of stages to which the development process must conform. In reality, stages may merge, the sequence of stages may vary and, almost always, the development process recycles back and forth between the stages. But the underlying ideas behind such stage models are widespread. For example, a common method of describing the product or service development process is to liken it to a funnel. The mouth of the funnel, being wide, can accommodate many alternative designs for the product or service. Indeed, theoretically, there will always be an infinite number of ways in which the benefits required from a product or service design can be delivered, even if some are only minor variants on each other. As the development process progresses, some design operations are discarded. There may be formal 'filters' at various points in the funnel whose sole purpose is to exclude some of the options. These filters often represent 'screens' which evaluate alternative designs against criteria of market acceptability, technical capability, financial return, and so on. Eventually, only one design option remains which is then developed into its final form. The whole process moves from a broad concept capable of infinite interpretation at one end of the funnel to a fully formed and specified design at the other.

Just as the stage model in Figure 12.5 was a simplification, so is the concept of the development funnel. Do not expect that all product and service development will conform to the obvious and regular funnel shape as shown in Figure 12.8(a). Most developments do not look like this, and more to the point, *nor necessarily should they.* Rather than see the funnel as a prescription for how development should be, it is

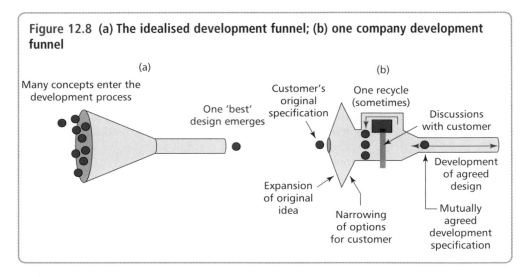

Figure 12.8 (a) The idealised development funnel; (b) one company development funnel

better to see it as a metaphor for the design process which can be reshaped to reflect how the development process itself can be designed. The implication of this is that, even if an organisation does not want to progressively reduce its new product and service ideas using a perfectly smooth funnel, it certainly needs to understand what shape of funnel it really does want.

Example

Consider the following quote from the vice president in charge of product development in a company which makes advanced and customised electronic devices:

> *'Our customers put business our way mainly because we are experts in taking their problems and solving them. They usually give us an initial specification to which we design, then at some time in the future they approve the design and we start to manufacture for them. What we have learnt to do right at the start of the development process is deliberately expand the number and scope of ideas beyond that which the customer first gives us. This can often result in a more creative solution than the customer had originally envisaged. After all, they are not the experts in this technology, we are. The trick is to not let this period last too long before we start narrowing down to two or three options which we can present to the customer. It is important to get to this stage before the customer's own internal deadline. That gives us time to refine ideas after we have presented them. Some designs will be recycled at this point if the customer wants a further development, but we have a rule that we only ever recycle once. From experience, if the customer wants further substantial changes then they are not even sure in their own mind what they really want. After this stage we go into the final development of a single design tied to a very tight specification agreed between ourselves and the customer.'*

Figure 12.8(b) illustrates how this particular executive saw the development funnel in her company. It may not be the perfect funnel of the textbooks, but it is well defined, well understood in the company, and can be easily communicated to the customer.

Simultaneous development

Earlier we described the development process as a set of individual, predetermined stages. Sometimes one stage is completed before the next one commences. This step-by-step, or *sequential*, approach was traditionally the typical form of product/service development. It has some advantages. It is easy to manage and control development projects organised in this way because each stage is clearly defined. In addition, each stage is complete before the next stage is begun, so each stage can focus its skills and expertise on a limited set of tasks. The main problem of the sequential approach is that it is both time consuming and costly. Any difficulties encountered during one stage might necessitate the design being halted while responsibility moves back to the previous stage. Yet often there is really little need to wait until the absolute finalisation of one stage before starting the next. Perhaps while generating the concept, the evaluation activity of screening and selection could be started. It would have to be a crude evaluation maybe, but nevertheless it is likely that some concepts could be judged as 'non-starters' relatively early on in the process of idea generation. Similarly, during the screening stage, it is likely that some aspects of the developing product or service will become obvious before the phase is finally complete. The preliminary work on these parts of the design could be commenced before the end of the final screening and selection process. In other words, one stage commences before the previous one has finished, so there is *simultaneous* or *concurrent* work at the stages. (See Figure 12.9.)

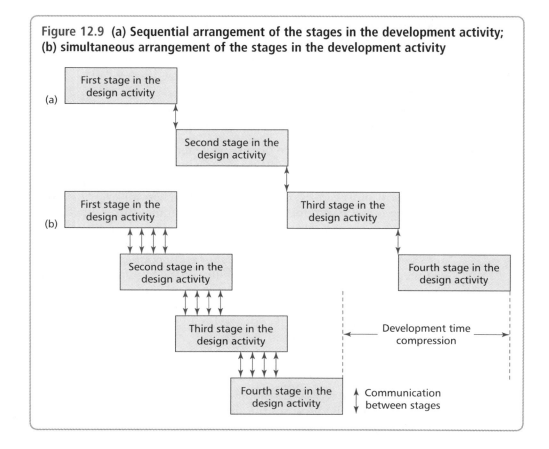

Figure 12.9 (a) Sequential arrangement of the stages in the development activity; (b) simultaneous arrangement of the stages in the development activity

We can link this idea with the idea of uncertainty reduction discussed earlier. We made the point that uncertainty reduces as the design progresses. This also applies to each stage of the design, so uncertainty regarding the concept reduces through the concept generation stage, uncertainty about the preliminary design reduces through that phase, and so on. If this is so, then there must be some degree of certainty which the next stage can take as its starting point prior to the end of the previous stage. In other words, designers can be continually reacting to a preceding stage. However, this can only work if there is effective communication between each part of the stages.

A market requirements perspective on product and service development

Products and services are developed to satisfy market needs. It follows then that an important way of judging the effectiveness of the product and service development process is to judge how it performs in terms of quality, speed, dependability, flexibility and cost. These performance objectives have just as much relevance for the production of new product and service ideas or designs as they do for their ongoing production once they are introduced to the market. There is, however, a difference in judging how development processes satisfy market needs. When customers are both familiar and relatively satisfied with existing products and services they find it difficult to articulate their needs for novel products or services.[9] Customers often develop an enhanced understanding of their own needs only when they come into direct contact with the product or service and start to use it. Many software companies talk about the 'I don't know what I want but I'll know when I see it' syndrome, meaning that only when customers use the software are they in a position to articulate what they do or don't require.

Quality of product and service development

In Chapter 1, when we were discussing generic performance objectives, quality was not easy to define precisely. It is no easier when we are looking at the quality of product and service development. Yet, again, as when we are looking at it in its generic sense, most of us can recognise high quality when we see it. It is possible to distinguish high-quality product and service development from low-quality product and service development (although this is easier to do in hindsight). A useful approach if we wish to judge ongoing product and service development is to use the distinction between *market requirements quality* and *operations resource quality*. By market requirements quality we mean the ability of the output from the product or service development process (its final design) to meet the requirements of the company's intended market position. Operations resource quality indicates the extent to which the final design of the product or service allows the exploitation of the capabilities of the company's processes.

Speed of product and service development

Fast product and service development has become the norm in many industries. Sometimes this is because the pressures of market competition have forced companies to capture the markets' imagination with the frequent introduction of new offerings. Consumer electronics, for example, significantly increased the rate of new product introduction during the 1980s and 90s. Sometimes it is the result of fast-changing consumer fashion. Getting to market quickly in order to capture a trend is important in many sectors of the garment and toy industries, for example. Sometimes fast development is the result of a rapidly changing technology base. Personal computers need to be updated frequently because their underlying technology is constantly improving. Sometimes all of these pressures are evident, as in many Internet-based services, for example. But no matter what pressures have motivated organisations to speed up their development processes, many have discovered that fast development brings a number of specific advantages.

- *Early market launch* – The most obvious advantage of an ability to develop products and services speedily is that they can be introduced to the market earlier and thus earn revenue for longer. Not only that, but if the product or service is the first of its type into the market, initially it has a hundred per cent market share, and customers may subsequently be reluctant to move to a competitor. Moreover, new offerings often can command price premiums.

- *Starting development late* – An alternative way of deploying a fast development advantage is by starting the development process late rather than introducing a product or service early. In some markets this has advantages, especially those where either the nature of customer demand or the availability of technology is uncertain and dynamic. In both cases fast development allows design decisions to be made closer to the point at which they are introduced to the market.

- *Frequent market stimulation* – Short development times allow the introduction of new or updated products or services more frequently. With a given set of development resourcing, if it takes 12 months to develop a new product and service, a company can only introduce a new or updated offering every 12 months. A six-month development process doubles their potential for making an impact in the market.

- *More opportunities for innovation* – In markets where the underlying 'technology' base is moving fast, it may be important to have frequent opportunities to introduce these new technologies as often as possible. Short development time with frequent updates produces more windows of opportunity for this type of innovation.

Dependability of product service development

Fast product and service development processes which cannot be relied on to deliver innovations dependably are, in reality, not fast at all. Development schedule slippage can extend development times, but worse, a lack of dependability adds to the uncertainty surrounding the development process. Conversely, processes that are dependable give stability and minimise development uncertainty. Yet this poses a problem for most development processes. Unexpected technical difficulties, innovations that do not work or have to be modified, suppliers who themselves do not deliver solutions on time, customers or markets that change during the development process itself, and so on, all contribute to an uncertain and sometimes ambiguous environment. Certainly professional project management of the development process can help to reduce uncertainty. At least it should minimise the risk of internal disturbance to the development process if effective project management can prevent (or give early warning of) missed deadlines, detect bottlenecks and spot resource shortages. External disturbances to the process, however, will remain. Again, these may be minimised through close liaison with suppliers and effective market or environmental monitoring. Nevertheless, unexpected disruptions will always occur and the more innovative the development, the more likely they are to occur. This is why flexibility within the development process is one of the most important ways in which dependable delivery of new products and services can be ensured.

Flexibility of product and service development

Flexibility in new product and service development is usually taken to mean the ability of the development process to cope with external or internal change. The most common reason for external change is because the market in general, or specific customers, change their requirements. This may be prompted by their own customers and markets changing, or because developments in competitors' products or services dictate a matching or leapfrogging move in specification. Internal changes could include the emergence of superior materials or technical solutions. One suggestion for measuring development flexibility is to compare the cost of modifying a product or service design in response to such changes against the consequences to profitability if no changes are made. The higher the cost of modifying a product or service in response to a given change, the lower is the development flexibility.[10]

Two trends in many markets make development flexibility particularly important. The first is the pace and magnitude of environmental change. Although flexibility may not be needed in relatively predictable environments, it is clearly valuable in more fast-moving and volatile environments. The second factor, however, which amplifies environmental volatility is increasing complexity and interconnectedness of products and services. A bank, for example, may bundle together a number of separate services for one particular segment of its market. Privileged account holders may obtain special deposit rates, premium credit cards, insurance offers, travel facilities, and so on together in the same 'product'. Changing one aspect of this bundle may require changes to be made in other elements. So extending the credit card benefits to include extra travel insurance may also mean the redesign of the separate insurance element of the package.

One of the biggest benefits from development flexibility is that it can reduce development risk. Much development risk derives from the changes that occur during the development period. At the beginning of the development time, managers will presumably form a view concerning customer requirements, available technologies, and specification of competitor products and services. During the development period any, or all, of these might change. Customers may change their mind, either because their needs have changed or because they did not understand their own needs in the first place. The boundary of what was technologically possible may change as new technologies come onto the market, and competitors introduce rival products and services with superior or different performance. Development flexibility can help to minimise the impact of such occurrences.

Product development at Microsoft[11]

The software industry has, especially over the past ten years, posed new challenges for product and service development. Both user requirements and the underlying technological possibilities for software products are turbulent and difficult to predict. Furthermore, the products themselves are complex and frighteningly interconnected in their internal structure. Making changes to one part of a software product during the development process will almost certainly affect other parts, though exactly how is difficult to predict. Above all, software products are big and getting bigger. Some Microsoft products from the early 1980s had fewer than 100,000 lines of code. The first Windows NT in 1993 had about 4.5 million lines of code and Windows 95 (introduced in 1995) has 11 million lines of code. Similarly, teams of developers who once numbered ten or twenty can now number many hundreds.

At Microsoft a strategy for coping with such difficult development products has emerged. It consists of two main clusters of ideas. The first defines the approach the company takes to conceptualising the overall development task and allocating resources to its various stages. The second concerns the company's approach to managing the development process itself on a day-by-day basis.

The first part of the strategy has been referred to as *focus creativity by evolving features and fixing resources.* This consists of a number of ideas, including the strict prioritisation of individual features within the product, the most important being developed first. Without such prioritisation development can drag on, always a tendency in software development, especially when customer requirements and technologies are moving rapidly. Brief vision statements for each part of the project help to define more detailed functional specifications needed to determine resources, but not so detailed as to prevent the redefinition of development objectives as the project progresses. (Often feature sets can change by over 30 per cent during development.) A modular architecture for the product as a whole facilitates incremental change involving the addition or deletion of individual features. An important element in this part of Microsoft's strategy is its rule to 'fix' project resources early in the development process. This limits the number of people and the time available for each part of the development, encouraging the individual development teams to abandon features if development times slip (not necessarily harmful because of the strict prioritisation). It also focuses the team's creativity towards achieving a 'working' (if not perfect) version of the product which can be made ready for market testing.

The second part of the Microsoft strategy has been referred to as *do everything in parallel with frequent synchronisations.* This is an attempt to tackle the dilemma of ensuring development discipline and order without inhibiting the developers' creativity. Big projects do need clearly defined development phases and task allocation, but over-specifying a project structure does not encourage innovation. Microsoft uses relatively small teams of three to four hundred developers who synchronise their decisions very frequently, often every day. These synchronisations, called 'builds', always occur at a fixed time (usually 2 p.m. or 5 p.m.). Staff are free to work flexibly and contribute their development to the project only when they have something to add. Developers submit their work at the fixed 'build' time. This then allows the various bits of code to be recompiled (put together) by the end of the day or the start of the next day. Testing and debugging can then commence. This frequent synchronisation allows individual teams to be creative and to change their objectives in line with changing circumstances but, at the same time, ensures a shared discipline. Even so, it is necessary to stabilise the design periodically through the use of intermediate 'milestones'. Each milestone marks the completion of a cluster of components. Providing such 'finish points' reduces the number of components being developed in parallel and makes the project easier to control.

The newspaper metaphor

Not all aspects of a development programme need to be flexible. Some aspects of a product or service may be judged unlikely to change over the development period, whereas others may be particularly difficult to forecast. It would seem sensible, therefore, to delay decisions regarding the uncertain elements until as late as possible in the process and build in sufficient flexibility in these elements rather than 'waste' it on the more stable elements. This is exactly how a daily newspaper designs its content. Special feature sections may be planned several weeks in advance and may even be printed well before their publication. Similarly, regular sections such as television times and advertisements are prepared several days before the newspaper is due to come out. On the day of publication, several stories may be vying for the front page. This is where flexibility is needed. The more flexible is the news desk in taking in new news and deciding the layout and priority of stories, the later the decision can be made and the more current the newspaper will be. Thus, in the development of any product or service, the more stable elements can be designed (in terms of making decisions around their form) well in advance, with their specification fixed early in the process. Other elements of the design can remain fluid so as to incorporate the latest thinking and then fixed only at the last moment.[12]

Incremental commitment

One method of retaining some flexibility in development processes is to avoid yes/no decisions. Alternative and parallel options can be progressed in stages. So, for example, an idea might be given approval to move to the next stage with no implied commitment to develop that idea through to the end of the project. One often-quoted example concerns the development of the Boeing 777. Unusually for this type of product, the drawing which defined some parts had six or seven 'release levels'. This means that rather than confirming the final design of a part, it would be done in stages. So the design may be given approval for purposes of purchasing test materials but not for purposes of confirming tool design. This provided a more flexible way of delaying decisions until the last minute without holding up the whole development process.

Cost of product and service development

The cost of developing products and services is conventionally analysed in a similar way to the ongoing cost of producing the goods and services. In other words, cost factors are split up into three categories: the cost of buying the inputs to the process, the cost of providing the labour in the process, and the other general overhead costs of running the process. In most in-house development processes the latter two costs outweigh the former. As with day-to-day production of products and services, however, it is perhaps more revealing to consider how the other performance objectives drive cost:

- *Quality* – 'Error-free' processes reduce reworking concepts and designs.
- *Speed* – Fast development can use resources for shorter periods.
- *Dependability* – On-time development provides process stability, allows efficient resource planning and prevents expensive launch date slippage.

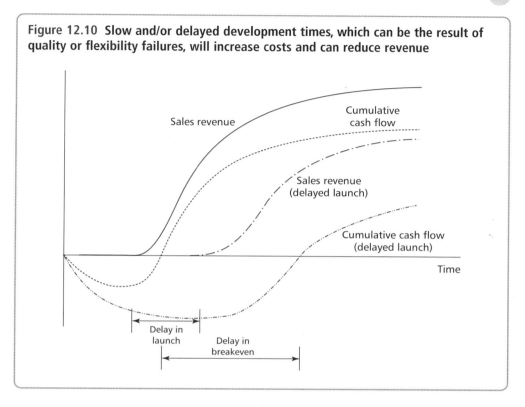

Figure 12.10 Slow and/or delayed development times, which can be the result of quality or flexibility failures, will increase costs and can reduce revenue

- *Flexibility* – The ability to delay design decisions can ensure the most appropriate options being chosen, preventing the costs of changing direction in the development.

One way of thinking about the effect of the other development performance objectives on cost is shown in Figure 12.10. Whether through quality errors, intrinsically slow development processes, a lack of project dependability, or delays caused through inflexible development processes, the end result is that the development is late. Delayed completion of the development results in both more expenditure on the development and delayed (and probably reduced) revenue. The combination of both these effects usually means that the financial breakeven point for a new product or service is delayed far more than the original delay in the product or service launch.

An operations resources perspective on product and service development

An operation's resource perspective on product and service development involves examining the decision areas which we would normally use but applying them specifically to the development process. This is not difficult since all the categories can be applied directly. The capacity of the organisation's development processes needs managing over the long term, choices need to be made about whether some activities are performed in-house or subcontracted, investments in process technology are becoming an increasingly important element in managing new product and service development, and the organisation of the development process has become an important factor in managing the development process. Furthermore, behind each of these decisions lies the general objective of nurturing and exploiting the organisation's capabilities.

Product and service development capacity

As in any other process, the management of capacity involves deciding on the overall level of activity which an operation can support and also deciding how that level of support can be changed in order to respond to likely changes in demand. Essentially all the issues discussed in Chapters 4 and 5, in the context of the whole operation, also apply to the product and service development process. However, remember that the development process is a service in that it creates and works with knowledge for the benefit of its (usually internal) customers. This means that such options as building up an 'inventory' of designs is not usually feasible as such. Storing knowledge in a relatively developed form, however, may be possible. Indeed, in many ways, the whole development process can be characterised as building up and then deploying 'inventories' of design-based knowledge. Similarly, a 'capacity lagging' strategy (see Chapter 5) is not usually practical. The whole ethos of product and service development is one of broadly anticipating market requirements and attempting to bring ideas to market as early as possible. Deliberately planning to have a level of design capacity lower than the likely demand for such development rather implies extended time-to-market performance.

Uneven demand for development

The central issue for managing product and service development in many organisations is that the internal 'demand' for such development is uneven. Even in very large companies the rate of new service or product introduction is not constant. The

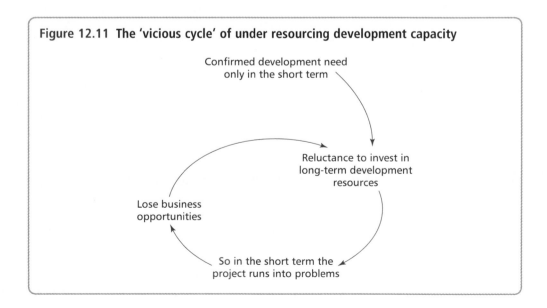

Figure 12.11 The 'vicious cycle' of under resourcing development capacity

need for product/service innovation is likely to be dictated by several complex and interrelated market factors. This may lead to several new offerings being introduced to the market close together, while at other times little development is needed, thus posing a resourcing problem. The capacity of a firm's development capability is often difficult to flex. The expertise necessary for development is embedded within designers, technologists, market analysts, and so on. Some expertise may be able to be hired in as and when it is needed, but much development resource is, in effect, fixed. Such a combination of varying demand and relatively fixed development capacity leads some organisations to be reluctant to invest in development capacity because they see it as an under-utilised resource. This may lead to a vicious cycle in which, although there is a short-term need for development resources, companies fail to invest in those resources because many of them (such as skilled development staff) cannot be hired in the short term, which leads to development projects being under-resourced with an increased chance of project overrun or failure to deliver appropriate technical solutions. This in turn may lead to the company losing business or otherwise suffering in the marketplace, which makes the company even less willing to invest in development resources. (See Figure 12.11.)

Product and service development networks

Most interest in supply networks has focused on the flow of parts, products (and occasionally services). Recently interest has also started to focus around the

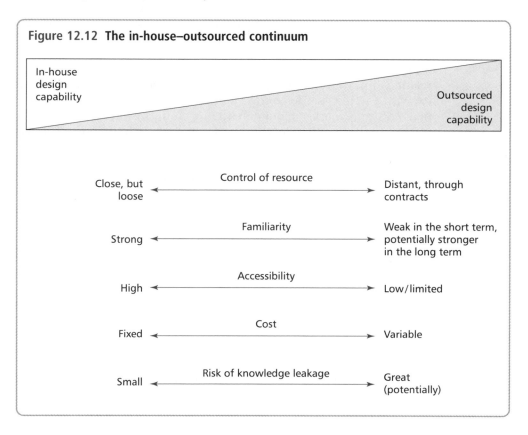

Figure 12.12 The in-house–outsourced continuum

In-house design capability

Outsourced design capability

	Control of resource	
Close, but loose	← →	Distant, through contracts
Strong	Familiarity ← →	Weak in the short term, potentially stronger in the long term
High	Accessibility ← →	Low/limited
Fixed	Cost ← →	Variable
Small	Risk of knowledge leakage ← →	Great (potentially)

exchange of product and service development *knowledge*, and the integrating of suppliers into the innovation process. This network of knowledge exchange is sometimes called the 'design (or development) network' or 'design chain' and in many ways the operations strategy decisions concerning conventional supply networks are also reflected in development networks. Two decisions in particular do much to determine the effectiveness of development networks. The first is the extent of vertical integration – the decisions of how much development to do in-house and how much to subcontract. The second is how to manage the relationship between the 'players' (most notably, customers and suppliers) in the network.

In-house and subcontracted development

Companies position themselves on a continuum of varying degrees of design engagement with suppliers. At one extreme, a firm may retain all the necessary design capabilities in-house, while at the other end, it outsources all its development work, acting only as a focal point for the coordination of the design process. Between these extremes there exist options with varying degrees of internal and external design capability. In general, though, few companies are at the extremes of this continuum since process development necessitates some kind of interaction.

Figure 12.12 shows some of the more important factors that will vary depending on where an organisation is on the in-house versus outsourced design capability spectrum. Design resources will be easy to control if they are kept in-house because they are closely aligned with the company's normal organisational structures, but control should be relatively loose because of the extra trust present in working with familiar colleagues. Outsourced design requires greater control and, because it has to be applied at a distance, contracts, often with penalty clauses for delay, may be needed.

However, penalty clauses and contracts do not help to build long-term partnership relationships. In-house design has an advantage here because of its strong familiarity with the rest of the company's product or service range, operations processes, materials and market requirements. In contrast, outsourcing design can mean a weaker understanding in the short term, though if long-term relationships do develop, product and service familiarity will become stronger. The underlying capabilities built up through the development activity are generally assumed to be highly accessible when the development is done in-house. It is more difficult to provide access to tacit knowledge when it is housed outside the organisation. One motive behind companies investing heavily in common computer-aided design systems with their design suppliers is to ensure better accessibility. The overall cost of in-house versus outsourced development will vary, depending on the firm and the development project. An important difference, however, is that external developments tend to be regarded as a variable cost. The more external resources are used, the more the cost will be. In-house development is more of a fixed cost. Indeed a shift to outsourcing may occur because fixed development costs are viewed as too great. Paradoxically though, as external sourcing of development becomes an integral part of a company's strategy and relationships become stable, costs tend to be more or less fixed. Finally, a major driver of this decision can be the risk of knowledge leakage. Firms become concerned that experience gained through collaboration with a supplier of development expertise may be transferred to competitors. Again there is a paradox here. Companies usually outsource development primarily *because* of the supplier's capabilities which are themselves an accumulation of specialist knowledge from working with a variety of customers. Without such knowledge 'leakage' the benefits of the supplier's accumulated development capabilities would not even exist.[13]

Involving suppliers in development

The nature of the relationship between a supplier of product or service design services is not the same as when a supplier (even the same supplier) is providing product or services on an ongoing basis. For example, a component manufacturer, asked by a customer to design a new part, is providing a service rather than making a physical product. Even a supplier of services, in designing a new service for a customer, is engaged in a one-off (or at least relatively infrequent) exchange with its customer, in which its own knowledge is embedded in the design. In fact, a development relationship between customer and supplier is very similar to that between professional service firms, such as lawyers or consultants, and their clients. When choosing suppliers of design and development knowledge, companies often use criteria such as experience, trust, technical knowledge and 'relationship': a very similar list to that used to select their accountancy firm and their legal representatives.[14]

Characterising development relationships as professional services has practical implications, especially for suppliers. First, it emphasises the importance of customer perception of the 'process' of development as well as the final design which emerges from the process. Frequently demonstrating expertise during the development process allows suppliers to build their 'technical' reputation. Second, just as professional services, such as accountants, keep 'client files' which detail all contacts with individual clients, so design suppliers can use similar client knowledge management to manage the development of the relationship with customers. Third, it broadens the nature of contact with customers to include a more general responsibility for the development of relationships among other sources of expertise in the network. This has implications for the way suppliers might organise their design activity, for example in the way they attempt to respond to change in client needs during the creation of the design service, or in the use of implicit 'service guarantees'.

Theory Box **Guest engineers**[15]

One particular organisational mechanism that is becoming widely used, especially in the method of overcoming some of the problems of outsourcing design, is the *guest engineer*. These are technical specialists who reside, for at least part of their time, within their customer's organisation. However, confusingly, there are several terms in use to describe such engineers, each with a variety of implied roles. Furthermore, the term is sometimes used to refer to customer engineers who temporarily reside within a supplier firm. The concept of *guest engineering* has existed in the automotive industry (amongst others) since the 1950s. Their origins seem to have been with Toyoda Machine Tools, who used them in their sister company Toyota. Their responsibility was not only to maintain the machines supplied to Toyota, but also to convey detailed feedback to Toyoda Machine Tools so that their products could be continuously improved. The use of resident engineers is now common practice for Japanese vehicle manufacturers; Honda, for example, introduced them into their simultaneous engineering teams in the later 1970s. Today, Toyota insists that suppliers assign engineers to Toyota's technical centre in Toyota City, where they are given desks and co-located with Toyota's engineers, even if they are already located nearby. The main benefit is that complex, dynamic information can be communicated directly to suppliers, and any errors can be discovered early in the development process. As customers and suppliers increasingly

▶

collaborate in design and production, the role of resident engineers has become more prevalent, both at the request of customers and through mutual agreement from closer working relationships.

Now a variety of types of guest engineer are used in several industries. Figure 12.13 defines four types of guest engineers defined by their location and the primary focus of their work:

Figure 12.13 A broad typology of guest engineers

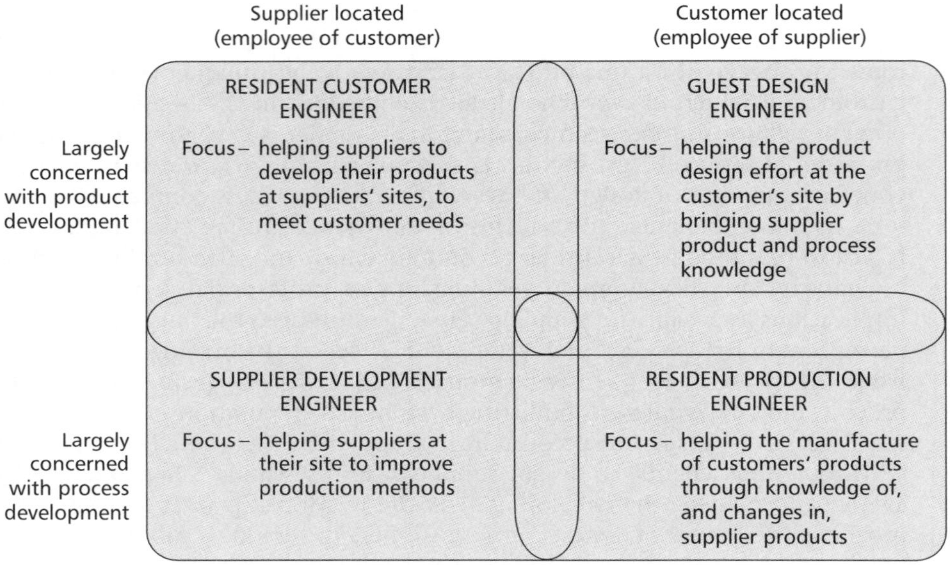

	Supplier located (employee of customer)	Customer located (employee of supplier)
Largely concerned with product development	**RESIDENT CUSTOMER ENGINEER** Focus – helping suppliers to develop their products at suppliers' sites, to meet customer needs	**GUEST DESIGN ENGINEER** Focus – helping the product design effort at the customer's site by bringing supplier product and process knowledge
Largely concerned with process development	**SUPPLIER DEVELOPMENT ENGINEER** Focus – helping suppliers at their site to improve production methods	**RESIDENT PRODUCTION ENGINEER** Focus – helping the manufacture of customers' products through knowledge of, and changes in, supplier products

- *Guest design engineer* – A supplier design engineer who collaborates with the customer design team to solve various design problems, ensures conformance to target costs, and brings a knowledge of component technology and its related manufacturing requirements to the customer's total product design effort.

- *Resident operations engineer* – A supplier engineer who reports back any problems, and resolves quality issues at the customer site. This type of engineer may suggest design changes and may try to learn about the customer's long-term development strategy. He or she may also spend time representing customers' problems at the supplying operation.

- *Supplier development engineer* – A customer employee who works with the supplier to improve the supplier's processes, and to help achieve total quality, cost and delivery requirements. (Sometimes referred to as kaizen engineer, site engineer, or factory engineer.)

- *Resident customer engineer* – A customer employee who works most of the time with a supplier, partly to understand the operations implications of customer-initiated changes in specification, but primarily to focus on the development of the supplier's product or service.

Involving customers in development

Few people know the merits and limitations of products and services better than the customers who use them. An obvious source, then, of feedback on product or service performance will be those who regularly use (or have ceased using) them. Different types of customer have the potential to provide different types of information. New users can pinpoint more attractive product and service features; those who have switched to a competitor offering can reveal its problems. A particularly interesting group of customers are the so-called 'lead users'.[16] Lead users have requirements of a product or service which will become more general in a market, but they are aware of these needs well ahead of the rest of the market. They also are users who will benefit significantly by finding a solution to their requirements. This may prompt them to develop or modify products or services themselves rather than wait for them to become commercially available. One reported example of lead-user research[17] concerns a new product development manager at Bose, the high-quality hi-fi and speaker company. On visiting his local music store, his professional ear noted the high quality of the background music being played. Investigating, he found that the store manager was using Bose speakers designed for home use but had attached metal strips around the speaker boxes so that they could be suspended close to the ceiling of the store. Inspired by this, Bose built prototypes of speakers which would satisfy the need for quality in-store speakers. These were taken back to the music store for further testing and eventually led to the company successfully entering the market for high-fidelity background music speakers.

Product and service development technology

One of the more significant changes in product and service development has been the growing importance of 'process' technology within the development process. Until relatively recently, although product/service technology knowledge was an important input into the development activity, technology used to process this knowledge was relatively unusual. It was limited to testing and evaluation technologies such as the mechanical devices which would simulate the stresses of everyday use on products such as automobiles or sports shoes, often testing them to destruction. Now process technologies are much more common, especially those based on computing power. For example, simulation software is now common in the design of everything from transportation services through to chemical factories. These allow developers to make design decisions in advance of the actual product or service being created. They allow designers to work through the experience of using the service or product and learn more about how it might operate in practice. They can explore possibilities, gain insights and, most important, they can explore the consequences of their decision decisions. In that sense, simulation is often a predictive rather than an optimising technology.

Computer-aided design (CAD)

Perhaps the best-known process technology in product development is computer-aided design (CAD). CAD systems store and categorise product and component information and allow designs to be built up on screen, often performing basic engineering calculations to test the appropriateness of proposed design solutions. They provide the computer-aided ability to create a modified product drawing and allow conventionally used shapes to be added swiftly to the computer-based representation of a product. Designs created on screen can be saved and retrieved for later use; this enables a library of standardised part and component designs to be built up. Not only can this dramatically increase the productivity of the design process but it also aids the standardisation of parts in the design activity. Often CAD systems come with their own library of standard parts.

Knowledge management technologies

In many professional service firms, such as management consultancies, service development involves the evaluation of concepts and frameworks which can be used in client organisations to diagnose problems, analyse performance and construct possible solutions. They may include ideas of industry best practice, benchmarks of performance within an industry, and ideas which can be transported across industry boundaries. However, the characteristics of management consulting firms are that they are geographically dispersed and rarely are staff at their offices. The consultants spend most of their time in client organisations acquiring knowledge day by day. Yet at the same time it is vital for such companies to avoid 'reinventing the wheel' continually. Any means of collectivising the cumulative knowledge and experience within the organisation must greatly assist the development of new concepts and frameworks. Most consultancy companies attempt to tackle this problem using knowledge management routines based on their intranet capabilities. This allows consultants to put their experience into a common pool, contact other staff within the company who have skills relevant to a current assignment, and identify previous similar assignments. In this way information is integrated into the ongoing knowledge development process within the company and can be tapped by those charged with developing new products.[18]

The significance of most of these development technologies is that they help to reduce the impact both of uncertainty and complexity. Simulation technologies allow developers to reduce their own uncertainty of how products and services will work in practice. Similarly, knowledge management systems consolidate and juxtapose information on what is happening within the organisation, thus presenting a more comprehensive vision and reducing uncertainty. CAD systems also help to deal with complexity by storing data on component details as they develop through various interactions. The absolute size and interrelatedness of some large products required sophisticated CAD systems if they are to be developed effectively. One of the most reported examples was the development of Boeing's 777 aircraft. The powerful CAD system used on this project was credited with Boeing's success in being able to involve its customers in the design process, allow more product configuration flexibility (such as the proportion of seats in each class, etc.), and still bring the huge project successfully to completion.

Simulation in the America's Cup[19]

One of the best-known uses of simulation for success in the sporting world came in the 1995 America's Cup. The America's Cup is a yacht race, originally founded in 1851 by the Royal Yacht Squadron of England. An American boat won that first race and from that point the race acquired its name. American boats continued to win the race for the next 132 years until 1983 when an

Australian boat, using a radical new design, captured the trophy. This focused even greater attention on to the design of the boats and the next ten years saw the incorporation of formal experimentation, testing and computer-based simulation during the design processes which were attempting to come up with world-beating yacht designs. By the 1995 contest, various potential challengers for the trophy were using different types of computer simulation to analyse the structural characteristics of a design, simulate the flow of water over the 'critical surfaces' and predict how the yacht would behave under different wind and sea conditions. It had been found that, although simulations were not always totally accurate, they had a number of advantages over the alternative experimental technique of using scale models in wind tunnels and towing tanks. This had proved an expensive technique and even with the large budgets available for America's Cup yacht designs, teams could rarely afford more than 20 or so prototypes to be tested in this way. Simulation provided both faster and cheaper feedback to the designers. Unfortunately, the advanced simulation programs required a considerable amount of computing power. For this reason, teams often formed partnerships with organisations who could provide advanced computing facilities. The New Zealand team partnered with Silicon Graphics, the Australian team used the facilities of the Sun computing company, and an American team obtained over $1 million worth of computer time with a group of partners that included the aircraft manufacturer Boeing and the supercomputer manufacturer Cray.

The eventual winner in January 1995 was the boat designed by Team New Zealand. Not only was this one of the very few non-American boats ever to win the cup in its history, but they won by a clear 5–0 margin. Much of their success was put down to their use of simulation-based experiments during the process which culminated in their final design. Although using cycles of frequent simulation and feedback, they were careful to blend their own practical experience with the more theoretical information coming from the simulations. Dave Egan, Team New Zealand's head of simulation, was careful to put the role of their computer-based experiments in perspective. *'In practice, if you start with a bad design, simulation won't get you anywhere near a good one. Some of the other (design) syndicates let. . . simulation . . . drive their process. The Australians, for example, had some really deep simulation experts, and see where that got them.'* (In one of their early races against Team New Zealand, the Australian boat sank!)

The organisation of product and service development

Chapter 10 described organisational structure as the way in which resources were clustered together and the nature of the relationship between each cluster. We also described several organisational forms, together with their merits and drawbacks. Amongst the criteria which are used to assess the effectiveness of different organisational forms, two in particular are important to product and service development – specialisation and integration. Specialisation is important because it encourages the depth of knowledge and technical understanding which is required in a concentrated form during the development process. Because of the (normally) finite time allowed for product and service development, technical knowledge needs to be deployed in a concentrated manner during limited windows of opportunity. Clustering resources around technical specialisms encourages the development of such concentrated knowledge. Integration is important because both product and services are composed of smaller components or subsystems. Coordinating the efforts of developers in different parts of a project and integrating their technical solutions in such a way as to reflect the market priorities within the development project is clearly an important aspect of any organisational structure. Both these criteria need to be incorporated in the organisational structure which is built to support a development project.

Project-based organisation structures

The total process of developing concepts through to market will almost certainly involve personnel from several different areas of the organisation. Most functions will have some part to play in making the decisions which will shape a final design. Yet any development project will also have an existence of its own. It will have a project name, an individual manager or group of staff who are championing the project, a budget and, hopefully, a clear strategic purpose in the organisation. The organisational question is which of these two ideas – the various organisational functions which contribute to development, or the development project itself – should dominate the way in which the development activity is managed? In Chapter 10 we described the matrix form of organisation as a compromise between two (or more) approaches to clustering resources. It is an ideal model to examine the debates over an appropriate organisational form for development projects. Here the two conflicting approaches are the functional (specialist) dominated structure, and the project (or programme) dominated structure.

In a pure functional organisation all staff associated with the design project are

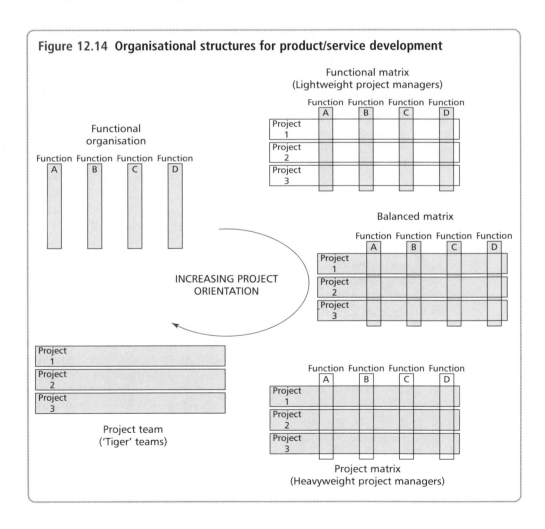

Figure 12.14 Organisational structures for product/service development

based unambiguously in their functional groups. There is no project-based group at all. They may be working full-time on the project but all communication and liaison is carried out through their functional manager. The project exists only because of agreement between these functional managers. At the other extreme, all the individual members of staff from each function who are involved in the project could be moved out of their functions and perhaps even physically relocated to a 'task force' dedicated solely to the project. The task force could be led by a project manager who probably holds all the budget allocated to the design project. Not all members of the task force necessarily have to stay in the team throughout the development period, but a substantial core might see the project through from start to finish. Some members of a design team may even be from other companies. In between these two extremes there are various types of 'matrix' organisation with varying emphasis on these two aspects of the organisation. (See Figure 12.14.) And, although there are, in practice, an infinite number of structures, five stereotypical positions on the continuum are often discussed:

- *Functional organisation* – The project is divided into segments and assigned to relevant functional areas and/or groups within functional areas. The project is coordinated by functional and senior management.

- *Functional matrix* (or *lightweight* project manager) – A person is formally designated to oversee the project across different functional areas. This person has limited authority over functional people involved and serves primarily to plan and co-ordinate the project. The functional managers retain primary responsibility for their specific segments of the project.

- *Balanced matrix* – A person is assigned to oversee the project and interacts on an equal basis with functional managers. This person and the functional managers jointly direct work flow segments and approve technical and operational decisions.

- *Project matrix* (or *heavyweight* project manager) – A manager is assigned to oversee the project and is responsible for the completion of the project. Functional managers' involvement is limited to assigning personnel as needed and providing advisory expertise.

- *Project team* (or *tiger* team) – A manager is given responsibility for a project team composed of a core group of personnel from several functional areas and/or groups, assigned in a full-time basis. The functional managers have no formal involvement.

... but then Netscape changed[20]

It was an archetypal, loosely organised collective of free spirits. They were the kind of development group which was always associated with software developers working on the frontier of their science (or art?). They had free soft drinks permanently available for the developers, brought their pets into work, kept beds under their desks for those times (not unusual) when they would work extended periods to crack a particularly intriguing bug. They had a web cam constantly updating a picture of their fish tank. They built a scale model of the Golden Gate Bridge across part of their headquarters, made entirely of soft drink cans. They embedded secret jokes into their code for the amusement of the faithful. Above all else, they were dedicated, innovative and creative. They (and all their followers) called their product Mozilla, after the cartoon lizard-like creature which was their mascot.

▶

Everyone else called their company Netscape. They were the first to develop a web search engine, at least in the form we know them today. It was based on a web browser called Mosaic written by the National Centre for Supercomputing, from where most of the original development team came. Like much of the web's software at the time, the Mozilla browser was free, reflecting the anti-big business culture of many pioneering development groups. Maybe change was inevitable, and change it did. Commercial pressures started to curb the slightly anarchic culture of the developers. In 1998 the web cam was turned off. The company's web site became almost indistinguishable from other corporate sites. By the end of the year Jim Clark, the CEO of Netscape, sold the company to AOL, regarded by some as the symbol of big business in the Internet world. Several of Netscape's founding developers left (setting up their own web site, www.exmozilla.org). As one web site devoted to images of the Mozilla cartoon had it, *'Mozilla was the mascot of the Netscape company in the early days; he gradually went away, because he was scared of the pinstriped suits.'*

Effectiveness of the alternative structures

Although there is no clear 'winner' amongst the alternative organisational structures, there is wide support for structures towards the project rather than the functional end of the continuum. In one widely respected study, Professors Clark and Fujimoto argued that heavyweight project manager structures and dedicated project teams are the most efficient forms of organisation for product competitiveness, shorter lead-times and technical efficiency.[21] Other studies, although sometimes more equivocal, have shown that, in terms of the best total outcome from the development process, structures from balanced matrix through to project teams can all give high success rates. Perhaps of more interest is the suitability of the alternative structures for different types of product or service development project. Matrix structures are generally deemed to be appropriate for both simple and highly complex projects. Dedicated project teams, on the other hand, are seen as coming into their own especially in highly complex projects.

Yet again, there are advantages in functionally based development structures. In Chapter 10 we discussed how clustering resources around a functional specialism helped the development of technical knowledge. Some organisations do manage to capture the deep technological and skills development advantages of functional structures, while at the same time coordinating between the functions so as to ensure satisfactory delivery of new product and service ideas. Perhaps the best known of these organisations is Toyota, the Japanese car giant. They have a strong functionally based organisation to develop their products. It adopts highly formalised development procedures to communicate between functions and places strict limits on the use of cross-functional teams. But what is really different is their approach to devising an organisational structure for product development which is appropriate for them. The argument which most companies have adopted to justify cross-functional project teams goes something like this:

Problems with communication between traditional functions have been the main reasons for, in the past, failing to deliver new product and service ideas to specification, on time and to budget. Therefore let us break down the walls between the functions and organise resources around the individual development projects. This will ensure good communication and a market-oriented culture.

Toyota and similar companies, on the other hand, have taken a different approach. Their argument goes something like this:

> The problem with cross-functional teams is that they can dissipate the carefully nurtured knowledge that exists within specialist functions. The real problem is how to retain this knowledge on which our future product development depends, while overcoming some of the traditional functional barriers which have inhibited communication between the functions. The solution is not to destroy the function but to devise the organisational mechanisms to ensure close control and integrative leadership which will make the functional organisation work.[22]

SUMMARY ANSWERS TO KEY QUESTIONS

Why is the way in which companies develop their products and services so important?

Competitive markets and demanding customers require updated and 'refreshed' products and services. Even small changes to products and services can have an impact on competitiveness. Markets are also becoming more fragmented, requiring product and service variants developed specifically for their needs. At the same time, technologies are offering increased opportunities for their exploitation within new products and services. Nor can one always separate the development of products and services on the one hand from the development of the processes that produce them on the other. Thus product and service development influences and is influenced by almost all other decisions and activities within the operations function.

What process do companies use to develop products and services?

There is no single product and service development process as such. However, there are many stage models which attempt to define and describe the various stages which a process should include. Typical of these stages are such activities as concept generation, concept screening, preliminary design, design evaluation and improvement, prototyping and final design, and developing the operations process. It is important to remember, though, that although these stages are often included (either formally or informally) within an organisation's product or service development process, they do not always follow each other sequentially. In reality the process may recycle through stages and even miss some out altogether. A common metaphor to illustrate the process is that of the 'funnel of development'. Again, though, the idea of many ideas passing through a funnel, being periodically screened and a single product or service design emerging from the end, is itself a simplification.

How should the effectiveness of the product and service development process be judged in terms of fulfilling market requirements?

The market effectiveness of any product or service development process can be judged in the same way as the day-to-day operations processes which produce the products and services themselves. That is, the development process can be judged in terms of its quality, speed, availability, flexibility and cost. Development projects must be error free, fast to market, deliver on time, retain sufficient flexibility to change as late as possible in the process, and not consume excessive development resources.

What operations resource-based decisions define a company's product and service development strategy?

Again we can classify the decisions around the product or service development process in the same way as we can classify the decisions that specify the resources for day-to-day operations process. The overall development capacity of an organisation needs to be managed to reflect fluctuating demand for development activities, decisions must be made regarding the outsourcing of some, or all, of the development activity as well as the nature of the relationships with development 'suppliers', technologies such as computer aided design and simulation may be required to aid the development process, and the resources used for development need to be clustered into some form of organisational structure.

CASE EXERCISE – What would you do?

Project Orlando at *Dreddo Dan's*

'Most people see the snack market as dynamic and innovative, but actually it is surprisingly conservative. Most of what passes for product innovation is in fact tinkering with our marketing approach, things like special offers, promotion tie-ins and so on. We occasionally put new packs round our existing products and even more occasionally we introduce new flavours in existing product ranges. Rarely, though, does anyone in this industry introduce something radically different. That is why this project is both exciting and scary.'

Monica Allen, the technical vice-president of PJT's snack division, was commenting on a potential new product to be marketed under PJT's best-known brand, *Dreddo Dan's Snacks*. The new product development project referred to was internally known as Project Orlando (no one could remember why). The project had been running officially for almost three years but had hitherto been seen as something of a long shot. Recent technical breakthroughs by the project team now made the project look far more promising and it had been given priority development status by the company's board. Even so, it was not expected to come to the market for another two years.

'Orlando' was a range of snack foods which had been described within the company as 'savoury potato cookies'. Essentially they were one and a half inch discs of crisp, fried potato with a soft dairy cheese-like filling. The idea of incorporating dairy fillings in snacks had been discussed within the industry for some time but the problems of manufacturing such a product were formidable. Keeping the product crisp on the outside yet soft in the middle, while at the same time ensuring microbiological safety, would not be easy. Moreover, such a product would have to be capable of being stored at ambient temperatures, maintain its physical robustness and have a shelf life of at least three months. Enough of the technical problems associated with these requirements had been solved by the Project Orlando team for the company to have real confidence that a marketable product would eventually emerge. It would, however, be the most important new product development in the company's history.

'The main problem with this type of product is that it will be expensive to develop and yet, once our competitors realise what we are doing, they will come in fast to try and out-innovate us. Whatever else we do we must ensure that there is sufficient flexibility in the project to allow us to respond quickly when competitors follow us into the market with their own "me-too" products. We are not racing against the clock to get this to market, but once we do make a decision to launch we will have to move fast and hit the launch date reliably. Perhaps most important, we must ensure that the product is 200 per cent safe. We have no experience in dealing with the microbiological testing which dairy-based food manufacture requires. Other divisions of PJT do have this experience and I guess we will be relying heavily on them'. (Monica Allen)

Monica, who had been tasked with managing the now much expanded development process, had already drawn up a list of key decisions she would have to take:

● How to resource the development project – The division had a small development staff, some of whom had been working on Project Orlando, but a project of this size would require extra staff amounting to about twice the current number of people dedicated to product development.

● Whether to invest in a pilot plant – The process technology required for the new project would be unlike any of the division's current technology. Similar technology was used by some companies in the frozen food industry and one option would be to carry out trials at these (non-competitor) companies' sites. Alternatively, the Orlando team could build their own pilot plant which would enable them to experiment in-house. As well as the significant expense involved, this would raise the problem of whether any process innovations would work when scaled-up to full size. However, it would be far more convenient for the project team and allow them to 'make their mistakes' in private.

● How much development to outsource – Because of the size of the project, Monica had considered outsourcing some of the development activities. Other divisions within the company might be able to undertake some of the development work and there were also specialist consultancies who operated in the food processing industries. The division had never used any of these consultancies before but other divisions had occasionally done so.

● How to organise the development – Currently, the small development function had been organised around loose functional specialisms. Monica wondered whether this project warranted the creation of a separate department independent of the current structure. This might signal the importance of this project to the whole division.

Further reading

Baldwin, C.Y. and K.B. Clark (1997) 'Managing in an age of modularity', *Harvard Business Review*, September–October.

Bowers, M. (1989) 'Developing new services: improving the process makes it better', *The Journal of Services Marketing*, Vol. 3, No. 1.

Bruce, M. and W.G. Biemans (1995) *Product Development*, Wiley, Chichester, UK.

Clark, K.M. and T. Fujimoto (1991) *Products Development Performance*, Harvard Business School, Boston.

Cross, R. and L. Baird (2000) 'Technology is not enough: improving performance by building organisational memory', *Sloan Management Review*, Spring.

Iansiti, M. and J. West (1997) 'Technology integration: turning great research into great products', *Harvard Business Review*, May–June.

Leonard-Barton, D. (1992) 'Core capabilities and core rigidities: a paradox in managing new product development', *Strategic Management Journal*, Vol. 13, pp. 11–125.

Pisano, G.P. (1997) *The Development Factory*, Harvard Business School Press, Boston.

Sanchez, R. (1995) 'Strategic flexibility in product competition', *Strategic Management Journal*, Vol. 16, No. 2.

Smith, P.G. and D.G. Reinertsen (1991) *Developing Products in Half the Time*, Van Nostrand Reinhold, New York.

Taylor, A. 3rd (1997) 'How Toyota defies gravity', *Fortune*, Vol. 136, No. 18, December.

Trott, P. (1998) *Innovation Management and New Product Development*, Financial Times-Prentice Hall, Harlow, UK.

Wheelwright, S.C. and K.B. Clark (1995) *Leading Product Development*, The Free Press, New York.

Notes on the chapter

1 Schnaars, S.P. (1994) *Managing Imitation Strategies*, The Free Press, New York.

2 Source: Company information.

3 Baldwin, C.Y. and K.B. Clark (1997) 'Managing in an age of modularity', *Harvard Business Review*, Sept–Oct.

4 Mass customisation was first fully articulated in Pine, B.J. (1993) *Mass Customisation: The new frontier in business competition*, Harvard Business School Press, MA. Also see Hart, C.W.L. (1995) 'Mass customisation: conceptual underpinnings, opportunities and threats', *International Journal of Service Industry Management*, Vol. 6, No. 2.

5 Ahlström, P. and R. Westbrook (1999) 'Implications of mass customisation for operations management', *International Journal of Operations and Production Management*, Vol. 19, No. 3.

6 Lehnerd, A.P. quoted in Pine, B.J. (1993) op.cit.

7 Source: *The Economist* (1997) 'Sold with an American accent', 27 Sept.

8 Based on Slack, N., S. Chambers and R. Johnston (2001) *Operations Management*, Financial Times-Prentice Hall, UK.

9 von Hippel, E. (1988) *The Sources of Innovation*, Oxford University Press, New York.

10 Thomke, S. and D. Reinertsen (1998) 'Agile product development', *California Management Review*, Vol. 41, No. 1.

11 Sources: Company documents and Cusumano, M.A. (1997) 'How Microsoft make large teams work like small teams', *Sloan Management Review*, Fall.

12 Thomke, S. and D. Reinertsen, op.cit.

13 The above discussion is based on Twigg, D. (1997) 'A Typology of Supplier Involvement in Automotive Product Development', Warwick Business School Research Paper No.271.

14 Haywood-Farmer, J. and J. Nollet (1991) *Serviced Plus: Effective service management*, Marin Boucherville, Quebec.

15 Based on Slack, N. and D. Twigg (2000) 'The organisation of external resources through guest engineering', *International Journal of Innovation Management*, Vol. 3, No. 1.

16 von Hippel, E., J. Churchill and M. Sonnack (1998) *Breakthrough products and services with lead user research*, Oxford University Press.

17 Von Hippel, E. *et al.*, op.cit.

18 Iansiti, M. and A. MacCormack (1997) 'Developing products on internet time', *Harvard Business Review*, Sept–Oct.

19 MacCormack, A. and M. Iansiti (1996) 'Team New Zealand (A) and (B)', Harvard Business School Case 9-697-040.

20 Source: O'Brien, D. (2000) 'The rise and fall of Mighty Mozilla', *Sunday Times*, 10 Sept.

21 Clark, K.B. and T. Fujimoto (1991) *Product Development Performance*, Harvard Business School Press.

22 Sobek, D.K. II, J.K. Licker and A.C. Ward (1998) 'Another look at how Toyota integrates product development', *Harvard Business Review*, July–August.

THE PROCESS OF OPERATIONS STRATEGY

The precise nature of any 'real' strategy will inevitably vary from organisation to organisation but there are a number of issues which are common to many of them. Part 3 of this book will focus explicitly on exploring the process of operations strategy – what reconciling market requirements and operational resources actually means in practice. It will do this by taking different 'slices' through the process of formulating and implementing operations strategy.

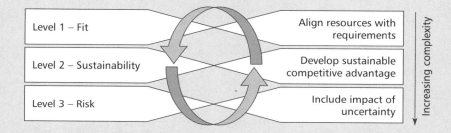

- Chapter 13 will focus upon the first objective of reconciliation, namely, the achievement of some kind of 'fit' between what the market wants and what the operation can deliver.

- Chapter 14 looks at 'sustainability' – achieving 'fit over time', especially the static (barriers to entry and imitation) and dynamic (capabilities and innovation) implications of sustainability.

- Chapter 15 examines how an understanding of risk can be incorporated within the process of operations strategy.

Operations strategy and 'fit'

Introduction

In this chapter we treat the first 'level' of operations strategy analysis – achieving 'fit' between the company's resources and processes on one hand and the requirements of its market positioning on the other (Figure 13.1). This has been a repeated theme in this book and clearly is at the heart of operations strategy as we see it. In effect, achieving 'fit' is the first stage in achieving reconciliation between operations resources and market requirements. Linking an operations strategy specifically with market positioning is important because operations cannot simultaneously support all possible ways of competing. The type of resources and processes which are designed to produce exceptionally low-cost products and services, for example, cannot also be exceptionally good at providing support for other ways of competing. (Note we are saying they cannot be *exceptionally* good, we are not saying that they have to be bad at any of them.) Similarly, from an operations resource perspective, it is important to seek out markets which enable the organisation to exploit its distinctive operations capabilities. The practice of achieving 'fit' is the attempt to bring these two perspectives together.

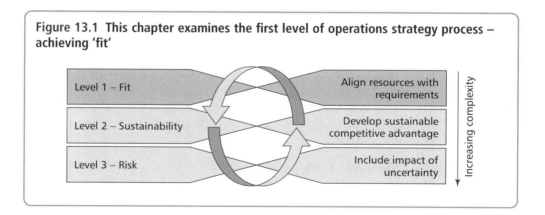

Figure 13.1 This chapter examines the first level of operations strategy process – achieving 'fit'

- *What do we mean by 'doing' operations strategy?*
- *What is 'fit' in operations strategy, and why is it important?*
- *How do we know when an operations strategy has achieved 'fit'?*
- *What practical frameworks exist to help achieve 'fit'?*
- *What are the practical challenges for achieving 'fit'?*

'Doing' strategy or 'thinking' strategy

It might seem surprising to find a whole section of this book dedicated to the 'process of operations strategy'. Is this just another potential contradiction? Strategy, after all, is broad, abstract, concerned with generalities rather than details – almost theoretical in nature. Operations is about doing the things that produce goods and services. Strategy is cerebral, operations is practical. But this is a contradiction which has been evident throughout almost every chapter of this book. Moving on to discuss the *process* of operations strategy merely brings the tension between the strategic and operational aspects of operations management to the fore. In this, and the following two chapters, we will deal with some practical aspects of managing operations at a strategic level. This does not mean that we shall avoid broad concepts. But we shall concentrate more on actually 'doing something' with them rather than just 'thinking and talking' about them. And while readily acknowledging that any 'real' operations strategy will vary from organisation to organisation, many of the formulation activities of operations strategy *processes* are common to many organisations.

Some initial challenges

Before embarking on an examination of the concept of 'fit' in operations strategy, it is worthwhile identifying some of the practical difficulties that face any operations strategy process. These challenges apply to all three of the levels of analysis we are dealing with in this part of the book. But they first become evident when dealing with this first level.

Scope and unit of analysis

One organisation's sub-strategy for operations will be another organisation's entire business strategy. For example, a medium-sized hotel chain can quite clearly consider its operations strategy as being concerned with the way it manages all its resources which produce its services. The scope of any operations strategy analysis would cover all the resources owned or controlled by the company. Each of the decision areas which we dealt with in Part 2 of the book would have some relevance for the analysis. But what of the far larger hotel and leisure group? One that has several types of hotel, branded in different ways and offering different types of service? It may also have theme parks, sports centres and other related businesses. Furthermore, it might both own and manage some of its resources while, in other parts of the group, it runs businesses which are owned by other people (a practice common in the hotel industry). How does this business start to consider its operations strategy? Including all the resources owned or managed by the group under one operations strategy is obviously out of the question. Different parts of the group will have different markets, different visions, serve different sets of customers and operate in different parts of the world. On the other hand, formulating an operations strategy for a single hotel within one part of the group might make no sense if the overall strategic objectives of that part of the group also apply to other hotels.

Drawing a sensible boundary for an operations strategy analysis is therefore an important issue. Ideally, whatever resources lie within the boundary of analysis should have common, overall strategic objectives. This obviously makes the task of establishing a coherent operations strategy more straightforward. However, in practice, this is not always easy. Often the answer is defined in terms of the process of doing the analysis itself. Put simply, if putting an operations strategy together is difficult, then maybe you've got the boundary wrong. If it is not possible to devise a strategy which both corresponds to strategic objectives and is internally coherent, one possible reason is that the operations strategy is attempting to span too great a range of strategic objectives.

What is 'operations'

The objectives, tasks and activities we have defined as 'operations' do not always match a coherent organisational function. Although many service organisations do have an explicit operations function, the notion of separating out the service 'product' from its production and delivery 'processes' is sometimes conceptually difficult. This can lead to a blurring between the boundaries of operations strategy, other functional strategies and the entire business strategy. Even in manufacturing businesses, where the idea and title 'operations' is more common, there are considerable overlaps between, say, Human Resource strategy, Engineering strategy and what we have included in Operations strategy. We would contend that including *all* the resources that produce the organisation's services and products within an operations strategy is usually the best starting point.

How explicit

An operations strategy only exists formally in the documented decisions and actions agreed by whatever decision-making body drives the formulation process. But not every detail of an operations strategy is completely explicit. The degree to which it is made explicit is itself a formulation decision. Making an operations strategy analysis complex does not necessarily make it a better analysis. Indeed, many operations deliberately leave the overall direction of strategy quite 'light' in order to encourage creativity and dynamic problem solving.

The role and position of operations

In Chapters 10 and 11 we discussed the organisational role of the operations function, and the way in which the expectations which the rest of the organisation had for it influenced its contribution to overall strategic success. Clearly operations' role and expected contribution will shape the way in which it devises strategy. For example, if, historically, the contribution of operations has been poor and the expectations which the rest of the organisation have of it are consequently low (what, in Chapter 11, we noted as Hayes and Wheelwright's *Stage 1*), strategy will be mainly concerned with stopping holding the organisation back. This will include examining the root causes of the (probably numerous) operations failures, establishing 'base level' operations processes, bringing process technology investment up to a minimum level, and so on. Conversely, where the operations function is looked to as the main driver of the organisation's strategic direction (Hayes and Wheelwright's *Stage 4*), operations strategy formulation will be very different. Here the operations function will be looking for creative ways in which to leverage its superiority: redefining its customers' and suppliers' understanding of their relationships, timing each new innovation to maximise strategic advantage, and so on.

Although it may seem trivial, the physical position of the operations function in the organisation can also impact on the way it devises strategy. Operations managers run operations, and operations are often geographically dispersed. The simple task of bringing together operations expertise from around the world needs to be done in a planned and formal manner. Even shared databases and conference calls are not as free-form as the more *ad hoc* strategy making which can occur when all the relevant managers occupy the same corridor. Moreover, traditionally, the operations function has fewer indirect analyst-type jobs. Operations managers who directly manage ongoing processes have to make a deliberate decision to leave those processes to indulge in 'strategy making'. Functions such as marketing, who traditionally have more indirect roles, rarely face this problem.

Emergent strategies

Defining the *content* of an operations strategy is a necessary first step, but it is only the first step. The process of operations strategy puts those content decisions together. However, content decisions are not always clear. The exact timing of capacity change, the precise set of suppliers to partner with, the details of organisational structure, and so on might only be decided in vague terms. This is because the future is uncertain and the response of operations resources sometimes unclear. The details of content decisions may emerge only over time. Similarly, day-to-day operational experience in dealing both with markets and resources can lead to such a degree of 'refinement' of content decisions that the decision is in effect changed completely. This emergent aspect of the strategy process cannot be ignored in practice. This is why our definition of operations strategy does not view resources and requirements as naturally congruent but rather emphasises an *ongoing* process of reconciliation between them. Such an approach is more practical because at its heart lies the recognition that many environmental and operational variables are unknown in advance (and, in some cases, unknowable). This means that many strategic operations decisions will be made over time regardless of the formal formulation process.

Operations strategy as 'fit'

The concept of operations strategy is based upon the active process of reconciliation between operational resources and market requirements. This is essentially another way of describing the inherent challenges in achieving 'fit' – the notion that a successful firm should align itself with its external environment. It is now so widely accepted that it has entered the realms of managerial 'common sense':

a simple though profound core concept is at the heart of many organisation and management research findings ... The concept is that of fit among an organisation's strategy, structure and management processes. Successful organisations achieve a fit with their market environment and support their strategies with appropriately designed structures and management processes.[1]

Fit – a reminder

Figure 13.2 illustrates the concept of fit which we introduced in Chapter 2. The vertical dimension represents the nature and level of market requirements either because they reflect the intrinsic needs of customers or because their expectations have been shaped by the firm's marketing activity. This includes such factors as:

● strength of brand/reputation;

● degree of differentiation;

● extent of plausible market promises.

Movement along the dimension indicates a broadly enhanced level of market performance or market capabilities.

The horizontal scale represents the level and nature of the firm's operations resource and processes capabilities. This includes such things as:

● the performance of the operation in terms of its ability to achieve competitive objectives;

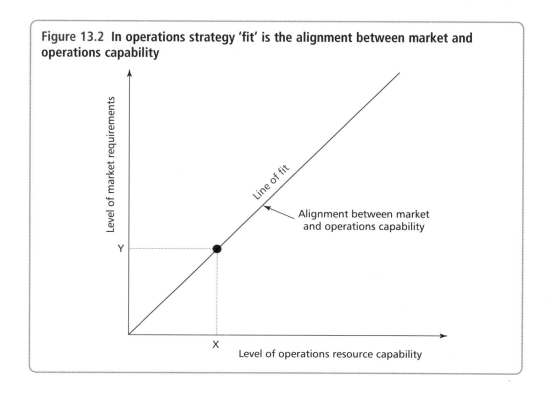

Figure 13.2 In operations strategy 'fit' is the alignment between market and operations capability

- the efficiency with which it uses its resources;
- the ability of the firm's resources to underpin its business processes.

Again, movement along the dimension indicates a broadly enhanced level of 'operations performance' and operations capabilities.

The purpose of 'fit' is to achieve an approximate balance between 'market performance' and 'operations performance'. So when fit is achieved firms' customers do not need, or expect, levels of operations performance which it is unable to supply. Nor does the firm have operations strengths which are either inappropriate for market needs or remain unexploited in the market. The diagonal line in Figure 13.2 therefore represents a 'line of fit' with market and operations in balance. Be careful, however, in using this diagrammatic representation. It is a conceptual model rather than a practical tool. We have deliberately been vague in calibrating or even defining precisely the two axes in the figure. The model is intended merely to illustrate some ideas around the concept of fit (and in the next two chapters, the concepts of sustainability and risk).

What should fit with what?

Two basic modes of fit can be identified. Firstly, and most commonly, an operation can seek to identify existing market requirements and then align its resources to match them. This approach has a number of intrinsic advantages, not least of which is the sheer availability of practical tools and techniques for classifying and identifying market requirements. This model also falls neatly into the traditional hierarchy of strategies (discussed in Chapter 1) whereby operations' role is to support predetermined market decisions. Despite the dominance

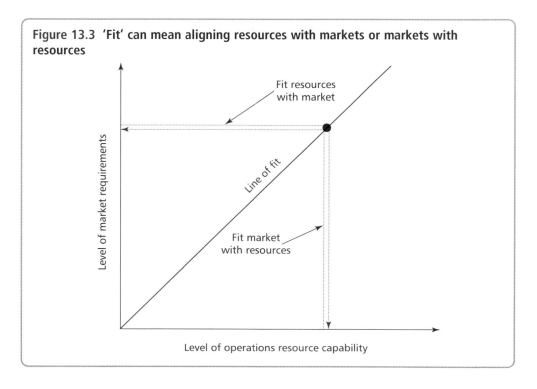

Figure 13.3 'Fit' can mean aligning resources with markets or markets with resources

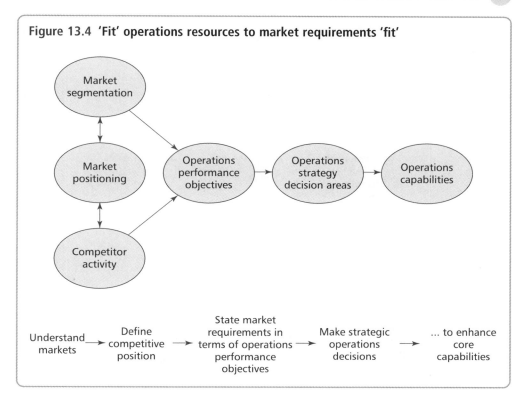

Figure 13.4 'Fit' operations resources to market requirements 'fit'

Understand markets → Define competitive position → State market requirements in terms of operations performance objectives → Make strategic operations decisions → ... to enhance core capabilities

of this approach, it is important to mention the second mode whereby an operation analyses its resources and then seeks market opportunities that fit well with it (see Figure 13.3).

It is not surprising that the majority of models for operations strategy development start with market requirements and work through to the implications for operations resources. After all, all businesses have markets. They may not always be well understood and the business may not be good at identifying which part of a market it is trying to serve. However, all businesses have some idea of the requirements of their market. But, not every business understands its operations capabilities and many may not even have any 'distinctive' capabilities. While we have continually stressed the importance of leveraging operations capabilities into the marketplace, this does presuppose that a business has some operations capabilities worth leveraging.

The implication of this is that at relatively low levels of fit between market requirements and operations resource capabilities, the concept of fit has to be largely market driven, that is, resources are shaped in order to fit with market requirements. Such an approach would start with a formal statement of market positioning as derived from an organisation's understanding of the market segments it wishes to address and the activities of its competitors. Following on from this, generic operations performance objectives would be used as a device to translate market positioning into a statement of market requirements which was understandable and useful to the operations function. These objectives would influence the various operations strategy 'content' decisions which in turn, over time, shape the operations capa-

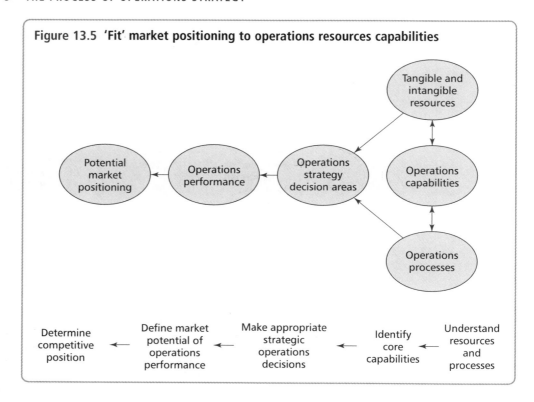

Figure 13.5 'Fit' market positioning to operations resources capabilities

bilities. As we shall see later, the practical frameworks designed to help formulate operations strategy are based on this approach which is summarised in Figure 13.4.

At higher levels of fit where demanding levels of market requirements are being matched with unique and strategic operations resources capabilities, it is those capabilities themselves that may dictate the search for markets which can fully appreciate them. Figure 13.5 illustrates this operations resource perspective approach. Here the operations capabilities embedded within its tangible and intangible resources and its operations processes are articulated. The operations strategy 'content' decisions are made with the objective of enhancing the strategic capabilities of the organisation. These result in a particular set of operations performance objectives which define a potential set of market positions. The final market positioning strategy which is selected under a 'pure' version of this approach is the one that best exploits the organisation's core capabilities.

Fit with broad environmental changes

The idea of fit between markets and resources can be demonstrated at different levels and over different time-scales. Over the long term, both market and general environmental factors can influence the way in which a company shapes its resources. For example, as automobile manufacturers go, Volvo (now part of the Ford Motor Company) has been one of the most innovative in terms of designing novel operations processes for making its vehicles. The box on Volvo briefly describes a number of Volvo's innovative plants.

Twenty-five years of manufacturing innovation at Volvo[2]

Before the early 1970s, Volvo's main plant was its Gothenberg complex. It was, at the beginning of this period, a relatively traditional plant using conventional assembly lines where individual workers are responsible only for their own stations tasks. But the Gothenberg plant looked dated in 1970 when all eyes were focused on a bold new experiment at Kalmar.

Kalmar (early, mid-1970s)

Kalmar marks the first of Volvo's moves away from the traditional plant. The essence of the plant was to break up the 'big factory' long assembly line into small 'mini factory' workshops, each of which was responsible for part of the car's assembly. Most spectacularly, the assembly line itself was scrapped and cars were moved about the factory on independently moving trolleys. Each independently powered trolley moved within and between the workshops. Small buffers of part-completed products between sections allowed the operators in each section to decide how they wanted to work on the cars. Significantly, although it was possible to have completely parallel working, which would have allowed operators to work together to complete the whole of their task, this was almost never done. Most operators preferred to work using mini-assembly lines within each section. What was radically new was the use of ergonomically designed tilting systems which allowed cars to be moved to positions convenient for working on. Volvo moved to this design of process for one overriding reason – to attract workers into the factories. At the time, car assembly work was so unattractive that there were no indigenous Swedish workers in some parts of the Gothenberg plant. Low unemployment and strong growth in the economy combined with a social reluctance to work on repetitive tasks made recruitment difficult. Paradoxically, the intense publicity surrounding such a novel design of car plant proved to be one of the main deterrents to Kalmar attracting local workers. The sheer number of visitors coming round the plant angered and distressed the operators (who at one stage took to throwing peanuts at the visitors like monkeys might in a zoo).

Uddevalla (mid-1980s)

The Uddevalla plant was designed so that 48 teams of operators in parallel built the whole car. Operators were 'car builders', not 'assembly workers'. The fully integrated teams were completely responsible, not only for building the car, but for many other indirect tasks such as quality, planning and, most radically of all, liaising with the customer sales end of the business. At the time, business was booming but the company were having some quality problems. They wanted highly skilled workers with personal dedication who would ensure the manufacture of high-quality products. They also wanted to exploit this aspect of production through 'customer car' programmes whereby customers could actually see their own car being built. This would in turn encourage personal responsibility among operators. Uddevalla also attracted considerable publicity:

> In a trial run, Roger Holtback, President of Volvo Car Corp., exchanged his usual Saville Row suit for overalls and assembled a car all by himself at a new plant in Uddevalla, Sweden. Holtback managed to drive off the finished Volvo 740 though it was by no means free of defects ... Still, this 1987 experiment reinforced Volvo's radical decision to mass-produce the mid-line 740 at Uddevalla without using assembly lines. (*Business Week*, 28 August 1989)

The type of production at Uddevalla was called by some 'neocraft' production, although in many ways it was relatively high-tech. For example, the materials handling devices to solve the logistics problems of getting all the parts to all 48 teams were sophisticated. Capital expenses at the plant were further increased by the necessity of providing all 48 teams with a full set of tooling required to do all the tasks necessary in assembling the car.

Gent (late 1980s)

In parallel with the Kalmar and Uddevalla experiments, Volvo's plant at Gent in Belgium had been slowly adopting the principles of lean production which would eventually kill off the two more radical plants. It was the first plant outside Japan to be awarded the Total Productive Maintenance (TPM) award. It had also developed a form of teamwork, while still retaining the traditional line process design. The major motivation behind Volvo's decision to give the Gent plant new models in the late 1980s was quite simply its combination of low cost and high quality. Its use of 'internal customer concepts' and 'continuous improvement' through total productive maintenance and total quality management was out-performing any of Volvo's other plants. This, at a time when the cost and quality performance levels of Japanese-owned factories were making for intense competition in the automobile market.

Born (mid-1990s)

The Born plant was different again. While maintaining a line-based process design and the type of teamwork based on the process which had been developed at Gent, it was a joint venture with Mitsubishi, the Japanese car maker. This meant it had to manufacture two different cars in the same plant. It managed this by carefully separating the common and the unique features of each product, and designing flexible processes. The main implication of the move to more flexible joint production with another company concerned the operations management of the plant. They now had to cope with a far more complex operations environment. Not only were there more types of model and engine etc. to programme into the plant, but, at times, there was some conflict to be resolved between Volvo and Mitsubishi's sales demands. The reason why the two companies cooperated had much to do with their size. By world standards Volvo was a small car manufacturer while Mitsubishi's European sales were, in world terms, low. Both had to devise a way of making relatively small volumes of vehicles economically. Sharing fixed assets and retaining flexibility between the two vehicles allowed them to do this.

Volvo's fit with its environment

Although small by international standards, Volvo's factory at Kalmar was a radical experiment in trying to make car assembly attractive to an increasingly reluctant and discriminating workforce. While its design was clearly a product of Scandinavian social ethics, the business motivation was more hardnosed. In the long term, Volvo figured, they could not continue to manufacture in Sweden without making their factories more attractive to potential workers. The Uddevalla plant was to some extent a further step along this same path. Again, its design reflects its Scandinavian social context. However, now there is also a more recognisable external business objective – to enhance quality levels of Volvo's products in the quality-sensitive market they had chosen to compete in. In fact the Uddevalla plant was closed down in its original form in May 1993. Called by some an 'heroic failure', it still has its defenders, especially amongst some Swedish academics. Yet its productivity never came close to matching the levels of what was now the dominant operations paradigm for car assembly – lean production. Uddevalla's defenders claim that it was never given a fair chance because volumes never reached the levels intended. The plant never produced at much more than half its design capacity. Whether it was the inherent costliness of this form of production which prevented Volvo pricing their cars at a level which would have increased volume, or whether demand in the market by that time was such that the plant could never hope to compete, is a matter of some argument. What was undisputable, however, was the startlingly better performance of the 'lean production influenced' plant at Gent. Although this plant had been slowly developing its lean production capabilities, it became central to Volvo's strategy when the competitive environment became tougher with the high-quality, low-cost capabilities of Japanese manufacturers. In this regard, for once, Volvo was adopting broadly the same operations strategy as most Western automobile manufacturers. They broke away from the crowd again, however, when they opened their joint venture with Mitsubishi at Born. This time, the efficiency, speed and quality objectives had been supplemented by the need to be flexible. Especially for a relatively small automobile company, flexibility in terms of being able to adjust product mix and volumes had become essential.

What is important here is not so much the individual operations strategies within each of these Volvo plants, but rather the way in which operations resources were shaped and deployed (often in a highly innovative manner) *to fit in* with changes in its social and business environment. This is an important point to make about the nature of fit. Over time, organisations which understand their environment will naturally attempt to shape their operations resources and processes accordingly. Admittedly, not all will act fast enough and not all will be as innovative as Volvo. But, in the long term the concept of fit is a natural business process. Table 13.1 summarises Volvo's strategies within its alternative plants.

Fit with generic competitive position

Whereas the Volvo example above shows fit as almost a 'natural' process, the concept of fit is also important in understanding more deliberative strategic decisions. Aligning any operations resources with its intended market position (the 'market led' view of fit) is an important element in most companies' operations strategy. In detail there are an infinite number of ways a firm may choose to compete. Different markets with different customer groups and competitor behaviour will all produce a different set of competitive options. However, according to the leading strategy academic Michael Porter, underneath them all there are broadly three 'generic' types of competitive strategy which describe how companies present themselves (or their products and services) to their customers *in comparison with their competitors*.[3]

Cost leadership

The aim of cost leadership strategy is to reduce the cost of producing and delivering products and services below that which competitors can achieve. This cost advantage can then be used either to reduce prices and gain business from competitors, or alternatively to earn a higher profit margin by keeping prices the same as competitors. Often a cost advantage can be used to obtain both advantages. That is, reduce prices in order to discomfort competitors while, at the same time, earning higher profit margins which may be invested to achieve other types of competitive advantage such as higher-quality products and services.

Differentiation

Differentiation strategies are those where, by studying customers' needs and preferences, companies are able to incorporate elements into their products and services which customers find particularly attractive compared with those on offer from competitors. When enough customers are sufficiently attracted to the differentiated products and services, the company may use the advantage to:

- build brand loyalty, giving a continuity and robustness in the marketplace;
- charge a premium price for its products and services;

Table 13.1 **Evolution of operations fit at Volvo**

Resources and processes at each Volvo plant	Why? – Strategic objectives
Kalmar (1973)	
Broke up the line	Attract staff
Created 'small factories'	Social ethics
Used 'auto carriers'	
Ergonomic work position	
Reduced pacing	
Uddevalla (1987)	
Staff build complete cars	Quality
Car builders, not assembly workers	Social ethics
Results-oriented teams	
Parallel working	
High customer contact	
Gent (1988)	
Started in 1965	Cost
Lean production approach late 1980s onward	Quality
KLE (quality, delivery, economy)	Speed
Multi-skilled online teams	Inter-plant competition
Internal customer concepts	
Born (1996)	
Joint venture	Flexibility
Volvo + Mitsubishi	Common processes
Product technology – Volvo	World-class efficiency
Process technology – Mitsubishi	Product and brand integrity
Netherlands govt. partners	
'Uniqueness around conformity'	

● gain more market share because of the attractiveness of its products and services; or

● some combination of the above.

Focus

A focus strategy involves selecting a narrow part of the total market and developing products and services in such a way that they concentrate on the needs of customers in that segment. Appealing to customers in niche markets could be done using either of the previous two strategies. That is, the company could offer either lower costs than competitors in that market niche, or a set of differentiated products and services.

The implications for operations strategy

The different strategies described above will require different things from the operations function of any company that pursues them. From an operations strategy viewpoint, our interest in different types of competitive strategy is that it helps us progress towards giving the operations function some guidance as to how they can contribute to supporting the requirements of the market. As such, it is an important link in the translation process between market needs and operations objectives.

For a *low-cost* strategy the implications for operations are straightforward. Low cost means that operations must be efficient and productive in the way they manage their processes. It also means that operations must consider changing the design of their products and services to simplify their production and delivery. Perhaps they may even consider reducing the range in order to reduce operations complexity, and so on. A *differentiation* strategy will also place specific demands on the operations function, though their exact nature will depend on how differentiation is to be achieved. For example, if differentiation is achieved through customising products and services to customers' exact requirements, then operations flexibility is likely to be particularly important. If enhanced product and service features are to be included, then operations will need to be able to respond quickly and reliably to their introduction. High-quality products and services will imply the development of error-free processes, and so on. Similarly, for a *focus* strategy, operations will have to be able to produce a performance which corresponds to the required market position. The point here is not so much what the link between market positioning and

Table 13.2 Implications of Porter's three approaches to competitive strategy

	Low cost	*Differentiation*	*Focus*
Target market	*Broad target*	*Broad target*	*Narrow target*
Competitive position	Achieve lower costs than competitors.	Offer customers something which they value and which competitors cannot offer.	Concentrate on serving niche market with either low-cost or differentiated products and services.
Products and services	Acceptable but basic product and service with few features that increase cost.	Products and services with enhanced features that are different to those offered by competitors.	Adapted or customised products and services which centre on the needs of niche customers.
Market strategy	Understanding what not to cut from product and service offerings to maintain value to customers while emphasising the virtue of features that help keep costs low.	Understand what features customers are prepared to pay for, emphasise these differentiating features and establish the premium price customers will pay for them.	Understand the specific needs of the niche, concentrate on serving that niche over time and emphasise the ability of the company to serve that niche.
Operations objectives	Continuous emphasis on low cost of production and delivery without abandoning essential product and service features.	Depends on how differentiation is to be achieved; could be enhanced product and service quality, range, speed of delivery, specification etc., but will probably need operations to be innovative.	Depends on strategy to achieve focus, but it is important that operations concentrates on a narrow range of performance objectives which correspond to needs of the market.

operations objectives is, rather it is that there *is* a link. Put simply, different ways of competing in the marketplace imply different demands and different types of performance from the operations function. Table 13.2 summarises the three approaches to competitive strategy and their implications for the operations function.

Fit with a specific competitive position

Examining the concept of fit at a general environmental level over time, as we did with the Volvo example, and relating generic competitive positions with their resource implications both help us to understand the nature of fit. At a more pragmatic level, however, we need to understand how an individual company's specific competitive position can be reflected in its operations strategy. To do this, let us take the first of three looks in this part of the book at one of the best-known companies in the world – IBM (see the box on International Business Machines [A]).

International Business Machines [A]

In 1980 the US corporation International Business Machines (universally known by its acronym, IBM) posted profit figures of $3.6 billion. On 11 July 1983, *Time* magazine described IBM as the 'colossus that works', echoing a widely held belief that this massive company was probably the best-managed organisation in the world. Consultants and academics flocked to IBM and offered a wide range of explanations for its world domination. At that time 'Big Blue' (derived from the ubiquitous corporate uniform of a dark blue suit worn with a white shirt and dark tie) had over 300,000 staff, assets of $27 billion, sales of $26 billion and was widely viewed as one of the world's greatest companies. IBM is a long-established firm. It began life as the Computing-Tabulating-Recording Company in 1911 (this firm was formed by the merger of three others with complementary products), eventually changing its name (under the leadership of Thomas Watson Sr.) to IBM in 1924. It was under the leadership of Thomas Watson Jr. (CEO from 1956 to 1971), however, that the modern firm really began to emerge.

In 1965 (less than a decade after mainframe technology first emerged commercially) the 'general purpose' IBM system 360 was on sale to a wide range of users. IBM was not the first firm to produce mainframes but became a first mover in the industry by following an operations strategy based upon economies of scale. They invested heavily in product-specific integrated production technology (in addition to extending their already developed sales and marketing network). The firm's operations included the research, design, manufacture and maintenance of a range of computer equipment and associated software but their core profitability was built around the global mainframe market. Their operations strategy in this crucial market was based around two key elements:

● *Production efficiency* – In the late 1970s IBM made a series of huge capital investments (large-scale capacity strategy) in the latest process technology. This allowed them to become one of the highest-quality and lowest-cost producers in the industry.

● *Vertical integration* – IBM was the world's largest producer (exploiting scale and process technology again) of memory chips and then installed all its productive output into its own machines.

By 1980, the firm was number one in a market that was by then worth $50 billion worldwide. At the same time, they established an equally dominant position in the market for lower-priced (application-specific) minicomputers.

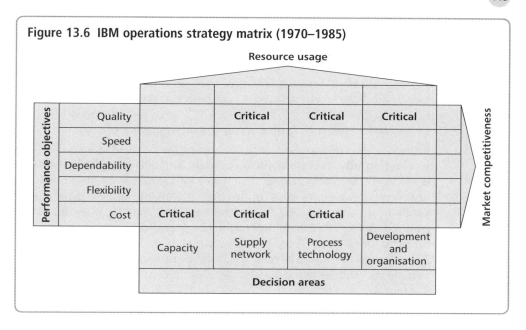

Figure 13.6 IBM operations strategy matrix (1970–1985)

IBM, in its early and middle years, is often cited as an example of the benefits to be gained from 'fit'. It is fascinating to note that IBM was not really known for any specific product innovation or organisational form, but it was widely viewed as simply being good at everything it did. The matrix (Figure 13.6) shows how its operations strategy provides a strong degree of fit with the dominant market requirements of cost and quality. In the mainframe (and linked minicomputer) market, there were relatively few suppliers providing broadly similar levels of product specification. As a result, combining IBM's extensive sales, marketing and support network with an operations strategy that ensured well-designed, reliable (and/or maintainable) product widely available at competitive prices offered IBM a 'tight fit' with their core market. There was also a significant first-mover advantage effect because, once installed, the nature and cost of the product meant that customers tended to become locked in to a specific supplier.

Of course, history did not end in 1983 and we will return later to discuss the rollercoaster aspects of its more recent history but it is still instructive to turn the clock back to the mid-1980s. It is useful to derive an approximate operations strategy matrix for the firm.

'Fit' is both a static and a dynamic concept

Although the advantages of fit might seem obvious, and are widely accepted managerial common sense, the underlying concept is not necessarily as straightforward as it sounds. This is because 'fit' is both a *static* attribute and a *dynamic* process. For example, an online share trading operation may question the 'outcome' of its operations strategy by asking, 'how good are our back-office operations at delivering the response time which our share trading market requires?' Answering this question would involve drawing a connection between the way in which the share trading back-office operations are organised and their market performance. However, another legitimate question is, 'how long will it be before our investment in state-of-the-art processing technology has an impact?' Here the question is more to do with the dynamic *process* of achieving fit. It concerns *how* the new processing technology is being used in practice to extend the capabilities of the operation. As an illustration of this, it is interesting to look at one of the dominant strategic operations issues of the past 20 years – lean production.

Lean production as 'static outcome' and 'dynamic process'

A decade ago the lean production concept was viewed as a counter-intuitive alternative to traditional manufacturing models. Today it is arguably *the* paradigm for many operations, the influence of which can be found in a wide range of manufacturing and service strategies. The originators of lean initiatives formulated the 'operating problem' as an unceasing battle against waste, making it seem axiomatic that 'lean' implied 'better'. Yet 'lean' operations is only a description of the state of the operation. It does not tell us anything about how to achieve or maintain this status. Nevertheless, it was shown that (during the late 1980s and early 1990s) Japanese vehicle assemblers were much more productive than their Western counterparts. Largely this was seen to be the result of their 'lean production' model which related operations-led competitive advantage to three key principles:

1 improved flow of material and information across business functions;

2 an emphasis on customer pull rather than organisational push shop-floor control;

3 a commitment to continuous improvement enabled by people development.

These principles were strongly influenced by Toyota and the work of Taiichi Ohno in particular. When this celebrated engineer wrote his book (after retiring from the firm in 1978) he was able to portray Toyota's manufacturing plants as embodying a coherent production approach. This was both a powerful advertisement for Toyota's competence and appealed to the social scientists, industrial engineers and consultants seeking a systematic explanation for Toyota's success. However, this encouraged observers to focus in on the specific techniques of lean production and de-emphasised the impact of 30 years of 'trial and error'. The success of Toyota was as much to do with the *process of fit*, in so much as they worked over time to ensure alignment between their intended market position and their operations resources, as it was with the specific outcomes of their production systems. Maybe the real achievement of Toyota was not so much what they did but how they did it.

The level of fit

Because it is very difficult to predict the precise impact that operational change will have upon the organisation, the dynamic process of fit is inevitably difficult to manage. Moreover, the requirements of the marketplace are not themselves static but prone to evolve and, in the presence of competitive action, shift quite radically. Add to this that very few operations serve only one narrow market and it becomes clear why so few operations exhibit 'tight fit' with their external environments. As a result of these internal and external change processes, operations inevitably exhibit different degrees of fit over time. At certain points in time an organisation may well exhibit 'tight fit' between its underlying operational resources and the requirements

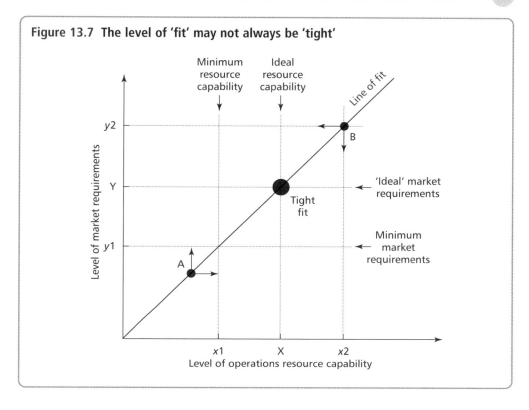

Figure 13.7 The level of 'fit' may not always be 'tight'

of the marketplace. However, it is more likely that there will always be some degree of increased alignment necessary.

In many instances an operation will find itself in position A in Figure 13.7. It will fall short of delivering the requirements that the market requires (Y) because it lacks sufficient operational capability (X). The important issue here will be to identify what really are the minimum market requirements ($y1$) and therefore the minimum level of resource capability ($x1$) necessary to meet them. Many organisations, however, will wish at least to meet, and possibly exceed, the specific criteria required by their market. Given the uncertainty surrounding both any interpretation of market requirements and any understanding of underlying resource capability, it may even seem desirable to provide 'excess' resource capability. This is shown in position B in Figure 13.7. Such excess capability ($x2$) might seem to be a utopian position and 'over deliver' ($y2$) market requirements to the extent that it can readily 'delight' the customer. However, occupying position B may restrict resource availability for other critical activities. In this respect there is probably also a maximum dimension associated with any appropriate performance envelope.

Comprehensive, coherence, correspondence and criticality

Back in Chapter 2 we introduced the idea of the *operations strategy matrix*. We suggested that, because it emphasised the intersections between what is required from operations (in terms of the relative priority which should be given to each

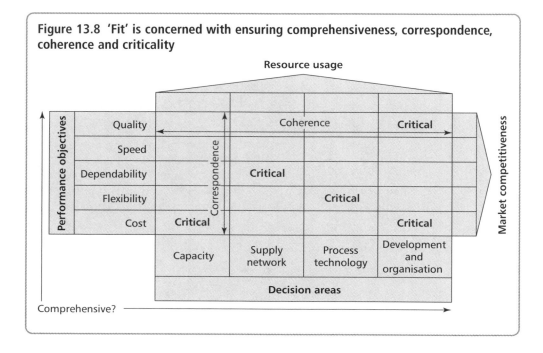

Figure 13.8 'Fit' is concerned with ensuring comprehensiveness, correspondence, coherence and criticality

performance objective) and how the operation tries to achieve this through the choices made in each decision area, it was a useful device to describe any organisation's operations strategy. At least it could act as a checklist to ensure that the organisation had been reasonably comprehensive in considering different aspects of its operations strategy. In fact we can use the matrix to go further than merely describe an operations strategy. We can use it to question, develop and even formulate strategies. Indeed, using the matrix to check for comprehensiveness could be considered the first step in a formulation process. Here we will use the matrix to explore some of the most basic aspects of operations strategy formulation (see Figure 13.8):

1 exploring what it means for an operations strategy to be *comprehensive*;

2 ensuring there is internal *coherence* between the different decision areas;

3 ensuring that decisions taken as part of the operations strategy process *correspond* to the appropriate priority for each performance objective;

4 highlighting which resource/requirement intersections are the most *critical* with respect to the broader financial and competitive priorities of the organisation.

Comprehensive

In seeking to achieve operations fit, this notion of 'comprehensiveness' is a critical first step. Business history is littered with world-class companies that simply failed to notice the potential impact of, for instance, new process technology, or emerging changes in their supply network. Also, many attempts to achieve fit have failed because operations have paid undue attention to only one of the key decision areas. As an illustration of both how the matrix can act as a checklist for comprehensiveness and the impact of overlooking key decision areas, it is interesting to turn to one of the key strategic operations challenges of the past two decades – *improving quality* through Total Quality Management (TQM).

Improving quality through TQM

The past 20 years, however, have seen the emergence of quality as a major competitive challenge. In the early 1980s many observers documented major quality gaps between US and European companies on one hand, and Japanese companies on the other. A boom market emerged for quality-related advice and guidance. Much of this market was satisfied by traditional suppliers of business advice such as consultants and academics. However, in addition, many companies who had themselves embarked early on quality-related initiatives also attempted to sell such expertise. For example, by the end of the 1980s managers at the (now) well-known US utility company Florida Power and Light (the first non-Japanese winner of the prestigious Deming quality prize) estimated that 90 per cent of the Fortune 100 companies had attended their monthly seminars. Indeed, to cope with the demand Florida Power and Light (FPL) set up a subsidiary consulting operation, Qualtec. Yet despite FPL's devotion to quality and its considerable performance achievements, it is not clear how positive the effect was upon its bottom-line performance. In her book *Fad Surfing in the Boardroom*,[4] Eileen Shapiro describes how staff of the Florida Public Service Commission quickly began complaining that local taxpayers should not have to pay for FPL's dash for the Deming prize.

The popularity of TQM means that nearly all service and manufacturing operations have now been exposed to some form of strategic quality improvement programme. But by no means all such initiatives have been successful. Many have lost their impetus over time. Various researchers and consultants have put forward prescriptions on how to avoid what has been described as *total quality disillusionment*.[5] Many of these prescriptions stress that operations quality programmes should be both strategic and comprehensive. In other words, if one applied the operations strategy matrix to such an initiative, we would expect to see a spread of activities (albeit of differing priority) at the intersections with each of the decision areas. To test this assertion out, read the Practice Box on Deming's 14 points.

Practice Box **Deming's 14-point quality programme[6]**

W. Edwards Deming, considered in Japan to be the father of quality control, asserted that quality starts with top management *and is a strategic activity*. It has been claimed that much of the success in terms of quality in Japanese industry was as the result of his lectures to Japanese companies in the 1950s.[7]

Deming's 14-point model is, in many ways, both a crystallisation of his lifetime of work in the improvement area and (because it was published relatively late in the quality boom) a summary of some other authorities' ideas on quality improvement. In order to translate these different elements onto the operations strategy matrix, we have listed each of Deming's 14 points followed by the operations strategy decision areas to which they relate.

1 Plan for a long-term commitment to quality [*Development and organisation*].

2 Quality must be built into the processes at every stage [*Process technology, Supply network, Development and organisation*].

▶

3 Cease mass inspection [*Process technology, Supply network, Development and organisation*].

4 Do not make purchase decisions on price alone [*Supply network, Development and organisation*].

5 Identify problems and work continuously to improve the system [*Supply network, Development and organisation*].

6 Implement SPC and quality training [*Process technology, Development and organisation*].

7 Institute leadership and a human-centred approach to supervision [*Development and organisation*].

8 Eliminate fear [*Supply network, Development and organisation*].

9 Break down barriers between departments [*Supply network, Development and organisation*].

10 Stop demanding higher productivity without the methods to achieve them [*Capacity strategy, Process technology, Supply network, Development and organisation*].

11 Eliminate performance standards based solely on output [*Capacity strategy, Process technology, Supply network, Development and organisation*].

12 Remove barriers to pride in workmanship [*Development and organisation*].

13 Institute education and self-improvement programmes [*Development and organisation*].

14 Create a top management structure that emphasises the above 13 points every day [*Development and organisation*].

Figure 13.9 To be strategic, quality initiatives need to comprehensively cover all decision areas

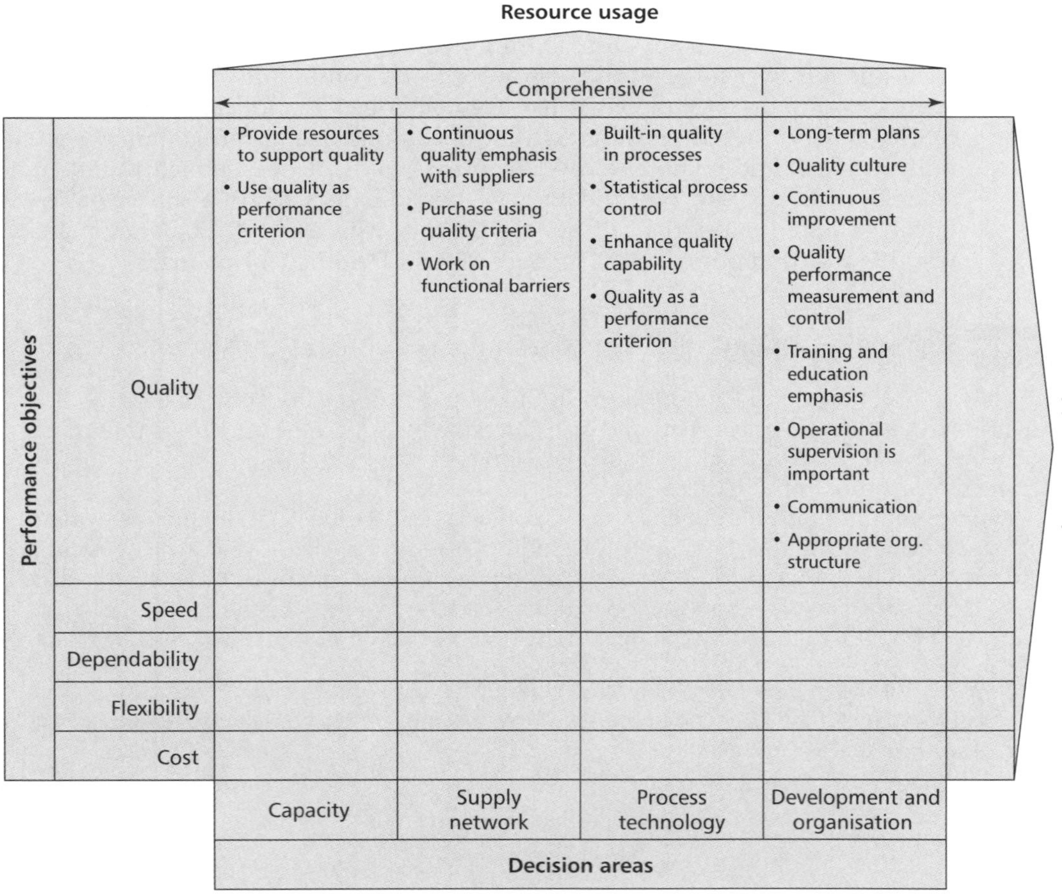

Resource usage

Comprehensive

Performance objectives		Capacity	Supply network	Process technology	Development and organisation	Market competitiveness
	Quality	• Provide resources to support quality • Use quality as performance criterion	• Continuous quality emphasis with suppliers • Purchase using quality criteria • Work on functional barriers	• Built-in quality in processes • Statistical process control • Enhance quality capability • Quality as a performance criterion	• Long-term plans • Quality culture • Continuous improvement • Quality performance measurement and control • Training and education emphasis • Operational supervision is important • Communication • Appropriate org. structure	
	Speed					
	Dependability					
	Flexibility					
	Cost					

Decision areas

The matrix in Figure 13.9 summarises Deming's points in each decision area and illustrates that the Deming points are comprehensive, though heavily emphasising the infrastructural aspects of operational change. However, changing behaviours and beliefs is not easy and requires constant emphasis over an extended period of time. The individual operations strategy matrix is essentially a 'snapshot' in time but for a strategy to be truly comprehensive, the different elements must not only be in place, but be in place over time.

Coherence

In the above discussion of making a strategy comprehensive we stressed how important it was to consider the dynamic process of implementation over time. As a comprehensive strategy evolves over time, different tensions will emerge that threaten to pull the overall strategy in different directions. This can result in a loss of coherence. Coherence is when the choices made in each decision area do *not* pull the operation in different directions. For example, if new flexible technology is introduced which allows products or services to be customised to individual clients' needs, it would be 'incoherent' to devise an organisation structure which did not enable the relevant staff to exploit the technology because it would limit the effective flexibility of the operation. For the investment in flexible technology to be effective, it must be accompanied by an organisational structure which deploys the organisation's skills appropriately, a performance measurement system which acknowledges that flexibility must be promoted, a new product/service development policy which stresses appropriate types of customisation, a supply network strategy which develops suppliers and customers to understand the needs of high-variety customisation, a capacity strategy which deploys capacity where the customisation is needed, and so on. In other words, all the decision areas complement and reinforce each other in the promotion of that particular performance objective. The main problem with achieving coherence is that so many decisions are made which have a strategic impact, it is relatively easy to make decisions which inadvertently cause a loss of coherence.

Correspondence

Equally, an operation has to achieve a correspondence between the choices made against each of the decision areas and the relative priority attached to each of the performance objectives. In other words, the strategies pursued in each decision area should reflect the true priority of each performance objective. So, for example, if cost reduction is the main organisational objective for an operation then its process technology investment decisions might err towards the purchase of 'off-the-shelf' equipment from a third-party supplier. This would reduce the capital cost of the technology and may also imply lower maintenance and running costs. Remember, however, that making such a decision will also have an impact on other performance objectives. An off-the-shelf piece of equipment may not, for example, have the flexibility that more 'made-to-order' equipment has. Also, the other decision areas must correspond with the same prioritisation of objectives. If low cost is really important then one would expect to see capacity strategies which exploit natural economies of scale, supply network strategies which reduce purchasing costs, performance measurement systems which stress efficiency and productivity, continuous improvement strategies which emphasise continual cost reduction, and so on.

Criticality

In addition to the difficulties of ensuring coherence between decision areas, there is also a need to include financial and competitive priorities. Although all decisions are important and a comprehensive perspective should be maintained, in practical terms some resource/requirement intersections will be more critical than others. The judgement over exactly which intersections are particularly critical is very much a pragmatic one which must be based on the particular circumstances of an individual firm's operations strategy. It is therefore difficult to generalise as to the likelihood of any particular intersections being critical. However, in practice, one can ask revealing questions such as, 'If flexibility is important, of all the decisions we make in terms of our capacity, supply networks, process technology, or development and organisation, which will have the most impact on flexibility?' This can be done for all performance objectives, with more emphasis being placed on those having the highest priority. Generally, when presented with a framework such as the operations strategy matrix, executives can identify those intersections which are particularly significant in achieving fit.

Formulation models for fit

At some time, most organisations will want to formulate their own operations strategy to cope with what they see as their individual competitive circumstances. There are many alternative procedures which have been suggested as providing the outline framework for developing an operations strategy. Most consultancy companies have developed their own frameworks, as have several academics. It would be too lengthy a process to describe many of these frameworks. Most of them are surprisingly similar anyway. Therefore, we will confine ourselves to describing a couple of contributions from academics in the area. Two well-known procedures are briefly described here to give the flavour of how operations strategies are formulated in practice. These are the *Hill framework* and the *Platts–Gregory procedure*.

The Hill framework

One of the first, and certainly most influential, approaches to operations strategy formulation (although once again its development is largely connected with manufacturing operations) is that devised by Professor Terry Hill of Templeton College, Oxford. The 'Hill framework' is illustrated in Figure 13.10. Hill's model, which is here adapted to the terminology used in this book, follows the well-tried approach of providing a connection between different levels of strategy making. It is essentially a five-step procedure. Step one involves understanding the long-term corporate objectives of the organisation so that the eventual operations strategy can be seen in terms of its contribution to these corporate objectives. Step two involves understanding how the marketing strategy of the organisation has been developed to achieve corporate objectives. This step, in effect, identifies the products/service markets which the operations strategy must satisfy, as well as identifying the product or service characteristics such as range, mix and volume, which the operation will be required to provide. Step three translates marketing strategy into what we have called performance objectives. These are the things which are important to the

Figure 13.10 The Hill framework of operations strategy formulation

Step 1	Step 2	Step 3	Step 4	Step 5
Corporate objectives	Marketing strategy	How do products or services win orders?	Operations strategy	
			Process choice	Infrastructure
• Growth • Profit • ROI • Other 'financial' measures	• Product/ service markets and segments • Range • Mix • Volumes • Standardisation or customisation • Innovation • Leader or follower	• Price • Quality • Delivery speed • Delivery dependability • Product/service range • Product/service design • Brand image • Technical service	• Process technology • Trade-offs embodied in process • Role of inventory • Capacity, size, timing, location	• Functional support • Operations planning and control systems • Work structuring • Payment systems • Organisational structure

operation in terms of winning business or satisfying customers. Hill goes on to divide the factors that win business into order-winners and qualifiers (we explained this distinction in Chapter 2). Step four is what Hill calls 'process choice'. This is similar, but not identical, to the decision areas of capacity, supply networks and process technology. The purpose is to define a set of structural characteristics of the operations which are coherent with each other and correspond to the way the company wishes to compete. Step five involves a similar process but this time with the infrastructural features of the operation (broadly what we have called 'development and organisation' decisions).

Hill's framework is not intended to imply a simple sequential movement from step one to step five, although during the formulation process the emphasis does move in this direction. Rather, Hill sees the process as an iterative one, whereby operations managers cycle between an understanding of the long-term strategic requirements of the operation and the specific resource developments which are required to support strategy. In this iterative process the identification of competitive factors in step three is seen as critical. It is at this stage that any mismatches between what the organisation's strategy *requires* and what its operation can *provide* become evident.

The steps in the Hill framework are closely related to classic corporate planning methodologies (with clear separations of responsibility, strong functional tasks, etc.) but Hill argues that whereas the first three elements are treated as interactive and iterative, the final two are commonly presented as straightforward, linear, logical implementation issues. This echoes the early works of Wickham Skinner who argued that operations was too often 'missing' from the corporate strategy debate.[8]

By stressing the iterative nature of his framework, Hill emphasises the need to improve the critical relationship between operations and marketing (too often a 'fault-line' in businesses) and facilitates this process by providing a framework that helps to simplify the complexity of manufacturing operations. This is essentially a mechanism for ensuring the coherence and correspondence of the overall strategy.

Furthermore, he stresses that these reviews should not be static in so far as they should consider both existing products and plans for future products. This allows considerations of product (and process) life cycle to be included. With finite resources available, the framework can highlight some of the trade-offs that exist in any operations strategy.

The Platts–Gregory procedure

Although superficially similar to the Hill framework, the work of Ken Platts and Mike Gregory of Cambridge University adds at least one crucial element missing from Hill – namely a form of prioritisation based upon an assessment of relative, competitive performance. The overall framework comprises three distinct stages (see Figure 13.11).

- Stage 1 involves developing an understanding of the market position of the organisation. Specifically it seeks to identify the factors that are 'required' by the market and then compares these to a level of achieved performance.

- Stage 2 seeks to identify the capabilities of the operation. Decision categories (similar to those developed by Hayes and Wheelright) are provided to help managers classify current operations practice and then link these practices to the priorities identified in stage 1.

- Stage 3 is the least structured of the elements, encouraging managers to review the

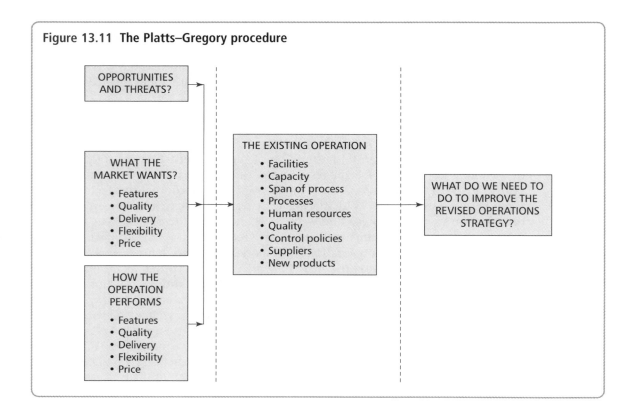

Figure 13.11 The Platts–Gregory procedure

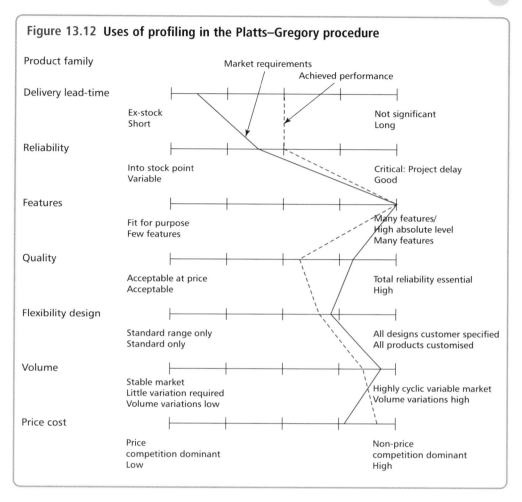

Figure 13.12 Uses of profiling in the Platts–Gregory procedure

different options they have for improvement and developing a new operations strategy – against the backdrop of market criteria.

Like many of the practical quality methodologies, the Platts–Gregory procedure develops a 'gap-based' model for driving improvement. Here the gap is between customers' view of what is important and the way in which the operation actually performs. In this way it is similar to the importance–performance matrix described in Chapter 11. But instead of a matrix the procedure uses profiles of market requirements and achieved performance to show up the gaps which the operations strategy must address. Figure 13.12 illustrates the use of these profiles.

Common elements of operations strategy procedures

The two formulation procedures described here are broadly representative of those available. Yet neither includes all the various points and issues which, taken together, operations strategy formulation procedures address. Typically, many of the formulation processes include the following elements:

- A process which formally links the total organisation strategic objectives (usually a business strategy) to resource-level objectives.

- The formal listing of performance objectives as a translation device between market positioning objectives and operations strategy.

- A step which involves judging the relative importance of operations performance objectives in terms of customer preference.

- A step which includes assessing current achieved performance, usually as compared against competitor performance levels.

- An emphasis on operations strategy formulation as an iterative process.

- The concept of an 'ideal' or 'greenfield' operation against which to compare current operations. Very often the question asked is, *'If you were starting from scratch on a greenfield site how, ideally, would you design your operation to meet the needs of the market?'* This can then be used to identify the differences between current operations and this 'ideal' state.

- A 'gap-based' approach. This is a well-tried approach in all strategy formulation which involves comparing what is required of the operation by the marketplace against the levels of performance which the operation is currently achieving.

Practical challenges for achieving fit

Although it is very easy to argue why fit is a good thing, the practical challenges associated with achieving and maintaining fit are immense. Nor can the idea of fit be separated from the challenges of implementing the strategies intended to achieve it.

A large number of authors, writing about all forms of strategy, have discussed the importance of effective implementation. This reflects an acceptance that no matter how sophisticated the intellectual and analytical underpinnings of a strategy, it remains only a document until it has been implemented. More directly related to our discussions, for instance, Ken Platts of Cambridge University has written about the nature of the operations strategy formulation process. His generic description of the process is labelled the five P's.[9]

1 *Purpose* – As with any form of project management, the more clarity that exists around the ultimate goal, the more likely it is that the goal will be achieved. In this context, a shared understanding of the motivation, boundaries and context for developing the operations strategy is crucial.

2 *Point of entry* – Linked with the above point, any analysis, formulation and implementation process is potentially politically sensitive and the support that the process has from within the hierarchy of the organisation is central to implementation success.

3 *Process* – Any formulation process must be explicit. It is important that the managers who are engaged in putting operations strategies together actively think about the process in which they are participating. Indeed, this final section of the book describes our conceptualisation of the operations strategy 'process'. The three levels of analysis that we propose (fit, sustainability and risk) are intended to provide a relatively comprehensive coverage of the critical issues.

4 *Project management* – There is a cost associated with any strategy process. Indeed, one of the reasons why operations have traditionally not had explicit strategies relates to the difficulty of releasing sufficient managerial time. The basic disciplines of project management, such as resource and time planning, controls, communication mechanisms, reviews, and so on, should be in place.

5 *Participation* – Intimately linked with the above points, the selection of staff to participate in the implementation process is also critical. So, for instance, the use of external consultants can provide additional specialist expertise, the use of line managers (and indeed staff) can provide 'real world' experience and the inclusion of cross-functional managers (and suppliers etc.) can help to integrate the finished strategy.

In the rest of this chapter we will illustrate specific issues related to the two dimensions of the operations strategy matrix (resources and requirements) and then conclude with a discussion of some of the generic obstacles to change that exist.

Analysing market requirements

It is beyond the scope of an operations strategy book to explore the many practical models that exist to help practitioners assess the requirements of the marketplace. There is a rich and sophisticated literature on marketing stretching back over the history of modern business. However, simply because there are many highly structured, rational models for analysing the external environment, this does not imply that these analyses are foolproof. No matter how complex and detailed the model, regardless of how much time and effort is invested in the data collection, it is still an ambiguous and unreliable process. For example, the box on 'New Coke' provides an illustration of how even the most sophisticated consumer companies can get their interpretation of 'what the market wants' completely and utterly wrong! Despite the application of expensive and sophisticated analyses to a market that they had served for nearly 100 years, the Coca-Cola Corporation got this new product wrong. Of course, the episode was not a total disaster as it effectively served to re-affirm in the public's mind the popularity of the original product. Indeed, conspiracy theorists argued that this was always the firm's intention, the whole process being in effect an expensive and elaborate marketing gimmick!

The practical reason for emphasising the problems with this process is to help reinforce the balanced nature of the reconciliation between the resources and requirements. Although analysis of the marketplace is generally characterised by better tools and techniques, in reality both are characterised by ambiguity and uncertainty.

Remember New Coke?[10]

Coca-Cola was first invented in 1886 and since that time has proved to be not only an extremely successful product but has become a global symbol for the United States. Despite this iconic status, Pepsi – Coca-Cola's main rival in the so-called 'soft drinks' market – has also established a very powerful market position. The rivalry that exists between these two huge US corporations is legendary and has on more than one occasion led to major marketing innovations. However, in April 1985, Coca-Cola shifted the focus of their innovative activity from marketing to actual product development and launched 'New Coke'.

In 1979, Coke's lead over Pepsi in the US market had fallen to just 4 per cent – despite the fact

▶

that Coca-Cola spent a lot more money on advertising. The idea of a completely new product emerged after a series of marketing analyses revealed that in a blind tasting, a majority of consumers actually preferred the taste of Pepsi (in a curious echo of Pepsi's own 'taste test' advertising campaign). Project Kansas (as the new product development project was known) started in 1982 under the personal guidance of the Chief Executive, Roberto Goizueta. It began by asking approximately 2000 consumers hypothetical questions around the idea that Coke had a new ingredient to make it taste smoother. Surprisingly, only 11 per cent of those interviewed expressed any concern with this move. Still, the company proceeded cautiously and over the next 12 months, executives toured the United States to 'test new TV commercials' with a variety of focus groups. At the end of these sessions, it was suggested to the participants that a great new formula was being introduced for an unnamed but long-established product. When asked if they would buy this variant, the answer was an unequivocal 'no' if the unnamed product was Coca-Cola. Despite this apparent setback, the technical development continued and in late 1984 (by which time Coke's lead over Pepsi had reduced to 2.9 per cent), the firm's technical division came up with a formula that they felt certain would 'beat Pepsi'. The new version was sweeter and less fizzy than the original. Introduced to the public in a series of blind taste tests, the new flavour began consistently outscoring Pepsi. The largest-ever consumer test was carried out – comprising 191,000 people (aged between 13 and 60) across 13 different US cities – and 61 per cent of those involved preferred the new product. In total, $4 million was spent over two years investigating the exact requirements of the marketplace. The results of this analysis made the senior managers incredibly confident in their new product and the decision was taken that it would completely replace the original flavour. On 23 April 1985, Coca-Cola launched 'New Coke' to over 700 journalists across the States. The CEO confidently claimed that this was the 'surest move ever made'.

The launch was a big news story – indeed it was estimated that within 24 hours of the press launch, 81 per cent of the US population knew of the change. However, the media reaction was largely negative and as people realised that the new product was intended as a complete replacement for the 99-year-old original, complaints began to pour in. In May, 5000 calls a day were being taken at Coke HQ and almost 40,000 letters were received. By June the number of calls had risen to 8000 and a pressure group, The Old Coca-Cola Drinkers of America, had been formed. Now suddenly, the firm's own market research was also providing nothing but bad news. By the beginning of July, only 30 per cent of those surveyed admitted to liking New Coke.

The negative impact of the change began to spread. Coca-Cola's bottlers demanded the return of the traditional formula. People began stockpiling the original and its unofficial price began to rise. In a panic, the firm altered the flavour to give it more acidity but this was too little, too late to have any real impact. On 11 July 1985, Coke executives admitted that they had made a mistake and apologised to the public, promising the continued production of the original recipe. By the end of April 1986, New Coke had less than 3 per cent of the total market.

Analysing operational resources

It can be difficult to analyse the external environment despite the widespread availability of practical tools and techniques designed to help in this process. But it can be even more difficult to analyse the 'inside' of the organisation. This aspect of strategy formulation is not supported by many practical frameworks. In fact Birger Wernerfelt, one of the first academics to advocate a resource-based view of the firm, argued that conceptually we tend to treat organisational resources as an *'amorphous heap'*.[11] As the discipline/function that is in many ways the closest to organisational resources, some operations authors have added descriptive depth to our understanding of the resource base of the firm. Hayes and Wheelwright,[12] for instance, articulated the common-sense notion that most companies consider themselves to be particularly good in specific activities, whereas they try to avoid head-to-head competition in others. They use the term 'distinctive competence' to describe those unique operational 'aspects' through which the firm competes.

Despite this, most of the practical operations strategy models remain based on an 'outside-in' view of formulation. Although resources/competences/capabilities, etc. concepts are regularly employed in discussions of operations' strategic role, the advice available on the central practical issues of precise definition and identification remains limited. More than 20 years ago, US academic Howard Stevenson carried out an investigation into the utility of one of the most widely applied strategy management tools – SWOT analysis. This mechanism explicitly links internal (strengths and weaknesses) and external (opportunities and threats) factors. He highlighted how SWOT analysis was extremely difficult to incorporate into an effective planning process. Nevertheless, the 'strengths and weaknesses' part of SWOT is a starting point for the analysis of operations resources. Table 13.3 lists some possible operations factors which might be included in such an analysis.

Although only a selection of general strengths and weaknesses, many weaknesses (in Table 13.3) are simply a lack of a particular strength, for example having 'in-house operations expertise' is a strength, while not having it is a weakness. But other strengths may conflict with each other. So achieving good 'economies of scale' can

Table 13.3 Some possible operations-related factors in a SWOT analysis

Strengths

- Economies of scale
- Ability to adjust capacity
- Reserve capacity
- Appropriate locations
- Long-term supplier relationships
- Supply market knowledge
- Supply chain control
- Advanced process technology knowledge
- In-house process technology development capability
- Flexible organisational structure
- In-house operations expertise
- Continuous improvement culture
- Effective product and service development processes

Weaknesses

- Uneconomic volume
- Under-utilisation of capacity
- Insufficient capacity
- Inappropriate locations
- Lack of power in supply market
- No long-term supply relationships
- Old process technology with poor performance
- No capability to improve 'off the shelf' process technology
- Rigid organisation or decision-making structure
- No in-house operations expertise
- Static levels of operations performance
- Poor product and service development skills

leave the operation open to 'under-utilisation of capacity' if demand drops. Similarly, 'resource capability' is only a strength if there are greater benefits of capturing extra demand than there are costs of providing the excess capacity. What are strengths in one set of circumstances could be weaknesses in another. It is important, therefore, to clarify the assumptions under which such lists are derived.

Although every SWOT analysis will be unique to the operation for which it is being devised, some general hints have been suggested that will enhance the quality of the analysis.[13]

- Keep it brief: pages of analysis are usually not required.
- Relate strengths and weaknesses, wherever possible, to key factors for success.
- Strengths and weaknesses should also be stated in competitive terms, if possible. It is reassuring to be 'good' at something, but it is more relevant to be 'better than the competition'.
- Statements should be specific and avoid blandness: there is little point in stating ideas that everyone believes in.
- Analysis should distinguish between where the company *wishes to be* and where it *is now*. The gap should be realistic.
- It is important to be realistic about the strengths and weaknesses of one's own and competitive organisations.

Classifying resources

In this book we distinguish between the *strategic* resources that potentially underpin competitive advantage and those resource inputs such as fuel, raw materials, 'off-the-shelf' technology, for which an open market exists. Already in this book we have employed a framework (scarcity, immobility, inimitability and substitutability) that helps us to distinguish between these different types of resources and in the next chapter we will discuss in more detail how these dimensions can be applied in a practical manner. At this point, however, we will focus on one of the real challenges associated with analysing the resource base of the firm, namely how to consider these less tangible assets. Throughout our discussions of capacity, process technology, supply networks, product development, etc. we have sometimes emphasised the criticality of the 'softer' aspects of operations, including skills, knowledge, experience, reputation, learning and relationships. But too often operations strategy is driven by a 'rough-cut' approach to financial accounting which only values those tangible assets that are traditionally listed on a balance sheet.

Practice Box ## Calculating intangible value (CIV)

While there are clearly established rules for calculating the residual value of tangible assets (i.e. machinery, computer equipment, land, buildings), one of the greatest challenges for any operation is to place a market value on the intangible (skills, knowledge, experience, etc.) resources in its possession. One very simple measure of intangible value is the difference between its market value (price per share × total number of issued shares) and the book value (everything that is left on a balance sheet after debt is removed). The problem with such a metric is that it can be influenced by factors that have nothing to do with the performance of the firm (i.e. interest rate changes, accounting procedures under- or over-valuing asset prices). In an attempt to develop a more firm-specific metric of intangible value, NCI Research – a firm affiliated to the Kellogg School of Business at Northwestern University – developed the following method. [In his book *Intellectual Capital*, Thomas A. Stewart has applied the method to the published accounts of Merck, the pharmaceutical company.][14]

1 Calculate average pre-tax earnings for three years [$3.694 billion].

2 Obtain (from the balance sheet) the average year-end tangible assets for three years [$12.953 billion].

3 Divide earnings by assets to get the return on assets [29%].

4 Find the industry average ROA for the same three years [pharmaceuticals = 10%]. However, if a company's ROA is *below average* then the RCI method does not work.

5 Calculate the 'excess return'. Multiply the industry ROA [10%] by the firm's average tangible assets [$12.953 billion]. This tells us what the average company would earn from that level of assets.

6 Subtract this value from your firm's pre-tax earnings (step 1). This is how much more your firm earns (before tax) from its assets than the industry average [$2.39 billion excess].

7 Calculate the three-year average tax rate and multiply this by the excess return. Subtract the result from the excess return (step 6) to give the aftertax result [average tax rate = 31%, giving a premium of $1.65 billion attributable to their intangible assets].

8 Calculate the net present value of the premium [using an arbitrary 15% this gives a figure for Merck of $11 billion].

This is what NCI call the 'calculated intangible value' of the organisation. It is a measure of the firm's 'ability to use its intangible assets to outperform other companies in its industry'.

Techniques like the CIV (see the Practice Box) are important, less because they give us a specific value but more because they provide a mechanism for introducing some competitive comparability into discussions of the firm's underlying resource base. The technique was developed nearly ten years ago in order to help knowledge-intensive start-ups borrow capital (when they had very few tangible assets to act as collateral). With such companies it is particularly important to evaluate intangible resources and include them in the exploitation of their operations strategies.

Obstacles to change

There are limits to the ability of any organisation to fit itself to changing environmental requirements. This is because in any complex system there are certain resources and processes that tend to prevent adaptation/innovation rather than enable it, or, in other words, organisations are subject to a wide range of inertial forces. The dictionaries tend to define inertia as *'the tendency to continue in the same state [or] to resist change'* and as we discuss the practical challenges of achieving operational fit, it is important to explore the sources of inertia. Before doing this, however, we will briefly turn our attention to one of the most infamous recent examples of an operation that was unable to overcome inertia and adapt itself to a new set of market requirements. The company is one we have already discussed in this chapter, IBM, and the specific example relates to the years between 1980 and the mid-1990s when Big Blue struggled to adapt to the world of the PC.

International Business Machines [B]

Throughout the 1970s and early 1980s IBM enjoyed a position of nearly complete market fit (as described earlier in this chapter). The firm entered the 1990s, a decade widely predicted to see a global explosion in computer applications, as the largest computer firm in the world and in 1990 it made $6 billion profits. Incredibly, just two years later in 1992, the firm posted the largest loss in American corporate history – a staggering $4.97 billion! The share price collapsed from over $100 dollars to less than $50 and that same year the firm (with its reputation for staff commitment and career longevity) was forced to make nearly 50,000 people redundant.

Of course, such a dramatic reversal of fortune does not truly happen overnight and in IBM's case their fall from a position of business 'super-stardom' reflected a series of poor corporate decisions over the previous decade. As discussed earlier, IBM's operational 'fit' was primarily with the mainframe market and, although still a valuable and profitable business, the global computer industry was rapidly shifting towards smaller, personal computers. IBM launched their first PC in 1981 and it proved to be a great success, yet as they attempted to further exploit this market opportunity they made two fundamental errors of judgement relating to software (the Microsoft DOS and Windows operating systems) and hardware (the Intel 80386 microprocessor).

● At the beginning of the 1980s, IBM passed up their option to acquire the operating system that evolved into DOS (Disk Operating System), leaving Bill Gates to buy it for only $75,000. This has now entered folklore as one of the greatest business mistakes, but in a similar vein, IBM signed a joint development agreement with Microsoft in 1985 that did not include their new project, Windows.

● Intel's 80386 chip promised to be the fastest, most powerful processor on the market but IBM prevaricated over the decision to purchase this chip. Through this action they diminished their influence over the company that would eventually dominate PC hardware standards and in 1986 allowed Compaq (at that time another small firm) to launch a vastly superior 80386-based machine directly against IBM's PC range.

In addition to these specific managerial blunders, changes in IBM's approach to its 'core' mainframe market also impeded the development of its PC business. IBM had traditionally leased many of its mainframes but in the early 1980s, the decision was taken to encourage customers to buy their machines outright. Although initially this gave a great boost to the firm's revenues, its longer-term impact was largely negative. Their renowned sales force no longer achieved commission through keeping established customers happy but rather through finding new buyers. At the same time, the sales commission on a mainframe was so much greater than that on a PC that there was little incentive to exploit existing relationships to promote PC sales.

It is easy to forget that in 1980 Microsoft was a start-up with fewer than 50 staff (IBM had over a quarter of a million employees) and that despite phenomenal growth, by 1982 the combined market capitalisation of both Intel and Microsoft was only about one-tenth of IBM's. Today the advantage of small innovative units is clear, but two decades ago this was not the dominant logic of business. We will return in the next chapter to the practical mechanics of innovation (and discuss how IBM 'came back from the brink') but IBM's fall from grace provides an invaluable example for developing an analysis of the different mechanisms that cause operational inertia.

The dangers of tight fit

It is almost a truism that any successful organisation contains the seeds of its own downfall. This phenomenon has been explored by a number of authors, most recently by Dorothy Leonard[15] when discussing the relationship between what she calls core capabilities and core rigidities. Leonard offers the following extremely apposite quote from John F. McDonnell of the McDonnell Douglas Corporation to illustrate the phenomenon of success-enabled inertia:

> While it is difficult to change a company that is struggling, it is next to impossible to change a company that is showing all the outward signs of success. Without the spur of a crisis or a period of great stress, most organisations – like most people – are incapable of changing the habits and attitudes of a lifetime.

But why should this be so? Surely success generates revenue and profits that in turn can be invested in the future of the firm? If we explore the impact of high levels of success we can discern a number of specific structural issues that can increase the level of inertial forces at play. For instance:

- *Operations' resource profile* – Once an investment has been made in either tangible or intangible assets, this inevitably influences subsequent decision making. It is fairly obvious how certain assets are dedicated to specific tasks and not readily transferable, but more broadly the whole profile of an organisations operations strategy can create inertial forces. For instance, IBM's vertically integrated production system made them the largest chip manufacturer in the world. This technological independence had an inevitable influence upon their delayed decision to purchase Intel's market-leading 80386 chip. Similarly, the agreement with Microsoft that overlooked Windows was internally justifiable because at that time the software was just a prototype and they had their own system in development.

- *Investment bias* – Operations will tend to invest further in those resource/ requirement intersections that have proved successful. Regardless of whether this takes the form of extra capacity, additional R&D expenditure or staff recruitment etc., investment here appears to offer a more reliable return. Given a finite resource base to draw upon, other aspects of the operation can easily suffer comparative neglect.

- *History* – Organisations become constrained by their own history. Once systems and procedure and 'ways of working' are established, it becomes difficult and expensive to change them. So, for example, even though IBM invented both floppy and hard drive technology, the firm saw itself as 'a supplier of integrated systems' and therefore it did not sell these components – effectively leaving other firms to make a fortune from their invention.

- *Organisational structures/Political forces* – Often overlooked in rational discussions of operations management, political forces have an enormous influence. In all operations there are individual managers and influential groups who compete for resources (see Investment bias above) with their different priorities, opinions and values. In an organisation the size of IBM (in the mid-1980s) the combination of a cumbersome organisational structure (a single hierarchy for the whole business) and political machinations effectively killed off their entry into the PC market. Their first model, in 1981, had been very successful but the supposedly mass-market PC Jr. model (intended for launch in July 1983) was delayed by senior management interference. They introduced an inferior keyboard, scrapped plans to sell it in department stores, missed the crucial Christmas sales period and gave it too high a price. A year later, they dropped the price, sold through different outlets and realised it was too late – their competitors had developed new, more appealing models. The 'Jr.' tag was withdrawn in 1985.

Inertial forces need to be understood if their negative impact is to be overcome. In the next chapter we will explore some of the positive benefits of inertia in developing sustainable competitive advantage.

SUMMARY ANSWERS TO KEY QUESTIONS

What do we mean by 'doing' operations strategy?

Although operations strategy is (like much of operations management) essentially a practical issue, it does need thinking about in so much as there are general issues to resolve before we can do anything practical. The boundary within which an operations strategy is to be formed must be decided. Should the boundary be around a single site?, a single company?, a division?, or the whole group? The answer is largely pragmatic. If it is difficult to put together a meaningful operations strategy, one reason may be that the boundaries have been drawn too widely or too narrowly. The word 'operations' may also cause difficulty. In many (often service) companies there is no such function. Remember our definition of operations, though, those parts of the organisation which produce and deliver goods and services. Anything falling within this definition can be subjected to an operations strategy analysis. The role and position of the operations function may also influence the nature of its strategy. Operations which have a largely defensive role are less likely to produce innovative strategies than those where the function has already proved its worth in the company. Even the physical requirements of collecting operations managers together can be a problem. Often they are geographically spread and busy managing their own operations. Finally, it also must be recognised that notwithstanding our description of formal operations strategy procedures, many strategic decisions will emerge informally over time.

What is 'fit' in operations strategy, and why is it important?

Fit is the state where an operation's capabilities match the requirements of its market. Its operations resources therefore are aligned with its external environment. It is important because it is the operationalisation of our definition of operations strategy – the reconciliation of market requirements and operations resources. In practical terms, most organisations will attempt to make their operations resources fit the requirements of their market. That is, they will start from a market perspective and work through to defining required operations capabilities. However, at higher 'levels of fit' an organisation may start from the perspective of the unique capabilities of its operations and then attempt to leverage these into appropriate market positionings.

How do we know when an operations strategy has achieved 'fit'?

The extent of fit within an organisation's operations strategy can be assessed by analysing it using the operations strategy matrix. Perfect fit (in a static sense) is when all intersections on the operations strategy matrix are understood, so the strategy is comprehensive, there is internal coherence between the different decision areas in that the decisions taken in every area influence performance objectives in the same way, within each decision area the strategies correspond to the relative priorities of the company's performance objectives, and the critical intersections on the matrix are understood and identified.

What practical frameworks exist to help achieve 'fit'?

There are many and various frameworks put together by consultancy companies and academics. Two typical ones are the Hill framework and the Platts–Gregory procedure. Both are market driven in the sense that they start from a market perspective and work inwards towards the operations resources.

What are the practical challenges for achieving 'fit'?

Although most frameworks start with the requirement to understand markets, this is not always straightforward. Markets are, by their nature, dynamic and companies frequently mistake market reaction. Similarly, understanding operations resources is not straightforward. In particular, understanding the nature and value of intangible assets can be problematic. Also, the sheer inertia of organisations makes implementing strategic decisions difficult. In large companies especially, radical new changes in markets or internal technologies can often be underestimated.

CASE EXERCISE – What would you do?

The Focused Bank

It is only three years since e1 bank was first formed as a joint venture between 6th National Bank of Luxembourg and Aurora, a leading provider of outsourcing services to the financial sector. The strategic intent was to become an early-entrant into the exclusively online retail banking firm operating in the UK and Ireland. Although not expected to register any real profit for five years, the bank's tightly defined operational and market proposition ensured that all customers contributed to an ongoing operating profit. In its first year the new bank signed up only 25,000 customers. However, as household Internet usage continued to grow rapidly, aggressive price-related marketing (lower loan and higher savings interest rates) and a developing reputation for dependability (a form of early-mover advantage) meant that after 30 months the bank had passed the 0.5 million customer mark.

Since UK deregulation in 1986, a range of new entrants (building societies, supermarkets, insurance providers, etc.) had made the retail banking sector increasingly competitive. Despite these pressures, the industry continued to generate significant profits and remain highly attractive to shareholders. For instance in the first six months of 1997, the year that e1 was launched, the overall sector index rose by almost 50 per cent. At the time, most of the established 'high street' banks were talking a great deal about the potential impact of the Internet on their core service delivery (see the table detailing average cost per transaction) but most were still a long way from launching a fully online option.

Despite this initial success, the past six months have seen their rate of customer growth begin to flatten off. As increasing numbers of customers can access Internet-based

Transaction type	Branch	Telephone	ATM	PC banking	Internet
Cost (£)	0.67	0.34	0.17	0.01	0.006

services, more and more competitors have entered the market, including, perhaps most significantly, the long-established high street banks. Having established a strong presence in the retail market by exploiting core operational strengths, the firm began to consider how they could build new markets and as a result e1's CEO, Kevin Tilly, hired James Phillips from an international consulting firm to head up a new product development process. After an in-depth market analysis, the decision was taken to explore the potential of the corporate services market. As James explains, there were very good reasons for choosing this particular segment:

> 'Like our attack on retail banking, this is a market with – largely the same – well-established players who quite frankly charge a lot of money and provide very ordinary service. The tragic thing is that our analyses suggested that the big players didn't make anywhere near the money they could out of these customers simply because they were so inefficient. This meant that our core strengths could be leveraged effectively. Several of the key corporate clients banked with us as individuals and in focus groups expressed surprise that we didn't offer our services to different customer groups.'

Starting with a small pilot service (three clients) the firm began, in early 1999, to offer corporate services. They hired a team of eight corporate banking specialists from one of the established players and invested substantial time and energy in defining and meeting the needs of these new 'premium' clients. After six months they had added 15 new clients, 7 new staff and were establishing a new reputation in the marketplace. James Phillips recognised, however, that they needed to add several new services, hire more staff and open a dedicated London office if they were truly to realise their potential. A special meeting was convened to discuss the project and seek approval for further expansion investment. It did not proceed quite as James had expected, as the following excerpts illustrate.

> 'As you know, these clients are paying a lot of money for the services we offer. They came to us because of our high-tech reputation but they will only stay if we build strong relationships. This means more staff and better facilities. Similarly, some of them are hinting that we don't offer the full range of products. This is not a problem yet and, as I have explained to them, with our expertise I see no reason why they shouldn't get exactly what they want. They were very impressed by this kind of commitment.' (James Phillips, New Product Director)

> 'You all know we needed to grow rapidly in order to be viable in the medium term! When we first started, our unique proposition was enough to win us new customers but the big players are no longer as hopeless as they once were! I see this experiment as an unambiguous success and fully support James' request for further investment.' (Mary Walsh, Marketing Director)

> 'I think that no one disputes the growth argument, the question is how do we achieve it? We founded the business on a simple proposition and I think that we're in danger of destroying that with this new venture. What James seems to be saying is that they like what we do but can we change it all!' (Bernard Williams, Operations Director)

> 'you've all seen the numbers, you know that basic account opening rates of growth are slowing, I thought that this was what I had been hired to do, quite frankly I can't see why this is even an issue!' (James Phillips, New Product Director)

Neither Bernard nor James was willing to compromise on his position. As a result, the meeting became somewhat acrimonious and Kevin Tilly proposed a short analysis of the overall viability and impact of the new venture.

Further reading

Cole, R.E. (1998) 'Learning from the quality movement: what did and didn't happen and why', *California Management Review*, Vol. 41, No.1, Fall, pp. 43–73.

Fine, C.H. and A.C. Hax (1985) 'Manufacturing strategy: a methodology and an illustration', *Interfaces*, Vol. 15, No. 6.

Hannan, M.T. and J. Freeman (1977) 'The population ecology of organizations', *American Journal of Sociology*, Vol. 82, pp. 929–964.

Hayes, R.H. and S.C. Wheelwright (1984) *Restoring our Competitive Edge: Competing through manufacturing*, Wiley, New York.

Hayes, R.H., S.C. Wheelwright and K. Clark (1998) *Dynamic Manufacturing*, The Free Press, New York.

Hill, T. (1993) *Manufacturing Strategy: The strategic management of the manufacturing function*, Macmillan, Basingstoke, UK.

Skinner, W. (1979) *Manufacturing in the Corporate Strategy*, Wiley, New York.

Voss, C.A. (1992) *Manufacturing Strategy*, Chapman & Hall, London.

Notes on the chapter

1 Miles, R.E. and C.C. Snow (1984) 'Fit, failure and the hall of fame', *California Management Review*, Vol. 26, pp. 10–28.

2 Based on Karlsson, C. (1996) 'Radically new production systems', *International Journal of Operations and Production Management*, Vol. 16, No. 11.

3 Porter, M.E. (1985) *Competitive Advantage: Creating and Sustaining Superior Performance*, The Free Press, N.Y.

4 Shapiro, E. (1996) *Fad Surfing in the Boardroom*, Capstone, Oxford.

5 Oakland, J.S. (1993) *Total Quality Management*, 2nd edn, Butterworth Heinemann, London.

6 Deming, W.E. (1986) *Out of Crisis*, MIT Centre for Advanced Engineering Study, Boston, USA.

7 Oakland, J.S. (1993) op.cit.

8 Skinner, W. (1969) 'Manufacturing – missing link in corporate strategy', *Harvard Business Review*, May–June.

9 Mills, J., M. Bourne, K. Platts and M. Gregory (1999) 'Competence in a Service Network', in Bartezzaghi, E. (Ed) *Managing Operations Networks*, EUROMA, Politechnico di Milano.

10 Pendergrast, M. (1993) *For God, Country and Coca-Cola*, Phoenix Books.

11 Wernerfelt, B. (1984) 'A Resource-based Theory of the Firm', *Strategic Management Journal*, Vol. 13, pp. 111–125.

12 Hayes, R.H. and S.C. Wheelwright (1984) *Restoring our Competitive Edge*, Wiley, New York.

13 Lynch, R. (1997) *Corporate Strategy*, Financial Times-Prentice Hall, UK.

14 Stewart, T.A. (1998) *Intellectual Capital*, Nicolas Brearly Publishing, Naperville, IL.

15 Leonard-Barton, D. (1992) 'Core capabilities and core rigidities: a paradox in managing new product development, *Strategic Management Journal*, Vol. 13, pp. 111–125.

Operations strategy and 'sustainability'

Introduction

In the previous chapter we mentioned that analysing fit is difficult in most organis-ations because of the complexity of simply describing operations resources and market requirements. If these elements are difficult to describe at any given point in time, they become even harder to 'pin down' as they evolve and modify in a dynamic organisational and environmental context. Yet operations strategy must not only maintain fit, it must also extend the level of fit over time. This represents the second 'level' of operations process – sustainability. In this chapter, we will dis-cuss the practical mechanisms that operations can deploy to develop sustainability – in other words to achieve 'fit over time' (Figure 14.1). We will begin by looking at the 'static' barriers to entry and imitation that can be used to prevent erosion of an existing competitive advantage. These help to minimise the impact of external and internal dynamics on fit. Then, we turn our attention to the processes whereby an operation can harness innovation to achieve higher levels of fit.

Figure 14.1 This chapter examines the second level of the operations strategy process – achieving sustainability

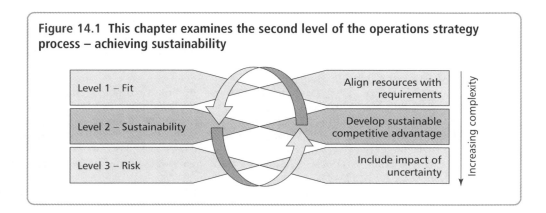

- *Why should an operations strategy consider sustainable competitive advantage?*
- *What internal and external mechanisms help create 'static' sustainability?*
- *How does an operation develop and exploit 'dynamic' sustainability?*
- *What are some of the key practical challenges associated with sustainability?*

Sustainability

Organisations are, in the majority of cases, as mortal as the people who create and run them. Why is this? Why is it that those firms that last for many years are the exception rather than the rule? Returning to our 'resource and requirements' model, the obvious explanation is that firms fail to reconcile the two because, as the previous chapter suggested, it is all too easy either to misinterpret customer requirements or fail to develop the requisite operational capabilities. Most new business ventures fail to make it past their first year. At the same time, history is littered with companies that had their moment of competitive glory and then faded or disappeared for ever. These are organisations that may have effectively reconciled operational resources and market requirements to achieve fit *at one point in time*, but then failed to *sustain* this operating position. And while many other factors, such as macroeconomic shifts and exchange rate fluctuations, also have a huge influence on

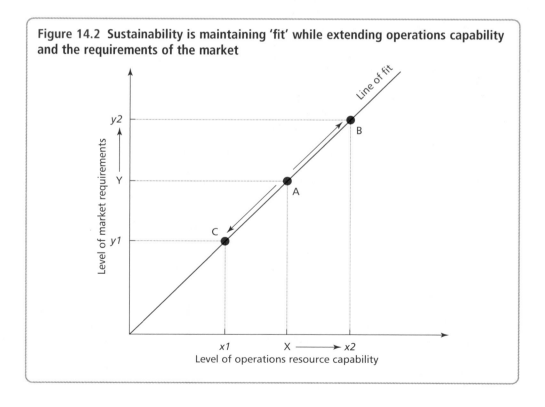

Figure 14.2 Sustainability is maintaining 'fit' while extending operations capability and the requirements of the market

the success of organisations, the ongoing battle to reconcile resources and requirements to achieve sustainable fit is clearly of great importance.

Sustainability is 'fit over time'

Put in terms of operations resources and market requirements, we define sustainability as the achievement of 'fit over time'. After all, operations strategy formulation should not be a one-off event. Strategies will be formed repeatedly over time in order to take into account changes in both operations resources and market requirements. At each of these 'formulation episodes' (which may be both frequent and informal), a key objective is likely to be the retention of 'fit'. Sometimes this will mean maintaining fit during an increase in both operations resource capabilities and market requirements. This is shown as the progression from A to B in Figure 14.2 (moving the level of resource capability from X to *x2* and market requirements from Y to *y2*). At other times, sustainability may mean retaining 'fit' at point A or even occasionally managing the transition to point C (with resource capability reduced to *x1* as market requirements decline to *y1*).

Static and dynamic sustainability

Figure 14.2 presents an idealised form of capability development exactly in line with evolving market requirements. More realistically, even the most successful long-run firms will experience differing degrees of fit between market requirements and their operational resources. The case of CAG, the domestic waste-recycling firm in the Netherlands, illustrates how operations strategy can develop over a ten-year period (described in the box).

Clean and Green (CAG) Recycling Services

With the widespread adoption of technologies like fax machines, photocopiers, laser printers, etc., paper usage for most firms exploded, leaving them with vast quantities of paper to dispose of. Recognising this requirement as a potential opportunity for a new business, 'Clean and Green' began operating in late 1990 as a venture in and around the town of Maastricht – initially targeting medium-sized businesses with a confidential paper removal and recycling service. Figure 14.3 illustrates their initial operations strategy matrix with critical intersection.

The idea was to allow businesses to dispose of their paper without worrying about negative environmental impact (in effect CAG were also offering intangible enhancement to their clients' reputation for citizenship) while also preventing confidential information leaks. As a support to their relatively focused operations, their marketing effort emphasised the quality and dependability of the service. Initially, the operation consisted of dedicated collection receptacles and a number of vehicles (capacity and process technology decisions). Additionally, the firm made special contractual arrangements with paper producers (a supply network decision). This 'start-up' phase lasted for about three years as they acquired a growing reputation and incrementally increased their capacity.

The firm entered the next distinct phase of their development in late 1993. The Netherlands is an environmentally aware society and many people are conscious of the impact that their consumption patterns have on the broader environment. Green politics are influential at the national and local level and this means that many publicly provided recycling services have also been developed. Having built up a reputation with local businesses over a three-year period, the firm was

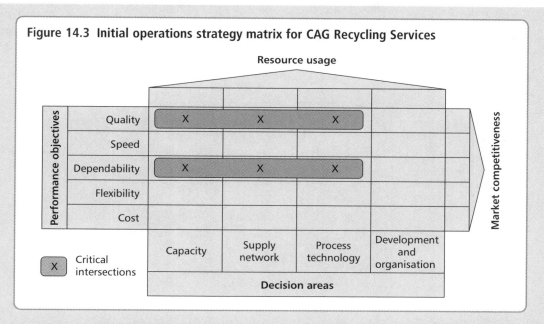

Figure 14.3 Initial operations strategy matrix for CAG Recycling Services

invited by a consortium of local authorities to tender for a domestic paper collection contract. Figure 14.4 illustrates how their operations strategy evolved to cope with these new requirements.

In essence, this was not just an increase in requirements but also a very different kind of market. It required them to collect and recycle a wider range of paper from more sites and without any value being placed upon the confidentiality of their service. They needed to add capacity and enhance their process technology in order to both increase flexibility and reduce costs. After nego-

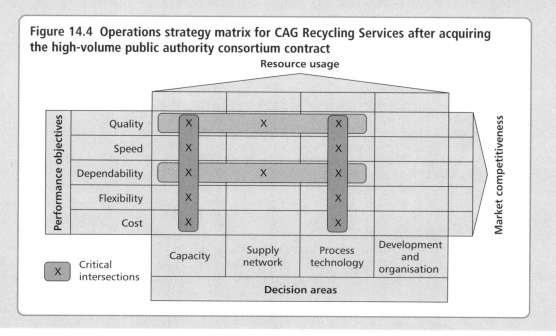

Figure 14.4 Operations strategy matrix for CAG Recycling Services after acquiring the high-volume public authority consortium contract

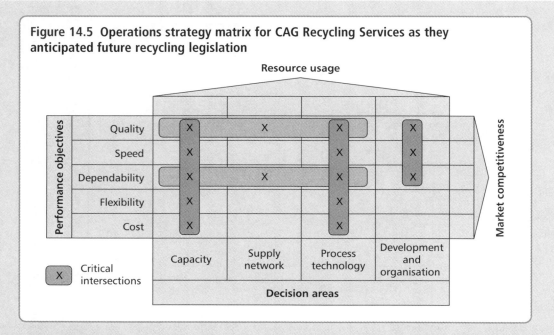

Figure 14.5 Operations strategy matrix for CAG Recycling Services as they anticipated future recycling legislation

tiating with the consortium (who were keen to assist in the development of a range of potential contractors), they were awarded a contract with an understanding that it would take almost 12 months to acquire and develop the requisite operational capability. After the award of this first very large contract, CAG won more public and private work and over time both added extra capacity and introduced other types (different materials etc.) of recycling process. This was an essentially incremental process over a period of about four years, leveraging and developing existing capability while introducing new relationships with other physical recycling plants.

In 1998, the firm took its most significant strategic decision – a gamble on future recycling legislation in The Netherlands and the rest of Europe. Over an 18-month period they invested heavily in a 'complete recycling' capability which allowed them to collect a large percentage of all recyclable household waste. This meant extra collection capacity (vehicles and staff), different collection and sorting systems and new external relationships (including political lobbying). In particular, growth of the firm and the nature of the work meant that significantly more temporary staff were employed. This necessitated the introduction of new control and training systems (see Figure 14.5).

Future legislation was likely to 'require' much higher levels of domestic waste to be recycled which would introduce a step change in market requirements. Unlike their previous experience, in trying to achieve a sustainable advantage for this new market, they deliberately developed capability before the market required it.

CAG over time

The operations strategy matrix to describe CAG's changing issues over time allows us to see how different resource and requirement issues become more or less important as the company develops and allows us to discuss the complexity, coherence and comprehensiveness of the overall strategy. However, it does not fully capture the balancing act of reconciliation over time. Figure 14.6 is an attempt to represent this dynamic process.

Figure 14.6 Fit over time at CAG Recycling Systems

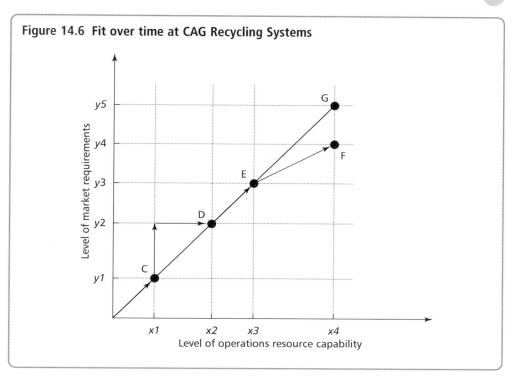

CAG were the first firm in their geographical area to offer a confidential and environmentally friendly paper disposal service and therefore the initial level of market requirement (shown as level $y1$ on Figure 14.6) exactly matched the operation's capability to deliver ($x1$). This 'start-up' phase is represented on the above figure by the transition to position C. Having built up a reputation with local businesses over a three-year period, the firm was invited by a consortium of local authorities to tender for a much larger single contract (market requirement, $y2$). They were awarded a contract with an understanding that it would take them a number of months to acquire and develop the requisite operational capability ($x2$). This transition from points C to D on the diagram is shown as a shift to the left of the 'line of fit' – indicating that initially they had insufficient capability for the market requirements.

After the award of this first large contract, the firm won more and more similar public and private work and over time (requirements shifting from $y2$ to $y3$) added gradually to its underlying capabilities. This incremental growth phase is represented by the transition from point D to E. The next fundamental strategic decision taken by the firm was to invest heavily in a 'complete recycling' capability ($x3$). This allowed them to present a more extensive market offering ($y3$). It was then their strategic assumption (also their active lobbying strategy) to look for the introduction of new legislation that would in effect introduce a step change in market requirements ($y5$). On the diagram, position F is to the right of the 'line of fit' (this indicates that they only currently need to meet $y4$ requirements) but they anticipate rapidly leveraging (i.e. moving to position G) these capabilities once the new market requirements are introduced.

The CAG example is interesting for a number of reasons. Generally, it reinforces the point that even the most successful and apparently problem-free development paths include times of mismatch between resources and requirements. More specifically, it illustrates the two basic models for assuring sustainability that we will discuss in this chapter:

● the use of 'static' mechanisms which defend a given position;

● the use of 'dynamic' mechanisms which encourage innovation and change.

'Static' sustainability at CAG

An operation can seek to identify the *market isolating* (barriers to entry) and *resource isolating* (barriers to imitation) mechanisms that minimise change and act to keep a lock on a specific resource/requirement position. We will consider such approaches to be essentially *static* in so far as they seek to exploit existing market positions and resource deployments. In the CAG case, first-mover advantage in a specific geographical area effectively locked out other competitors. In resource terms, the distribution of dedicated recycling facilities (i.e. specially designed receptacles for paper) proved an effective barrier to entry.[1] The early contractual arrangements with suppliers reduced their bargaining power (and effectively prevented them from moving upstream into this business) and the deliberate co-production between CAG and its clients of an environmental reputation also reduced their bargaining power.

'Dynamic' sustainability at CAG

Ultimately, even in the most isolated of market niches, customer requirements evolve and, as a result, operational capabilities also need to evolve. Secondly therefore, achieving sustainability also requires operations strategy to engage with the *dynamic* processes of innovation and change. Despite all the barriers to entry and imitation that CAG created and/or exploited during their 'start-up' phase, their growth plans required them to enter new markets and develop both related and entirely new capabilities. This required them to actively embrace risk and uncertainty, especially with their later strategies which anticipated future legislation.

Theory Box | **The Red Queen effect**

The constant battle to survive in a competitive marketplace reflects an almost biological view of competition (if you have the superior capabilities, you will probably survive, but it won't get any easier!). Once practical and theoretical discussions turn to questions of sustainability and long-run survival in a competitive environment, the comparisons with biology become apparent. There is, for instance, a whole field of academic study called evolutionary economics that draws explicitly on concepts from the biological sciences. One of the most widely employed metaphors is that of the 'Red Queen' effect.

Popular science writer Matt Ridley describes (in his conveniently titled book *The Red Queen*) how in 1973, Leigh Van Valen was searching for a way to describe the discovery that he had made while studying marine fossils. He had established that no matter how long a family of animals had already existed, the probability that the family will become extinct is unaffected. In other words, the struggle for survival never gets easier. However well a species fits with its environment it can never relax. Although there are legitimate difficulties in accepting that competitive survival in a business context is quite the 'fight to the death' of the biological world, the analogy that Van Valen drew has a strong resonance with business realities. He recalled that in *Alice's Adventures Through The Looking Glass*, she had encountered living chess pieces and, in particular, the Red Queen.

'Well, in our country', said Alice, still panting a little, 'you'd generally get to somewhere else – if you ran very fast for a long time, as we've been doing'. 'A slow sort of country!' said the Queen. 'Now, here, you see, it takes all the running you can do, to keep in the same place. If you want to get somewhere else, you must run at least twice as fast as that! (Lewis Carroll, 1871)

In many respects this is like business. The strategy that proves the most effective is the one that people will try to block or imitate. Innovations are soon countered in response by others that are stronger. The quality revolution in manufacturing industry, for example, is widely accepted, but most firms that have survived the past 15 years (in the automotive sector, for example) now achieve much higher levels of quality performance, reflecting greater depth of operational capability. Yet their relative position has in many cases not changed. Their competitors who have survived have only done so by achieving similar levels of quality themselves.

'Static' mechanisms: Barriers to replication and barriers to entry and imitation

There is nothing really static about any industry or resource characteristics – they are all subject to dynamic forces of varying intensity. However, the label static is useful because it reflects a category of strategic decision that exploits existing market and capability conditions as sources of sustainability rather than seeking to change the operation in order to deliver innovative value propositions. 'Static' mechanisms for achieving sustainability are concerned with preventing competitors from attacking existing market and resource positions, rather than trying to move to an entirely new position. So to some extent, it is a defensive rather than offensive approach.

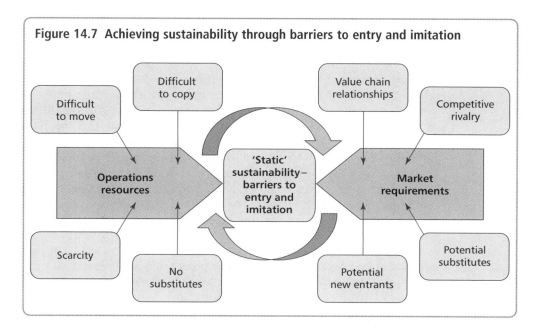

Figure 14.7 Achieving sustainability through barriers to entry and imitation

Nevertheless, it is an approach to sustaining competitiveness which is much practised by many companies. Figure 14.7 illustrates the different internal and external mechanisms that we will discuss in this section.

Internal mechanisms

We have used the idea before that operations resources can be considered particularly valuable if they are scarce, difficult to move, difficult to copy or difficult to find substitutes for. Because they are difficult to replicate, such resources act to sustain competitive advantage by preventing competitors replicating their advantage. The possession of a resource that customers directly value (for example, a prime beachfront location for a restaurant) or that contributes to the production of a product/service they value (for example, a skilful chef cooking excellent seafood) has valuable benefits (customers will choose your restaurant over rivals). Furthermore, if that resource is *scarce* then the competitive benefits are fairly obvious (customers are unable to find a comparable alternative to your restaurant). One difficulty is that as soon as the chef gets a reputation, he or she will either be offered higher wages to move to another establishment, or alternatively might decide to set up on their own. Longer-term competitive benefits will therefore only be accrued if the resource is *difficult to move* (owning the location is more durable than hiring a particular chef). There is also the chance that rivals will simply seek to develop their own equivalent resources. Again the strongest long-term benefits will come if the resource is not just scarce but also *difficult to copy* (if your chef has 'name recognition' or even his or her own TV series, it is difficult to copy what is in effect a unique brand). Even if all these factors are met, there is still always the threat that rivals will simply develop an alternative (for example, hire a newly qualified chef from the same school as yours and offer him or her the same facilities, promote him or her, use fresher, more expensive ingredients etc.). In such a competitive battle, the harder it is to *create a substitute*, the better.

External mechanisms

The dominant idea behind much of the work which has attempted to understand how companies can sustain competitive advantage by defending their external position is based on the 'structure–conduct–performance' paradigm. This assumes that the overall performance of a firm will depend on how well its conduct (that is, its strategy and its actions) takes into account the specific structure of the industry in which it is competing. In particular, the work of Michael Porter has been hugely influential in understanding this view. His distillation of industrial organisation economics into a series of practitioner-orientated frameworks has become particularly widespread. Porter's generic strategies[2] (cost leadership, product differentiation, cost focus, differentiation focus) were treated in the previous chapter. And although his work has been criticised[3] for implying a rigid separation of industry sectors, underestimating the value of being 'stuck in the middle', and underplaying the difficulties of learning and implementation, it offers a very useful external perspective on sustainable advantage. As Porter himself argues, the goal of strategy is *'to find a position in an industry where a company can best defend itself against these competitive forces or can influence them in its favour'*. The forces Porter refers to can be summarised as (a) the bargaining power of *suppliers* and *buyers*; (b) the threat of potential *market entrants*; (c) the threat of *substitute products/services* and (d) the challenge from *existing competitive rivals*.

Table 14.1 offers some illustrations of how operations strategy can exploit both internal and external strategic attributes of sustainability.

Table 14.1 Internal and external 'static' mechanisms of sustainability

Internal	Notes
Scarcity	Scarce operational resources might include bespoke production facilities in industries like petrochemicals and pharmaceuticals, where first-mover advantage often generates superior returns. Other scarce resources might include experienced operational staff embodying tacit knowledge developed over time (such resources confer a considerable advantage in the IT sector, for instance) or a proprietary product/service database (capturing knowledge over time) etc.
Difficult to move	Any operational resource (i.e. process technology) developed in-house cannot be accessed without purchasing the entire company – such purchases are not uncommon, of course. Interestingly, market and societal dynamics have led to greater labour mobility (either intentionally or through downsizing!) and this means that critical skills and experiences can move to rivals quite easily. This has meant more complicated contracts constraining subsequent employment and a rapid rise in wages. The resources that are the most difficult to move are therefore those that 'don't walk on legs' and are tied somehow into the operation. The attraction of any form of interconnection with other resources and processes (i.e. management system/culture rather than an individual manager etc.) helps to explain the increased emphasis being placed upon infrastructure development to retain skills and knowledge etc.
Difficult to copy	Although underpinned by many of the same dynamics as mobility, the relative imitability of a resource is an equally important characteristic. In the hugely competitive confectionery market, for instance (Mars versus Cadburys etc.), there is almost pathological secrecy associated with specific proprietary production processes. Any 'learning curve' effects that might exist in operations (i.e. semiconductor manufacture) can offer competitors a difficult barrier to overcome if they try to emulate an application. Equally, formal legal protection can make systems more difficult to copy, even though the patent application process is long, often expensive and may attract greater competitive risk than simply having better site security.
Difficult to create a substitute	Given all the advantages conferred by the above mechanisms, no operation wants its operational resources simply to become irrelevant through the introduction of a substitute (or simple alternative). Market-based dynamics can help here. So, for instance, EDI-type proprietary connections can integrate customers and suppliers. It also introduces extra switching costs (i.e. if we are already connected to Wal-Mart, why invest in a rival's set of requisite systems'), help to establish de-facto standards and can therefore prevent rivals offering substitute services. Interestingly, the advantages offered by the open protocols of the Internet make switching and hence substitution a great deal easier.

External	Notes
Bargaining power of buyers and suppliers	Operating at the critical point of the value chain can reduce suppliers' bargaining power. In other words, if an operation is a demand aggregator (e.g. supermarkets) and controls access to 'the market' then other firms are effectively compelled to supply. Suppliers are able to exploit similar strategies if their products/services are seen as vital elements of the value proposition – thus reducing the buyers' market power. The 'Intel Inside' marketing campaign is an example of such a strategy at work.
The threat of potential market entrants	The threat posed by new entrants can be dramatically reduced if firms exhibit a number of different operational characteristics, for example if an operation exploits *economies of scale* (e.g. steel production traditionally required vast integrated plants to permit profitable production; utility provision and telecommunications networks had similar characteristics). In addition to economies of scale, *economies of scope* can restrict new entrants. Often it is not enough to have a specific capability; sustainable success depends upon complementary assets and capabilities in marketing, distribution, after-sales service, etc. Of course, strategies aimed at effectively locking out competitors can be limited by monopoly-restricting legislation. As the Microsoft 'antitrust' battle demonstrated, however, the distinction between a legitimate search for sustainable advantage and illegality can be a fine one. ▶

Table 14.1 continued

External	Notes
The threat of substitute product and/or services	The diminution of any threat from substitute products/services (see also the 'no available substitutes' resource category) is essentially an extension of the mechanisms associated with barriers to new entry (see above). More specifically related to products and services, however, if the operation has been able to establish a dominant *technological standard* (e.g. Microsoft with DOS and Windows), this can be a major barrier to entry. This is especially true if protected by patents. Some industry sectors are more reliant upon patent protection (e.g. pharmaceuticals) than others (e.g. commodities like pulp and paper). This is probably because it is more difficult to 'get around' a clearly specified chemical compound than other forms of innovation.
The challenge from existing competitive rivals	The challenge from existing rivals is strongly influenced by all of the resource categories discussed above. Additionally, operations jealously guard secrets to prevent rivals gaining comparable advantage. In response most firms dismantle rival products/sample services to try to establish the nature of the process, what innovations are present etc. A clear corollary of secrecy, the strength of patent protection has a huge influence on minimising competitive rivalry. It is of course a problematic process as it takes a long time and involves public discussion of key elements of the innovation.

International Business Machines [C]

Although business failures are often portrayed as the consequences of particularly poor decision making, a richer, more detailed explanation is normally more instructive. As discussed in the two boxes in the previous chapter, on entering the personal computer market IBM were able to draw on a powerful reputation and brand name, fundamental technological 'know-how' and an organisational capability in new product development. These 'resources' were initially extremely valuable but inside ten years their apparent value had dramatically diminished – despite an almost exponential growth in demand for PC products. The demand growth led to many new entrants producing what were widely known as 'clones' because they adopted the open technological standards created by IBM. Although consumers were initially suspicious, many of these products proved themselves reliable (often at a considerably lower price) and new brand names began to develop. This process eroded both the scarcity and inimitability of critical IBM resources. Likewise, its renowned organisational capabilities were easily surpassed by smaller, more entrepreneurial firms and, as the market matured, substitute capabilities, such as low-cost manufacturing, became more and more important. Finally, as competitors attacked IBM's sources of competitive advantage, most of the remaining value in the PC product was appropriated by Intel and Microsoft, the critical suppliers who owned the microprocessor and operating system technology respectively. Here, even the most strategic resources eroded over time. During this relatively extended period (from the mid-1970s to the late 1980s) it is difficult to imagine that IBM's technical and strategic staff were unable to forecast the changes occurring in their industry. Yet how difficult it proved to do anything about it.

Dynamic mechanisms: Innovation and change

In addition to exploiting existing barriers to entry and imitation, operations can raise their game through innovation and change in order to achieve sustainability. Doing this involves the operation actively moving up the line of fit and achieving a balance between market requirements and operations resources *at a higher level*. There are many organisational theories and concepts that have explored the nature and practical implications of innovation and change, most of which are beyond the scope of this book. But the debate within economic theory about the nature and impact of innovation, involving the ongoing discussion as to whether successful innovation should be radical, is important. (See the Theory Box on Schumpeterian and Austrian theories of innovation.)

What is not in question however, is that strategies of innovation and change lie at the heart of achieving sustainable operational advantage. For instance, prior to the launch of the Federal Express 'next day' delivery *service* (*'for when it absolutely, positively has to be there overnight'*) market analyses suggested that few organisations needed such a fast and dependable service.[4] Indeed, traditional postal delivery pricing models were based on just two variables – weight and size. Once launched, however, early adopters of the service, such as global industrial firms and professional and financial services, obtained competitive advantage from the speed and dependability benefits of overnight mail. As a result, increasing numbers of firms began to use the service. Although rivals eventually began to imitate the services, for a number of years this radical operating innovation (followed by focused incremental capability refinement) proved to be hugely profitable for Federal Express, who in effect had gone to market with an entirely new set of capabilities delivering significantly improved speed and dependability performance.

Theory Box | **Schumpeterian and Austrian theories of innovation**

These two schools of thought echo other 'strategic' arguments about the nature of leadership versus the nature of management ('the entrepreneur' versus 'the administrator'), or the creation of new profit potential versus maximal exploitation of existing profit streams.

Celebrated economist Joseph A. Schumpeter wrote extensively about how certain activities result in major innovations that increase or create systemic uncertainty and introduce major gaps between followers and leaders. In other words, innovation results in the change **of** an operating situation. Although writing in the first half of the twentieth century, the impact of these ideas was limited until nearly 100 years later. By that time a combination of resource-based and entrepreneurial theory had combined with longitudinal studies that identified how *ad hoc* and discontinuous the innovation process really was. In the face of such unpredictable and disrupting shocks, existing skills and know-how can rapidly become redundant and fundamentally new capabilities are required. This process will inevitably involve entering the 'black box' of uncertainty where at least some reliance will have to be placed upon luck and intuition.

> [The entrepreneur] must still foresee and estimate on the basis of his experience. But many things must remain uncertain, still others only ascertainable within wide limits, some can perhaps only be 'guessed' . . . action must be taken without working out all the details of what is to be done. Here the success of everything depends upon intuition, the capacity of seeing things in a way which afterwards proves to be true, even though it cannot be established at the moment, and of grasping the essential fact, disregarding the unessential, even though one can give no account of the principles by which this is done. (Schumpeter, 1934, p. 85)[5]

The so-called Austrian school, on the other hand, emphasised the 'equilibrium' effects of innovation. They held that profitable discoveries could flow from the more gradual discovery of mismatches and gaps in the market. In other words, innovation results from changes

▶

within an operating situation. This is essentially an incremental view of innovation. The 'space' between an operation's current and its required knowledge will be bridged by the internal actions of managers. However, if the space between existing and required knowledge is too large then attempts at renewal and creation are likely to fail. This suggests (albeit rather fatalistically) that in certain circumstances, an operation is doomed (because of its resources, processes and routines) to fail to respond to external changes and threats. In many ways it does not matter if these two perspectives are mutually exclusive or, as some authors[6] have argued, are essentially complementary. Together they highlight the complexity and challenge associated with both conceptualising and effecting innovation.

Learning, appropriation and path dependency

For any operation to achieve 'dynamic' sustainability, its operations strategy needs to address three important issues:

- How can an operations strategy encourage the *learning* necessary to make sure that operations knowledge is carried forward over time?

- How can an operations strategy ensure that the organisation *appropriates* (captures the value of) the competitive benefits which are derived from any innovations?

- How can an operations strategy take into account the fact that innovations have a momentum of their own and are strongly *path dependent* (they are influenced by what has happened before)?

Organisational learning

In uncertain environments any organisation's ability to pre-plan or make decisions in advance is limited. This suggests that rather than adhering dogmatically to any single predetermined plan or goals, it is also necessary to be capable of adapting to the unpredictability of events. And, the more uncertain the environment, the more an operation needs to emphasise this form of strategic flexibility to build on its ability to learn from events. Generally this strategic flexibility depends on a learning process which concerns the development of insights and knowledge, and establishes the connections between past actions, the results of those actions, and future intentions. Moreover, for learning to be possible, there has to be some form of interaction, whether that be interaction between the organisation and its environment, or more internally focused interaction between changes to resources and their consequences. This is the type of interaction we discussed in Chapter 11 when discussing improvement. The crucial issue here is an essentially pragmatic and practical one, 'how does an operations strategy encourage, facilitate and exploit learning, in order to develop strategic sustainability?' Initially this requires us to recognise that there is a distinction between single- and double-loop learning.[7]

Single-loop learning

Single-loop learning is a phenomenon which is widely understood in operations management. In terms of an input/output transformation process, it occurs when

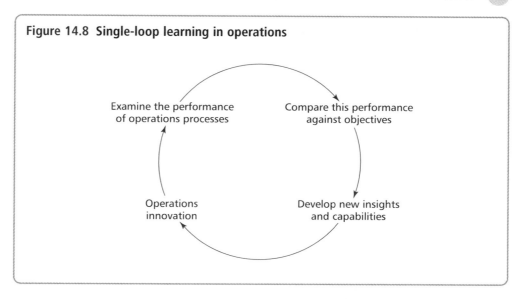

Figure 14.8 Single-loop learning in operations

there is repetitive association between input and output factors. Statistical process control, for instance, measures output characteristics from a process, such as product weight, telephone response time, etc. These can then be used to alter input conditions, such as supplier quality, manufacturing consistency, staff training, with the intention of 'improving' the output. In Chapter 11 we have indicated how such forms of control provide the learning which can form the basis for strategic improvement. This is called *single-loop learning*. Every time an operational error or problem is detected, it is corrected or solved, and more is learned about the process, but without questioning or altering the underlying values and objectives of the process. (See Figure 14.8.)

Single-loop learning is of great importance to the ongoing management of operations. The underlying operational resources can become proficient at examining their processes and monitoring general performance against generic performance objectives (cost, quality, speed, etc.), thereby providing essential process knowledge and stability. Unfortunately, the kind of 'deep' system-specific process knowledge that is so crucial to effective single-loop learning can, over time, help to create the kind of inertia that proves so difficult to overcome when an operation has to adapt to a changing environment. Compare the situation with that of a sportsman. Imagine a professional tennis player in the early 1980s (before the introduction of new materials in racket design) who has developed a devastatingly fast service game with his wooden racket. He wins nearly all of his points on serve, becomes known for his serve and practises his serves the entire time. In a tight game situation he relies on his service to give him a boost. Knowing this, his opponents cannot give up on trying to win service points, but they also begin to look for other weaknesses and probe these consistently. They develop specific game plans to attack his back-hand stroke-play. Then, with the introduction of new carbon-fibre and graphite technology into the game, suddenly everyone is serving 10 per cent faster and because serving is now a slightly different (and slightly easier) process, the relative advantage of his serve is radically diminished. It is then and only then that he really notices the relative weaknesses of his game in other areas and finds that he rapidly

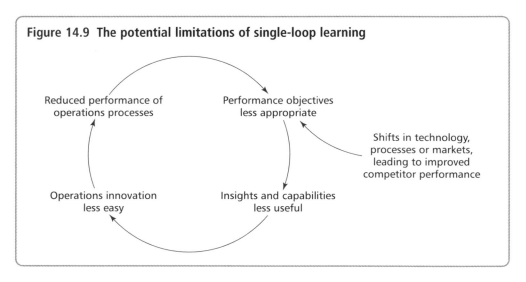

Figure 14.9 The potential limitations of single-loop learning

goes from being one of the best players on the tour to struggling to qualify. In this way a core capability based on single-loop learning can become a 'rigidity' and then a major weakness. All effective operations are better at doing what they have done before and this is a crucial source of advantage. But while an operation develops its distinctive capability only on the basis of single-loop learning, it is exposing itself to risks associated with the things that it does not do well (see Figure 14.9).

Sustainable operations strategies therefore also need to emphasise learning mechanisms that prevent the operation becoming too conservative and thereby effectively introduce delays and inappropriate responses to major change decisions.

Changing the game at Royal Dutch/Shell[8]

It is not enough simply to identify good ideas from the external environment; operations that seek to become truly innovative also have to establish mechanisms to encourage entrepreneurial behaviour. This is not simply to generate new ideas but also helps the operation overcome some of the obstacles to change. Royal Dutch/Shell set out to encourage innovation and change with the GameChanger process.

As one of the world's largest operations, Royal Dutch/Shell employs more than 100,000 people all around the world in a range of mainly oil-related businesses (from exploration and production through to petrochemicals). Once celebrated for their analytical investment appraisal techniques and scenario planning approaches, by late 1996 several senior managers had begun to realise that core divisions were unlikely to meet their financial targets simply through further rationalisation (of operating and R&D investment etc.). Tim Warren, the director of research and technical services in Shell's Explorations and Production division, was particularly convinced that the firm needed to explore entirely new business opportunities and different operating models.

As an initial experiment, Tim encouraged his staff to spend up to 10 per cent of their time thinking about 'non-linear' ideas. The results of this low-key initiative were felt to be very disappointing and this led to a more structural innovation, the creation of a panel with $20 million to allocate to 'rule-breaking, game-changing' ideas. Anyone, from any part of Shell, could submit ideas to the panel, thus avoiding the usual bureaucratic and time-consuming investment appraisal process. Once again, just having money available for wild ideas did not immediately generate much enthusiasm or an overwhelming flow of initiatives. This was the genesis of the

GameChanger process. Under the guidance of consulting firm Strategos, a three-day 'Innovation Lab' was developed to help employees have radical thoughts.

At the workshop, participants were encouraged to learn from innovations outside the oil industry, how to challenge industry conventions and how to conceive of novel applications for extant competences. Then put together in small groups, individuals submitted their ideas over networked computers – a process that by the end of the day had generated 240 ideas. A set of screening criteria were selected, 12 ideas nominated and groups of volunteers agreed to support each one. Seventy-two people volunteered for the first lab and many of those that turned up were people few senior managers would have imagined as budding entrepreneurs. After the success of the first lab, a second one was arranged for a month later, producing similar results.

Recognising that there was also a need to provide institutional support for the ideas, internal payments were immediately made to cover the time of the employees involved with the ideas development teams. Another five-day 'Action Lab' (again designed in collaboration with Strategos) was used to help develop meaningful business plans for the ideas and then after some further testing, a 'venture board' reviewed them. The GameChanger panel met weekly to discuss new submissions. Ideas that were accepted received funding within 10 days and were given a few months to prove the concept workable. In its first two years of existence, about a quarter of the ideas that were given funding ended up in an operating unit. Others were carried forward as R&D projects (30 per cent of Tim Warren's R&D budget was allocated to GameChanger ideas) and others written off as interesting but unsuccessful experiments. By early 1999, four of the company's five largest growth initiatives had come from the process.

Double-loop learning

Single-loop learning is defined as essentially operational learning that does not question underlying values and objectives. In an operations strategy context, double-loop learning, by contrast, would question fundamental objectives, service or market positions or even the underlying culture of the operation. This kind of learning implies an ability to challenge existing operating assumptions in a fundamental way, seeking to re-frame competitive questions and remain open to any changes in the competitive environment. But being receptive to new opportunities sometimes requires the abandonment of existing operating routines at certain points in time – sometimes without any specific replacement in mind. This is difficult to achieve in practice, especially as most operations tend to reward experience and past achievement (rather than potential) at both an individual and group level. Figure 14.10 illustrates double-loop learning.

St. Luke's (see box) is an example of an organisational culture that sought to encourage double-loop learning. It eliminated many of the traditional organisational control mechanisms that can inhibit creativity and devolved both information and decision making to front-line staff. The common bond of share ownership both allowed and encouraged a strong emphasis on performance and altered the significance of the traditional 'pay packet' metric. Maybe the agency was lucky and only really knew economic 'good times' but even growth brings its own challenges. As more staff are added to the operation, can they all be accommodated inside the radical structure? Also, double-loop learning can have dysfunctional effects. Questioning norms and values, encouraging dissent from established ways of working or simply spending too much time 'thinking instead of doing' can create instability, because double-loop is a cognitive process compared with the very

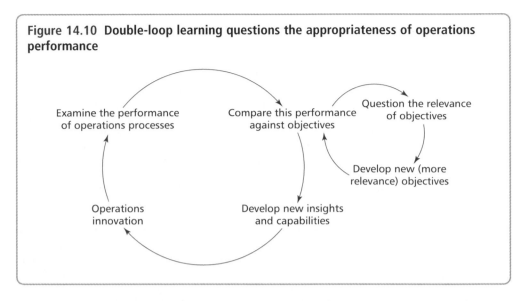

Figure 14.10 Double-loop learning questions the appropriateness of operations performance

practical basis of single-loop learning. In organisations like St. Luke's every decision had to be negotiated and this usually slows things down. Operations with an entrepreneurial culture with traditional command and control structures can move fast; inclusive cultures can initially be slower. Even within an inclusive culture, low levels of trust and defensive behaviour can emerge – especially if growth leads to the rapid addition of new employees. In fact the St. Luke's example may be difficult to apply to a classic mass operation. In an organisation with high levels of staff turnover and where individual staff members have less direct market value, opportunities for the creation of trust and open communication are more limited. Even in a small knowledge-creating business like St. Luke's, too much double-loop learning can create instability as a consequence of over-reactions and over-analysis. The operation can become prone to the exaggeration of small errors and overly responsive to fads and fashions. If an operation (like an individual) is particularly sensitive to its environment and at the same time prone to introspection, it can become difficult to distinguish noise from 'real' issues.

St. Luke's[9]

St. Luke's, an advertising agency based in London, started as a relatively small firm employing fewer than 100 people, but grew rapidly and won a number of prestigious awards. Originally the London office of the US firm Chiat Day, it began operating as a stand-alone firm in the summer of 1995. In addition to being an archetypal member of what has been called the 'knowledge economy', St. Luke's adopted a range of fascinating organisational structures intended to maximise the innovative potential of the whole operation, in other words to encourage double-loop learning. The business was founded by two managers from the Chiat Day agency, Andrew Law (who had been in charge of new business acquisition) and David Abraham (an account director). Chiat Day (established in 1968) had also been known in the past as an early adopter of new organisational ideas – pioneering open plan offices and 'hot desks' where no employee had dedicated office space – but in late January 1995, Chiat Day was bought out by the massive Omnicom agency.

As long ago as 1992, Law and Abraham (the founding managers) had proposed that Chiat Day reinvent itself as an ethical advertising agency that worked with its clients in different ways. Although Jay Chiat rejected this notion, a more limited application of their ideas in the London office was credited with winning new business and Andrew Law being invited to sit on the board of the US parent (Chiat Day Inc.). On being told of the Omnicom acquisition on 30 January 1995, Law was given the classic post-merger job of rationalising operations between their London office and the London office of former rival TBWA (also owned by Omnicom). Preferring not to become part of a much larger organisation (and conglomerate), Law and Abraham, together with their creative colleagues, decided that they wanted to establish an entirely new agency. Although now owned by a firm with vast financial resources, they argued that the firm had no real assets other than its creative personnel and that without their commitment and relationships, the firm had no real value. In potentially high-risk negotiations, the US company was keen to avoid the adverse publicity of conflict with staff in a major sub-unit of the firm they were in the process of acquiring. They agreed to sell the London office to Law and Abraham for a nominal fee of £1 (and a seven-year profit share worth an estimated £1.2 million!).

Although this represented the opportunity to become very wealthy, the two had not forgotten their aspiration to create a firm with a very different corporate culture – one that encouraged creativity and openness. They felt that the ownership structure of the business had to reflect this spirit of cooperation and therefore they needed some form of employee ownership. Although company lawyers encouraged them to adopt the traditional public limited form, the finance director discovered a rarely used structure known as a **Q**ualified **E**mployee **S**hare-Ownership **T**rust or Quest. The new firm was officially launched in October 1995 with employees (regardless of seniority or length of service) sharing 30 per cent of the start-up share capital. More shares are awarded to employees each year but the intent is that the trust will always have a majority.

St. Luke's took care of its corporate governance through a five-strong board (also known as the Quest) which was directly elected by the staff. The Quest, which met about once every two weeks, set leave (maternity and illness), employment and contract practices. Although any member of staff could attend the Quest, monthly 'Flag' Meetings were used for most strategic debates. At these informal and enthusiastic meetings, the shareholders reviewed and rewarded work and discussed new business opportunities. Traditional hierarchy was deliberately challenged at St. Luke's with little formal supervision of work and structural innovations such as having different junior members of staff chairing 'start-the-week' meetings each Monday morning. Although the Finance director set the overall pay growth for the year, peer and colleague appraisal was used to determine specific pay rises.

The notion of the open plan office was taken even further at St. Luke's. The building was organised around dedicated client brand management rooms and meetings about each client's account took place in 'their' rooms. All staff carried personalised mobiles allowing them to be contacted no matter where they were in the building and worked at large, communal tables where no one had a regular work space. At 5.30 every evening, the office manager came around with '5.30 boxes' to clear away work left at the tables. To aid relaxation the building included a 'womb', a round room decorated in rich red velvet where staff could retire to surf the Internet, play games and chat.

Balancing single- and double-loop learning

An operation needs both the limited single-loop learning, so it can develop specific capabilities, and the more expanded experience of double-loop learning. Single-loop learning is needed to create consistency and stability. At the same time, operations need double-loop learning for continual reflection upon their internal and external objectives and context. There has to be a continual balancing act if a sustainable position is to be developed. An operation may even have distinct phases or locations where it emphasises single or double-loop learning. For example, in 1999, J.P. Morgan & Co. decided that they should offer online financial services to some of North America's estimated 7 million millionaires. Senior managers recognised that they would not be able to create the service they needed at their Manhattan base. They would not be able to hire the right people or, within their existing structures, develop quickly or flexibly enough. So a wholly owned subsidiary, *Arrakis* (named after a planet in the science fiction novel, *Dune*), was formed and located on the edge of the MIT campus in Cambridge, Massachusetts. Like St. Luke's, the emphasis was on informal creativity with *'weekly movie nights, a "napatorium" for the odd snooze and a visiting masseuse'*.[10] J.P. Morgan wanted the creativity of a dot-com start-up without the risks of using a small supplier who might eventually 'leak' their innovations to competitors.

More commonly, however, companies will periodically engage in double-loop learning, searching to challenge accepted values and objectives while at the same time maintaining some (single-loop) operational routines. (See Figure 14.11.) Inevitably perhaps, this means a degree of tension between preservation and change. For an operations strategy this tension is particularly keenly felt. The need for managers to question and challenge what is currently practised is clearly important but at the same time, operations are largely responsible for delivering the already established organisational mission. These arguments echo the debate in Chapter 10 on the nature and role of the operations function within the broader organisation (i.e. should it be an implementer, supporter or driver of strategy?). For instance, Celltech, the European biotech firm (described in the box), shows how an organisation's approach to organisational learning can be deliberately altered over time.[11] In this case, the firm made a strategic shift from an essentially single-loop mode of operations – emphasising the increasingly effective *exploitation of* existing knowledge (using and developing things that are already known) – to a more double-loop mode – *exploration for* new knowledge.[12]

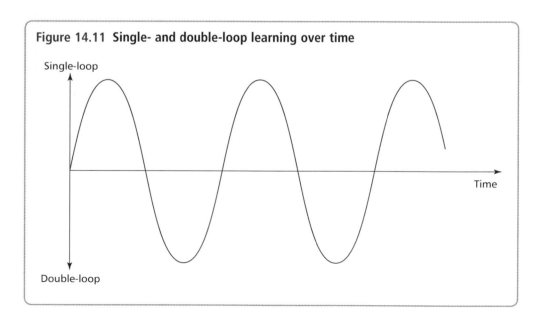

Figure 14.11 Single- and double-loop learning over time

Celltech plc[13]

In 1990, Celltech was a privately owned business and was in serious financial difficulties. By February 1999, it had been listed on the London Stock Exchange for six years and had a market capitalisation of $502 million.[14] During this period, under the leadership of its second CEO, the firm shifted its focus from contract manufacturing and onto drug discovery and development. The Celltech story – and its lessons for organisational learning – can be divided into four distinct phases:

- Formed in the 1980s, Celltech spent most of its first decade comprising two distinct businesses: contract manufacturing and research (the Biologics business) and in-house research and development of novel therapeutic drugs (the Therapeutics business). Although not structurally separate, they had distinct objectives and operational characteristics. The original corporate strategy sought to cover the costs of in-house R&D with revenues generated from doing contract research for other firms. During this period the firm developed very strong capabilities. For instance, in the contract manufacturing area technical capabilities grew up centred on recombinant DNA and antibody technologies. This capability was centred on the *exploitation* of extant knowledge and incremental knowledge growth through (single-loop) 'learning by doing'.

- Between 1990 and 1992, a new CEO joined the firm with a vision for the firm in terms of innovative drug development. The firm was formally divided into two divisions and the Therapeutics division was expanded. The percentage of turnover devoted to their in-house R&D grew rapidly and the intent was to develop a capability in the creation of innovative drugs from discovery through to regulatory clinical trials.

- Celltech's third period lasted until 1996. This was essentially a period of balance between exploiting the existing capabilities in Biologics and the ongoing development of new capabilities in Therapeutics. In particular, this period saw the development of a new collaborative development strategy with large pharmaceutical firms. These relationships brought a number of advantages: (a) expertise in the planning and conduct of clinical trials in order to expedite new drug approvals; (b) strength in the launch and marketing of new products and (c) external validation of Celltech's development capabilities. Additionally, in market terms, the firm was able to appropriate value from its knowledge base before reaching the end market via 'milestone' payments from its collaborators.

- The fourth period up to 2001 began with the sale of the Biologics division in 1996 for £50 million. With the disposal, the firm had, in six years, converted itself into a focused R&D operation. Such an operation requires knowledge from various disciplines (molecular biology, chemistry, etc.) to be combined into capabilities centred on knowledge *exploration*.

Of course, presenting the Celltech story in a linear fashion doesn't necessarily give any feel for the inherent difficulties and challenges as it developed its capabilities. Although both 'learning as exploration' and 'learning as exploitation' are critical for long-run survival, exploitation often dominates exploration. This is because exploitation generates clearer, earlier and closer feedback than exploration. It corrects itself sooner and yields more positive returns in the near term. During the first phase of the Celltech story we can see evidence of this. The firm was easily able to gauge the value of any incremental improvement (driven by single-loop learning) in their contract manufacturing capabilities because of rapid feedback from the marketplace. Exploration is an inherently more uncertain and ambiguous process. For Celltech, feedback from the market about its exploration capabilities is a much more drawn out and risky process. The discovery of a compound usually takes many years. Only one in a thousand are estimated to make it through to clinical trials and only 20 per cent of those eventually make it to the market. The cost of taking a drug through the entire process has been estimated to be in the region of $300–$500 million.

Appropriating competitive benefits

One of the most surprising aspects of innovation is that, even if change works, and even if a market is created for a new product or service, there is no guarantee that the innovating operation will benefit commercially from the results. A critical question to ask in all strategic decisions is, 'who actually captures the profits?' Powerfully innovative firms like Xerox in the US (who invented many of the core personal computer and interface application concepts) and EMI in the UK (who developed one of the most widespread medical revolutions – magnetic resonance imaging) both failed to gain full competitive benefit from their efforts. The issues of appropriation (i.e. getting the benefit from innovation) are particularly significant for operations strategy because, as we discussed in Chapter 6, 'partnership' relationships have become more important. Products and services are often developed jointly with customers,[15] and companies are increasingly actively sharing knowledge with suppliers. For example, firms such as Bose and Honeywell have adopted particularly close relationships with suppliers, often involving exchanges of key staff. It is argued that the benefit for the customer is instant access to 'rich' supplier expertise on a range of current and future product issues. The main benefit for the supplier is the 'opportunity' to learn of 'potential' new contracts.[16] Issues of long-term intellectual property rights can become very difficult to manage in such circumstances.

AutoElectrics

AutoElectrics are a family owned, UK-based business employing 430 people in the manufacture of electrical sub-assemblies for automotive control systems. In 1991 the firm had (at the behest of their largest customer) invested heavily in automation to improve quality and reduce unit costs. In this redesign they received a great deal of assistance from customer supplier development units. Although the changes effectively tied them into this OEM's production system (altering core manufacturing, order fulfilment and IT processes), in the short term it was seen as a great success. 'Work In Process' levels reduced, quality improved and fewer people were employed making higher volumes. In 1992 and 1994 the firm won customer 'best supplier' awards.

By 1996, continued pressure on their automotive market margins encouraged the firm to explore new business opportunities – deciding on controllers for food dispensing systems. The product technology was similar but the systems had to be fixed in aluminium housings. In order to control both quality and delivery reliability the decision was taken to acquire a local fabrications business. The explicit intent was to exploit their lean production expertise to 'bring this old metal-basher into the 21st century!' By 1998, after expending lots of investment on the site, 85 per cent of the original staff had left, inventory and defect levels were higher than before and throughput time had increased by almost 40 per cent.

When examining their operational data, AutoElectrics made dramatic operational improvements (i.e. 60 per cent reduction in process inventory) and yet they appear to have been unable to 'appropriate' these savings. They had some sales growth but profitability has been squeezed (profit reduced by 29 per cent over a five-year period). When asked about this phenomenon, the Finance Director was very direct:

> '[The OEM] steal it! Any real savings that we make are accounted for in next year's sales contract . . . we have preferred supplier status and a provisional three-year rolling contract and our side of the bargain is keep reducing costs and improving performance.'
>
> This, combined with the cost of their investments (their automation programme and later their acquisition), put severe pressure on the firms profitability. More than one industry observer has argued that the firm is only viable because it is privately owned.

For example, AutoElectrics (see box) failed to appreciate how, in a strongly interdependent network of firms, competitive benefits from any capability developments, such as cost reductions and quality improvements, can easily accrue to the firm with the greatest market power in the network. All firms (but small intermediates in particular) not only need technical and production competences but also have to highlight their constant evolution to key customers, so that they are in a strong position continuously to demonstrate the added value of the relationship.[17]

Path dependencies

As we have said before, 'history matters' when it comes to operations strategy. Very few operations have a completely blank sheet (or 'greenfield' scenario) when it comes to options and choices. Current resource and requirement positions act to constrain the future development paths, or trajectories, of the operation. In other words, operations capabilities are *path dependent*. For example, when chemical giant Monsanto first embarked upon their strategy to develop a biotechnology business, they had great difficulties in hiring new staff because they had no pre-existing capabilities for new staff to join, hence no visible career path, no guarantee of

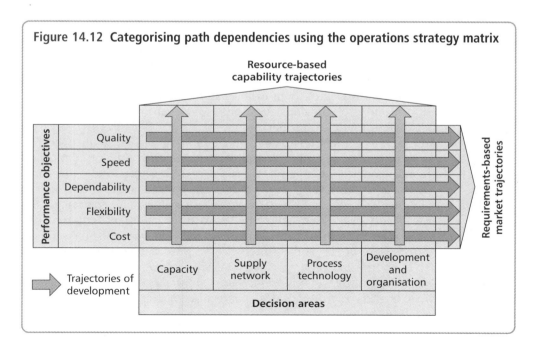

Figure 14.12 Categorising path dependencies using the operations strategy matrix

appropriate facilities, rewards and recognition and so on (Monsanto is discussed further in the next chapter). As we saw in the Celltech box, these path dependencies are not insurmountable but any analysis of the mechanisms for developing sustainable fit requires us to take them into account (see Figure 14.12).

Development trajectories

The influence of path dependency on sustainability is best summed up by the idea of capability and market *trajectories*. An operation may have been pursuing a particular strategy in each of its decision areas over a period of time. The pattern of these decisions will have become well established within the decision-making culture of the operation to the extent that the pattern of decisions may have established its own momentum. The organisation may have developed particular skills at making decisions to support its strategies. It probably will have become used to building upon the learning which it acquired from previous similar decisions. The decision area has developed its own trajectory. This may have both positive and negative effects. For example, a clothing retailer may have developed a product and marketing strategy which ideally captures the design and image values of the time. However, it knows that it will have to act quickly to establish itself in the high streets and shopping malls. It therefore embarks on an operations strategy which includes aggressive capacity expansion. The result is that the company do indeed succeed in capturing significant and profitable market share. For one or two years their skills at identifying, acquiring and commissioning new stores is a major factor in their ongoing success. However, their competitors soon start to adopt a similar expansion strategy and the company find it increasingly difficult to maintain their market share. Yet the policy of capacity expansion is so entrenched within the company's decision making that it continues to increase its floor space beyond the time when it should have been consolidating, or even reducing, its overall capacity. The trajectory of its capacity strategy, which was once a significant advantage, is now in danger of undermining the whole company's financial viability. What was once a *core capability* of the company has become a *core rigidity*.[18]

The same idea applies to the performance objectives which reflect market requirements. If an operation is used to thinking about quality, or speed, etc. in a particular way it will find it difficult to reconsider how it thinks about them internally and how it communicates them to its customers. Again, there is a momentum based on the trajectory of previous decisions. And again, this can have both positive and negative effects. Strong market-based trajectories can both lead to market success and expose companies to market vulnerability when challenged by radically new products and services. For example, Digital Equipment Corporation once dominated the minicomputer market. It was renowned for understanding its customers' requirements, translating these into products which matched its customers' requirements, and developing operations to support its product/market strategy. But eventually it was its very expertise at following its existing customers' requirements that caused it to ignore the threat from smaller and cheaper personal computers. Clayton Christensen, of Harvard Business School, has studied companies who found themselves in this position: '... *precisely because these firms listened to their customers, invested aggressively in new technologies that would provide their customers more and better products of the sort they wanted, and because they carefully studied market trends..., they lost their positions of leadership...there are times at which it is right not to listen to customers...*'[19]

The innovator's dilemma [20]

Both market and capability trajectories are brought together in what Christensen calls the innovator's dilemma, the dilemma being that, especially when faced by radical shifts in the technological or operating model of a product or service, meeting long established customer needs can become an obstacle, rather than an enabler, of change. Christensen divides technologies into *sustaining* and *disruptive* technologies. Sustaining technologies are those that improve the performance of established products and services along the same trajectory of performance which the majority of customers have historically valued. Disruptive technologies are those that, in the short term, cannot match the performance that customers expect from products and services. They are typically simpler, cheaper, smaller and sometimes more convenient, but they do not often provide conventionally enhanced product or service characteristics. However, all technologies, sustaining or disruptive, will improve over time. Christensen's main point is that, because technology can progress faster than the requirements of the market, disruptive technologies will eventually enter the zone of performance which *is* acceptable to the markets (see Figure 14.13).

One example Christensen uses is that of the electric car. At the moment, no electric car can come close to the performance characteristics of internal combustion engines. In that sense, this technology is not an immediate threat to existing car or engine manufacturers. However, the electric car is a disruptive technology in so

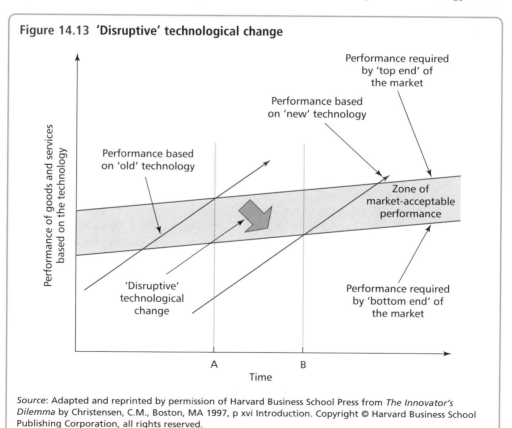

Figure 14.13 'Disruptive' technological change

much as its performance will eventually improve to the extent that it enters the lower end of the acceptable zone of performance. Perhaps initially, only customers with relatively undemanding requirements will adopt motor vehicles using this technology. Eventually, however, it could prove to be the dominant technology for all types of vehicle. The dilemma facing all organisations is how to simultaneously improve product or service performance based on sustaining technologies, while deciding whether and how to incorporate disruptive technologies.

Practical challenges of sustainable fit

In the previous chapter we began to discuss the importance of implementation in operations strategy. The practical themes we explored when discussing fit (the role of project management, the difficulty of analysing resources and markets, etc.) are equally relevant when developing strategies that seek to achieve fit over time. But also two further challenges must be included. The first is concerned with the sources of sustainability, the second with managing the dynamics of innovation.

The challenge of analysing capabilities

The idea of core capabilities is central to understanding how operations strategy can be sustained over time. But the idea of operations capabilities is not a straightforward one. Capabilities derive from strategically important assets – those which are scarce, difficult to move, difficult to copy and difficult to substitute for. But these types of assets are, by definition, more difficult to manage than those assets which are well understood, widely available and easy to copy. Practical analysis and implementation that is based upon a concept that is so ambiguous is therefore not always easy. However, it is possible to highlight a number of critical issues.

- Definitions (such as, *what is capability?*) can be important. As one confused engineer once exclaimed to one of the authors, *'this is very difficult you know, you don't walk around the factory and bang your head on the core capabilities of the firm!'*. Yet they do exist, and identifying them is an obvious first step in nurturing them. While complex definitions of different types of capability can be used, the more abstract the definition, the less likely it is that managers will find it useful. This drastically reduces the legitimacy of any decisions based upon the analysis and makes it harder for the dynamics of capability development to be incorporated on an ongoing basis. Therefore, if possible, keep definitions of capability as simple as is practical.

- Much of the competence and capability literature regularly use the words 'core' or 'distinctive' to add extra emphasis to those capabilities that are *most* important to the business. Indeed the most celebrated of these authors, Prahalad and Hamel,[21] only use the phrase 'core competence'. Their implicit warning is to focus on the very few capabilities which really are 'core' to the sustainability of the operation.

- Articulating capabilities in very abstract terms may capture their essence but can make them difficult to use. Some degree of operationalisation is usually necessary. Collis and Montgomery[22] hint at this practical challenge when they argue that *'evaluating whether Kraft General Foods or Unilever has better consumer marketing skills may be impossible, but analysing which is more successful at launching product-line extensions is feasible'.* In many ways such analyses are essentially forms of internal benchmarking and, as with that process, the greater the level of detail, the greater the cost and time necessary to perform the analysis.

- The level of aggregation in how capabilities are defined is also critical. For instance, while one might reasonably assert that Sony's core capability is 'miniaturisation', this may be too generic for Sony's managers to act upon. Again Collis and Montgomery[23] illustrate this challenge with the example of a manufacturer of medical diagnostics test equipment that had defined its core capability as 'instrumentation'. Such an intuitively obvious definition was too broad for managers to act upon. Analysing to greater levels of disaggregation, however, revealed that their strength was mainly the result of competitive advantage in designing the human/machine interface. In order to exploit and deepen this competence, the firm hired ergonomists and set out to design a product for the fast-growing general practitioner market where the equipment would not be operated by skilled technicians.

- The practical consequences of identifying the 'core' capabilities within an operation is usually that additional resources will be acquired and deployed. This is clearly a political issue within the organisation. It can alter power balances, bolstering one set of managers, perhaps at the expense of others. It is important therefore to understand that asking managers to judge core capabilities is inevitably a political process. In one workshop, for example, a senior information technology (IT) manager was asked to rate the importance of 'managerial IT skills, knowledge and experience'. The answer was an unsurprising 'absolutely critical!'

The influence of time and timing

Because sustainability is 'fit over time', there has to be an explicit time dimension to any assessment of it. For example, firms like Intel and Dell in the computer industry might, at any point in time, possess a significant design and manufacturing performance advantage over their competitors. Unfortunately, in their hyper-competitive markets the danger is that their advantage will be quickly 'competed away', with sustainability measured in months rather than years.

Resource life cycles

Jeffrey Williams published a study of sustainability patterns in a range of industries.[24] He proposed a model classifying capability-based advantages according to how fast they can be duplicated, focusing on the time-based interdependencies between organisational resources and the environment. Nothing lasts for ever, and competitive success inevitably attracts imitators who offer superior product features or lower prices. Yet despite this truism, it is also clear that some organisations are able to sustain the advantages of their products and services for much longer than others. For instance, throughout the 1990s, why was it that, in the PC industry, certain products like Microsoft's Office Suite of programs were highly stable, with functionality and prices essentially unchanged during more than ten years, whereas physical products sold by IBM, Compaq, Apple, etc. could last less than one year? In attempting to explain these and other differing patterns of sustainability, the following typology of resource life cycles offers some interesting insights:[25]

Slow cycle

Products and services in this class (Microsoft Word, British Airways flights through Heathrow) reflect resource positions that are strongly shielded from competitive pressures by mechanisms that are durable and enduring. In economic terms, such resources exploit scarcity characteristics that are derived from factors that are impossible (or at least extremely difficult) to imitate, such as unique geographical locations, long-standing brand reputations, personal client relationships, etc. Although being the first mover into a resource/market position is not a guarantee of advantage, in certain markets it can lead to incredibly sustainable positions.

Standard cycle

Products and services in this class (General Motors' cars, McDonald's fast food, Visa credit card services) exploit less specialised resources and therefore face higher levels of resource imitation pressure. Firms in this position often face direct competition over extended periods of time and this encourages a kind of trench warfare between established rivals (automobiles, banking, branded food, soft drinks, etc.). As a result, successful companies tend to emphasise discipline (control and coordination) in operations and products tend to be standardised for production at high volumes (product/service line rationalisations are common in this type of firm) and are strongly market share oriented. The huge financial and organisational commitments that derive from such strategies mean that firms tend to tread very carefully over their competitive territory. Indeed, efforts to streamline these operations and make them more lean can, if duplicated by rivals (and this is what normally happens!), bring on even more intense resource-imitation pressures – creating fast-cycle markets that they are poorly equipped to deal with.

Fast cycle

Products and services in this class (Sony Walkman, Intel microprocessors, Nokia mobile telephones, corporate financial instruments) face the highest levels of resource imitation pressure. Such products/services are often idea driven and their economic half-life (the rate of product profit margin reduction minus reinvestment expenditure) is typically less than two years. Once established, these products do not require complex operations to support them and are increasingly outsourced to low-cost, focused producers. To maintain sustainable fit, these firms must master competitive routines associated with innovation and time to market. In his article, Williams asks 'how is a 1 Mbyte DRAM chip like a Cabbage Patch doll?'. Both products derive their value from the idea and information content is (unless protected by patents) inherently unsustainable.

The implications for management could seem counter-intuitive for operations managers used to emphasising speed and efficiency as key strategic goals. They include:

● *Determining the correct speed for innovation* – Too much innovation can become distracting for both the operation and its customers. The correct speed of innovation should depend upon the sustainability of the firm's resources. Williams cites the example of the Campbell Soup Company, which during the 1980s launched 300 products in a five-year period. Only a few were successful and the firm had to, according to CEO David Johnson, 'fight the motherhood of innovation'.

- *Resource cycles should influence diversification* – Business history is littered with examples of firms such as many defence contractors, who attempt to shift from their own 'slow cycle' markets into seemingly attractive 'medium cycle' or even 'fast cycle' markets. Their lack of understanding and capabilities in dealing with faster resource/requirement dynamics leaves them with over-engineered products, missed development lead-times, exorbitant production costs, etc. The key lesson becomes, 'beware of hidden barriers to entry'.

- *Look out for cycle time shifts* – Not all changes necessarily drive markets towards higher rates of imitation. For instance, the advent of hub and spoke control in airports gave less dominant regional airlines an invaluable source of competitive advantage over the major carriers. However, regardless of the direction of change, such shifts can be difficult to adjust to and therefore need to be actively sought out and analysed. At the same time, as in the airline example, they also represent major opportunities.

SUMMARY ANSWERS TO KEY QUESTIONS

Why should an operations strategy consider sustainable competitive advantage?

There is really no alternative to considering sustainability if an organisation wishes to survive. Even if an operation's ambitions are not to raise its level of fit to higher levels of market requirements and operations capabilities, it needs to ensure that its position is not eroded. This is, in itself, sustainability, the achievement of fit over time. Maintaining an existing market requirements and operations capability balance is a 'static' approach to sustainability. Attempting to raise both operations capabilities and market requirements through a process of innovation is called a 'dynamic' approach to sustainability.

What internal and external mechanisms help create 'static' sustainability?

Two sets of mechanisms are used to prevent competitors attacking existing market and resource positions (as opposed to moving to an entirely new position). Internal mechanisms try to erect barriers to imitation. Operations resources which are considered *strategic resources* are some combination of scarce, difficult to move, difficult to copy, and difficult to find substitutes for. This makes them difficult to replicate. External mechanisms refer to those things that provide a 'barrier to entry'. This involves finding a position in a market which can be defended against competitive forces. Porter recommends analysing markets in terms of the bargaining power of suppliers and buyers, the threat of potential market entrance, the threat of substitute products or services, and the challenge from existing competitive rivals.

How does an operation develop and exploit 'dynamic' sustainability?

Dynamic sustainability involves innovation and change. Three issues in particular are important in encouraging innovation-based sustainability. These are learning, appropriation and path dependency. Organisational learning is important because the process of innovation involves increasing one's understanding of both markets and capabilities even when they are themselves changing over time. The important distinction here is between single-loop learning which creates in-depth knowledge assuming stable objectives, and double-loop learning which questions and learns about the objectives themselves. Both types of learning are necessary for innovation. Appropriation means making sure that the value of innovation is captured within the firm. A danger to the innovative organisation is that other players in a market (such as customers or suppliers) can gather the value of innovation to themselves. The idea of path dependencies stresses the importance of past decisions on a company's ability to make decisions about its future. All companies will have a number of development trajectories defined by patterns of decisions made in the past. Changing these trajectories can be difficult because they are deeply embedded in the decision-making values and culture of an organisation. Trajectories which are too strongly established can make a core capability into a core rigidity.

What are some of the key practical challenges associated with sustainability?

Two challenges in particular are important in analysing sustainability. The first is that capabilities themselves are not always obvious. Because capabilities derive from assets which are scarce, difficult to move, difficult to copy and difficult to substitute for, they are more difficult to manage than assets which are well understood. Although there are many practical difficulties to identifying core capabilities, it is important to have some understanding of them because they are often the basis for innovation. The second issue is that the capabilities underpinning some types of product and service are inherently more difficult to copy (and therefore sustainable) than those within other companies. Firms that produce fast-, medium- or slow-cycle products and services find it difficult to shift from one category to another.

CASE EXERCISE – What would you do?

Clever Consulting

The Clever Consulting Company (CCC) was first established in October 1994 when four business school finance faculty decided to '*try and do it for real ... and also make a lot more money!*'. The firm was not entirely independent. The idea was created with the support of their university's business development scheme, whereby for an equity stake and some supervisory influence, the university provided the opportunity, continued association with the university name and some basic facilities.

The original operation comprised the four partners, four consultants (all recent MBA graduates who had been taught by the academics), three analysts (recent first-degree graduates from the university) and one person providing administrative and secretarial support. At the start of the venture, none of the partners was firmly established as the leader, they were all first among equals.

'During the first 18 months everything went incredibly smoothly ... the initial proposition was to leverage our academic credibility and functional expertise in order to give us a niche position and the market responded. We began with one big bank as a client but very quickly we undertook two or three smallish projects for other clients

who without exception came back to us with larger and longer projects. No-one minded putting in the hours . . . which frankly were often crazy . . . I guess that in those early days commitment and creativity drove growth.' (Managing Partner)

By the end of the second full year of trading, however, it became clear that the firm's flat managerial structure was unsustainable, especially in their dealings with the university parent and other equity holders. Although the firm continued to grow organically, November 1996 saw the firm enter into a prolonged period of leadership crisis. Eventually one of the partners was firmly established as the Managing Partner but it was not a smooth transition. For nearly a year there was personal and professional conflict within the firm, making it difficult for the firm to address strategic growth and corresponding structural issues. Evidence for the impact of this crisis on CCC's business can be seen in the annual revenue figures. The years immediately before the crisis saw growth of 55 per cent and 66 per cent whereas during this difficult period growth fell to 17 per cent. While apparently respectable, this was considerably less than their growth target and at the same time a number of operational initiatives floundered. Recruitment, training and promotions became difficult and plans to develop a web-based infrastructure for capturing project knowledge were postponed indefinitely. The crisis of leadership was only partially resolved when, in April 1997, two of the founding partners returned to full-time academia in different institutions. A year later the third founding partner retired.

During the last two financial years CCC's revenues have grown by an impressive 93 per cent and 113 per cent, arguably a demonstration of the benefits of clear managerial direction. Unfortunately, this level of growth has simply served to reinforce many of the structural and infrastructural challenges ignored over the last two years. What kind of consulting operation was CCC and what kind did it want to become? It seemed clear that depending on the type of work the firm undertook/received, different structures would be needed – with a range of operational implications. For instance, the more procedural or routine consulting work becomes, the higher the analyst/partner ratio. Consequently, intense competition for career progression up to partner level is created and staff turnover in this type of firm is very high. If staff turnover is high then preventing valuable knowledge from leaking out of the firm becomes critical. Similarly, too complicated a mix of different types of assignments can make capacity planning extremely complex etc. While the Managing Partner had very clear views on the nature of the dilemma they faced, she was less certain about the strategy they should follow.

'I love this business and believe that we have created something special here. I want to build a firm that will still be here in ten years' time but I know that in order to develop truly sustainable competitive advantage we have to get over a number of obstacles . . . Operationally we need to decide what kind of consulting firm we are going to be. I read a book recently[26] *that summed it up very effectively. There is the kind of consulting work that comprises a large 'grey matter' quotient; the work with a large 'grey hair' quotient; and work where the problem is recognised, well understood and just needs 'bright' people resource thrown at it. I believe that we began life as a combination of the first two but over time . . . and with our senior people problems. . . I have tried to steer us towards the first rather than second mode of operation. The future might be different again?.'*

Further reading

Bessant, J., S. Caffyn and J. Gilbert (1996) 'Learning to Manage Innovation', *Technology Analysis and Strategic Management*, Vol. 8, No. 1.

Christensen, C.M. (1997) *The Innovator's Dilemma: When new technologies cause great firms to fail*, Harvard Business School Press, Boston, MA.

Leonard-Barton, D. (1995) *Wellsprings of Knowledge: Building and sustaining the sources of innovation*, Harvard Business School Press, Boston, MA.

Porter, M. (1980) *Competitive Strategy*, Free Press, New York.

Tidd, J., J. Bessant and K. Pavitt (1997) *Managing Innovation: Integrating technological, market and organisational change*, Wiley, Sussex, UK.

Utterback, J. (1994) *Mastering the Dynamics of Innovation*, Harvard Business School Press, Boston, MA.

Von Hippel, E. (1988) *The Sources of Innovation*, MIT Press, Cambridge, MA.

Notes on the chapter

1 This expensive strategic decision was inspired by the successful deployment (albeit one that has subsequently caused a great deal of legal furore) of proprietary freezers by the ice cream industry.

2 Porter, M. (1980) *Competitive Strategy*, Free Press, New York.

3 See for instance Tidd *et al.* (1997) pp. 67–69, op.cit.

4 See James Gleick's fascinating book, *Faster* (Little Brown, 1999) for an exploration of the societal issues raised by the speed revolution.

5 Schumpeter, J.A. (1934) *The Theory of Economic Development*, Harvard University Press, Cambridge, MA.

6 Most notably, Tushman M. L. and Anderson P. (1986) 'Technological Discontinuities and Organisational Environment', *Administrative Science Quarterly*, Vol. 31, pp. 439–465, who observed, in their studies of product innovations, indications that technology proceeds through relatively long periods of incremental improvement, punctuated by occasional competence destroying changes.

7 Argyris, C. and D. Schon (1978) *Organisational Learning*, Addison-Wesley, Reading, MA.

8 For more details of the 'GameChanger' concept see Hamel, Gary (1999), 'Bringing Silicon Valley Inside', *Harvard Business Review*, September–October, pp. 71–84.

9 The information for this example was drawn primarily from Chapter 6 of Leadbeater, C. (1999) *Living on Thin Air: the new economy*, Viking, London, pp. 65–69. See also www.stlukes.com.

10 Quote from 'Building the Anti-J.P. Morgan', *Business Week*, September 18, 2000, p. 64.

11 Source: McNamara, P. (1999) *Genetic Engineering News*, 19(4), pages 20, 27 and 37.

12 Levinthal, D. (1993) 'The Myopia of Learning', *Strategic Management Journal*, No. 14, pp. 95–112.

13 The information for this example was drawn from the following paper. McNamara, P. and C. Baden-Fuller (1999) 'Lessons from the Celltech Case: Balancing Exploration and Exploitation in Organizational Renewal', *British Journal of Management*, Vol. 10, pp. 291–307.

14 It is interesting to note that despite this renewal in shareholder value, Celltech was actually marginally profitable in 1990 whereas between 1990 and 1998 they posted cumulative net losses of £75.9 million.

15 Lewis, M. (2000) 'Lean Production and Sustainable Competitive Advantage', *International Journal of Operations and Production Management*, Vol. 20(8).

16 Dixon, L. and A.M. Porter (1994) *JITII: A revolution in buying and selling*, Cahners Publishing, Newton, MA.

17 See Ramsay, J. (1995) 'Purchasing Power', *European Journal of Purchasing and Supply Management*, 1(3), pp. 125–138 and Lorange, P. (1996) 'Interactive Strategy – Alliances and Partnerships', *Long Range Planning*, 29(4), pp. 581–583 for more discussion of these themes.

18 This idea is pursued in the context of product development by Dorothy Leonard in Leonard-Barton, D. (1992) 'Core Capabilities and Core Rigidities: A paradox in managing new product development', *Strategic Management Journal*, Vol. 13, pp.111–125.

19 Christensen, C.M. (1997) *The Innovator's Dilemma: When new technologies cause great firms to fail*, Harvard Business School Press, Boston, MA.

20 This discussion is based on Slack, N., S. Chambers and R. Johnston (2001) *Operations Management*, 3rd edn, Financial Times-Prentice Hall, UK.

21 Prahalad, C.K. and G. Hamel (1990) 'The core competencies of the corporation', *Harvard Business Review*, May–June.

22 Collis, D.J. and C.A. Montgomery (1998) *Corporate Strategy: Resources and scope of the firm*, Irwin, Boston.

23 Collis and Montgomery, op.cit.

24 Williams, J. ((1992) 'How sustainable is your competitive advantage?', *California Management Review*, Vol. 34, No. 3.

25 Williams, op.cit.

26 Maister, D. (1993) *Managing the Professional Service Firm*, Free Press, New York.

Operations strategy and 'risk'

Introduction

An important element in any operations strategy is the risk associated with getting 'operations things' wrong. At a strategic level, there are risks deriving from a failure to achieve fit between operations resources and market requirements. At a more operational level, some operations are inherently dangerous, with processes which contain specific hazards that can injure employees. Yet operations-related failures, whether relatively minor or completely catastrophic, and the negative consequences of such failures, are rarely formally considered during operations strategy formulation. Maybe this is not surprising. Few managers like to discuss 'downsides' in public, and being responsible for a perceived failure is not traditionally viewed as a good springboard for career acceleration. In this chapter, we will discuss some practical mechanisms that operations can deploy to incorporate notions of risk into operations strategy (Figure 15.1). We will distinguish between those 'pure' risks which can result only in negative consequences and those more 'speculative' risks where things could go right or wrong. These are any capability development process which seeks to obtain operations fit over time. Pure risks need to be prevented, mitigated or, in the worst case scenario, recovered from. The downsides of risks have to be correctly analysed and, where possible, minimised. More importantly, both types of risk need to be incorporated into operations strategy formulation and implementation.

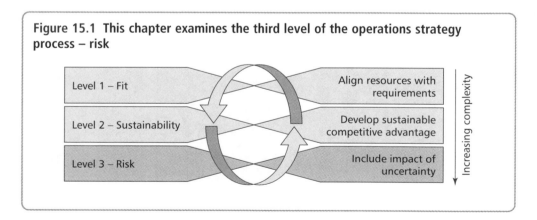

Figure 15.1 This chapter examines the third level of the operations strategy process – risk

Level 1 – Fit	Align resources with requirements
Level 2 – Sustainability	Develop sustainable competitive advantage
Level 3 – Risk	Include impact of uncertainty

Increasing complexity

Risk is an important element in the process of operations strategy

In the previous chapter, we explored achieving sustainable fit. But what remained largely absent was any explicit discussion of the impact of risk. Yet most organisations recognise that operations-related hazards potentially can impact upon their continued viability. It is surprising, therefore, that risk has not traditionally been treated in a comprehensive manner within operations strategy. Certainly we have discussed the implications of making inappropriate decisions within some of the content areas we treated in Part 2 of this book. We looked at the negative consequences of investing in too much or too little capacity, for example. Yet, when it comes to formulating operations strategy it is unusual to see risk treated systematically as an important issue. Partly this is because usually risk is seen exclusively as something to be avoided. And most managers are normally interested in what went right rather than what went wrong. For instance, few operations spend money benchmarking themselves against poorer performers. Yet operations, tacitly at least, accept that learning from experience is critical. Organisations embrace continuous improvement programmes,[1] with a presumption of a cycle of learning and experimentation. For example, process technology is tested in pilot experiments that will (if they are true experiments) sometimes fail. Firms like Sony and 3M are reported[2] as deliberately pursuing products that will be market or technological failures just for the learning they will obtain from the experience.

There is also an emerging competitive, technological, social and political environment that is raising the importance and impact of operations-related risk. For example, when web-based ordering was introduced in order to minimise transaction costs, it opened up new competitive models, and exposed basic inadequacies in order fulfilment processes. Many of the (then) newly launched online retail propositions (toys, consumer electronics, foodstuffs, etc.), regardless of whether they were brand new firms or the online divisions of established retailers, suffered stockouts, delays and poor order compliance during their first crucial Christmas period. Indeed, in any period where technology is changing fast, operations strategy decision making becomes increasingly risky. Similarly, where market requirements and expectations are volatile, general market uncertainty raises the importance of formally including risk in operations strategy analysis.

The risks of lack of fit over time

In the previous two chapters we have used the simple device of comparing market requirements against operations resource capability. Figure 15.2 illustrates how deviating from the line of fit can be regarded as incurring risks to the operation. We shall

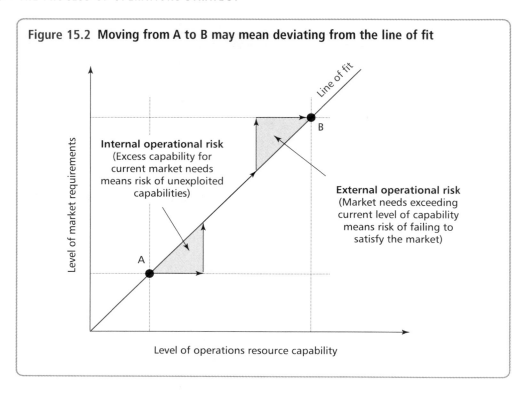

Figure 15.2 Moving from A to B may mean deviating from the line of fit

Internal operational risk
(Excess capability for current market needs means risk of unexploited capabilities)

External operational risk
(Market needs exceeding current level of capability means risk of failing to satisfy the market)

Line of fit

Level of market requirements

Level of operations resource capability

use this idea again later in the chapter, but for now it is worth observing that the less certain and predictable it is for an operation to reposition itself on either of the two axes of Figure 15.2, the more likely is deviation from the line of fit and therefore the greater the exposure to risk.

Types of risk

Before we can usefully incorporate risk into any operation strategy formulation process, we have to understand the risks which operations can create and to which operations may be exposed. A descriptive typology can be developed using the operations strategy matrix. Figure 15.3 illustrates the scope and importance of operations-related risk. Potentially every intersection on the matrix represents a source of operations-related risk. Some will be catastrophic but all can be important and warrant consideration. The box on Barings Bank illustrates a specific incident which we use to not only describe, but analyse operations-related risk.

Figure 15.3 Examples of the scope and importance of operations-related risk

On 2 December 1984, the dependability of production technology and global operating practices became the subject of international debate when, as a result of a faulty pipe-washing operation, the *Union Carbide* pesticide plant in Bhopal, India released large quantities of poisonous gas into the atmosphere. Estimates of the number of people killed range from 3 to 10 thousand. Significantly, the plant did not employ the same technology as that used in Europe and North America and had, since its inception, operated at less than 50 per cent capacity because of declining pesticide demand. The resultant cost pressures prompted managers to cut back expenditure on a range of facilities management practices (maintenance etc.).

On 11 May 1995, *ValuJet* flight 592 from Miami crashed shortly after take-off into the Florida Everglades. A firm that had aspired to be the Wal-Mart of airlines killed 110 passengers. The specific cause of the crash was an explosion (of oxygen generators being shipped for more cost-effective disposal in Atlanta) in the hold but the critical issue was one of negligence and poor safety and documentation systems. Flight refurbishment had been outsourced to SabreTech (allegedly) on cost grounds and the firm had not instituted sufficient quality checks and controls. Similarly, the explosive nature of the oxygen generators should have alerted someone amongst the ground staff, but, most disturbingly, an identical incident had occurred two years previously on the ground in California but no changes had been enacted

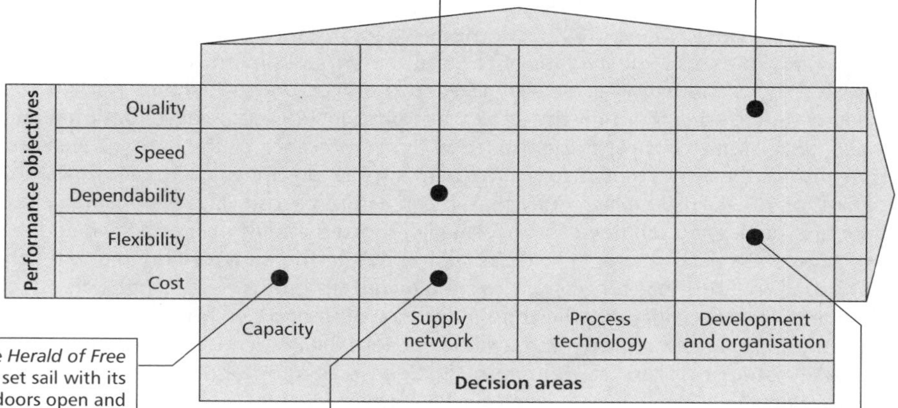

A matrix diagram with **Performance objectives** (Quality, Speed, Dependability, Flexibility, Cost) on the vertical axis and **Decision areas** (Capacity, Supply network, Process technology, Development and organisation) on the horizontal axis. Plotted points: Quality × Process technology; Dependability × Supply network; Flexibility × Development and organisation; Cost × Capacity; Cost × Supply network.

In March 1987, the *Herald of Free Enterprise* ferry set sail with its bow loading doors open and capsized outside Zeebrugge harbour (Belgium), resulting in 193 deaths. The official enquiry revealed that standard operating procedures had not been followed and that warning signals indicating open doors proved inadequate. Central to the failure, however, was the competitive nature of the industry and operational pressure to increase the level and utilisation of total productive capacity (turn-around time is waste etc.).

Nike, the sporting goods firm, developed an operations strategy whereby almost 95 per cent of manufacturing is carried out by subcontractors in low-wage areas, mostly in SE Asia. In 1996 they became the target of campaigns (including a Presidential commission) aimed at improving conditions in clothing sweatshops. The media also challenged the supply chain strategy. On 17 October 1996, Dan Rather and *48 Hours* criticised Nike on prime-time TV and the *Wall Street Journal* highlighted how only $1.66 of the $70 purchase price of a training shoe goes on direct labour costs.

In November 1994 an academic informed *Intel* that their new pentium processor had a minor mathematical flaw. The firm was confident and did not take the issue very seriously. The professor then used the Internet to establish if others had experienced the problem and received thousands of replies! Customers demanded a replacement product despite the firm's assurance that the problem was irrelevant to nearly all PC functions (affecting 1 in 9 billion calculations). The media coverage was scathing ('Intel…Exxon of the Chips industry'). Although, once a replacement policy was established (after IBM stopped shipping Pentium machines) only approximately 3 per cent of individual customers took up the offer, the problem eventually cost the firm a $475 million charge against earnings.

Barings Bank and Nick Leeson[3]

On 3 March 1995 Nick Leeson, the Singapore-based 'rogue trader', was arrested immediately after his flight from the Far East touched down in Frankfurt. Since 27 February, the world's financial community had been in shock after Barings (famously known as the British Queen's Bank) collapsed following the 'discovery' of massive debts. Leeson spent nearly nine months in a German jail before finally being returned to Singapore to stand trial. During this period, auditors, regulators and legislators learnt a lot more about the real life working of international financial operations. Although most of the blame for the crash should be placed upon Leeson (whose increasingly risky and fraudulent deals eventually cost Barings $1.3 billion), inadequate systems for monitoring their trading operations were also blamed.

In 1984 Barings spent £6m on a small team of dealers who were experts in Pacific Rim stocks. This stand-alone group, eventually to become Barings Securities Limited (BSL), made massive profits on the 'bullish' Japanese stock market and underwent massive growth. By 1989 it was returning more than half the entire Baring Group's profits. As a result, the Securities business spawned 21 offices in 19 countries. But all good things come to an end; eventually profits within the group began to fall and by 1992 Barings Securities was reporting a loss. At that time, one of the Baring directors argued that the business had 'fingers in too many pies'. As a result of this poor performance, March 1993 saw the merger of Barings Securities and Baring Brothers (an action known as solo-consolidation) to form Baring Investment Bank (BIB). Although this had a financial logic, this action effectively created the structure that would allow Nick Leeson to get away with illicit dealing until the bank went bust. In 1993 solo-consolidation enabled Barings to make large loans to its constituent parts without reference to the Bank of England, which had a supervisory role with respect to overall banking risk positions, their key principle being that no bank should ever risk more money than it can afford to lose. Large exposures (more than 10 per cent of a bank's capital) need to be formally reported in writing, yet by the end of 1993 Barings' exposure was nearly 45 per cent of its capital. While the Bank of England was concerned about this situation, 'informal concessions' were allowed (the supervisor responsible for this concession resigned after the collapse, admitting ignorance of Baring's securities business).

In July 1992, Leeson opened the trading account 88888 as an 'error account'. An error account is usually used to record sales pending their investigation and clearance. The volume of such trades is normally small and they are quickly cleared from the account. However, Leeson from the outset used account 88888 inappropriately. By the time of the collapse the size of the positions booked in this account was so large that, when market prices moved unfavourably, it caused the collapse of the Baring Group. Funding for positions in the form of cash or securities deposited with an exchange is known as margin. A margin call is a demand from an exchange or broker/dealer for additional cash or collateral to cover that position. In order to finance the SIMEX (Singapore's exchange) margin deposits for account 88888 transactions, Leeson needed funds from other Baring companies. In January 1995, Coopers & Lybrand's annual audit of Baring's Singapore office account picked up a discrepancy in the accounts, so that Barings' management knew that there was a problem, but not exactly where it lay or its size. However, Leeson managed to evade the auditors' questions. Around the same time, SIMEX auditors identified a problem with the 88888 account. By February 1995, Barings Securities was severely worried by events. Up until February 1995, the position might have been recoverable, but thereafter the market fell persistently and losses in account 88888 mounted almost exponentially. Barings' fate was sealed by the absence of either the people or the systems needed to stop the flow of funds to Singapore. By that time the bank was *'like a colander, leaking funds to Leeson through a variety of orifices'*. No checks were carried out when money was transferred from one part of Barings to another. Because no apparent risk was involved, the job was allocated to junior clerks. Also, because no systems existed for detecting fraudulent activities, it was left up to individuals to pick up and interpret clues.

When Leeson had moved to Singapore in 1992 it had been envisaged that his trading role would be limited to executing orders placed by Baring Group companies elsewhere on behalf of external clients. However, by the end of 1993, Leeson was trading on behalf of the Baring Group itself (proprietary trading). By the end of 1994, it was considered that Leeson had become a major contributor to Baring Group profits. One adviser argued that because *'Leeson was authorised only to take large fully hedged positions . . . this strategy should have been . . . absolutely riskless'*. Nick Leeson's fraudulent activities began in August 1992. At about this time, a £2–3m deficit (most accounted for by 88888 account losses) was found by Barings staff in London, but account reconciliation was not rigorous and no action appeared to be taken. Leeson managed to get cash to fund his dealings and, by not hedging his Japanese options, effectively ignored the rules from the start. Profits were remitted to London by raiding account 88888. Settlements staff in Singapore made paper transfers of money to account 88888 at the end of each month so that it appeared in credit and then transferred funds back again at the start of the following month.

The factors contributing to catastrophic business failures have been summarised as a generic set of Human, Organisational and Technological (HOT) variables.[4] Human factors might include operator and managerial errors. Organisational factors might include inadequate resource allocations and cost pressures that curtail normal operating (i.e. safety) standards. Technological factors might include defective equipment and inadequate technical procedures. Using these dimensions we can begin to analyse the particular causes of the Barings debacle.

Human

Nick Leeson's book (and much of the media portrayal at the time) suggested that he was something of an innocent scapegoat for corporate greed. However, prior to his posting to Singapore, Leeson had applied to be registered as a trader in the UK but Barings had withdrawn this application after the SFA discovered that he had provided false information about a court debt judgement. He made a similar false statement in his application to SIMEX for registration as an Associated Person. These and other fraudulent activities (such as his rapid setting up and illegal use of the 88888 account) suggest that individual 'human' responsibility accounts for much of the Barings disaster. However, the bank's hiring, training and operating systems allowed these human failings to become important. Leeson was effectively entrusted with responsibility for front and back offices without adequate checks having been carried out on his activities or integrity. It is also self-evident that he was an amateur in the world of options. Every time he walked to the options pit he was declaring his ignorance of the market. Other options traders assumed he was selling on behalf of a rather stupid customer and piled in to take advantage of whoever it was. Similarly, Leeson's managers had limited experience in equity derivatives. Hence there was a limit to how they could function as the managers of a trader who did not candidly report his activities. It also seems likely that Barings London staff continued to oblige the requests for money from Singapore simply because they lacked understanding of the system used by the Singapore exchange.

Organisational

The process of solo-consolidation brought together two very different operating cultures. Traditional merchant banking operations involved advising clients on assets or acting as sellers of assets, whereas the securities business involved derivatives trading. Derivatives are more complex and therefore harder to understand. This problem was further exacerbated as experienced traders left the company, leaving traditional bankers in charge of derivative trading. There are echoes of traditional 'quality management' arguments about the risks in judging 'performance' exclusively on *outcomes* rather than *process*. The *process* by which those *outcome* performance measures are attained may become secondary to achieving them. Barings' remuneration policy gave directors and senior employees a significant direct interest in the Group's annual results. Group policy was that around 50 per cent of profits before tax went into a bonus pool, which was allocated according to the performance of each product group and the individuals within it. Although the Board of Banking Supervision report (1995) concluded there was no evidence that managerial judgements were inhibited by the possibility that their bonuses might be prejudiced, an industry benchmarking study showed that Barings remuneration levels were some of the highest among comparable institutions in the UK and USA. In addition to the performance measures in place, the bank employed a matrix management structure. This organisational form has many strengths but it can create ambiguities around who has the primary responsibility for monitoring the activities of an individual employee. There was confusion from the start of his appointment over to whom Leeson should report. He initially reported to Barings' London office but after a few months a memo was received from the Singapore office urging that Leeson should report there.

Technological

The Settlements back-office operations had never had a high priority in Baring Securities and resources were not committed to developing the global IT infrastructure that could enable management in London to know the firm's position anywhere in the world; nor was technology applied to the process of risk management. For instance, Leeson lacked even the most basic computer-based option-pricing model that might have helped him derive the correct price for market volatility.

Barings was by no means a 'one-off'. In June 1994, US investment bank Kidder Peabody had dismissed a trader for 'creating' $350 million of fake profits through false accounting. In October 1995, Daiwa Bank accused bond trader Toshihide Iguchi of having concealed trading losses worth over $1 billion over a period of eleven years. In June 1996, the head copper trader of Sumitomo Corporation was accused of having tried to manipulate the world copper market. In 1997, the UK's NatWest Group discovered a £706 million 'black hole' caused by one trader and the failure of their derivatives control mechanisms, and the Union Bank of Switzerland faced exactly the same problem twelve months later.[5] Although it might be attractive to emphasise the individuals who sought to 'break the bank', if we attach too much weight to the problems that exist at an individual level (the term 'rogue trader' suggests as much) more systems-based risk controls will not be developed.

Risk and uncertainty

The Barings story illustrates both uncertainty and risk. But it is important to draw a distinction between them. While they are intimately linked, they are not the same. Risks are the negative consequences of exposure to uncertainty.

To illustrate the difference between the two, compare two electricity generation plants.[6] One runs only on fuel oil and the other can use either oil or natural gas. They both perform the same operational task and they are both exposed to *uncertainty* associated with the price of fuel oil (i.e. this is a variable beyond the control of each generating unit) but the *risks* for each plant are very different. In the first case, oil price uncertainty underpins the operations risk profile. In other words, if the price increases too far then they cannot produce electricity at a profit and the only strategic options are to continue losing money or shut down. In the second case, their risks are determined by a combination of oil and gas price uncertainty and the deployment of an operational capability in response to changing events. In other words, if oil is unfavourably priced in comparison with gas, the operation can reduce risk (its potential exposure to negative consequences like losing money and/or closure) by switching to gas-based generation. Simply having the technological option to switch does not *by itself* reduce risk. The operation has also to be capable of switching between the two fuels quickly and cost-effectively. In other words, uncertainty is a key driver of risk but managers are also able to change the risk exposure of operational resources if they effectively analyse and deploy capability that allows them to adapt in the face of uncertainty.

Operations-related risk

There is no widely accepted definition for operations-related risk. In this chapter we will draw upon both operations strategy and risk management ideas in order to develop some theoretical and practical models which will help to incorporate risk into operations strategy. Before embarking on this process, however, we have to provide a working definition of operations-related risk:

> **Operations risk is the potential for unwanted negative consequences from an operations-related event.**

Once again we have drawn upon the process model widely employed in operations analysis shown in Figure 15.4. Except in this case an operations event is transformed into an outcome with negative consequences.

Although the operations strategy matrix and the HOT factors provide us with a useful starting point for reviewing the specific pathology of an operational failure, they represent an incomplete categorisation of operations strategy-related risks.

Pure and speculative risk

A useful distinction is that between *pure* risks, involving events that will produce the possibility only of loss, and *speculative* risks that emerge from competitive scenarios and hold the potential for loss or gain. A pure risk might be the risk that, while testing blood samples for HIV, a technician at a medical laboratory is involved in an

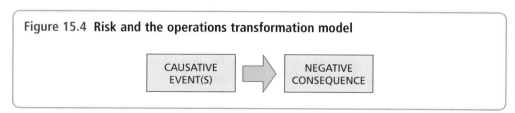

Figure 15.4 Risk and the operations transformation model

CAUSATIVE EVENT(S) → NEGATIVE CONSEQUENCE

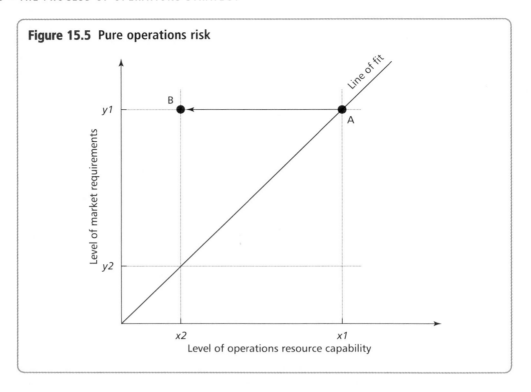

Figure 15.5 Pure operations risk

accident that leads to possible infection. A speculative risk might be the risk associated with developing a new computer-based diagnostics and information infrastructure to enable the laboratory to offer a range of profitable new services. The risk here is that the technology may not work (or not work on time or in budget) or that the market will not want to pay for the new services.

Pure risk

Pure operations-related failures include incidents (often the 'newsworthy' disasters) such as pollution, transportation failures, computer systems breakdowns and industrial accidents. In Figure 15.5 an operation (A) with capability ($x1$) satisfies a specific level of market requirement ($y1$). Following an operational failure (such as a chemical spill shutting a factory), the effective level of operational capability is radically reduced ($x2$). This leaves the firm at position B, incapable of satisfying its market requirement by an amount ($y1$-$y2$).

Such an operation is left facing the prospect of substantial losses and, in the case of a chemical spill, possible regulatory investigation. Although compliance with regulatory requirements is expensive and time-consuming, failure to comply can create significant pure risks such as legal and financial liabilities. Operations that are proven to be somehow negligent may also face massive compensation claims. For example, a Boeing employee who suffered from Repetitive Motion Disorders stemming from a poorly designed operating environment was awarded $1.6 million in damages.

Take a tablet and a glass of water ...

Two infamous examples illustrate both the seriousness and vulnerability of operations to 'pure' risks. For both Tylenol and Perrier, unexplained contamination had disastrous consequences.

Tylenol

On 29 September 1982, three people died in the US after consuming cyanide-contaminated Tylenol capsules. Testing and the discovery of further strychnine-laced capsules led *Johnson & Johnson* to recall 31 million products at a cost of over $100 million. Although sabotage was suspected, no one was charged and J&J brought the product back to market with tamper-proof packaging. Their response was lauded as a successful case of crisis management (market share regained in eight months). In February 1986, cyanide-laced Tylenol killed another woman and led to the discovery of more contaminated bottles. These were traced back to specific production facilities and another recall followed. Control systems were clearly incapable of preventing such incidents and therefore the capsule form was abandoned. These recall and retooling costs were estimated at over $150 million.

Perrier

In 1990, sparkling mineral water producer *Perrier* ordered a product recall as reports of benzene contamination emerged. To compound the problem, explanations of the source of the benzene differed: Perrier (US) reported it was an exclusively North American issue; Perrier (France) stated the source was a cleaning fluid used on the US bottling line; Perrier (UK) said they had no idea. Three days after the French announcement, it was established that the contamination had been caused by a failure to replace charcoal filters in the technology used to process source water. This failure proved to be a significant source of advantage for Perrier's rivals who rapidly gained much more market share.

Curiously, despite its much more serious human health implications, Johnson & Johnson's positive and open response to the Tylenol crisis did little long-term damage to the product or the parent brand and in the end came to be recognised as an example of crisis management 'best practice'. Conversely, the Perrier incident resulted in little actual harm to people but perhaps as a result of their confused and secretive corporate reaction, US consumer opinion swung against the brand and their previously dramatic growth profile came grinding to a halt! Not long after the incident, Swiss food giant Nestlé acquired the firm.

Speculative risk

Operations capabilities are a critical component in a firm's competitive advantage. However, when operations become central to strategic aspirations, then a range of associated 'speculative' risks emerge. Consider the capacity strategy decision in the semiconductor sector (mentioned in Chapter 4). A typical-sized 'fab' (fabrication) facility will cost nearly $2 billion yet the product it manufactures might be obsolete in three or four years' time. Or consider the product development process in the pharmaceutical industry. For every drug like Prozac earning billions of dollars per year, 50 per cent of new drugs make only $100 million, while the average cost of taking a drug through all of its developmental and trial phases is something like $300 million. Again, look at the generic representation of fit between capabilities and requirements in Figure 15.6.

An operation (at position C) that has achieved fit with its marketplace has the operational capability ($x3$) to meet a specific market requirement ($y3$). As market requirements (for example, product quality performance) shift ($y4$), the operation must

Figure 15.6 Speculative operations-related risk

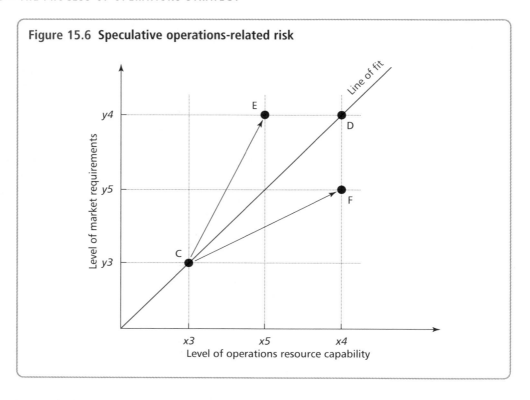

invest (*x4*) in its operations capability, in order to retain this level of fit (D). It might achieve this capability development by installing new process technology or investing in new quality control systems and staff training. This process raises speculative risks that the firm fails to meet these objectives and instead achieves a lower level of capability (*x5*) which positions it at (E). Alternatively, the firm predicts a certain market requirement (*y4*), successfully develops the capability (*x4*) to achieve fit (D) but discovers that the market has not moved as far as predicted (*y5*). In this case, the firm has an 'excess' level of capability (F). Although this might seem less serious, it involves opportunity costs, under-utilisation, potentially restricted flexibility, and so on.

Monsanto: Building capabilities for the future?

The Monsanto Chemical Works was formed to manufacture saccharin (an artificial sweetener) in 1901 in St. Louis, Missouri and by 1995 had grown to become the third-largest chemical firm in the US and the 145th-largest industrial company). An agriculture division was formed in the 1960s focused on inorganic fertilisers and plant growth regulators. Herbicides were a major part of Monsanto's success during the 1970s, with products like Lasso and Roundup – the latter going on to become the world's largest-selling herbicide. During the late 1970s, most commodity chemical producers were facing unprecedented international competition, much tougher domestic environmental legislation and the energy crisis. As a result, many of them began the search for higher-margin and patent-protected products. John Hanley became CEO of Monsanto in 1972, in the same year that the firm abandoned saccharin production because of intense Japanese competition. Encouraged by Ernest Jaworski of the Agricultural Products Division, he began to look seriously at the possibilities of cellular and molecular biology. In 1973, Jaworski received approval from the general manager of the agriculture company to go ahead with a project (staffed by about 35 scientists) to investigate the creation of plants with innate herbicide resistance. Jaworski himself saw this as the beginning of a much more ambitious project to develop new 'genetic' capabilities that would create true value for consumers and help Monsanto build new and sustainable sources of competitive advantage. Despite Jaworski's vision and Hanley's support, the biotechnology strategy was, until 1979, continuously at risk when competing with other research projects – often with nearer-term and more definite paybacks! In 1979, however, Howard Schneiderman (formerly Dean of Biological Sciences at the University of California at Irvine) was persuaded to join the firm as Vice-President for Research and Development. Together, Jaworski and Schneiderman set about realising CEO Hanley's vision of making Monsanto a world force in biotechnology in 5–10 years.

This was not straightforward. Without a strong reputation in the field, or the security of tenure of a faculty member, or the share options of a start-up venture, many scientists were reluctant to join the firm. Eventually, however, with assurances of cutting-edge research themes, long-term projects and continuous funding, Monsanto was able gradually to develop an internal R&D capability. Schneiderman realised that this was not quick enough and supported this process through a licensing agreement with Genentech. This firm had expertise in growth hormones and Jaworski was convinced that this collaboration would speed Monsanto's progress towards commercial applications of cow and pig growth hormones. In 1983, after preliminary safety and efficacy tests, Monsanto decided to develop a large-scale production process for bovine somatotropin (BST). Effective application of BST can increase the efficiency with which dairy cows convert feed into milk by about 10 to 25 per cent. Progress in animal agriculture was paralleled by progress in plant agriculture. In 1982, Jaworski's group performed the first genetic modification of a plant cell and by 1985 the group had genetically modified crops to resist the Roundup herbicide. Such a modified crop would allow for in-crop spraying of herbicide, removing the need (and diminishing the market) for different in-crop herbicides that are arguably more harmful to the environment.

The final element of Monsanto's biotechnology progress was in the area of human health and pharmaceuticals. Proteins could be produced in quantity for use in drugs such as insulin or interferon. In 1982, a Health Care Division was created to prepare the way for the acquisition of a pharmaceutical company. Like with the Genetech collaboration, this strategy recognised that internal capability development needed to coexist with the integration of external skills. Schneiderman argued: *'unless you build internal capabilities, you don't know the right price for technology that you acquire from the outside. You don't know whether a discovery is significant or durable or whether it is ephemeral.'* In 1985, G.D. Searle was bought for $2.7 billion (the price, at 5.5 times book value and 19 times earnings, was argued by some analysts to be over the top). This acquisition brought access to an already established distribution system. In addition they had to buy the NutraSweet brand artificial sweetener – managed at that time by Bob Shapiro. By the end of 1985, Monsanto as a corporation produced (and was organised around) a range of high-value agricultural products (including herbicides and seeds), industrial chemicals (including plastics and fibres), pharmaceuticals and food products. Although their diversity of product markets left Wall Street unsure of their overall corporate direction, the then CEO Richard J. Mahoney insisted that '*R&D wasn't part of the strategy, R&D was the strategy!*'.

Over the next decade, through further development and leveraging of R&D and an active acquisition and partnership strategy, Monsanto (now under the leadership of Bob Shapiro) developed what was arguably the most advanced technology capability for the production of genetically modified crops. In late 1998, analysts once again forecast a rosy future for a firm that had promised much over many years but too often disappointed. Unfortunately, 1999 was the year they became the subject of a global campaign by a variety of environmental pressure groups. The *New Yorker* (10 April 2000) quoted one of the firms opponents as saying 'this is about power…if you want to introduce new technology, you…are going to have to go through us. And if we don't approve, we are going to bring you down'. Only a few of the firms that invested heavily in genetic modification (GM) were subject to the same intense external scrutiny as Monsanto. The press-

▶

ure group Greenpeace deliberately selected them for their 'anti-GM' campaign and in doing so effectively increased media and consumer interest and thereby political interest in consumers. Interviewed in the *New Yorker*, Lord Melchett of Greenpeace argued *'Monsanto...is no worse than DuPont. But DuPont can survive without genetically modified organisms, and I don't think Monsanto can. So we have had an opportunity with them that we did not have with anyone else.'*

Risk at Monsanto

By December 1999, Monsanto announced that it was to merge with Pharmacia and Upjohn. Its share price had fallen from a high of $63 to $35. Arguments about technological endeavour, triggered in a Europe reeling from food and health scares, had overwhelmed the firm. As we can see from this example, the notion of speculative risk is very closely attuned to our idea of balancing market requirements and operational capabilities. Monsanto focused all their attention on the development of world-class capabilities – indeed they were recognised by several management academics as being very effective at this.[7] Look at Figure 15.7. Between 1985 and 1998, Monsanto continued to extend its capabilities (shifting $x6 \rightarrow x7$). In attempting to redefine an industry, they accepted that current market conditions (environmental legislation relating to traditional pesticides etc.) might mean that they were ahead of key customer requirements and that over time not all of the potential products generated would realise market value. In effect the firm accepted operations-related risk by committing investment to the development of 'excess' capability. Their intent was increasingly to leverage this capability (shifting from position G $\rightarrow$ H).

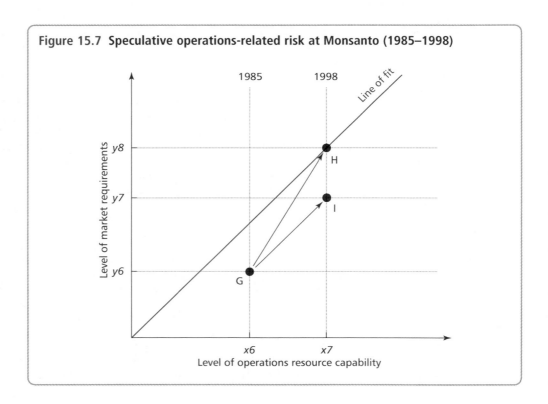

Figure 15.7 Speculative operations-related risk at Monsanto (1985–1998)

Monsanto quickly discovered that although some specific markets recognised the value of their genetically modified products ($y8$), with sales to US farmers for instance growing rapidly, the general 'end consumer' market had not moved as far ($y7$). They had only moved to position I. In many ways it seemed that the firm had not even considered this 'customer's customer' perspective. This is somewhat surprising given how well aware they were of the need to develop a positive reputation amongst the scientific community. Perhaps the fact that the firm had faced similar controversies in the early 1990s (over a growth hormone in milk production) led them to believe that the consumer and media interest would simply fade away after a while. Whatever the explanation, the collapse in the share price was a market recognition that if little value could be realised from all of their capabilities, it was not worth the risk of being in position I.

Pure and speculative risk as a continuum

The Monsanto example offers a good illustration of how pure and speculative risk exist on a continuum. Monsanto saw themselves as engaged in speculative (capability-developing) risk taking. However, it was this very process that triggered the pressure group campaigns which quickly became a pure risk. This is not uncommon. The competitive pressure to bring products and processes to market quickly (speculative risk) increases the potential for direct market and product failure (pure risks). So, in the mid-1970s as the breast implant market boomed, *Dow Corning* rapidly developed a silicone-based implant. By the 1980s anecdotal evidence of health problems led to a series of legal actions, by 1992 the US authorities blocked further sales and the firm halted production. By late 1994, the firm still faced thousands of lawsuits that eventually cost $3.2 billion to settle. Although the firm manufactured almost 5000 other products, in 1995 it was forced to file for bankruptcy reorganisation.

Cognition, context and control

Taking a 'risk' perspective on the process of operations strategy both adds a greater richness to the formulation activity and allows us to judge operations performance from a more realistic standpoint. But individual managers will often see risk in different ways. They will also attempt to manage it in different ways. To understand possible responses to risk in operations strategy we need to consider three sets of factors.

First, an operations strategy must consider how the real 'actors' in the operations (managers and staff, as well as current and potential customers, regulators, etc.) view risk. It is their *cognition* of risk which is significant because individuals do not always deal with risk in a rational manner.

Second, our perception of risk is strongly influenced by its business *context*. Therefore the internal (operations system) and external (customer and stakeholder) circumstances must be taken into account.

Third, because by definition a risk is something with unwanted consequences, it is something that we normally seek to *control*. However, the control of risk covers a range of different strategies, including prevention, mitigation and, at worst, failure recovery.

Risk cognition

Few operations are strangers to the process of risk assessment. It is increasingly a formal exercise that is carried out using standard frameworks and prompted by health and safety concerns, environmental regulations, and so on. These frameworks are similar to the formal quality inspection methods associated with quality standards like ISO 9000. They bring with them an implicit assumption of unbiased objectivity. However, individual attitudes to risk are complex and subject to a wide variety of biases and influences. For instance, in his book *Managing Technological Innovation* John Ettlie references what he describes as a little known but interesting empirical study into risk aversion amongst managers.[8] Figure 15.8 shows a simplified representation of the results, with larger scores on the vertical axis representing greater risk aversion.

It was found that older managers would be more risk averse (line A). However, closer analysis of the data revealed the more interesting result (line B). Risk aversion decreased sharply until about 35 but then levelled off until about 50 when risk aversion set in again. The study,[9] while somewhat dated (and drawing on an entirely male sample population), still offers interesting insight into the relationships that exist between risk cognition and the individual.

In fact many studies have demonstrated that people are generally very poor at making risk-related judgements. As an everyday illustration of this, consider the success of state and national lotteries. In nearly every case, the chances of winning (the benefits) are extraordinarily low, and the costs of playing sufficiently significant, to make the financial value of the investment entirely negative. If we broaden the analysis further, then participation can begin to seem foolhardy. For example, if players have to drive their car in order to purchase a ticket, they may be more likely to be killed or seriously injured than they are to win. Individual perceptions, or 'subjective' judgements, will probably not coincide with an expert, or 'objective', view.[10] As a result of this our view of risk also should include situations where strategic objectives are fully met but 'failure' still arises as a result of the consequences being

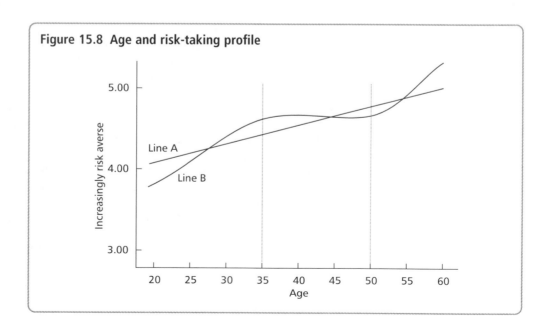

Figure 15.8 Age and risk-taking profile

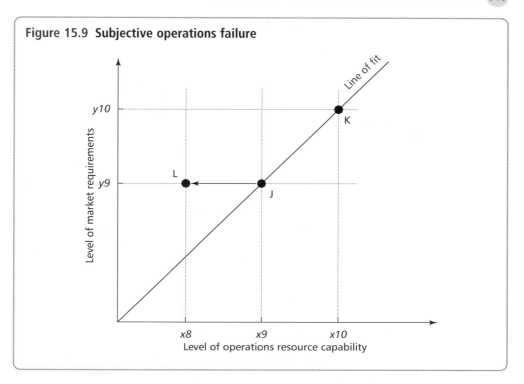

Figure 15.9 Subjective operations failure

judged to be inappropriate or undesirable by specific stakeholders. For instance, Figure 15.9 illustrates a traditional retail banking operation (J) facing a market requirement ($y9$) shifting towards telephone and Internet-based service delivery and, as a result, declining volumes of face-to-face transactions.

Given its current level of capability ($x9$), the most likely operations strategy response would be to close branch locations and instead create additional telephone and Internet channel capability ($x10$), thus satisfying the new market requirements (K). Successful implementation of such a strategy appears to offer entirely positive outcomes for the firm. For example, such things as improved efficiency, return on capital and share price, also perhaps more intangible benefits such as an enhanced industry reputation for embracing new technologies. Unfortunately, the same outcome may be viewed as entirely negative by, for instance, a group of elderly customers who distrust technology and who have been using local branches for all of their adult lives. Their specific market requirements have not changed ($y9$), they do not appreciate the new level of non-branch capability ($x10$) and therefore perceive the closures as a reduction of capabilities ($x8$, L) – in other words, a subjective operations failure.

To further complicate matters, individuals are often inconsistent about both subjective risk and expressed fears. The 'mad cow' BSE crisis in the UK led to a dramatic decline in the consumption of beef. Presumably many heavy drinkers and smokers gave up eating beef because of their health concerns! If we look at some examples of both objective and subjective risk assessments and commonly expressed fears we can see how often these three are at odds with each other (Table 15.1).

Table 15.1 Different combinations of risks and expressed fears

Objective risk	Subjective risk	Expressed fear	EXAMPLE
High	High	High	Someone driving a car too fast in icy and foggy conditions and their passengers expressing these concerns
High	High	Low	Construction staff fearing redundancy continuing to work on a building site despite the absence of adequate safety equipment
Low	High	High	Complaints about the safety of asbestos construction materials behind sealed surfaces
Low	Low	High	Staff exploiting safety concerns to gain non-safety improvements (when the actual risks and their perceptions of the risks are low)

Looking at the last two of these examples we can also see hints of how often 'objective' evaluations of risks can be used for 'political' (small p and large P) purposes. When oil and chemicals giant Royal Dutch/Shell took the decision to employ deepwater disposal in the North Sea for their Brent Spar Oil Platform, they felt that they were making a rational operational decision based upon the best available scientific evidence concerning environmental risk. Unfortunately, Greenpeace disagreed and put forward an alternative 'objective analysis' showing significant risk from deepwater disposal. Eventually Greenpeace admitted their evidence was flawed but by that time Shell had lost the public relations battle and had altered their plans. Brent Spar became an example, not of science-led environmental analysis, but rather a very public illustration of the political nature of objective risk analysis.

By considering the impact of cognitive limits and *bounded rationality* (i.e. people don't always make rational decisions) we are not abandoning risk management to the realms of chaos and irrelevance. Rather we are simply highlighting the limits of the highly rational models that often dominate operations strategy and risk analysis. For instance, Prospect Theory (see Theory Box) highlights how people tend to pay too much attention to dramatic low-probability events and overlook routine events.

Theory Box Prospect Theory[11]

One of the most influential theories of how individuals cope with risk is called Prospect Theory. It looks at how people make choices when faced with uncertain outcomes, by highlighting two factors that undermine the 'rational' model of decision making. First, emotions can undermine self-control and second, most individuals are unable to understand *fully* what is being dealt with in any given situation. When faced with uncertainty, as individuals we can fall back on our own observations of past experience. Unfortunately, most situations are so varied and complex that we cannot guarantee that we have drawn valid generalisations from what we observe. Kahneman and Tversky, who first formulated the theory, use the following question to illustrate how intuitive perceptions can mislead us. *Does the letter K appear more often as the first or third letter of English words?* Most people answer that it appears more often as the first letter whereas it actually appears as the third letter twice as often. They argue that this error can be explained because we find it easier to recall words with a certain letter at the beginning rather than elsewhere. This reliance upon what we might call judgement heuristics creates a number of subjective decision-making processes, including:

- Making inconsistent choices when faced by the same problem framed in a different way. We display risk-aversion when offered a choice in one setting and then become risk seeking when offered the same choice in another. In their first paper they described an experiment where subjects were asked to choose between an 80% chance of winning $4000 and a 20% chance of winning nothing, versus a 100% chance of receiving $3000. The risky choice has a higher probabilistic payoff of $3200 (0.8*4000=3200) but 80% of subjects chose the guaranteed $3000. In other words, people seemed to be risk averse. They then changed the game slightly and offered subjects the choice of an 80% chance of *losing* $4000 and 20% chance of breaking even versus a 100% chance of losing $3000. The risky choice now has the higher probabilistic loss, $3200, but in this context, 92% of subjects chose the gamble. In other words when the choice involves losses, people are risk-seekers, not risk averse. Tversky argues that this illustrates how people are not risk averse but loss averse. He speculates that this is because 'people are much more sensitive to negative than to positive stimuli . . . think about how well you feel today and then try to imagine how much better you could feel . . . there are a few things that could make you feel better but the number of things that would make you feel worse is unbounded'.

- We have trouble recognising how much information is enough and how much is too much. Indeed, research has suggested that additional information can actually get in the way of effective decision making. Tversky described another experiment involving 120 Stanford graduates. They were each asked to assess the likelihood of various possible causes of death. Each evaluated one of two different lists, the first listing specific causes (like heart disease, cancer, homicide, etc.) and the second offering generic headings (natural and unnatural causes). All participants vastly overestimated the probability of violent death and underestimated deaths by natural causes but most revealing is the difference between the two lists. The estimated probability of dying under either set of circumstances was higher when the circumstances were explicit as compared with the two generic headings.

These are only specific illustrations of Prospect Theory (and the large and rich vein of research that explores theories of choice and uncertainty) but they highlight how prevalent irrationality, inconsistency and incompetence are in decision making.

The context of risk determination

Earlier we considered how a bank shifting capacity away from high-street branches to telephone call centres could result in perceived negative consequences for some customers. Prospect Theory re-emphasises the idea that risk perceptions will be influenced by one's point of reference and context in general. In order to explore the influence of operating context in determining perceived negative consequences, it is instructive to look at an illustrative (pure risk) example.

Example – The Steel Company Inc.

Steel Company is a major manufacturer of electrical steels, whose product is used in a range of electrical motor applications by a number of global white goods manu-

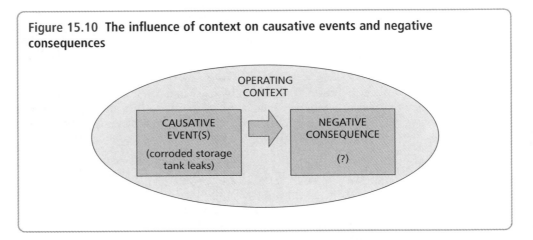

Figure 15.10 The influence of context on causative events and negative consequences

facturers (washing machines, refrigerators, etc.). A variety of process stages are used to impart the correct electrical properties to the sheet steel, including passing it through a chemical treatment tank (a process known as 'pickling'). This process was the source of an operational failure when one of their on-site chemical storage tanks developed a leak, as a result of unobserved corrosion. This kind of incident is a clearly identifiable hazard for any steel firm operating these types of process, but in order to analyse the risks associated with this event we also need to understand what the negative consequences might be (see Figure 15.10).

● A first attempt to define consequences might consider the chemical and biological nature of the specific spill and at the same time assess the risk of staff being exposed. Questions to be asked would include, 'who was working near the tank at that time?', and 'how long was it before the spill was detected?'. If we ascertain that no employees were exposed to the spill then we might conclude that, in the absence of any injuries, the negative consequences of the spill were minimal.

● Although the specific spill did not immediately harm employee health, it made an already contaminated site much worse. In this context, our definition of negative consequences needs to include the medium and long-term health consequences of the staff – thereby including some staff who were not even employed at the time of the incident.

● Unfortunately, the factory's location and the specific local geology also meant that the resulting site contamination eventually seeped into the local water supply. In this context, the local population also faces potentially serious short, medium and long-term negative consequences.

So, by broadening our conception of the operating context, we can arrive at different conclusions about negative consequences. The risk analysis has required us to think beyond the 'space and time' confines of the immediate spillage incident. In order to understand all of the possible 'levels of consequence' of such incidents, we might need to analyse all of the physical 'transmission' pathways for specific spill types. This will probably be defined by a complex mixture of operations-related factors such as the location of the tank, the duration of the leak before detection, and so on, and geographical/geological/chemical factors. Of course, this broadening out of our thinking should not stop at the geographical limits of physical contamination. Negative consequences are equally influenced by more subjective factors:

● The chemical leak was reported to the state regulatory authority that then engaged standard investigation procedures. The subsequent discovery of contamination of the local water supply triggered supplementary investigations by both the state and federal environmental agencies. Also, the announcement of the contamination and investigations triggered local and national media interest. Potential risks to staff health led to labour union interest and individual employees began to consider taking legal action against the firm. The regulatory and environmental dimension, combined with the high level of media interest, led to active pressure group and political involvement.

From this example it is clear that any assessment of negative consequences needs to include subjective stakeholder perspectives. Unfortunately, these are often inconsistent. For instance, in our analysis of Monsanto, even the pressure groups that attacked the firm admitted that its strategy was effectively indistinguishable from many of its rivals. However, Monsanto's difficulties suggest that the more focused the operation and the bigger the brand, then the bigger the news story and the greater the potential for realising subjective negative consequences from operations-related events.

Brand-based competition and operations-related risk

In many sectors, where intense competition leads to the rapid diffusion of innovation and 'commoditisation' of most product and service offerings, a strong brand can be the difference between competitive survival and failure. Unfortunately, despite the best efforts of clever advertising, most brands develop relatively slowly over time. If it is actively managed, a brand is heavily influenced by marketing activity. But it will also reflect the influence of past operations-related actions. The brand risk associated with operations failure is increasingly significant and needs to be constantly considered. Remember the Virgin train business described in Chapter 2 as an illustration of the impact of operations risk on brand. Under the auspices of the charismatic Richard Branson and a single logo, seemingly unrelated companies (drinks, airlines, music, cosmetics, wedding dresses, etc.) were brought together and became successful. However, when Virgin became an operator on Britain's privatised train system, operational problems quickly emerged. The firm performed badly in surveys and quickly became a byword for disappointing service. Although such difficulties may be inevitable when entering a new business, the company's widespread subjective association with operational failure became a threat to the whole brand.

The role of the media

An increasing number of operations and managers have been exposed to investigation by the print, television and online news media. Many of those who have received media attention complain of the superficial coverage the technical and operational issues received. If we examine the way in which a particular operational failure is presented by a respected news organisation (in this case BBC News) we can infer a number of more generic characteristics about the influence of the media context on risk assessments.

Lead Story, BBC1 News [27 April 1998][12]

VISUALS	News presenter in studio; Still photo of dead fish, belly up.
SCRIPT	(News presenter direct to camera) Environmental groups are increasingly concerned about the impact of poisonous flood water near Europe's biggest national park . . .
VISUALS	Still map of Spain indicating location of national park.
SCRIPT	. . .in southern Spain. Toxic waste escaped on Saturday from an industrial reservoir near the Corton Donana national park in Southern Spain, threatening to destroy plants and wildlife.
VISUALS	Return to still photo of dead fish, belly up.
SCRIPT	The surrounding farmland has been devastated. Local farmers say that it could cost them up to £8 million.
VISUALS	Video: close-up of boot turning over dead animal lying in mud.
SCRIPT	(Correspondent voice-over) This is the aftermath of the toxic spill; it has choked everything in its path.
VISUALS	Video: pull back from dead animal to couple walking in front of mud-devastated fields.
SCRIPT	For Jose Antonio Deluna and his wife Carmen, these are days of despair.
VISUALS	Video: Three panning distance shots of mud stretching into tree-lined distance.
SCRIPT	Much of their 30-hectare farm is now under a sea of mud. Jose Antonio should have started harvesting his peach crop this week, now he's afraid that he may never be able to work his land again.
VISUALS	Video: couple interviewed in front of muddied fields.
SCRIPT	(Voice of Jose Antonio with translator's voice-over) For us this is total ruin, this is our business and our home. We don't even know whether we will be able to stay living here because we won't be able to farm.
VISUALS	Video: aerial panning scenes of industrial reservoir and burst banks, following the sea of mud across devastated landscapes.
SCRIPT	(Correspondent voice-over) These pictures from the environmental group Greenpeace show how far the tide of toxic material has spread. They say it is a disaster for land and health. The full effects won't be known for five or six years.
VISUALS	Video: Greenpeace representative interviewed in front of lush green vegetation.
SCRIPT	(Eva Hernandez, Greenpeace representative) Heavy metals are now in this place, in the water, in the ground and only in a few years will we be able to know what is happening to the bird population, the fish population.
VISUALS	Video: mid-shot to close-up shot of dead fish belly up.
SCRIPT	(Correspondent voice-over) The cost of the toxic spill is high and rising . . .
VISUALS	Video: distance to mid-shots of birds circling to land on mud-covered fields.
SCRIPT	Voladin Apearsa, the Swedish mining company involved, are bringing in senior executives as a government enquiry begins.
VISUALS	Video: correspondent standing in front of mud-devastated fields.
SCRIPT	(Correspondent direct to camera) The problems here are just beginning. The toxic waste is continuing to seep into the soil. Hour after hour it is causing greater contamination. Local people say it's not only livelihoods that have been destroyed here, but lives too. Orla Guerin, BBC News, Seville.

The purpose of this analysis is not to dispute the environmental impact of the failure event. Rather, by looking more closely at this 'piece' we are able to discern a number of particular media characteristics:

- The images used as a backdrop to the story do not really provide any information (with the possible exception of the map of Spain) but rather serve to help authenticate the words and help provide a mood for the piece.[13]

- There is no coverage of what actually, operationally or technically, went wrong – perhaps because the cause is not yet fully established (there is mention of an enquiry) or is seen as too complex to explain in a short time.

- Despite the need for voice-over translation, the piece deliberately seeks out 'ordinary voices' to humanise the story – helping to increase the viewer appeal of the story? Interestingly, this presentation of diverse views could also be seen as reflecting the journalistic ideal of balance. This process sometimes means that equal weight is given to all available views – regardless of what technical specialists might see as a lack of specific competence to comment.

- The piece not only interviews a representative of, but also uses video (albeit acknowledged on screen) provided by, the environmental pressure group Greenpeace. This highlights how attuned to the priorities and requirements of the media many pressure groups are, often in direct contrast with the operations that they target in their campaigns.

This example reflects the fundamental operating characteristics of the modern media industry. Although reasonably transparent, they are constrained by the time imperatives of news production. There are competitive pressures for audience appeal and there may be ownership/editorial influences. Yet despite the obvious flaws and limitations of the process, over time the media will probably come to exert a stronger rather than weaker influence over calculations of risks and therefore operations strategy decisions.

> The experts respond to hazard; the public responds to outrage. When hazard is high and outrage is low, the experts will be concerned and the public will be apathetic. When hazard is low and outrage is high, the public will be concerned and the experts will be apathetic. (Dr Peter Sandman)[14]

Layers of context

Here we have barely scratched the surface of identifying and analysing those stakeholders who might have an influence on perceptions of negative consequences. Discussion of the legal and regulatory context for most operations strategy decisions could fill an entire book. The important point is to 'peel back the different layers' of operating context while analysing operations-related risks. Figure 15.11 presents the discussions of this section as a set of generic layers.

Controlling risk

Operations strategy practitioners are understandably interested in how an operation can avoid failure in the first place, or if it does happen, how they can survive any adverse conditions that might follow. In other words, how they can control risk. Figure 15.12 provides a simple structure for describing three generic mechanisms for controlling risk.

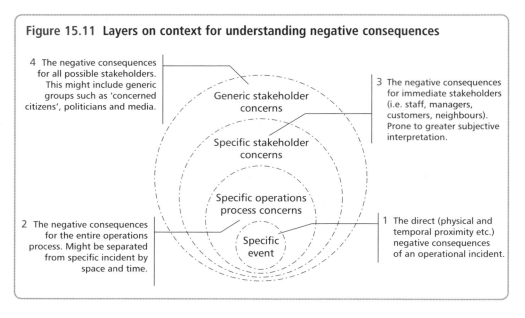

Figure 15.11 Layers on context for understanding negative consequences

4 The negative consequences for all possible stakeholders. This might include generic groups such as 'concerned citizens', politicians and media.

Generic stakeholder concerns

Specific stakeholder concerns

Specific operations process concerns

Specific event

3 The negative consequences for immediate stakeholders (i.e. staff, managers, customers, neighbours). Prone to greater subjective interpretation.

2 The negative consequences for the entire operations process. Might be separated from specific incident by space and time.

1 The direct (physical and temporal proximity etc.) negative consequences of an operational incident.

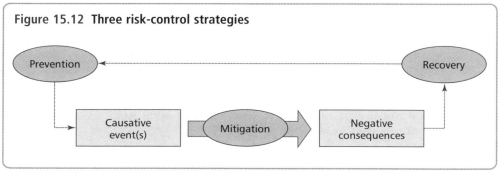

Figure 15.12 Three risk-control strategies

Prevention

Recovery

Causative event(s)

Mitigation

Negative consequences

- *Prevention strategies* – are where an operation seeks to completely prevent (or reduce the frequency of) an event occurring.

- *Mitigating strategies* – are where an operation seeks to isolate an event from any possible negative consequences.

- *Recovery strategies* – are where an operation analyses and accepts the consequences from an event but undertakes to minimise or alleviate or compensate for them.

Prevention strategies

It is almost always better to avoid failure and negative consequences than have to recover from them. There are many ways that managers can seek to prevent specific events from happening, but the classic approach is to inspect and audit operations activity. For instance, by emphasising its use of 'fair trading' principles, the high street retailer The Body Shop was able to develop its 'ethical' brand identity as a powerful advantage, but it also became a potential source of vulnerability. When in 1994 a journalist accused one of the firm's suppliers of using animal product testing, the rest of the media eagerly took up the story. To prevent this kind of accusation from resurfacing, the firm introduced a detailed (and expensive) auditing method to prevent any suspicion of unethical behaviour in their entire supply chain. Unfortunately, inspection and audit cannot, on their own, provide complete assurance that undesirable events will be avoided. The content of the audit has to be appropriate, the checking process has to be sufficiently frequent and comprehensive and the inspectors have to have sufficient knowledge and experience. In fact, too superficial an approach to inspection can create more problems than it solves (see the box on Met Life).

Failed controls at Met Life?[15]

In August 1993, Florida's Insurance Commissioner charged America's second-largest insurance operation, Metropolitan Life, with a number of regulatory violations. It was alleged that their agents in Tampa were misrepresenting life-insurance policies as savings products and had thereby 'stolen' $11 million from customers, many of whom were nurses.

Rick Urso ran the Tampa office. He had built it up from a one-man operation in 1983 to one of the firm's largest and most profitable (in 1990 and 1991, they won the Sales Office of the Year award). By 1993 Tampa employed 120 reps and 30 administrative staff. Rick himself became Met Life's third-highest paid employee, earning $1.1 million as a branch manager. The product that fuelled this great growth was a whole-life insurance policy (part life insurance and part savings) that required high premiums but only attracted limited interest payments. For the sales rep this product paid an extraordinary 55 per cent first year commission compared with, say, an annuity that paid only 2 per cent. Nurses appeared to be particularly drawn to the product's claims of life-long economic security (perhaps their points of reference were heavily influenced by their exposure to illness and death) and Urso instructed his salespeople to call themselves 'nursing representatives' and target people beyond the confines of Florida. Complaints began to emerge and in 1990, the Texas insurance commissioner warned Met Life about its strategy to target nurses. The firm responded by sending out two circular letters to its staff. This wasn't the only evidence of problems. An internal audit in 1991 argued that the *nursing representative* was a 'made-up title' and that *retirement savings policy* was an inappropriate label for the core product. Unfortunately, at the same time they congratulated the Tampa office for its contribution to firm profits. Only when the Florida investigation began did the firm's official attitude change. On the Monday after Christmas 1993, Rick Urso was fired! Met Life had initially denied any wrongdoing, then under increasing public pressure it agreed to pay out more than $40 million in fines and refunded premiums (at a cost expected to reach $76 million) to more than 92,000 policyholders. Five senior executives were fired or demoted, the Tampa office was closed, all seven of Urso's managers and several reps were dismissed. Policy sales in the following year fell by almost 25 per cent and Standard and Poor's downgraded the firms bond rating.

Met Life provides a good example of how a cursory internal audit can actually be damaging. The token effort of the 1991 audit sent (at best) mixed messages and at worst implied that this was acceptable practice – no matter what we have to say publicly! Moreover, the evidence of a weak attempt at control actually rendered the firm more vulnerable to future measures. Whatever the reality, the results of the audit gave the impression that the firm was deliberately overlooking issues. This did not just provoke regulator sanction, from the perspective of the bond market this raised concern about all other aspects of the operations controls. Therefore, because of these potential weaknesses, in addition to audit and inspection, operations also seek to design out common failure modes. For instance, a building surveying service might seek to replace the people in its drafting operations with new scanning and printing technology in order to improve process consistency and prevent common errors. Interestingly, this approach has strong echoes of the dominant logic in modern quality management, where designing out errors and avoiding waste are paramount concerns.

Mitigation strategies

Not all events can be avoided, but an operation can try to separate an event from its negative consequences (or isolate desirable from undesirable events). However, in some areas of operations management, relying on such mitigation, rather than prevention, is very unfashionable. For instance, 'acceptance sampling' and 'inspection' practices in quality management were based on the assumption that failures were inevitable and needed to be detected before they could cause harm. More modern total quality management places much more emphasis on prevention. Likewise in purchasing, one of the justifications for having multiple suppliers of the same sub-component was that, regardless of the nature of the causative event (industrial action, a fire, legislative action, etc.), it would reduce the potential impact of a supply failure. More recent ideas in purchasing focus on the partnership advantages of single suppliers. Yet mitigation can be a useful approach when used in conjunction with prevention, especially at a strategic level.

Example – Mitigating currency risk

As an illustration of risk mitigation in practice it is instructive to look at the way that an operation deals with exposure to currency fluctuations. Consider the example of a multinational consumer goods firm. After the collapse of communism in the early 1990s, like many other Western firms, they began to invest in the markets of the former Soviet Union. Their Russian subsidiary sourced nearly all products from its parent's factories in France and Germany, while its main rivals had manufacturing facilities in Russia. Conscious of the potential volatility of the 'new' rouble, the firm needed to minimise its operating exposure to a devaluation of the currency. Any such devaluation would leave the firm's cost structure at a serious disadvantage with respect to its rivals and without any real option but to increase their prices (already aimed at a premium, quality segment). In seeking to mitigate against the risk of devaluation, the firm could choose from among various financial and operations-based options. For example, financial tools were available to minimise currency exposure. Most of these allow the operation to reduce the risk of currency fluctuations but involve an 'up front' cost. Usually, the higher the risk the greater the up-front cost. Alternatively, the company may restructure its operations strategy in order to mitigate its currency risk. One option would be to develop its own production facilities within Russia. This may reduce, or even eliminate, the currency risk, although it will probably introduce other risks. A further option may be to form supply partnerships with other Russian companies. Again, this does not eliminate risks but can shift them to ones that the company feels more able to control. More generically, this issue of managing operating exposure through operational capabilities necessitates the creation of a portfolio of operations-based options. In this way risks can be balanced by, for instance, developing alternative suppliers in different currency zones, building up excess/flexible capacity in a global production network, and creating more differentiated products which are less price sensitive.

Recovery strategies

Recovery strategies can involve a wide range of activities. They include the (micro) recovery steps necessary to minimise an individual customer's dissatisfaction. This might include apologising, refunding monies, reworking a product or service, or providing compensation. At the same time, operations have to be prepared for the (macro) major crises that might necessitate a complete product recall or abandonment of service. The question that an operations strategy needs to consider is, 'at what point do we reach the limit of avoidance and mitigation strategies before we start to rely on recovery strategies?' It is helpful to use the concept of *coupling* as an analytical device for make this type of decision (see the Theory Box on 'loose and tight coupling').

Theory Box   **Loose and tight coupling**

Tight coupling is a term originally used to denote the absence of slack or buffer between the components of an engineering technology. As an operations process concept it is directly relevant to risk. Many advanced production systems emphasise greater integration and the removal of all forms of waste such as slack resources, thereby directly creating tighter coupling. Likewise, as supply bases are rationalised, inventory levels reduced and core services outsourced, supply networks have also become more tightly coupled. Although this can have considerable advantages, it can also reduce the ability to mitigate failure and therefore increase failure consequences.

Figure 15.13 describes a model of the likely risk-control consequences of different levels of operations coupling. The vertical axis describes the seriousness of the failure event (e.g. from minor capacity restriction to complete network shutdown). The horizontal axis is the degree

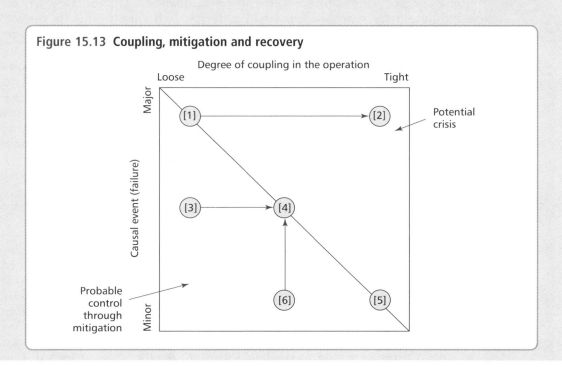

Figure 15.13 Coupling, mitigation and recovery

of coupling that the operations system exhibits. The diagonal between the two dimensions suggests the limit to the applicability of mitigation strategies, before the advent of crisis and reliance on recovery strategies.

In the upper left-hand corner of the matrix [1] a major failure will probably be so serious that it would be difficult to separate it from its consequences. There would be only very limited opportunity for mitigation. When such failures are more 'tightly coupled' to other systems (i.e. moving towards [2]), the effects of the failure are far more likely to 'ripple out' and have 'knock-on' consequences. For example, a failure could trigger stakeholder and media interest. In these cases, recovery strategies will predominate. Moving down the vertical axis, the scope and complexity of operations failure is reduced [3] and control through mitigation is more feasible. As coupling increases, however, the scope for mitigation decreases, and at [4] recovery becomes the only likely option. The bottom-right corner of the matrix [5] indicates how, in a tightly coupled operation, only minor negative outcomes can be tolerated before negative consequences are realised, mitigation becomes impossible and recovery is necessary.

Of course, an operation will need to establish the true seriousness of a failure event. For example, it needs to know whether an individual customer complaint is just an isolated incident [6] or the beginning of a major product recall [4].

It is increasingly common for operations to create crisis recovery teams (and rehearse major incidents) that are ready to swing into action when disaster strikes. In the absence of well-thought-out procedures, an operation can rapidly lose (or at least appear to lose) control of a recovery situation. In 1990, for instance, when Perrier was faced with claims of Benzene contamination in its products, the firm reacted quite quickly in ordering a recall. However, the firm's response to media enquiries and real concerns from customers was confused. Multiple lines of communication led to multiple explanations. Perrier in the US claimed that the contamination was limited to the US, Perrier UK protested ignorance of the situation and the French HQ claimed that the origin of the benzene was a cleaning fluid mistakenly used on a US bottling line. Three days later that story was changed again with the identification of the real problem: a failure to replace a charcoal filter used to remove impurities. In this case, just as in the Met Life example, Perrier's flawed recovery attempt (clearly overlooking critical problem analysis and communication issues) actually proved as damaging to its brand as the real failure event.

Practical challenges of risk

Managing pure risk

We defined a pure risk as one that produces the possibility of only loss. An immediate reaction is probably to avoid such risks completely and some pure risks do fall into an 'avoid if at all possible' category, especially high-probability incidents that will result in severe consequences such as loss of life or serious injury. However, not all pure risks are like this. For instance, there are many risks that might very occasionally result in a minor accident at work. While in theory it is important to eliminate as many pure risks as possible, if the cost of eliminating a hazard is prohibitive then most operations will make a rational choice to accept the risk. This raises an immediate practical issue, 'how do we know that we have identified all possible pure risks?'

Comprehensiveness

Several authors have developed frameworks to aid comprehensive and practical decision making over risk. One of the most comprehensive of these is the Reputation Assurance Framework developed by Glen Peters, a partner at the Pricewaterhouse Coopers consulting firm. In his book, *Waltzing with the Raptors* (1999), he proposed a model based around four key drivers of reputation: managerial action; environmental record; health and safety record; and effectiveness of communication. Some issues raised in this framework are summarised in Table 15.2. Not all of these 'drivers' will be equally important to all stakeholders. For instance, it is unlikely that a management consultancy business will be attacked for its environmental policies in the same way as petrochemical giants like Exxon have been.

Table 15.2 Some examples of actions which promote good operations reputation (based on the Reputation Assurance Framework)[16]

Driver of operations reputation	Examples of actions which promote good operations reputation
Managerial action	• Ensure a competitive return to shareholders. • Conserve, protect and increase operations assets. • Meet product/service standards and guarantees to customers. • Meet reasonable expectations of performance to customers such as continuity of supply, pricing, etc. • Maintain equality in pay and benefits for employees. • Respect staff union, religious and individual rights. • Anticipate and handle conflict such as industrial action, litigation, security, facility closure and so on sensitively. • Avoid all corrupt practices such as receiving gifts, insider trading, etc. • Deal with suppliers and partners in an equitable coercion-free manner. • Respect partners' tangible and intellectual property. • Encourage responsibility in partners and suppliers, including the meeting of shared standards. • Respect and promote human rights. • Respect cultural traditions and local laws. • Promote economic stability of local economy. • Promote fair trade.
Environmental impact	• Promote sustainable investment criteria. • Seek to minimise negative impact of all operations practices through such things as life-cycle design, restoration of natural resources, etc. • Encourage individual environmental responsibility amongst employees such as energy efficiency, total resource management, etc. • Foster environmental responsibility in suppliers and business partners. • Encourage sustainable development and conservation in society generally such as reducing the possibility of environmental risk. • Recognise all view points no matter how divergent by not dismissing or ignoring the opinions of environmental groups, etc.

▶

Table 15.2 continued

Driver of operations reputation	Examples of actions which promote good operations reputation
Drivers of operations' reputation Health and safety record	● Promote health and safety as a legitimate investment criterion by screening all investments for health and safety risk. ● Minimise negative impact of products and services on customers through ongoing 'stewardship' approach to products and services, recall and abandonment policies, etc. ● Provide appropriate working conditions for employees which minimise risks to health and safety. ● Encourage individual health and safety responsibility in the operation, including mental and physical health. ● Foster responsibility for health and safety in business partners and suppliers. ● Consider responsibility for health and safety in society in general. ● Put relevant compensation policies in place. ● Have disaster/crisis management strategies developed and rehearsed.
Effectiveness of communication	● Disclose relevant information in a truthful and timely manner. ● Respect customer privacy by ensuring confidentiality of data, etc. ● Be honest and open in all communications, especially in regard to specific complaints, etc. ● Respect employee privacy, including confidentiality of employment information. ● Ensure fair and open communication between and with suppliers and business partners. ● Operate full disclosure of relevant business information. ● Demonstrate respect for societal concerns.

This is an obvious comparison between the kind of self-assessment framework shown in Table 15.2 and those employed in quality management schemes. And the message is similar: without the right intent or sufficient commitment to the process, any self-evaluation can rapidly become a paper-based exercise in self-promotion. However, as part of a serious commitment to operations strategy development, such models can provide an invaluable input.

Managing speculative risks

Unlike pure risks, speculative risks hold the potential for loss or gain. This is the type of risk we are referring to when we talk about the relationship between risk and reward in business. In other words, risk as opportunity as well as risk as downside.

The risk-return evaluation

Potential operations strategy decisions involving risk can be evaluated in terms of their expected pay-off or return, and their risk may be represented by the spread of possible pay-offs. Figure 15.14 shows four process technologies, A, B, X and Y, plotted on a graph with the spread of pay-offs and the expected pay-off as the axes.

The top left-hand part of the graph represents an undesirable area where options have low expected pay-offs, yet run high risks. The bottom right-hand part of the

Figure 15.14 The risk-return diagram

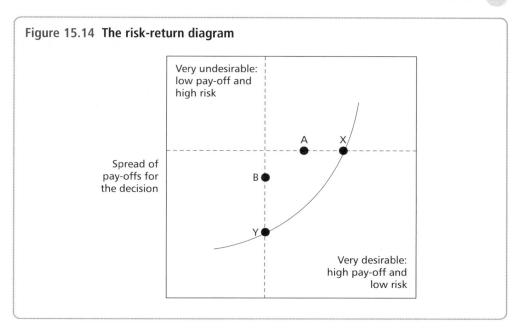

graph includes the extremely attractive options which give a high pay-off, but involve little risk. Somewhere between these two extremes will lie a line representing combinations of risk and pay-off which are the best that can be achieved in a particular decision. Options X and Y are contained in this set – sometimes called the *efficient frontier*. Any process technology that is positioned on the line *dominates* any other that lies towards the top left-hand part of the graph. So technology X dominates technology A (X gives a better pay-off for the same risk) and technology Y dominates technology B (Y gives a better pay-off for the same risk). The purpose of this type of analysis, even if done in an approximate manner, is to exclude possible decisions which are clearly dominated by others.

Using net present value (NPV)

Conventionally, the consideration of speculative risk for most operations investment decisions tends to focus on downsides. The use of net present value (NPV) calculations, for instance, where expected values from an investment are discounted back to represent the time value of money (i.e. $100 today is better than $100 in five years time), embodies this risk-averse attitude. (NPV was explained in Chapter 9.) Because decisions are made at a fixed point in time, the higher the uncertainty associated with a project, the higher the 'hurdle rate' will be set (the amount by which future value is discounted). The greater the discounting of future value, then the less attractive a project becomes and the less likely that the project will be approved. Recently though, this use of NPV has been criticised for underestimating the importance of capability development underpinned by learning by doing, experimentation, and the occasional 'intelligent failure'. Uncertainty, it is argued, also creates opportunities and therefore the practical challenge is to find ways of incorporating this value in risk analyses.

Real options and operations strategy

We began this chapter with an analysis of the catastrophic failure at Baring's Bank. It is therefore appropriate to conclude with mention of a practical model derived from the theory which underpins the kind of financial products that Nick Leeson so completely misunderstood – the 'real options' model.

In an earlier example of risk mitigation, *options* were briefly introduced as one potential financial solution for minimising operating exposure to currency fluctuations. In very general terms an option is the non-obligatory right to take some form of action in the future. On the stock market, an option could be the right to buy a specified stock at a specified price at a specified date. As such, the buyer will only exercise the option if the stock's value on that date is greater than that specified. The underlying logic which options employ, of actively embracing uncertainty as a source of value, is only just beginning to make an impact on strategic planning. This notion of what are termed 'real options' has implications for the way that managers think about a whole range of operations strategy decisions, such as capacity investment, flexibility, product/service and process development, strategic alliances and infrastructure development. It is particularly important for considering speculative risk and operations strategy.

Although initially derived from complex financial mathematics, at its heart the notion of real options is actually very simple – *uncertainty is good*. In their book, *Real Options*, Amram and Kulatilaka argue that traditional (e.g. NPV) models interpret higher levels of uncertainty as probably offering lower returns. By contrast, the real options approach views greater levels of uncertainty as actually opening up options to realise higher returns – *providing that managers are able to respond flexibly to unfolding events*.

They use a simple model, the 'cone of uncertainty', to illustrate how uncertainty relates to time (see Figure 15.15). The approach emphasises that the value of an investment can go up as well as down but that the highest and lowest values are unlikely. In fact, at each point in time there will be a range of options whose probability can be assumed to follow a normal distribution.

Given this uncertainty (with both positive and negative consequences) and the

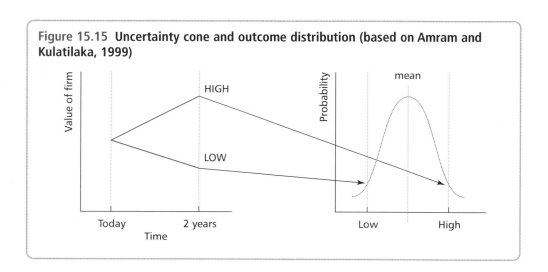

Figure 15.15 Uncertainty cone and outcome distribution (based on Amram and Kulatilaka, 1999)

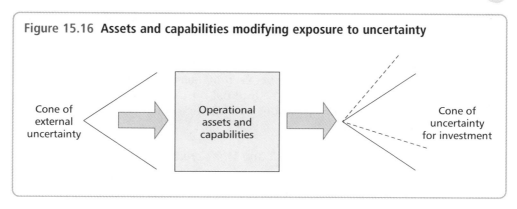

Figure 15.16 **Assets and capabilities modifying exposure to uncertainty**

existence of a range of options over time, operations strategy should not run away from uncertainty but rather seek to understand it. It should determine the degree of resource exposure and then respond through modified investments. In other words, the external uncertainties of market and economic growth do not only impact on the underlying assets and capabilities of the firm. By identifying and exploiting options, managers can reduce their exposure to negative outcomes and increase their exposure to positive outcomes. This has the effect of tilting the cone of uncertainty upward over time (see Figure 15.16).

Crossair[17]

In 1996, European airline Crossair began to invest in a project to be the first carrier to introduce a more advanced global positioning system (GPS) into their aircraft. This would have a range of advantages but in particular would allow their aircraft to land under difficult conditions at smaller airports with automatic guidance equipment. Although the technical elements of the project were demonstrated on time and pilot applications were successful, the overall implementation failed for a variety of reasons. In other words, the project was what would be called a failure.

However, not long after, in 1998, Crossair's aircraft supplier made the decision to abandon production of small commercial planes, leaving the firm needing to find a new supply partner. After an extensive search and extended negotiations, it was able to find another manufacturer who, despite their relatively small size, was willing to adopt them as a 'lead customer' with a strong influence on aircraft design. There was a range of motivations for the aircraft OEM but critical amongst them was Crossair's expertise in the next generation of GPS systems – the by-product of a failed project!

SUMMARY ANSWERS TO KEY QUESTIONS

Why should an operations strategy include considerations of risk?

Risk is an important element in operations strategy because many of the decisions within operations strategy formulation carry with them intrinsic risk. Business magazines are full of examples where operations-related decisions have gone wrong and caused harm to the organisation and society more broadly. More positively, risk is an important issue because operations can learn from mistakes provided that they are sensitive to the learning which can take place. Risk is also closely aligned to the whole idea of operations strategy – reconciling market requirements with operations resources. Any imbalance between market requirements and operations resources is, in itself, a risk. This may be internal operations risk (the risk of having excess capability) or external operations risk (the risk of market needs exceeding current operations capability).

What do we mean by risk and what are the generic types of risk?

Operations risk is the potential for unwanted negative consequences from an operations-related event. The factors which contribute to such risks can be human, organisational or technological (the so-called HOT variables). However, the main distinction between different types of risk is that between 'pure risk' and 'speculative risk'. Pure risks involve events that can produce the possibility only of loss, whereas speculative risks hold the potential for loss or gain. In fact, the two types of risk are really the extreme points on a continuum. Speculative risk (such as adopting a new technology) can often lead to pure risk (such as that technology failing in service).

How can an operation understand and articulate and control risk?

The three key issues here are cognition (how we think about risk), context (the situation in which the risks occur) and control (how do we reduce the negative effects of risk). Risk cognition is important because individuals see risks in very different ways. There can be major discrepancies between how we think about risk in an objective way, what our subjective view of risk is, and how we express our fear of the consequences. Understanding the context in which a risk takes place is important because it can determine how we view the consequences of negative events. Controlling risk can involve adopting prevention strategies (where an operation seeks to prevent a negative event occurring), mitigating strategies (where an operation seeks to isolate an event from any possible negative consequences), and recovery strategies (where an operation analyses and accepts the consequences from an event but undertakes to minimise or alleviate or compensate for them).

What are the practical challenges associated with measuring and controlling operations-related risk?

The main challenge in managing pure risk lies in identifying as many of the potential causes of risk as possible. There are many frameworks which help to do this. One is the Reputation Assurance Framework. However, these self-assessment frameworks need to be carried out with sufficient commitment to avoid them becoming ritual exercises. Speculative risks can be subjected to conventional financial tools such as risk-return evaluation and net present value (NPV) evaluation. More recently, 'real options' have been used to fully incorporate the more positive aspects of speculative risk in evaluation procedures.

Saunders Industrial Services

Saunders Industrial Services (SIS) began life as the classic family firm. Art Saunders' father had opened a small manufacturing and fabrication business in his hometown of Milwaukee on returning from duty in the Second World War. He had successfully leveraged his skills and passion for craftsmanship over many years while serving a variety of different industrial and agricultural customers. Art himself spent nearly ten years working as a production engineer for an automotive OEM but eventually returned to Milwaukee to take over the family firm. Exploiting his experience in mass manufacturing, Art spent more than 20 years building the firm into a larger-scale industrial component manufacturer but retained his father's commitment to quality and customer service. In 1985 he sold the firm to a UK-owned industrial conglomerate and ten years later in 1995 it had doubled in size again, and now employed approximately 600 people and had a turnover approaching $210 million. Throughout this 'third' period the firm had continued to target their products into niche industrial markets where their emphasis upon product quality and dependability meant they were less vulnerable to price and cost pressures. However, in 1992, in the midst of difficult economic times and widespread industrial restructuring, they had been encouraged to bid for higher-volume, lower-margin work. This process was not very successful but eventually culminated in a 1994 tender for the design and production of a core metallic element of a child's toy.

Interestingly, the client firm, KidCorp, was also a major customer for other businesses owned by SIS' corporate parent. They were adopting a preferred supplier policy and intended to have only one or two purchase points for specific elements in their global toy business. They had a high degree of trust in the parent organisation and on visiting the SIS site were impressed by the firm's depth of experience and commitment to quality. In 1995, they selected SIS to complete the design and begin trial production.

'Some of us were really excited by the prospect ... but you have to be a little worried when volumes are much greater than anything you've done before. I guess the risk seemed okay because in the basic process steps, in the type of product if you like, we were making something that felt very similar to what we'd been doing for many years.'
(Operations Manager)

'Well, obviously we didn't know anything about the toy market but then again we didn't really know all that much about the auto industry or the defence sector or any of our traditional customers before we started serving them. Our key competitive advantage, our capabilities, call it what you will, they are all about keeping the customer happy, about meeting and sometimes exceeding specification.'
(Marketing Director)

The designers had received an outline product specification from KidCorp during the bid process and some further technical detail afterwards. Upon receipt of this final brief, a team of engineers and managers confirmed that the product could and would be manufactured using an up-scaled version of current production processes. The key operational challenge appeared to be accessing sufficient (but not too much) capacity. Fortunately, for a variety of reasons, the parent company was very supportive of the project and promised to underwrite any sensible capital expenditure plans. Although this opinion of the nature of the production challenge was widely accepted throughout the firm (and shared by KidCorp and parent), it was left to one specific senior engineer to actually sign both the final bid and technical completion documentation. By early 1996, the firm had begun a trial period of full-volume production. Unfortunately, in this design validation process SIS had effectively sanctioned a production method that would prove to be entirely inappropriate for the toy market, but it was not until mid-1997 (16 months later) that any indication of problems began to emerge.

Throughout both North America and Europe, individual customers began to claim that their children had been 'poisoned' while playing with the end product. The threat of litigation was quickly levelled at KidCorp and the whole issue rapidly became a 'full-blown' child health scare. A range of pressure groups and legal damage specialists supported and acted to aggregate the individual claims and although similar accusations had been made before, the litigants and their supporters focused in on the recent changes made to the production process and in particular the increasing role of suppliers.

> '. . . it's all very well claiming that you trust your suppliers but you simply cannot have the same level of control over another firm in another country. I am afraid that this all comes down to simple economics, that KidCorp put its profits before children's health. Talk about trust . . . parents trusted this firm to look out for them and their families and have every right to be angry that boardroom greed was more important!'
> (Legal spokesperson for the litigants, interviewed on UK TV consumer rights show)

Under intense media pressure, KidCorp rapidly convened a high-profile investigation into the source of the contamination. It quickly revealed that an 'unauthorised' chemical had been employed in an apparently trivial metal cleaning and preparation element of the SIS production process. Although, when interviewed by the US media, the parent firm's legal director emphasised that there was 'no casual link established or any admission of liability by either party', KidCorp immediately withdrew their order and began to signal an intent to bring legal action against SIS and its parent. This action brought an immediate end to production in this part of the operation and the inspection (and subsequent official and legal visits) had a crippling impact upon the productivity of the whole site. The competitive impact of the failure was extremely significant. After over a year of production, the new product accounted for more than a third (39%) of the factory's output. In addition to major cash-flow implications, the various investigations took up lots of managerial time and the reputation of the firm was seriously affected. As the site operations manager explained, even their traditional customers expressed concerns:

> 'It's amazing but people we had been supplying for 30 or 40 years were calling me up and asking '[Manager's name] what's going on?' and that they were worried about what all this might mean for them . . . these are completely different markets!'

Further reading

Amram, M. and N. Kulatilaka (1999) *Real Options: Managing Strategic Investment in an Uncertain World*, HBS Press.

Augustine, N.R. (1995) 'Managing the Crisis You Tried to Prevent', *Harvard Business Review*, November–December, Reprint 95602.

McIntosh, M. (1998) *Corporate Citizenship – Successful Strategies for Responsible Companies*, Financial Times-Pitman, London.

Perrow, C. (1984) *Normal Accidents: Living with High Risk Technologies*, Basic Books, New York.

Peters, G. (1999) *Waltzing with the Raptors: A Practical Roadmap to Protecting Your Company's Reputation*, Wiley, New York.

Shrivistava, P., I.I. Mitroff, D. Miller and A. Miglani (1988) 'Understanding Industrial Crises', *Journal of Management Studies*, Vol. 25, No. 4, pp. 285–303.

Tversky, A. and D. Kahneman (1974) 'Judgement Under Uncertainty: Heuristics and Biases', *Science*, Vol. 185, pp. 1124–1131.

Weick, K.E. (1976) 'Educational Organizations as Loosely Coupled Systems', *Administrative Science Quarterly*, Vol. 21, pp. 1–19.

Weick, K.E. (1979) *The Social Psychology of Organizing*, McGraw-Hill, New York.

Weick, K.E. (1987) 'Organizational Culture as a Source of High Reliability', *California Management Review*, Volume XXIX, No. 2. Winter, pp. 112–127.

Notes on the chapter

1 Interestingly, Karl Weick (1979) has argued that the concept of continuous improvement is a sensible method for motivating action because by encouraging 'small wins' it helps to overcome the natural aversion to failure associated with large changes.

2 See Nonaka and Takeuchi (1995), *The Knowledge Creating* Company, Oxford University Press, New York, p. 139.

3 The information in this case is drawn primarily from Leeson's own book, *Rogue Trader* (1996), Warner Books, and (the more objective) *The Collapse of Barings: Panic, Ignorance and Greed* by Stephen Fay (1996), Arrow Books.

4 See Shrivastava *et al.* (1988) 'Understanding Industrial Crises', *Journal of Management Studies*, Vol. 25, No. 4, p. 290.

5 See *The Economist* (14 February 1998) for more details.

6 This is based upon an example given in Amram, M. and N. Kulatilaka (1999) *Real Options*, HBS Press.

7 See, for instance, pages 114–115 in Leonard, D. (1995) *Wellsprings of knowledge*, HBS Press.

8 Ettlie, J. (1998) *Managing Technological Innovation*, Free Press, New York.

9 Vroom, V.H. and B. Pahl (1971) 'The relationship between age and risk taking among managers', *Journal of Applied Psychology*, Volume 55, No. 5, pp. 399–405.

10 This distinction between objective and subjective risks and expressed fears is drawn from Waring, A. and I. Glendon (1998) *Managing Risk*, International Thompson Business Press. The examples are based upon those given in Waring, A. (1996) *Safety Management Systems*, Chapman and Hall.

11 The description of Prospect Theory is drawn from Peter Bernstein's excellent book about risk, *Against the Gods: The Remarkable Story of Risk*, Wiley and Sons (1996).

12 This example was transcribed in Cottle, S (2000) 'TV news, Lay voices and the visualisation of risks', pp. 29–40, in Allan, S., B. Adam and C. Carter (eds) *Environmental Risks and the Media*, Routledge, UK. This article, and the rest of the book, offers an informative assessment of the media portrayal of specific (in this case environmental) risks, drawing heavily on the notion of 'manufactured risk' introduced by Ulrich Beck in his book, *The Risk Society* (1992 in translation), Sage, UK.

13 Cottle (p. 41) notes how the Greenpeace representative is interviewed against a lush green backdrop – perhaps to serve as a further contrast with the barren images of the industrial accident.

14 Speaking at a Royal Institute of International Affairs, Energy and Environmental Programme Workshop in Oslo, April 1997. Quoted in Mitchell, J (ed.) (1998) *Companies in a World of Conflict*, Earthscan Publications, London.

15 Details of the Met Life case are drawn from Chapter 15 of Hartley, R.F. (6th edition, 2000) *Management Mistakes and Successes*, Wiley.

16 Peters, G. (1999) *Waltzing with the Raptors: A practical road map to protecting your company's reputation*, Wiley, New York.

17 Loch, C. (1999) 'Cross-Air', INSEAD Case Study, available through the Case Clearing House, Cranfield University, UK.

Index

Note: Page references in *italics* refer to Figures; those in **bold** refer to Tables